December 10–12, 2012
Toronto, Ontario, Canada

I0038159

Association for Computing Machinery

Advancing Computing as a Science & Profession

VRST'12

Proceedings of the 18th ACM Symposium on
Virtual Reality Software and Technology

Sponsored by:
ACM SIGCHI and ACM SIGGRAPH

Supported by:
Graphics, Animation and New Media Network of Centres of Excellence, University of Ontario Institute of Technology, Universität Würzburg, and York University

Association for Computing Machinery

Advancing Computing as a Science & Profession

The Association for Computing Machinery
2 Penn Plaza, Suite 701
New York, New York 10121-0701

Notice to Past Authors of ACM-Published Articles

ACM intends to create a complete electronic archive of all articles and/or other material previously published by ACM. If you have written a work that has been previously published by ACM in any journal or conference proceedings prior to 1978, or any SIG Newsletter at any time, and you do NOT want this work to appear in the ACM Digital Library, please inform permissions@acm.org, stating the title of the work, the author(s), and where and when published.

ISBN: 978-1-4503-1768-9 (Digital)

ISBN: 978-1-4503-1469-5 (Print)

Additional copies may be ordered prepaid from:

ACM Order Department
PO Box 30777
New York, NY 10087-0777, USA

Phone: 1-800-342-6626 (USA and Canada)
+1-212-626-0500 (Global)
Fax: +1-212-944-1318
E-mail: acmhelp@acm.org
Hours of Operation: 8:30 am – 4:30 pm ET

ACM Order Number: 609123

Printed in the USA

General and Program Chairs' Welcome

It is our great pleasure to welcome you to the *2012 ACM Symposium on Virtual Reality Software and Technology – VRST'12*. VRST has become one of the major scientific events in the area of virtual reality since its debut in 1994 in Singapore. The symposium continues its tradition as an international forum for the presentation of research results and experience reports on leading edge issues of software, hardware and systems for Virtual Reality. The mission of the symposium is to share novel technologies that fulfill the needs of Virtual Reality applications and environments and to identify new directions for future research and development. VRST gives researchers and practitioners a unique opportunity to share their perspectives with others interested in the various aspects of Virtual Reality and owes its existence to a vibrant and productive research community. This year, VRST was held December 10-12, 2012 in Toronto, Ontario, Canada.

The call for papers attracted 88 submissions from Asia, Europe, Australia, and North and South America in all areas of Virtual Reality research. Particular attention was given to work on system with a special track focusing on architectures, frameworks, reusability, adaptivity, and performance testing and evaluation. An international program committee consisting of 16 experts in the topic areas and the three program chairs handled the highly competitive and selective review process. Almost every submission received four or more reviews, two from members of the international program committee and two from external reviewers. Reviewing was double-blind, where only the program chairs and the program committee member assigned to identify external reviewers knew the identity of the authors.

In the end, the program committee was able to accept 25 out of 88 submissions, which corresponds to an acceptance rate of 28%. For posters, 15 out of 32 submissions will appear in the proceedings. The topics range from tracking, augmented and mixed reality, interaction, navigation and locomotion, collaboration, haptics, simulation, agents and behaviors to two sessions for a systems track. We hope that these proceedings will serve as a valuable reference for Virtual Reality researchers and developers.

Putting together the content for *VRST'12* was a team effort. We first thank the authors for providing the content of the program. Special thanks go to the members of the international program committee, who successfully dealt with a reviewing load that was substantially larger than predicted. We also thank the external reviewers. Bill Kapralos and Faisal Qureshi handled the posters and also had to deal with a larger than expected number of submissions. We would also like to thank Andrew Hogue for developing and updating the conference website and Faisal Qureshi as conference treasurer. The local organization team deserve many thanks for organizing the event. James Stewart from PCS assisted by providing and maintaining the reviewing system. Adrienne Griscti and Lisa Tolles from ACM and Sheridan Proceedings Service helped greatly to create the proceedings in a timely manner. Our universities, the University of Ontario Institute of Technology, University of Würzburg, and York University and colleagues supported us in this endeavor. Finally, we thank the sponsoring organizations, the ACM Special Interest Groups on Graphics and Human-Computer Interaction (SIGGRAPH, SIGCHI), and the Graphics, Animation, and New Media Network of Centres of Excellence (GRAND NCE) for support.

We hope that you will find this program interesting and thought-provoking and that the symposium will provide you with a valuable opportunity to share ideas with other researchers and practitioners from institutions around the world.

Mark Green
VRST'12 General Chair
University of Ontario,
Institute of Technology, Canada

Wolfgang Stuerzlinger
VRST'12 Program Co-Chair
York University, Canada

Marc Erich Latoschik
VRST'12 Program Co-Chair
University of Würzburg, Germany

Bill Kapralos
VRST'12 Program Co-Chair
University of Ontario,
Institute of Technolgy, Canada

Table of Contents

Session 5: Move It (Interaction)

Session 6: Where And How (Locomotion and Collaboration)

Session 7: Dreaming Big (Systems Track: System Engineering)

Session 8: The Ins and Outs (Tracking)

Posters

VRST'12 Symposium Organization

General Chair: Mark Green *(University of Ontario Institute of Technology, Canada)*

Program Chairs: Wolfgang Stuerzlinger *(York University, Toronto, Canada)*
Marc Erich Latoschik *(University of Würzburg, Germany)*
Bill Kapralos *(University of Ontario Institute of Technology, Canada)*

Poster Chairs: Bill Kapralos *(University of Ontario Institute of Technology, Canada)*
Faisal Qureshi *(University of Ontario Institute of Technology, Canada)*

Publicity Chair: Andrew Hogue *(University of Ontario Institute of Technology, Canada)*

Treasurer: Faisal Qureshi *(University of Ontario Institute of Technology, Canada)*

Steering Committee: George Baciu *(The Hong Kong Polytechnic University, Hong Kong)*
Steven Feiner *(Columbia University, USA)*
Mark Green *(The University of Ontario Institute of Technology, Canada)*
Yoshifumi Kitamura *(Tohoku University, Japan)*
Rynson Lau *(City University of Hong Kong, Hong Kong)*
Daniel Thalmann *(Nanyang Technological University, Singapore)*
Michael Zyda *(University of Southern California, USA)*

Program Committee: Roland Blach *(Fraunhofer, Germany)*
Wolfgang Broll *(TU Ilmenau, Germany)*
Gery Casiez *(University of Lille, France)*
Pablo Figueroa *(Universidad de los Andes, Colombia)*
Rainer Herpers *(Bonn-Rhine-Sieg University of Applied Sciences, Germany)*
Andrew Hogue *(University of Ontario Institute of Technology, Canada)*
Gudrun Klinker *(Technical University of Munich, Germany)*
Manfred Lau *(Lancaster University, UK)*
Jean-Luc Lugrin *(Teesside University, UK)*
Dirk Reiners *(University of Louisiana, Lafayette, USA)*
Frank Steinicke *(University of Würzburg, Germany)*
Evan Suma *(University of Southern California, USA)*
Rob Teather *(York University, Toronto, Canada)*
Robert van Liere *(Centrum Wiskunde & Informatica, Amsterdam, The Netherlands)*
Chad Wingrave *(University of Central Florida, Orlando, USA)*
Gabriel Zachman *(Clausthal University, Germany)*

Additional reviewers:

Bruno Arnaldi	Raphael Grasset
Clemens Arth	Philippe Gravez
Sabarish Babu	Mark Green
George Baciu	Martin Hachet
Patrick Baudisch	Patrick Hartling
Günther Bauernfeind	Frank Haselberger
Stephan Beck	Jan Herling
Johannes Behr	Michikata Hirose
Miklas Bergou	Victoria Interrante
Allen Bierbaum	Joe Istead
Mark Billinghurst	Wei Ji
Renaud Blanch	Bernhard Jung
Martin Bleichner	Bernhard Kainz
Mark Bolas	Saad Khattak
Gerd Bruder	Peter Khooshabeh
Gerd Bruder	Luv Kohli
Sarah Buchanan	Stefan Kopp
Daniel Buckstein	Regis Kopper
Matthias Bues	Ernst Kruijff
Thomas Butkiewicz	Alexander Kulik
Jeff Cashion	Yoshihiro Kuroda
Romain Cavagna	Markus Lappe
Joaquim Bento Cavalcante-Neto	Florian Larrue
Jian Chen	Rynson Lau
Mehdi Chouiten	Anamary Leal
Joon Chuah	Vincent Lepetit
Julien Cordry	Erich Leung
Brent Cowan	Rob Lindeman
Jeff Craighead	Benjamin Lok
Carolina Cruz-Neira	Kok-Lim Low
Mirabelle D'Cruz	John Lucas
Raimund Dachselt	Anatole Lécuyer
Gerwin de Haan	Wendy Mackay
Konstantinos Derpanis	Nadia Magenat Thalmann
Arindam Dey	David Mainzer
Stephen DiVerdi	Jonathan Marbach
Ralf Doerner	Treib Marc
Andreas Duenser	Maud Marchal
Thierry Duval	Mark Mine
Florian Echtler	Betty Mohler
Arjan Egges	Matthias Mueller
Francois Faure	Abdeldjallil Naceri
Angus Forbes	Nassir Navab
Nikos Frangakis	Luciana Nedel
Bernd Froehlich	Carsten Neumann

Additional reviewers
(continued):

Mohammad Obaid	Sharon Stansfield
Jarrell Pair	Anthony Steed
Byron Perez	Oliver Stefani
Valeria Petkova	Wen Tang
Jonas Pfeil	Mina Tawadrous
Thomas Pietrzak	Franco Tecchia
David Pizzi	Veronica Teichrieb
Nicholas Polys	Bruce Thomas
Andreas Pusch	Marcus Toennis
John Quarles	Henrik Tramberend
Bruno Raffin	Helmuth Trefftz
Andrew Raij	Dimitar Valkov
Gerhard Reitmayr	Manuel Veit
Bernhard Riecke	Jeffrey Ventrella
Mikko Rissanen	David Waller
Marcel Ritter	Andreas Weber
Rafael Roberto	Rene Weller
Nicolas Roussel	Mary Whitton
Roy Ruddle	Michael Williams-Bell
Emanuele Ruffaldi	Chen Yan
Dieter Schmalstieg	Yuting Ye
Rene Schubotz	Chris Zerebecki
Marco Schumann	Caroline Ziemkiewicz
William Sherman	Stefanie Zollmann
Ferdi Smit	

VRST 2012 Sponsors & Supporters

Sponsors:

Supporters:

Generating Diverse Ethnic Groups with Genetic Algorithms

Tomas Trescak
IIIA, Artificial Intelligence
Research Institute
Spanish Research Council
Barcelona, Spain
ttrescak@iiia.csic.es

Anton Bogdanovych,
Simeon Simoff
MARCS Institute
University of Western Sydney
NSW, Australia
a.bogdanovych@uws.edu.au
s.simoff@uws.edu.au

Inmaculada Rodriguez
Applied Mathematics
Department
University of Barcelona
Barcelona, Spain
inma@maia.ub.es

ABSTRACT

Simulating large crowds of virtual agents has become an important problem in virtual reality applications, video games, cinematography and training simulators. In this paper, we show how to achieve a high degree of appearance variation among individual 3D avatars in generated crowds through the use of genetic algorithms, while also manifesting unique characteristic features of a given population group. We show how virtual cities can be populated with diverse crowds of virtual agents that preserve their ethnic features, illustrate how our approach can be used to simulate full body avatar appearance, present a case study and analyze our results.

Categories and Subject Descriptors

H.5.1 [**Multimedia Information Systems**]: Artificial, augmented, and virtual realities

Keywords

Crowd Simulation, Genetic Algorithm, Avatar Appearance

1. INTRODUCTION

Virtual worlds and 3D games use 3D avatars[1] for user's physical representation in the virtual space as well as for simulating computer-controlled non-player characters. 3D avatars are also widely used in the movie industry, training simulators and health systems. In most instances, such avatars are manually designed, but often there are situations when such manual design is not practical. The most common case when avatar design automation is required is when a large crowd of computer-controlled avatars must be simulated to perform a particular group activity.

As an example of automatic crowd generation, one of the most popular solutions in the movie industry, is to utilize

---

[1]3D avatar is an animated, emotive, complex model representing a user in a graphical form that ranges from actual resemblance of the human user to a talking fish or a robot.

Massive[2] software that offers facilities for creating a given number of avatar clones and further modification of those clones by introducing a slight variation into their appearance features. This technique was widely used in Peter Jackson's The Lord Of The Rings film trilogy[3] for simulating battles.

The approach in generating crowds, taken by systems like Massive, is to use a number of manually created avatar shapes and randomly modify some shape parameters and textures to introduce the variety. To avoid non-plausible distortions of the resulting shapes, the features being changed are often limited to randomly selecting a clothing texture from a predefined list or modifying the height and width of the avatar. Thus, such systems are limited in terms of introducing a variety into crowds.

What is often desired in crowd simulation - is to have a diverse crowd with representatives of various genders and age groups, having different appearance, while still consistently maintaining the distinct features of their ethnic group. Simulating such diverse groups requires identifying the characteristic features that represent a given population and defining the acceptable range of variation in these features, as well as their intelligent manipulation. When generating crowds of avatars in an automatic fashion, without satisfying these conditions, either the believability of the crowd appearance or its diversity will be very limited.

Nowadays, most modern game engines and virtual worlds offer facilities to design parametric avatars [15], where avatars can be edited using hundreds of individual parameters (head shape, nose length, eye size, etc.). Such parametrisation offers enormous flexibility in generating unique avatar crowds and calls for revisiting existing crowd generation techniques.

Having parametric avatars allows to go beyond standard randomization techniques [18] for the crowd simulation. We suggest to introduce diversity into avatar appearance by mimicking genetic rules of reproduction present in nature. Under normal circumstances, humans and animals, when producing their offsprings, manage to achieve enough variety in the appearance of their children, while also preserving their distinct personal and ethnic characteristics, as well as ensuring that their body shape and facial features remain within the acceptable range of variation for the given species.

Thus, in this paper, we introduce an algorithm that generates visually unique avatars following the representations and techniques used in genetic algorithms theory [7] (e.g. crossover and mutation). This algorithm generates individuals that respect the visual, racial, cultural and behavioural

---

[2]http://www.massivesoftware.com/ (last access 07/2012)
[3]http://www.lordoftherings.net/ (last access 07/2012)

features of a defined population as well as genetic inheritance of these features. Using genetic mutation, we add novelty to generated avatars. In addition to the visual aspects of crowd simulation, our approach is also applicable to generating unique personalities of virtual agents.

Our work focuses on generating large crowds, where each individual is a unique, distinguishable member of some ethnic group (see Figure 1). It should not be treated as an attempt to closely mimic genetic reproduction found in nature. Simulating the underlying processes behind forming body tissues and bone structure based on the DNA code is quite complicated, as those mechanisms are not yet fully understood and are not computationally feasible at present. Instead, our algorithm uses the same basic principles, but deals with a high-level representation of genetic code and a very straight-forward technique for manipulating it to produce the desired changes in the avatar appearance.

Figure 1: Generating Diverse Ethnic Groups

In our approach, we first isolate and quantify visual features of an avatar (e.g. nose width) and then use approaches and techniques from *genetic algorithms* rather than mimicking biological behavior. Genetic algorithms belong to the field of *evolutionary computing* where computational approaches in optimization seek inspiration from evolution and genetics.

Isolation and quantification of visual features of an avatar can be a tedious process, but by doing so we can achieve a great level of detail and variety in generated avatars [10]. For example, for heads of human avatars some can represent the craniofacial measures quantified by their minimal and maximal values [21, 20]. Limiting these features by an interval allows us to better control the appearance of an avatar, prohibiting the creation of unwanted (e.g. implausible) results. Also, we can combine them to represent physical properties (e.g. fatness), or even emotions (e.g. happiness). Another possibility is to define different intervals of quantification for visual features of children and adults.

A big advantage of isolating visual features is the reusability with different 3D models. It also becomes possible to manipulate non-human 3D models while using the same basic principles (e.g. manipulate a visual feature of eye-size in a 3D model of an animal).

When visual features are isolated and quantified, all their values for an individual are extracted to form the *chromosome*. A specific value of a visual feature is named *gene*. Genetic algorithms provide different operators that combine (i.e. crossover) and manipulate (i.e. mutation) parent chromosomes to generate their children with a defined level of novelty. Next, we explore the related work in avatar generation, describe our approach and discuss experimental results.

2. RELATED WORK

Avatar generation and crowd generation methods vary in how to model a single individual and in the approach of making every crowd member unique. In one of the first attempts to generate a population of unique 3D characters, [4] created a system that generated facial models. The model was based on randomization of anthropometric measures applied to B-spline surfaces. Later, [2] used Principal Component Analysis (PCA) to analyze datasets of facial features to extract base vectors from the face, and used these vectors to generate new, unique faces. This work was extended by [1] to generate the whole body of an avatar. A different approach was taken by [12] and [18] who used variance of attachments and textures over a predefined set of avatars, where avatars mainly differed in size and the type of textures, while still appearing as clones that undergone a minor modification.

In other works, authors considered different means of crowd generation and isolated specific visual parameters (i.e. body and clothing) which deform related 3D models. The values of these parameters can be randomized in order to produce unique crowd members [16] [11].

Identification of such visual parameters inspired researchers to encode their values into genetic structures and apply genetic algorithms theory to generate unique crowd members. Ventrella [19] was one of the first to discuss the possibilities of storing and modifying the avatar properties in a "chromosome", represented by an array of integer values and then modifying those properties to generate a 2D sketch of an avatar with different appearances. Technological details of this work, however, were not explained and the main focus was limited to generating a single avatar, not a crowd [19].

While Ventrella worked with 2D sketches a similar approach was taken by [10] to generate 3D avatars. Authors in [10] presented a method for encoding a rigged 3D avatar into a list of bones and their dimensions with further modification of those using genetic principles. The resulting avatar generation method often produced unrealistic body shapes and was intended to be used in a supervised manner, where a user was presented with a large list of possible avatars and was expected to manually select the most suitable one.

The most similar work to our approach was done by [21, 20], who investigated generating an avatar's appearance using genetic inheritance principles. Genetic inheritance was approached from the biological perspective, where each child chromosome holds a copy of mother's and father's chromosome. During the reproduction process, child chromosomes were duplicated, combined and then split into four "gametes". Through the process called "fecundation" a father gamete and a mother gamete are combined to produce the new child's chromosomes. The parents' gene values from the chromosome are combined to visualize the final value. This method relied on direct modification of 3D meshes and was limited in the number of parameters that can be modified, and similar to [10] often produced non-plausible results.

We advance existing work by applying genetic algorithms rather than mimicking biological evolution like [21]. Similar to [10], we encode visual properties as genes, which form chromosomes, but rather than using meshes or bones - we rely on fully parametric avatars. We use genetic operators to generate new, unique individuals, which due to parametric nature will be limited to plausible characters. Our contributions include the definition of new techniques applied during replication, such as deep inheritance, which provides the possibility of inheritance of features from indirect ancestors. Another contribution is the definition of genotype rules, which can define key ethnic features that have to be preserved during replication, or dependencies between visual features, e.g. making an avatar fat. As a result, we can generate ethnic crowds with a high degree of variation across hundreds of body features, while also maintaining the similarity with avatar ancestors in a classical genetic sense. This allows us to simulate avatar groups of unlimited size, where every individual has a unique appearance, while at the same, is identifiable as the member of its ethnic group based on characteristic appearance features.

3. AVATAR GENERATION

In this section, we propose a general-purpose model for automatic generation of 3D avatars, which can be deployed in modern video games or virtual worlds. This model is not limited to human avatars and can be used with other avatar types (e.g. humans, animals, fishes, robots, orcs) as long as they have distinguishable *visual features*. Next, we focus on generating individual virtual agents with unique appearance from a small sample of manually designed avatars.

3.1 Genetic algorithms

Genetic algorithms (GA) belong to the larger class of evolutionary algorithms, which generate solutions to optimization problems using techniques inspired by natural evolution, such as *inheritance, mutation, selection,* and *crossover*.

In the history of evolutionary computing, four important paradigms served as a base activity of the field: genetic algorithms [7], genetic programming [9], evolutionary strategies [14] and evolutionary programming [5]. Their differences lie within the terminology behind the algorithms, the reproduction operators and selection methods. In our work, we use the terminology and procedures from genetic algorithms.

A traditional genetic algorithm defines and manipulates individuals at the level of their *chromosomes*, where a chromosome is represented as a *fixed-length bit string*. Each position in the string is assumed to represent a particular feature of an individual, called *gene*. Usually, the string is "evaluated as a collection of structural features of an individual, which have little or no interactions" [17]. To produce a new generation of individuals, we combine parent's chromosomes using a *crossover* operator. Combining parent's genes allows gene *inheritance*. To introduce novelty in the population, we apply *mutation* to the current chromosome.

Genetic algorithms are employed in numerous fields, such as *search, optimization* and *machine learning* [6]. In most of these cases GA are used as a search heuristic that mimics the process of natural evolution. In this approach, the GA are treated as an optimization algorithm utilizing a fitness function to *select* a partial solution of the original problem, till reaching some predefined threshold for suboptimal solution.

In our approach, we are not using GA as an optimization algorithm. This is why we do not use the *selection* and focus only on *crossover, mutation* and *inheritance*. In the following sections, we provide the formal representation of genetic data and operators. Then we contemplate our design

of deep inheritance, also called gene skipping, and explain the generation algorithm.

3.2 Formal Representation of Genetic Data

In this section, we formalize genetic concepts used during the avatar generation process. First, we define visual information or definable visual traits of an avatar. For the purpose of generation of unique avatars such information needs to: (i) express the specific appearance trait of an individual and (ii) must be quantifiable. Therefore, this information must hold the quantifiable visual descriptors of an individual. For example, "height" visual descriptor can be quantifiable by a numeric interval, from 0 to 100, with 0 being short to 100 being tall (respecting the natural height of humans). Moreover, a visual descriptor can quantify the shape, texture or color of an avatar's body part. We define the visual descriptor as the *visual feature* (see Table 1):

Definition 1. *A* **visual feature** *holds a quantifiable descriptor of a body part of an avatar. It is defined as* $vf = \{$Id, Name, Value, Interval, Minimum, Maximum$\}$ *where:*

1. *Id is a unique integer identifier,* $id \in \mathbb{I}$

2. *Name is a string that identifies the visual feature,* $name \in \mathbb{S}$

3. *Interval defines the range of visual feature values with textual descriptor of Minimum value (e.g. short) and Maximum value (e.g. tall).*

Id	Name	Interval	Minimum	Maximum	Gene
33	Height	[0,100]	Short	Tall	81
45	Nose Size	[0,100]	Small	Big	21
67	Arm Length	[0,100]	Short	Long	27
80	Gender	{0,1}	Male	Female	1

Table 1: Examples of definitions of visual features

Using our approach, each avatar is first described by a list of *visual features*. These features should thoroughly characterize its appearance. When such list is defined, we quantify the values of visual features into *genes*. Genes are real or boolean values of visual features, which allow us to perform genetic operations, such as crossover and mutation.

Definition 2. *A* **gene** $g \in \mathbb{R} \cup \mathbb{B}$ *represents a real or boolean value of the visual feature* $g = vf_{value}$ *(i) to quantify the presence of the visual feature,* $g \in \mathbb{B}$; *(ii) to quantify the strength or a position of a feature (e.g. height with values close to minimum representing short avatar and values close to maximum representing a tall avatar),* $g \in \mathbb{R}$.

The ordered set of avatar's genes is called *chromosome*. A chromosome holds the complete genetic information of an individual. Order of the genes in a chromosome is specified by *genomic sequence*.

Definition 3. *A* **genomic sequence** *defines the genetic composition of a chromosome of a specific group, forming a representative gene ordering of a species or group. A genomic sequence* GS *for a chromosome of length* n *is a set of indexes which define the ordering of genes in the chromosome:* $GS = \{i_1, i_2 \ldots i_n\}$.

Definition 4. A **chromosome** of length n, c_n, is an ordered list of n genes $g_1, g_2 \ldots g_n$, where gene order is given by a genomic sequence GS, that is $c_n = \{g_{i_1}, g_{i_2} \ldots g_{i_n}\}$ where $i_1, i_2 \ldots i_n \in GS$.

A chromosome identifies all visual features of an individual; thus, it is possible to analyze chromosomes of an existing population and identify the genes that are common for a specific ethnic group. These genes are marked as ethnic-specific and they are modified only steadily during the reproduction, in order to maintain the ethnic-specific features.

Furthermore, to operate with the genetic inheritance in population we store all the parent-child relationship information in a *genealogy tree*. As a result, it allows us to navigate within the relationships of the population. This tree provides information on ancestors or siblings of the generated avatar and provides access to their chromosomes. Its name comes from the graphical representation where the family ancestors are visualized in the tree-like structure, also called as *family tree*. A *genealogy tree* is usually represented as a directed acyclic graph (see Figure 4).

3.3 Formal Definition of Genetic Operators

In our approach, we first define the initial population, that characterizes the base groups of population. Members of these groups have distinguishable visual features that define such group (e.g. asians with asian eyes, africans with african skin). Then, we use this characteristic information to create new individuals. Therefore, we may refer to our generation process as to *reproduction*. During reproduction, we use the information stored in *chromosomes* of parents and combine and modify them using a *genetic operator* to reproduce chromosomes of new unique individuals.

In the previous section, we have formalized genetic concepts related to the reproduction process, that is *genes*, *chromosome*, *genomic sequence* and *genealogy tree*. In the following sections, we define all the genetic functions and operators. Such operators are responsible for *crossover*, *mutation* and *inheritance* of genetic information from parents. Moreover, we introduce the *genotype rule* a mechanism to explicitly control the generation process, preserve the group characteristic visual features and introduce relationships between genes. Our algorithm first combines parent chromosomes using the *crossover* operator and then uses *gene skipping* to inherit some genes from its deeper ancestors. Next, to introduce novelty, it *mutates* the produced chromosome. Finally, using a set of predefined *genotype rules*, it adjusts this chromosome to respect the population group properties.

3.4 Crossover

Crossover is a genetic algorithm operator that is used to vary and combine the genetic information stored in chromosomes from one generation to the next one [17]. Analogous processes from biology are *genetic reproduction* and *biological crossover*. In this process, a crossover function selects and combines the genes from one or more parents to create a new child chromosome. We formalize different crossover operators. Some operators (i.e. clone, split) are traditional, coming from the genetic algorithm theory, some are defined by us to meet our needs (i.e. exchange, fuzzy). The first traditional crossover operator is *clone* operator, which copies the genetic information directly from one of the parents.

Definition 5. Given the mother chromosome c^m consisting of genes $c^m = g_1^m g_2^m \ldots g_n^m$ and the father chromosome c^f consisting of genes $c^f = g_1^f g_2^f \ldots g_n^f$ a **clone** operator $\oplus^q : C \times C \to C$ is defined as $c^m \oplus^q c^f = g_1^q g_2^q \ldots g_n^q$ where q is either denoting mother (m) or father (f) genes.

Cloning is the simplest and fastest crossover technique, but it does not provide many functionalities in mixing genetic information from parents. The simplest crossover operator that allows us to combine this genetic information is the *split* operator (in GA terminology also known as one-point crossover [17]). Figure 2 contemplates the operation of the split operator. This technique splits the chromosome after a specific gene, called *split point*, and all genes on the left of this split point are copied from one parent, and all genes on right are copied from the other one. The split point specifies a *father-mother ratio*, r^{fm}, meaning what percentage of genes should be copied from mother and which from father. The split technique is applicable to more parents, where we select one split point for each additional parent. Formally:

Definition 6. Given the mother chromosome c^m consisting of genes $c^m = g_1^m g_2^m \ldots g_n^m$ and the father chromosome c^f consisting of genes $c^f = g_1^f g_2^f \ldots g_n^f$ and the split point $0 \leq s \leq n$, a **split** operator $\ominus : C \times C \to C$ is defined as $c^m \ominus c^f = g_1^m g_2^m \ldots g_s^m g_{s+1}^f \ldots g_n^f$

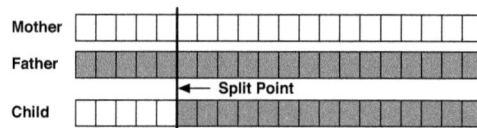

Figure 2: Crossover technique called "split"

Previous crossover operators allow none, or very limited mechanisms for combining and experimenting with genetic information from parents. A flexible crossover operator, is the *exchange operator*. This operator combines parents' chromosomes by randomly selecting two complementary subsets of genes from parents and joining them. Formally:

Definition 7. Given the mother chromosome c^m consisting of genes $c^m = g_1^m g_2^m \ldots g_n^m$, the father chromosome c^f consisting of genes $c^f = g_1^f g_2^f \ldots g_n^f$ and the exchange selection function $e : G \times G \to G$ that for input father and mother genes outputs only one of them, we define a crossover **exchange** operator $\otimes : C \times C \to C$ as $c^m \otimes c^f = e(g_1^m, g_1^f) \cdot e(g_2^m, g_2^f) \ldots e(g_n^m, g_n^f)$.

The process of gene exchange is shown in Figure 3, clearly marking genes selected from mother and from father. The number of genes selected from the father and mother is controlled by the *father-mother ratio*.

For our purposes, we define a new crossover operator named *probabilistic fuzzy operator*. This operator is similar to *exchange* operator, but rather to copy the exact values of parent genes it combines values in the interval given by the values of genes from the father and mother. This operator brings even more variety into the generation process. We use this operator to evaluate our approach in Section 4.

Definition 8. Given the mother chromosome c^m consisting of genes $c^m = g_1^m g_2^m \ldots g_n^m$, the father chromosome c^f

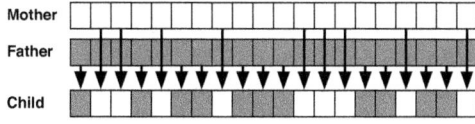

Figure 3: "Gene exchange" crossover technique

consisting of genes $c^f = g_1^f g_2^f \ldots g_n^f$, the parent *gene selector function* $s_{rfm}^i : 2^G \rightarrow \{0,1\}$ which for position i, where $0 \leq i \leq n$, selects either mother or father gene depending on probability given by the father-mother ratio r^{fm} and the *fuzzy function* $f : \mathbb{I} \rightarrow \mathbb{R}$ which for gene on position i selects a random value in the interval given by $f(i) = [s(i), (g_i^m - g_i^f)/2]$, we define a **fuzzy** crossover operator $\oslash : C \times C \rightarrow C$ as $c^m \oslash c^f = f(1) \cdot f(2) \ldots f(n)$.

We can define even more crossover operators, but for our purposes, the split, exchange and fuzzy are enough. An example of custom crossover operator would take the arithmetic average of mother and father gene values.

3.5 Inheritance and Gene Skipping

Looking at ourselves in the mirror and analyzing our visual appearance, most probably we find visual traits from our parents. Nevertheless, many of our traits go even deeper into our ancestry tree, and sometimes we look more similar to our grandparents than to parents. Inheriting visual and behavioral features from our predecessors is possible due to a process called *gene skipping*. Although, sometimes our visual features have little similarity with our ancestors and are the result of *mutation* or are altered by some external factor (see Section 3.6).

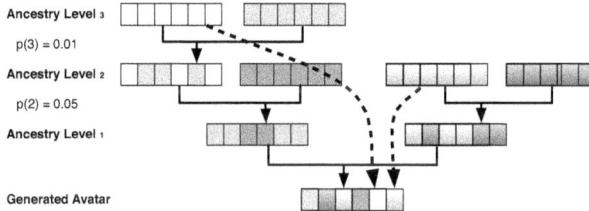

Figure 4: "Gene skipping", where $p(n)$ denotes the probability of inheriting gene from ancestry level n

Gene skipping is a natural genetic process that occurs during the reproduction process, when we obtain the genetic information from our deeper ancestors. Such genetic information does not only alter our appearance, but also behavior, personality and predispositions.

Figure 4 contemplates the process of gene skipping. In our approach, this process becomes active after combining chromosomes using a crossover operator. For each gene in the chromosome, we evaluate the possibility of inheriting this gene from our ancestors. The probability value is bound to an *ancestry level*. Ancestry level of our parents is 1. Our grandparents are our second closest ancestors, their level is 2, great-grandparents have level 3 and so on. For a given gene, we define the probability of skipping it from a predecessor in ancestry level n as a quadratic function

$p(n) = \frac{1}{5 \times 2^n}$, where $n \geq 2$. We have not found unified and exact values of such probabilities in the literature; therefore, we have modelled it to reflect the quadratic decrease with relation to older ancestors. In this manner, there is a 5% probability of inheriting a given gene from our grandparents, 2.5% from our great-grandparents, 1.25% from great-great-grandparents. The gene skipping technique introduces an interesting level of variability of avatar appearance. Next, we present another genetic operator called *mutation*, which further extends the variability of generated results.

3.6 Mutation

In genetic algorithms, mutation is a genetic operator used to provide diversity from one generation to the next. Mutation alters one or more gene values in a chromosome from its initial state. Using mutation, the solution may change entirely from the previous solution. Hence a genetic algorithm can come to improved solutions using mutation [6].

We use mutation to bring more variability to generated avatars, allowing them to have new visual traits, unknown to their ancestors. In our case, mutation is performed by randomly selecting a specific number of genes and modifying their values. The new value is either random, or taken from a specific interval (e.g. $\pm$ 20% of parent value). The mutation level is expressed by the percentage of the mutated genes from the total number of genes. In the bottom of the Figure 7, we see a woman avatar, PintoLae2 that is significantly different from his parents due to the high level of mutation set to generate this avatar.

3.7 Genotype Rules

In genetics, the *genotype* is a genetic makeup of a cell, an organism, or an individual. In another words, it is a measurement of how an individual differs within a group of individuals or species. We have borrowed this specific term for a mechanism that allows us to define the characteristics of individuals or population groups, using *genotype rules*.

We propose *genotype rules* to provide precise control over values of individual genes during the reproduction process. It is a powerful mechanism, that allows us to define the characteristics of a population group and to maintain their significant traits (e.g. asian eyes). Moreover, genotype rules can specify the relationship between genes. Such rule can, for example, force the inheritance of a group of genes only from one parent, depending on the gender of the generated avatar. Further we illustrate it on an example of generating female avatars with "ideal" breast-waist-hip proportions.

A genotype rule modifies the gene value of the reproduced chromosome depending on the other gene values stored in this reproduced chromosome, as well as gene value stored in any of its ancestors. Genotype rules use the *selection function* that allows them to select the gene value from its own chromosome or from a chromosome of a specific relative. The input of this selection function for gene n is a string, which encodes the full path to the given individual.

Definition 9. A **gene selector function** $s_g : \mathbb{S}^* \rightarrow \mathbb{R}^*$ is a recursive function which returns the value of a specific gene g from one or several relatives. Relatives are selected depending on the *input string* s in the form $s = X_1 \cdot X_2 \cdot \ldots \cdot X_m$ where $X_{k|k \leq m} \in \{self, parent, child, sibling\}^*$. Values of X_k represent standard tree node selection functions and their concatenation specifies the path to specific relatives.

5

Examples of *input strings* S^*, to the gene selector function follow the subscript notation (i.e. $selectionFunction_{geneName}$) with the gene name *geneName* of some selected individual appearing under the selection function name *selectionFunction*:

Avatar: *self*
Father: $parent_{gender}$ = 'male'
All my brothers that are taller than me:
$sibling_{gender}$ = 'male' $\wedge$ $sibling_{height}$ > $self_{height}$

Definition 10. A **genotype rule** for gene g_i is a function $r_{g_i} : S_1 \times S_2 \times \ldots S_n \to \mathbb{R}$ which for a given input $s_1, s_2 \ldots s_n$, where $s_{k|k \leq n}$ is a gene selector function, returns the value of gene g_i.

Definition 11. A **genotype** is a set of genotype rules that characterizes a specific population group or an individual.

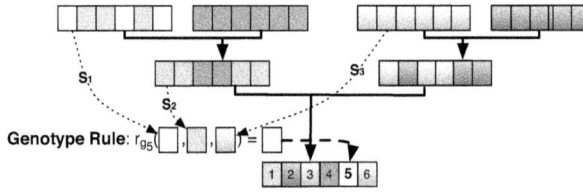

Figure 5: Selection process for rule $r_{g_5} : S_1 \times S_2 \times S_3$

Figure 5 contemplates the process of selection of genes for the genotype rule evaluation. Next, we show an example of how the genotype is used to characterize a population group and to specify a gene relation. For clarity, we do not use the number index of a gene r_{g_i} but the name of related visual feature r_{gender} that represents gene g_i.

Example: Ideal ratio

In this example we generate female avatars with breast-waist-hip ratio of (90-60-90). These dimensions are specified with four rules, where the diversity of generated values are respected by using them as measure to the new "ideal" proportions.

1. r_{gender} = "female"

2. $r_{breasts} = \frac{3}{8}(s_{breats}(self) + s_{waist}(self) + s_{hip}(self))$

3. $r_{waist} = \frac{2}{8}(s_{breats}(self) + s_{waist}(self) + s_{hip}(self))$

4. $r_{hip} = \frac{3}{8}(s_{breats}(self) + s_{waist}(self) + s_{hip}(self))$

The first rule defines that all generated avatars will be female. The remaining rules encode that breasts should be $\frac{3}{8}$ (same as $\frac{90}{240}$) of the ratio and hip $\frac{2}{8}$ of the ratio and waist $\frac{3}{8}$ of the ratio. This example shows how easily we can model relations between genes.

3.8 Algorithm

Algorithm 1 uses all the mechanisms introduced in the previous section. First, it combines the chromosomes from *father* and *mother*, using a specific *crossover operator* and creates a new child *chromosome*. Second, if allowed, performs a *gene skipping* using the new chromosome and information stored in the *genealogy tree*. Gene-skipping uses

pre-defined probabilities to decide if a given gene should be skipped. Third, the algorithm *mutates* a specific amount of genes in the new chromosome. This amount is set by the *mutation level*. At last, the chromosome is modified according to *genotype rules*. The algorithm repeatedly executes all rules till no change in chromosome is detected. The generated chromosome contains all the information about visual appearance of a new unique 3D avatar. The values of genes of generated chromosomes are used to render the new avatar.

Algorithm 1: Algorithm for generating an avatar

Input: genealogyTree, mother, father, crossover operator, fatherMotherRatio, mutationLevel, skipGenes, genotype rules

Output: Chromosome representing a new unique 3D avatar

begin
    // combine parent chromosomes
    chromosome ← Crossover (crossoverType, fatherChromosome, motherChromosome, fatherMotherRatio);
    // gene skipping
    if skipGenes **then**
        chromosome ← SkipGenes (genealogyTree, chromosome);
    // mutate chromosome
    chromosome ← Mutate (chromosome, mutationLevel);
    // adjust chromosome according to genotype
    // execute the rules till no change is performed
    repeat
        adjusted ← *false*;
        foreach *(rule* ∈ genotype) **do**
            adjusted = adjusted ∨ ExecuteRule (rule, chromosome);
    until *adjusted* = *false*;
    return chromosome

Figure 6 shows the interface of the Genetic Mixer tool[4], that implements all the features of the presented Algorithm 1. We used the Genetic Mixer to generate examples in Figure 7.

Figure 6: Interface of the Genetic Mixer tool

Next, we evaluate the variability of the generated avatars and the performance of the algorithm.

4. EVALUATION

We have evaluated the generation algorithm on the diversity of the resulting avatar crowd depending on different

---

[4]see supporting video at http://youtu.be/Re7oVUFGis4

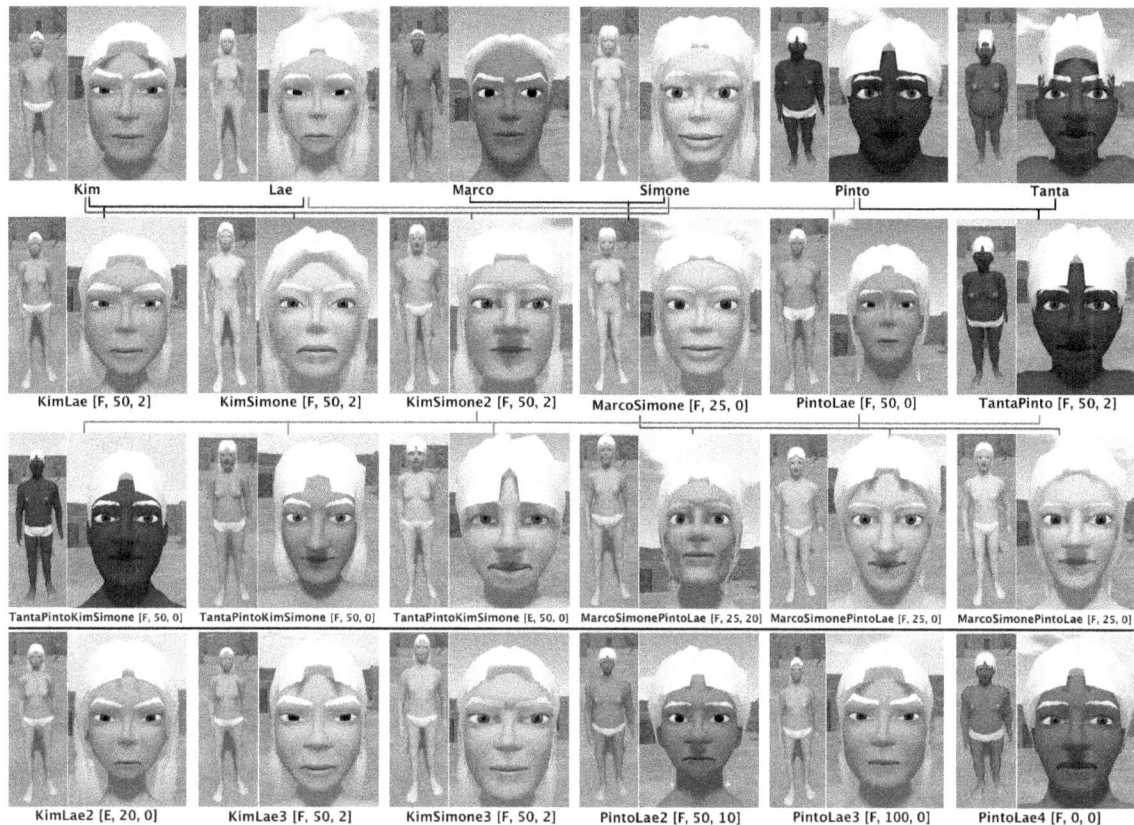

Figure 7: Avatars generated using our method. The top row forms the start population. The label of every figure contains following information: *Name [crossover, father-mother ratio, mutation level]*

input parameters of the algorithm, that is crossover operator, father-mother ratio and mutation level. We have also tested if characteristic ethnic features of individuals are preserved within their children. Some members of the resulting generated crowd are shown in Figure 7.

For our purposes, we have manually designed six avatars, three females and three males that form the base population of our virtual world. Two avatars are asian (Kim and Lae), two are african (Pinto and Tanta), one caucasian (Simone) and one arab (Marco).

To highlight our approach to identifying characteristic appearance features - we have designed the base population so that every avatar has white hair colour. One of the hypotheses that was tested during evaluation is that our algorithm will correctly identify this appearance feature as being characteristic for the given ethnicity and no or little mutation will be performed in relation to this feature, so that it is preserved in every member of the generated crowd.

We have isolated 200 visual features of each avatar, that are provided by OpenSimulator[5] and that define shape, skin, eyes and hair. Each of these visual features represents a gene in an avatar's chromosome. For the generation, we have used two crossover operators, *fuzzy* (marked as F in the avatar captions) and *exchange* (marked as E in the avatar caption). We have used different father-mother ratios and different mutation level. Each generated child is named by

combining the father's and mother's name (e.g. child of Kim and Lae is named KimLae).

In the first row of Figure 7, we see all six avatars from our base population. In the second row, we see their children. Our system was able to correctly identify hair color as an important characteristic feature of the generated ethnicity, so all the generated avatars have white hair. KimLae was generated using the *fuzzy* with the ratio set to 50%. We can clearly see the resemblance from both father and mother. She has her father's eyes, but her mother's chin. Nose width is somewhere between father and mother. We can clearly see that she is asian. The same parameters were set for TantaPinto and we can see that she is black, resembling both parents. If we now focus on KimSimone and her brother KimSimone2, we see that they are both generated using the same parameters with significantly different results. This is due to the random nature of fuzzy operator and the use of *mutation*, which was set to 2%. When we look at the grand-kids of the base population avatars we can see how their visual features are combined.

In the last row we present a selection of avatars that we generated during the generation of 3000 avatars from our base population. PintoLae2 is significantly different from others due to the high level of mutation set to 10%. It's evident from the results that the algorithm generates a large variety of visually acceptable avatars respecting the genetic inheritance of ancestor features. Although, we were able to generate 3000 avatars, we are unable to display them all at

---

[5]http://www.opensimulator.org (last access 09/2012)

once, as we are limited by the capabilities of the OpenSimulator allowing to host a maximum of 100 avatars, but recent research on using Distributed Scene Graphs (DSG) [8] allowes simultaneous participation of thousands of users.

We have also measured the average speed of generation of one avatar during the generation of crowd of avatars. The speed of the algorithm linearly depends on the length of the chromosome, that is its time complexity for m agents is $O(m \times n)$ with respect to the length of a chromosome n. We have generated 3000 different avatars, using the most complex *fuzzy* operator with mutation level set to 2% and on average the algorithm generated a new avatar in 305 ms. The generation was performed on a MacBook Pro with 2.6 GHz Intel Core 2 Duo processor and 4GB of RAM.

5. CONCLUSION AND DISCUSSION

We have presented an algorithm for generating a diverse ethnic group of unlimited size from a small sample of manually designed 3D avatars. Genetic principles of inheritance, crossover and mutation are applied to the sample population to create new visually unique group members. Predefined genotype rules allow us to preserve important appearance features that are characteristic for the given ethnicity.

Generating large ethnic groups is important in domains like virtual heritage [3], where not only avatars must look different, but also have to appear as members of the same culture. In virtual heritage it is often needed to interact with individual avatars and inspect them at close proximity, so the use of cloning or colour substitution (as in [13]) is not sufficient as it is likely to be noticed. Also, introducing diversity by using a fully random approach to modifying individual parameters (as in [10]) may result malformed avatars and would modify the important appearance features that define the ethnicity of the simulated group.

It is important to mention that in simulating ethnic groups it is undesired for generated agents to have very close resemblance with their "genetic parents". Thus, the proposed genetic algorithms approach is also more beneficial than a biological approach of [21] as it results increased diversity, more transparent execution and better control over results.

The key drawback of our method is that it requires to have avatars defined in parametric form and to allow for quick modification of individual avatar parameters on the fly. However, many modern game engines, virtual worlds as well as popular 3D modelling packages support parametric avatars and provide the corresponding visual tools.

Future work includes extending this approach to generating agents with diverse personalities, as well as conducting an advanced study similar to [13], where the diversity of the generated avatars, resemblance with ancestors and preservation of ethnicity are evaluated in a more formal manner.

6. ACKNOWLEDGMENTS

This work was supported by the Digital Humanities Research Program of School of Computing, Engineering and Mathematics in the University of Western Sydney, as well as Consolider (CSD2007-002), TIN2009-14702-C02-01/02 and TIN2011-24220 Spanish Research Projects.

7. REFERENCES

[1] B. Allen, B. Curless, and Z. Popović. The space of human body shapes: reconstruction and parameterization from range scans. In *SIGGRAPH 2003 Papers*, pages 587–594, New York, NY, USA, 2003. ACM.

[2] V. Blanz and T. Vetter. A morphable model for the synthesis of 3d faces. In *SIGGRAPH 2009 Papers*, pages 187–194, New York, NY, USA, 1999. ACM.

[3] A. Bogdanovych, K. Ijaz, and S. Simoff. The City of Uruk: Teaching Ancient History in a Virtual World. In *IVA 2012 Conference*, pages 28–35. Springer, 2012.

[4] D. DeCarlo, D. Metaxas, and M. Stone. An anthropometric face model using variational techniques. In *SIGGRAPH 1998 Papers*, pages 67–74, New York, NY, USA, 1998. ACM.

[5] D. Fogel. *Evolutionary Computation*. IEEE Press, New York, 1995.

[6] D. Goldberg. *Genetic algorithms in search, optimization, and machine learning*. Addison-wesley, 1989.

[7] J. H. Holland. *Adaptation in natural and artificial systems*. MIT Press, Cambridge, MA, USA, 1975.

[8] Intel. Intel increases opensim avatar capacity 20 fold. http://www.hypergridbusiness.com/2011/06/intel-increases-opensim-avatar-capacity-20-fold/.

[9] J. Koza. *Genetic Programming: On the Programming of Computers by Means of Natural Selection*. MIT Press, Cambridge, MA, 1992.

[10] M. Lewis. Evolving human figure geometry. Technical report, Ohio State University, 2000.

[11] N. Magnenat-Thalmann, H. Seo, and F. Cordier. Automatic modeling of virtual humans and body clothing. *Journal of Computer Science and Technology*, 19(5):575–584, 2004.

[12] J. Maim, B. Yersin, and D. Thalmann. Unique character instances for crowds. *Computer Graphics and Applications, IEEE*, 29(6):82–90, 2009.

[13] R. McDonnell, M. Larkin, B. Hernández, I. Rudomin, and C. O'Sullivan. Eye-catching crowds: saliency based selective variation. *ACM Trans. Graph.*, 28(3):55:1–55:10, July 2009.

[14] I. Rechenberg. *Evolutionsstrategie. Optimierung technischer Systeme nach Prinzipien der biologischen Evolution*. Frommann Holzboog, 1973.

[15] S. Robbins and M. Bell. *Second Life For Dummies*, chapter 5.2: Editing Your Avatar's Appearance. Wiley, 2008.

[16] H. Seo and N. Magnenat-Thalmann. An automatic modeling of human bodies from sizing parameters. In *Proceedings of the 2003 symposium on Interactive 3D graphics (I3D'03)*. ACM, 2003.

[17] S. Sivanandam and S. Deepa. *Introduction to genetic algorithms*. Springer Verlag, 2007.

[18] D. Thalmann. *Crowd simulation*. Wiley Online Library, 2007.

[19] J. Ventrella. Avatar Physics and Genetics. In *VW '00: Proceedings of the Second International Conference on Virtual Worlds*. Springer-Verlag, 07 2000.

[20] R. C. C. Vieira, C. A. Vidal, and J. B. Cavalcante-Neto. Reproducing virtual characters. *Computers and Graphics*, 36(2):80 – 91, 2012.

[21] R. C. C. Vieira, C. A. Vidal, and J. B. C. Neto. Simulation of genetic inheritance in the generation of virtual characters. In *Proceedings of Virtual Reality (VR'10) Conference*, pages 119–126. IEEE, 2010.

Bridging the Gap between Visual Exploration and Agent-Based Pedestrian Simulation in a Virtual Environment

Martin Brunnhuber
VRVis Research Center
Donau-City-Strasse 1
Vienna, Austria
brunn@vrvis.at

Helmut Schrom-Feiertag
Austrian Institute of
Technology
Giefinggasse 2
Vienna, Austria
helmut.schrom-
feiertag@ait.ac.at

Christian Luksch
VRVis Research Center
Donau-City-Strasse 1
Vienna, Austria
luksch@vrvis.at

Thomas Matyus
Austrian Institute of
Technology
Giefinggasse 2
Vienna, Austria
thomas.matyus@ait.ac.at

Gerd Hesina
VRVis Research Center
Donau-City-Strasse 1
Vienna, Austria
hesina@vrvis.at

ABSTRACT

We present a system to evaluate and improve visual guidance systems and signage for pedestrians inside large buildings. Given a 3D model of an actual building we perform agent-based simulations mimicking the decision making process and navigation patterns of pedestrians trying to find their way to predefined locations. Our main contribution is to enable agents to base their decisions on realistic three-dimensional visibility and occlusion cues computed from the actual building geometry with added semantic annotations (e.g. meaning of signs, or purpose of inventory), as well as an interactive visualization of simulated movement trajectories and accompanying visibility data tied to the underlying 3D model. This enables users of the system to quickly pinpoint and solve problems within the simulation by watching, exploring and understanding emergent behavior inside the building. This insight gained from introspection can in turn inform planning and thus improve the effectiveness of guidance systems.

Categories and Subject Descriptors

I.3.7 [**Computer Graphics**]: Three-Dimensional Graphics and Realism—*Visible line/surface algorithms*; I.6.7 [**Simulation and Modeling**]: Simulation Support Systems—*Environments*

Keywords

Human perception and performance, perceptual validation, virtual environments, pedestrian simulation, wayfinding

1. INTRODUCTION

Agent-based pedestrian simulations in virtual environments have recently become a powerful tool for planning and improving barrier-free environments in public buildings due to advances in both algorithms and available hardware solutions (see, e.g. [3]). Unfortunately, most of these simulation systems rely on a very simplified abstraction of the most active human sense during a way-finding process: the visual system. While this simplification may be sufficient to simulate an "average" person, the limitations associated with such approaches affect the proper simulation of handicapped or impaired people, whose visual scene perception and movement behavior differs significantly – although barrier-free access is of highest importance for them.

Another limiting aspect in this research field is the difficult analysis and interpretation of the simulation results: Due to the abstraction of the scene (e.g. to keep the simulation complexity within reasonable limits), usually only simple 2D visualizations are provided, making it hard to understand behavior and decision-making of an agent visually, and therefore leaving the interpretation of simulation results to an experienced expert in this field.

We propose a novel way to increase the importance of visual aspects in the field of agent-based pedestrian simulation by combining it with techniques from the area of Computer Graphics. By applying strategies for visibility calculations in semantically annotated 3D scenes as an additional input to the simulation system, autonomous way-finding and decision-making can be brought to a new level by taking plausible human visual perception into account. Moreover, we show how to visualize both simulation and visibility data in an interactive 3D environment, making it possible to easily understand the behavior of the simulated agent(s), verify the correctness and quality of the simulation, improve the simulation parameters through the gained insights, and simplify the planning and improvement of barrier-free buildings.

The application of our system is demonstrated in a real world example: The railway station "Vienna North" in Austria has been virtually reconstructed and semantically tagged, and used in a simulation scenario with both a walking person and a wheel chair driver as virtual agents.

The main contributions in our presented approach are therefore based on the interdisciplinarity prevalent in the system:

- We propose a 3D visibility evaluation method based on hardware-accelerated real-time techniques, that extends the typical 2D pedestrian simulation by introducing a plausible three-dimensional model for human visual perception as additional input for simulated agents.

- Together with semantic annotations in the 3D scene, this improved visual perception system supports decision-making in the pedestrian simulation, enabling a more realistic human movement behavior than in a simplified 2D abstraction.

- Finally, a real-time 3D visualization of simulated trajectory and visibility data helps to understand behavior and decisions of virtual agents and to verify and improve the simulation parameters and quality.

2. RELATED WORK

While the usage of computer graphics hardware to support decisions made by virtual agents in a person path simulation in a 3D environment *visually* is a new concept, there are still various publications and techniques related to our presented technique.

2.1 Visibility

Calculation of visibility is a major research topic in computer graphics as it is on the one hand needed for 3D applications to run efficiently and on the other hand to compute various visual effects (e.g. shadows). Especially culling techniques such as *frustum or occlusion culling* as described by Akenine-Moeller et al. [1] are widely used in 3D applications. An overview of visibility algorithms for walkthrough applications is given by Cohen-Or et al. [6]: They show various examples of visibility tests in computer graphics and indicate that occlusion culling and shadow algorithms have a lot in common – a fact that is heavily exploited in our work.

Ray tests are a further well-known technique for visibility calculation in computer graphics: An aggressive approach which is shown by Wonka et al. [21], where guided rays are used to detect visible triangles with a low amount of errors. A related approach to finding visibility of regions inside public buildings was presented by Brunnhuber et al. [5], where rays are used to mark visible regions of a complete crowd over a period of time. Their method requires a long processing time and produces only an approximative visualization of visibility. The view blocking aspects of other persons do not receive any attention in their work, but the views of every simulated person are accumulated into a so-called visibility map in order to point out well-noticed parts of the environment.

Shadows are essential for a realistic look of a rendered image. In [9], a recent state-of-the-art overview on techniques

and research in real-time shadows is given. Shadow mapping, a widely used real-time shadow technique, was first presented 1978 by Williams [20] and consecutively refined in terms of quality and hardware adoptions. The basic idea is to first store a discretized version of the scene depth rendered from the light source view into a texture and then compare its distance to the light source with the stored depth values for each screen space fragment. Whenever the stored distance is smaller, the fragment lies in shadow. Hourcade and Nicolas [12] propose to store object IDs in the texture instead of depth values, so that the shadow evaluation is only based on an ID comparison, making the use of a depth bias unnecessary. In our work, this approach is used in different variations. A key novelty in our work is the transfer of the basic idea of the shadow mapping algorithm, i.e. the hardware-accelerated mapping of a texture containing visibility from a certain view point to the domain of person path simulations, where it is used for visibility identification of objects in a 3D environment.

2.2 Crowd Rendering

Tecchia et al. [17] describe several aspects and methods used for crowd rendering. Topics like collision detection and behavior modeling are tackled in this work, explaining the major aspects of crowd rendering in a detailed way. In our work, we use the technique described by Dudasch [7] to visualize large crowds with DirectX *hardware instancing* and animation data provided by a texture-lookup.

2.3 Simulation

Recent advances in computational technologies have led to the development of application-specific simulation models focusing on different aspects of the collective behavior, using different modeling techniques. It can be distinguished roughly between two broad areas of crowd simulations. The first area is high-quality visualization for movie productions or games, where usually realism of the behavior model is not the priority (for a survey see [18]). These applications aim at a convincing visual result.

The second group focuses on realism of behavioral aspects with usually simple 2D visualization like evacuation or crowd dynamic simulations. In this area, the behavior represented in the simulations is usually restricted to a narrow range with efforts to quantitatively validate the fit of results to real-world observations of particular situations [19]. Visualization is used to help understanding simulation results, but it is not crucial and in most cases a schematic representation with colored dots is used.

Techniques employed in both areas can be distinguished between the different levels of description related to Mirosław [14] ranging from *macroscopic models* that do not distinguish individuals and describes characteristics at the level of flow-speed-density equation (such as the models implemented in Pedflow, Space Syntax methods, Pedroute), *mesoscopic models* at the level of the statistical description and *microscopic models* at the level of interacting entities using cellular automata such as STEPS, PedGo or the social force paradigm such as Legion, the pedestrian module of VISSIM and CAST. Agent based microscopic modeling is an approach for simulating pedestrians as single autonomous individuals by supplying a detailed representation of their behavior, including decisions on various levels (e.g. related to orientation and navigation) and interactions with other pedestrians in the crowd. The goal is to reproduce realistic single autonomous and emergent collective crowd behavior.

Compared to other models, social force-based models have been found to describe pedestrian behavior more realistically [2]. The most prominent social force model is Helbing's model [10] which is also used in the presented approach. This model has been calibrated and adapted to real world data by Johansson et al. [13]. The social force model was also extended by Musse to include individualism [4]. Pelechano et al. [15] merged rule-based and social force-based models and incorporated psychological state into the pedestrian simulation model. Shao and Terzopoulos [16] used a complex cognitive and behavior model for planning, but did not attempt realistic small-scale motion behavior like the social force model.

Many currently available simulation models are based on the assumption that all pedestrians know the infrastructure and consequently all pedestrians choose the fastest path to reach their goal.

Not every pedestrian is familiar with the infrastructure and wayfinding abilities are influenced by a number of physical, psychological, and physiological factors that will influence the ability of people to detect and correctly interpret the information conveyed by the signs. It is therefore important to include wayfinding in pedestrian simulation to achive realistic simulation results.

3. SYSTEM OVERVIEW

The presented work is separated into three modules: *Visible Object Identification*, *Simulation*, and *Visualization*. The data flow is depicted in Figure 1. For each simulation cycle, the positions of the simulated persons (*agents*) are sent together with a query for visible objects of a certain person (*viewer*) to the *Visible Object Identification* module (see Section 4). The visible object identification uses the 3D model of the environment to provide visibility information of objects to the *Simulation*.

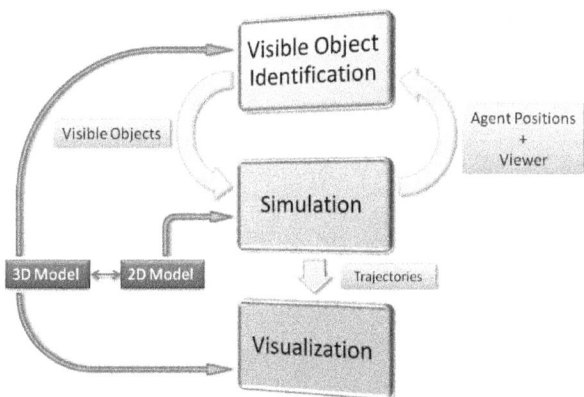

Figure 1: Visual description of the System which combines a pedestrian simulation using real-time rendering techniques to identify visible objects in a virtual 3D environment and a visualization module for visibility exploration and evaluation of the simulation results.

This information is used by the *Simulation* to calculate the next position of the viewer in a correlating 2D model (see Section 5). The simulation saves trajectory data of

each single simulated agent and sends it to the *Visualization* module, where corresponding walking paths are visualized in the 3D model, making a visual evaluation of the results possible (see Section 6). Together with the visualization of the calculated 3D visibility of the environment, decisions made inside the simulation can easily be reproduced and understood.

The visualization module in the described system provides two different modes to show and explore visibility: The *viewing field visualization* shows visible regions of the viewer from a certain time step of the simulation. It is possible to step through time interactively to explore the data in a 3D environment and retrace decisions made in the simulation. The *attention region visualization* shows visibility over a time range of interest. Accumulated visibilities are shown in this view to see which regions are in main focus of the viewer and which ones are barely recognized during his way through the building. Section 6 describes both visualization modes in more detail.

4. VISIBILITY CALCULATION

The definition of an extended visibility model to emulate human sight in a virtual 3D environment is a major extension for an improved simulation with plausible behavior inside unfamiliar public buildings. By extending commonly used 2D methods with three-dimensional visibility information, occluding objects, moving crowd and access to semantic information can be taken into account in a realistic way.

4.1 Visibility Model

To describe the identification of objects, a visibility model based on the research of Xie et al. [22] has been defined. In the used model, objects in the center of a person's field of view should be recognized with full visual power (i.e. a defined value of perception - full visual power describes regions which are completely recognized by the viewer). The outer border of the viewing field is bound by an ellipse with a horizontal and vertical viewing angle (α, β) where visual power reaches zero. A falloff of visual power is modeled by a density function v dependent on the location relative to the center of the viewing field. Figure 2 illustrates this model. In the implemented examples the density function v describes a linear falloff over the viewing field, and the angles (α, β) have been set to $(50°, 30°)$.

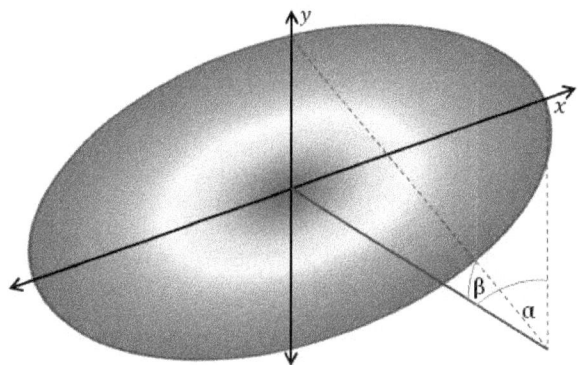

Figure 2: Model of the visual power density function v over an elliptic viewing field parameterized by the angles (α, β).

In the presented approach, visibility of an object i is assumed to be equivalent to its projected area in the viewing field weighted by the described visual power v at each differential surface fragment $p(x, y)$. The accumulated result described by the surface integral over the projected visible object in Equation 1 gives an absolute visibility value per object V_i. This allows the simulation to decide together with additional semantic information whether an object is recognized or not.

$$V_i = \iint\limits_D v(x, y) \cdot p(x, y) \mathrm{d}x \mathrm{d}y \qquad (1)$$

4.2 Crowd Rendering on Various Paths

Inclusion of crowd rendering in the visualization and visibility object identification leads to a more realistic analysis of the viewer's environment recognition. The simulation calculates every position of the viewer person and the crowd to get point lists for the visualization of movement over time. For accurate visibility on the paths all simulated persons are handled. In order to animate large numbers of individuals we use DirectX *hardware instancing* as described by Dudasch [7]. With this method, the same pedestrian model is efficiently reused multiple times at varying locations with different parameters. Individual animation data is provided by a lookup-texture containing key-frame transformations.

With the described techniques a realistic environment for the viewer person inside a crowd is created. Pedestrians may block the viewing field of the viewer and visibility visualization and calculation for simulation becomes more realistic.

4.3 Visible Object Identification

A 3D model of the environment allows to accurately calculate possibly visible parts within that model from a single viewpoint. Object IDs are set for every object reasonable for decisions of the viewer in the simulation. These IDs are connected to semantic information to identify the reaction on the object recognized. The concept of visibility calculation for lights in real-time rendering applications - "Whatever the light sees is illuminated; what it does not see is in shadow." [1] - has been adapted for the calculation and visualization of visibility. In particular, an ID-based approach similar to the technique of Hourcade and Nicolas [12] is used.

The viewer is the reference point of the visibility calculation and can be seen as a light source. The GPU is used to rasterize visible objects with the ID values from a viewpoint into an ID buffer. Therefore the simulation is able to make decisions based on recognized items. The viewing field of the viewer is bound by a horizontal and vertical angle α and β defining a perspective projection P. Together with the position of the head $\mathbf{l}$ and viewing direction $\mathbf{e}$, which define a view-space V, an image as seen by the viewer can be rendered using the view-projection transformation VP. The visibility model is used to accumulate a meaningful visibility value per object: Each pixel in the rendered image represents a discrete visible surface fragment of an object with equal area in the viewing field. The given weight of the viewing density function v at the pixel location adds viewing power to the visibility value of the object defined by the ID of the rendered pixel. Summing all discrete visibility values of an object requires grouping and accumulation of all pixels of the rendered image. This is no typical rendering step, but with GPGPU computations of modern graphics hardware this task can be processed in real-time.

The visibility value gives an absolute measurement of the objects visibility. From the object ID, the simulation retrieves additional predefined semantic information, and together with the distance from the viewer, the position of the object center and its viewing angle, an object can be identified as a sign and whether it is close enough to be read or not as mentioned by Xie et al. [22]. With the ID identification it is additionally possible to set any object of interest for the scene. The viewer is able to handle different tasks like buying a ticket at a railway station or to look for a shop to get something to eat. Such information is important for the simulation which is based on the defined needs of the viewer to decide his way realistically based on the seen environment.

5. VISIBILITY AIDED SIMULATION

Pedestrian motion behavior is often described in three different levels [11]. The *strategic level* determines the arrival time of the pedestrian at the infrastructure, its entry position and the pedestrian's goal (e.g. going to the train). In our case this level is not modeled but the origin and the final goal (e.g. getting a certain train) are predefined. The *tactical level* describes the route a pedestrian will choose to move through the infrastructure. This is where the 3D visibility calculation as described in Section 4.3 comes into play by making it possible for a pedestrian to select a way based on his current view. The *operational level* calculates the actual movements towards the next goal, including collision avoidance. In this work, an agent-based approach is used to assign and vary the characteristics of individual pedestrians as required. The model development will be supported by empirical data collection providing data of people's real life bahavior. This empirical data collection enhances the understanding of parameters and their influence to individuals' decisions to choose a certain route.

5.1 Operational Level

Human motion on an operational level is modeled based on a social force model [10]. Force models provide explicit equations for the movement of pedestrians. They are defined in continuous time and space by providing differential equations for the acceleration of an agent. Acceleration is then integrated once in order to obtain velocity, and integrated twice in order to obtain the new position of the agent. Using an analogy from physics, acceleration is identified with force. Different forces act on each agent i as follows:

$$F_i = F_i^a + F_i^p + F_i^w, \qquad (2)$$

where F_i^a denotes the attractive force directed towards the pedestrian's goal, F_i^p denotes the repulsive forces directed away from other pedestrians and F_i^w prevents the pedestrian from colliding with walls or other obstacles. As a first approximation the same equations are used for modeling pedestrian and wheel chair movements varying two parameters: 1) The desired speed of the agent on which the attractive force is depending and 2) the body height on which the repulsive forces are depending.

5.2 Tactical Level - Wayfinding

Route planning and navigation are intuitive skills for pedestrians, but it is no easy task to simulate these abilities in a virtual environment. In conventional simulation models the fastest path is computed or stochastic rules are applied to get a route from the origin to the destination.

For the tactical level field tests at the train station Vienna North using thinking aloud voice recording and time-motion tracking were made. A detailed description of measuring behavior can be found in [8]. The results identified elements of the orientation system in the built environment that respondents use to navigate.

In the proposed approach the cognition of guidance systems is modeled using insights from field tests and creates the possibility to simulate agent navigation through an unknown infrastructure using present signage. No routing graph has to be defined in advance, only the visual information obtained from the 3D model is used to find the route to the destination. The order of tasks (e.g. buying a ticket, getting departure information) which has to be performed by the agent on his way through the station is predefined. Paths between goals have to be found according to the following wayfinding algorithm: Whenever the agent cannot see the next goal (i.e. the location of the next task) from his current position he looks (see previous section) for the nearest sign which is close enough to be readable and indicates the direction to the next goal. If he cannot find any appropriate sign he moves on with current speed and direction for one simulated second and then starts his search again. After finishing a task when no information referring to the next goal is available the agent moves back to the last visited sign. Information about the visible environment is gained by using visibility calculation and information identification as described in section 4.3.

6. VISUALIZATION

For a proper exploration of visible regions and recognized areas during the simulation, two visualization modes have been developed.

6.1 Viewing Field

An explorative 3D visualization of the viewer's sight at a specified time step is the first mode in the presented system. The computation of this visualization is similar to the visibility calculation in Section 4.3 using an ID buffer. The visual power as described in the model of Section 4.1 is visualized in real-time. According to the visibility model, the visibility value of a surface fragment is dependent on its projected area in the viewing field. Since the visualization is directly applied on the object surface in 3D, the projected area in the viewing field of a person at location $\mathbf{l}$ is calculated with the fragment position $\mathbf{f}_p$ and its orientation $\mathbf{f}_n$ as follows:

$$p(f) = \frac{\mathbf{f}_n \mathbf{s}}{d^2}, \quad \text{where} \quad d = |\mathbf{l} - \mathbf{f}_p| \text{ and } \mathbf{s} = \frac{\mathbf{l} - \mathbf{f}_p}{|\mathbf{l} - \mathbf{f}_p|}, \quad (3)$$

where d is the distance and $\mathbf{s}$ is the normalized direction vector to the viewers head at l. The projected area $p(f)$ is then weighted by the visual power density function v which is evaluated in the parameterized viewing field (Figure 2). Therefore the surface fragment position f_p is transformed by the view projection transformation VP giving the location used to calculate the visual power.

The resulting values are normalized depending on a user specified parameter which defines a distance that still allows recognition of an area in the center of the viewing field. This allows to visualize recognition of different types of objects,

e.g. a sign is specified to be readable at a distance of 10 meters. The visual power in visible regions is colored based on a one dimensional transfer function. Figure 3 shows the viewer and the color coded region in sight. Another person blocks the sight of the viewer, but the sign at the exit is still perfectly recognized. By the exploration of the viewer walking around in the public building, while his viewing field is visualized, decisions made by the simulation can be explored.

Figure 3: A viewer looks to the exit of the station - his view is partly blocked by another person.

6.2 Attention Regions Visualization

The attention regions visualization is based on the viewing field visualization described above, but shows the accumulated visibility of the viewer person over time. Although this is a computationally expensive task, the time required for computing is relatively short (see Section 7.2) due to further exploitation of hardware acceleration, and depends on the number of time-steps in the specified range. The GPU is used to store the accumulated visibility power in a previously assigned texture atlas, allowing real-time exploration after precomputation.

In contrast to the single time step visualization, the computation is performed in texture space. Therefore, for each texel in the texture atlas, the corresponding surface position $\mathbf{f}_p$ and orientation $\mathbf{f}_n$ need to be precomputed. For every time step, a visibility calculation like in the first visualization mode takes place and the results are accumulated. Occlusion is again calculated using the shadow mapping algorithm. While the evaluation of a single time step can be performed in real-time, this visualization is calculated at a rate of several hundred time-steps per second.

7. RESULTS

The combined approach of simulation and visualization makes it possible to evaluate visibility of the guidance system and to show areas with leaks of guidance information for people unfamiliar with the infrastructure, especially for elderly and handicapped people with reduced reception capabilities. The agent moves through the station using the described wayfinding algorithm depending on the visibility of the guidance information. This could be shortened by a reduced agent vision or a very dense crowd, especially for wheel chair drivers with a lower point of view. The used 3D environment including 3D human models for the simulated agents gives the opportunity to calculate possibly occluded sections from one viewpoint realistically.

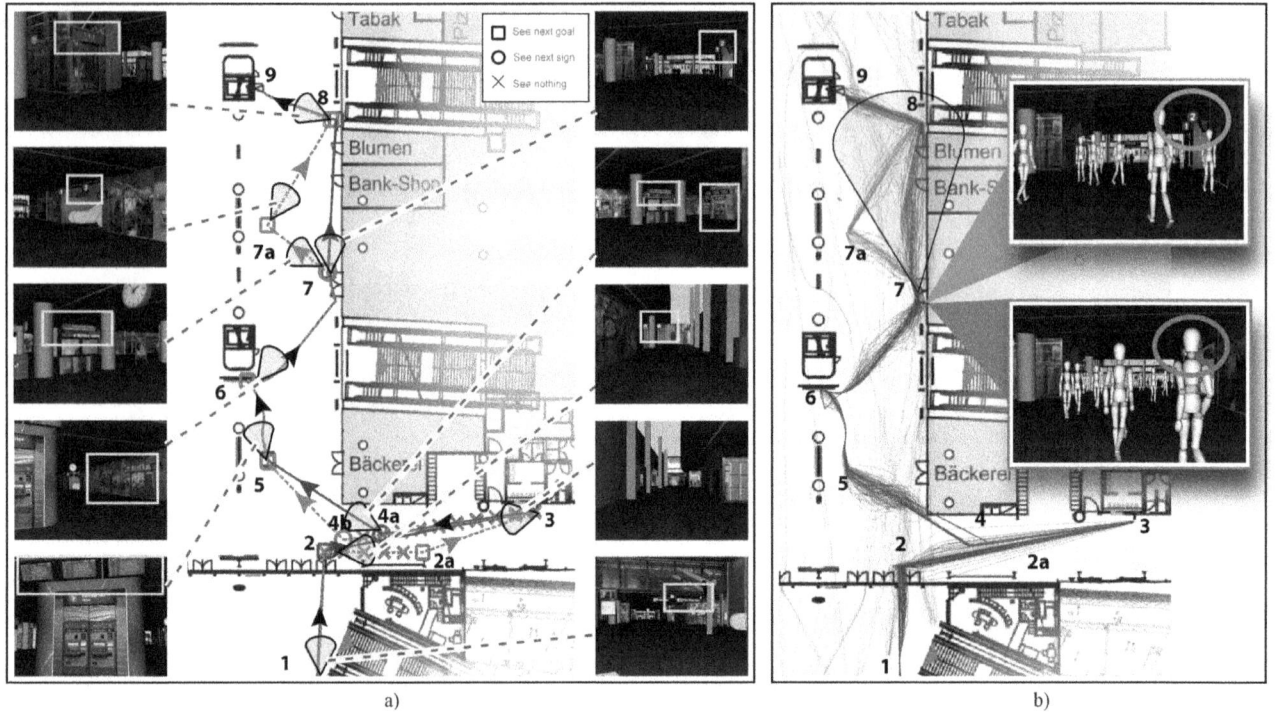

a)   b)

Figure 4: Trajectories of simulated wheel chair drivers. The left hand side (a) shows a scenario in the empty hall comparing full (blue) and reduced reception capabilities (red), Circles indicate positions where the agents can read a sign, squares where the agent can see the next goal and 'x' where the agent cannot find any helpful information and therefore moves on. The right hand side (b) shows the morning peak hour scenario with direct routes (blue) and detours to point 7a (red), caused by the occlusions of signage through the dense crowd.

We show the results achieved with the visibility aided simulation in Section 7.1, and discuss the visual output and the performance of the visualization in Section 7.2.

7.1 Visibility Aided Simulation Results

In order to demonstrate the wayfinding algorithm's applicability to real-world environments, different scenarios have been simulated and the results are shown in Figure 4. All scenarios are based on the same tasks: A wheel chair driver starting at the elevator exit into the main hall of the "Praterstern" station has to reach the train to "Stockerau". Apart from getting the departure information and buying a ticket, he needs to go to the toilet and wants to get some snacks for the journey. The order of activities is predefined: First go to the toilet (3), then buy the ticket (6), look for a monitor to get the departure information, go to the supermarket (7) and finally, use the elevator (9) that brings you up to the platform where the train is departing.

The three scenarios for the wheel chair driver differ in the level of crowdedness and the agent's vision: Scenario 1) empty hall, full vision with no visual impairments, scenario 2) empty hall, half vision meaning half of the viewing distance shown in 4a and scenario 3) crowded hall according to the morning peak (7:15-8:15), full vision to show the applicability of the approach for occlusions in crowds.

Figure 4a) shows the results of the first two scenarios. In both cases the agents start at position 1 where they can get an overview of the hall. The overhead sign which indicates the direction to the toilet at position 2 is readable for both

of them. Having walked past the sign they both stop and search for the toilet in the given direction. The agent with full vision can read the sign at entrance of the toilet at position 3 already from here and moves directly to the toilet. The agent with reduced vision moves on in the given direction searching five times for the toilet until position 2a where he can read the toilet sign at position 3. Leaving the toilet both agents cannot find any helpful information. Therefore they move back to the last visited sign. At position 4a the agent with full vision can already read the sign at position 5 which indicates the direction to the ticket machine. The second agent needs to move to position 4b where he is near enough to read the sign at position 5. Having reached position 5 both can see the ticket machine at position 6 where they buy their tickets. Since a monitor is mounted above the ticket machine they get the departure information there as well. The train to "Stockerau" is leaving at platform 2. From position 6, the entrance of the supermarket at position 7 is visible for both and they move directly there. Leaving the supermarket the agent with full vision can read the sign at the staircase to platform 2 (position 8), the second agent can only read the sign at position 7a which indicates the direction to platform 2. At position 7a he can read the sign at position 8 as well. Having realized that at position 8 there are only stairs and escalators they look around and find the elevator to platform 2 at position 9.

Figure 4b) shows the results of the third scenario where the agent with full vision is moving through the hall during the morning peak hour (7:15-8:15). Hundred simulation runs with slightly different start times were selected and the trajectories are plotted in the single figure (blue lines) to show the differences in dense crowds (light gray lines). In all runs the trajectories till the supermarket (position 7) are identical among each other and also with the trajectory of the agent with full vision in Scenario 1. The only difference at position 4 after the toilet back to the main hall comes from the occlusion of the sign at position 5 through the pedestrian flow crossing in front of the agent.

After leaving the supermarket at position 7, the agents are following different paths. In 59 of the 100 simulation runs the agent had free sight to the platform 2 sign at position 8 (see red circle in the upper screen-shot) and moves on like in scenario 1 (blue path). Whereas, for the agent in the other 41 simulation runs the sign is occluded behind one or more pedestrians and therefore the agent makes a detour via the sign at position 7a (red path) which indicates the direction to platform 2. The two screenshots in Figure 4b) shows the two different situations with free sight and occlusion through to other pedestrians to the sign.

Each scenario showed different routes compared to the shortest route due to differences in the range of vision and crowdedness. Especially for wheelchair users crowdedness has a significant impact. In 41% of our simulation runs crowds occlude signage or form obstacles leading to a higher rate of maneuver, longer routes and travel discomfort. The approach has shown to be capable of simulating handicapped people finding their way through a transport infrastructure using signage information only and provides an outlook about the impact of occlusions through dense crowds.

7.2 Visualization Results

During our tests for the *Attention Regions Visualization* (Section 6.2), the system needed about 1.3 seconds to accumulate 750 timesteps, using a shadow map resolution of 512x512 pixels and a 2048x2048 pixel texture atlas. The testing system was a PC with an Intel Core2Quad processor with 2.83 GHz, 8 GB RAM and a Geforce GTX 280 Graphics Card with 1 GB RAM. The main scene was the model of the mentioned railway station Vienna North with more than 140000 triangles.

Figure 5: Color-coded visualization of the station over the whole simulated time-range showing the degree of the viewer's attention at different regions.

Figure 5 shows a section of the guidance system in the second visualization mode. The ticket machine and the moni-

tors above are coded in red, meaning well recognized by the viewer. Information tables and the guidance system above did not get much attention. If this sign had been important for the viewer to perform his given task (e.g. finding a ticket machine on the way to the bus station), this would indicate a problem in the guidance system. Figure 6 gives another example of visualized attention regions during a simulated walk to the bus station

8. CONCLUSION AND FUTURE WORK

The presented work shows a prototype which combines human behavior simulation with real-time rendering and visualization. This cooperation of modern technologies of different disciplines enables an agent to find its way autonomously through a building based on visible information. The developed prototype has been applied to a realistic scenario to demonstrate the functionality of the algorithms. A 3D model of a railway station creates the basis for visibility calculation and visualization. 3D rendering including human 3D models representing the simulated agents gives at the one hand the opportunity for the simulation to calculate possibly occluded sections from a viewpoint realistically and at the other hand to explore the simulation results and to analyze the efficiency of the guidance system in public buildings.

Figure 6: Attention regions in the station visited by a simulated viewer. Computation time for time-ranged based visualization: 1.3 sec including 750 time-steps in a scene with about 140.000 triangles

Visible regions in public buildings can furthermore not only be seen as guidance systems, but also as an indicator for the quality of locations where advertisements and shops are placed. This and similar analyses can easily be performed with the help of the visualized quantifications of human perception.

The calculation of visible sections can probably be improved by using psychological effects, like attention. Lighted or animated signs for example catch the focus of people, and active search for guidance system elements leads to different regions of interest. Another interesting aspect of human vision is how long an object is in focus and if visibility was long enough for recognition. The presented approach already includes this aspect with the attention region visualization. With advanced techniques in the field of temporal coherence it might be possible to explore such regions in real-time and include time dependent object recognition in the simulation.

Using visualization tools to improve a simulation seems to be a promising start for further research – especially in the case of understanding and analyzing movements of impaired people. While visual analysis of simulated trajectories and views of a person in a wheelchair has already given new insights and made it possible to improve the corresponding simulation parameters, our visual object identification system could easily be extended to account for visually impaired people (e.g. near-sighted persons could be simulated by reducing the visual power for objects in far distance, ...), having an immediate positive impact on the planning of easily accessible public buildings.

Visualization of visibility and the calculation of recognized objects in a virtual environment could moreover be used in different simulation scenarios. Traffic simulations might be improved with a derivation of the presented approach to see if cars are recognizable in narrow curves or to evaluate the positions of signs on streets.

9. ACKNOWLEDGMENTS

This work is part of the project MASIMO and has been funded by the research program line ways2go within the framework of the Austrian strategic initiative IV2Splus Intelligent Transport Systems and Services plus under the project number 819192.

10. REFERENCES

[1] T. Akenine-Möller, E. Haines, and N. Hoffman. *Real-Time Rendering 3rd Edition*. A. K. Peters, Ltd., Natick, MA, USA, 2008.

[2] D. Bauer. Comparing pedestrian movement simulation models for a crossing area based on real world data. In R. D. Peacock, E. D. Kuligowski, and J. D. Averill, editors, *Pedestrian and Evacuation Dynamics*, pages 547–556. Springer US, Boston, MA, 2011.

[3] N. Brändle, T. Matyus, M. Brunnhuber, G. Hesina, H. Neuschmied, and M. Rosner. Realistic interactive pedestrian simulation and visualization for virtual 3D environments. In *Proceedings of the 15th International Conference on Virtual Systems and Multimedia*, 2009.

[4] A. Braun, S. R. Musse, L. P. L. d. Oliveira, and B. E. J. Bodmann. Modeling individual behaviors in crowd simulation. In *16th International Conference on Computer Animation and Social Agents (CASA 2003)*, page 143, Los Alamitos, CA, USA, 2003. IEEE Computer Society.

[5] M. Brunnhuber, G. Hesina, R. F. Tobler, and S. Mantler. Interactive person path analysis in reconstructed public buildings. In *Proceedings of the 2009 Spring Conference on Computer Graphics*, SCCG '09, pages 145–150, New York, NY, USA, 2009. ACM.

[6] D. Cohen-Or, Y. L. Chrysanthou, C. T. Silva, and F. Durand. A survey of visibility for walkthrough applications. *IEEE TRANSACTIONS ON VISUALIZATION AND COMPUTER*, 9(3), 2003.

[7] B. Dudash. Animated crowd rendering, 2007.

[8] V. Egger, H. Schrom-Feiertag, L. Ehrenstrasser, and G. Telepak. Creating a richer data source for 3d pedestrian flow simulations in public transport. In *Proceedings of the 7th International Conference on Methods and Techniques in Behavioral Research*, MB '10, pages 20:1–20:4, New York, NY, USA, 2010. ACM.

[9] E. Eisemann, M. Schwarz, U. Assarsson, and M. Wimmer. *Real-Time Shadows*. A.K. Peters, 2011.

[10] D. Helbing and P. Molnar. Social force model for pedestrian dynamics. *Physical Review E*, 51:4282–4286, 1995.

[11] S. P. Hoogendoorn and P. Bovy. Pedestrian route-choice and activity scheduling theory and models. *Transportation Research, Part B: Methodological*, 38:169–190, 2004.

[12] J. C. Hourcade and A. Nicolas. Algorithms for antialiased cast shadows. *Computers & Graphics*, 9(3):259–265, 1985.

[13] A. Johansson and D. Helbing. Analysis of empirical trajectory data of pedestrians. In W. W. F. Klingsch, C. Rogsch, A. Schadschneider, and M. Schreckenberg, editors, *Pedestrian and Evacuation Dynamics 2008*, pages 203–214. Springer Berlin Heidelberg, Berlin, Heidelberg, 2010.

[14] L. Mirosław. Microscopic, mesoscopic and macroscopic descriptions of complex systems. *Probabilistic Engineering Mechanics*, 26(1):54–60, Jan. 2011.

[15] N. Pelechano, J. M. Allbeck, and N. I. Badler. Controlling individual agents in high-density crowd simulation. In *Proceedings of the 2007 ACM SIGGRAPH/Eurographics symposium on Computer animation*, pages 99–108, San Diego, California, 2007. Eurographics Association.

[16] W. Shao and D. Terzopoulos. Autonomous pedestrians. *Graph. Models*, 69(5-6):246–274, 2007.

[17] F. Tecchia, C. Loscos, and Y. Chrysanthou. Visualizing crowds in real-time. *Computer Graphics Forum*, 21:753–765, 2002.

[18] D. Thalmann and S. R. Musse. *Crowd simulation*. Springer, 2007.

[19] P. A. Thompson and E. W. Marchant. Testing and application of the computer model 'SIMULEX'. *Fire Safety Journal*, 24(2):149 – 166, 1995.

[20] L. Williams. Casting curved shadows on curved surfaces. *SIGGRAPH Comput. Graph.*, 12:270–274, August 1978.

[21] P. Wonka, M. Wimmer, K. Zhou, S. Maierhofer, G. Hesina, and A. Reshetov. Guided visibility sampling. *ACM Trans. Graph*, page 502, 2006.

[22] H. Xie, L. Filippidis, S. Gwynne, E. R. Galea, D. Blackshields, and P. J. Lawrence. Signage legibility distances as a function of observation angle. *Journal of Fire Protection Engineering*, 17(1):41–64, Feb. 2007.

Real-time Physical Modelling of Character Movements with Microsoft Kinect

Hubert P. H. Shum
School of Computing, Engineering and
Information Sciences
Northumbria University
Newcastle, United Kingdom
hubert.shum@northumbria.ac.uk

Edmond S. L. Ho
Department of Computer Science
Hong Kong Baptist University
Kowloon Tong, Hong Kong SAR
edmond@comp.hkbu.edu.hk

ABSTRACT

With the advancement of motion tracking hardware such as the Microsoft Kinect, synthesizing human-like characters with real-time captured movements becomes increasingly important. Traditional kinematics and dynamics approaches perform sub-optimally when the captured motion is noisy or even incomplete. In this paper, we proposed a unified framework to control physically simulated characters with live captured motion from Kinect. Our framework can synthesize any posture in a physical environment using external forces and torques computed by a PD controller. The major problem of Kinect is the incompleteness of the captured posture, with some degree of freedom (DOF) missing due to occlusions and noises. We propose to search for a best matched posture from a motion database constructed in a dimensionality reduced space, and substitute the missing DOF to the live captured data. Experimental results show that our method can synthesize realistic character movements from noisy captured motion. The proposed algorithm is computationally efficient and can be applied to a wide variety of interactive virtual reality applications such as motion-based gaming, rehabilitation and sport training.

Categories and Subject Descriptors

I.3.7 [**Computer Graphics**]: Three-Dimensional Graphics and Realism—*Virtual reality*

Keywords

Real-time motion synthesis, Microsoft Kinect, physical simulation, virtual reality

1. INTRODUCTION

Synthesizing natural movements for virtual characters has been an active research area in past decades. In particular, using captured human motion to control virtual characters

is getting more popular, thanks to the advancement of motion acquisition hardware. However, many kinematics-based control algorithms such as Motion Graph [12] require carefully crafted/cleaned motion. When synthesizing character movements from a stream of real-time captured motions such as those from the Microsoft Kinect, the result is usually sub-optimal due to the noise and incompleteness of the data. Simply replaying the captured motions would result in jittery movements and awkward joint orientations. Furthermore, the synthesized characters cannot react to external forces or interact with physically simulated objects, which degrades the user experience in virtual reality applications.

On the other hand, dynamics controllers that are originally proposed for robotic controls provide alternative methods to synthesis realistic character movements. Locomotion controllers such as [5] can track a series of postures and optimize for dynamically stable movements. The synthesized characters are guaranteed to be physically correct and can response to external perturbations. The major problem is that users have limited control over the resultant movements, since the simulation is strictly governed by physical laws. Some movements such as standing with one leg are very difficult to be dynamically reproduced without accurate information about the body mass and fictional force. Furthermore, motion captured from real-time systems usually contains a lot of noise, which can dramatically weaken the balance of the dynamically simulated character.

In this paper, we propose a unified framework to control characters with real-time captured motion from the Microsoft Kinect. We propose to track an input motion with a physically simulated character. Unlike the robotics simulation algorithms that use joint torques to drive a robot, our method controls the character with external forces and torques computed by a PD controller, which supports the balance of the character and enables it to perform any posture. Our method combines the advantage of kinematics and dynamics simulation. On one hand, it creates smooth and plausible movements that tightly resemble the user performed motions. On the other hand, it allows the simulated character reacting to external forces and interacting with the virtual environment.

The major problem of controlling characters with live captured motion from Kinect, or any capturing systems in general, is the noise and the incompleteness of the motions. During capture, some joint information may be missing because of occlusion or the restricted capturing volume. What is worse is that the number of tracking points in Kinect is very limited. Losing one point practically means losing both position and orientation of one joint, making it impossible to control a complete virtual character. To tackle this problem, we propose an efficient method based on Principal Component Analysis (PCA) to search for a similar posture in a motion database and substitute the missing information. This ensures the robustness of the system and relieves the requirement of clean input motion.

Experimental results show that realistic character movements can be synthesized from noisy captured motion. As the characters are physically synthesized, they react to external forces, and can interact with virtual objects. The proposed algorithm is computationally efficient, and can simulate multiple characters in real-time. Apart from motion-based gaming, our system is best to be applied in virtual reality applications such as those involving rehabilitation and sport training.

The rest of the paper is organized as follow. We first review the related works in motion synthesis based on user control signals and physical simulations in Section 2. We then explain the modelling of the physical environment in Section 4. We further explain the construction and usage of the motion database in Section 5. The core of the framework explained in Section 6 is a posture solver that involves both positional controls and rotational controls. Section 7 details how to improve the accuracy of the simulation with motion retargeting. Section 8 presents the experimental results. Finally, in Section 9, we conclude the paper, as well as discuss the limitations and future research directions.

2. RELATED WORK

Controlling the movement of virtual characters has been a popular research area in last two decades. The existing motion synthesis techniques can be divided into two categories: data-driven approaches and physics-based simulations. We first review the previous work in using live captured body movements of the user for controlling virtual characters. Then, we review researches in dynamics simulations using the proportional-derivative (PD) controller, which is a fast and effective way to simulate human motions.

2.1 Intuitive Control for Virtual Characters

Controlling the full body motion of the virtual characters is a challenging problem as the number of Degrees of Freedom (DOF) of the character is usually high. While techniques such as Motion Graphs [11, 12] have been widely used for controlling characters with pre-captured motions, they control characters with offline captured motions. In this research, we are more interested in algorithms that can deal with live captures.

Previous works try to control the full body motion with low-dimensional signals such as the positions of a few reflective markers [3], the readings of a small number of inertial sensors attached to the upper body [14], and the readings from a few 3D accelerometers attached to the limbs [23, 25]. The motion of the character can be estimated by referencing a motion database according to the low-dimensional signals. However, the resultant quality depends heavily on the size and quality of the database, as only a limited DOF are captured during run-time. With the Microsoft Kinect, it is now possible to capture motion with more DOF that can contribute to the synthesis quality. Shiratori et al. [22] propose to attach Wii controllers on a user's legs and synthe-

size walking cycle directly by extracting physical parameters from the input signals. However, the algorithm is specific for locomotion, making it difficult to be applied in other kinds of VR applications.

On the other hand, live performance of the user has been used for controlling the virtual character by full body motion capture [10, 13, 17, 21]. While we share similar interests with [13, 17] in controlling virtual characters using the live performance of the user to interact with the objects in the virtual world, our method tackles some of the problems that have not been addressed and explored in the previous works. In [17], the live performance is captured by an optical motion capture system. With the large number of markers used, the positions and orientations of the body segments can be calculated even when some markers are occluded. However, for affordable devices such as the Microsoft Kinect, the number of tracked points is extremely limited. Liu and Zordan [13] try to apply pre-recorded motions in a database with Kinect to simulate more realistic movements. However, it is unclear how the motion database is constructed and how it affects the quality of the resultant motion.

2.2 PD Controller for Physics-based Systems

In physics-based simulations, forward dynamics has been used extensively for gait simulations [19, 26]. One of the popular implementations of these systems is the proportional-derivative (PD) controller. A wide variety of motion can be synthesized with the controller, such as walk-to-run and run-to-walk transition [7, 22], as well as walking with different step length [8]. Usually a finite state machine is used to connect multiple PD controllers and handle the transition between controllers. Apart from locomotion, athletic motions such as cycling and handspring vaulting [9], and somersault motion [18] can be generated. Such systems require a certain amount of manual design to create different types of motions. PD control is also suitable to generate responsive motions such as the falling back motions when one is being pushed [27].

Since generating realistic full body motions require carefully designed dynamics systems, it is proposed to control characters by simply tracking captured human movements, such that the movements can react to external forces [1]. To speed up the simulations, simplified polygons model can be used to represent the characters with high degrees of freedom [16]. In this research, we use PD controller to track a posture that is computed from the captured motion and the best matched motion from a motion database.

3. SYSTEM OVERVIEW

The overview of our proposed method is shown in Figure 1. At every time-step, the posture of the user is captured by Kinect. The streamed postures contain only limited number of joints and are usually incomplete due to occlusion. We propose to search for a matching posture in a motion database to provide a reasonable estimation on the missing information. The Kinect posture, database posture and optional environment constraints are fed into a physical simulator as positional and rotational constraints. The simulator then solves for the final posture and simulates the resultant scene.

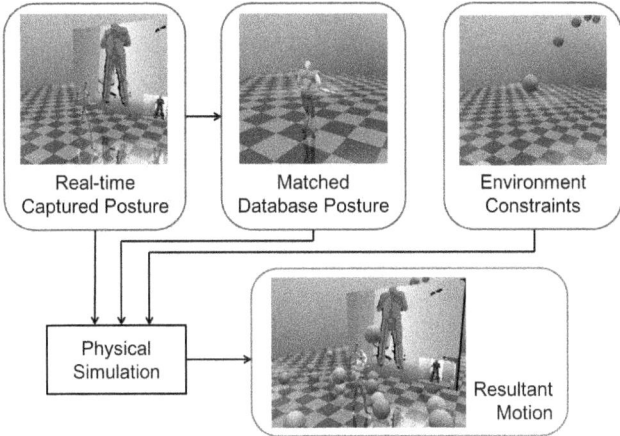

Figure 1: The overview of our proposed framework.

3.1 Contributions

We have two major contributions in this paper:

- We propose a unified framework, which combines positional controls and rotational controls, to model character movements in a physically simulated environment based on real-time captured motions. On one hand, simulated characters can resemble any posture produced by the users similar to kinematics motion synthesis. On the other hand, they response to external forces and are capable of interacting with virtual objects as in dynamics simulations.

- Motions captured from real-time system such as the Microsoft Kinect usually do not provide the necessary degree of freedom (DOF) required to control a virtual character. This is because of the limited number of tracking joints and the occluded/noisy joints that cannot be captured. We propose to substitute missing DOF from a motion database by searching for the best matching posture. To enhance the computational efficiency, we implement the database in a reduced space using Principal Component Analysis (PCA).

4. PHYSICAL WORLD MODELLING

In this section, we describe how we model the characters and the environment in the simulator.

We use the Open Dynamics Engine [24] to simulate the physical world. Each character is represented by 19 body segments and 20 joints according to the Kinect skeleton definition. Since Kinect does not enforce the bone length, we set the size and the mass of each segment according to [2]. Segments are modelled with capsules for efficient collision detection, and the joints are modelled with ball joints which indicating that each segment has 3 degrees of freedom in rotation. Although it is possible to model some specific joints such as the elbows and the knees with hinge joints to enhance the realism of the characters, the system will need to solve an inverse kinematic problem to calculate the orientation of their respective parent joints (i.e. the shoulder and the hips), which increases the computational cost. The trade off between the enhancement of realism and computational efficiency shall be adjusted according to the availability of computational resources.

Environment objects in our systems are modelled with primitive shapes. We create an infinity large plane in the ODE world as the floor plane, which provides supporting force to the characters and the objects. Gravity is implemented such that when no control force is applied, the characters and objects fall onto the ground naturally.

5. REFERENCE MOTION SELECTION

In this section, we present the process of selecting a reference posture that is the most similar to the posture captured from Kinect. We will explain the proposed method to construct the motion database, enhance the computational cost by dimensionality reduction techniques and select the best matching posture.

5.1 Motion Database Construction

Here, we explain how we compose our motion database.

We create the motion database by motions captured from a commercial optical motion capture system. We retarget the captured motions to the character definition explained in Section 4 using commercial software. We also remove the global rotation along the vertical axis and the global 3D translation for normalization. Each posture is represented by a set of joint positions (P_d), as well as a set of joint rotations along the joint axes (Θ_d). To enhance the efficiency of run-time database searches, we calculate the sum of squared differences of joint positions, and remove similar poses if the differences is smaller than a predefined threshold.

The motions that should be contained in the database depend on the target application. The idea is that we compose a database with the motions that the users are expected to perform. In our implementation, our database includes boxing motions, sword fighting motions, walking motions, as well as general exercising motions. The unfiltered database contains roughly 1500 postures, which is then filtered into around 300. Our database is relatively compact due to the scope of the target motion. However, if the application requires the user to perform a large variety of motion, such as dancing in different style, a larger database will be needed.

5.2 Motion Comparison

Here, we explain how we apply PCA to reduce the computational cost of database searches with the Kinect input.

During run-time, we obtain a set of joint positions (P_k) from Kinect, and retrieve the best match poses from the database (P_d). While we can consider the P_k and P_d as two point clouds and conduct motion comparison [11], this costs computational power unnecessarily, as there exists an intrinsic redundancy among the joints in the postures. We proposed to reduce the dimensionality of the motions by PCA to improve the performance of database queries. In other words, we reduce P_d into a reduced representation P_{dr}. During run-time, the projection matrix calculated by PCA is used to reduce the Kinect joint positions P_k into P_{kr}. We then conduct a search to find the most similar posture between P_{dr} and P_{kr}, by considering their sum of squared differences. Although more dedicated algorithms such as k-d tree can further speed up the searching process, we find that brute force searches in the reduced space is fast enough for real-time applications. In our implementation, P_d has 60 dimensions and P_{dr} has 7. Please refer to Section 8.4 for the analysis on deciding the optimal dimension of the reduced space.

In the situation when a joint is missing in the data obtained from Kinect due to occlusions or the restricted capture volume, we assume the joint position to be the mean value of that joint from all posture in the database, and compose P_{kr} accordingly. Empirically, we find that this assumption works well in database queries even when a few joints are missing.

6. POSTURE SOLVER

In this section, we explain how we combine the Kinect posture, database posture and optional environment information into a set of constraints. We separately control the target positions and the target rotations along the joint axes, and solve for the final posture with the physical simulator. At the end of this section, we discuss why our hybrid controller is superior to a pure positional/rotational controller.

6.1 Positional Constraints

Here, we explain how we generate positional constraints by combining the Kinect posture and the database posture. Then, we present the optional constraints that can be obtained from the environment. Finally, we give details on how to calculate the control forces to satisfy the positional constraints.

At each frame, we obtain a set of joint positions P_k from Kinect. Since P_k may be incomplete due to the run-time tracking error, we substitute the missing joint positions from the matched database posture P_d that is found as described in the previous section, and create the resultant set of positions P_e. Notice that P_e is an invalid posture in which segment lengths are not maintained, as it is created by simply replacing missing joints with those in P_d. Thus, we cannot directly force the character to perform P_e. Instead, we consider P_e as a set of positional constraints defined for every joint, and implement a tracking system to track the constraints.

We can include optional constraints based on the requirement of the application or the environment. For example, we can change the target location of a hand in a reaching motion such that the character can touch a virtual object. In such a case, we replace some DOF in the positional constraints defined in P_e with a calculated position. Notice that we only need to adjust the subset of joints that are explicitly related. For example, adjusting the positional constraint of the hand in a reaching motion results in the corresponding movement of the lower arm and the upper arm. The major advantage of using positions, instead of rotations, to represent the constraints here is that they are more trivial to human understanding and facilitate easier motion editing.

With the positional constraints expressed in P_e, we calculate the control force for each joint, and drive the character to fit into all constraints. In each time step, the control force is calculated by a PD controller:

$$F = K_e(p_{target} - p_{current}) + K_d(p'_{target} - p'_{current}) \quad (1)$$

where p_{target} is the target position of a joint defined by P_e, $p_{current}$ is the current position of the joint, p'_{target} and $p'_{current}$ are the respective derivatives, K_e is the elasticity gain and K_d is the damping gain. A high K_e can improve the responsiveness of the character, while a high K_d produce more stable movements. We manually tune the smallest possible K_e and K_d, as a system with high control forces is

usually not stable, and use the pair to control all joints. Furthermore, the magnitude of the resultant force F is bounded by a predefined value to avoid unexpected high control force while the target values are very different from the current ones.

Notice that positional constraints implemented with control forces are not guaranteed to be met in the final result. If we wish to ensure meeting a specific constraint, we have to further define a virtual ball joint to connect the joint with a constraint position, which can either be on another object or in the empty space. This allows the constrained joint to rotate around the target position, but not moving away from it, even when forces are applied. Notice that if too many virtual joints are created, there may be incompatibility among them, such as fixing the feet on the floor while requiring the hand to move to an unreachable position. In such a situation, the posture solver will fail and the segment lengths will no longer be maintained.

In our implementation, we use virtual joints to fix the supporting feet on the floor. At the moment when the constraint positions of the feet touch the floor, we use virtual joints to fix it until the constraint positions move away from the floor. Furthermore, we use virtual joints to emulate the effect when a character holds an object such as a mace by fixing the hand with the object. When solving for the final posture, ODE maintains virtual joints as hard constraints, and coordinates other available DOF to achieve the desired movement. Empirically, we found that applying virtual joints on end effectors produces plausible results.

6.2 Rotational Constraints

Here, we explain the rotational constraints that control the rotation of joints along the joint axes.

To control a full character, apart from the positional constraints explained in the previous section, we also need the joint orientations. We define the rotation along the joint axes obtained from Kinect as Θ_k. Due to the limited number of tracking points in Kinect, Θ_k is incomplete whenever one or more point is not tracked.

Since the matched database posture P_d is similar to the Kinect one P_k, it is reasonable to assume that the corresponding rotational information, Θ_d, is similar to Θ_k as well. We substitute the missing DOF of Θ_k with those in Θ_d, and create the resultant set of rotation along the joint axes, Θ_e.

We formulate the control torque in ODE for each joint with a PD controller:

$$T = K_\epsilon(\theta_{target} - \theta_{current}) + K_\delta(\theta'_{target} - \theta'_{current}) \quad (2)$$

where θ_{target} is the rotation of a joint along the joint axis defined in Θ_e, $\theta_{current}$ is the current rotation, θ'_{target} and $\Theta'_{current}$ are the respective derivative, K_ϵ and K_δ are the hand tuned elasticity gain and damping gain. Similar to the force calculation, the torque T is bounded by a predefined value.

6.3 Physical Simulation

Here, we describe how ODE handles the control forces and torques to simulate the final posture.

For each joint, we apply the control forces calculated in Equation 1 to control the 3D translation, and the control torques calculated in Equation 2 to control the rotation along the joint axis, as shown in Figure 2(a). The physical simulation engine ODE maintains the segment length

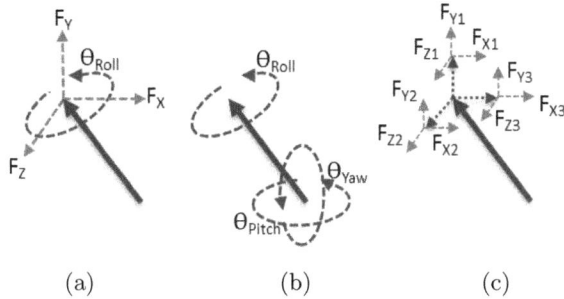

Figure 2: Different control schemes for a joint, with the red arrows representing positional control, and the blue arrows representing rotational control. (a) The proposed control scheme based on 3D positional control and rotational control along the joint axis. (b) Pure rotational control. (c) Pure positional control by sampling extra control points with fixed offsets.

and segment connectivity defined by joints while applying the control forces and torques. The resultant posture is the equilibrium state of the character and it represents the posture that can satisfy most of the constraints.

In case a character is being pushed or hit, extra control force is applied to simulate the impact. Since the segment length is fixed, when a force is applied to a joint, the rest of the joints will be dragged to such a direction. The advantage of using PD controller for tracking the live performance in physical simulation is that the virtual character can adapt to unexpected collisions in the environment while trying to track the target posture given by the user. As a result, realistic movements of the virtual character responding to a dynamic environment can be generated.

Although it is possible to obtain all 3 dimensions of rotation and use Equation 2 to control the overall system as shown in Figure 2(b), we found that the result is suboptimal. This is mainly because the actual segment movement after rotating the joint depends on the length of the joint, while human is sensitive to positional movements. Thus, to obtain the best result, K_ϵ and K_δ have to be tuned individually for each joint, as opposed to using the same value of gains for all joints in our system. Furthermore, positional based requirements for specific joints, such as fixing the supporting feet on the floor, will require solving an inverse kinematic problem, which requires extra computational effort.

Similarly, it is possible to sample multiple control points based on fixed offsets from a joint to represent its rotation along the joint axis as shown in Figure 2(c). Then, we can use Equation 1 to model all constraints. However, this increases the complexity of the system unnecessarily, and is likely to result in unstable simulations in the physical engine due to the large number of constraints. In our system, we construct a unified framework taking into account both controlling forces and rotational torques along the joint axes, with the latter being a supporting element. We find that it works efficiently and the gains in the equations can be tuned with ease.

7. MOTION RETARGETING

In this section, we explain how we retarget the Kinect pos-

ture into a standard size to further improve the performance of the system. While previous works [4, 6] can retarget motion for characters of different sizes, our retargetting algorithm is significantly simpler and efficient. This is because (1) the characters that we consider have the same joint hierarchy definition, and (2) our posture solver provide support for inverse kinematic, thus we do not need to solve it during the retargetting stage.

Since Kinect does not maintain the bone lengths of the tracked character, users with different body size have different character dimensions. In addition, the bone lengths may change during a capture session when the joint positions are not accurately recognized. To improve the stability of the simulation, we retarget the Kinect posture into the character dimensions we defined in ODE such that database matching (Section 5) and constraints definition (Section 6) can be more accurate.

Without loss of generality, for a Kinect joint i with position P_k^i and its parent joint j with position P_k^j, we calculate the normalized directional vector:

$$d_k^i = \frac{P_k^i - P_k^j}{|P_k^i - P_k^j|} \qquad (3)$$

The retargeted position of the joint i is calculated as:

$$P_{k'}^i = P_{k'}^j + d_k^i \times L(i, j) \qquad (4)$$

where $P_{k'}^j$ is retargeted position of the parent joint j, $L(i, j)$ indicates the bone length between joint i and j designed for the virtual character. Since the retargeted position of a joint depends on its retargeted parent joint, this process have to be started with the joint in the top level of the body structure hierarchy.

8. EXPERIMENTAL RESULTS

In this section, the results generated using our method are presented. We first show the motions created by our method in different scenarios. Next, we evaluate the database matching accuracy. The readers are referred to the attached video for the results.

All experiments ran in real-time on a computer using a single thread of an Intel i7-2600K processor. The proposed method is implemented on Windows with Visual C++, and Microsoft Kinect SDK [15] version 1.5 is used to obtain the live captured motion stream.

8.1 Interacting with Boxes

In the first experiment, the character was controlled by the user to lift and carry a bulky box as shown in Figure 3(a). Notice that as our character was physically simulated, the hand of the character did not penetrate the boxes upon contact, even when the raw Kinect posture illustrated by the yellow skeleton did. Also notice that although the Kinect posture had significant size difference with the simulated character, the resultant motion appears natural due to the motion retargeting process.

In the second experiment, a large number of boxes were added to the virtual environment at random locations. The virtual character was controlled by the user to interact with the boxes by body movements such as punching, kicking and walking, as shown in Figure 3(b). The masses of the boxes were set to be small to magnify the effect of impacts.

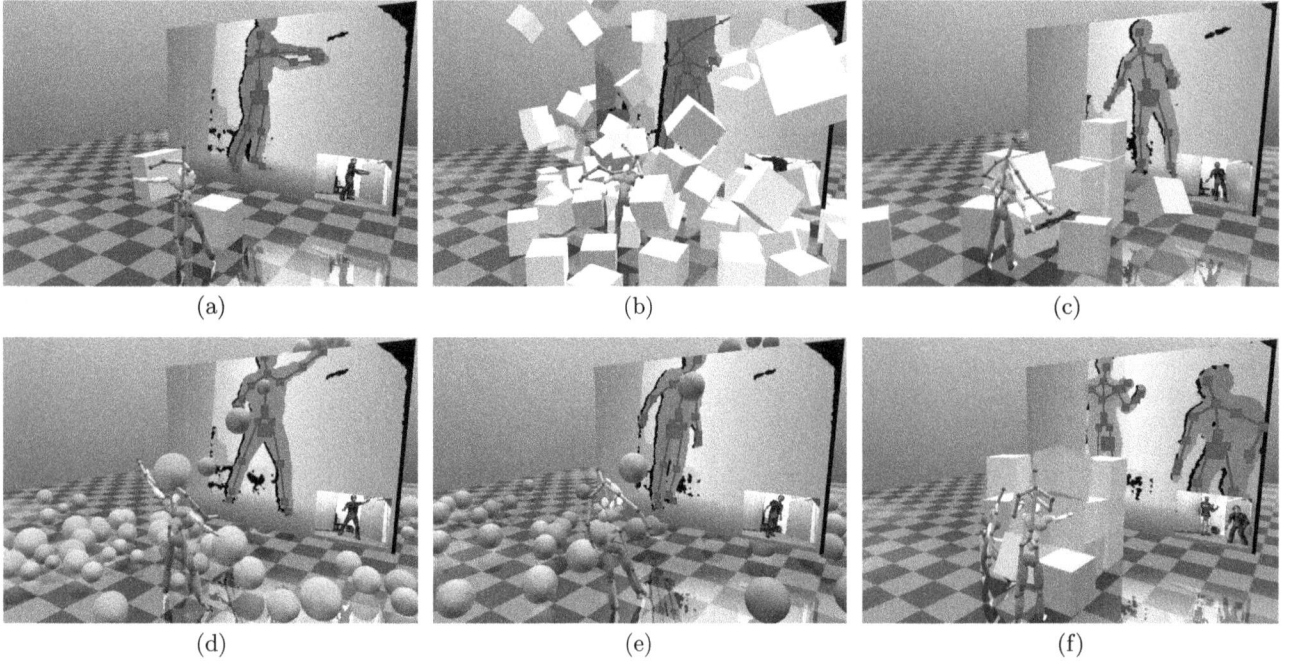

(a)   (b)   (c)

(d)   (e)   (f)

Figure 3: (a) The user controls the virtual character to grab and carry a box. (b) The virtual character interacts with a large number of boxes in the environment. (c) A simulated mace is attached to the hand of the character with a virtual joint. (d) The user controls the virtual character to interact will the balls. (e) Dodging motion is synthesized automatically by positional constraints. (f) Two characters are controlled by two users simultaneously.

In the third experiment, a physically simulated mace was connected to the hand of the character with a virtual joint as described in Section 6.1. The movement of the simulated mace was computed based on the motion of the character's hand, as well as the collision with other objects. The user controlled the character to interact with the boxes with the mace as shown in Figure 3(c). Notice that since the mace had a mass itself, it affected the hand movement of the character, which was similar to a human swinging a heavy object in the real world.

8.2 Interacting with Balls

In the first experiment, a large number of balls with random sizes shot towards the virtual character. The user tried to control the movements of the virtual character to interact with the balls as shown in Figure 3(d). Notice that when the balls hit the virtual character, the effect of external impacts applied onto the body segments was synthesized naturally.

We further show an example of automatically controlling a subset of body segments subject to selected external events. Specifically, we enabled the character to dodge an incoming object by raising its arms. To simulate such an effect, we set the target positions of the forearms around the head as positional constraints when the balls arrive. Figure 4(a) and (b) show the motions synthesized without and with the automatic dodging feature respectively using a non-user controlled T-pose, in which the arms of the character were extended outwards.

We applied the automatic dodging feature for a user controlled character as shown in Figure 3(e). By enabling this feature, the virtual character can automatically react to the balls shooting towards its head. This feature is particu-

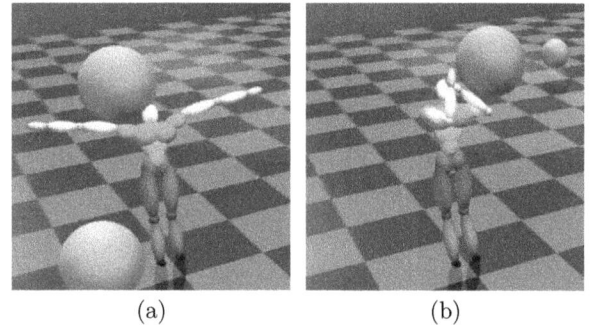

(a)   (b)

Figure 4: Motion synthesized (a) without the auto dodging feature. (b) with the auto dodging feature.

larly useful when the users do not want to control all the body segments by himself/herself, as well as synthesizing the reflective motions of human to increase the realism of the virtual character.

8.3 Multi-character interactions

In this experiment, two users interacted indirectly with each other in the virtual world by throwing boxes to each other (Figure 3(f)). Notice that with a single Kinect, it is difficult to capture close interaction due to occlusion. More research is needed to enhance the performance for tracking multiple interacting users.

8.4 Performance Evaluation

Here, we evaluate the effectiveness of using PCA to reduce dimensionality of the postures and the impact on the quality of posture matching. We also discuss the computation cost of the system.

We record 600 frames of motion performed by a user with Kinect. Then, we reduce the dimensionality of the database motions and the Kinect motion to a specific value between 1 and 60, and perform motion matching. Finally, we compute the different between the retrieved database posture and the Kinect posture in the full dimensional space. The posture errors in a frame f is computed by:

$$e(f) = \sum_{i=1}^{60} (P_k^i - P_d^i)^2 \tag{5}$$

where 60 is the total number of joints in the full dimensional space, i is the joint index, P_k^i and P_d^i are the 3D locations of the i-th joint in the Kinect and selected database posture in the full space respectively. The percentage of error is calculated by:

$$\frac{\sum_{f=1}^{n} e_r(f) - \sum_{f=1}^{n} e_{60}(f)}{\sum_{f=1}^{n} e_{60}(f)} \times 100\% \tag{6}$$

where f is the frame number, $n = 600$ is the total number of frames, e_r is the posture error found using r dimensions matching with Equation 5, e_{60} is the posture error with the full 60 dimensions.

The results are plotted as the red line in Figure 5. It shows that when the dimensionality is significantly reduced, there is a high error rate as expected. However, the rate drops below 3% when the dimensionality is reduced to 7. Since then it decreases slowly when the dimensionality increases. Based on the results, we decide that reducing the dimensionality of the motion search space to 7 can balance the trade-off between efficiency and accuracy. The finding agrees with the work from Safonova et al. [20].

The average computational time required for searching the database and synthesizing the motion for a single character is plotted as the blue line in Figure 5. When using 7 dimensions, the time required is roughly 0.65 ms, in which 0.10 ms is for database search and 0.55 ms is for motion synthesize. The time for motion synthesize does not change significantly for different degree of freedom. When comparing to the full dimension search, 24% of computational cost is saved if 7 dimensions is used.

Notice that performance mentioned above does not consider the time required to obtain data from Kinect, as well as to render the outcome. With everything included, the computational cost is roughly 8.5 ms per frame when using 7 dimensions. This means that the system can run 4 times faster than real-time, although the frame rate is limited by Kinect in practice.

9. CONCLUSIONS AND DISCUSSIONS

In this paper, we proposed a unified framework to track live captured motions from Kinect using physically simulated characters. Our framework can synthesize any posture efficiently using external forces and torques calculated from a PD controller. To overcome the problem of missing DOF of the postures captured from Kinect, we further proposed to select an appropriate posture from a dimensionality reduced motion database to estimate the required information. We demonstrated that the proposed PCA-based motion selection approach is computationally efficient while keeping the matching error under a reasonable level. Experimental

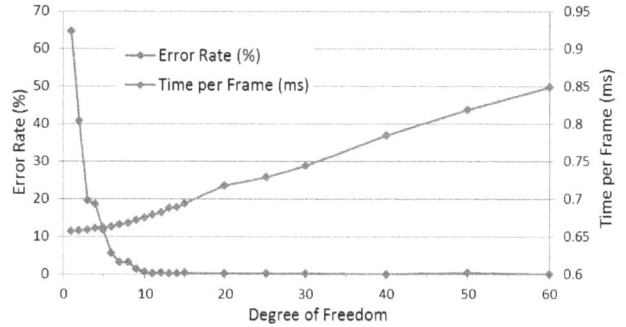

Figure 5: The results of posture matching error and computational cost with respect to the corresponding dimensionality of the postures.

results show that our method robustly synthesized the user controlled characters that interact with virtual objects in a physically simulated environment, even when the motions captured from Kinect were very noisy.

While Kinect is used as the motion capture system in this paper, our proposed framework is general and can be applied with different hardware. For example, in traditional optical motion capture system, it is very common that some track points are missing due to tracking error. Our system can substitute the missing DOF from a matched posture and synthesize stable character movements in real-time. Similarly, the framework can be applied to synthesize full body movement from the Wiimote controllers, although further research is required to effectively find a matching posture from the extremely limited DOF provided from these controllers.

While we show the effectiveness of the proposed method, there are some limitations. First of all, the database posture matching process becomes inaccurate when the number of joints recognized by Kinect is dropped significantly. This usually happen when capturing the whole body rotation of the user. As a common limitation of any single camera motion capture system, when the user is not facing the camera, the captured motion becomes inaccurate since a large portion of body segments are occluded. One possible solution is incorporating multiple cameras in a capturing session.

The accuracy of the database searches also depends on the content of the database. If the user performed motion is very different from those in the database, the returned posture may not match the input motion well. However, we observe that most applications have their own set of target objectives, which can help to identify the target motion that should be included in the database. In the future, we are interested in a more sophisticated motion completion scheme such as taking into account the temporal coherency of the joint locations. Another interesting direction is to integrate non-vision based motion capture devices, such as inertial sensors, into our proposed method to improve the robustness of the framework.

10. ACKNOWLEDGMENTS

We would like to thank the anonymous reviewers for their constructive comments and suggestions. We also thank Mr. Chris Blythe for his help in producing the demonstration video and revising the paper.

11. REFERENCES

[1] Y. Abe and J. Popović. Interactive animation of dynamic manipulation. In *SCA '06: Proceedings of the 2006 ACM SIGGRAPH/Eurographics symposium on Computer animation*, pages 195–204, Aire-la-Ville, Switzerland, Switzerland, 2006. Eurographics Association.

[2] H. G. Armstrong. Anthropometry and mass distribution for human analogues. volume 1. military male aviators, 1988.

[3] J. Chai and J. K. Hodgins. Performance animation from low-dimensional control signals. In *SIGGRAPH '05: ACM SIGGRAPH 2005 Papers*, pages 686–696, New York, NY, USA, 2005. ACM.

[4] K.-J. Choi and H.-S. Ko. On-line motion retargetting. In *Proceedings of the 7th Pacific Conference on Computer Graphics and Applications*, PG '99, pages 32–, Washington, DC, USA, 1999. IEEE Computer Society.

[5] S. Coros, P. Beaudoin, and M. van de Panne. Generalized biped walking control. *ACM Trans. Graph.*, 29(4):130:1–130:9, July 2010.

[6] M. Gleicher. Retargetting motion to new characters. In *Proceedings of the 25th annual conference on Computer graphics and interactive techniques*, SIGGRAPH '98, pages 33–42, New York, NY, USA, 1998. ACM.

[7] J. Hodgins. Biped gait transitions. *Robotics and Automation, 1991. Proceedings., 1991 IEEE International Conference on*, pages 2092–2097 vol.3, 9-11 Apr 1991.

[8] J. Hodgins and M. Raibert. Adjusting step length for rough terrain locomotion. *Robotics and Automation, IEEE Transactions on*, 7(3):289–298, Jun 1991.

[9] J. K. Hodgins, W. L. Wooten, D. C. Brogan, and J. F. O'Brien. Animating human athletics. In *SIGGRAPH '95: Proceedings of the 22nd annual conference on Computer graphics and interactive techniques*, pages 71–78, New York, NY, USA, 1995. ACM.

[10] S. Ishigaki, T. White, V. B. Zordan, and C. K. Liu. Performance-based control interface for character animation. *ACM Trans. Graph.*, 28(3):61:1–61:8, July 2009.

[11] L. Kovar, M. Gleicher, and F. H. Pighin. Motion graphs. *ACM Trans. Graph.*, 21(3):473–482, 2002.

[12] J. Lee, J. Chai, P. S. A. Reitsma, J. K. Hodgins, and N. S. Pollard. Interactive control of avatars animated with human motion data. *ACM Trans. Graph.*, 21(3):491–500, 2002.

[13] C. Liu and V. Zordan. Natural user interface for physics-based character animation. In J. Allbeck and P. Faloutsos, editors, *Motion in Games*, volume 7060 of *Lecture Notes in Computer Science*, pages 1–14. Springer Berlin Heidelberg, 2011.

[14] H. Liu, X. Wei, J. Chai, I. Ha, and T. Rhee. Realtime human motion control with a small number of inertial sensors. In *Symposium on Interactive 3D Graphics and Games*, I3D '11, pages 133–140, New York, NY, USA, 2011. ACM.

[15] Microsoft Corporation. Kinect for windows SDK programming guide version 1.5. 2012.

[16] H. Mitake, K. Asano, T. Aoki, S. Marc, M. Sato, and S. Hasegawa. Physics-driven multi dimensional keyframe animation for artist-directable interactive character. *Computer Graphics Forum*, 28(2):279–287, 2009.

[17] N. Nguyen, N. Wheatland, D. Brown, B. Parise, C. K. Liu, and V. Zordan. Performance capture with physical interaction. In *Proceedings of the 2010 ACM SIGGRAPH/Eurographics Symposium on Computer Animation*, SCA '10, pages 189–195, Aire-la-Ville, Switzerland, Switzerland, 2010. Eurographics Association.

[18] R. Playter and M. Raibert. Control of a biped somersault in 3d. *Intelligent Robots and Systems, 1992., Proceedings of the 1992 lEEE/RSJ International Conference on*, 1:582–589, 7-10 Jul 1992.

[19] M. H. Raibert and J. K. Hodgins. Animation of dynamic legged locomotion. *SIGGRAPH Comput. Graph.*, 25(4):349–358, 1991.

[20] A. Safonova, J. K. Hodgins, and N. S. Pollard. Synthesizing physically realistic human motion in low-dimensional, behavior-specific spaces. In *SIGGRAPH '04: ACM SIGGRAPH 2004 Papers*, pages 514–521, New York, NY, USA, 2004. ACM.

[21] H. J. Shin, J. Lee, S. Y. Shin, and M. Gleicher. Computer puppetry: An importance-based approach. *ACM Trans. Graph.*, 20(2):67–94, Apr. 2001.

[22] T. Shiratori and J. K. Hodgins. Accelerometer-based user interfaces for the control of a physically simulated character. In *SIGGRAPH Asia '08: ACM SIGGRAPH Asia 2008 papers*, pages 1–9, New York, NY, USA, 2008. ACM.

[23] H. P. H. Shum, T. Komura, and S. Takagi. Fast accelerometer-based motion recognition with a dual buffer framework. *The International Journal of Virtual Reality*, 10(3):17–24, September 2011.

[24] R. Smith. Open dynamics engine, 2008. http://www.ode.org/.

[25] J. Tautges, A. Zinke, B. Krüger, J. Baumann, A. Weber, T. Helten, M. Müller, H.-P. Seidel, and B. Eberhardt. Motion reconstruction using sparse accelerometer data. *ACM Trans. Graph.*, 30(3):18:1–18:12, May 2011.

[26] M. Van De Panne. Parameterized gait synthesis. *Computer Graphics and Applications, IEEE*, 16(2):40–49, Mar 1996.

[27] V. B. Zordan and J. K. Hodgins. Motion capture-driven simulations that hit and react. In *SCA '02: Proceedings of the 2002 ACM SIGGRAPH/Eurographics symposium on Computer animation*, pages 89–96, New York, NY, USA, 2002. ACM.

OmniKinect: Real-Time Dense Volumetric Data Acquisition and Applications

Bernhard Kainz, Stefan Hauswiesner, Gerhard Reitmayr, Markus Steinberger,
Raphael Grasset, Lukas Gruber, Eduardo Veas, Denis Kalkofen, Hartmut Seichter,
and Dieter Schmalstieg
Institute for Computer Graphics and Vision, Graz University of Technology
Inffeldgasse 16, A-8010 Graz, Austria
\<author-last-name\>@icg.tugraz.at

ABSTRACT

Real-time three-dimensional acquisition of real-world scenes
has many important applications in computer graphics, computer vision and human-computer interaction. Inexpensive
depth sensors such as the Microsoft Kinect allow to leverage the development of such applications. However, this
technology is still relatively recent, and no detailed studies
on its scalability to dense and view-independent acquisition
have been reported. This paper addresses the question of
what can be done with a larger number of Kinects used
simultaneously. We describe an interference-reducing physical setup, a calibration procedure and an extension to the
KinectFusion algorithm, which allows to produce high quality volumetric reconstructions from multiple Kinects whilst
overcoming systematic errors in the depth measurements.
We also report on enhancing image based visual hull rendering by depth measurements, and compare the results to
KinectFusion. Our system provides practical insight into
achievable spatial and radial range and into bandwidth requirements for depth data acquisition. Finally, we present a
number of practical applications of our system.

Categories and Subject Descriptors

C.0 [**Computer Systems Organization**]: System architectures; D.4.7 [**Organization and Design**]: Interactive
systems; C.4 [**Performance of Systems**]: Performance attributes

Keywords

depth sensors; 4D reconstruction; Microsoft Kinect

1. INTRODUCTION

The Microsoft Kinect has profoundly changed the possibilities of sensing for games or Virtual Reality applications.
Previously, inexpensive and thus scalable sensing technology was primarily based on affordable digital video cameras, making computationally expensive image processing

necessary. With a Kinect device, direct depth sensing and
video capture immediately deliver rich information on the
scene structure without intensive processing at a competitive price. Not surprisingly, many researchers have taken
advantage of this opportunity, and we see a proliferation of
research projects that rely on this technology.

A single Kinect can deliver enough information to let a
user control a character in a video game with body movements or resolve real time occlusion of video-see through
Augmented Reality (AR) applications. However, the scope
of potential applications is ultimately limited by the view-
dependent nature of the sensor and the fact that it samples
surfaces at a finite resolution. Scalability by using data from
multiple Kinects is therefore a prime research topic for improving the quality of acquisition and reconstruction with
such a device.

For applications that demand fully view-independent and
dense surface reconstruction of dynamic scenes in real time,
multiple Kinects can be clustered and their output combined. This approach is still inexpensive, at least for professional applications. However, building such a setup is not
necessarily trivial, as a number of conceptual and technical challenges in the system design must be overcome. In
this paper, we report on the construction and evaluation
of OmniKinect, a system using multiple Kinects for real-
time dense volumetric acquisition. We describe the challenges in making such a system work in practice. In particular, we describe the efforts taken in making our hardware
setup flexible and scalable. We also report on an improvement technique to allow real-time fusion of sensor readings
from multiple Kinects, and on an image-based rendering approach enhanced by depth information. Both algorithms
are versatile tools for the processing of combined RGB-D
data. Finally, we illustrate our work with several application examples, which previously would have been very hard
or impossible to achieve.

2. RELATED WORK

Multi-view stereo systems: Before affordable depth
sensors became available, systems with multiple video cameras were used to reconstruct and render dynamic 3D scenes.
Early approaches extended the concept of feature-based stereo
matching to multiple cameras [5]. GPU-based implementations work by, for example, using plane sweep algorithms [22]
to achieve interactive frame rates.

In many applications, only a defined foreground object is
of interest. If the foreground object or the background can

be segmented in the multiple camera images, shape-from-silhouette algorithms can be used to reconstruct a coarse hull of the object fast [2]. GPU-based implementations can speed up the process considerably [10]. For applications that intend to render the reconstructed object without an explicit 3D model, image-based visual hull (IBVH) rendering [13] circumvents the explicit reconstruction of a 3D mesh or voxel grid by directly computing a depth map of the scene object from the desired viewpoint. A similar approach is used for 3D TV based on camera arrays [14].

Single and multi-depth sensor systems: The capabilities of the Microsoft Kinect have been already explored for a variety of applications. For example, a single Kinect already enables high-quality real-time human pose estimation [18]. Kinect-based body scanning [19] also enables virtual try-on applications at low costs. Newcombe et al. have shown with their work on KinectFusion [15] that dense volumetric reconstructions can be created in real time. Because the Kinect is so inexpensive, combining multiple devices has also been investigated for different research projects. For example, Wilson *et.al.* [21] and Berger *et.al.* [1] use up to four depth sensors to monitor a room. Both ensure that the reconstruction light patterns do not overlap, to avoid interferences of the structures light patterns emitted by multiple sensors. Maimone and Fuchs [11] propose advanced hole filling and meshing techniques to use a multi-Kinect setup for telepresence applications. Other approaches use different modulation frequencies per camera [8, 6], which is not possible when using Kinect depth sensors.

The problem of overlapping reconstruction light pattern has been solved by Maimone *et.al.* [12] and Butler *et.al.* [3] with a similar approach. Letting the whole RGB-D camera vibrate at a relatively high frequency blurs the light pattern for other, concurrently capturing sensors. The rigid connection of the vibrating sensor and the light pattern supports a clear reconstruction without interferences from other Kinects. In OmniKinect, we altered this approach slightly to gain more flexibility, as detailed in Section 3.

The FreeCam system [9] combines color cameras and depth cameras in a system for free-viewpoint rendering. They use a multi-camera rig instead of a full capturing room.

3. OMNIKINECT SYSTEM

The OmniKinect system provides a way to capture, record and stream information using a multiple Kinect sensors infrastructure, for both static or dynamic sensors. We propose a hardware setup and a list of software tools that can be used for a large number of applications. Our software tools include a set of basic capturing tools (record, filter, export) and a set of high level software components (tracking, visual hull rendering), which have been optimized for this specific system.

Setup overview: Our basic setup consists of an extensible, ceiling mounted aluminum frame with rigidly fixed vertical rods at regular distances. We have attached Kinect for Windows devices to the rods with stiffened foot joints. To reduce interferences between the Kinects, the rods are equipped with vibrators. In contrast to previous work [12, 3], we do not mount the vibrators directly onto the Kinects but on the supporting structure. This has various advantages: First, we do not have to disassemble the Kinects and demount their foots to mount the vibrators at a center position and ensure a stiff mounting. We have also tried a

mounting on top of the Kinect, which revealed to be hard to control and to mount because of the bent shape of the Kinect and which produces much more image blurring than in our setup. Second, we can adjust and fine-tune the vibration amplitude by the position of the Kinect. Since the rods are not mounted on the floor, they vibrate at a higher amplitude near to their end/bottom, where the vibrator is mounted. The vibrator frequency can be controlled by an adjustable power supply.

Currently, our setup uses eight vibrating rods. Additional rods can be inserted with just a few simple steps in less than five minutes. To reduce clutter and to allow defined lighting conditions, we have surrounded the setup by two layers of curtains. We have measured the light filter effect of each curtain and can adjust the layers to reduce the incoming light by approximately 25% (one layer) or 50% (two layers). Figure 1(a) shows a schematic illustration of our setup and Figure 1(b) shows the current implementation of this setup.

Mounting: We use 1400mm long, 40×40mm *profile 8* pieces from *item Industrietechnik GmbH* (http://www.item24.de) as vertical rods on a 3450×3600mm ceiling mounted frame. The rods are mounted by using right-angled butt-fastening with T-slot nuts in the ceiling mount, to allow a rigid but slightly moveable connection for the vibration. Figure 1(a) shows the details for this approach. It is also possible to move one additional non-vibrating Kinect freely, as the reconstruction patterns of all mounted Kinects are blurred out by the Maimone/Butler method.

Vibrators and frequency control: Maimone *et al.* [12] do not give a lot of details for their choice of vibrators, hence we have experimented in the same way as Butler *et al.* [3] with different engines and offset weights to gain the optimal result. We finally chose an Igarashi *N2738-51* 12V motor with max. 14800rpm (idle running), 0.90Ncm torque and max. 11.8W output, a grub screw shaft connector, a 10g item "T-slot nut 8 St M8" as offset weight and hot glue as safety fixation. The engine's shaft connector is screwed into the thread of the T-nut. The vibrators are mounted with hot glue and tape to the vertical rods.

All vibrators are driven by a parallel circuit at slightly different frequencies, due to different cable lengths. In the final setup, we operate the vibrators between 7200 and 10200rpm, which corresponds to a vibration frequency for each motor between 120 and 170Hz. The final frequency adjustment has to be done manually, to reduce randomly occurring resonances with the mounting and therefore blurry RGB images for certain Kinects. Usually, 150Hz produces no disturbing resonances for our setup. Note that we use a higher frequency than proposed in [3], due to our vibrator mounting. We cannot measure the absorption caused by the vertical rods. Therefore we assume that the actual Kinect vibration in our setup is approximately at the same frequency as proposed by Butler *et al.* [3] ($60 - 80Hz$).

Display device: To allow real-time visual feedback for various applications, we use a large TV LCD screen display, which can be freely positioned within our setup.

Control unit: As a control unit, we use an off-the-shelf PC with an ASUS Sabertooth X58 mainboard (two on-board USB 2.0 controllers and one USB 3.0 controller), an Intel Core i7 980X processor, 16 GB RAM, an NVIDA Quadro 6000 graphics card and four additional VIA USB 3.0 controllers. We also use powered USB extenders. Note that for the setup of multiple Kinects, only the number of physical

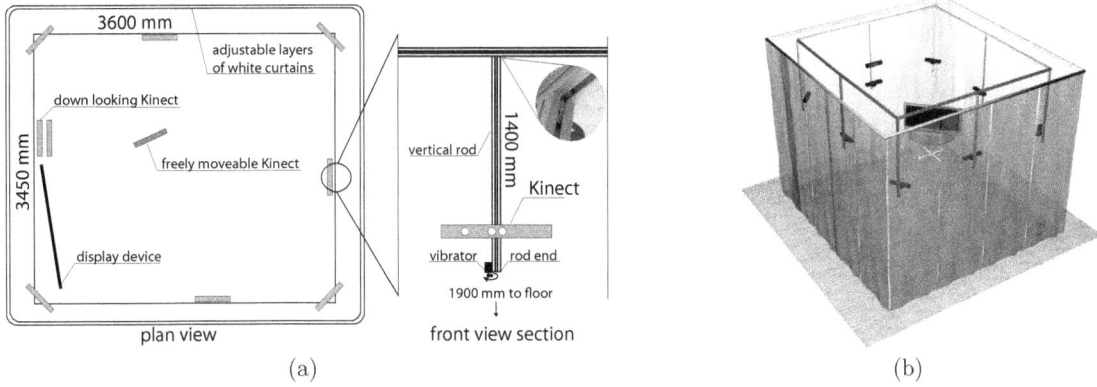

Figure 1: Plan views (a) and 3D overview (b) of our OmniKinect setup. In (a), vibrating Kinects are marked green and not vibrating Kinects red.

USB controller chips is important and not the number of USB ports. With this system, we can successfully operate 12 Kinects if only the RGB or the depth stream is used and 7 Kinects if both streams are used. This is mainly due to the limited bandwidth of the mainboard's south-bridge controller. As driver, we can use either the Microsoft Kinect SDK Driver, or, as for most of our example applications, the OpenNI (http://openni.org) PrimeSense Driver.

Calibration: We considered intrinsic, extrinsic, and depth calibration parameters.

As intrinsic camera parameters, we use the values given in the Microsoft Kinect SDK. However, for most of our target applications, we also need an initial extrinsic camera calibration for each Kinect.

We obtain extrinsic camera parameters using a $1300mm$ high calibration target, shown in Figure 2 with StbTracker [20] targets. Each of the target's 3 sides ($400 \times 500mm$) has 4 marker. The back-projection error for this target is in the sub-pixel range and can therefore be neglected.

The external calibration is computed on the RGB camera image. The depth image is transformed into the coordinate system of the RGB image by using the static transformation given by the OpenNI or Microsoft Kinect SDK.

Additionally, we provide a method to overcome depth inaccuracies between the Kinects. Each Kinect generates slightly different depth values, which can lead to holes or overlaps for the resulting reconstructions. For applications that require highly accurate multi-depth measurements, we perform an additional inter-Kinect depth calibration step using a red sphere ($\varnothing 120mm$), which is moved through the reconstruction volume (Figure 2 (c)). This sphere is segmented in the RGB image stream, and by mapping the depth stream onto the RGB stream also its depth values are obtained. Relying on the extrinsic and intrinsic calibration of the statically mounted cameras, the sphere's position in the room is triangulated. For each Kinect, the depth error d_{err} for one measurement is computed, taking the difference between the Kinect's estimated depth value d_{in} and the depth value obtained by the triangulated position of the sphere. After estimating depth errors for the entire calibration sequence, we fit a three dimensional polynomial function f_{err} (with the pixel coordinates p_x, p_y, and d_{in} as input) to the depth errors:

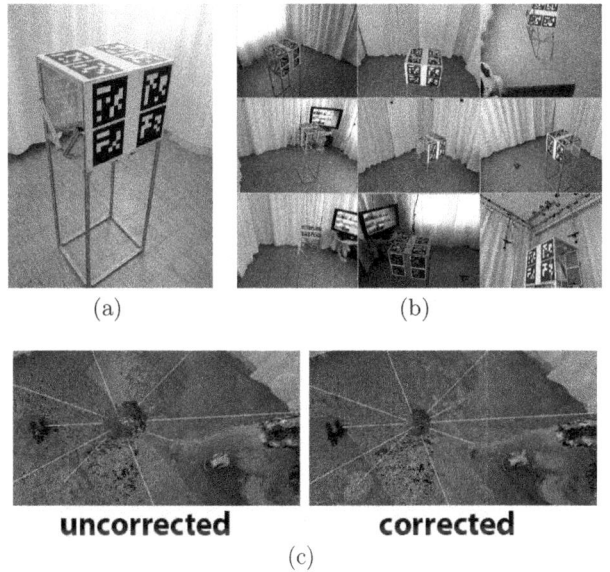

Figure 2: The StbTracker calibration target ($1300 \times 400 \times 500mm$) to gain initial extrinsic camera parameters (a) and the initial calibration view (b) showing the coordinate frame center for one example configuration using nine Kinects. (c) shows a point cloud rendering of the depth calibration target before (left) and after (right) correction with the camera viewing rays (white lines).

$$f_{err}(p_x, p_y, d_{in}) = \sum_{x,y,z} p_x^x \cdot p_y^y \cdot d_{in}^z \cdot c_{x,y,z} \overset{!}{=} d_{err}, \qquad (1)$$

with the exponents x, y, z running from zero to a maximum degree of four. According to our measurements, a maximum exponent of 1 for x, 1 for y, and 3 for depth works already sufficiently well and does not suffer from over-fitting. The polynomial coefficients $c_{x,y,z}$ are obtained by an SVD decomposition and stored in a calibration file. Using the coefficients the estimated depth error for unseen inputs can be computed efficiently. Adding this estimate to the reported depth value of the Kinect yields the corrected depth value $d_{out} = d_{in} + d_{err}$. Using a single 3D polynomial guarantees a smooth transaction between neighboring locations.

Note that this approach needs to be carried out only once, even if the setup is changed slightly, as the depth calibration is obtained for each individual Kinect and it is only parametrized by the local pixel coordinates and the depth estimate. In principle, it would be possible to mount such spheres statically in our setup and to evaluate their position continuously. However, this does not seem to be necessary, as the depth error is not time varying. Additionally, such a setup would significantly reduce the available leeway.

Recording and playback: We use the OpenNI recorder and player feature to record or play back a sequence for each Kinect. Thereby, the maximum movement speed of objects is limited by the capture rate of the depth sensor, which is currently 30 frames per second.

Costs: Including all Kinects, the PC, the mounting and the motors, our whole system can be built with less than 5000 USD.

4. HIGH LEVEL COMPONENTS

4.1 OmniKinect fusion

Our experiments have shown that a straight forward fusion of depth maps from different sources is not possible, mainly due to the variations in the depth map accuracy between different Kinects. The user could use our extended polynomial calibration method from Section 3. However, this method might not always be feasible because of sparsely overlapping field-of-views within the sensor arrangement and the generally high time-effort for the calibration procedure. Therefore, we have extended the KinectFusion algorithm presented by Newcombe et al. [15] to work properly also with simultaneous uncorrected input streams from multiple Kinects. This approach uses only an initial extrinsic pose estimation of the cameras. We introduce an additional step for the algorithm as shown in Figure 3, which uses a smoothed histogram volume of truncated signed distance functions (TSDF) [4] to filter outlier measurements of the signed distance field before a temporal smoothing. In this way, persistent outliers due to variations in the registered pose or depth accuracies are removed, yielding a more robust estimate of the surface generating a complete and accurate reconstruction of the observed volume.

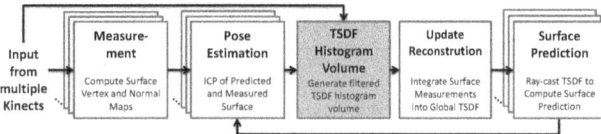

Figure 3: Overall system workflow for the modified KinectFusion algorithm [15] to support multiple simultaneous Kinects with different inaccuracies. The additional step is marked as red center square.

In our technique, we introduce a new volume consisting of a discrete histogram for the TSDF per voxel. We calculate the TSDF similar to Newcombe et al. with a ramp length of $\pm\mu$. The true surface is assumed to lie within this interval. Therefore, the TSDF $f_{R_k}(v, d)$ at a voxel v for device d with

a distance η to the measured depth is given as

$$f_{R_k}(v, d) = \Psi(\eta) = \begin{cases} \min(1, \frac{\eta}{\mu}) & \text{if } \eta \geq -\mu \\ null & \text{otherwise.} \end{cases} \quad (2)$$

$\Psi(\eta)$ lies in the interval $[-1, 1]$ and is positive in free space, negative behind the surface. Instead of a direct weighted integration into the TSDF volume, we count the values of $\Psi(\eta)$ from each depth map at a voxel v in one histogram $\Theta(v)$ per voxel and increment the corresponding histogram bin with λ:

$$\begin{aligned} \Theta_i(v) &= \Theta_i(v) + \lambda, \lambda = 1 \\ i &= \left\lfloor (f_{R_k}(v, d) + 1) * \frac{K}{2} + 0.5 \right\rfloor. \end{aligned} \quad (3)$$

The number of bins K can be freely chosen and defines another level of under-sampling for the TSDF. To allow a good coverage of zero-crossings, it is sufficient to choose this value as a small odd number. During our experiments, $K = 5, 7, 9, 11$ provided good results. Because of this discretization step, the histogram transformation behaves like an infinite impulse response (IIR) filter. The more bins are used for the histogram, the better edges and details are represented.

After the TSDFs of all input devices have been evaluated, each histogram bin is filtered separately with a three-dimensional bilateral filter to obtain a discontinuity preserving TSDF histogram volume with reduced noise per layer θ_i of $\Theta(v)$ between the measurements of the separate Kinects:

$$\theta_i(v) = \frac{1}{W} \sum_{q \in \mathcal{V}} \mathcal{N}_{\sigma_s}(\|v - q\|_2)\mathcal{N}_{\sigma_r}(\|\theta_i(v) - \theta_i(q)\|_2)\theta_i(q), \quad (4)$$

for each voxel $v = (x, y, z)^T$ in the volume domain $v \in \mathcal{V} \in \mathbb{R}^3$, $\mathcal{N}_\sigma = exp(-t^2\sigma^{-2})$ (spatial domain $\mathcal{N}_{\sigma_s}$ and intesity range domain $\mathcal{N}_{\sigma_r}$) and W as a normalization constant. Note, that this filter is very similar to the bilateral depth map filter of [17] in $\mathbb{R}^2$, but performed in $\mathbb{R}^3$ at this point. A subsequent maximum search per voxel histogram gives a robust estimate of the underlying TSDF volume value because it acts like a majority vote decision or IIR filter.

The histogram bins $\Theta_i(v)$ are normalized to the upper limit of the used data structure for the filter step. The actual value of the histogram bins does not influence the following steps, because we transform the index of the maximum of these histograms back into a regular TSDF volume ψ, using weighted averaging for this integration. Thereby, we use the inverse transform to Equation 3:

$$\begin{aligned} \psi(v) &= -1 - \frac{1 - 2\alpha}{K}, \text{with } K \neq 0 \text{ and} \\ \alpha &= \arg\max_i(\theta_i(v)) \end{aligned} \quad (5)$$

We integrate that value into the final TSDF volume $F_{R_k}(v)$ with weighted averaging by storing a weight $W_k(v)$ with each value:

$$\begin{aligned} F_{R_k}(v) &= \frac{W_{k-1}(v)F_{k-1}(v) + W_{R_k}(v)\psi(v)}{W_{k-1}(v) + W_{R_k}(v)} \\ W_k(v) &= W_{k-1}(v) + W_{R_k}(v) \end{aligned} \quad (6)$$

where $W_{R_k}(v) = 1$. Originally, this weight is proportional to $\cos(\tau)/R_k(x)$, where τ is the angle between the associated pixel ray direction and the surface normal measurement. Newcombe et al. [15] showed that a simple average with $W_{R_k}(v) = 1$ provides good results. Our tests showed the same good performance with $W_{R_k}(v) = 1$. A similar weight can be used to increase the count in a histogram bin in Equation 3 by setting $\lambda = \lfloor 1 + |\cos(\tau)/R_k(x)| + 0.5 \rfloor$. With this approach, the tracking and reconstruction performance can be improved for certain scenes.

Note, that we do not reproduce the exact values of the input TSDF from Equation 3 in Equation 5. We are only interested in the majority vote for a zero-crossing of the different input devices. Therefore, exact numerical values are not necessary. The second volume implements a temporal smoothing, filtering temporal noise in the depth values.

With our method the standard KinectFusion *pose estimation* step can overcome calibration inaccuracies and disagreements of the depth sensors by adjusting the cameras' positions and orientations to positions in space, where most Kinects agree in their measurements. Furthermore, the vibration of the Kinects does not impair the transformation of the depth values into the static frame of reference because the vibration frequency is much higher than the image acquisition rate and possibly remaining artifacts are filtered out by integration over time. Figure 5 in Section 5.1 shows a comparison between a straight forward application of the original KinectFusion algorithm and OmniKinect fusion.

4.2 3D video and free viewpoint rendering

Capturing and rendering 3D videos is an important component of a variety of applications. For example, in 3D teleconferencing each participant needs to be rendered as seen from the observer's viewpoint. For digital entertainment and virtual try-on applications, a user wants to see herself immediately on a screen, immersed in a virtual world and augmented with virtual objects. To demonstrate the utility of the suggested system for these applications, we have implemented a free viewpoint rendering algorithm to display the 3D scene interactively.

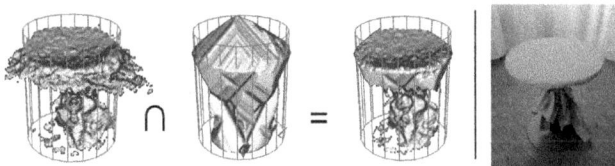

Figure 4: **Free-viewpoint rendering of a static round table. From left to right: Point cloud rendering directly from Kinect depth maps suffers from low-quality edges. Visual hulls, on the other hand, have sharp edges, but not enough concavities. By intersecting the two surface representations, we are able to achieve a much more desirable result. The red cylinders indicate the ground truth diameter of the table on the right.**

The image-based visual hull (IBVH) algorithm reconstructs and renders 3D objects from silhouette images. It is very efficient compared to stereo matching techniques. Additionally, it has the advantage of avoiding an explicit intermediate data representation, such as a voxel grid (as computed by KinectFusion) or mesh. It derives output depth maps directly from silhouette images and thus only computes surface regions that are actually visible. It can therefore provide pure dense image synthesis faster than with KinectFusion.

The IBVH algorithm produces depth maps of the object with clear edges, watertight topology, and no noise, even when using cheap cameras. However, it does not incorporate the depth data that is available in our system: it was designed to work with standard color cameras. Therefore, it fails to reconstruct some of the concavities.

In contrast to color images, depth maps from Microsoft Kinect are rather noisy and suffer from occlusions at depth discontinuities. At the same time, they convey more information about the shape of the scene. To get the advantages from both depth map-based rendering and image-based visual hull rendering, we combine the strengths of both approaches as follows.

Silhouette-carved point clouds: A prerequisite for visual hulls are silhouette images. To obtain silhouette images, the scene needs to be captured without foreground objects before the visualization starts. We use background subtraction based on color- and depth values to segment foreground objects. This method is more robust than relying on color or depth alone.

Our first method to incorporate visual hull information into point-based rendering is to carve the point clouds on the image planes by only considering depth values that are inside the silhouettes. Silhouettes are calculated by using binary foreground masks, which can be generated by using the aforementioned background subtraction. During our experiments we observed that some of the depth values are outliers even though they are inside their respective silhouettes.

Visual hull-carved point clouds: The visual hull of an object is a conservative surface estimate: It contains the whole object plus space that does not belong to the object. To remove low-quality depth values that caused noise in the silhouette-carved approach, we restrict the point cloud from all Kinects to the 3D space that is covered by the visual hull.

To do so, we perform IBVH rendering followed by point splatting to get both surface estimates. Then, all point splats are culled against the visual hull surface at that pixel. The result can be seen in Figure 4: concavities are reconstructed while sharp and precise edges are preserved.

5. EVALUATION AND RESULTS

5.1 OmniKinect fusion performance

To evaluate the performance of the OmniKinect fusion algorithm from Section 4.1, we have recorded several static scenes and compared their reconstruction results to a direct adaptation of the KinectFusion algorithm. The direct method integrates the TSDF values of each Kinect into a common volume with atomic operations. Figure 5 shows a comparison of horizontal and vertical slices through the TSDF volumes of these two approaches with a selected scene, which contains a simple box. Another qualitative comparison is given in Figure 6, using a reconstruction of the resulting zero-level set of the same round table object as shown in in Figure 4. Both reconstructions used the same parameters with $\mu = 0.1[m]$ and a TDFS size of 256^3 for the surface predictions, which were dumped after 10 frames. The corrugated regions in Figure 5 are the curtains around the setup.

Our additional computations introduce an average overhead of $3 - 9ms$ for the TSDF histogram evaluation per Kinect and $7 - 16ms$ for the histogram filtering, depending on the volume size and number of used histogram bins. A detailed run-time analysis for the original KinectFusion

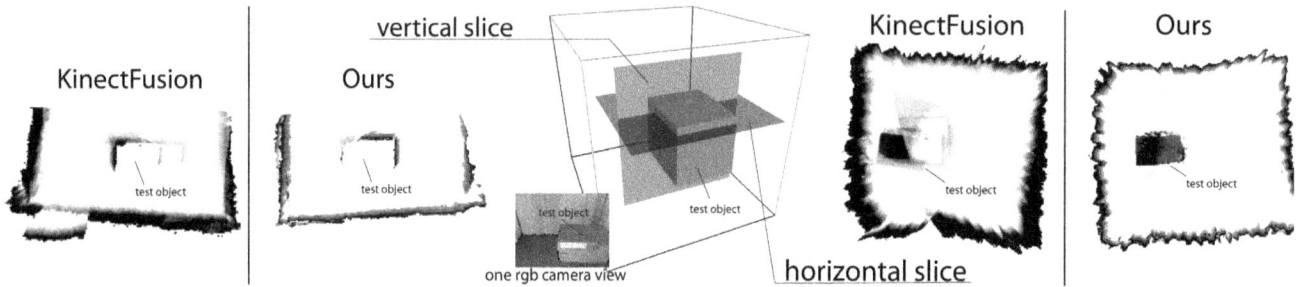

Figure 5: Overview over one of the test scenes using a large brown cardboard box and a comparison between cutting planes of the TSDF of a straight forward application of the KinectFusion algorithm to our approach.

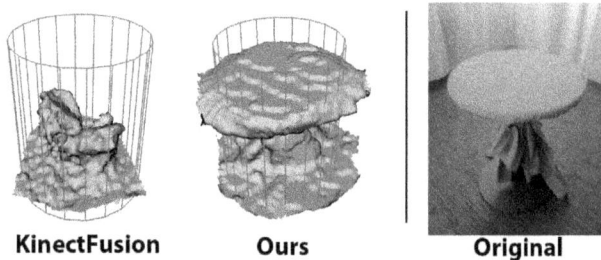

Figure 6: A qualitative comparison of the zero-level set resulting from the direct application of Kinect-Fusion and our approach with the same object as shown in Figure 4 after 10 frames of recording time. For the direct approach (left), no clear zero-crossing can be extracted for the table surface. Similar to Figure 4, the red cylinders indicate the ground truth diameter of the table on the right.

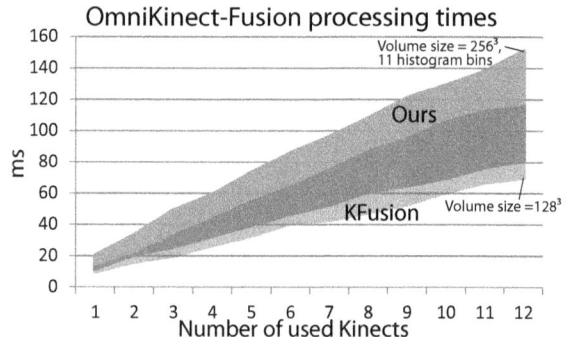

Figure 7: Evaluation of different configurations of OmniKinect fusion (green) compared to a straight forward implementation of the KinectFusion algorithm for multiple Kinects (blue). The KinectFusion range covers tests with TSDF volume sizes between 128^3 and 256^3. The tests for our method cover the same TSDF volume sizes. Additionally histograms with 5, 7, 9 and 11 bins have been measured for these volume sizes.

algorithm with multiple Kinect support and our system is given in Figure 7. We have performed our tests on a Nvidia GTX680 and average the overall processing times over 50 full computation cycles.

5.2 Free viewpoint rendering performance

To evaluate the quality of the OmniKinect setup, we captured an object of known size: a table with circular top (see Figure 4). We then reconstructed and rendered the object with a varying number of sensors with two methods: visual hulls and point cloud rendering.

Figure 8 shows the results. For two Kinects, the point cloud that is rendered from the depth data is already quite good when compared to the visual hull. One, two or even three silhouette images do not contain enough information to reconstruct such a surface in a meaningful way.

For a larger number of sensors, the rendering quality of the visual hull improves. It surpasses the quality of point cloud rendering at the edges of the object. The reason for this is that the Kinect cameras can be calibrated intrinsically and extrinsically very exactly, which directly translates to precise visual hull edges.

IBVH avoids explicit data representations and is output-driven: for every output pixel exactly one surface intersection is computed. Invisible parts or backsides of the object are not computed, which makes it very efficient. Point splatting is also a very efficient algorithm because modern GPUs are built for fast geometry transformations. The required

scatter operation is also significantly faster to compute with recent CUDA versions. As a result, the visual-hull carved point cloud algorithm takes around 40 ms to compute on an Nvidia Quadro 6000 at a resolution of 1000×1000 pixels using 7 Kinects.

6. APPLICATIONS

In this section, we present selected application examples that leverage the OmniKinect system.

Full body scanning: An obvious application for our OmniKinect-fusion algorithm is detailed smooth body capturing. The user or dummy is placed in the center of the room and the zero-level set of the TSDF volume is extracted as soon as sufficient integration quality has been reached. During our tests, we have achieved good results already after 5-10 frames. Figure 9 shows an example for that use case.

Consistent photometric registration: Photo-realistic AR requires a geometric and a photometric model of the real world, so that virtual objects can be embedded consistently with the real environment. For example, virtual and real objects should mutually occlude each other, and cast shadows upon each other. Using the OmniKinect fusion detailed in section 4.1, high quality geometric information of the real scene can be obtained almost instantaneously. To

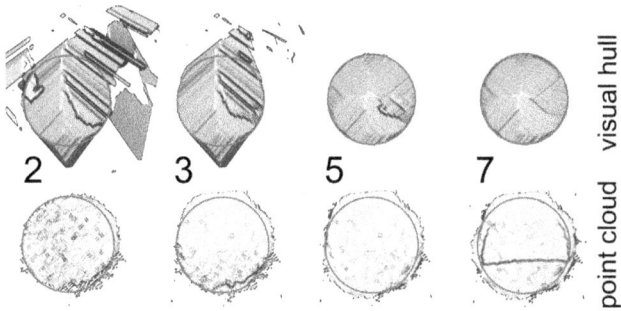

Figure 8: The top row shows visual hull rendering, the bottom row point cloud rendering for a varying number of Kinects. The red circle indicates the ground truth diameter of the reconstructed object.

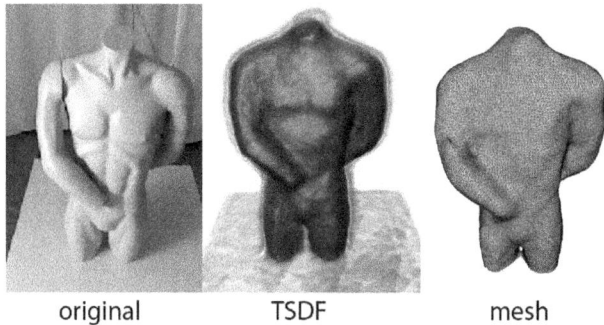

original   TSDF   mesh

Figure 9: Example of a dummy body-scan application using OmniKinect fusion after ten frames integration time. A volume rendering of the resulting TSDF volume is shown in the center and the resulting mesh of the zero-level set at the right.

acquire an estimate of the real-world illumination in real time, previous approaches have relied on special light probe devices, such as a mirror ball or an omni-directional camera. OmniKinect's high quality volumetric model allows to use the scene itself as a light probe, and infer the current illumination from observations of the scene.

As proof of concept, we implemented a photometric registration application (Figure 10). For the light estimation, we simultaneously observe the reflection of the incident light on the scene geometry from multiple views. This allows measuring all outgoing light from the scene, which can be interpreted as a hemisphere of illumination directions. The final result is a combination of all light estimates from each camera view. For efficient real time computation, the illumination is represented using Spherical Harmonics.

X-ray visualization in Augmented Reality: Live volumetric representations of a real scene allow advanced X-ray visualizations in AR. Rather than simply combining virtual and real objects, we can leverage the volumetric representation to modify the appearance of a real object with respect to other real objects.

For example, X-ray visualization can make a real object translucent and show another real object occluded by the first one. Because the whole working volume is available in real time, both the occluder and the occluded can be dynamic, animated objects such as moving human beings.

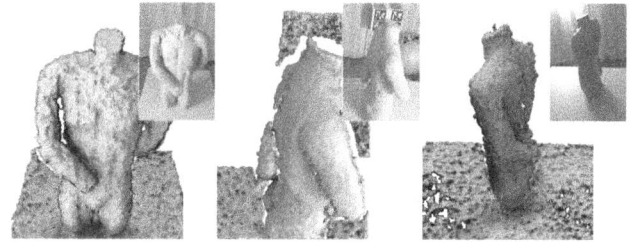

Figure 10: The three images show the reconstruction of the scene lit by the estimated environment light. For better comparison the input images of the camera are added as small inserts in the upper right corner. Note that the light situation is the same for all three images.

Technically, any combination of real and virtual views can be rendered to separate frame buffers, and then blended in a final step relying on a G-buffer approach [7]. Multiple objects can be extracted from the OmniKinect reconstruction using an appropriate segmentation method, for example by giving a bounding volume for a static object or by comparing a scene with and without a particular object. The object can then be rendered separately, and treated differently in the compositing, for example by modulating transparency.

Figure 11: X-Ray visualizations: see-through-me demo by segmenting a person (left), see inside the box with free-hand Kinect (middle), by comparing minimal differences in two scenes and using OmniKinect to see behind an object (right).

3D Magic Book: The OmniKinect setup can create a 3D AR Magic Book. Similar to 3D Live [16], we can record movement sequences and play them back in an AR environment. As our system is simpler to use, it can be easily deployed and provide a way to create a personalized 3D photo-book, a three-dimensional extension of online photo-book creation tools. The accompanying video presents an example of playing an AR book of a Karate training. Each of the sequences has been exported separately in an offline process, converted to a point cloud and saved to a compressed format supporting animation.

3D Magic Mirror: OmniKinect combined with a 3D autostereoscopic display can be used for a Magic Mirror metaphor where the user interacts with the reconstructed sequence (see Figure 12). Especially in sports that require specific postures the trainee can directly observe the scene in full 3D. Furthermore, the OmniKinect fusion reconstruction can be used to create a real-time differential 3D reconstruction to analyze diverging movements.

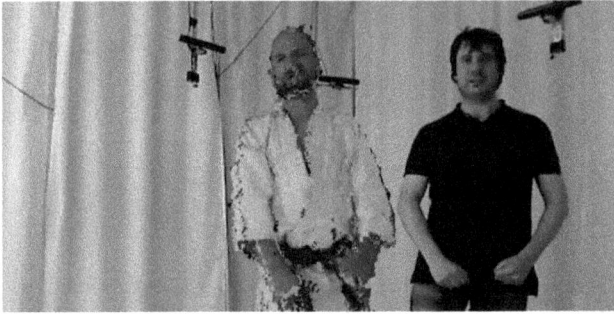

Figure 12: MagicMirror using the OmniKinect for generating a virtual trainer.

7. CONCLUSIONS

We have presented an easy-to-build, flexible, and affordable system for real-time 3D reconstruction and free-viewpoint rendering of real-world scenes. While conceptually simple, the calibration and fusion of data from multiple depth sensors requires careful design and deployment of the hardware setup and advanced algorithms for data processing and analysis. We have successfully improved the KinectFusion algorithm to accommodate multiple sensors simultaneously. Using this foundation, it is easy to implement depth segmentation algorithms and geometrically aware AR for dense dynamic scenes.

For 3D video capture and free-viewpoint rendering of moving and deforming objects, we introduced visual-hull carved point cloud rendering. It combines the advantages of image-based visual hull and point cloud rendering: precise edges and support for concave objects.

As future work we will conduct more thorough quantitative and qualitative evaluations, and investigate more applications. Currently, we are also working on an automatic marker-less online depth value correction, which will ease the initial calibration procedure significantly.

Acknowledgments: This work was supported by the Christian Doppler Laboratory for Handheld Augmented Reality, the Austrian Science Fund (FWF): P23329 and P24021, and the Austrian Research Promotion Agency (FFG) under the BRIDGE program, project 822702 (NARKISSOS).

8. REFERENCES

[1] K. Berger, K. Ruhl, C. Brümmer, Y. Schröder, A. Scholz, and M. Magnor. Markerless motion capture using multiple color-depth sensors. In *Proc. VMV 2011*, pages 317–324, Oct. 2011.

[2] E. Boyer. A hybrid approach for computing visual hulls of complex objects. In *Proc. IEEE CVPR*, pages 695–701, 2003.

[3] A. Butler, S. Izadi, O. Hilliges, D. Molyneaux, S. Hodges, and D. Kim. Shake'n'sense: reducing interference for overlapping structured light depth cameras. In *Proc. CHI '12*, pages 1933–1936, 2012.

[4] B. Curless and M. Levoy. A volumetric method for building complex models from range images. In *Proc. SIGGRAPH '96*, pages 303–312, 1996.

[5] U. Dhond and J. Aggarwal. Structure from stereo-a review. *IEEE Trans. on Systems, Man and Cybernetics*, 19(6):1489 –1510, nov/dec 1989.

[6] L. Guan, J.-S. Franco, and M. Pollefeys. 3D Object Reconstruction with Heterogeneous Sensor Data. In *Proc. 3DPVT*, 2008.

[7] D. Kalkofen, E. Mendez, and D. Schmalstieg. Comprehensible visualization for augmented reality. *IEEE TVCG*, 15(2):193–204, 2009.

[8] Y. M. Kim, D. Chan, C. Theobalt, and S. Thrun. Design and calibration of a multi-view TOF sensor fusion system. In *Proc. IEEE CVPR Workshops*, pages 1 –7, June 2008.

[9] C. Kuster, T. Popa, C. Zach, C. Gotsman, and M. Gross. Freecam: A hybrid camera system for interactive free-viewpoint video. In *Proc. VMV*, 2011.

[10] M. Li. *Towards Real-Time Novel View Synthesis Using Visual Hulls*. PhD thesis, Universität des Saarlandes, 2004.

[11] A. Maimone and H. Fuchs. Encumbrance-free telepresence system with real-time 3D capture and display using commodity depth cameras. In *Proc. ISMAR '11*, pages 137–146, 2011.

[12] A. Maimone and H. Fuchs. Reducing interference between multiple structured light depth sensors using motion. In *Proc. IEEE VR*, pages 51–54, 2012.

[13] W. Matusik, C. Buehler, R. Raskar, S. J. Gortler, and L. McMillan. Image-based visual hulls. In *Proc. ACM SIGGRAPH '00*, pages 369–374, 2000.

[14] W. Matusik and H. Pfister. 3D TV: a scalable system for real-time acquisition, transmission, and autostereoscopic display of dynamic scenes. In *Proc. SIGGRAPH '04*, pages 814–824, 2004.

[15] R. A. Newcombe, S. Izadi, O. Hilliges, D. Molyneaux, D. Kim, A. J. Davison, P. Kohli, J. Shotton, S. Hodges, and A. Fitzgibbon. Kinectfusion: Real-time dense surface mapping and tracking. In *Proc IEEE ISMAR '11*, pages 127–136, 2011.

[16] S. Prince, A. D. Cheok, F. Farbiz, T. Williamson, N. Johnson, M. Billinghurst, and H. Kato. 3D Live: Real Time Captured Content for Mixed Reality. In *Proc. IEEE ISMAR '02*, page 7, 2002.

[17] C. Rhemann, A. Hosni, M. Bleyer, C. Rother, and M. Gelautz. Fast cost-volume filtering for visual correspondence and beyond. In *Proc. IEEE CVPR '11*, pages 3017–3024, 2011.

[18] J. Shotton, A. Fitzgibbon, M. Cook, T. Sharp, M. Finocchio, R. Moore, A. Kipman, and A. Blake. Real-time human pose recognition in parts from single depth images. In *Proc. IEEE CVPR'11*, 2011.

[19] J. Tong, J. Zhou, L. Liu, Z. Pan, and H. Yan. Scanning 3d full human bodies using kinects. *IEEE TVCG*, pages 643–650, 2012.

[20] D. Wagner, T. Langlotz, and D. Schmalstieg. Robust und unobtrusive marker tracking on mobile phones. In *Proc. IEEE ISMAR'08*, pages 121–124, 2008.

[21] A. D. Wilson and H. Benko. Combining multiple depth cameras and projectors for interactions on, above and between surfaces. In *Proc. ACM UIST '10*, pages 273–282, 2010.

[22] R. Yang, G. Welch, and G. Bishop. Real-time consensus-based scene reconstruction using commodity graphics hardware. In *Proc. Computer Graphics and Applications 2002*, pages 225 – 234, 2002.

iAR: an Exploratory Augmented Reality System for Mobile Devices

Nils Karlsson
Imaging and Computer Vision
Siemens Corporate Research
and Technology
Princeton, NJ, USA

Gang Li
Imaging and Computer Vision
Siemens Corporate Research
and Technology
Princeton, NJ, USA

Yakup Genc
Imaging and Computer Vision
Siemens Corporate Research
and Technology
Princeton, NJ, USA

Angela Huenerfauth
User Experience Design
Siemens Healthcare
Diagnostics
Flanders, NJ, USA

Elizabeth Bononno
User Experience Design
Siemens Healthcare
Diagnostics
Flanders, NJ, USA

ABSTRACT

In this paper we propose an exploratory augmented reality(AR) system for mobile devices. A hybrid system of 3D object detection and 3D tracking is used to rapidly localize the object in the scene. Based on randomized tree classifier, object detection supports large viewpoint changes. While edge-based 3D tracking provides efficient computation and better accuracy for pose estimation of incremental motions. The result is an augmented reality system that works well with large viewpoint variance and has superior accuracy. Using a mobile device such as iPad or iPhone, our system further provides exploratory capability using their touch screen and wireless connectivity. The user is able to interact and explore the 3D object on the image or video, and collaborate with a remote user. Extensive experiments with different subjects demonstrate that the proposed system advances the state-of-the-art in augmented reality with novel and intuitive applications.

Categories and Subject Descriptors

I.4.8 [**Image Processing and Computer Vision**]: Scene Analysis—*Tracking*; H.5.1 [**Information Interfaces and Presentation**]: Multimedia Information Systems—*Artificial, Augmented, and Virtual Realities*

Keywords

Augmented reality; computer vision; 3D object detection; 3D tracking; mobile; collaborative AR; interaction techniques

1. INTRODUCTION

Augmented reality(AR) is a very active research area [2, 14, 8]. With the availability of smart phones and tablet devices equipped with cameras and high speed processors, real-time markerless augmented reality applications are now becoming available. Mobile devices such as smartphones provide the best way of introducing AR to the mass market, due to the readily availability of these devices [22]. In this paper we propose an exploratory augmented reality system for mobile devices, where a hybrid system of 3D object detection and 3D tracking is used to rapidly localize the object in the scene. Based on randomized tree classifier, object detection supports large viewpoint changes. While edge-based 3D tracking provides efficient computation and better accuracy for pose estimation of incremental motions. The result is an augmented reality system that works well with large viewpoint variance and has superior accuracy. This novel system utilizes the camera, touch screen, processing power and wireless connectivity of a hand held device. With the proposed system it is possible to localize (by detection or tracking) one or several objects of varying size in real-time. Once the object is localized at all times in the camera view, the system uses the camera pose to augment the scene. (see Figure 1).

This novel system utilizes the camera, touch screen, processing power and connectivity of a hand held device. Using a touch screen adds more functionalities to an AR system. In addition to overlay textual information and graphics with regards to the object it also adds a more intuitive way of interacting with the object. By touching on different parts of the object in the image or video, there is a myriad of possibilities. The second layer of utilizing a hand held device is the use of its wireless connectivity. By having an up-link to a server or to the cloud we also introduce novel ways of collaborating in exploring an object and the environment around it using AR. These novel ways of using the capabilities of the hand held devices are discussed later in this paper. We call our system iAugmentedReality(iAR).

Figure 1: In Augmented Reality a stream of incoming images (Top) is overlayed with some graphical information (Bottom). In this example a complex diagnostic machine (Siemens VersaCell) is tracked and a 3D model is overlayed on top of the camera feed.

1.1 Related work

The iAR system has three key components: pose estimation, interaction, and collaborative AR.

Pose estimation has been studied extensively in computer vision [4, 16]. To recover camera pose, model edges or points in 3D can be used for tracking. Drummond and Cipolla [3] and Lepetit and Fua [11] use model edges, where Illc et al. [6, 7] exploit model edges derived from implicit surface representation. Vacchetti et al. [21] reply on model points. Independently, pose estimation can be achieved by first extracting feature descriptors (e.g. SIFT [15]) and then classify using machine learning techniques [12, 24]. Klein and Murray [9] propose an impressive parallel tracking and mapping (PTAM) algorithm for augmented reality, where both pose estimation and mapping are addressed.

Interaction techniques have also been researched [25]. Some of the first mobile AR systems used mobile trackballs, trackpads and gyroscopic mice to handle 2D pointing tasks [22]. Schmalstieg et al. [18] implemented an interaction panel in which the user can manipulate an objects in an augmented reality space. On mobile devices with touchscreens Wagner et al. [23] developed the "The Inivisible Train" project and used markers to allow users interact with augmented train tracks using the touch screen. In addition, interaction techniques have also been researched in AR games [10].

Collaborative AR was first developed in the mid 90s with "The Studiersube" [19] and "Shared Space" [1] projects demonstrating the collaborative possibilities of AR. Henrysson et al. [5] developed a game called AR Tennis on a mobile phone that augmented a tennis court allowing two players to play against each other. Reitmayr and Schmalstieg [17] used a wearable computer and marker based approach that allowed for collaboration between a mobile and a stationary user.

2. SYSTEM OVERVIEW

Figure 2 shows an overview of the iAR system. A mobile device equipped with a camera continuously captures images and sends them to a PC connected through Wifi. The PC performs pose estimation via tracking or detection. If the tracking fails the system switches to the slower detection mode (that covers larger viewpoint variance). By sending the stream of images to a PC allows for faster computation than what would be possible on the device itself. The PC then renders an augmented view and sends the rendered image back to the mobile device where it is rendered on the screen.

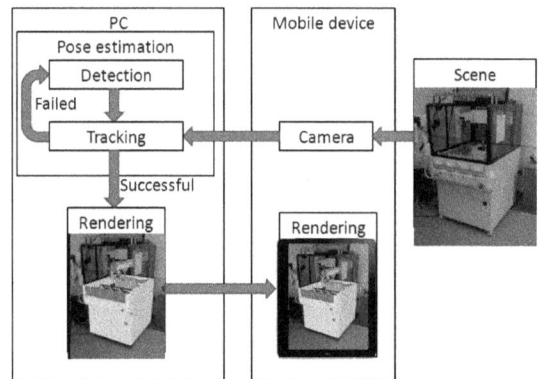

Figure 2: Overview of the iAR system.

3. ALGORITHM

The key to Augmented Reality (AR) is for every frame to estimate object to camera pose, traditionally known as the pose estimation problem [4]. The goal is to determine the relative pose between the object and the camera coordinate system, i.e. rotation $\mathbf{R}_i$ and translation $\mathbf{T}_i$ for the i-th image:

$$s\mathbf{u}_i = \mathbf{K}(\mathbf{R}_i\mathbf{X} + \mathbf{T}_i) \qquad (1)$$

where $\mathbf{X} = (X, Y, Z)^T$ is any scene point, $\mathbf{u} = (u, v, 1)^T$ is its image point represented in homogeneous coordinates, $\mathbf{K}$ is the internal calibration matrix and it is determined offline, and s is a scalar.

In the proposed method, this is achieved through a hybrid system where either 3D object detection or edge-based 3D tracking is utilized (see Figure 2).

3.1 3D Object Detection

The detection algorithm uses feature point extraction and randomized trees classification [12] to detect and localize objects in 3D. A training phase is first performed where one

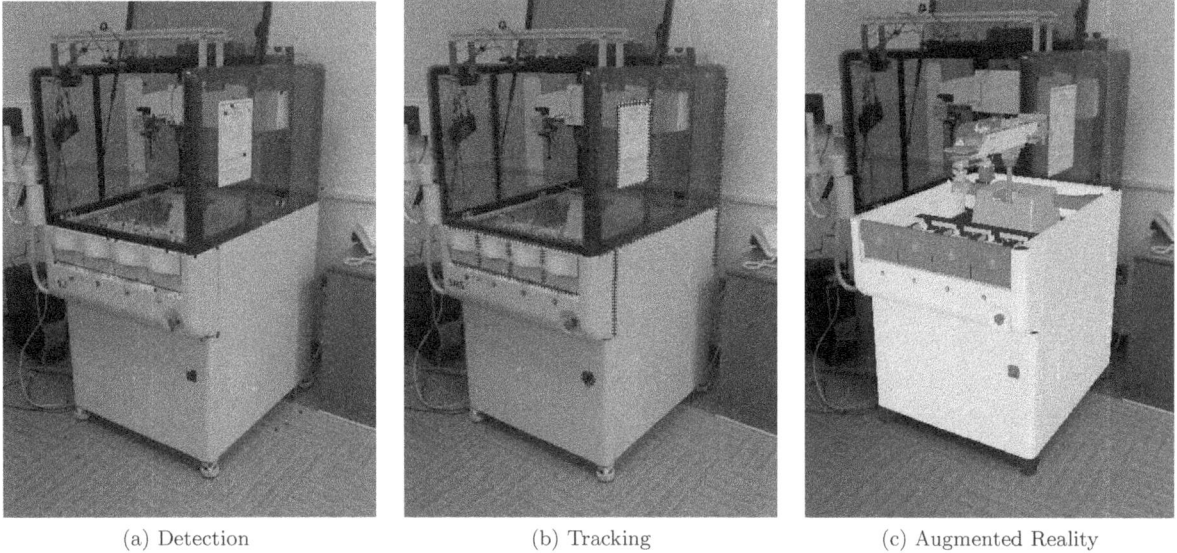

(a) Detection (b) Tracking (c) Augmented Reality

Figure 3: The proposed system is a hybrid system. When large viewpoint change occurs, object localization relies on 3D object detection (as shown in (a)), where the green dots show inliers of feature points and red dots show outliers. Otherwise, when incremental motion occurs object localization is obtained through edge-based 3D tracking (as shown in (b)), which is much faster and more accurate for pose estimation. The red line segments are the edges we use for tracking. When tracking fails, our system automatically converts to the detection mode. In our experiments the proposed hybrid system is able to transition smoothly between these two modes. (c) Augmented reality using recovered camera pose.

or several training images is taken and the algorithm extracts a number of feature points from this image. These prominent keypoints on the object model form a set $\mathbf{K} = \{\mathbf{k}_1, \mathbf{k}_2, ..., \mathbf{k}_N\}$. The feature points are extracted using a scale invariant approach. Once the feature points are extracted a number of synthetic views are created for each feature point and a patch around it. By assuming low curvature, the feature points and the patch around them can be treated as locally planar and by doing affine transformations all the possible views of these patches can be synthesized. At runtime, feature points are extracted and matched to the training set, where wide baseline point matching is cast as a classification problem. We use randomized trees [12] where we observe robust performance and reasonable speed (about 100 milliseconds per frame). Given an input patch $\mathbf{p}(\mathbf{k}^{input})$ centered at a keypoint $\mathbf{k}^{input}$ extracted from the input image, we wish to decide whether its appearance can be matched to a keypoint $\mathbf{k}_i$ in the set $\mathbf{K}$ so that a proper class label $Y(\mathbf{p}) \in C = \{-1, 1, 2, ..., N\}$ can be assigned to $\mathbf{p}(\mathbf{k}^{input})$, where -1 label denotes there is no match. Since Y cannot be observed directly, we need to build a classifier $\hat{Y}$ such that $P(Y(\mathbf{p}) \neq \hat{Y}(\mathbf{p}))$ is small.

In randomized trees, each internal node encodes a simple test that splits the space of image patches. Each leaf node contains an estimate based on training data of the posterior distribution over the classes. Classification for a new patch is obtained by dropping the patch down the tree and performing a simple test at each node that determines whether it goes to the left sub-tree or the right sub-tree. When it arrives at a leaf node, it is assigned probabilities of belonging to a class depending on the distribution stored in the leaf. Specifically, the tree leaves store posterior probabilities $P_{\eta(l,\mathbf{p})}(Y(\mathbf{p}) = c)$, where c is a label in $\mathbf{C}$ and $\eta(l, \mathbf{p})$ is the leaf node of tree T_l reached by patch $\mathbf{p}$. These proba-

bilities are evaluated at training as the ratio of the number of patches of class c in the training set that reach η and the total number of patches that reach η. As in [12], $\mathbf{p}$ is classified via considering the average of the probabilities $P_{\eta(l,\mathbf{p})}(Y(\mathbf{p}) = c)$:

$$\hat{Y}(\mathbf{p}) = \arg\max_c p_c(\mathbf{p}) = \arg\max_c \frac{1}{L} \sum_{l=1,...,L} P_{\eta(l,\mathbf{p})}(Y(\mathbf{p}) = c)$$
(2)

where $p_c(\mathbf{p})$ is the average of the posterior probabilities of class c and constitutes a good measure of the match confidence. We determine in training a threshold T_c to decide whether to consider a match correct (inlier) or incorrect (outlier).

The tests performed at each node is just a simple binary test by checking the difference of intensities of two pixels $\mathbf{m}_1$ and $\mathbf{m}_2$ taken in the neighborhood of the keypoint [12]:

$$C_2(\mathbf{m}_1, \mathbf{m}_2) = \begin{cases} \text{If } \mathbf{I}_\sigma(\mathbf{p}, \mathbf{m}_1) \leq \mathbf{I}_\sigma(\mathbf{p}, \mathbf{m_2}), & \text{go to left child} \\ \\ \text{otherwise}, & \text{go to right child} \end{cases}$$
(3)

where $\mathbf{I}_\sigma(\mathbf{p}, \mathbf{m})$ is the intensity of path $\mathbf{p}$ at pixel location $\mathbf{m}$, after smoothing by a Gaussian convolution to reduce image noise. This is essentially a test on the polarity between the two locations $\mathbf{m}_1$ and $\mathbf{m}_2$.

3.2 3D Tracking

While the detection method described above can cover a large range of viewing conditions, both speed and pose estimation accuracy can be improved when incremental motions occur to known camera poses. We adopt an edge-based 3D tracking method [11, 3]. Given a calibrated camera and a

35

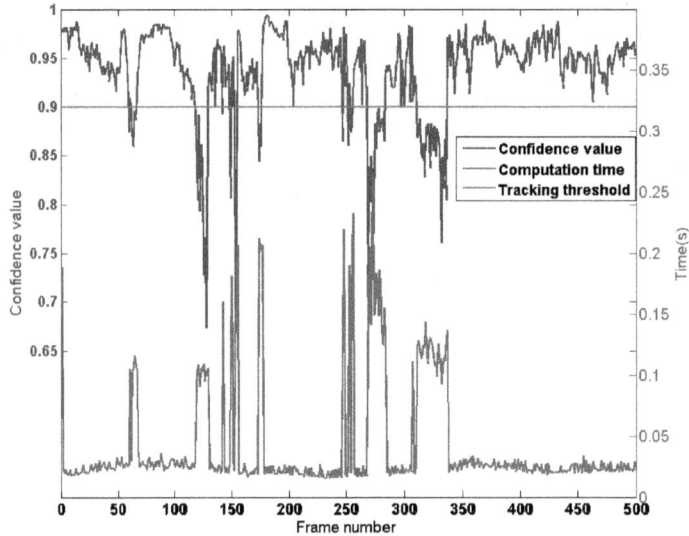

Figure 4: Tracking confidence values (in blue) and running time (in green) over a dataset of 500 frames. As our 3D edge-based tracking is much faster and more accurate for pose estimation, when tracking achieves high confidence value (larger than 0.9) we consider tracking successful. When tracking fails, our system automatically converts to the detection mode, which works for much larger viewpoint change and provides re-initialization to the tracker.

known 3D object in the scene, these techniques find out the pose of the camera with respect to the object through optimization. In particular, we apply an edge-based 3D tracking method [3] where each frame takes only about 5 milliseconds. We optimize our pose parameters using re-weighted least squares for an error function defined over edge matching scores. Due to space limitation we will not explain in details about this step but refer to published work such as [3, 11, 13]. The method involves the following logical steps:

(1) *Pose initialization.* An initial estimate of the pose for the current frame is obtained as the correctly estimated pose from the previous frame. If this is not available (e.g. tracking failure) or it is the first frame, 3D detection (as explained in the previous subsection) will provide the pose initialization.

(2) *Sampling.* 3D edges are sampled such that their projections are equally spaced in the image plane. Visibility study is also performed to ignore invisible points.

(3) *Projection.* Sampled 3D edge points are projected into the image.

(4) *Feature detection.* Edge candidates are detected in the current image.

(5) *Feature matching.* Match edge profiles of sampled points to tentative correspondences in current image. This is performed efficiently along the normal direction of the projected edges.

(6) *Optimization.* Minimize a cost function whose global minimum corresponds to the correct pose for the current image. A robust method [20] is adopted to iteratively solve a weighted least square optimization problem. This yields robust estimation of the pose.

Steps (5) and (6) are iterated until convergence is achieved.

4. A HYBRID SYSTEM: EXPERIMENTAL RESULTS

The proposed system has been tested extensively. Figure 3 shows the two modes of our system. When large viewpoint change occurs, object localization relies on 3D object detection (Figure 3(a)), where the green dots show inliers of feature points and red dots show outliers. Otherwise, when incremental motion occurs object localization is obtained through edge-based 3D tracking (Figure 3(b)), which is much faster and more accurate for pose estimation. The red line segments are the edges we use for tracking. When tracking fails, our system automatically switches to the detection mode. In our experiments the proposed hybrid system is able to transition smoothly between these two modes. As a result, the proposed system can cover large areas for motion and at the same time be computationally very efficient.

Figure 4 shows tracking confidence values (in blue) and running time (in green) over a dataset of 500 frames calculated on a PC with a 3.00GHz Dual-core processor. As our 3D edge-based tracking is much faster and more accurate for pose estimation, when tracking achieves high confidence value (larger than 0.9) we consider tracking successful. When tracking fails, our system automatically converts to the detection mode, which works for much larger viewpoint change and provides re-initialization to the tracker. As a result, our system is both computationally efficient and at the same time works within a large area (e.g. 180 degrees of horizontal motion with training done at only one viewpoint). As a simple extension, we can train our classifier at multiple viewpoints to support even larger motion range.

Figure 5 is the detection and tracking result over a dataset of 100 frames where every 3rd frame is plotted. Shown are

36

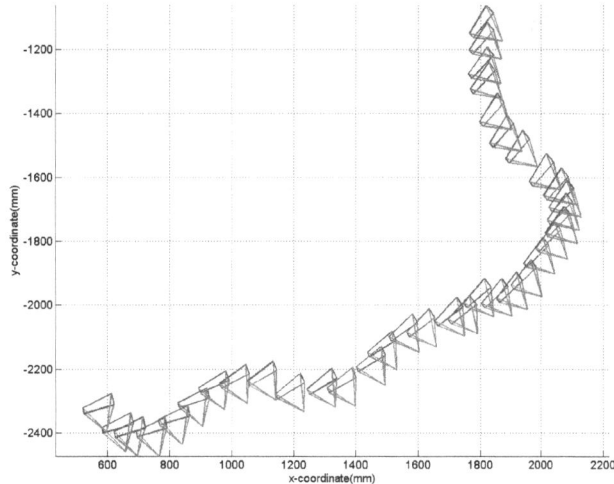

Figure 5: Detection and tracking results over a dataset of 100 frames where every 3rd frame is plotted. Shown are recovered camera poses using the proposed hybrid system. In this dataset the camera/iPad followed a smooth trajectory from the upper right to the lower left (in the X-Z plane) while moving away or toward the object. This plot suggests that the recovered poses are accurate.

recovered camera poses using the proposed hybrid system. In this dataset the camera followed a smooth trajectory from the upper right to the lower left (in the X-Z plane) while moving away or toward the object. This plot suggests that the recovered poses are accurate.

Since no ground truth is available for a quantitative error analysis, we manually select a few points from the model and their corresponding image points to obtain pose estimation. Table 1 shows the error between the pose estimated using tracking for 5 frames compared with "ground truth" acquired manually. The error is defined in two parts, translation error and rotational error defined as the angle between the estimated pose and ground truth. Given that the object is about 3 meters away from the camera we can see the proposed system is able to recover pose accurately.

Framer number	Translation error(mm)	Error in angle(degree)
1	11.7179	1.4714
2	14.4503	1.6139
3	10.9212	1.6498
4	0.8882	3.8101
5	13.1888	2.7206

Table 1: Translation and rotation error for 5 frames compared to ground truth.

Other objects have also been experimented with the proposed system. Figure 6 shows the iAR system running with a Siemens Acuson S2000 ultrasound machine.

5. NOVEL APPLICATIONS USING TOUCH SCREEN AND WIRELESS CONNECTIVITY

Our system was implemented on an iPhone and an iPad (Figure 7). Using a mobile device such as a smartphone

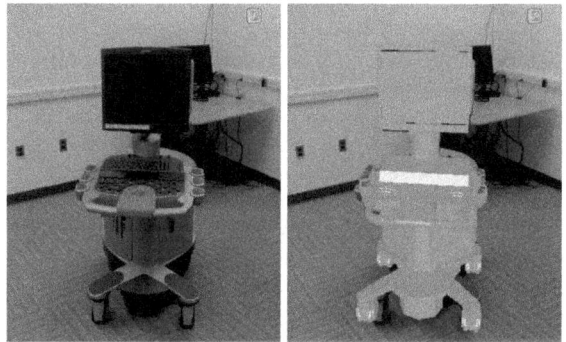

Figure 6: Siemens Acuson S2000 ultrasound system with augmented reality overlay.

adds a new layer to augmented reality. In our iAR system we utilize the touch screen and the wireless connectivity of modern mobile devices to explore novel ways of using AR. Below follows an explanation of the different features introduced to our system. Notice that our iAR system is different from the highly successful PTAM system of Klein and Murray [9], where an environment map is built in parallel with tracking. In stead, our system utilizes the known 3D model (or content) of the object, classically known as model-based vision. In addition to traditional graphics rendering of augmented reality, this further provides the possibility of interacting and exploring the object.

5.1 Exploratory Augmented Reality: Exploration and Interaction Using the Touch Screen

A touch screen introduces a more intuitive way of interacting and exploring the object. The coordinates of a press on the touch screen are mapped from image coordinates to

Figure 7: The iAR system running on an iPad and an iPhone.

world coordinates using the estimated camera pose and a 3D model of the object/scene. By knowing the physical layout of the object (and on a larger scale even the surroundings can be used), it is possible to map the coordinates of a press on the screen to the world coordinates of the object in the scene. The user can press on any part of the object to trigger an action related to that specific part of the scene. The implemented system accomplishes this by using a ray-shooting function in OpenGL. Below follows the different implemented touch screen related features of the iAR system:

(1) Parts information: By pressing on a part of an object on the screen, specific information related to that part is presented on the device in the form of a 3D model and textual information. The 3D model can be rotated and zoomed using the touch screen (see Figure 8).

(2) See-through: Using a detailed model of the interior and exterior of the object, the user can click on a part of the object to make it transparent, giving an "x-ray" view enabling the user to see the interior of the model (see Figure 9). This can be used for educational purposes or for maintenance.

(3) Virtual layout planning: The user can manipulate the scene by adding objects to the scene, by pressing on a location the user can add non existing objects to the scene (see Figure 10). This allows the user to see how an object would fit into the environment/scene to be used for example in planning the layout of a room.

(4) Animation: The user can press on a part of an object or on controllers on the screen to make it stop or start an animation (Figure 11). This is also useful in education and training.

(5) Snapshot: By pressing a button on the screen the most recent image from the camera stream is feazed, achieving the "pause" effect. So the user does not have to point the camera at the object but instead can use one still image and be free to explore and interact with the object and environment.

5.2 Multi-Way Communication for Remote Interaction

Using the wireless connectivity of a hand-held mobile device allows augmented reality to be used as a tool in two-, or multi-way communication. In the iAR system two users are able to interact with each other using augmented reality (Figure 12). A remote user receives the live stream of images sent from the mobile device. The remote user can then manipulate the object in similar ways as the local user holding the hand held device. Using all of the tools mentioned

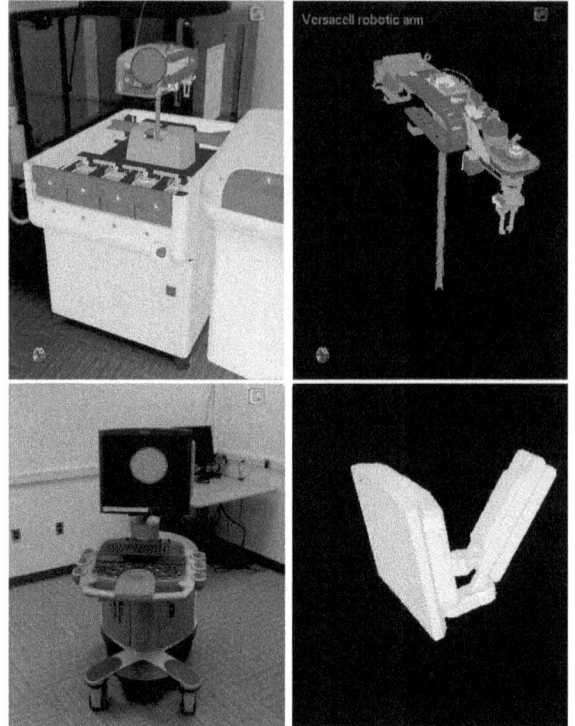

Figure 8: (Left) The user presses, represented by the big red circle, on the robotic arm (top) and the monitor (bottom) of a machine. (Right) A 3D model exploration interface appears where the user can navigate and interact with this part using the touchscreen.

above, the remote user can manipulate the environment and the object graphically (or with audio or text) to interact with the local user.

By clicking on any point in the image, the remote user will add an arrow to this specific location in the scene, this can be seen in Figure 12. The 2D image coordinates are mapped to 3D world coordinates and the arrow remains in the same location as the local user moves around. The remote user can guide the local user with the mobile device to a certain spot. This can be especially useful for maintenance where an expert user can point to any location to where repairs need to be done. Combined with the see-through (or x-ray) view even parts inside the object can be pointed to easily.

6. SUMMARY

In this paper we present an exploratory augmented reality system for mobile devices. The system uses a hybrid of edge-based 3D tracking (very fast – about 5 milliseconds per frame) and 3D object detection based on randomized trees (that covers much larger viewing range, but with slower speed at about 100 milliseconds per frame). In addition, in this exploratory augmented reality system the user can actively explore the scene through mobile devices with touch screens such as iPad or iPhone, which is a novel interaction method in augmented reality. Finally, multi-way communication further enhances with remote interaction, where remotely located server or human expert can interact back to

Figure 9: (Left) The user presses a part (represented by the red circle). (Right) The user sees the interior of the machine for the area pressed. The scroller on the left controls the level of transparency of the exterior casing of the object. On the top row the entire bottom part of the casing becomes transparent. In the bottom a slightly different approach is used, no overlay is displayed until the user presses somwhere on the object and consequently is able to see inside the machine.

the mobile device user for instruction, guidance, or collaboration.

Acknowledgments

We thank Yanghai Tsin, Hesam Najafi, Serhan Gurmeric, and Hongze Zhao for their contributions.

7. REFERENCES

[1] M. Billinghurst, S. Weghorst, and T. Furnes. Shared space: An augmented reality interface for computer supported collaborative work. In *Proc. Collaborative Virtual Environments*, 1996.

[2] A. I. Comport, E. Marchand, M. Pressigout, and F. Chaumette. Real-time markerless tracking for augmented reality: The virtual visual servoing framework. *IEEE Trans. on Visualization and Computer Graphics*, 12(4):615–628, 2006.

[3] T. Drummond and R. Cipolla. Real-time visual tracking of complex structures. *IEEE TPAMI*, 24(7):932–946, 2002.

[4] D. A. Forsyth and J. Ponce. *Computer Vision: A Modern Approach*. Prentice Hall, 2003.

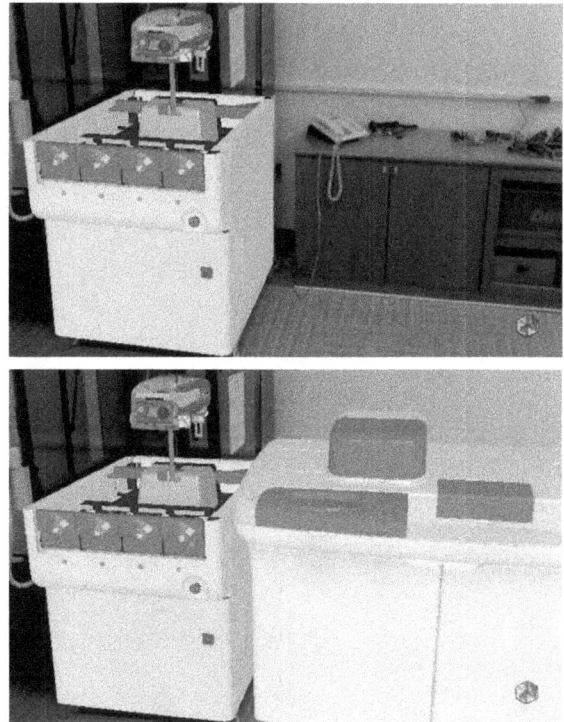

Figure 10: The augmented view can further be expanded by having the user add objects in the environment that don't exist. (Top)Only the 3D model of the object is rendered. (Bottom) The user has, using the touch screen, chosen to add another object on the right side of the object.

[5] A. Henrysson, M. Billinghurst, and M. Ollila. Face to face collaborative ar on mobile phones. In *Proc. International Symposium on Augmented and Mixed Reality*, 2005.

[6] S. Ilic, M. Salzmann, and P. Fua. Implicit surfaces make for better silhouttes. In *Proc. CVPR*, 2005.

[7] S. Ilic, M. Salzmann, and P. Fua. Implicit meshes for effective silhouette handling. *IJCV*, 72(2):159–178, 2007.

[8] S. Kim, C. Coffin, and T. Hollerer. Relocalization using virtual keyframes for online environment map construction. In *Proc. ACM Symposium on Virtual Reality Software and Technology*, 2009.

[9] G. Klein and D. Murray. Parallel tracking and mapping for small AR workspaces. In *Proc. International Symposium on Mixed and Augmented Reality*, 2007.

[10] K. Kuikkaniemi, M. Turpeinen, A. Salovaara, T. Saari, and J. Vuorenmaa. Toolkit for user-created augmented reality games. In *Proc. International Conference on Mobile and Ubiquitous Multimedia*, 2006.

[11] V. Lepetit and P. Fua. Monocular model-based 3D tracking of rigid objects: A survey. *Foundations and Trends in Computer Graphics and Vision*, 1(1), 2005.

[12] V. Lepetit and P. Fua. Keypoint recognition using randomized trees. *IEEE TPAMI*, 28(9):1465–1479, 2006.

[13] G. Li, Y. Tsin, and Y. Genc. Exploiting occluding

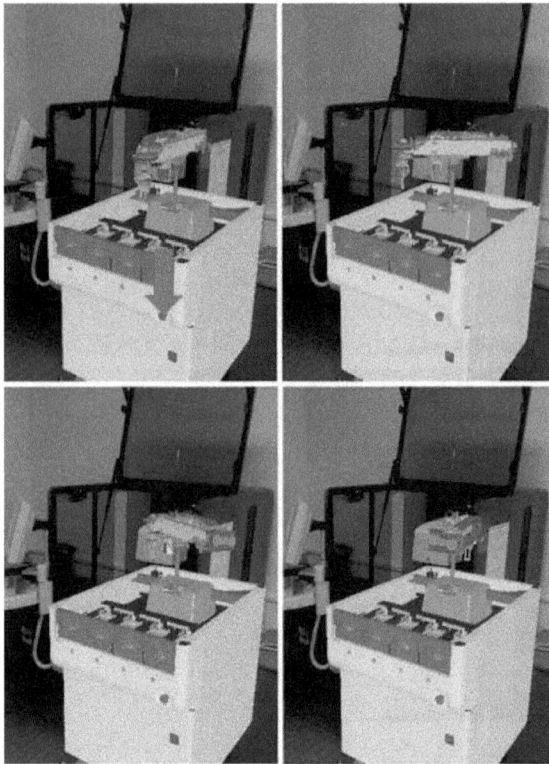

Figure 11: The user presses the red button on the machine and an animation starts where the robotic arm rotates 180 degrees.

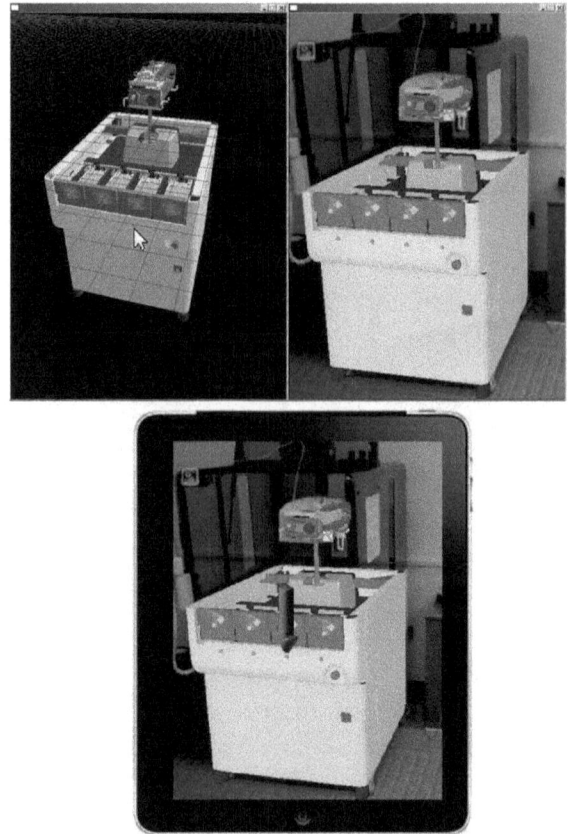

Figure 12: (Top) User interface for a remote user on a PC. The remote side has two views: (Left) a 3D environment where the remote user can navigate the 3D object freely; and (Right) the incoming stream of images sent from the mobile device of the local user. When the remote user clicks on a certain point on the 3D model (indicated by the mouse cursor in the top left) an arrow will appear on the screen for both the remote user and the local user.

contours for real-time 3D tracking: A unified approach. In *Proc. ICCV*, 2007.

[14] J. P. Lima, V. Teichrieb, J. Kelner, and R. W. Lindeman. Standalone edge-based markerless tracking of fully 3-dimensional objects for handheld augmented reality. In *Proc. ACM Symposium on Virtual Reality Software and Technology*, 2009.

[15] D. G. Lowe. Distinctive image features from scale-invariant keypoints. *IJCV*, 60(2):91–110, 2000.

[16] C.-P. Lu, G. D. Hager, and E. Mjolsness. Fast and globally convergent pose estimation from video images. *IEEE TPAMI*, 22(6):610–622, 2000.

[17] G. Reitmayr and D. Schmalstieg. Mobile collaborative augmented reality. In *Proc. International Symposium on Augmented Reality*, 2001.

[18] D. Schmalstieg, A. Fuhrmann, and G. Hesina. Bridging multiple user interface dimensions with augmented reality. In *Proc. IEEE International Symposium on Mixed and Augmented Reality*, 2000.

[19] Z. Szalavari, D. Schmalstieg, A. Fuhrmann, and M. Gervautz. Studierstube-an environment for collaboration in augmented reality. *Virtual Reality Systems, Development and Applications,*, 3(1):37–49, 1998.

[20] Y. Tsin and T. Kanade. A correlation-based approach to robust point set registration. In *Proc. ECCV*, 2004.

[21] L. Vacchetti, V. Lepetit, and P. Fua. Stable real-time 3D tracking using online and offline information. *IEEE TPAMI*, 26(10):1385–1391, 2004.

[22] D. van Krevelen and R. Poelman. A survey of augmented reality technologies, applications and limitations. *The International Journal of Virtual Reality*, 9(2):1–20, 2010.

[23] D. Wagner, T. Pintaric, F. Ledermann, and D. Schmalstieg. Towards massively multi-user augmented reality on handheld devices. In *Proc. International Conference on Pervasive Computing*, 2005.

[24] D. Wagner, G. Reitmayr, A. Mulloni, T. Drummond, and D. Schmalstieg. Pose tracking from natural features on mobile phones. In *Proc. IEEE International Symposium on Mixed and Augmented Reality*, 2008.

[25] F. Zhou, H. B.-L. Duh, and M. Billinghurst. Trends in augmented reality tracking, interaction and display: A review of ten years of ismar. In *Proc. IEEE International Symposium on Mixed and Augmented Reality*, pages 193–202, 2008.

FlyVIZ: A Novel Display Device to Provide Humans with 360° Vision by Coupling Catadioptric Camera with HMD

Jérôme Ardouin[1]   Anatole Lécuyer[2]   Maud Marchal[2]   Clément Riant[3]   Eric Marchand[2]
ESIEA - INSA - Inria   Inria - IRISA   INSA - IRISA - Inria   ESIEA   IRISA - Inria

ABSTRACT

Have you ever dreamed of having eyes in the back of your head? In this paper we present a novel display device called FlyVIZ which enables humans to experience a real-time 360° vision of their surroundings for the first time. To do so, we combine a panoramic image acquisition system (positioned on top of the user's head) with a Head-Mounted Display (HMD). The omnidirectional images are transformed to fit the characteristics of HMD screens. As a result, the user can see his/her surroundings, in real-time, with 360° images mapped into the HMD field-of-view. We foresee potential applications in different fields where augmented human capacity (an extended field-of-view) could benefit, such as surveillance, security, or entertainment. FlyVIZ could also be used in novel perception and neuroscience studies.

Categories and Subject Descriptors

B.4.2 [Input/Output and Data Communications]: Input/Output Devices. -Image display: I.4.1 [Image Processing and Computer Vision]: Digitization and Image Capture. -Imaging geometry.

General Terms

Design

Keywords

Display device; 360° vision; catadioptric camera; panoramic images; Head Mounted Display

1. INTRODUCTION

People are familiar with sophisticated optical devices and can use them to adapt their vision to various uses. For instance, microscopes and telescopes are classical optical devices that can magnify small or distant objects. These devices map a small part of the Field of View (FoV) to a larger one. Such mapping process decreases the effective FoV of the user.

The human field of view is limited to 180 degrees horizontally and 110 degrees vertically. Increasing the natural FoV is actually very difficult to achieve with traditional optical devices. In this paper, we introduce a display device which can enhance the human FoV, and enable a 360° horizontal FoV (80° vertically with our system). This novel device (see Figure 1), called FlyVIZ, is based on three components: (1) an acquisition system (e.g., a catadioptric sensor, on top of the user's head, for capturing 360° images), (2) a Head-Mounted Display (HMD) to display the processed image to the end-user in real-time, and (3) a computer vision algorithm to map the captured 360° images to the shape and dimensions of HMD screen).

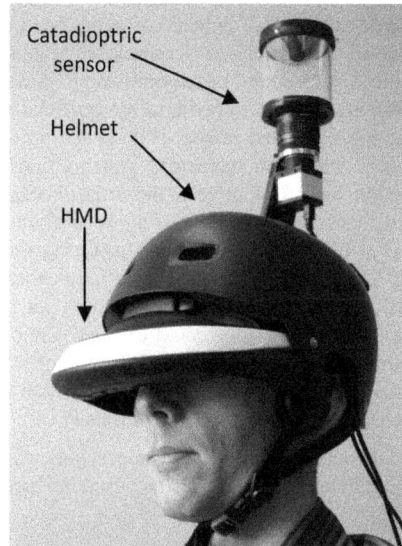

Figure 1: FlyVIZ prototype and proof-of-concept.

In the remainder of this paper we first review related work. Second, we describe the global concept of FlyVIZ and its main components. Then, we present a proof-of-concept prototype and detail the proposed hardware and the real-time image processing algorithm. Finally, we discuss the performances and potential uses of our novel approach.

2. RELATED WORK

A HMD is a display device, worn on the head or as part of a helmet, which has a small display in front of one (monocular HMD) or both eyes (binocular HMD). The typical horizontal FoV of research or commercial HMDs ranges from 24° to 187°. Efforts are regularly made to extend the FoV of HMDs. As an example, Sensic company notably proposed an approach based on a mosaic of small screens [1], that are able to extend the FoV while maintaining good resolution at the same time. The field of view of an HMD is also a critical parameter from a human perception perspective. When a 1:1 scale is used with a limited FoV, HMD users tend to complain, and often feel like they are looking through a keyhole.

The combination of HMDs with panoramic cameras has been scarcely studied up to now. Few examples exist in the tele-operation field. In [2], Nagahara et al. coupled a panoramic imaging sensor with a wide-FoV HMD for the purpose of remote exploration/visualization. The HMD was coupled with a head tracker, so that the user could explore the remote 360° FoV by turning his/her head. The image displayed in the HMD was not a panoramic image and the remote 360° FoV was sequentially explored. A similar system can be found in [3] for visual surveillance and remote monitoring. In Virtual Reality

---

[1] ardouin@esiea-ouest.fr
[2] {alecuyer, mmarchal, marchand}@irisa.fr
[3] riant@et.esiea-ouest.fr

applications, a similar process of exploration of the virtual world is adopted [4]. The virtual 360° FoV is explored sequentially thanks to a head tracker (ie. a device able to capture the user head orientation) and turning head movements. Interestingly enough, Fiala and Roth demonstrated the benefit of using a remote panoramic imaging system for tele-operation [5]. In particular, it removes the need for a closed-loop feedback for the remote low-FoV camera, and then reduces the overall latency.

The distortion or extension of human vision has been investigated in several scientific fields such as Neuroscience (e.g., for studying visual perception and brain adaptation using prisms [6]), or Augmented Reality (e.g. by superimposing artificial information onto the naturally perceived images [7]). In the artistic domain, some performers have also developed systems that can extend human vision. In his 3RDI project, the artist Wafaa Bilal, was equipped with a camera on the back of his head giving a reversed point of view of his everyday life and displaying images to the audience [8]. The Crew Company coupled a panoramic sensor with an HMD and a head tracker. They could set up different performances in which the user could explore part of remote or recorded panoramic videos (similarly to the tele-operation systems aforementioned). Finally a similar artistic experience was built to play with the feeling of "presence" of the users [9].

To the best of the authors' knowledge, no previous work proposed a display to experience full 360° vision of one's surroundings in real-time.

3. THE "FlyVIZ" CONCEPT

With FlyVIZ, our objective is to enhance the natural human field of view. We intend to reach a full 360° FoV of the user's surroundings, in real-time. This would fulfill a dream of humans: to be able to "see behind their back" or see like some animals, such as flies, with a wider FoV, even reaching a fully panoramic vision. This objective is obviously difficult to achieve using simple and traditional optical devices. However, an image processing approach connecting an image acquisition system with a head-mounted display could suit our purpose. As illustrated in Figure 2, three main functions should drive the design of such a system. First it has to capture omnidirectional information/images from the user's environment (image *acquisition*). Second, it has to transform this view into a meaningful representation (image *transformation*). Finally, it has to display this view to the user (image *presentation*). The *Image acquisition* can be done with a catadioptric sensor, i.e., the combination of a camera with a mirror. Various shapes of mirrors could be used such as parabolic, hyperbolic, or spherical mirrors. Composite sensors could also be used, i.e., a set of multiple cameras assembled in a circle or sphere to cover the 360° FoV. The *Image transformation* requires a

processing unit to carry out the necessary computations. This can be a laptop, a netbook, a wearable computer or dedicated hardware (ASIC). Smartphones with enough processing power could also fit. The *Image presentation* can be made using a Head-Mounted Display, but specific video glasses could also be suitable. As a complementary requirement, the whole system must preferably be wearable and compatible with the user's locomotion.

Proof of concept: In this paper, we describe a first prototype of the FlyVIZ concept that is displayed in Figure 1. The image acquisition step is achieved with a catadioptric sensor [10] made up of a hyperbolic mirror and a traditional 6mm-lens mounted on a CCD camera (IDS μEye 2210). The image acquisition system is mechanically attached on a helmet. Figure 3 displays a typical image acquired by this system. The panoramic images are acquired in the head reference frame (and so, it does not require head tracking). The image transformation is done on a laptop computer worn by the user in a backpack. The image presentation is done by means of a HMD (SONY HMZ-T1).

4. PROCESSING OF 360° IMAGES

In this section we further detail the image transformation process that is a key component of our system. The purpose of the image transformation algorithm is to transform the acquired image (Figure 3) into an image that can be displayed in the HMD. A comprehensible representation of the environment is targeted, i.e., a projection which can be effectively perceived by the user. With our approach, each pixel displayed in the HMD has to be mapped to its corresponding location in the acquired image. The image transformation is achieved in two successive steps, which correspond to two different projections:

1. Projection between a location on the final displayed image and a direction of the space ;

2. Projection between a direction of the space and its respective location in the acquired image.

For the first projection, the mathematical formulation of the problem consists in mapping all the space directions onto a plane. Mapping one direction of the 3D space is equivalent to map a point from a unit sphere onto a plane [10]. This mapping problem (and its inverse problem) has been widely studied by mathematicians and cartographers [11]. We use the plate carrée cylindrical projection [11] (aka. the equirectangular projection) that is widely used both in cartography and panoramic imaging. Although the plate carrée projection generates some distortions at poles, it preserves the shapes along the 0° parallel. This is known to strongly help the overall human interpretation of the final view.

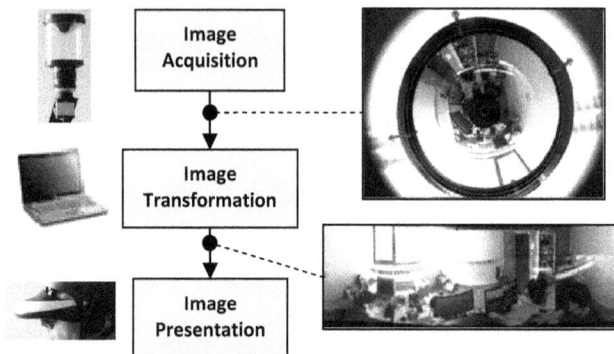

Figure 2: FlyVIZ components

Figure 3: Image provided by the catadioptric system.

The second projection corresponds to the calibration of our optical system. The equations map a 3D space vector to its corresponding location in the acquired image. Details on the modeling and the calibration of catadioptric sensors can be found in [10] and [12]. A practical implementation can also be found in [12]. In our setup we use a dedicated sensor calibration algorithm available in the OCamCalib toolbox [12]. The procedure takes about 15 minutes, and does not require to be fulfilled again, as soon as the optical alignment of the camera lens and the mirror is preserved. The calibration parameters are then stored and can be used later, at runtime.

Mathematically, the whole process can be described as follows:

$$\begin{pmatrix} x \\ y \end{pmatrix} \xrightarrow{P} \begin{pmatrix} \lambda \\ \varphi \end{pmatrix} \xrightarrow{S} \begin{pmatrix} X \\ Y \\ Z \end{pmatrix} \xrightarrow{M} \begin{pmatrix} x' \\ y' \end{pmatrix} \qquad (1)$$

Thus, in the first step of our image transformation algorithm, a pixel with coordinates (x,y) is transformed to (λ,φ) with the plate carrée inverse projection (P) which is a simple affine transformation that remaps the x coordinates to $[-\pi,\pi]$ and y to $[-\pi/2,\pi/2]$. Then, the 3D space vector (X,Y,Z) is deduced from the parameterized form of the sphere equation (S).

$$\begin{pmatrix} X \\ Y \\ Z \end{pmatrix} = \begin{pmatrix} \cos(\varphi)\cos(\lambda) \\ \cos(\varphi)\sin(\lambda) \\ \sin(\varphi) \end{pmatrix} \qquad (2)$$

Finally, the associated coordinates in the input image (X',Y'), are computed from (X,Y,Z), using the camera model (M) [12].

At runtime, each raw image is acquired from the catadioptric sensor and uploaded into the video memory as a texture buffer. A full-screen quad is then rasterized by using a dedicated fragment program on GPU. To transform the raw image into the final unwrapped image, the fragment program has to handle the two mappings described earlier: the plate carrée projection and the catadioptric camera model. For each processed pixel in the final image, (λ,φ) coordinates are deduced from UV coordinates of the full screen quad. The corresponding 3D vector is computed using the inverse mapping of the plate carrée projection. This vector is then used to address the input image according the catadioptric camera model [12]. This texture look up is done using hardware texture linear filtering to maintain smoothness over the final image. Both the raw panoramic image addressing and the plate carrée cylindrical projection are implemented at a fragment level. Such an implementation thus benefits from the parallel processing power available in modern GPUs and optimizes computation performances.

5. SYSTEM PERFORMANCES

Our prototype is based on an HMD with a FoV of 45° and a 16:9 aspect ratio (ref. SONY HMZ-T1). This aspect ratio fits relatively well with the properties of the plate carrée projection that constrains the displayed image to an aspect ratio of 2:1. Taking our optical setup into account, the final image is displayed in the HMD with 360° horizontal FoV and 80° vertical FoV (Figure 4). Our image transformation algorithm is implemented in C++ using OpenGL API and the GLSL shading language. We have benchmarked our algorithm on two different platforms with both a high (laptop) and low computational performances (netbook). The resulting frame rates obtained in HMD are given in Table 1. With a high-end laptop, the frame rate is far above the refresh rate of the camera (60Hz). But even with a low-cost netbook, the refresh rate meets a real-time constraint (24Hz). The overall latency of the system (end to end from acquisition to display) has been measured by taking pictures of a precision clock and its image processed by the system and displayed in the HMD. The value seen through the HMD was then subtracted to the directly observed value. With this procedure, we found an average latency of 83 ms.

Table 1: Computation performance (frame rates)

Hardware	CPU	GPU	Frame Rate (Hz)
15' laptop	i7-2820QM 2.30GHz	Quadro 2000M	480
12' netbook	ATOM D525 1.8GHz	ION2	24

6. SYSTEM IN USE

The FlyViz system is fully operational and has been tested by multiple users and in different conditions (e.g., indoor or outdoor). We can use different illustrative scenarios as illustrated in Figures 5 and 6.

During these tests, users get used within the first 15 minutes of practice, letting them to smoothly move in their environment. Users also get used to the new visual feedback loop of their arms and hands, letting them open doors or grasp objects. In these cases, depth perception is altered since binocular vision is not available, but as suggested by Cutting [13], users seem to be able to base depth evaluation on the other depth cues (motion parallaxes, etc.). For the main user, a first scenario consists in grasping an object (a stick) held out by another person. Without moving his/her head, the user instantly perceives the position of the stick and can grab it, even when it is located out of his/her natural field of view. In a second scenario, the user is walking and must avoid some balls thrown at him/her, with balls sometimes being thrown from behind. A third scenario consists in driving a car on a parking lot, being able to see both the external environment and the car interior at the same time (Figure 5). During several tests, the device has been worn for more than an hour, without motion sickness or particular visual fatigue.

Figure 4: Image displayed in the HMD corresponding to the transformation of the raw image of Figure 3.

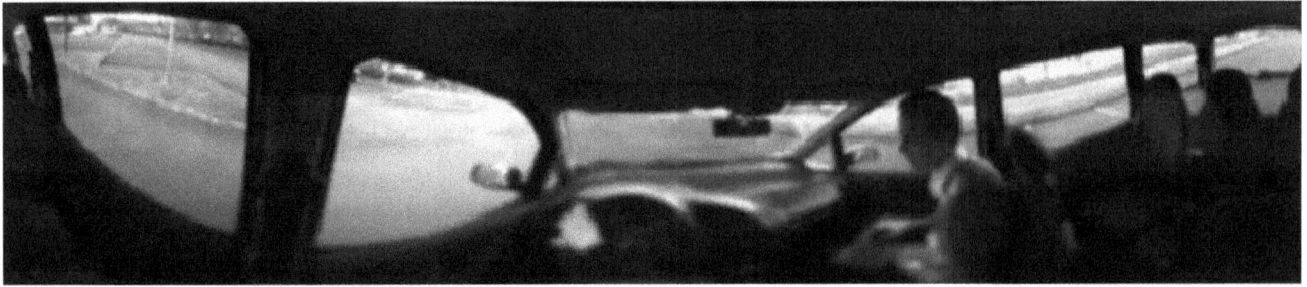

Figure 5: Third illustrative scenario: driving a car on a parking lot (HMD view).

The main discomfort came from the unbalanced weight of the headset (helmet, camera, optics and HMD: 1650g). Future work is of course necessary now to evaluate the learning process, user perception, and the potential exploitation of 360° vision in various tasks, which is not the focus of this paper.

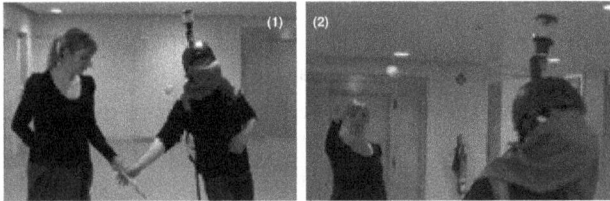

Figure 6: Two illustrative scenarios.
(1) Catching a stick out of the natural field of view,
(2) avoiding a ball thrown from behind.

7. CONCLUSION AND PERSPECTIVES

This paper has introduced FLyVIZ: a novel display device to augment humans with 360° vision. FlyVIZ astutely connects a panoramic camera and a head-mounted display to present images with 360° horizontal field-of-view in real-time. A proof-of-concept system was developed based on a catadioptric system with a standard camera and a commercial HMD. An image processing algorithm based on a plate carrée projection was developed to transform the acquired images into images compatible with HMD screens and aspect ratio. Our software implementation benefits from parallel processing power provided by modern GPUs. On a standard laptop, the system reaches a frame rate of 480Hz and 83ms latency. The operability of the FlyVIZ prototype has been illustrated in different indoor or outdoor scenarios. For example users have been able to enjoy grasping an object held out behind their back without turning their head. The FlyVIZ concept and prototype are patent pending.

There are different application fields that could benefit from an enhanced FoV. In safety and security applications, soldiers, policemen or firemen could benefit from omnidirectional vision to avoid potential dangers or locate targets more rapidly. In less critical situations, some surveillance applications with a high visual workload, in all directions of space for instance, could also be concerned, such as for traffic regulation. Considering the novel perceptual experience proposed, FlyViz could also be transformed into entertaining applications and devices, as well as experimental materials for new perception and neuroscience studies.

Future work: We foresee different paths for extensions and improvements. First, other projections and mapping methods could be tested with other geometric properties (conformal (preserving angles), equidistant, equal area, etc). These properties could influence the usability of the presented view according to a specific usage scenario. Moreover, instead of directly providing a 360° horizontal FoV, we could use a "split-screen" approach and

different viewports on the image, such as using "driving mirrors" (rear and/or lateral mirrors). Other hardware components (camera and HMD) could also be tested with different aspect ratio or resolution characteristics. High dynamic range image sensors could also dramatically improve the final image quality. Then, augmented reality applications based on FlyVIZ could be proposed, for instance for improving perception of 360° vision with superimposed virtual cues.

8. REFERENCES

[1] Sensic piSight technical specifications. http://www.sensics.com

[2] H. Nagahara, Y. Yagi, M. Yachida, "Wide Field of View Head Mounted Display for Tele-presence with An Omnidirectional Image Sensor, *Int. Conf. on Computer Vision and Pattern Recognition Workshop*, 2003

[3] Y. Onoe, N. Yokoya, K. Yamazawa, H. Takemura, Visual surveillance and monitoring system using an omnidirectional video camera, *Int. Conf. on Pattern Recognition,* 1998

[4] D. A. Bowman , E. Kruijff , J. J. LaViola , I. Poupyrev, 3D User Interfaces: Theory and Practice, *Addison Wesley Longman Publishing*, 2004

[5] M. Fiala, G. Roth, Automatic Alignment and Graph Map Building of Panoramas, *IEEE Int. Workshop on Haptic Audio Visual Environments and their Applications*, 2005

[6] C. S. Harris, Perceptual adaptation to inverted, reversed, and displaced vision, *Psychological Review*, Vol 72(6), 1965

[7] W. Barfield , T. Caudell, Fundamentals of Wearable Computers and Augmented Reality, *Lawrence Erlbaum Associates,* 2000

[8] W. Bilal. 3RDI project. http://www.3rdi.me

[9] K. Vanhoutte, N. Wynants, Pending presence: negotiating the space in-between, *in Space cowboys: how art creates, networks and visualises hybrid spaces*, R. van Klaveren ed. Genk, Media and Design Academy, 2009

[10] S. Baker, S. Nayar. A theory of catadioptric image formation, *Int. Conf. on Computer Vision,*, 1998

[11] J. P. Snyder, Map Projections: A Working Manual, *USGS Professional Paper*, 1987.

[12] D. Scaramuzza, A. Martinelli, R. Siegwart, A Flexible Technique for Accurate Omnidirectional Camera Calibration and Structure from Motion, *IEEE Int. Conf. of Vision Systems*, 2006

[13] J. E. Cutting, How the eye measures reality and virtual reality, *Behavior Research Methods, Instruments & Computers* Vol 29, 1997

Online Real-Time Presentation of Virtual Experiences for External Viewers

Kevin Ponto
University of
Wisconsin-Madison
Madison, WI 53715
kbponto@wisc.edu

Hyun Joon Shin [*]
Ajou University
Suwon, Korea
joony@ajou.ac.kr

Joe Kohlmann
University of
Wisconsin-Madison
Madison, WI 53715
jkohlmann@wisc.edu

Michael Gleicher
University of
Wisconsin-Madison
Madison, WI 53715
gleicher@cs.wisc.edu

ABSTRACT

Externally observing the experience of a participant in a virtual environment is generally accomplished by viewing an egocentric perspective. Monitoring this view can often be difficult for others to watch due to unwanted camera motions that appear unnatural and unmotivated. We present a novel method for reducing the unnaturalness of these camera motions by minimizing camera movement while maintaining the context of the participant's observations. For each time-step, we compare the parts of the scene viewed by the virtual participant to the parts of the scene viewed by the camera. Based on the similarity of these two viewpoints we next determine how the camera should be adjusted. We present two means of adjustment, one which continuously adjusts the camera and a second which attempts to stop camera movement when possible. Empirical evaluation shows that our method can produce paths that have substantially shorter travel distances, are easier to watch and maintain the original observations of the participant's virtual experience.

Categories and Subject Descriptors

H.5.1 [**Information Presentation**]: Multimedia Information Systems—*Artificial, augmented, and virtual realities*

Keywords

Virtual Reality; Viewpoint Similarity; Camera Motion; Stabilization; Observation.

1. INTRODUCTION

Monitoring the experiences of a user in a virtual environment is generally useful for spectators, scientists, architects, and designers.

---

[*]Work performed as a visiting professor at the University of Wisconsin-Madison.

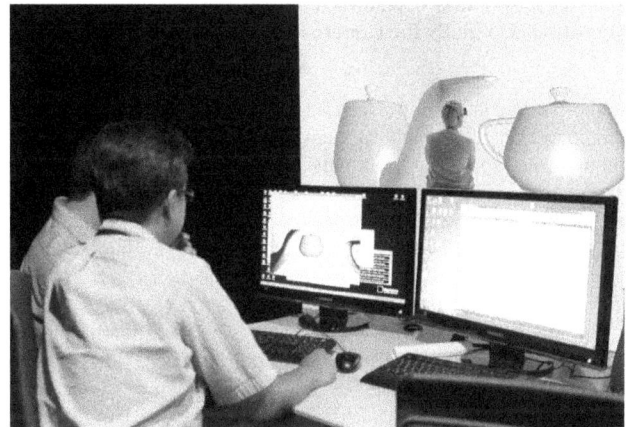

Figure 1: External viewers often find it difficult to observe the experience of a virtual participant due to the perceived unnaturalness of the egocentic camera movements. Our method is able to make these external views easier to watch by minimizing camera movement while maintaining the context of the participant's observations.

While some virtual reality hardwares allow external viewers to see both the individual and the projection, enclosed environments such as a C6 CAVE or a HMD provide little means to ascertain insight into the participant's virtual experience. In these cases, the traditional means in which viewers can gain an understanding of the user's experience is through the replication of the user's egocentric perspective. Unfortunately, this egocentric view is often difficult to watch as it is filled with movements that feel unnatural and unmotivated to an outside viewer [16].

In this paper, we introduce methods for creating camera views for external viewers based on the experience of a participant in a virtual environment. The methods operate online[1] in real-time[2], creating a camera path that meets two goals: conveying what the participant is seeing and providing camera movement that is easy to watch for external viewers. These two goals are often in conflict

---

[1]We define an online algorithm as an algorithm which must process input sequentially without knowledge of future inputs.
[2]We define real-time as an algorithm that runs at interactive rates.

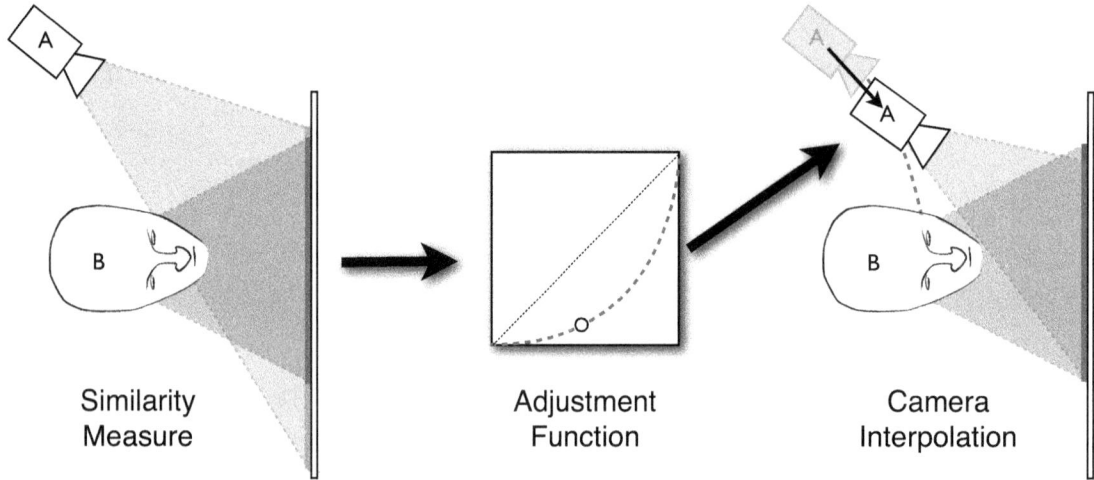

Figure 2: The system consists of three components for each point in time. First the similarity between the camera and the participant's viewpoint is determined. From this, an adjustment function is computed to determine the amount the camera should be repositioned. Finally the camera in moved in order to achieve a better view by interpolating it towards the participant's viewpoint.

as the participant's control can lead to movements that they can anticipate (since they control them), but will appear as unnatural, unmotivated, and jerky to an outside viewer. Therefore, methods for creating views for external viewers must balance between being faithful to the participant's path, which fully conveys what they are seeing but may be difficult to watch, and simplifying the camera path to create an easy to watch video, at the expense of not conveying the participant's full view information.

Our approach to external view synthesis balances fidelity (conveying what the participant sees) with watchability by using a content-dependent metric that limits the amount of motion of the camera based on how similar what it sees is with what the participant's camera sees. This effectively removes camera motions that are not necessary to show what the participant is seeing. Unlike a pure filter-based approach, our method will produce sharp camera motions if they are necessary for conveying content. The method operates on a per-frame basis, moving the camera towards the participant's view at each time step. The amount that the camera is allowed to move in each step is controlled by the view content similarity metric.

The contribution of this paper is a method for creating a watchable external view that conveys the experience of a virtual environment participant, online and in real-time. While the problem of effective external view creation has been considered in prior work, our approach is the first that operates online in real-time, and thus can serve important applications where observation occurs during the participant's experience. Our method builds on a prior view-dependent metric to provide an adaptivity that would not be possible with simple filtering. We demonstrate the effectiveness of our approach through quantitative assessment and through a crowd-sourced user study. Our study shows that our method is able to produce paths that are easier to watch while maintaining the content of the original participant's observations.

2. RELATED WORK

Our work is inspired by recent results in video stabilization that show that optimization can explicitly balance between motion smoothness and faithfulness to the original camera [8, 9]. Unlike our work,

these approaches use off-line optimizations and focus on challenges unique to 2D video stabilization.

Techniques to stabilize imagery in an online real-time fashion have been used in a variety of fields. Hansen et al. developed methods to stabilize satellite imagery in order to generate a larger photo mosaic [10]. Many researchers have used filtering techniques to stabilize video sequences in real-time [2, 6, 18, 21]. This type of filtering has become a particular focus for researchers dealing with mobile platforms [12, 15]. Others have used real-time stabilization as a means of treatment. For example, Pothier et al. used real-time image stabilization and augmented reality eyewear in the treatment of Oscillopsia for patients with bilateral vestibular loss [17]. Unfortunately, these types of image stabilization techniques generally do not handle the high-frequency movements of egocentric data gracefully [16].

Sensor fusion along with Kalman filtering has proven to be extremely useful to help stabilize the view of the participant in a virtual environment [7, 24]. These techniques are now common for commercial grade tracking equipment [14]. This type of filtering is unfortunately incredibly dependent on the conditions of the environment [6] and may therefore require parameters to be tuned for every different environment in order to be effective.

Researchers have studied changing the virtual perspective as a means to present different views of a virtual environment. Salamin et al. studied whether a participant inside of a Virtual and Augmented Reality situation would prefer to see themselves from a 3rd or 1st person perspective [19]. The authors found that the preferred perspective was very dependent on the task the participant was asked to accomplish. Yang and Olson tested whether 3rd party commanders were able to direct more efficiently with either ego- or exo-centric viewpoints [23]. Their results also showed very mixed results, with ego-, exo-, or tailing cameras performing better depending on the situation. As the viewpoints were not being generated from a tracking device, no stabilization was needed.

A variety of methods to automatically position virtual cameras have been developed based on different types of constraints. Christie et al. provide a survey paper outlining these various techniques [3]. The major motivation of our work comes from Ponto et al. who were able to show that egocentric viewpoints could be processed in order to create replay videos that were more effective at communicating participants' experiences in virtual environments for outside observers [16]. The authors' method decoupled the egocentric viewpoint from the replay camera path in order to minimize the camera movement and more effectively place the camera. Salient camera positions were determined using clustering by comparing viewpoints using a content dependent Viewpoint Similarty metric [16]. The authors demonstrated that their methods were able to outperform simple filtering techniques in terms of their ability to convey content. Due to the offline nature of their algorithms, the techniques could not be implemented for an online application where future data are unavailable. We use the authors' similarity metric and presentation style as motivation for the development of our own online real-time algorithms.

3. OUR METHOD

Our basic idea is to produce a novel camera path in an online real-time manner by adjusting the camera only when necessary to maintain the content of the participant's observations. To do this, our method consists of three components as shown in Figure 2. First we determine the similarity between the viewpoints of the participant and viewer. From this similarity, we determine how much viewer's viewpoint should be adjusted. Finally camera the is repositioned by interpolating its previous position with the current participant's viewpoint.

3.1 Viewpoint Similarity

We chose to use the Viewpoint Similarity metric, described by Ponto et al. [16], as it provide a means to rapidly compare the content seen by two different viewpoints using a flashlight analogy. The method is based on a variant of shadow mapping [22], thus providing an efficient means for implementation on the GPU.

The method first computes the visibility of one viewpoint (B) in the context of the other viewpoint (A) as shown in Equation (1).

$$V(A,B) = \sum_{p=0}^{N} \frac{L(A_p, B_p)}{N}, \qquad (1)$$

where $L(A_p, B_p)$ is a visibility function for a pixel, p of B in A and N is total number of pixels in the view. This function can be easily implemented on the GPU using occlusion queries [16]. As $V(A,B)$ is not equivalent to $V(B,A)$, the Viewpoint Similarity metric between A and B is defined as a weighted sum of the two viewpoints' relative visibilities:

$$S(A,B) = w_A V(A,B) + w_B V(B,A). \qquad (2)$$

We use this computation to determine similarity between the viewpoints of the participant and the viewer. From Equation (2), we set A to the participant's viewpoint and B to the current state of viewer's viewpoint, with the weights according to the scheme shown in [16]. This similarity is used to adjust the camera position as shown below.

3.2 Adjustment Function

After computing the Viewpoint Similarity, we create an adjustment function which indicates how much the camera's viewpoint should be altered. If the two viewpoints are highly similar, we can assume that camera needs very little adjustment. Conversely, if the two viewpoints are highly dissimilar, the camera viewpoint will need to be greatly repositioned. For our purposes, we have created two adjustment profiles, the Continuous Adjustment Profile (CAP) and the Stopping Adjustment Profile (SAP).

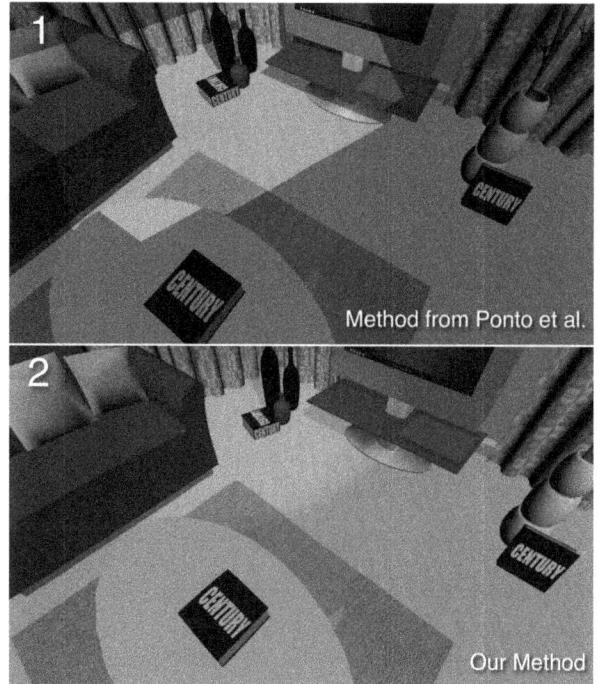

Figure 3: (Top) The rectangular light used by Ponto et al. with sharp edges of the light was shown to be distracting for viewers when both the camera and light were moving [16]. (Bottom) Our method using a gradual falloff to provide probabilistic information as to where the participant was looking proved to be less distracting for the same situation.

The CAP is designed to prioritize maintaining a camera position that is able to convey the content that the participant seeing over easing the camera movement. For the CAP, we define u, the interpolation parameter as

$$u = k(1 - S(A,B)). \qquad (3)$$

For this equation, the variable k defines a sensitivity parameter, which is adjustable by the participant. This value determines the maximum step size for each time step, meaning if two viewpoints are entirely dissimilar, this would be the max amount the camera should be adjusted. In practice we found the inverse of the rendering frame-rate to be a useful default value.

While this first function constantly adjusted the camera position to increase the view similarity, others have shown that is useful to stop the camera movement when possible to help external viewers understand the virtual experience more effectively [8, 16]. Therefore, we introduce another profile, SAP, which prioritizes generating easy to watch camera movement over maintaining the precise view that the participant is seeing. For SAP, the interpolation parameter u, is defined as:

$$u = nk(1 - S(A,B))^n. \qquad (4)$$

As the similarity value is normalized between zero and one, raising it to a large power will assure that highly dissimilar values will still adjust the camera, while marginally dissimilar values will not. As this function decreases camera movement, we also multiply the function by the exponent to ensure proper sensitivity.

In practice, both profiles have their advantages and disadvan-

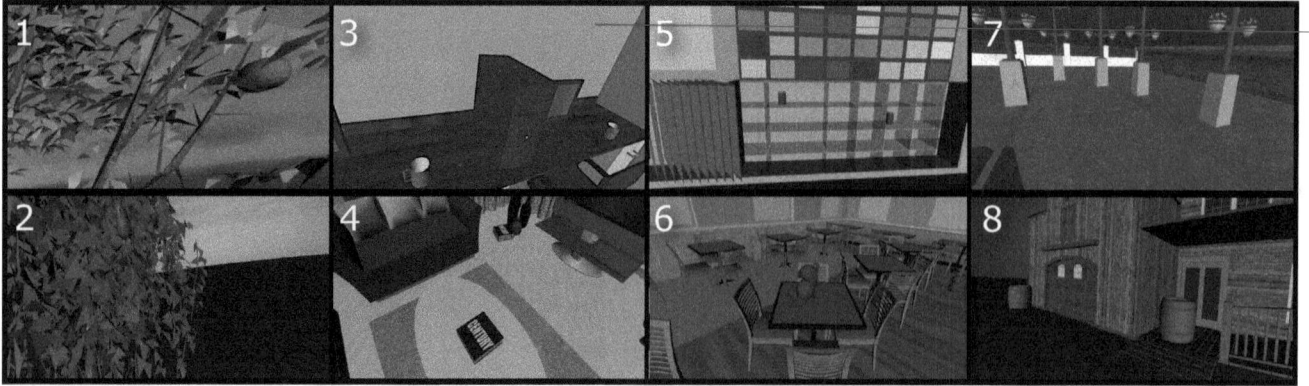

Figure 4: Images taken from the eight different scenarios for the participant to locate virtual objects.

tages. In Section 4.2 we evaluate both methods to inform the choice between them and the selection of their parameters.

3.3 Camera Interpolation

After determining the adjustment amount, we move the camera by interpolating between its previous position and the participant's viewpoint.

We adopt exponential maps for performing these interpolations as they rely on directly manipulating the viewing transforms, as opposed to interpolating the various camera components independently. Exponential maps accomplish this by performing linear interpolation operations in the logarithm space of the matrices [1]. We chose to use exponential maps as opposed to parameter interpolation as, in common cases, they do a better job of keeping points of interest centered in view, as shown by Hawkins and Grimm [11]. It is worth noting that as the interpolated amounts are often quite small, the difference between parameter interpolation and exponential maps is likely negligible. After interpolation we remove camera roll to produce views that are level in the horizontal axis, following the practices of Ponto et al. [16].

Equation (5) demonstrates how $A(t)$, the next position of viewer's viewpoint, is calculated given the viewpoint of the viewer ($A(t - \Delta t)$) updated previously, participant's viewpoint ($B(t)$), and the adjustment parameter (u) determined from Section 3.2.

$$A(t) = e^{(1-u)\log A(t-\Delta t) + u \log B(t)}. \quad (5)$$

While this method does not have any explicit easing parameters as were shown in [8] and [16], some smoothing will happen naturally assuming that the viewpoints do not change too rapidly. For instance, as the participant slowly changes their view, the Viewpoint Similarity will also decrease, thereby increasing the interpolated step-size. Conversely, as the viewpoints become more similar, the Viewpoint Similarity metric will also increase, thus decreasing the interpolated step-size.

3.4 Presentation

As shown by Ponto et al., manipulating a camera path may reduce an external viewer's understanding of the participant's experience [16]. To reduce this artifact, the authors drew a rectangular light representing the participant's viewpoint as shown in Figure 3-1 to provide the viewer with a clear representation of where the participant is looking. However, this rectangular light with a sharp cutoff was shown to be distracting when the light and the camera were moving at the same time. Furthermore, the field of view represented by the rectangle did not precisely match that of the partici-

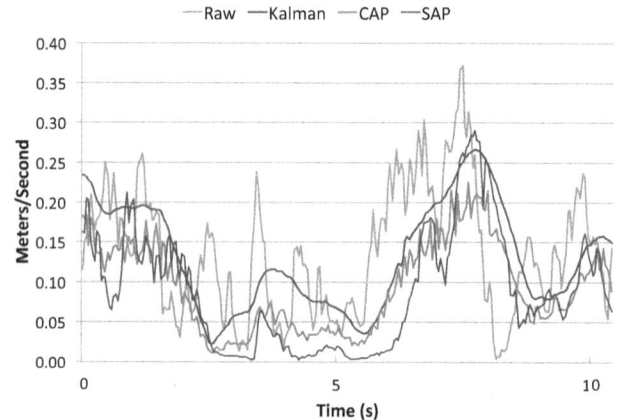

Figure 5: Velocity profile for approximately 10 seconds of a participant walking around a virtual tree (Scene 1). As shown, our method reduces the magnitude of the velocity compared to the Raw or Kalman filtered camera path.

pant's perspective. We instead created a virtual light with a gradual fade-off to provide probabilistic information as to where the participant was looking, as shown in Figure 3-2. This proved to also be less distracting for the viewer when the camera was in motion.

4. RESULTS

The goal of our method was to produce new camera paths in an online real-time fashion that reduce the camera movement, thus making them easier to watch without obscuring content from the raw camera path. In order to determine if our methods achieved these objectives, we first generated camera paths by asking participants to walk around in a fully enclosed C6 CAVE and find a particular type of objects within one of several virtual environments. This task was asked only as a means to generate paths and the performance of the participant to find these objects in the virtual environment was not evaluated.

The eight scenes in which participants were asked to locate objects are shown in Figure 4. The scenes could be grouped into four classes: small scale walk-around, small interior environments, large interior environments, and larger outdoor spaces. In the first group, the participants were tasked with counting apples (Figure 4-1) and birds in a dense bush (Figure 4-2). The small interior environments included an office with coffee mugs (Figure 4-3) and

Camera Travel Distance [m] (Distance / Raw)			
Scene	Raw	Kalman	CAP	SAP
1	5.0	4.4 (.88)	3.2 (.64)	2.8 (.56)
2	14.3	12.6 (.88)	11.2 (.78)	9.4 (.66)
3	9.8	9.1 (.93)	6.1 (.62)	4.5 (.46)
4	11.3	11.3 (1.0)	9.3 (.82)	7.3 (.65)
5	31.1	31.0 (1.0)	26.5 (.85)	25.8 (.83)
6	27.9	30.3 (1.1)	25 (.90)	24.1 (.86)
7	33.5	33.5 (1.0)	29.5 (.88)	26.9 (.80)
8	90.1	100.1 (1.1)	85.0 (.94)	85.7 (.95)
Average Ratio		.99	.81	.72

Table 1: **Camera movement metrics for 30 seconds of each scene for each method. Note that while the Kalman filter has very mixed results in reducing camera travel distance, our methods are able to consistently reduce the distance the camera traveled. This reduction in the camera travel distance did not result in a loss of content as shown by our user study.**

a living room with books (Figure 4-4). In the two larger interior spaces, the participant was tasked with locating toys in a small restaurant (Figure 4-5) and cans in a store (Figure 4-6). For the last group, we created a park scene with light posts (Figure 4-7) and an old western town with barrels (Figure 4-8).

During these tasks, participants' head positions and orientations were recorded for further analysis. To assess the relative performance of our method to other approaches, we considered four different on-line methods.

The first path consisted of the raw egocentric viewpoint, which is used for external viewers in most of practical implementations. For the second path, we adopted a Kalman filter with constant velocity models for camera position and orientation [20]. The filter parameters including measurement errors and process errors, were set to be enough to suppress high-frequency components in raw camera movements while preserving its important features without significant delay. The third path was constructed using the CAP method (Equation (3)) with k set at 0.016. The fourth path was constructed using SAP method (Equation (4)) with k set at 0.016 and n set at 64. Each of the four methods was applied to the traces of from all of the scenes.

4.1 Performance

While the Kalman filter requires very little computation overhead to process, the CAP and SAP methods due incur some computational penalties. To compute the Viewpoint Similarity, the scene must be rendered from both the camera and the participant positions, thus requiring a second render of the geometric models. Secondly, the Viewpoint Similarity metric requires a screen-space computation to be completed for each comparison (Equation (2)). Finally, the flashlight overlay (Figure 3) requires one final screen-space pass. We rendered each of the eight scenes into a 960x540 sized window on a computer equipped with an Intel Xeon 2.67 GHz CPU, 24 GB RAM, and an Nvidia Quadro 5000 GPU. We were able to achieve a rendering rate greater than 60 Hz for both the CAP and SAP method.

While the end goal of our method is to produce camera paths that are easier to watch, the total path length traveled by the camera provides an accessible, quantitative assessment of camera motion. Videographers are generally encouraged to use camera motion sparingly [8] and it has been shown that simpler and shorter camera paths are desirable because they are easier to watch [16].

To test whether the CAP and SAP methods did reduce the camera movement, we monitored the change in camera position at each time step for each of the methods. Figure 5 shows an example velocity profile demonstrating that both the CAP and SAP methods tend to have a lesser velocity compared to Raw or Kalman filtered camera paths.

Table 1 shows the distance the camera traveled for each of the methods, as well as its ratio compared to the original camera path. As shown, the Kalman filter does not affect the amount the camera travels compared to the Raw path on average for the listed experiences. This makes sense as the Kalman filter is targeted to remove the high-frequency components of the camera movement and thus can overshoot the targeted camera motions. The CAP and SAP methods both reduce the distance the camera traveled in all eight scenes, with the SAP method able to reduce the camera motion by over 50% for some scenes. Further discussion of this result will be given in Section 5.

4.2 Study

We designed a study to test whether the CAP and SAP methods were able to create a better viewing experience without obscuring information. Our hypothesis was that viewers should be able to perform the same counting tasks asked of the participant in the virtual environment based solely the visual images being shown to them. We hypothesized that our method could improve the viewing experience for our study subjects, allowing them to complete the counting tasks more easily and with more confidence, and without reducing their performance compared to viewing the raw camera path.

We ran the experiment through Amazon Mechanical Turk, following the practices described by Kittur et al. [13] and Downs et al. [5]. Specifically, we chose a standard rate of pay and created questions to verify that the participant was human, had the technical ability to participate, and was actively engaged. Subjects were compensated based on an estimate that the experiment would require approximately 15 minutes of their time.

After completing questions about demographic information, the subjects were shown eight videos corresponding to a randomly selected scene and method. The order of the videos and methods was randomly selected so that each subject would see each scene once and each method twice. The study subjects were asked to count the same objects that the participant was asked to count inside of the virtual environment. After watching each video, the participant was asked to input their counted value and input a prominent floating word from the video as an engagement check. The participant was then asked a series of questions about the camera movement, the difficulty of the task, and their confidence in their answers. Each question was answered on a five point Likert scale. The study attracted 24 subjects and all subject's data were used.

We found that subjects were generally able to count the objects accurately, with subjects able to produce the correct result 57% of the time. We found no significant difference in the error of the object count between the methods. We also found no significance between the error count and the scene being shown. The result confirms our hypothesis that subjects can complete the same counting task and that the CAP and SAP methods did not obscure the content of the original observations.

Figure 6 shows graphs for each of the subjective questions asked in the study. We note that while these questions used a five-point Likert scale, research has shown Likert scales to be an approximate of a continuum [4]. As shown, the CAP and SAP methods were able to perform well in all of the categories listed.

We found that subjects rated the calmness of the camera move-

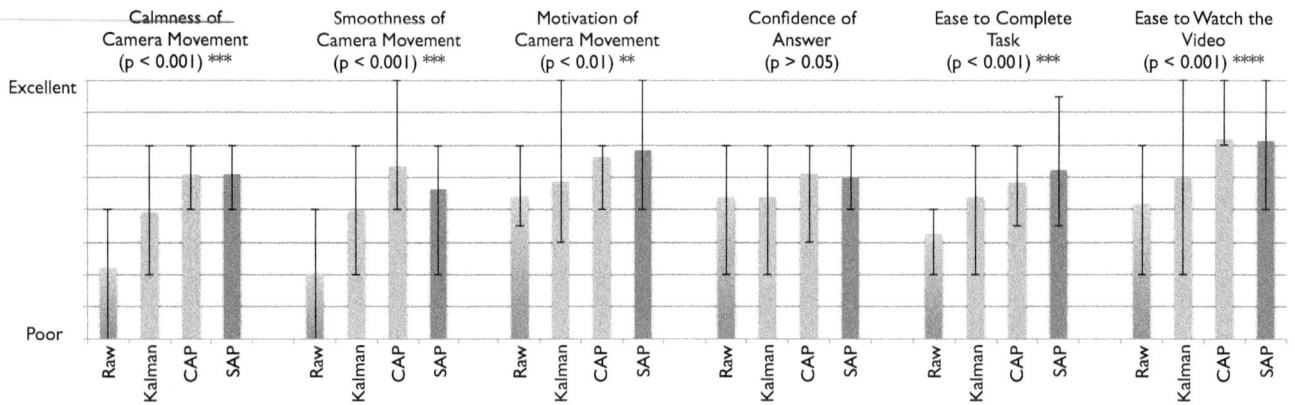

Figure 6: Graphs for each of the subjective questions asked in the study. The results proved to be statistically significant, with the only exception for the subjects' confidence in their answers. The bars show the first and third quartiles.

ment to be statistically significant, $F(3, 188) = 18.105$, with Tukey post-hoc analysis showing the CAP and SAP methods to be significantly better than the Kalman and Raw methods. Subjects' ratings of the smoothness of the camera movement also proved to be statistically significant, $F(3,188) = 19.385$, with Tukey post-hoc analysis showing the CAP and SAP methods to be significantly better than the Raw method and the CAP method to be significantly better than the Kalman method. Subjects' ratings of the motivation of camera movement proved to be statistically significant, $F(3,187) = 4.4988$, with Tukey post-hoc analysis showing the CAP and SAP methods to be significantly better than the Raw method.

We also found that subjects rated the ease with which they could accomplish the counting task to be statistically significant, $F(3,188) = 5.9002$, with Tukey post-hoc analysis showing the CAP and SAP methods to be significantly better than the Raw method. Finally, we found subjects' ratings of the ease to watch the video were statistically significant, $F(3,188) = 7.1315$, with Tukey post-hoc analysis showing the CAP and SAP methods to be significantly better than the Raw method. We did not find a significant difference for subjects' confidence for answering the questions about the number of objects in a scene. These results confirmed our hypothesis that viewers would find the CAP and SAP methods easier to watch and find the task easier to accomplish. While we did see a higher confidence for answering the questions with the CAP and SAP methods, the result was not statistically significant.

5. DISCUSSION

From the results of our study, we feel that both the CAP and SAP methods are superior to the standard method of presenting views using raw egocentric camera motion. The SAP method slightly out-performed the CAP method in most metrics with the exception of the smoothness test, which is to be expected. From this result it would be interesting to study a variety of settings for the exponential parameter, n, in the SAP method.

The results of our study show that the CAP and SAP methods perform equally well in comparison to the Raw path in terms the counting of objects, thus indicating that our method does not obscure the content of the original path. While it was outside of the scope of this paper, it would be interesting to determine if any method would be able to outperform the original observations. Although we did not see any significant difference between the methods for the correctness of the counting task, we think it is worth mentioning that the variance in the error of the normalized object

count is smaller with the SAP method (0.010) compared to the Raw, Kalman and CAP methods (0.032, 0.026, and 0.020 respectively).

As shown in Figure 6, the subjects were not significantly more confident in their answers with the path from either CAP or SAP method than the others. However, we found no correlation between the subject's confidence in their answer and the correctness, suggesting that self-reported confidence is not a good predictor of performance for this task.

Another interesting finding is that geometric smoothness does not always coincide with perceptual smoothness. While the velocity profile of the Kalman filter appears to be smoother than either the CAP or SAP methods, the subjects rated the camera movements of both CAP and SAP methods to be more calm and/or smooth.

The fact that CAP and SAP methods reduced the distance the camera traveled is of interest when coupled with the fact that the CAP and SAP methods did not cause a reduction in observed content. In this regard, many of the camera motions in the Raw path can be viewed as unnecessary in terms of communicating content and can be removed as was done in the CAP and SAP methods. Furthermore, the CAP and SAP paths produced significantly higher ratings of the camera movement when compared to the Raw path, matching the results of Ponto et al. which found that simplified paths were generally easier to watch [16].

While this distance metric only accounts for changes in position, a variety of other distance metrics could take orientational changes in the camera as well. While future work may analyze different methods to quantify camera movement, these new distance metrics would only provide a new source for comparison and would not affect the resulting paths from the CAP or SAP methods as they used screen space constraints.

It should also be noted that the experience for the participant in the virtual environment and the subject viewing the paths on a 2D monitor were quite different. Our method aims to present the experience of a participant in a highly immersive environment to an external observer with substantially less immersive capabilities. Future work will explore how to convey virtual experiences to an external participant in a second highly immersive environment.

For all results of our paper we used a GPU implementation that utilized an offscreen buffer with the same sized window. However, this may be undesirable in situations with extremely complicated scenes, ultra-high-resolution displays, or lower-end graphical hardware. By reducing the size of the buffers used to store the depth maps for the participant's view and the camera's view, both the scene rendering and pixel-wise comparisons can done more rapidly. As shown in Ponto et al., reducing the size of these buffers can greatly increase performance without affecting results [16].

6. CONCLUSIONS

We created a novel method for presenting the experience of a participant in a virtual environment to external viewers in an online real-time fashion. Our method uses a content dependent metric to determine how much the camera should be adjusted on a per-frame basis. Our method is able to greatly reduce the camera movement over time and is thusly able to provide camera paths that are easier and more pleasing to watch while maintaining the content of the participant's original observations. Future work will explore using other viewing perspectives, such as an over the shoulder viewpoint, and will investigate methods to change the camera's field of view dynamically.

7. ACKNOWLEDGMENTS

We would like to acknowledge the support of the the Living Environments Laboratory, the Wisconsin Institute for Discovery, and the CIBM training program. This project was supported in part by NLM award 5T15LM007359 and NSF awards IIS-0946598, CMMI-0941013, and IIS-1162037. We would specifically like to thank Patricia Brennan, Kendra Jacobsen, Andrew Morland, and Ross Tredinnick for their support and assistance.

8. REFERENCES

[1] M. Alexa. Linear combination of transformations. *ACM Trans. Graph.*, 21:380–387, July 2002.

[2] H.-C. Chang, S.-H. Lai, and K.-R. Lu. A robust real-time video stabilization algorithm. *Journal of Visual Communication and Image Representation*, 17(3):659 – 673, 2006.

[3] M. Christie, R. Machap, J. marie Norm, P. Olivier, and J. Pickering. Virtual camera planning: A survey. In *In Proceedings Smart Graphics*, pages 40–52. Springer, 2005.

[4] J. Dawes. Do data characteristics change according to the number of scale points used? *International Journal of Market Research*, 50(1), 2008.

[5] J. S. Downs, M. B. Holbrook, S. Sheng, and L. F. Cranor. Are your participants gaming the system?: screening mechanical turk workers. In *Proceedings of the 28th international conference on Human factors in computing systems*, CHI '10, pages 2399–2402, New York, NY, USA, 2010.

[6] S. Ertürk. Real-time digital image stabilization using kalman filters. *Real-Time Imaging*, 8(4):317 – 328, 2002.

[7] E. Foxlin. Inertial head-tracker sensor fusion by a complementary separate-bias kalman filter. In *Virtual Reality Annual International Symposium, 1996., Proceedings of the IEEE 1996*, pages 185 –194, 267, mar-3 apr 1996.

[8] M. L. Gleicher and F. Liu. Re-cinematography: Improving the camerawork of casual video. *ACM Trans. Multimedia Comput. Commun. Appl.*, 5:2:1–2:28, October 2008.

[9] M. Grundmann, V. Kwatra, and I. Essa. Auto-directed video stabilization with robust L1 optimal camera paths. In *Computer Vision and Pattern Recognition (CVPR), 2011 IEEE Conference on*, pages 225–232. IEEE, 2011.

[10] M. Hansen, P. Anandan, K. Dana, G. van der Wal, and P. Burt. Real-time scene stabilization and mosaic construction. In *Applications of Computer Vision, 1994., Proceedings of the Second IEEE Workshop on*, pages 54 –62, dec 1994.

[11] A. Hawkins and C. M. Grimm. Camera keyframing using linear interpolation of matrices. *journal of graphics, gpu, and game tools*, 12(3):55–69, 2007.

[12] Y. Kim, V. Jayanthi, and I. Kweon. System-on-chip solution of video stabilization for cmos image sensors in hand-held devices. *IEEE transactions on circuits and systems for video technology*, 21(10):1401–1414, 2011.

[13] A. Kittur, E. H. Chi, and B. Suh. Crowdsourcing user studies with mechanical turk. In *Proceeding of the twenty-sixth annual SIGCHI conference on Human factors in computing systems*, CHI '08, pages 453–456, New York, NY, USA, 2008.

[14] J. Liang, C. Shaw, and M. Green. On temporal-spatial realism in the virtual reality environment. In *Proceedings of the 4th annual ACM symposium on User interface software and technology*, UIST '91, pages 19–25, New York, NY, USA, 1991.

[15] C.-T. Lin, C.-T. Hong, and C.-T. Yang. Real-time digital image stabilization system using modified proportional integrated controller. *Circuits and Systems for Video Technology, IEEE Transactions on*, 19(3):427 –431, march 2009.

[16] K. Ponto, J. Kohlmann, and M. Gleicher. Effective replays and summarization of virtual experiences. *Visualization and Computer Graphics, IEEE Transactions on*, 18(4):607 –616, april 2012.

[17] D. D. Pothier, C. Hughes, W. Dillon, P. J. Ranalli, and J. A. Rutka. The use of real-time image stabilization and augmented reality eyewear in the treatment of oscillopsia. *Otolaryngology – Head and Neck Surgery*, 2012.

[18] K. Ratakonda. Real-time digital video stabilization for multi-media applications. In *Circuits and Systems, 1998. ISCAS '98. Proceedings of the 1998 IEEE International Symposium on*, volume 4, pages 69 –72 vol.4, may-3 jun 1998.

[19] P. Salamin, D. Thalmann, and F. Vexo. The benefits of third-person perspective in virtual and augmented reality? In *Proceedings of the ACM symposium on Virtual reality software and technology*, VRST '06, pages 27–30, New York, NY, USA, 2006.

[20] H. J. Shin, J. Lee, S. Y. Shin, and M. Gleicher. Computer puppetry: An importance-based approach. *ACM Trans. Graph.*, 20(2):67–94, Apr. 2001.

[21] C. Wang, J.-H. Kim, K.-Y. Byun, J. Ni, and S.-J. Ko. Robust digital image stabilization using the kalman filter. *Consumer Electronics, IEEE Transactions on*, 55(1):6 –14, february 2009.

[22] L. Williams. Casting curved shadows on curved surfaces. *SIGGRAPH Comput. Graph.*, 12:270–274, August 1978.

[23] H. Yang and G. M. Olson. Exploring collaborative navigation:: the effect of perspectives on group performance. In *Proceedings of the 4th international conference on Collaborative virtual environments*, CVE '02, pages 135–142, New York, NY, USA, 2002.

[24] S. You and U. Neumann. Fusion of vision and gyro tracking for robust augmented reality registration. In *Virtual Reality, 2001. Proceedings. IEEE*, pages 71 –78, march 2001.

Dense Depth Maps from Sparse Models and Image Coherence for Augmented Reality

Stefanie Zollmann
Graz University of Technology
Inffeldgasse 16, 8010 Graz
Graz, Austria
zollmann@icg.tugraz.at

Gerhard Reitmayr
Graz University of Technology
Inffeldgasse 16, 8010 Graz
Graz, Austria
reitmayr@icg.tugraz.at

ABSTRACT

A convincing combination of virtual and real data in an Augmented Reality (AR) application requires detailed 3D information about the real world scene. In many situations extensive model data is not available, while sparse representations such as outlines on a map exist. In this paper, we present a novel approach using such sparse 3D model data to seed automatic image segmentation and infer a dense depth map of an environment. Sparse 3D models of known landmarks, such as points and lines from GIS databases, are projected into a registered image and initialize 2D image segmentation at the projected locations in the image. For the segmentation we propose different techniques, which combine shape information, semantics given by the database, and the visual appearance in the referenced image. The resulting depth information of objects in the scene can be used in many applications, including occlusion handling, label placement, and 3D modeling.

Categories and Subject Descriptors

H.5.1 [**Multimedia Information Systems**]: Artificial, Augmented and Virtual Realities; I.4.6 [**Image Processing and Computer Vision**]: Segmentation

General Terms

Theory

Keywords

Augmented Reality, Depth Map Estimation, Segmentation

1. INTRODUCTION

Geographic information systems (GIS) store a large amount of geo-referenced information about indoor and outdoor environments. Commercial as well as governmental suppliers offer a wide range of data including mapping information, infrastructure data, and building plans. User generated map data, such as OpenStreetMap, provide access to detailed 2D information on building outlines, street curbs and other features in the environment. Utility companies have extensive GIS databases of their infrastructure comprising pipes, cables, and other installations, as well as objects in the surroundings, including street furniture, trees, walls, and again buildings. Due to the geo-referenced character of this data, it is natural to create Augmented Reality (AR) visualizations for it. Application areas include the visualization of GIS data for infrastructure maintenance [14], agricultural data [8], or scientific data [11]. Unfortunately, the GIS data provided by most suppliers is geometrically sparse. Objects are represented by simple geometric primitives such as points, lines or polygons, usually representing only the 2D projections of the real objects onto a map ground plane. Even if a height value is stored, it only represents the point or line on the surface of the earth but does not describe the whole 3D shape. In this paper, we refer to such models as *sparse models* (Figure 1, (Left)) similar to sparse point clouds created by image-based reconstruction methods.

Without accurate information about the height, dimensions or extend of an object it becomes difficult to use this model data for advanced AR techniques that require dense models. For example, correct occlusion management between objects in the real environment and virtual geometry (Figure 1, (Right)) requires a detailed model of the real environment. Ideally, it is accurate enough to create a pixel-accurate occluder mask or depth map of the scene. Other uses include phantom geometry for interaction with the real scene or rendering realistic shadows and lighting effects between the real and virtual objects. The sparse model data afforded by GIS databases and similar engineering representations cannot provide this fidelity by itself.

This paper describes a method to combine sparse GIS data with information derived from real world imagery in order to infer a dense depth map (Section 3). Sparse 3D model data is transformed into 2D shape priors in the current camera frame guiding an appearance-based image segmentation (Section 4). We describe different image segmentation methods and their integration with the prior data to compute a segmentation of the real world objects corresponding to the model prior (Section 5). The result of our approach is a dense depth map representing real world objects (Section 6 and Figure 1, (Middle)). The dense depth map can then be used for occlusion management, visualization or to determine more exact extends of objects (Section 7).

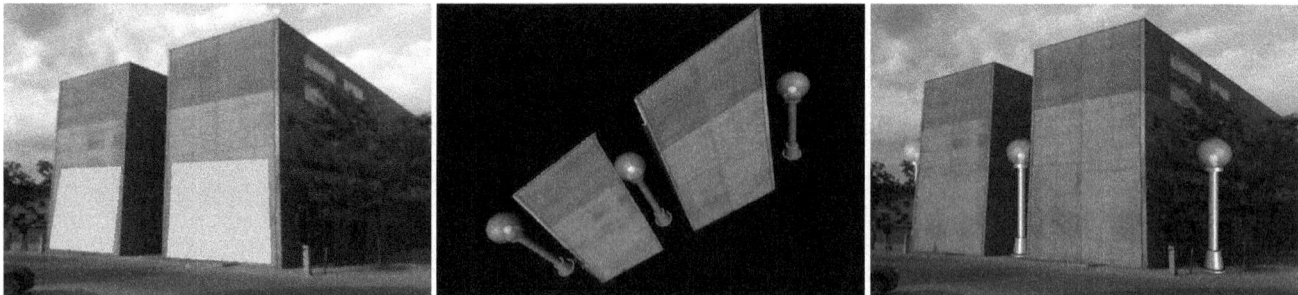

Figure 1: (Left) Sparse GIS model data overlaid over a registered view. (Middle) Segmentation of the registered view derived from the sparse model. (Right) Correct occlusion with virtual geometry using the derived depth map.

2. RELATED WORK

Creating 3D model information from images is a traditional research area in computer vision. However, many techniques require data such as multiple images with known camera poses, expensive computation or specialized hardware such as stereo cameras or depth sensors to create dense depth maps of images. Our work focuses on outdoor AR systems which may not support most of these approaches. Therefore we aim to determine depth maps from single images without specialized hardware, but by reusing other information.

For creating depth information from a single image Hoiem et al. [5] proposed a method for the automatic creation of photo pop-up models. The result of their method was a billboard model, which was created by mapping discriminative labels to parts of the image and applying different cutting and folding techniques to them. Since this method was limited to work only for selected scenes without foreground objects, Ventura et al. proposed a method for supporting the cutting and folding by an interactive labeling of foreground objects [18]. Another technique to create pop-up objects was introduced by Wither et al. [19]. For their approach the authors used depth samples produced by a laser range finder as input for a foreground background segmentation. Using the segmentation and the known depth sample they are able to propagate depth to each image pixel. The idea of our work is to create these kind of pop-up models automatically, without being limited to selected scenes or using user input or an additional laser range sensor.

In 3D reconstruction, several research groups already used external input to improve the results of Structure from Motion (SfM) approaches, for instance 2D outlines drawn by the user [15] or prior knowledge about the architecure [1]. Grzeszczuk et al. replaced the interactive input by information from GIS databases allowing for a fully automatic approach [4]. However, outdoor AR users are usually visually observing the scene from one location by rotating and afterwards moving on to the next position; observing by moving from location to another location is rather rare. Therefore, it would be difficult to create large image sets from different viewpoints as input for a SfM approach. But Grzeszczuk's work motivated us to use GIS data as additional input for a depth from single image approach.

The basic idea of our method is to combine depth information from a GIS database with a single camera image to map depth information to selected parts of the image. To find the corresponding pixels in the registered camera view a segmentation has to be computed. Typically, segmentation methods work with user input that provides sample information about foreground and background [13]. To implement a fully automatic approach, we replaced the user input with input from the GIS database.

The results of our dense depth map estimation can be used for different visualization techniques in AR, such as occlusion refinement or X-Ray visualization. Examples of information from camera images used for occlusion handling in AR include edges [7] and salient information [12, 21]. The lack of accurate or dense 3D information of the scene motivated our investigations. With the method that we propose in this paper, we can create additional information about the 3D scene structure that can help to improve the occlusion management.

3. APPROACH

Our method uses the combination of GIS information and a geo-registered image given by an AR system to segment the input image (see Figure 2 for an overview). From the GIS data, (1) we generate sparse prior 3D models that are projected into the camera image and (2) seed an automatic segmentation process with shape and appearance priors. (3) The segmentation process returns an image area that corresponds to the 3D model feature and is taken as the true object outline in the image. The object outline is back-projected onto a plane representing the depth of the sparse 3D feature. From multiple such features and assumptions on the ground plane and the scene depth, (4) we create a coarse pop-up like depth map of the input image (Figure 2, (Right)).

A building, for example, is usually only represented as the 2D projection of the walls onto the map reference plane in the GIS. Thus, we only have information about the location and extend of the intersection between walls and ground, but not the actual height or overall shape of the building. Assuming a certain minimal building height, we can create an impostor shape that represents the building up to that height (e.g. 2m). This shape will not correspond to the true building outline in the input image, but is enough to provide both shape and appearance priors. Its shape and location already provide a strong indication where in the image the segmentation should operate.

In general, segmentation splits the image into a foreground object and background based on visual similarity, i.e. sim-

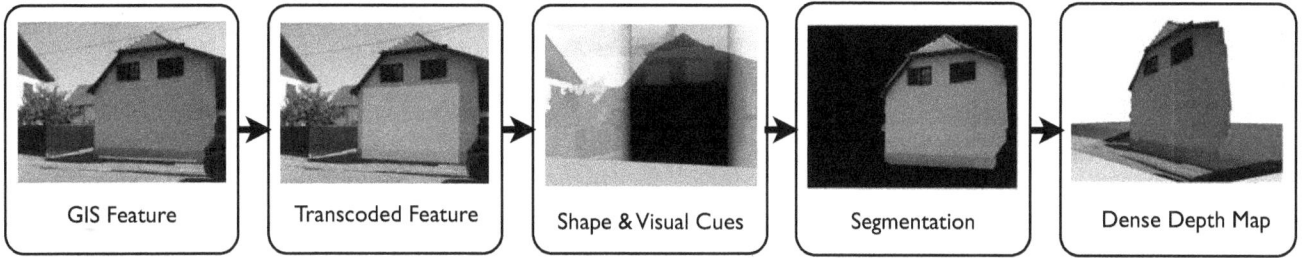

Figure 2: Overview of our approach. The AR system provides a registered background image, which is combined with GIS model data to derive visual and shape cues and guide a 2D segmentation process. From the segments and the corresponding 3D location a dense 3D depth map is formed.

ilar colors in the image. Through sampling the pixel colors in the re-projected shape, we create an initial color model for the foreground object. This input is similar to the user input in interactive segmentation methods as they provide foreground and background color models. The result of the segmentation labels image pixels as either belonging to the object of interest, or not. Together with the depth information, the object pixels are used to create a flat model of the object of interest which can be textured by the camera image or used to render a depth map for occlusion effects.

4. CUES FROM SPARSE MODELS

The first step in our method is the extraction of the cues from the GIS. The sparse 3D model obtained from a typical GIS database will provide the following inputs:

- A supporting shape onto which the segmentation is projected

- Seed pixel locations that inform a foreground color model for the segmentation

- Additional energy terms to steer the segmentation

4.1 Support shape

Typical GIS or engineering model usually contain only sparse and abstract geometric representations of real world objects. Therefore, we need to use additional information about the represented object and the application to create an approximate support shape.

Despite the sparseness of the geometric features, they usually transport a lot of meta-information, such as a label representing a type (wall, street curb, tree, fire hydrant) and specific parameters (diameter of a pipe, type of tree). We use this additional semantic information to arrive at an approximate geometric shape.

For simple augmented or virtual reality visualizations, GIS database features are usually transcoded using the geo-referenced positions and their semantic labels to assign some predefined 3D geometry and parameterize it with the available position data [14]. Additional parameters that are required for the visualization are configured in advance by expert users. For instance, all features with the semantic label "tree" are transcoded to a 3D cylinder and positioned at the reference point. The radius and height of the cylinder are fixed parameters configured for the particular transcoding operation.

To create a support shape from a feature, we employ a similar transcoding step. In contrast to pure visualizations,

we are only interested in obtaining an estimate for the shape and location of the object in the image. For example, a building wall is defined as a horizontal line in the GIS. Because it is a wall, we extrude it vertically to create a vertical support plane for it.

Due to the missing information in the database, some dimensions are less constrained then others. For the building wall in the example given above, the ground edge of the wall and the extension in the horizontal direction are well defined, while the height is essentially unknown. Therefore, we create geometry that is conservative and should only cover an area in the image that we can be certain belongs to the real object.

4.2 Visual cues

The 2D location information provided by the support shape alone is not enough input for a good segmentation. Good visual cues are essential to obtain an accurate segmentation of the image. Appearance information cannot be inferred from the database, because the semantic labels give no further information about the appearance of a feature. However, projecting the transcoded geometry into the image allows the sampling of pixels in the coverage area to extract a foreground appearance model of the object's segment. This model can include gray values, color values in different color spaces, texture information, or binary patterns as described by Santner et al. [13].

To avoid the influence of noise and inaccurate shape priors we apply an over-segmentation to derive visual cues. For that purpose, we use the superpixel algorithm described by Felzenszwalb et al. [2], because it provides the over-segmentation based on a perceptually natural grouping and it is fast to compute. Now, image statistics are calculated

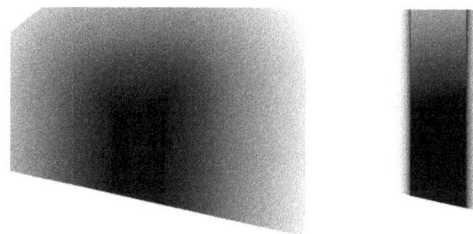

Figure 3: Distance-transform of shape cue. Left: Isotropic distance transform of shape cue. Right: Anisotropic distance transform of shape cue.

on individual superpixels. We use the average L*a*b-value and the texturedness of each superpixel as the appearance model.

4.3 Spatial cues

Besides an appearance model and a seed location from the support shape, the location and area potentially covered by a feature in the image should also be taken into account. We assume that objects have a compact and simple-connected shape and are not spread over multiple disconnected areas in the image.

To model this assumption, we introduce a spatial energy term in the segmentation that only selects pixels as foreground, if the energy for their location is low. The simplest such terms is the indicator function for the projection of the support shape itself. However, a sharp boundary would defeat the purpose of the segmenting the object from the image, therefore we create a fuzzy version of the projected shape by computing a distance transform of the projected shape (see Figure 3, (Left)). This fuzzification ensures that the segmented boundary will take the appearance model into account and not simply coincide with the reprojected shape.

4.4 Uncertainty

Furthermore, the shape and location of a feature is often not accurately known, and therefore the shape and location of the feature is uncertain. Again, we model this uncertainty through blurring the spatial energy term accordingly.

For example, tracking inaccuracies might lead to wrong re-projection of the feature, thus shifting the object boundary arbitrarily within a certain radius. To model this effect, we apply an isotropic distance function with radius σ representing the tracking error in image coordinates.

On the other hand, the shape of a feature is not fully known from the GIS information alone. For example, walls and buildings have unknown heights, even though the baseline and horizontal extend is well defined by the 2D outline. Here we assume a reasonable minimal height (e.g. 2m) and create extrusions of the foot print up to that height. Additionally, we perform a distance transform only in the unknown direction - up in this case. This creates a sharp spatial energy term in the known directions, but a soft energy in the unknown directions and results in an anisotropic distance transform of the shape cue (Figure 3, (Right)). Overall this makes the segmentation robust against these unknown parameters.

5. SEGMENTATION

Based on the extracted cues, we continue with the segmentation of the input image into foreground objects corresponding to the data given by the model database. For this step we experimented with two different methods. Both methods use the same input from the projected, transcoded GIS data and compute the same output, a segmentation labeling every pixel as part of the object of interest or not. The two methods offer a trade-off between complexity and quality of the segmentation.

The input consists of the visual and spatial cues as described in Section 4. Each set of cues defines a cost function for every pixel in the image describing the likelihood that this pixel is part of the foreground object.

The re-projected and transformed support shape defines a likelihood function f_{shape}. Pixels that are located far from

Figure 4: Segmentation results. (Left) Segmentation based on the Greedy method, some parts of the roof are missing. (Right) Segmentation based on the Total Variation approach.

the input shape get a lower probability than pixel located close to the input shape or that are located inside the input shape. Uncertainty is encoded in the distance transformed input as well as detailed in section 4.4.

Visual cues are represented as the mean feature vector $V(S)$ averaged over all pixels in a set S. This set may be defined differently, based on the segmentation algorithm. The likelihood function $f_{vis}(p)$ of a pixel p is then given as the squared euclidean distance of the pixel's feature vector to the mean feature vector

$$f_{vis}(p) = \|V(p) - V(S)\|^2. \qquad (1)$$

5.1 Greedy algorithm

The first segmentation method is a greedy approach and calculates the final segmentation by operating on the superpixel representation. All image segments that are covered by the shape cues seed a region growing algorithm and are labeled as foreground object. The region growing enforces connectivity to obtain a single object. The set of foreground segments is called L.

For a segment s that is adjacent to one or more segments $n \in L$, we define the likelihood function $f_{vis}(s)$ for the visual cues as the minimal distance between the feature vector of the segment and all neighboring foreground segments.

$$f_{vis}(s) = \min_{n \in L} \|V(s) - V(n)\|^2 \text{ where } n \text{ neighbors } s. \qquad (2)$$

The labeling $L(s)$ is then given by summing the likelihoods of the distance transform $f_{shape}(s)$ averaged over the segment and the visual similarity $f_{vis}(s)$ as defined in (2) to a single cost function $C(s)$ for the segment s

$$C(s) = f_{shape}(s) + f_{vis}(s), \qquad (3)$$

and thresholding the cost function to decide the label:

$$L(s) = \begin{cases} 0, & \text{if } C(s) \geqslant T \\ 1, & \text{if } C(s) < T. \end{cases} \qquad (4)$$

This decision is iterated until no new segments are labeled as foreground. The result of the Greedy segmentation method is a binary labeling that describes whenever an image segment belongs to the object of interest or not (Figure 4, left). The disadvantage of this method is that it is not searching for an optimal solution.

5.2 Total variation approach

The second method computes the segmentation based on minimizing a variational image segmentation model [17]. Total variation has already been successfully applied for interactive image segmentation [13]. Since this method tends to find very accurate object segmentations based on minimal user input, we decided to use this approach and replace the interactive input with input from the GIS database. To apply the variational method, we need to define a per-pixel data term similar to the cost function for each segment in section 5.1.

The variational image segmentation minimizes the following energy function $E(u)$ over a continuous labeling function $u(x, y)$ that maps every pixel to the interval $[0, 1]$ indicating if it is foreground (as 0) or background (as 1):

$$\min_{u \in [0,1]} E(u) = \int_\Omega |\nabla u| d\Omega + \int_\Omega |u - f| d\Omega. \quad (5)$$

The first term is a regularization term minimizing the length of the border between the segments. The second term is the data term given by the function $f(x, y)$ indicating how much a pixel belongs to the foreground (0) or background (1).

We define the data-term $f(x, y)$ again based on the shape cues and visual cues presented in section 4:

$$f(x, y) = \alpha f_{shape}(x, y) + (1 - \alpha) f_{vis}(x, y) \quad (6)$$

$$= \alpha f_{shape}(x, y) + (1 - \alpha) \|V((x, y)) - V(S)\|^2. \quad (7)$$

$V(S)$ is averaged over the set of all segments covered by the initial shape cues. The function $f(x, y)$ is further normalized by its maximum value to serve as a data term in (5). The parameter α weights the influence between shape or visual cues. The output of the Total Variation approach is a smooth labeling function $u(x, y)$ that is thresholded at 0.5 to obtain a binary labeling. The final binary labeling provides a pixel accurate representation of the foreground object (Figure 4, (Right)).

6. GEOMETRY CREATION

The resulting binary image serves now as input to calculate a 3D depth map that can be used for different purposes such as visualization or occlusion management. It is a 2D representation describing the parts of the image belonging to the sparse model given by the GIS database and has to be converted into 3D geometry.

For this purpose we use the support shape extracted in section 4.1 and compute the final geometry by back-projecting the outline of the segmented object onto the support shape. First, the outline of the segmentation is extracted from the image by tracing the points on the border in either clockwise or counterclockwise order. The result is a list of ordered pixels forming the outline. Next, we setup a plane containing the support shape and aligning the plane with vertical direction of the world to obtain an upright representation. The individual pixels of the segmentation outline are back-projected into 3D rays through the inverse camera calibration matrix and intersected with the plane. This intersection establishes the 3D coordinates for the pixels that are combined to create a 3D face set. To obtain a full dense representation, we also add a representation of the ground, either derived from a digital terrain model or by approximating the average height with a single plane.

To use the 3D geometry for visualization, or model-based tracking a textured 3D geometry is necessary. Our approach uses projective texture mapping to correctly project the camera image back onto the 3D geometry (see Figure

Figure 5: Extracted pop-up model created with our method for the image shown in the inset.

5). Therefore we set up the texture matrix to use the same camera model as the calibrated real camera.

7. RESULTS

To analyze the results that we achieve with of our approach, we computed the accuracy of the results under different conditions and compared the accuracy of the Total Variation approach with the Greedy method.

7.1 Accuracy

We tested the accuracy of the dense depth estimation against a 3D reconstruction of building as ground truth. The 3D reconstruction was created using a structure-from-motion pipeline on images acquired with an octo-copter [6]. The 3D reconstruction from the SFM pipeline is rather sparse, therefore to create more ground truth data, a semi-dense

Figure 6: Computation of segmentation error. (Left) Reprojected 3D points of the point cloud. (Middle) Computed filled polygon of the reprojected points. (Right) Extracted segmentation.

Figure 7: Segmentation results for selected offsets. (Left) Segmentation result for 0.5m offset. (Right) The segmentation with an 1m offset shows a larger error, but still an visually acceptable result.

point cloud is computed from this sparse representation by applying the method of Furukawa et al. [3]. Known GPS positions of the octo-copter allow geo-referencing the point cloud and aligning it with known GIS data. As input to the dense depth estimation we used a geo-referenced 2D CAD plan of the the building provided by a construction company and geo-referenced images of the building.

To determine the accuracy of the dense depth estimation, we use the 3D point cloud as a ground truth. Points corresponding to objects of interest are manually selected from the point cloud and compared to the dense depth map computed by the Total Variation approach (see Figure 6). To compare ground truth and dense depth map we first computed for each point of the object, if its projection on the plane of the estimated pop-up model is inside the polygon describing the outline of the extracted object or not. The accuracy value for the *inlier* estimation is then given by the amount of inliers divided by the number of points. Since this measurement can only provide information if the extracted object is big enough, but not if the outline of the extracted object is similar to the reference object, we compute a second value, the *segmentation error*. The segmentation error is computed by calculating the difference in pixel between the extracted polygon and the polygon created by re-projecting the 3D points and computing the outline of the resulting 2D points.

These measurements also allow us to compute the registration accuracy that is required by our approach to produce reliable results. To determine this accuracy value, we created an artificial location offset of the input data and calculated the inliers and the segmentation error. As excepted the results show that with increasing offset errors the accuracy of the result is decreasing (Figure 8). But we can also show that with an offset of 0.5 m for all directions, still segmentation errors below 15% can be reached. Even for 1m

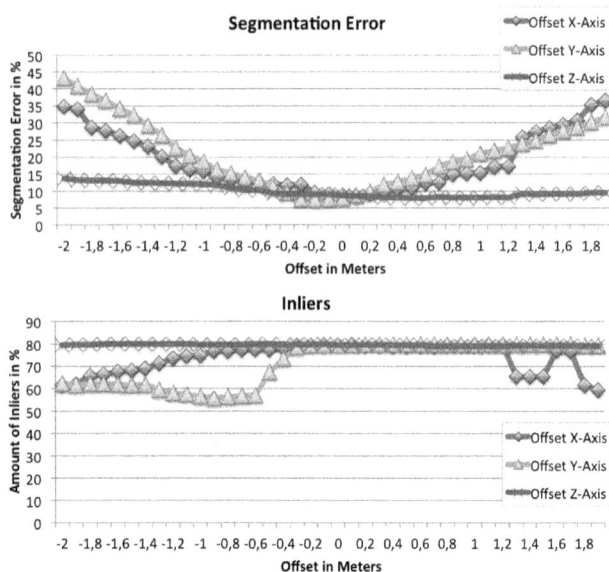

Figure 8: Accuracy measurements for different offsets. (Top) The segmentation error decreases with decreasing offsets. (Bottom) The amount of inliers is increasing with decreasing offsets.

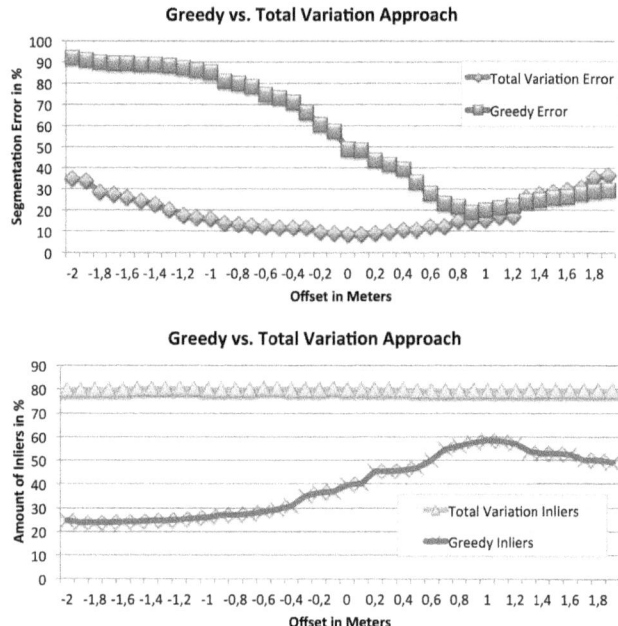

Figure 9: Accuracy measurements both segmentation methods. The segmentation error for the Total Variation method is lower than for the Greedy method. Bottom: The amount of inliers is higher for the Total Variation method.

offset the segmentation errors are below 20%. As shown in Figure 7 the segmentation results are still visually acceptable. This level of accuracy can be easily obtained by using a L1/L2 RTK receiver as we use in our outdoor AR setup.

7.2 Comparison of segmentation methods

So far, we determined the accuracies that can be achieved by using the Total Variation approach. Furthermore we used the accuracy values to analyze the difference between the Greedy and the Total Variation approach. We used the same methods to determine the segmentation error as well as the amount of inliers as described in the previous section. As shown in Figure 9 the segmentation error for the Greedy method is much higher than for the Total Variation approach. Also the amount of inliers is much lower than for the Total Variation approach. This shows that the accuracy of the Total Variation method is higher than for the Greedy approach.

8. APPLICATIONS

The dense depth maps created by the introduced approach support several applications such as the on-site creation of pop-up models (Figure 5), which can later be used for AR and VR visualizations. Furthermore, dense depth maps can help to improve the scene comprehension (Figure 10), the in-place surveying and annotation (Figure 11, (Left) and (Right)) or the relighting in outdoor AR where usually no accurate dense depth model is available. In the following we will discuss some of these application scenarios and show results of the application.

Figure 10: Occlusion management. (Left) The spatial relationship between real and virtual objects is complicated to understand when using a simple overlay. (Middle) X-Ray visualization using the pop-up model of the building for blending. The blending is only done for occluded elements to provide additional depth cues. (Right) X-Ray visualization using the pop-up model combined with a checkered importance mask.

Figure 11: Using the dense depth maps in other applications: (Left) Annotating a building. The dense depth map allows to make annotations spatially consistent. (Middle) Labeling. The dense depth maps helps to filter visible labels (marked red) from invisible (marked black). (Right) Surveying. The user can interactively survey parts of the building by using the dense depth map as interaction surface.

8.1 Occlusion management for AR

X-Ray AR allows to make occluded invisible virtual information visible. This kind of visualization often comes with the problem of wrong depth perception due to missing depth cues. For instance, Figure 10 (Right) shows a simple overlay of a mix of virtual occluded and virtual non-occluded information over a camera image of the real world. Due to missing occlusion cues it is hard to understand the spatial layout of real and virtual objects.

Dense depth maps allow to decide whether virtual content is occluded or visible and allows to visualize this information using different visualization techniques (Figure 10, (Middle), where only occluded points are rendered transparent or Figure 1, where occluded points are not rendered to improve the spatial perception). Furthermore the dense depth maps allow to apply advanced occlusion management techniques similar to the ones presented by Mendez and Schmalstieg [10]. In their paper they proposed the usage of importance maps to improve depth perception in X-Ray Augmented Reality. This technique requires a phantom representation of the scene, which is usually not available. For this purpose we can use the dense depth maps of each object as the corresponding phantom object (Figure 10, (Right)).

8.2 Annotations

Another application that can benefit from our approach are annotations of the real world. Previous systems are working image-based allowing only to view the annotations from a specified location [9] or using additional input devices such as laser range finders [19] to determine the depth

of an object of interest. Wither et al. also proposed an approach for using additional remote views of the scene [20] to determine the 3D position of an annotation. The dense depth maps created by our approach allow to create georeferenced annotations without additional measurement devices and without interacting in remote views of the scene (Figure 11, (Left)).

Another problem of label placement in standard AR browsers is that all available labels for the user's position are shown. This results in cluttered views, where the user may have difficulties associating labels with the environment. By creating dense depth maps using our method, we are able to display only relevant, visible labels for the current view (Figure 11, (Middle) shown in red).

8.3 Surveying application

Surveying is an important task for a lot of architectural and construction site tasks. Usually, people have to make use of extensive equipment. The dense depth map allows the user to survey real world objects in an Augmented Reality view. For instance to survey the width and heights of windows, the user can select 3D points directly on the facade of the building by calculating the intersection point between the dense depth map of the facade (Figure 11, (Right)). In this way polygons can be created and the length of line segments can be determined.

9. CONCLUSION AND FUTURE WORK

This paper presented an automatic method to create a dense depth map in AR applications, when only sparse 3D model data is available. By initializing a segmentation algorithm with projections of the sparse data, we can obtain more accurate representations of the 3D objects and build a pop-up model. We demonstrated different application areas for our results, such as occlusion cues for AR scenes, annotation and surveying.

Whereas the results of the dense depth maps can be used in AR in real-time, the current implementation of the calculation does not operate in real-time as both the super-pixel segmentation and the final variational method do not run at interactive frame rates. We aim to overcome this limitation through incremental computation of the super-pixel segmentation [16] and relying on frame-to-frame coherence to reuse results from the last frame, as well as application of the variational optimization to the superpixels directly. This would reduce the complexity of the problem by several orders of magnitude.

Finally, we are planning to investigate the different application scenarios of the dense depth maps with expert users from the construction and engineering industries to obtain information about the applicability in real-world scenarios.

10. ACKNOWLEDGMENTS

This work was supported by the Austrian Research Promotion Agency (FFG) FIT-IT projects Construct (830035) and SMARTVidente (820922). The authors wish to thank Thomas Pock for his valuable support for the Total Variation method.

11. REFERENCES

[1] A. R. Dick, P. H. S. Torr, and R. Cipolla. Modelling and interpretation of architecture from several images. *Int. J. Comput. Vision*, 60(2):111–134, Nov. 2004.

[2] P. F. Felzenszwalb and D. P. Huttenlocher. Efficient graph-based image segmentation. *Int. J. Comput. Vision*, 59(2):167–181, Sept. 2004.

[3] Y. Furukawa, B. Curless, S. M. Seitz, and R. Szeliski. Towards Internet-scale multi-view stereo. In *Proc. CVPR*, pages 1434–1441. IEEE, June 2010.

[4] R. Grzeszczuk, J. Kosecka, R. Vedantham, and H. Hile. Creating compact architectural models by geo-registering image collections. In *Proc. 3DIM*, 2009.

[5] D. Hoiem, A. A. Efros, and M. Hebert. Automatic photo pop-up. *ACM Transactions on Graphics (TOG)*, 24(3):577, 2005.

[6] A. Irschara, V. Kaufmann, M. Klopschitz, H. Bischof, and F. Leberl. Towards fully automatic photogrammetric reconstruction using digital images taken from UAVs. In *Proc. ISPRS*, 2010.

[7] D. Kalkofen, E. Mendez, and D. Schmalstieg. Comprehensible visualization for augmented reality. *IEEE TVCG*, 15(2):193–204, 2009.

[8] G. R. King, W. Piekarski, and B. H. Thomas. Arvino: Outdoor augmented reality visualisation of viticulture GIS data. In *Proc. ISMAR '05*, pages 52–55, Washington, 2005. IEEE.

[9] T. Langlotz, D. Wagner, A. Mulloni, and D. Schmalstieg. Online creation of panoramic augmented reality annotations on mobile phones. *IEEE Pervasive Computing*, 11(2):56–63, 2010.

[10] E. Mendez and D. Schmalstieg. Importance masks for revealing occluded objects in augmented reality. In *Proc. VRST '09*, pages 247–248. ACM, 2009.

[11] A. Nurminen, E. Kruijff, and E. Veas. Hydrosys: a mixed reality platform for on-site visualization of environmental data. In *Proc. W2GIS'11*, pages 159–175. Springer, 2011.

[12] C. Sandor, A. Cunningham, A. Dey, and V. Mattila. An Augmented Reality X-Ray system based on visual saliency. In *Proc. ISMAR '10*, pages 27–36. IEEE, 2010.

[13] J. Santner, T. Pock, and H. Bischof. Interactive multi-label segmentation. In *ACCV'10*, pages 397–410. Springer, 2011.

[14] G. Schall, S. Junghanns, and D. Schmalstieg. The transcoding pipeline: Automatic generation of 3d models from geospatial data sources. In *Proc. GISCIENCE 2008*, 2008.

[15] S. N. Sinha, D. Steedly, R. Szeliski, M. Agrawala, and M. Pollefeys. Interactive 3d architectural modeling from unordered photo collections. In *SIGGRAPH Asia '08*. ACM, 2008.

[16] J. Steiner, S. Zollmann, and G. Reitmayr. Incremental superpixels for real-time video analysis. In *Proc. CVWW 2011*, February 2-4 2011.

[17] M. Unger, T. Pock, W. Trobin, D. Cremers, and H. Bischof. Tvseg - interactive total variation based image segmentation. In *Proc. BMVC 2008*, 2008.

[18] J. Ventura, S. DiVerdi, and T. Höllerer. A sketch-based interface for photo pop-up. In *Proc. SBIM '09*, pages 21–28. ACM, 2009.

[19] J. Wither, C. Coffin, J. Ventura, and T. Hollerer. Fast annotation and modeling with a single-point laser range finder. In *Proc. ISMAR '08*, pages 65–68. IEEE, 2008.

[20] J. Wither, S. DiVerdi, and T. Höllerer. Annotation in outdoor augmented reality. *Computers & Graphics*, 33(6):679–689, Dec. 2009.

[21] S. Zollmann, D. Kalkofen, E. Mendez, and G. Reitmayr. Image-based ghostings for single layer occlusions in augmented reality. In *Proc. ISMAR '10*, pages 19–26. IEEE, Oct. 2010.

Achieving Robust Alignment for Outdoor Mixed Reality using 3D Range Data

Masaki Inaba
The University of Tokyo
Tokyo, Japan
inaba@cvl.iis.u-
tokyo.ac.jp

Atsuhiko Banno
Advanced Industrial Science
and Technology
Ibaraki, Japan
atsuhiko.banno@aist.go.jp

Takeshi Oishi
The University of Tokyo
Tokyo, Japan
oishi@cvl.iis.u-
tokyo.ac.jp

Katsushi Ikeuchi
The University of Tokyo
Tokyo, Japan
ki@cvl.iis.u-tokyo.ac.jp

ABSTRACT

Mixed reality (MR) technology can be applied to various applications such as architecture, advertising, and navigation systems, so the desire to utilize MR in outdoor environments has been increasing. In order to utilize MR, it is necessary to achieve alignment super imposing virtual contents in the desired position. However, because light changes continually in outdoor environments, and the appearance of real objects changes also, in some cases the previous image-based alignment methods do not work well. In this paper, a robust image-based alignment method to be used in outdoor environments is proposed. In the proposed method, the albedo of real objects is estimated using 3D shapes of these objects in advance, and the appearance is reproduced from the albedo and current light environment. The appearance of real objects and reproduced image becomes close, so a robust image-based alignment is achieved.

Categories and Subject Descriptors

H.5.1 [**Multimedia Information Systems**]: Artificial, augmented, and virtual realities

Keywords

Mixed Reality, Augmented Reality, Alignment, 3D Range Data, Albedo, Analysis by Synthesis

1. INTRODUCTION

Mixed reality (MR) is the technique to combine the real world and the virtual world by superimposing virtual contents onto the real world. By using MR technology, users can experience virtual contents as though they existed in the real world through a head mounted display (HMD), a smartphone, or some other device. MR technology can be applied to many fields such as education, architecture, medical treatment, advertising, navigation systems, and entertainment. So there is much research on MR [2,3].

In recent years, considering the many possible applications, desire to utilize MR in outdoor environments as well as in indoor environments has been increasing. Applications using outdoor MR technology include virtual completion of outdoor building and virtual outdoor advertising. In addition, virtual restoration of lost cultural assets has attracted interest. By superimposing a 3D CG model restored using CAD into the real world, users can watch restored cultural assets in their actual setting, so they can feel that they are present [10, 18, 26].

One of the issues to be solved for seamless MR is geometric registration. Geometric registration is necessary to achieve alignment between a real object and a virtual object. In order to achieve this alignment, estimation of the camera position and pose is necessary. The processes to calculate absolute camera parameters and relative camera parameters are hereinafter referred to as **global alignment** and **local alignment**.

In this paper, by using a dense 3D shape of the real environment (3D model) retrieved by laser range sensor [9], a robust image-based alignment method for light changing is proposed because light changes continually in an outdoor environment. The following describes the gist of the proposed method.

First, the reflectance (albedo) of real objects is estimated from a 3D model and omnidirectional image measurement in advance [17]. Thus, a 3D model with albedo is created using texture mapping. This makes it possible to achieve robust feature-matching for light changes and to estimate the exact camera position and pose. In global alignment, the appearance is reproduced by radiosity from the 3D model with albedo and current light environment, and correspondences between the camera image and reproduced appearance are searched using natural features.

In local alignment, by projecting natural features of a previous camera frame on a 3D model, a 3D natural features map is generated in real time. Because these natural features are extracted from the camera image in the current light environment, the feature-matching between the current camera frame and the previous camera frame is easy, so camera position and pose are estimated relatively. By repeating the camera parameters estimation and natural features projection, a robust local camera position and pose tracking is possible. However, errors of camera parameters estimation are accumulated using only local alignment. So the appearance is reproduced in real time by simple shading from the 3D model with albedo and current light environment, and global realignment is tried at the same time. If the feature-matching between the current camera frame and reproduced appearance is successful, global realignment is performed, and it is possible to eliminate the accumulated error.

This paper is organized as follows. Chapter 2 introduces related research on alignment, and describes the problems of previous methods and the significance and purpose of this study. Chapter 3 describes the proposed method of robust global alignment and local alignment for light changes using a 3D model with albedo. Chapter 4 shows the effectiveness of the proposed method by evaluation experiments. Chapter 5 contains the conclusion and future issues.

2. RELATED WORK

In order to achieve alignment, it is necessary to acquire the camera position and pose, and continue to match the coordinate systems of the real world and the virtual world. There are various studies to estimate the camera position and pose, and the technologies that have attracted attention recently are the feature-based method, the 3D map-based method, and the analysis by synthesis (AbS)-based method.

2.1 Feature-based Method

Feature-based Methods use visual tracking to estimate camera pose. Diverdi et al [7] use Lucas and Kanade's optical flow [14] by Shi and Tomasi's good features [23], on the other hand Wagner et al [27] use Fast corner tracking [20]. These methods can estimate camera pose in real time. But, feature-based methods cannot estimate camera position, so they must be combined with inertial sensor, and so on [5, 21]. Further, estimation errors accumulate little by little.

2.2 3D Map-based Method

In 3D map-based methods, a 3D range map of local point features is constructed from camera images. The camera position and pose can be estimated from the 2D-3D correspondences between the camera image (real world) and the 3D features map (virtual world).

A method called PTAM (Parallel Tracking And Mapping) [11] uses visual SLAM (Simultaneous Localization And Mapping) to perform 3D range mapping of environment and camera parameter estimation at the same time by tracking local point features of the camera image. In this approach, it is possible to achieve rough local alignment without prior information using only one camera. As a method similar to PTAM, DTAM (Dense Tracking and Mapping) [15] has been proposed. PTAM adopts a stereo method using only feature points, but DTAM adopts a stereo method using all the pixels of the camera image. By creating a dense depth map, the accuracy of alignment improves. However, in these methods, since there is no prior information of the real world, the virtual contents have to be placed roughly, so exact alignment between real objects and virtual objects is difficult. In addition, errors accumulate gradually.

Taketomi et al [25] propose a method to create a 3D landmark database of local point features by calculating the 3D position using SfM (Structure from Motion) in advance. The camera position and pose estimation is carried out by feature-matching between the camera image and the 3D landmark database. A highly accurate global alignment can be achieved in real time using this method. However, if the light environment of the current camera image is very different from that of the database image due to time or weather, feature-matching is difficult because appearance of these images is different. In particular, because light changes continually in outdoor environments, this is a fatal problem.

Figure 1: Real object and 3D model

2.3 Analysis by Synthesis-based Method

Analysis by synthesis-based methods use 3D CAD models of real objects. The flow of 3D model rendering, feature-matching between the rendered image and the camera image, feature projection to 3D model, and camera parameter estimation is repeated.

Reitmayr et al [19] use a textured 3D model of the surrounding environment. In this method, edges and shape of the rendered image and the camera image are extracted and matched. Then, these features are projected back to the 3D model, so 2D-3D correspondences are acquired. This method achieves sufficiently accurate alignment in real time. In [30], 3D line model is created, and edges and shape are used as features similarly. This method is more faster than the method of Reitmayr et al. But edges and shape are weak against the occlusion, and cannot be used for the objects that have few edges.

In [12, 24], local point features are used instead of edges. These methods also achieve precise alignment in real time. Local point features are robust against the occlusion, but computational cost is high. In addition, these methods do not consider the influence of the light sources. So, if the light environment changes, feature-matching cannot work well.

Schumann et al [22] use a 3D model with diffuse parameters and try to achieve tracking by AbS under the assumption that the 3D model can be rendered in the current light environment. In order to estimate camera position and pose, various local feature-based methods are compared and the similarity-based method is considered. However, these methods cannot run in real time. Further, the creation of a 3D model with diffuse parameter, the rendering of a 3D model in the current light environment, and light environment estimation are not achieved in this study.

From the above, in this research, it is proposed to achieve a markerless absolute alignment method that is robust for light changing. The proposed method is based on the AbS method and considers the effect of light sources.

3. METHOD

In order to achieve geometric registration, it is necessary to always obtain the camera position and pose. By using a color image and a 3D model acquired in advance, in addition to the input camera image, global alignment and local alignment are achieved. The color image and the 3D model acquired in advance are hereinafter referred to as the database.

If the color image and the 3D model in the database are calibrated, by searching correspondences between the input camera image and the database image, camera parameters can be estimated, and global alignment can be performed. By using an existing feature point extraction method, correspondences can be automatically extracted from the two images, but if the light environment is very different, correct feature-matching becomes difficult. In such a case, the camera parameters estimation will fail and the virtual contents cannot be superimposed on the desired position.

In the proposed method, the database image is converted to a reproduced image that has the same light environment as the input camera image does. The reflectance (albedo) of real objects is estimated from the database image and the 3D model in advance [17], and the appearance in the current light environment is reproduced from the albedo. Since the light environment of the reproduced appearance is similar to that of the input camera image, the appearance of the two images becomes close, and feature-matching becomes easy.

By mapping the natural features of the input image to the 3D model after the initial global alignment, a 3D natural features map is created in real time, so local alignment is achieved. Feature-matching is easy because the natural features are extracted from the current appearance. However, the error of the camera parameters estimation will accumulate. So appearance is reproduced by simple shading in real time, and global realignment is attempted at the same time.

3.1 Database Creation

The database comprises the color image and the 3D model of the real object (Fig. 1). The color image is obtained by shooting multiple times while changing the shutter speed using an omnidirectional camera so as to be an HDR (High Dynamic Range) image that has a wide brightness range. The 3D model is acquired by a laser range sensor. The camera parameters of the HDR image are calculated in the coordinate system of the 3D model by acquiring correspondences manually. Then, the calibration of the color image and the 3D model is performed.

3.1.1 Albedo Estimation

The albedo of real objects is estimated using the method of Okura et al [17]. Under the narrow-band camera assumption, the camera sensitivity can be approximated by the Dirac delta function, so the wavelength of the light source is constant [29]. Therefore, when k means the channel of RGB, the intensity of camera image I_k is represented by the following equation:

$$I_k = \tau_k S_k E_k \qquad (k = \{r, g, b\}) \qquad (1)$$

τ_k is the camera gain, S_k is the albedo value, E_k is the illuminance value.

In order to estimate the albedo value S_k from the above equation, it is necessary to determine the illuminance value E_k on the surface of the real object. Illuminance value E_k is calculated by the radiosity method using IBL (Image-Based Lighting) [6]. IBL can be performed using the obtained omnidirectional HDR image as a light environment map with the rendering software Radiance[1], hereinafter referred to as **Radiance**. By setting the albedo value to 1.0 at the surface of the 3D model in the rendering, the illuminance image I'_k can be generated by the following equation:

$$I'_k = \tau_k E_k \qquad (2)$$

Because the brightness distribution of the light source and the real object is acquired by the same omnidirectional camera, camera gain τ_k of Eq. (1) and Eq. (2) are equal. The albedo value S_k of

[1]http://radsite.lbl.gov/radiance/

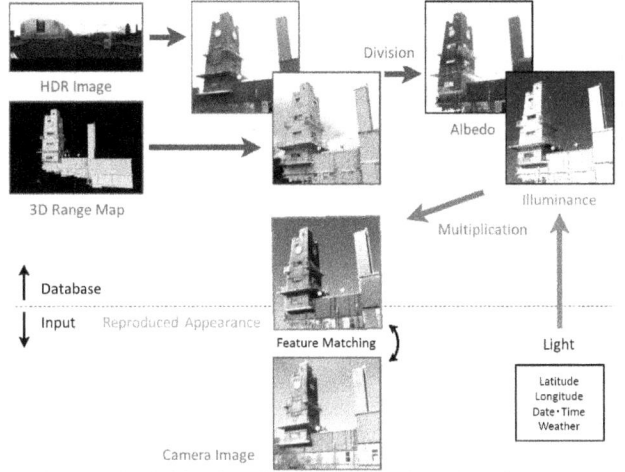

Figure 2: Process of global alignment

the real object is obtained by the following equation:

$$S_k = \frac{I_k}{I'_k} \qquad (3)$$

The albedo image is obtained in this way, and the 3D model with albedo is created by texture mapping.

3.2 Global Alignment

Fig. 2 shows the process of the proposed method from appearance reproduction to global alignment.

3.2.1 Appearance Reproduction

First, given as parameters the date, time, weather, and GPS information when performing global alignment, the sky light environment is simulated using Radiance, and then the illuminance value E_k is calculated from the 3D model. This method has the advantage that there is no need to shoot the HDR image in order to acquire the light environment. In addition, the reproduced appearance is only used for feature-matching by natural features, so it is not necessary to reproduce the exact light environment at the time of obtaining the input camera image. Using the albedo value S_k in the database and the illuminance value E_k, appearance is reproduced from Eq. (1).

3.2.2 Feature Matching

Feature-matching between the input camera image and the reproduced appearance is performed by natural features. It is necessary to obtain a sufficient number of correct correspondences for accurate camera parameters estimation in feature-matching. So removal of incorrect correspondences is attempted based on the RANSAC (RANdom SAmple Consensus) method [8] using epipolar constraint.

Because calibration between reproduced appearance and 3D model has been taken, 2D-3D correspondences of the input camera image and 3D model are obtained from the results of feature-matching of the input image camera and the reproduced appearance.

3.2.3 Camera Parameter Estimation

The camera parameters are calculated from n 2D-3D correspondences. It is desirable that the number of correspondences n is 6 or more. Internal camera parameters P are assumed to be known by

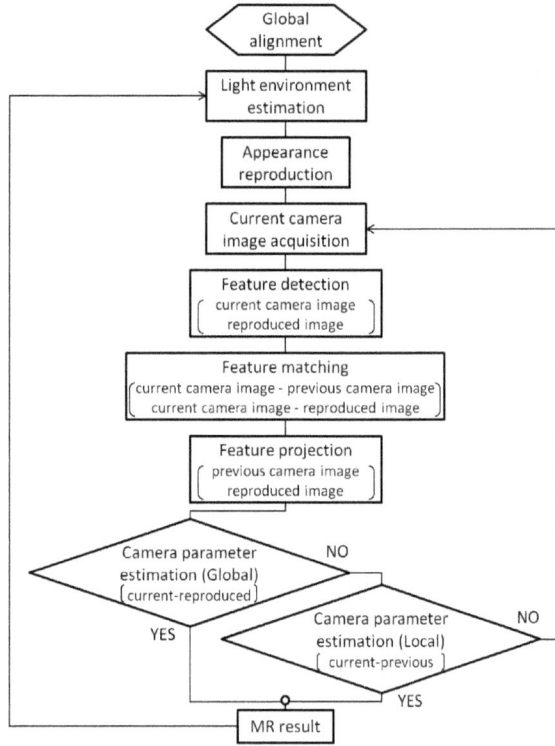

Figure 3: Flowchart of local alignment

3.3.1 Camera Tracking

By mapping natural features of the previous camera frame to a dense 3D model, a 3D natural features map is generated in real time. Because the calibration of previous camera frame and 3D model has been completed posteriorly, 3D coordinates can be obtained easily at the feature points of the camera image. In addition, due to natural features from the current appearance, feature-matching between the current camera frame and previous camera frame is easy, so the camera position and pose can be obtained from Eq. (5).

By repeating the camera parameters estimation and the feature projection, robust local camera position and pose tracking is possible. However, since the error of the camera parameters estimation in each frame accumulates, a gap is formed gradually. In order to eliminate this error, it is necessary to perform global realignment.

3.3.2 Global Realignment

In order to eliminate the error, appearance is reproduced in every frame as well as the global alignment, and the absolute alignment is tried by feature-matching using reproduced appearance. Because it is necessary to reproduce appearance according to the movement of the camera, appearance reproduction must be done in real time. However, because there is high computational cost in reproducing appearance by radiosity, real-time processing is difficult. Accordingly, appearance is reproduced in a short time by simple shading based on the reflection model of Lambert. In addition, light distribution is necessary in order to perform the shading, and light environment must be estimated for each frame because it always changes due to the movement of clouds and sun in an outdoor environment. There are various methods, but the proposed method estimates the light environment directly using the sky zenithal image acquired by a fisheye camera, an omnidirectional camera, or some such device [10]. Estimated light environments are also used to achieve photometric registration in MR.

The 3D model with albedo is rendered from the estimated camera parameters and light environment to reproduce appearance. If a sufficient number of accurate correspondences is acquired between the current camera frame and the reproduced appearance, global realignment is performed, and it is possible to eliminate the errors. In addition, using the fact that the calibration between the previous camera frame and reproduced appearance is performed roughly, the removal of incorrect correspondences is carried out by the geometric relationship between the current camera frame and previous camera frame in feature-matching. In this way, even if correct correspondences are considerably less with respect to incorrect, only the correct correspondences are extracted well.

4. EXPERIMENT

In order to verify the effectiveness of the proposed alignment method, experiments of the alignment between the real object and the 3D model were conducted under different light environments. In this experiment, the building was used as shown in Fig. 1 and the PC spec was CPU: Intel Core2Duo T8300 2.40GHz, RAM: 4GB, GPU: nVIDIA GeForce8800M GTX 512MB.

4.1 Database Creation

The omnidirectional HDR color image and the 3D model were necessary to build the database. Ladybug3 of Point Gray Research[2] was used to acquire the omnidirectional HDR color image. HDS3000 Leica Geosystems[3] was used as the laser range sensor to obtain the

the method of Zhang [31]. External camera parameters are configured by the translational component T for camera position and the rotational component R for camera pose. In order to determine the external camera parameters R, T, linear estimation is performed following the method of Weng et al [28]. Then, external camera parameters R, T are calculated by minimizing the sum of squares of the reprojection error F_i using the linear estimation result as the initial value.

$$F_i = \begin{bmatrix} u_i \\ v_i \\ 1 \end{bmatrix} - P \begin{bmatrix} R^\top & -R^\top T \end{bmatrix} \begin{bmatrix} X_i \\ Y_i \\ Z_i \\ 1 \end{bmatrix} \qquad (4)$$

$$\{R, T\} = \arg\min_{R,T} \sum_i^n \|F_i\|^2 \qquad (5)$$

(u_i, v_i) are the 2D coordinates in the input camera image, and (X_i, Y_i, Z_i) are the corresponding 3D coordinates in the 3D model. The method of Levenberg-Marquardt is used for nonlinear optimization calculation.

3.2.4 Model Transformation

By converting the 3D model coordinate system using external camera parameters R, T, it is possible to adapt the coordinate systems of the real world and the virtual world. By these processes, it is possible to realize absolute alignment between the real objects and the virtual contents.

3.3 Local Alignment

After global alignment, it is necessary to keep track of the camera position and pose by local alignment. Fig. 3 shows the flow of local alignment.

[2]http://www.ptgrey.com/products/ladybug3/
[3]http://hds.leica-geosystems.com/en/5574.htm

(a) database image   (b) illuminance image   (c) albedo image

Figure 4: Albedo estimation result (11:30AM, 16th of December, sunny)

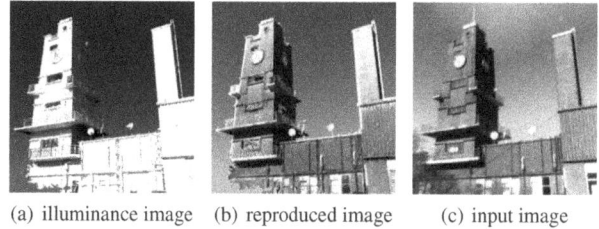

(a) illuminance image   (b) reproduced image   (c) input image

Figure 6: Appearance reproduction result by radiosity (11:30AM, 8th of December, sunny)

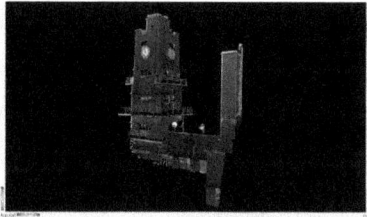

Figure 5: 3D model with albedo

3D model, and the integration of multiple distance data was carried out [16]. The 3D model has one million points. The camera parameters of the HDR image were estimated by giving 2D-3D correspondences between the HDR image and the 3D model manually.

Fig. 4 shows the result of albedo estimation. Although the HDR image had a clear difference in intensity between the front and side, the albedo image did not have that much difference. In addition, the 3D model with albedo was created by texture mapping using estimated albedo (Fig. 5). In the manner as described above, the database of omnidirectional HDR image and albedo image with 3D coordinate value was constructed.

4.2 Global Alignment

4.2.1 Appearance Reproduction

The input image was taken at a different time and date, and under different weather conditions. The illuminance image was generated using Radiance from the date, time, weather, and GPS information at the input image acquisition, and appearance was reproduced by the multiplication of the albedo image and illuminance image.

Fig. 6 shows the results of appearance reproduction by radiosity. Since the shading of the reproduced appearance is similar to that of the input image, the appearance was reproduced with correct shade and shadow. However, the process of appearance reproduction by radiosity took several minutes.

4.2.2 Feature Matching

The comparison of feature-matching between the previous method using a simple input image and the proposed method using reproduced appearance was performed. The resolution of all images is 600×600 pixels. SIFT [13], SURF [4], and CSIFT (Colored SIFT) [1] were used as the method of natural feature extraction. CSIFT is an illumination invariant feature. The number of correspondences and computational time were evaluated using images with the different light environment.

Table 1, 2 and Fig. 7, 8 show the results of feature-matching after the removal of incorrect correspondences based on the epipolar constraint by RANSAC. First, in Table 1 and Fig. 7, since the

appearance of the input image and database image was not very different, correct correspondences were obtained sufficiently to estimate the camera parameters in both the proposed method and previous method. On the other hand, in Table 2 and Fig. 8, since the appearance of the input image with deep shade was very different from that of database image, correct correspondences were not obtained in the previous method. Because there were too many incorrect correspondences as opposed to correct correspondences, the removal of incorrect correspondences by RANSAC did not work well. However, since the appearance of the input image and reproduced image became close, many correct correspondences could be obtained using the proposed method, so the proposed method was shown to be effective. In addition, correct correspondences were not obtained by CSIFT in either case.

The reason for failure by CSIFT as shown in Fig. 7(c), 8(c) was thought to be a feature of a building image that had little texture where the boundary almost disappeared by removing the light environment information. In other words, it can be said that in this case, the light environment information is very important to obtain correspondences, so the proposed method to reproduce appearance was considered to be reasonable. Correspondences could be obtained from around the edge with deep shading as shown in the Fig. 8(a), 8(b). Therefore, the proposed method uses the information for 3D geometric structure as well as information about the texture of the object. Considering the number of correspondences and computational time, the proposed method using SURF was fast and sufficient.

4.2.3 Camera Parameter Estimation

The accuracy of the camera parameters estimation was evaluated by the success rate of alignment and average of reprojection error represented by Eq. (5). The resolution of camera image is 640×480 pixels. If the average of reprojection error was less than 3 pixels, alignment was regarded as a success.

As the result of 100 trials, the average of reprojection error was 120 pixels, and alignment success rate was 4% in the previous method. On the other hand, the average of reprojection error was 2.5 pixels, and alignment success rate was 89% in the proposed method, so the effectiveness of the proposed method was confirmed. Fig. 9 shows the result of the correct alignment by the proposed method. The 3D model was superimposed to the same position as the real object, so the coordinate systems of the real world and the virtual world were calibrated.

4.3 Local Alignment

Because the local camera position and pose tracking must be performed in real time, it was necessary to perform feature-matching in real time. So CUDASURF[4] implemented by GPGPU was used.

---

[4] http://www.d2.mpi-inf.mpg.de/surf

Table 1: Comparison of feature matching (input image: 09:30AM, 8th of December, sunny. database image: 11:30AM, 16th of December, cloudy.)

	SIFT +previous	SIFT +proposed	SURF +previous	SURF +proposed	Colored SIFT
correspondences	31	24	14	15	0
calculation time[sec]	1.5	2.0	0.7	1.0	1.8

Table 2: Comparison of feature matching (input image: 11:30AM, 8th of December, sunny. database image: 11:30AM, 16th of December, cloudy.)

	SIFT +previous	SIFT +proposed	SURF +previous	SURF +proposed	Colored SIFT
correspondences	0	42	0	63	0
calculation time[sec]	1.8	2.4	1.0	1.2	2.4

(a) SURF matching between input image and database image

(b) SURF matching between input image and reproduced appearance

(c) Colored SIFT matching between input image and database image

Figure 7: Feature matching result (input image: 09:30AM, 8th of December, sunny. database image: 11:30AM, 16th of December, cloudy.)

(a) SURF matching between input image and database image

(b) SURF matching between input image and reproduced appearance

(c) Colored SIFT matching between input image and database image

Figure 8: Feature matching result (input image: 11:30AM, 8th of December, sunny. database image: 11:30AM, 16th of December, cloudy.)

(a) MR Result

(b) SURF matching between camera image and reproduced appearance by radiosity

Figure 9: Global alignment result

(a) MR Result

(b) SURF matching between current camera image and previous camera image

Figure 10: Local alignment result

Table 3: Processing times of each step

each step	time[msec]
light environment estimation	10
appearance reproduction by simple shading	180
CUDASURF detection	50
feature-matching + RANSAC	60
feature projection	10
camera parameter estimation	10
total	320

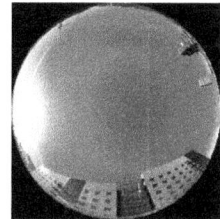

(a) MR Result (b) Light environment

(c) SURF matching between camera image and reproduced appearance by simple shading

Figure 11: Global realignment result

Fig. 10 shows the results of the local alignment. Enough correspondences between the current camera image and previous camera image were obtained, and the tracking by the proposed method was shown to work well (Fig. 10(b)). However, the errors of the camera parameters estimation accumulated as time increased, so deviation would arise little by little (Fig. 10(a)). If feature-matching using reproduced appearance by simple shading was successful, global realignment was performed as shown in the Fig. 11, so it is possible to prevent the accumulation of errors. Table 3 shows the processing times of each step. The local alignment ran at about 3fps, so it cannot be said to be running in real time. The appearance reproduction, feature detection, and feature matching must be more efficient.

5. CONCLUSION

In this paper, a robust alignment method for light changes in an outdoor environment is proposed.

By using the 3D model of the surrounding environment, the albedo of real objects is estimated, and the appearance in current light environment is reproduced by radiosity from the albedo, so robust feature-matching for light changes is achieved. This makes it possible to achieve robust global alignment even in an outdoor environment. As an experiment result, if the light environment was very different, the alignment success rate of the previous method was

4%. On the other hand, that of the proposed method was improved by up to 89%.

In addition, by projecting natural features of the camera image to a 3D model in each frame, robust local alignment is achieved. Moreover, by generating reproduced appearance by simple shading as well as global alignment, global realignment is performed and the accumulation of errors is eliminated during local camera position and pose tracking.

Several issues need to be dealt with in the future. It is necessary to further evaluate the proposed method in various light environments. Also, the processing of each step must be speeded up more. In addition, in the appearance reproduction by simple shading, in order to estimate the light distribution, the sky zenithal image was acquired directly. However, because some areas of sky image, such as the sun, are saturated, estimated light distribution is not exact.

By solving this problem, the quality of the reproduced appearance will increase, and then the accuracy of the global realignment will increase also.

6. ACKNOWLEDGMENTS

This research received support from Digital Museum Project of Ministry of Education, Culture, Sports, Science and Technology, and Green ICT Innovation Promotion of Ministry of Public Management, Home Affairs, Posts and Telecommunications.

7. REFERENCES

[1] A. E. Abdel-Hakim and A. A. Farag. Csift: A sift descriptor with color invariant characteristics. *Computer Vision and Pattern Recognition*, 2:1978–1983, 2006.

[2] R. Azuma. A survey of augmented reality. *Presence-Teleoperators and Virtual Environments*, 6(4):355–385, 1997.

[3] R. Azuma, Y. Baillot, R. Behringer, S. Feiner, S. Julier, and B. MacIntyre. Recent advances in augmented reality. *Computer Graphics and Applications*, 21(6):34–47, 2001.

[4] H. Bay, T. Tuytelaars, and L. Van Gool. Surf: Speeded up robust features. *European Conference on Computer Vision*, pages 404–417, 2006.

[5] G. Bleser and D. Stricker. Advanced tracking through efficient image processing and visual-inertial sensor fusion. *Virtual Reality Conference*, pages 137–144, 2008.

[6] P. Debevec. Image-based lighting. *Comput. Graph. Appl.*, 22(2):26–34, 2002.

[7] S. DiVerdi, J. Wither, and T. Hollerei. Envisor: Online environment map construction for mixed reality. *Virtual Reality Conference*, pages 19–26, 2008.

[8] M. A. Fischler and R. C. Bolles. Random sample consensus: a paradigm for model fitting with applications to image analysis and automated cartography. *Commun. ACM*, 24(6):381–395, 1981.

[9] K. Ikeuchi, A. Nakazawa, K. Hasegawa, and T. Ohishi. The great buddha project: Modeling cultural heritage for vr systems through observation. *International Symposium on Mixed and Augmented Reality*, page 7, 2003.

[10] T. Kakuta, T. Oishi, and K. Ikeuchi. Fast shading and shadowing of virtual objects using shadowing planes in mixed reality. *The Institute of Image Information and Television Engineers*, 62(9):1466–1473, 2008.

[11] G. Klein and D. Murray. Parallel tracking and mapping for small ar workspaces. *International Symposium on Mixed and Augmented Reality*, pages 1–10, 2007.

[12] V. Lepetit, L. Vacchetti, D. Thalmann, P. Fua, and C. Vrlab. Fully automated and stable registration for augmented reality applications. *International Symposium on Mixed and Augmented Reality*, pages 93–102, 2003.

[13] D. G. Lowe. Distinctive image features from scale-invariant keypoints. *International Journal of Computer Vision*, 60:91–110, 2004.

[14] B. D. Lucas and T. Kanade. An iterative image registration technique with an application to stereo vision. *DARPA Image Understanding Workshop*, pages 121–130, 1981.

[15] R. A. Newcombe, S. J. Lovegrove, and A. J. Davison. Dtam: Dense tracking and mapping in real-time. *International Conference on Computer Vision*, 1(6):2320–2327, 2011.

[16] T. Oishi, R. Sagawa, A. Nakazawa, R. Kurazume, and K. Ikeuchi. Parallel Alignment of a Large Number of Range Images. *3-D Digital Imaging and Modeling*, pages 195–202, 2003.

[17] S. Okura, R. Kawakami, and K. Ikeuchi. Simple surface reflectance estimation of diffuse outdoor object using spherical images. *Asian Conference on Computer Vision, Workshop on Multi-dimensional and Multi-view Image Processing*, 2007.

[18] G. Papagiannakis, S. Schertenleib, B. O'Kennedy, M. Arevalo-Poizat, N. Magnenat-Thalmann, A. Stoddart, and D. Thalmann. Mixing virtual and real scenes in the site of ancient pompeii. *Computer Animation and Virtual Worlds*, 16(1):11–24, 2005.

[19] G. Reitmayr and T. W. Drummond. Going out: Robust tracking for outdoor augmented reality. *International Symposium on Mixed and Augmented Reality*, pages 109–118, 2006.

[20] E. Rosten and T. Drummond. Machine learning for high-speed corner detection. *European Conference on Computer Vision*, pages 430–443, 2006.

[21] G. Schall, D. Wagner, G. Reitmayr, E. Taichmann, M. Wieser, D. Schmalstieg, and B. Hofmann-Wellenhof. Global pose estimation using multi-sensor fusion for outdoor augmented reality. *International Symposium on Mixed and Augmented Reality*, pages 153–162, 2009.

[22] M. Schumann, S. Achilles, and S. Müller. Analysis by synthesis techniques for markerless tracking. *Virtuelle und Erweiterte Realität, 6. Workshop der GI Fachgruppe VR/AR*, 2009.

[23] J. Shi and C. Tomasi. Good features to track. *Computer Vision and Pattern Recognition*, pages 593–600, 1994.

[24] G. Simon. Tracking-by-synthesis using point features and pyramidal blurring. *International Symposium on Mixed and Augmented Reality*, pages 85–92, 2011.

[25] T. Taketomi, T. Sato, and N. Yokoya. Real-time geometric registration using feature landmark database for augmented reality applications. *SPIE Electronic Imaging*, 7238, 2009.

[26] V. Vlahakis, N. Ioannidis, J. Karigiannis, M. Tsotros, M. Gounaris, D. Stricker, T. Gleue, P. Daehne, and L. Almeida. Archeoguide: An augmented reality guide for archaeological sites. *Computer Graphics and Applications*, 22(5):52–60, 2002.

[27] D. Wagner, A. Mulloni, T. Langlotz, and D. Schmalstieg. Real-time panoramic mapping and tracking on mobile phones. *Virtual Reality Conference*, pages 211–218, 2010.

[28] J. Weng, P. Cohen, and M. Herniou. Camera calibration with distortion models and accuracy evaluation. *Pattern Analysis and Machine Intelligence*, 14(10):965–980, 1992.

[29] J. A. Worthey and M. H. Brill. Heuristic analysis of von kries color constancy. *J. Opt. Soc. Am. A 3*, pages 1708–1712, 1986.

[30] H. Wuest, F. Wientapper, and D. Stricker. Adaptable model-based tracking using analysis-by-synthesis techniques. *Computer analysis of images and patterns*, pages 20–27, 2007.

[31] Z. Zhang et al. A flexible new technique for camera calibration. *Pattern Analysis and Machine Intelligence*, 22(11):1330–1334, 2000.

HapSeat: Producing Motion Sensation with Multiple Force-feedback Devices Embedded in a Seat

Fabien Danieau[*]
Technicolor R&I
Cesson-Sévigné, France

Julien Fleureau
Technicolor R&I
Cesson-Sévigné, France

Philippe Guillotel
Technicolor R&I
Cesson-Sévigné, France

Nicolas Mollet
Technicolor R&I
Cesson-Sévigné, France

Marc Christie
IRISA, MimeTIC Team
Rennes, France

Anatole Lécuyer
INRIA, VR4I Team
Rennes, France

ABSTRACT

We introduce a novel way of simulating sensations of motion which does not require an expensive and cumbersome motion platform. Multiple force-feedbacks are applied to the seated user's body to generate a sensation of motion experiencing passive navigation. A set of force-feedback devices such as mobile armrests or headrests are arranged around a seat so that they can apply forces to the user. We have dubbed this new approach *HapSeat*. A proof of concept has been designed which uses three low-cost force-feedback devices, and two control models have been implemented. Results from the first user study suggest that subjective sensations of motion are reliably generated using either model. Our results pave the way to a novel device to generate consumer motion effects based on our prototype.

Categories and Subject Descriptors

H5.2 [**Information interfaces and presentation**]: User Interfaces. - Haptic I/O.

General Terms

Design, Experimentation

Keywords

sensation of motion, force-feedback, haptic seat, audiovisual experience

1. INTRODUCTION

Motion simulation is usually provided by a motion platform [8]. Typically the user's whole body is moved to generate various sensations such as accelerating, falling or passing

---

[*]email: fabien.danieau@technicolor.com

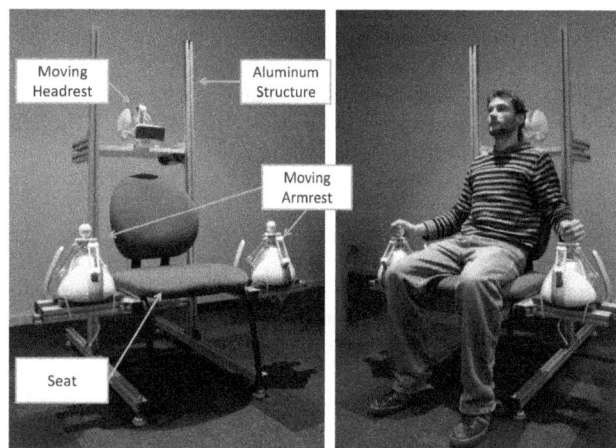

Figure 1: **Prototype of the HapSeat. Left: seat structure with 3 force-feedback devices. Right: the system in use.**

over bumps. While these devices generate a realistic sensation of motion with 6DoF, they are not designed for domestic settings and they are too expensive for the mass consumer market. Immersive experiences with motion effects are thus currently limited to amusement parks or "4D Cinemas".

In this article we present the *HapSeat*, a novel approach for producing motion sensations in a consumer settings using multiple force-feedback devices embedded in a seat. Three low-cost actuators which simulate 6DoF effects of motion are used. The motion effect is generated by adjuncts to the structure of the chair rather than moving the whole chair. A proof-of-concept prototype has been designed and constructed, which uses actuators held by an armchair-shaped structure (see figure 1). Two models to control the device has been implemented: a *Physical Model* which computes forces supposed to be felt during a movement, and a *Geometrical Model* which modifies the structure to match the position and posture that characterize a movement.

A user study was conducted to assess this approach. Participants reported a sensation of motion. When applied to a passive navigation simulation in a real or virtual environment, our results show that the *HapSeat* increases the quality of the user experience. We considered four factors in the measurement of the QoE: realism (of the simulation), sensory (involvement of the sense of touch), comfort and satisfaction.

In this paper we first review the literature on **human motion perception** and motion simulators (section 2). Then the *HapSeat* is introduced in section 3 while section 4 details the proof of concept. The user study is discussed in section 5. Finally a conclusion and perspectives are provided in section 6.

2. RELATED WORK

2.1 Human motion perception

The perception of motion is a complex sensation resulting from the integration of multiple perceptive inputs from different systems: visual, auditory, vestibular and kinesthetic [1, 4]. The visual system contributes to this perception by providing an estimation of distances between the body and landmarks. A displacement of the body will modify these distances and add the perception of self-motion. Moving visual cues can often trigger a sensation of self-motion even though the viewer is stationary [10]. This illusion is called vection. The auditory system may also contribute to this perception by locating the body relative to "acoustic" landmarks [15].

But the main contributor to the perception of motion is the vestibular system. Located in the inner ear, this organ is composed of three orthogonally-oriented semi-circular canals and two otolith organs. The canals allow rotational movements to be detected while otolith organs contribute to the perception of linear accelerations.

Finally, it is interesting to note that haptic cues provided by the kinesthetic system also influence the sensation of motion. The kinesthetic system provides information about limb positions. When an elevator goes up, one feels the motion thanks to the proprioceptive receptors in joints and muscles of the legs. The tactile sense also provides information about motion: internal receptors detect movements of visceral organs and act as accelerometers. These visceral graviceptors are especially to be be found in the region of the kidney. The somatosensory system indicates the direction of gravity through pressure patterns all over and inside the body [14].

2.2 Motion simulators

Motion simulators are well-known devices designed to make the user feel motion. They are intensively used in driving or flight simulators for training purposes. Most are based on a Stewart's platform [3], a 6 Degrees of Freedom (DoF) platform driven by 6 hydraulic cylinders. A motion simulator is basically a seat attached to this kind of platform. While the user navigates the virtual environment, the seat moves to generate a sensation of motion. These systems are often used in virtual reality rooms or 4D cinemas but few are designed for the end-user consumer.

To the best of our knowledge, the D-Box company[1] is one of the few actors in this market, having developed an armchair placed on four actuators that is suitable for an end-user's living-rooms. This seat generates 3DoF motion effects (pitch, roll and heave) for movie viewing and consumer applications. Despite this attempt to succeed in the consumer

environment, this chair remains expensive and limited to 3DoF motion effects.

The sensation of motion can also be induced in a less invasive way by force-feedback devices that simulate the kinesthetic system. Ouarti et al. applied a force to users' hands as they watched an optic flow stimulus [9]. The system was expected to generate an illusion of motion with force-feedback: when the interface pulled the user's hand, the user experienced a sensation of forward motion. Similarly, Danieau et al. used a 3DoF force-feedback device to induce the sensation of global movement in a video [2]. This system was designed to enhance audiovisual content as a cheaper alternative to motion platforms, but the movement simulated was limited to 3DoF (translations only).

The use of haptic illusions to enhance the audiovisual experience has also been explored by Israr et al., who designed a chair with several vibration devices embedded at different locations [5]. Actuators in the chair were activated in such a way that the user felt a continuous stimulus. Though no effect of motion was claimed in this study, Riecke et al. have showed that vibrotactile feedback may generate a vection effect by improving the realism of the simulation [11].

To sum up, there remains an important gap between haptic devices which do not, or only partially simulate, a sensation of motion, and complex simulators which are efficient in conveying motion but remain expensive and not well adapted to the consumer environment. We propose our *HapSeat* as a solution to fill this gap.

3. HAPSEAT: A NOVEL APPROACH FOR SIMULATING 6DOF MOTION

We propose to enhance the experience of passive navigation in virtual or cinematic content using 6DoF motion effects generated by multiple force-feedback devices. Instead of moving the whole user's body as on motion platforms, only some parts of the body are stimulated. As described in section 2.1, the perception of motion results from the stimulation of various parts of the body (vestibular system, visceral organs, kinesthetic system). Our approach is built on the hypothesis that local haptic cues suffice to trigger a sensation of self-motion.

Previous work has shown that a 3DoF force-feedback applied to a user's hand may simulate a 3DoF motion effect in a video viewing context [2]. But the simulated motion is limited to 3DoF (translations). Using only one or two 3DoF force-feedback devices is not sufficient to invoke a 6DoF sensation of motion [13] (translations and rotations). Extending the approach to three 3DoF devices in order to apply three force-feedback stimulus to the user's body offers the possibility of simulating a global 6DoF effect of motion. A plane looping sensation could be simulated by pulling the head backward and lifting both arms simultaneously, while a car braking could be simulated by pushing both the head and hands forward.

This concept can be extended by stimulating other regions of the body, using 5x3DoF devices for instance.

4. PROOF OF CONCEPT

The prototype developed as a proof of concept relies on three actuators. Two stimulate the user's hands, while a third stimulates the head. As the vestibular system is lo-

---

[1]http://www.d-box.com

cated in the head, stimulating this part of the body should heighten the illusion of simulated motion.

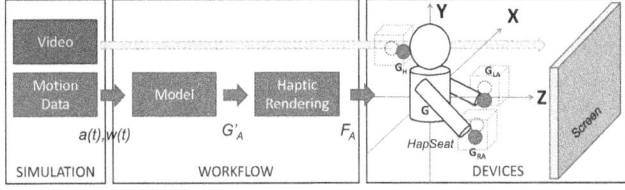

Figure 2: Simulating 6DoF motion with 3x3DoF force-feedback devices. While the three local devices are moving, the user is expected to feel a sensation of motion in relation to the visual content.

Figure 2 shows a schematic representation of the concept and offers an introduction to our notation. The motion description associated with a simulation is transmitted to a model at each instant t which computes the ideal position G'_A for each local actuator A. This position is then rendered by the haptic rendering algorithm as a force F_A. Each step of this workflow is detailed in this section.

4.1 Prototype of the HapSeat

An aluminum structure was designed to allow the positioning of the three actuators around an ordinary chair. The user passively rests his or her head and hands on each of the 3DoF actuators while watching a projection on a screen positioned in front of the chair (see figure 4). The head actuator is equipped with a block of foam for the user's comfort.

At rest (no rendered motions), the three actuators (H), (LA) and (RA) maintain the head, right arm and left arm of the user at the central positions G_H, G_{LA} and G_{RA} respectively. When the simulation starts, each actuator generates 3DoF forces on its respective body part within the limits of the cubic workspaces in figure 2.

Our current prototype uses three Novint Falcons[2] actuators. These devices are robust, relatively cheap and the forces generated are appropriate for safe movement of the user's head and hands.

4.2 Motion data

We focus on the case of a first person point-of-view simulation, whose intention is to mimic for the user the sensation of motion that the principal actor would have felt at the time of its recording. The audiovisual content is augmented with extra data describing the motion in terms of the linear acceleration $a(t)$ and the angular velocity $w(t)$. Let us define F_N as the navigation frame of the actor and F_B the frame associated with his body, centered on a point C (his chest for instance). The actor's motion is modeled as a rigid body motion described by two quantities $a(t) = [a(C \in F_B|F_N)]_{F_B} = \{a_x(t), a_y(t), a_z(t)\}^t$ (the gravity being removed [12]) and $w(t) = [w_{F_B/F_N}(t)]_{F_B} = \{w_x(t), w_y(t), w_z(t)\}^t$ (where the $[x]_F$ notation designates the vector x expressed in the frame F).

This kind of content can be easily produced by a video camera equipped with an inertial measurement unit. Danieau et al. used this setup to capture first-person point of view videos [2]. The capture device was attached to an actor's torso to record both his movement and a video of his field

of view. Therefore $a(t)$ and $w(t)$ describe the motion of the actor.

4.3 Models for motion simulation

Each actuator (H, LA, RA) moves to create the feeling of 6DoF global motion modeled by the quantities $a(t)$ and $w(t)$ as if the motion of the main actor was mapped onto them. Two models to control the device were devised. The first model is based on a *Physical Model*. The related acceleration applied to some parts of the body of the actor (here the head, left hand and right hand) are derived from the parameters of the global motion, $a(t)$ and $w(t)$ and then reproduced on the user by the corresponding actuators. The second model, referred to as *Geometrical Model*, aims at reproducing the position and attitude of the main actor on the basis of a more metaphorical paradigm.

4.3.1 Physical Model

In this model the accelerations felt by the main actor at his head, P_H, and at his left and right shoulders, P_{LS} and P_{RS}, are computed through a rigid body approach, where the motions of the hands are considered equivalent to the movements of the shoulders. Knowing $a(t)$ and $w(t)$ at the origin of his body frame F_B, the accelerations of a new point P of the rigid body may be computed by the following mechanical relation (time derivation of the kinematic torsor):

$$[a(P \in F_B|F_N)]_{F_B} = a(t) + \frac{dw}{dt} \wedge \overrightarrow{GP} + w \wedge (w \wedge \overrightarrow{GP}) \quad (1)$$

The new position G'_A for an actuator A is the formulated in terms of displacement from its initial and central position G_A by:

$$\overrightarrow{G_A G'_A} = \begin{bmatrix} s_x & 0 & 0 \\ 0 & s_y & 0 \\ 0 & 0 & s_z \end{bmatrix} \quad (2a)$$

$$(a(t) + \frac{dw}{dt}(t) \wedge \overrightarrow{GP_A} + w(t) \wedge (w(t) \wedge \overrightarrow{GP_A})) \quad (2b)$$

where G'_A is the new application point at time t, and s_x, s_y, s_z are scaling factors which map the actual motions of the three actuators in their workspaces. Those scaling factors are computed so as to use the workspace of the actuator in an optimal way. This involves compromises between the use of the largest possible space, so as to have a larger amplitude in the final rendering, while avoiding any saturation. These scaling factors are computed is a preprocessing step that consists of finding the maximal amplitude of the acceleration rendered by the actuator.

In this context the new application points G'_H, G'_{LA} and G'_{RA} are computed from the intial points G_H, G_{LA} and G_{RA}, and $s_x = s_y = s_z$.

4.3.2 Geometrical Model

This second model aims to make the chair reproduce the position and posture of the moving actor during the simulation. Two kinds of motion will be rendered: linear accelerations and orientation changes. The linear acceleration rendering is simply performed by a simultaneous translation of each of the different local actuators along the 3D vector given by $a(t)$. The scene pose changes rendering is trickier. It makes the assumption that the rotation speed of the current scene, modeled by $w(t)$, may be rendered by

---

[2]http://www.novint.com

71

rotating the position of the three actuators around the center modeled by a point G located near the user's sternum (see figure 2) and with a 3D angle modeled by w. Then the faster the object is turning, the bigger the angle of rotation. Moreover, if the rotation stops (i.e. $w(t) = 0$), the actuators are at rest.

The new position G'_A of the actuator A for a rotation around G can be expressed:

$$\overrightarrow{GG'_A} = (R_x(w_x(t))R_y(w_y(t))R_z(w_z(t)))\overrightarrow{GG_A} \quad (3)$$

i.e.:

$$\overrightarrow{G_A G'_A} \doteq \overrightarrow{GG'_A} - \overrightarrow{GG_A} \quad (4a)$$

$$= (R_x(w_x(t))R_y(w_y(t))R_z(w_z(t))) - I_3)\overrightarrow{GG_A} \quad (4b)$$

where R_x, R_y and R_z are the 3D rotation matrices around their respective X, Y and Z axes and I_3 is the identity matrix of R^3.

A complete 6DoF motion is a combination of linear accelerations and rotations. A function f is proposed to model the incorporation of both these types of information in our system. The proposed system has intentionally decoupled the linear motions from the rotational ones. This assumption is somewhat unrealistic from a mechanical point of view, but nevertheless makes sense in the context of passive navigation. If the motion to be rendered is a pure translation or a pure rotation, this decoupling is not a restriction. The difficulty arises when the motion to be rendered is a combination of translation and rotation. We make the assumption that a user would unconsciously expect to feel the dominant motion in the scene more strongly.

Then, if G_A represents the new position of the actuator A at time t and G_A its initial position, we have:

$$\overrightarrow{G_A G'_A} = f(\begin{bmatrix} s_x & 0 & 0 \\ 0 & s_y & 0 \\ 0 & 0 & s_z \end{bmatrix} a(t), \quad (5a)$$

$$(R_x(m_x w_x(t))R_y(m_y w_y(t))R_z(m_z w_z(t)) - I_3)\overrightarrow{GG_A}) \quad (5b)$$

with

$$f(B, C) = \frac{\|\vec{B}\|B + \|\vec{C}\|C}{\|\vec{B}\| + \|\vec{C}\|} \quad (6)$$

From this equation, the new application points G'_H, G'_{LA} and G'_{RA} are computed from the initial points G_H, G_{LA} and G_{RA}.

In addition, s_x, s_y, s_z on one hand and m_x, m_y, m_z on the other hand represent different scaling factors to map the actual motion represented by the couple $(a(t), w(t))$ in the workspace of the different actuators. As previously described, those scaling factors are computed so as to use the workspace of each actuator in an optimal way. More precisely, computing the scaling factors m_x, m_y and m_z is one using a preprocessing step that consists of in finding the maximal amplitude f with respects to the values of $a(t)$ and $w(t)$ over the whole time interval. An exhaustive numerical analysis is thus performed to find the joint optimal discretized values m_x, m_y and m_z. Several solutions may be admissible in the parametric space and the one that offers the best isotropic behavior is selected.

4.3.3 Output of the models

A comparison of the outputs of the models is described in this section to highlight their main differences. The outputs of simple translations and then rotations are compared together.

A linear forward acceleration on the Z axis can be described by $a(t) = \{a_x(t) = 0, a_y(t) = 0, a_z(t) = t\}^t$ and $w(t) = \{w_x(t) = 0, w_y(t) = 0, w_z(t) = 0\}^t$. Such a movement is rendered in the same way by both models. All actuators are moving simultaneously along the Z-axis as if the user were being pushed forward. The same behavior is observed for the other translations on Y and X axes. In these cases, the user is pushed upward or pulled toward the left side.

Secondly self-rotations are tested. For instance a left rotation around the Y-axis can be described by $a(t) = \{a_x(t) = 0, a_y(t) = 0, a_z(t) = 0\}^t$ and $w(t) = \{w_x(t) = 0, w_y(t) = \frac{t^2}{2}, w_z(t) = 0\}^t$ (the angular acceleration $w'(t)$ is linear). In this case (see figure 3), the outputs of the models are different. With the *Physical Model* the user's hands are moving along the X-axis toward the center while the head is not moving. With the *Geometrical Model*, the right hand is going forward (Z-axis) and the left hand is going backward (Z-axis) while the head slightly moves to the right side (X-axis). The same behavior is observed for rotations on other axes: the *Physical Model* renders self-rotation by an attraction of each part of the body toward the center G and the *Geometrical Model* renders them with desynchronized movements.

A 6DoF movement that combines translations and rotations is thus managed differently by each model depending on the amount of rotations.

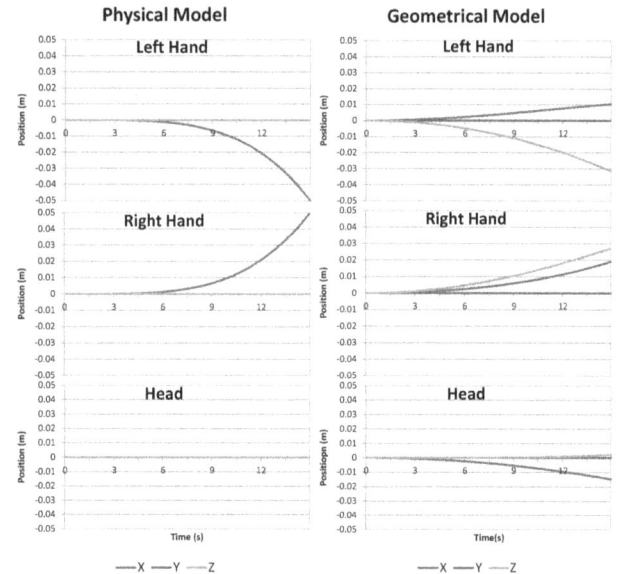

Figure 3: Output of the models (*Physical* on the left, *Geometrical* on the right) for a left rotation around Y-axis of 15 seconds. The position in meters is plotted for each actuator LA, RA and H, and for each axis.

4.4 Haptic Rendering

Whatever the model selected to control the chair, for each instant t of the simulation, each actuator A (namely H, LA

and RA) has to be in its targeted position G'_A (namely G'_H, G'_{LA} and G'_{RA}).

Most force-feedback devices (such as Novint Falcons) are impedance haptic devices, and the position of the actuator is thus not directly controllable. Indeed this kind of device is designed to sense the current position of the actuator and to provide a reaction force to the user. A classical spring-damper model may be used to control these devices in pseudo-position. The force F_A applied to an actuator A is computed by:

$$F_A = k(G'_A - P_A) - dV_A \qquad (7)$$

where G'_A is the targeted position, P_A the current position of the actuator, V_A its velocity, k the spring constant and d the damping constant.

4.5 Provisional Conclusion

The models and the rendering algorithm were integrated to a home-made multimedia player that allowed the haptic rendering on three force-feedback devices to be synchronized with the audiovisual playback. The haptic loop runs at 1KHz and the value of the force F_A is updated at each instant t. The control software is written in C++ and runs on an ordinary personal computer.

Our initial tests showed that the force capabilities and workspaces of the Novint Falcons were sufficient to move the user's head and hands. Our system enables the experience of novel motion sensations when viewing virtual navigation (see figure 4).

Figure 4: The user, comfortably installed on our device, is experiencing passive navigation enhanced by a haptic effect of motion.

5. USER STUDY

A user study was conducted to evaluate the quality of the simulated motion and to quantify its impact on the user's perceived quality of experience (QoE).

17 participants took part in the study, aged from 21 to 54 ($\bar{x}$=36.11 σ_x=11.11). Five were female, two participants were left-handed and one already used a Novint Falcon device. The pilot study was presented as a single experiment lasting 20 to 30 minutes. Each participant was first introduced to the Novint Falcon and given a demonstration of its

force capabilities. This step aimed to reduce the "surprise effect" for novice users. Participant was asked to passively experience each stimulus (see figure 4 and section 5.1) and then answer a questionnaire (see section 5.3).

5.1 Sequences: Haptic-Audiovisual Contents

Two driving sequences were created to test our device, and evaluate the sensation of motion and quality of experience (see figure 5). We generated two 1-minute videos and the associated descriptions of the global motion in terms of $a(t)$ and $w(t)$.

Our first sequence was a video of a **real car** driving session. Data was first captured using a front passenger equipped with a camera and an inertial measurement unit that sampled data at 30Hz.

The second sequence was a video of a **virtual car** racing video game. The main camera of the 3D simulation was placed inside the car in order to have a passenger point of view of the race. The visual output of the simulation was recorded while the accelerations and turn-rates of the car were extracted at 50Hz from the physics engine.

Figure 5: Haptic-Audiovisual contents. Left - Real video sequence of a car driving. Right - virtual car race.

5.2 Variables

To evaluate the quality of the simulated motion (and of the models) and the impact of this haptic feedback on the QoE, we defined four types of haptic feedback to be rendered with each sequence. **Physical Feedback**, computed from the physical model; **Geometrical Feedback** derived from the geometrical model; **No Haptic Feedback** in which only the audiovisual content was displayed, serving as a control to show how the other conditions impact on the QoE; and lastly **Random Haptic feedback** was provided. This random feedback was derived from low-pass filtered white noise (cutoff frequency $F_c = 0.5Hz$) played throughout the video. The amplitude of the signal was limited to the capabilities of the actuators. This last feedback was not synchronized to the video and was used to evaluate the effect of providing a continued haptic feedback.

All **height conditions** (two videos sequences x four types of haptic feedback) were presented in random order to the participants.

5.3 Measurement of QoE: questionnaire

A questionnaire was designed to evaluate the QoE of passive navigation enriched with haptic feedback. QoE relates to the subjective user experience with a service or an application [7]. This questionnaire was based on the four factors we wanted to evaluate [2]: realism, comfort, sensory and satisfaction. "Sensory" characterized how the haptic feedback contributed to the immersion. "Realism" describes the degree to which the simulation is realistic and consistent with the user's representation of the real world. This factor is particularly helpful in evaluating the quality of the simulated motion. "Comfort" measures how comfortable is the system. "Satisfaction" determines measures user enjoyment. Each factor was evaluated by questions rated on a **5-point scale**. A mean was calculated for each factor. The sum of the scores gave a global QoE score. Table 1 presents the questions used to evaluate the QoE.

Factor	Question
Realism	How much did this experience seem consistent with your real-world experiences?
	How strong was your feeling of self-motion?
Sensory	How much did the haptic feedback contribute to the immersion?
	Were the haptic and visual feedback synchronized together?
Comfort	Was the system comfortable?
	How distracting was the control mechanism?
Satisfaction	How much did you enjoy using the system?

Table 1: **QoE Qestionnaire. Each question is rated on a 5-point scale from 1 (Not at all) to 5 (Totally)**

5.4 Results

Two hypothesis are tested: the *HapSeat* enhances the quality of experience and generates a sensation of motion. Shapiro-Wilk and Bartlett tests were performed on our data and the normality and homoscedasticity for most distributions could not be assumed. Hence non-parametric tests were used to analyze the results presented in this section.

As described above, a score for the four factors, realism, sensory, comfort and satisfaction were obtained using a questionnaire (see figure 6 and table 2). The main result confirms our first hypothesis. Our device significantly enhances the quality of experience (Friedman Anova: $p = 8.44e^{-08} < 0.05$). The Wilcoxon test with the Holm-Bonferroni correction has been used for the post-hoc analysis (see table 3). With the haptic feedback computed from the *Physical* or *Geometrical* model, the QoE is significantly higher than without haptic feedback ($p < 0.05$). However the QoE of the *Geometrical Model* is not significantly different from the QoE of the *Physical Model* ($QoE_G = 15 \approx QoE_P = 14.20, p = 0.5575 > 0.05$). It seems that haptic feedback consistent with the video is necessary to improve the QoE: user scores for random feedback are not statistically different to the no feedback condition ($QoE_N = 8.36 \approx QoE_R = 9.45, p = 0.4816 > 0.05$).

This tendency is observable for three factors. Presenting users with haptic feedback computed from our models resulted in significant increases in their reporting of Realism (Friedman Anova, $p = 3.80e^{-08} < 0.05$), Sensory (Friedman Anova, $p = 7.02e^{-08} < 0.05$) and Satisfaction (Friedman Anova, $p = 3.86e^{-07} < 0.05$) scores. However Comfort remained equal for all conditions: the Friedman Anova is significant, $p = 1.27e^{-03} < 0.05$, but Wilcoxon tests cannot confirm this hypothesis, $p > 0.05$ (see table 3).

Finally no significant differences are found for the QoE of each model between the two sequences *Real Car* and *Virtual*

Car (Wilcoxon test, $p_{Geo} = 0.3933$ and $p_{Phy} = 0.4173 > 0.05$).

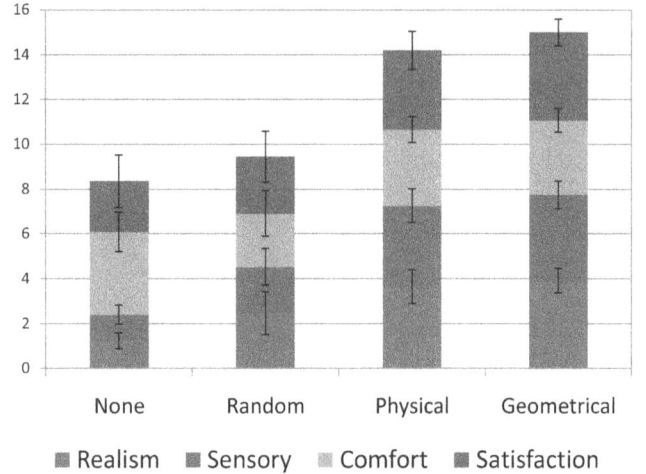

Figure 6: **Quality of experience. The haptic feedback provided by the Physical and Geometrical models significantly improves the QoE.**

Factor Model	QoE	Realism	Sensory	Comfort	Satisfact.	
None	8.3578	1.2353	1.1618	3.6961	2.2647	$\bar{x}$
	2.0741	0.3477	0.4325	0.8853	1.1608	σ_x
Random	9.4479	2.4688	2.0625	2.3854	2.5313	$\bar{x}$
	2.9550	0.9481	0.8190	1.0187	1.1324	σ_x
Physical	14.1961	3.6471	3.6176	3.4020	3.5294	$\bar{x}$
	2.5521	0.7451	0.7609	0.5790	0.8564	σ_x
Geo.	15	3.9167	3.8333	3.3166	3.9333	$\bar{x}$
	1.7904	0.5401	0.6099	0.5300	0.5936	σ_x
F. Anova	35.7534	37.3958	36.1324	15.7554	32.6279	χ^2
	3	3	3	3	3	df
	$8.44e^{-8}$	$3.80e^{-8}$	$7.02e^{-8}$	$1.27e^{-3}$	$3.86e^{-7}$	p
	***	***	***	*	***	sig.

Table 2: **Means ($\bar{x}$) and Standard deviations (σ_x) for each model with respects to each factor. A Friedman Anova ($\chi^2, df, p.value$) has been performed on each factor.**

In order to evaluate the second hypothesis, the answers to the two questions of the Realism factor were analyzed (see figure 7, Q1 on top and Q2 on bottom and table 4). The results from Q1 suggest that the simulated motion was perceived as realistic (Friedman Anova $p = 3.60e^{-05} < 0.05$). A Wilcoxon test with the Holm-Bonferroni correction was also performed on our data (see table 5). Again, no statistical difference between the *Physical* and *Geometrical* models is observed ($Q1_P = 3.6 \approx Q1_G = 3.8, p = 0.6356 > 0.05$) but they are significantly different from the *Random* and *None* conditions ($p < 0.05$). The results from Q2 follow the same pattern. Both models provided a strong sensation of motion, significantly higher than *Random* and *None* conditions (Friedman Anova $p < 0.05$, Wilcoxon tests $p < 0.05$).

5.5 Discussion

Our results suggest that the *HapSeat* does enhance the user experience during passive navigation simulation. Both rendering models significantly increased the QoE compared to the Random and None feedback conditions. Our results

QoE	Geometrical	None	Physical
None	$1.5e^{-05}$	-	-
Physical	0.5575	$6.5e^{-05}$	-
Random	$6.9e^{-05}$	0.4816	0.005
Realism	Geometrical	None	Physical
None	$5.3e^{-06}$	-	-
Physical	0.4336	$4.1e^{-06}$	-
Random	0.0005	0.0004	0.0028
Sensory	Geometrical	None	Physical
None	$5.5e^{-06}$	-	-
Physical	0.5169	$5.2e^{-06}$	-
Random	$4.6e^{-05}$	0.0004	0.0002
Comfort	Geometrical	None	Physical
None	0.1575	-	-
Physical	0.4927	0.1664	-
Random	0.0161	0.0064	0.0107
Satisfaction	Geometrical	None	Physical
None	0.002	-	-
Physical	0.4992	0.0095	-
Random	0.0037	0.4992	0.0273

Table 3: **Pairwise comparison of each model for each factor using Wilcoxon test with Holm-Bonferroni correction.**

Question Model	Q1	Q2	
None	1.2647	1.2059	$\bar{x}$
	0.5338	0.3976	σ_x
Random	2.1563	2.7813	$\bar{x}$
	0.9259	1.0483	σ_x
Physical	3.5588	3.7353	$\bar{x}$
	0.7045	0.8860	σ_x
Geometrical	3.8	4.0333	$\bar{x}$
	0.5606	0.6935	σ_x
F. Anova	20.4615	12.86	χ^2
	2	2	df
	3.60^{-05}	$1.61e^{-03}$	p
	***	*	sig.

Table 4: **Means ($\bar{x}$) and Standard deviations (σ_x) for each model with respects to Q1 and Q2. A Friedman Anova ($\chi^2, df, p.value$) has been performed on each question.**

How much did this experience seem consistent with your real-world experiences?

How strong was your feeling of self-motion?

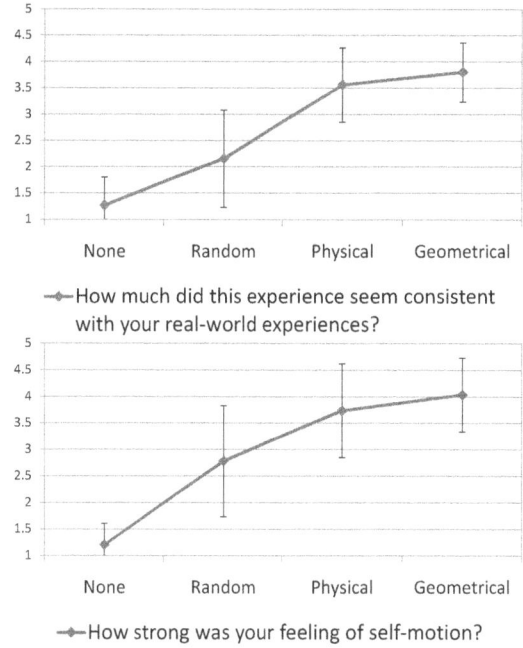

Figure 7: **Realism factor details. Users found the simulation realistic (top) and experienced a stronger sensation of self-motion (bottom).**

Q1	Geometrical	None	Physical
None	$4.5e^{-06}$	-	-
Physical	0.6356	$3.9e^{-06}$	-
Random	0.0002	0.0030	0.0005
Q2	Geometrical	None	Physical
None	$3.5e^{-06}$	-	-
Physical	0.3743	$3.5e^{-06}$	-
Random	0.0045	0.0001	0.0238

Table 5: **Pairwise comparison of each model for both question using Wilcoxon tests with the Holm-Bonferroni correction.**

also suggest that the synchronization of the haptic effect with the visual content is important.

In this study, no statistical differences are found between the models. This is probably due to the nature of the simulation (car driving) which does not fully exploit the 6DoF. Only translation (car acceleration) and rotation (turns) were included in the two sequence tested. More complex content, such as a plane or spaceship flight or a rollercoaster ride, might produce results that highlight differences between the models. In addition, the parameters of the models could be tuned to increase their differences. Each one is composed of several factors which impact the use of the workspace. The *Physical Model* could be also improved by modeling the segments and joints of the user's skeleton instead of treating the user as a single rigid body.

We observed that the simulated motion was not perceived in the same way by all participants. Some of them found that the haptic feedback computed from our models was reversed. For instance, they expected to be pushed backward instead of being pulled forward when the car (real or virtual) was moving straight forward. However this observation was not consistent among all users. Some participants expected to feel the reaction force instead of the acceleration only during turns, but found the feedback acceptable for linear translations, i.e. when the car was going straight forward. Though some participants seem to prefer a reversed force feedback in specific cases, this does not mean that the output of the models should necessarily be reversed. One might posit two user profiles "direct" and "reversed" to address this, it can certainly be said that the design of the associated haptic feedback is not straightforward. The perception of motion simulated by force-feedback devices require further evaluation. Studies are also needed to understand the influence of a haptic stimulus on the perception of a visual stimulus.

Our the device was reported as comfortable and user friendly. The perception of comfort was similar with and without haptic feedback, suggesting that no extra discomfort is introduced by the system. Nevertheless comfort could be improved, especially for the headrest. Some participants reported that the haptic feedback for the *real car* sequence contained too much vibration. This may be explained by the greater sensitivity of proximal joints to movement than distal joints [6]. Similar displacements are perceived more strongly on the head than on the hands. If this vibration that contribute to realism when perceived by the user's hand, might be too intense for the head. So far the haptic rendering for all actuators is the same. But dedicated algorithms could be implemented for each device. As a minimum, a low-pass filter could be applied on the output of the actuator H to reduce vibration.

6. CONCLUSION & PERSPECTIVES

We have presented the *HapSeat*, a novel approach to the simulation of 6DoF effect of motion. Instead of moving the whole user's body as it is traditionally done with motion platforms, we stimulate only parts of the body. Our hypothesis was that, coupled with a visual stimulus, these local stimulations could trigger a sensation of motion and thus improve the quality of experience.

Results of a user study show that the two control models, *Physical* and *Geometrical*, succeed at enhancing the quality of experience during passive navigation. Furthermore participants reported having experienced a realistic sensation of self-motion.

Future work to improve of the models and study of the user's perception of the simulated motion is planned. The prototype could be extended by adding more points of stimulation, for instance, for the legs. The input capabilities of the devices could be used to allow the user to interact with the simulation, offering the prospect of extending applications of the *HapSeat* to flight or driving simulators, teleoperation, etc.

To conclude, this original approach yields a new way to simulate a sensation of motion in a consumer environment and allows the creation of more immersive applications.

7. REFERENCES

[1] A. Berthoz. *The brain's sense of movement*. Harward University Press, 2000.

[2] F. Danieau, J. Fleureau, A. Cabec, P. Kerbiriou, P. Guillotel, N. Mollet, M. Christie, and A. Lécuyer. A framework for enhancing video viewing experience with haptic effects of motion. In *IEEE Haptics Symposium*, 2012.

[3] B. Dasgupta. The Stewart platform manipulator: a review. *Mechanism and Machine Theory*, 35(1):15–40, 2000.

[4] L. R. Harris, M. R. Jenkin, D. Zikovitz, F. Redlick, P. Jaekl, U. T. Jasiobedzka, H. L. Jenkin, and R. S. Allison. Simulating self-motion I: cues for the perception of motion. *Virtual Reality*, 6(2):75–85, 2002.

[5] A Israr and I. Poupyrev. Tactile brush: drawing on skin with a tactile grid display. In *CHI 2011*, pages 2019–2028. ACM, 2011.

[6] Lynette A Jones. Kinesthetic sensing. *Human and Machine Haptics*, 2000.

[7] K. Kilkki. Quality of experience in communications ecosystem. *Journal of universal computer science*, 14(5):615–624, 2008.

[8] S. D. Laycock and a. M. Day. Recent developments and applications of haptic devices. *Computer Graphics Forum*, 22(2):117–132, 2003.

[9] N. Ouarti, A. Lécuyer, and A. Berthoz. Method for simulating specific movements by haptic feedback, and device implementing the method, September 2009. French Patent $N°$ 09 56406.

[10] B.E. Riecke and J. Schulte-Pelkum. Using the perceptually oriented approach to optimize spatial presence & ego-motion simulation. Max Planck Institute for Biological Cybernetics, Technical Report $N°153$, 2006.

[11] Bernhard E. Riecke, Jörg Schulte-Pelkum, Franck Caniard, and Heinrich H. Bülthoff. Towards lean and elegant self-motion simulation in virtual reality. In *Virtual Reality*, pages 131–138, 2005.

[12] A. M. Sabatini. Quaternion-based extended kalman filter for determining orientation by inertial and magnetic sensing. *IEEE Transactions on Biomedical Engineering*, 53(7):1346–1356, 2006.

[13] A. Shah, S. Teuscher, E. McClain, and J. Abbott. How to build an inexpensive 5-dof haptic device using two novint falcons. In *Haptics: Generating and Perceiving Tangible Sensations*, pages 136–143, 2010.

[14] M. Trousselard, P-A. Barraud, V. Nougier, C. Raphel, and C. Cian. Contribution of tactile and interoceptive cues to the perception of the direction of gravity. *Cognitive brain research*, 20(3):355–62, 2004.

[15] A. Valjamae, P. Larsson, D. Vastfjall, and M. Kleiner. Travelling without moving: auditory scene cues for translational self-motion. *Proceeding of International Conference of Auditory Display*, 2005.

Simulation of Deformable Solids in Interactive Virtual Reality Applications

Wen Tang [*]
School of Computing, University of Teesside,
Middlesbrough,
United Kingdom, TS1 3BA

Tao Ruan Wan [†]
School of Informatics, University of Bradford,
Bradford, United Kingdom, BD7 1DP

ABSTRACT

Simulation of deformable objects has become indispensable in many virtual reality applications. Linear finite element algorithms are frequently applied in interactive physics simulation in order to ensure computational efficiency. However, there exists a variety of situations in which higher order simulation accuracy is expected to improve physical behaviors of deformable objects to match their real-world counterparts. For example in the context of virtual surgery, interactive surgical manipulations mandate algorithmic requirements to maintain both interactive frame rates and simulation accuracy, presenting major challenges in simulation methods. In this paper, we present an interactive system for efficient finite element based simulation of hyperplastic solids with more accurate physics behaviors compared with that of standard corotational methods. Our approach begins with a physics model to mitigate drawbacks of the corotational linear elasticity in preserving energy and momenta. A new damping model is presented which takes into account the differential of rotation to compensate the loss of momenta due to rotations. Thus, more accurate simulations can be achieved with this new model, whereas standard corotational methods using rotated damping to handle energy dissipation does not preserve momenta. We then present a real time simulation framework for computing finite element based deformable solids with full capability allowing complex objects to collide and interact with each other. A constrained system is also provided for robust control and the ease of use the simulation system. We demonstrate the parallel implementation to enable realistic and stable physics behaviors of large deformations capable of handling unpredictable user inputs in interactive virtual environments. The implementation details and insights on practical considerations in implementation such as our experience in parallel computation of the physics for

[*]w.tang@tees.ac.uk

[†]t.wan@bradford.ac.uk

mesh-based finite element objects would be useful for people who wish to develop real-time applications in this area.

Categories and Subject Descriptors

H.4 [**Information Systems Applications**]: Miscellaneous; D.2.8 [**Software Engineering**]: Physically based modeling;—*Computer Graphics*

Keywords

Physically based animation; Simulation and modeling; Interactive virtual reality technologies

1. INTRODUCTION

Simulating realistic behaviors of deformable solids is an active area of research with practical virtual reality based applications. Finite element algorithms are popular due to the ability of modeling complex physical behaviors of deformable objects by using only a small number of material parameters. When dealing with a variety of situations in which accurate physical simulations are important, a solid theoretical framework in engineering can also provide theorems with the potential to extend the finite element algorithms to higher order accuracy [3]. However, interactive virtual environments with large complex deformations and unpredictable arbitrary user inputs demand the robustness, efficiency as well as numerical stability of simulation algorithms to ensure that application contents are convincing without causing the system to crash or visual artifacts.

In this paper, we first propose a physics simulation model to account for the issue concerned with simulation accuracy when standard corotational linear finite element is used. Conservations of momenta are important in virtual reality applications where more accurate physical behaviors are prevalent, for instance in virtual surgery. The proposed model introduces a strain energy based damping model to handle energy dissipation such that momenta are preserved, whereas the standard corotational model adds damping forces by rotating the velocity gradient that is generally not diagonal and causes loss of momentum invariants. The energy based damping model computes the damping force according to the deformation happening in one simulation step with the differential of rotation to compensate the loss of momenta due to rotations. Thus, more accurate simulations can be achieved.

We then present a real time simulation framework for deformable solids, which include software components for mesh-based finite element method, a parallelization of physics computations, and constraint based control methods for user directed deformation manipulations, a valuable tool for facilitating interactive design and ease of use the simulation system. Simulation examples demonstrate the robustness of our approach with objects undergoing large deformations capable of handling unpredictable user interactions. It is necessary to take small time steps to ensure the numerical stability. Thus, computing complex phenomena such as large soft body deformations with arbitrary user interactions is especially computationally expensive. However, interactive virtual reality applications can benefit greatly from the opportunity offered by the multicore architecture of CPUs by parallelizing physics computations. We take a black-boxed approach to multithreading to achieve real time performances of the physics computation with stable and realistic collision responses.

2. ELASTICITY AND DISCRETIZATION

The core of the proposed simulation system is the finite element based physics modeling. Tetrahedral meshes are used with linear basis functions to describe the strain field as a piecewise constant over the object's mesh. The linear elasticity model has been extensively studied and became a standard method in computer graphics due to its computational efficiency [13, 7, 14, 3], producing a wide range of materials from hyperelastic to hyperplastic [21].

Let $\mathbf{u}$ be the vector of reference positions in the material space, and $\mathbf{x}$ the vector of deformed positions in the world-space. For a tetrahedral object with vertices indices i, j, k, l, the 3×3 shape matrix, $\mathbf{X}_m = [\mathbf{u}_j - \mathbf{u}_i \ \mathbf{u}_k - \mathbf{u}_i \ \mathbf{u}_l - \mathbf{u}_i]$, maps barycentric coordinates defined on the tetrahedron to a corresponding vector i in the material space, and the 3×3 shape matrix, $\mathbf{X}_w = [\mathbf{x}_j - \mathbf{x}_i \ \mathbf{x}_k - \mathbf{x}_i \ \mathbf{x}_l - \mathbf{x}_i]$, maps barycentric coordinates defined on the tetrahedron to a corresponding vector i in the world space. Linear basis functions are to collect these maps over all tetrahedra as a piecewise linear map. For an individual tetrahedron, the deformable gradient mapping from the material space to the world space is given by:

$$\mathbf{F} = \mathbf{X}_w \mathbf{X}_m^{-1} \qquad (1)$$

The linear elasticity approximates the Green-Lagrange strain $\varepsilon = (\mathbf{F}^T \mathbf{F} - \mathbf{I}) \approx (\mathbf{F}^T + \mathbf{F})/2 - \mathbf{I})$. The linearization leads to the definition for the deformation energy density as:

$$\mathbf{\Psi} = \mu \|\mathbf{F} - \mathbf{R}\|_F^2 + \lambda \frac{1}{2} \mathbf{tr}^2(\mathbf{R}^T \mathbf{F} - \mathbf{I}) \qquad (2)$$

where $\mathbf{\Psi}$ is a function of the deformation gradient alone, μ and λ are the Lame' coefficients, and $\mathbf{R}$ is the rotation from the polar decomposition of deformation gradient $\mathbf{F} = \mathbf{R}\mathbf{S}$ and $\mathbf{S}$ is a symmetric tensor, or a single value decomposition (SVD) of the gradient $\mathbf{F} = \mathbf{U}\hat{\mathbf{F}}\mathbf{V}^T$. In(2), the matrix norm $\|\mathbf{F} - \mathbf{R}\|_F^2 = tr[(\mathbf{F} - \mathbf{R})^T(\mathbf{F} - \mathbf{R})]$, $\mathbf{U}$ and $\mathbf{V}$ are the orthogonal rotation or the reflection, and $\hat{\mathbf{F}}$ is diagonal with positive diagonal entries.

Because SVD is much more expensive to compute than the polar decomposition, using the SVD at every time step for every tetrahedron could easily double the overall runtime or even more, hindering the real time performance of the system. A polar decomposition is used to remove the world space rotation of a tetrahedron to produce a symmetric $\mathbf{S}$. A robust simulation must also deal with degenerated or inverted elements [7, 18]. In the case of inverted elements, where $(\mathbf{detF} < 0)$, we first compute the full diagonalisation by invoking SVD to find $\mathbf{F} = \mathbf{U}\hat{\mathbf{F}}\mathbf{V}^T$ and to form the polar decomposition via $\mathbf{R} = \mathbf{U}\mathbf{V}^T, \mathbf{S} = \mathbf{V}\hat{\mathbf{F}}\mathbf{V}^T$ [?]. Therefore, the more costly SVD procedure is invoked only for $\mathbf{F}$ with a non-positive determinant.

The linear corotational finite element formulation presented in [17] has become a popular method in computer graphics as a specific treatments for the rotational invariant [7, 14], since the elastic energy of an isotropic material is invariant under the world and the material rotations. As the method proposed in [13] works on a node-based procedure which produces undesirable forces, we elect for a per-element based method [7]. Each deformation gradient can be decomposed into a rotation (or reflection) part and a matrix part that captures the deformation of the tetrahedron. Therefore, the modified strain measurement used in the corotated elasticity is defined as:

$$\varepsilon(\mathbf{R}^T\mathbf{F}) = \frac{1}{2}(\mathbf{R}^T\mathbf{F} + \mathbf{R}^T\mathbf{F}^T) - I = \mathbf{S} - I \qquad (3)$$

$$\sigma = \mathbf{R}[2\mu(\mathbf{S} - \mathbf{I}) + \lambda \mathbf{tr}(\mathbf{S} - \mathbf{I})\mathbf{I}]. \qquad (4)$$

where in equation (4), σ is the 1st Piola−Kirchhoff stress derived from a linear isotropic constitutive model.

3. THE MOMENTA CONSERVATION

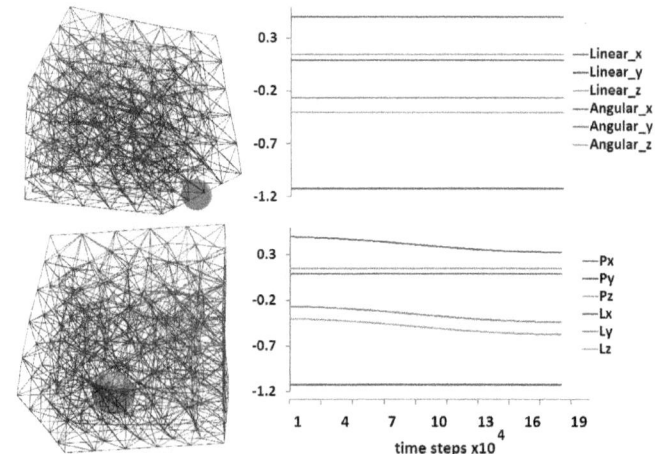

Figure 1: Angular and linear momenta behaviors of a cube given a non-zero initial position momentum. Both angular and linear momenta are preserved in the new approach (top image), whereas the loss of angular momenta are shown with corotational method (bottom image).

Solving a physical system of elasticity generally involves systems of differential equations. The accuracy of simulations is underpinned by mathematical models chosen to find solutions of the differential equations that are governing the physical system. In this regards, numerical techniques are crucial computational tools in computer simulations of deformable objects. More importantly, a mechanical system is characterized by *symmetries* and *invariants* (e.g., momenta) [15, 5]. Thus, preserving these geometric notions is of importance in capturing the underlying continuous motion in order to improve simulation plausibility and accuracy, albeit making approximations in numerical integrations is unavoidable. For example, classical methods such as fourth-order Runge-Kutta, implicit Euler, and more recently the Newmark scheme increase the approximation order by employing higher order differential terms in the integrator or taking two consecutive positions of the system to compute the next position [16].

In this section, we present geometric properties of finite element system of elasticity and describe how to increase the order of the simulation accuracy by introducing the differential of rotation to a corotational model with an energy based damping model. Given the energy density of equation (2), the deformation energy of an elastic body Ω can be computed as:

$$\mathbf{E} = \int_{\Omega} \mathbf{\Psi}(\mathbf{F}) dx. \tag{5}$$

The model domain Ω is discretized into tetrahedral elements with linear basis functions, so that the discrete version of equation (5) then becomes a sum of energies from each element E_e. A discrete force per node can in general be written as:

$$\mathbf{f_i} = -\frac{\partial E}{\partial x_i} = \sum_e (-\frac{\partial E_e}{\partial x_i}) = \sum_e f_i^e = \mathbf{R}\sigma(\mathbf{F}^e)\mathbf{B_i}. \tag{6}$$

where $\sigma(\mathbf{F}^e) := \partial\Psi/\partial\mathbf{F}$ and $\mathbf{B_i}$ is the constant vector of the area weighted normals (in the material coordinates) corresponding to the faces of the tetrahedron incident to each node. The equation of force equilibrium consists of the stiffness matrix $\mathbf{K}$, the Jacobian of the elastic force vector $\mathbf{f}$ w.r.t the world coordinates $\mathbf{x}$.

The geometric properties of a mechanical system is characterized by *symmetries* and *invariants* (e.g., momenta). As $\sigma(\mathbf{F}^e) := \partial\Psi/\partial\mathbf{F}$ is expressed in diagonal form in computation, the element stiffness matrices are symmetric and will preserve both linear and angular momenta. However, for damping the standard corotational methods adds damping forces by rotating the velocity gradient by the same U and V used to diagonalize deformation gradient. With standard corotational methods the damping stress is computed in the rotated frame by the rotated velocity gradient that in general is not diagonal, thus causing the loss of momentum invariant.

We use a damping model based on the strain energy to compute the damping force according to the deformation happening in one simulation step. Similar approaches termed as variational damping have been presented in [2, 9]. Chao expanded the variational integration introduced in [9] and described geometric structures of elastic deformation with representation of discrete differential geometry to produce elastic deformations. We invoke the Newton solver to compute the variational damping. Assuming state variables expressed in terms of per vertex momentum p, the

position x, and the velocity v, we compute discrete time steps $k \geq 0$ in the Newton solver to minimize energy:

$$\mathbf{w}(\mathbf{x}) = \frac{2}{h^2}(x-x^{(k)})^T M(x-x^{(k)}) + E(x) - \frac{2}{h}(p^{(k)})^T(x-x^{(k)}). \tag{7}$$

where h denoting the time step size, M the mass matrix, and E the elastic energy as defined in equation (5). With $x^* = argmin_x \mathbf{w}(\mathbf{x})$,, the transition $k \to k+1$ proceeds as:

$$v^{(k+1)} = \frac{2}{h}(x^* - x^{(k)}), \tag{8}$$

$$x^{(k+1)} = x^{((k))} + hv^{(k+1)}, \tag{9}$$

$$p^{(k+1)} = Mv^{(k+1)} - \frac{h}{2}\nabla E. \tag{10}$$

Newton iterations require the first order and the second order partial derivatives of the energy function E defined in equation (5) expressed in the stress tensor σ and the variation of the stress $\delta\sigma$ which depends on the differential of deformation gradient $\delta\mathbf{F}$ and the differential of rotation $\delta\mathbf{R}$. Taking differentials on equation (4) to obtain:

$$\delta\sigma = 2\mu(\delta(\mathbf{F} - \delta(\mathbf{R}) + \lambda\{tr(\delta(\mathbf{R}^T\mathbf{F}) + tr(\mathbf{R}^T\delta\mathbf{F})\}\mathbf{R}$$
$$+ \lambda tr(\mathbf{R}^T\mathbf{F})\delta\mathbf{R}$$
$$= \underbrace{2\mu\delta\mathbf{F} + \lambda tr(\mathbf{R}^T\delta\mathbf{F})\mathbf{R}}_{\text{the first part}} + \underbrace{\{\lambda tr(\mathbf{S} - \mathbf{I}) - 2\mu\}\delta\mathbf{R}}_{\text{the second part}} \tag{11}$$

The right hand side of equation (11) includes two parts: the first part is the tensor product between the differential of deformation gradients rotated by $\mathbf{R}$, the second part is the anti-symmetric part of the differential of rotation responsible for the conservation properties of the angular momenta, which has been omitted in standard corotational approaches. The differential $\delta\mathbf{F}$ of the deformation gradient can be computed from the displacement δx and we follow McAdams *et al* [12] to derive $\delta\mathbf{R}$ and we refer the interested reader to [12] and also its attached technical document for a detailed proof.

By invoke the Newton solver to compute the additional part (i.e.the second part) of the equation (11) with the differential of rotation, the physical behaviors of the deformation is compensated for the conservation of momenta. Figure 1 shows the tracking of momenta of an elastic body with some initial motion and deformation.

4. TIME INTEGRATION

Efficient time integration algorithms can greatly reduce computational overheads and enable real-time performances. Crucially the time integration is also closely related to the issue of numerical instability which causes unacceptable and unrealistic simulation effects. The restriction of an explicit Euler method on time step size is well documented, whereas full implicit integrations induce excessive damping to the simulation results [1]. The forward Euler method imposes stringent quadratic time step restrictions with dependence on damping forces. For stiff dynamic systems, an order of magnitude more steps are required. Therefore, a mixed explicit/implicit scheme is employed which is a good compromise with an explicit Euler step for elastic forces and an implicit backward Euler integration step for velocities upon which damping forces are dependent. In this way, forces that are independent of the velocity can be integrated efficiently, whereas the numerical stiffness of the system equations can be dealt with by implicit integration steps. The proposed integration scheme only uses a Newton solver for the velocity dependent damping forces, thus limiting the excessive artificial damping of a fully implicit scheme. The algorithm is described below with x denoting positions, v denoting velocities, and a as accelerations.

- $v^{n+1/2} = v^n + \frac{\Delta t}{2} a(t^n, x^n, v^n)$

- $x^{n+1} = x^n + \Delta t v^{n+1/2}$

- Compute rigid body collision detection with x^{n+1} and v^n; Finding final positions $\tilde{x}^{n+1}$ and modified velocities $\tilde{v}^n$

- $v^{n+1} = \tilde{v}^n + \frac{\Delta t}{2} a(t^{n+1}, \tilde{x}^{n+1}, v^{n+1/2})$.

The time step size in our simulation remains constant. A variable time step may be used. However, as the frame rate is unlikely to be a constant, unexpected numerical instability can occur. Instead, for each frame, we compute how many full Δt updates should be performed according to the time elapsed since the last frame, and perform multiple updates. The partial updates (less than Δt) are saved for the next frame. The value of Δt is chosen carefully in order to maintain an interactive simulation.

4.1 Collision detection and response

Deformable collision detection is an essential component in interactive physics simulations.

A summary of collision detection algorithms is presented in [19]. Among various methods, box hierarchies, distance fields, and spatial subdivisions are commonly used in computer graphics to facilitate the collision detection process. Furthermore, two main categories of methods for computing corresponding surface contacts and forces are available in the literature for resolving collision responses. The penalty method computes constraint forces to enforce the surface contact w.r.t. penetrating distances. These forces accelerate the system towards the desired configuration [4], whereas an alternative method is to employ an augmented Lagrangian formulation by introducing additional Lagrange multipliers to enforce contact constraints on the collision surface during the time integration step [1].

Computing collisions and responses is a time consuming task for deformable solids, especially for accurate collision resolutions due to additional restrictions on the time step length. In our simulation, the rigid body collision process is carried out by implementing a level-set algorithm by representing collision surfaces as implicit surfaces functions to facilitate efficient collision queries. Friction forces are implemented as a LCP solver. In addition, highly flexible structures such as deformable solids have the possibility colliding at multiple places. The bounding volume hierarchies [20] are not designed for deformable models due to the precomputed data. A stochastic collision approach with a two-steps scheme is used to process collisions and self-collisions. Firstly, we chose a pair of triangles randomly from a set of triangles to detect collisions between two triangle meshes of colliding objects. We then iteratively compute the local distance minimum by repeatedly replacing each triangle element by its topological neighbour with smaller distance compared to the other elements. If the distance is smaller than a given proximity threshold, a collision is detected. Secondly, when a collision occurs between two objects, a recursive algorithm is applied to search the neighbourhood for further possible collisions. This stochastic approach is based on the observation that collisions between deformable bodies are often grouped into collision clusters corresponding to colliding areas that can be identified efficiently through proximity search. In order to provide a robust collision response, collisions are propagated from the collision point to the vertices with a collision response applied to these vertices. Collision response is computed as a penalty force.

More specifically, collisions are handled by projecting each node of the element to the triangular surface mesh through the interpolation of barycentric coordinates of nodes within the owning tetrahedron. The level-set offers straightforward analytic expressions for computing the signed distance functions. A collision occurs whenever any node i penetrates collision objects. Thus, a collision response force is applied to move the node along the normal direction of the surface $\mathbf{n_i}$ according to the penetration distance (i.e. the velocity of the node $\mathbf{v_i}$ and the velocity of the rigid body $\mathbf{v}$). The collision force on a given node i is calculated as $\mathbf{F_n^i} = \mathbf{n_i}(\mathbf{v_i} - \mathbf{v})\frac{m}{\Delta t}$. For the frictional contact, we compute tangential velocities for both of the node point and the rigid body at the contact to find the relative tangential velocity $\Delta \mathbf{v_t}$. Both static and dynamic frictional forces are tested and the dynamic friction is given as $\mathbf{F_t^i} = -\mu \frac{(v_i - v) m \mathbf{n_i}}{\mathbf{v_t} \Delta t}$.

The collision handling is processed in the third step of the numerical integration step as described above, in which the final position of the node is calculated and the velocity of the node is modified. Figure 2 demonstrates the robust collision detections and responses for a complex mesh object that has multiple contacts to several collision objects. The responses to collisions include both penetration distance calculations and frictional contacts.

5. CONSTRAINTS

A hierarchical skeleton constraint system using kinematic motions to control the dynamic deformation of volumetric solids is developed to allow the interactive design and manipulation of deformable solids. Constraint based mesh deformation approaches have been presented previously for free-form deformations within discrete differential coordinates [23], for finite element deformations using the modal analysis with hardware accelerations [8], and more recently for animating character's skin deformation [11]. Our hierarchical constraint system consists of a set of joints acting as constraint nodes as controls. Each of the global transformation of a constraint node is computed through a recursive function. The hierarchical skeleton controls a sequence of simulation commands and drives the volumetric simulation through constraints. This enables essentially a skeleton driven deformations in our simulation examples. There are two types of constraints designed in our system namely positional and directional constraints. Constraint forces are computed and applied to tetrahedron nodes through these control nodes at each predefined and/nor instant user interactions.

Figure 2: An example scene of the collision detection and responses: a complex mesh structure has multiple collision contacts with several collision objects responding to both penetration forces and frictional forces.

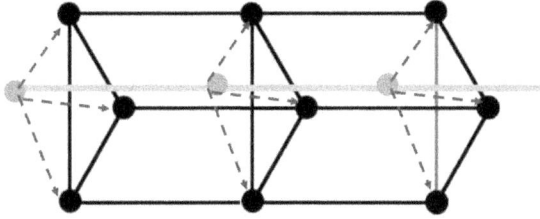

Figure 3: The hierarchical skeleton structure (the yellow line)consists of a set of constraint nodes (yellow points). Each constraint node is associated with a set of tetrahedral nodes (black points) and controls the motion of the tetrahedral nodes through constraint forces (green dashed lines).

Techniques for adding constraints to particle dynamics or Lagrangian dynamics were presented in [22]. Figure 3 depicts the control mechanism of the skeleton based constraint system in our system for simulating tetrahedron-based deformable solids.

5.1 Positional Constraints

From the traditional kinematics theory, we express the spatial velocity vector of a constraint node as a 6×1 vector, $\Psi = (\omega_x, \omega_y, \omega_z, v_x, v_y, v_z)$, where ω is the angular velocity and $\mathbf{v}$ is the linear velocity. Given the constraint node i, whose position is at $\mathbf{c}_i$, the velocity of the constraint node is defined as

$$\dot{\mathbf{c}}_i = [e]\mathbf{c}_i + \mathbf{v} = (-[\mathbf{c}_i]\mathbf{I})\Psi \qquad (12)$$

Here $[e]$ is a skew-symmetric 3×3 matrix acting on 3-vectors

$\mathbf{x}$ by $[e] \cdot \mathbf{x} = e \times \mathbf{x}$, and $\mathbf{I}$ is the the 3×3 identity matrix. Given a time step size $\triangle t$, the skeleton driven constraint means that the position of a constrained node in deformable objects at the next time step $(t+1)$ is transformed by its constraint node

$$\mathbf{C} = \mathbf{x}^{t+1} - \mathbf{v}^{t}\triangle t\Psi = 0 \qquad (13)$$

Therefore, the constraint nodes apply constraints to the tetrahedral nodes in world space, which offer animators control over the deformable objects. Thus, the acceleration of a constrained tetrahedron node that is enforced by the constraint node at a time step t is computed as

$$\ddot{\mathbf{x}} \approx \frac{1}{\triangle t}[\mathbf{v}^{t+1} - \mathbf{v}^{t}] \approx \frac{1}{\triangle t}(-[\mathbf{v}]\mathbf{I})(\Psi^{t+1} - \Psi^{t}) \qquad (14)$$

The constraint force applied on the tetrahedron node based on the Newton's law $\mathbf{F} = m\mathbf{a}$

$$\mathbf{f}_{\mathbf{pc}} \approx \frac{1}{\triangle t}m(-[\mathbf{v}]\mathbf{I})(\Psi^{t+1} - \Psi^{t}) \qquad (15)$$

This constraint force is the last force to be computed, after external and internal forces being obtained. The constraint force could be dependant on the total force that is already computed.

5.2 Directional Constraints

The computation of directional constraints is more involving than that of positional constraints, since the deformation enforced by directional constraints must be consistent with the corotational linear elasticity principle in removing artifacts caused by rotations. In doing so, we apply a rotational constraint to ensure that the rotational part R^{t+1} of the deformation of the constrained node at the simulation step $t+1$ is equal to the global rotation R_c^{t+1} of the skeleton node attached to it. The rotation caused by the constraint force is computed as $R_{f_c} = R_c^{t+1}(R^t)^{\mathrm{T}}$. The key idea of applying directional constraints is to keep the neighboring nodes in the same direction as the constrained node.

The constraint force to be applied to each node is separated into three distinct parts, each part acting towards the goal of keeping the same direction, i.e. the first part of the constraint force adds the correct force to rotate the neighboring nodes; the second part of the constraint force is the collinear projection of the total forces applied to a neighboring node to move the node along the constraint direction, and finally the third part of the constraint force compensates the initial velocity component of the node that is orthogonal to the constraint direction. We express the rotational constraint force as:

$$\mathbf{f_{rc}} = \underbrace{(\frac{\mathbf{x}^t R_c^{t+1} - \mathbf{x}^t}{\triangle t^2} m)}_{\text{the first part}} + \underbrace{(\mathbf{d} \cdot (\mathbf{f} \cdot \mathbf{d}) - \mathbf{f})}_{\text{the second part}} + \underbrace{(\frac{\mathbf{d} \cdot (\mathbf{v}^t \cdot \mathbf{d}) - \mathbf{v}^t}{\triangle t})m}_{\text{the third part}}$$

Figure 4: An example of the skeleton driven deformation.

Here $\mathbf{d}$ is the normalized direction vector. Similarly, the rotational constraint force is computed after external and internal forces being obtained and the constraint force could also be dependant on the total force that is already computed. Figure 4 shows an example of the skeleton driven deformation produced by both positional and rotational constraints.

6. PARALLELIZATION

Large soft body deformations are highly expensive to compute, since numerical stability of simulations requires small time integration steps, hindering interactive applications. The multi-core architecture of CPUs offers opportunities to the parallelization of physics computations. Simulations can benefit greatly from multithreading. Detailed analysis of the simulation code on modelling natural phenomena can be found in [6], which parallelizes the code on a simulated multicore architecture. Although this study was targeted for visual effects in films with no specific requirements for real-time computations, the analysis concerning bottlenecks and memory access patterns is equally applicable to a parallelized real-time physics simulation system.

In order to achieve the real-time performance for interactive deformable objects with realistic simulations,

it is possible to take the advantage of the multi-core architecture of modern computers with multithreading. In our implementation, the multithreading component used for safely parallelising physics computations offers significant advantages over serial implementations in terms of the computation performance. The diagonalisation process of the physics computation for each tetrahedron element described in previous sections is applied with multithreading operations to overcome the burden of computationally expensive SVD and polar decomposition processes through parallelizing.

A mesh data set is designed as tetrahedral batches and the multithreading component dedicates the tetrahedral mesh batches to a list of threads. Thread signals is also stored and the process is completely black-boxed for thread safe computations. Therefore, all the synchronization process is done internally and the user only calls one initialization and one update function at each simulation step. Tetrahedron batches are dispatched to each core for parallel computations. The assembling of stiffness matrix $\mathbf{K}$ takes a substantial amount of time, since for each element the computation is carried out independently, thus each group of the divided mesh elements can be computed by a dedicate thread. The row-compressed lists are also assembled independently by separate threads. To solve the system equation 7, the parallelized implementation distributes the row-vector multiplies over multiple threads and the block structure of the node-rows are computed simultaneously.

While multithreading computing the nodes, since a node can belong to several elements, care must be taken to ensure that the memory of same variables is not accessed by different threads at the same time. Otherwise, the result will be undefined. The strategy is to update the force applied to each node, while maintaining the independency of other variables (position, velocity, etc) so that values of these variables can be read safely. To avoid incorrect update for a node by different tetrahedra processed at the same time, a mutex (Mutual Exclusion) mechanism is used which allows only one thread to execute a section of the code at a given time, meanwhile other threads will have to wait until it finishes the task. This behavior is unfortunately not acceptable for the real-time physics computation, since the time taken by such synchronization process may almost cancel the benefit of parallel computations. The approach taken in our system is not to update the forces directly on the nodes soon after the thread finishing, but to write its value into a temporary buffer that duplicates the shared nodes. This buffer is then accessed after the parallel pass for updating each node safely.

Implementing a multithreaded system allows much larger deformable solids to be handled in real-time. Although the synchronization and reconstruction processes introduce a slight computation overhead, it is not a major problem as the performance gain is definitely noticeable. Figure 5 shows the computation time with up to 8 cores of threads being used for computing different meshes of varied sizes and geometric complexities. The system achieves just over 10 milliseconds performance for a large mesh and 2 milliseconds for a smaller object. However, the increase in performance is evident in this test with the number of processors being used, demonstrating a real-time interactive application for finite element based physics simulations.

Figure 6: Example scenes of animation sequences of two deformable solids.

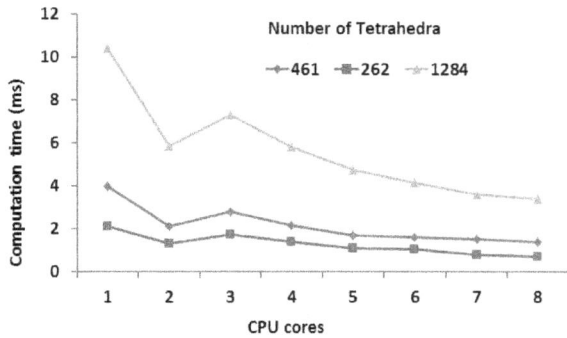

Figure 5: A test on multithreading computation with different mesh sizes and the number of threads being used.

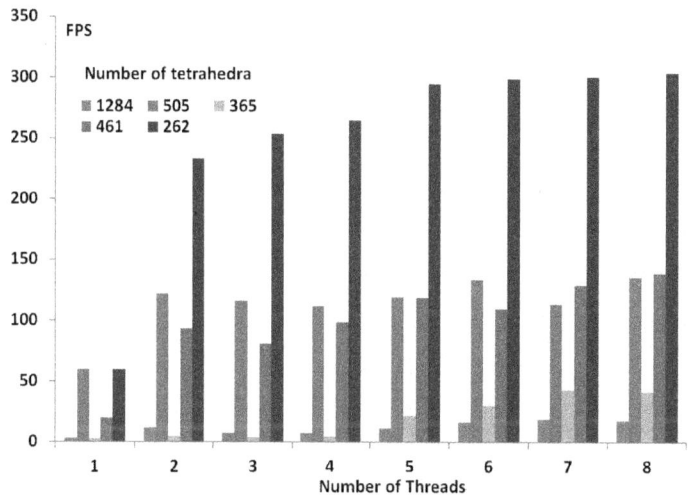

Figure 7: Frame rates test on multi-cores for different deformable solids with different number of tetrahedra.

7. RESULTS AND DISCUSSION

The system described here is a stand-alone physics engine for real-time simulating deformable solids, which can also be incorporated into other virtual reality simulation environments.

Figure 6 shows two representative animated scenes generated by our system. Additional examples are included in the accompanying video to this paper. We used the method described in [10] for tetrahedral mesh generation. With 8 cores multithreading computation, the physics simulation is generally reaching over 40 fps for large models such as the model shown in the bottom images of Figure 6. For the model shown in the top row of images that has relatively small number of elements, the computation is over 300 fps run on a 8-core Intel Xeon X5550 workstation. All simulations involved large numbers of inverted elements. The simulation example in Figure 6 has about 6 percent of the total degenerated tetrahedra. The plot in Figure 7 illustrates the simulation performance for a number of objects, some of which are illustrated in simulation examples as shown in Figures 2 to 6. The parallel multithreading realizes substantial gains over the serial processing of the code.

8. LIMITATIONS AND FUTURE WORK

The result of our integrated approach is an real-time simulation system that is suitable for interactive virtual reality applications with arbitrary user interactions as well as predefined constraint-based user controls. The simulation frame-work will be further extended for practical applications such virtual surgical simulations. The linear elastic model is extended and the model is stable and robust for simulating a wide range of deformation effects.

We have been focusing on optimizing for the CPUs, because much large and complex simulation scenarios can often run on clusters without GPUs. However, as the power of GPUs is increasingly recognized, it is important in our future work to experiment implementation with GPUs to compare the performance gains of GPUs with that of our optimized CPU code. The realism of simulations can be further improved by using accurate self-collision methods. Material anisotropy could be simulated by extending the constitutive model to include anisotropic components, however, we are yet to test Material anisotropic materials such as simulation of muscle tissues. We would also like to explore additional material features such as element splitting. In addition, the recent trend in finite element simulations is to use multigrid solvers for large scale computation, which might results in a under-performance to the size of the mesh that we can currently model in real-time, but for large scale simulations, multigrid solvers will indeed offer increased performance gain, which is definitely worth to explore in our future implementations.

9. REFERENCES

[1] D. Baraff. Linear-time dynamics using lagrange multipliers. In *Proceedings of ACM SIGGRAPH*, pages 137–146, 1996.

[2] I. Chao, U. Pinkall, S. Patrick, and P. Schröder. A simple geometric model for elastic deformations. In *Proceedings of ACM SIGGRAPH*, volume 29(4), pages 38:1–38:6, 2010.

[3] N. Chentanez, R. Alterovitz, D. Ritchie, L. Cho, K. K. Hauser, K. Goldberg, J. R. Schewchuk, and J. F. O'Brien. Interactive simulation of surgical needle insertion and steering. In *Proceedings of ACM SIGGRAPH*, pages 24(3):1–10. ACM Press / ACM SIGGRAPH, 2009.

[4] R. Goldenthal, D. Harmon, R. Fattal, M. Bercovier, and E. Grinspun. Efficient simulation of inextensible cloth. In *Proceedings of ACM SIGGRAPH*, volume 26, 2007.

[5] M. Hauth, O. Etzmuss, and W. Strasser. Analysis of numerical methods for the simulation of deformable models. volume 19, pages 581–600, 2003.

[6] J. C. Hughes, R. Grzeszczuk, E. Sifakis, D. Kim, S. Kumar, P. A. Selle, J. Chhugani, M. Holliman, and Y. K. Chen. Physical simulation for animation and visual effects: parallelization and characterization for chip multiprocessors. In *ACM SIGARCH Computer Architecture News*, volume 35, pages 220Ŭ–231, 2007.

[7] G. Irving, J. Teran, and R. Fedkiw. Invertible finite elements for robust simulation of large deformation. In *Proceedings of ACM SIGGRAPH / Eurographics Symposium on Computer Animation*, pages 131–140, 2004.

[8] D. James and D. K. Pai. Dyrt: Dynamic response textures for real-time deformation simulation with graphics hardware. In *In Proceedings of ACM SIGGRAPH*, pages 582–585. ACM Press / ACM SIGGRAPH, 2002.

[9] L. Kharevych, W. Y. Tong, E. Kanso, J. Marsden, P. Schröder, and M. Desbrun. Geometric, variational integrators for computer animation. In *Proceedings of the ACM SIGGRAPH/Eurographics Symposium on Computer Animation*, pages 43–52, 2006.

[10] B. M. Klingner and J. R. Shewchuk. Aggressive tetrahedral mesh improvement. In *Proceedings of the 16th International Meshing Roundtable (Seattle, Washington) October*, pages 2–23.

[11] A. McAdams, Y. Zhu, A. Selle, M. Empey, R. Tamstorf, J. Teran, and E. Sifakis. Efficient elasticity for character skinning with contact and collisions. In *Proceedings of ACM SIGGRAPH*, 2011.

[12] A. McAdams, Y. Zhu, A. Shlle, M. Empey, R. Tamstorf, J. Teran, and E. Sifakis. Efficient elasticity for character skinning with contact and collisions. Cambridge University Press, 2007.

[13] M. Müller, J. Dorsey, L. McMillan, R. Jagnow, and B. Cutler. Stable real-time deformations. In *Proceedings of ACM SIGGRAPH Symposium on Computer Animation*, pages pp.49–54. ACM, ACM Press / ACM SIGGRAPH, 2002.

[14] M. Müller and M. H. Gross. Interactive virtual materials. In *Proceedings of Graphics Interface*, pages 239–246, 2004.

[15] R. Parent. Computer animation: Algorithms and techniques. *Morgan Kaufmann, 2001*.

[16] W. H. Press, S. A. Teukolsky, W. T. Vetterling, and B. P. Flannery. Numerical recipes in c++: The art of scientific computing, 3rd ed. volume 30, page Article No. 37, 2011.

[17] C. C. Rankin and A. F. Brogan. An element independent corotational procedure for the treatment of large rotations. *ASME J. Press. Valve Techn*, 108(3):165–174, 1986.

[18] R. Schmedding and M. Teschner. Inversion handling for stable deformable modeling. In *The Visual Computer (CGI 2008)*, pages 625–633, 2008.

[19] M. Teschner, S. Kimmerle, B. Heidelberger, G. Zachmann, L. Raghupathi, A. Fuhrmann, M. p. Cani, F. Faure, N. Magnenat-thalmann, W. Strasser, and P. Volino. Collision detection for deformable objects. In *Eurographics State-of-the-Art Report*, pages 119–139, 2004.

[20] G. van den Bergen. Efficient collision detection of complex deformable models using aabb trees. volume 2, pages 1–14, 1997.

[21] M. Wicke, D. Ritchie, B. M. Klingner, S. Burke, J. R. Shewchuk, and J. F. O'Brien. Dynamic local remeshing for elastoplastic simulation. In *In Proceedings of ACM SIGGRAPH*, pages 1–11. ACM Press / ACM SIGGRAPH, 2010.

[22] A. Witkin. Physically based modeling: Principles and practice-constrained dynamics. In *Online Siggraph '97 Course notes*, 1997.

[23] S. Yoshizawa, A. Belyaev, and H. P. Seidel. Skeleton-based variational mesh deformations. In *Computer Graphics Forum (In Proceedings of EUROGRAPHICS)*, pages 255–264, 2007.

Real-time Simulation of Long Thin Flexible Objects in Interactive Virtual Environments

Tao Ruan Wan [*]
School of Informatics,
University of Bradford,
Bradford, United Kingdom,
BD7 1DP

Wen Tang [†]
School of Computing,
University of Teesside,
Middlesbrough,
United Kingdom, TS1 3BA

Dongjin Huang [‡]
School of Film and TV Arts
Technology, Shanghai
University
Shanghai, 200072, China

ABSTRACT

Many virtual reality-based applications involve simulations of micro-structures such as hair, fibers and textile yarns, as well as ropes, flexible wires and tubes. In virtual surgery, for example, flexible wires and tubes are common medical instruments and devices. Core to the simulations is the robust physics-based computation of elastic rods. In this paper, we present a volumetric finite element based approach to simulating rod-like objects with real-time performance suitable for interactive virtual environments. A sequence of Cosserat joints (tiny volumetric elastic joints) linked by rigid bar segments are used to compute the elastic rod objects. By construction, each of the joints is equipped with its own mass, degrees of freedom (DOFs) with a small volumetric deformation field to measure deformation energies due to stretching, shearing, bending, and twisting about the centerline curve of the long flexible object. Therefore, a generalized continuum formulation is derived to compute both bending and twisting deformations of elastic rods, resulting a simple and general simulation model to facilitate efficient physics computations, whereas conversional simulation methods for elastic rods require explicitly decoupling between bending and twisting deformations. In this paper, we show simulations of a wide range of object behaviors for interactive virtual reality applications.

Categories and Subject Descriptors

H.4 [**Information Systems Applications**]: Miscellaneous; D.2.8 [**Software Engineering**]: Physically based modeling;—*Computer Graphics*

[*]t.wan@bradford.ac.uk

[†]w.tang@tees.ac.uk

[‡]hdj@shu.edu.cn

Keywords

Physically-based simulation and modeling; Elastic rod; Interactive virtual reality

1. INTRODUCTION

Threads, ropes, and wires are common objects in virtual reality-based (VR) applications, for example, simulations of hair, textile fibers and yarns, and flexible wires and tubes for medical devices in virtual surgery [29]. However, despite the 1D geometric configurations, long thin and flexible objects are difficult to simulate. This is due to the fact that the geometric configuration of a rod-like object in space is governed by an intricately constrained physics system, in which the bending of the rod is coupled with the material twist around the object's centerline, which normally requires a decoupling scheme in simulation. In an interactive virtual reality environment where realistic simulations must be capable of handling unpredictable user interactions , numerical stability and computational efficiency are additional constraints.

In this paper, we present a volumetric finite element based model for simulating elastic rod objects. The physics simulation mode uses thin elastic joints termed as the Cosserat joints together with a set of ridgy bar elements to model a long thin flexible object. Each elastic joint is equipped with its own mass, the degrees of freedom (DOFs), deformation energies to model a small volumetric deformation field along any axis about the objects' centerline. Therefore, a general continuum formulation is derived to compute both bending and twisting deformations of elastic rod objects, resulting a simple and general simulation model, whereas conversional simulation methods for elastic rods require explicitly decoupling between bending and twisting deformations in order to facilitate efficient physics computations. Our model achieves efficient real-time computations by incorporating a set of rigid bar segments between the elastic joints to enforce the inextensible kinematic constraints. Based on the linear elastica theory, the proposed model is capable of simulating a wide range of physics behaviors such as large viscoelastic deformations, highly stretched and/or stiff non-stretching materials. Appendix presents the derivation of strain rates of joint elements in terms of the Kirchhoff rod model, a consequence of the theoretically grounded development of our real-time simulation model.

2. RELATED WORK

In the past, specialized methods have emerged for simulating elastic rods with compelling results. For example, the Lagrangian mechanics formulation was proposed to solve stiff underlying differential equations [27] and the use of the parallel transport for decoupling material twists from the bending [5]. Pai [24] used Newton iterations and line searching algorithm to solve stiff constrained differential equations for the static configuration of a Cosserat strand. A rigid body chain was used to compute the centerline curvature of an elastic rod by using differential algebraic equations [15]. The use of piecewise helix primitives to simulate hair strands was proposed in [7, 6]. The method of using quaternion as simulation DOFs to model the material twist required a small simulation time step to solve coupling constraints between the bending and the material twists [13, 28, 27], whereas Bergou *et al.* [5, 4] derived a discrete differential geometry formulation to solve the dynamic system of elastic rod efficiently with the use of parallel transport to decompose material twists from the bending.

We propose a general elastic rod model using volumetric elastic joints i.e. the Cosserat points. A long flexible object is represented by linking elastic joints between rigid edge elements. We depart from explicit material frame representations for material twists [5, 28], instead, use a generalized continuum formulation to solve both bending and twisting deformations. We show that bending strains of elastic joints can also represent material twists implicitly. In computer graphics, linear elasticity has become the basis for devising specialized methods for simulating long slender objects [10], fast deformable shells [9, 14] and deformable volumes [23, 16, 3]. The well-known volume growth limitations for large deformations using the linear elasticity were compensated for by co-rotational methods [19, 11, 17]. Networks of point masses were also popular for modeling elastica [2, 8, 26].

The theory of the Cosserat points has been developed to describe the motion of a material point equipped with its own mass, DOFs, and the elastic energy, which models small volumetric deformation field [25]. Martin *et al* [18] presented an accurate, unified treatment of elastica of different forms (solids, shells and rods) using the Cosserat points as elastic primitives called *elastons*. However, this method is non-real-time, since it requires neighborhood estimations. Cosserat points are commonly used in geophysics to add the stiffness of the linkage type of elements to analyze mechanics of solids [21].

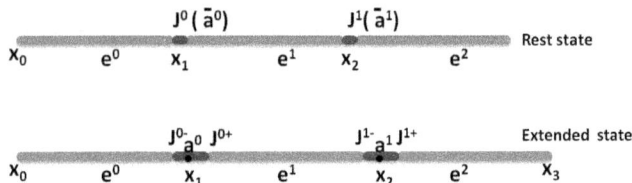

Figure 1: Notation: nodes, edges and joints.

3. DISCRETE CENTERLINE REPRESENTATION

In deriving system equations for simulation, we firstly consider a rod-like to be *inextensible*. The centerline of the object is a curve passing through the center of mass of every cross section of the object. Thus, the geometric configuration of the centerline in space describes the shape of the rod at a particular time frame. It is assumed that the length of the rod is significantly greater than its radius and is surrounded by a finite, but thin, elastic material twisting around the centerline. The rod, therefore, is a volumetric curve-like solid whose extent along $\mathbf{d}_1$, the tangent direction of the centerline, is much greater than along $\mathbf{d}_2$ and $\mathbf{d}_3$, the normal directions spanning the cross-sectional plane.

The centerline is represented as a chain of $(n+2)$ nodes $\mathbf{x}_0, ..., \mathbf{x}_{n+2}$, and $(n+1)$ straight edges $\mathbf{e}^0, ..., \mathbf{e}^{n+1}$ such that $\mathbf{e}^i = \mathbf{x}_{i+1} - \mathbf{x}_i$. In our inhomogeneous composition, we also place (n) elastic joints $\mathbf{j}^i, i \in [0, n]$ between the edge segments along the centerline (see Fig.1). Each joint is a volumetric elastic solid that produces strains along two normal directions spanning the cross sectional neighborhood, as well as a strain along the tangent direction of the centerline. Each edge is considered as a rigid bar segment that connects two joints by kinematic constraints.

4. VOLUMETRIC ELASTIC JOINTS

Our generalized continuum formulation does not explicitly represent the material twist using a material frame, instead, bending strains of thin elastic joints also incorporate a measurement for twisting deformations. Edge length constraints are maintained through a post integration step.

When the rod is in the rest state, the centre of mass of the joints $\bar{\mathbf{a}}^i, i \in [0, n-1]$ coincides with the centerline nodes, $\bar{\mathbf{x}}_i, i \in [0, n+1]$, where bar represents all quantities associated with the undeformed reference frame. When the material undergoes a deformation, the thin elastic joint has its two endpoints $\mathbf{j}^{i-}$ and $\mathbf{j}^{i+}$ constrained to edge segments $\mathbf{e}^i$ and $\mathbf{e}^{i+1}, i \in [0, n]$, respectively, and with its center of mass at $\mathbf{a}^i$ (see Fig.1).

4.1 Strains about the centerline

We begin with the classical theory of solid elastica [18] by considering a material whose undeformed positions $\bar{\mathbf{x}}(\xi)$ are parameterized by the curvilinear coordinates $\xi = (\xi_1, \xi_2, \xi_3)^T$, over the material domain Ω. When the material is deformed under external forces, the undeformed point $\bar{\mathbf{x}}(\xi)$ is moved to a new position taken into a account of the deformation in the world space $\mathbf{u}(\xi)$, such that:

$$\mathbf{x}(\xi) = \bar{\mathbf{x}}(\xi) + \mathbf{u}(\xi). \tag{1}$$

We choose a 3×3 linear Cauchy strain ε to measure the deformation

$$\epsilon_{ij} = \frac{1}{2}(\mathbf{u}_{,i} \cdot \bar{\mathbf{x}}_{,j} + \bar{\mathbf{x}}_{,i} \cdot \mathbf{u}_{,j}). \tag{2}$$

where the comma denotes partial differentiation, e.g. $\mathbf{u}_{,i} \equiv \partial\mathbf{u}/\partial\xi_i$, $\bar{\mathbf{x}}_{,j} \equiv \partial\bar{\mathbf{x}}/\partial\xi_j$, $\mathbf{u}_{,ij} \equiv \partial\mathbf{u}^2/\partial\xi_i\partial\xi_j$, and $\bar{\mathbf{x}}_{,i}$ and $\mathbf{x}_{,i}$ are the local frames of the undeformed and deformed configuration, respectively.

The constitutive law computes the 3×3 symmetric internal stress tensor σ for each material point based on the strain at that point. Assuming a Hookean material, it yields a linear relation between the stress and the strain:

$$\sigma = C(\epsilon). \qquad (3)$$

where $C = C_{ijkl}$ is the elasticity tensor contains the elastic coefficients (Young's modulus, Poisson's ratio) of the material. The stored elastic energy W is the integral of the volumetric energy density, over the material domain:

$$W = \int \epsilon_{ij} C_{ijkl} \epsilon_{kl} \, d\Omega, \qquad (4)$$

As a result of the deformation, forces on the nodes due to a strain correspond to the variational derivatives of the energy with respect to nodal positions $\partial W / \partial \mathbf{u}$. To compute the strain about the centerline, for small extents along both normals $\mathbf{d}_2$ and $\mathbf{d}_3$, we linearly approximate positions and displacements as:

$$\begin{aligned}
\bar{\mathbf{x}}(\xi) &\approx \bar{\mathbf{x}}(\xi_0) + \xi_2 \bar{\mathbf{x}}_{,2}(\xi_0) + \xi_3 \bar{\mathbf{x}}_{,3}(\xi_0), \\
\mathbf{u}(\xi) &\approx \mathbf{u}(\xi_0) + \xi_2 \mathbf{u}_{,2}(\xi_0) + \xi_3 \mathbf{u}_{,3}(\xi_0).
\end{aligned} \qquad (5)$$

Substituting into (2), performing the derivation of the small strain and discarding higher order terms in the thin direction $\mathbf{d}_2$ and $\mathbf{d}_3$ yield the linearized strain about the centerline as:

$$\varepsilon(\xi) \approx S(\xi_0) + \xi_2 B^2(\xi_0) + \xi_3 B^3(\xi_0), \qquad (6)$$

expressed in terms of the stretching strain as:

$$S_{ij} = \frac{1}{2}(\mathbf{u}_{,i} \cdot \bar{\mathbf{x}}_{,j} + \bar{\mathbf{x}}_{,i} \cdot \mathbf{u}_{,j}), \qquad (7)$$

and bending strains B^2 and B^3 along both normal directions $\mathbf{d}_2$ and $\mathbf{d}_3$ as:

$$\begin{aligned}
B^2_{ij} &= \frac{1}{2}(\mathbf{u}_{,i2} \cdot \bar{\mathbf{x}}_{,j} + \bar{\mathbf{x}}_{,i} \cdot \mathbf{u}_{,j2} + \mathbf{u}_{,i} \cdot \bar{\mathbf{x}}_{,j2} + \bar{\mathbf{x}}_{,i2} \cdot \mathbf{u}_{,j}), \\
B^3_{ij} &= \frac{1}{2}(\mathbf{u}_{,i3} \cdot \bar{\mathbf{x}}_{,j} + \bar{\mathbf{x}}_{,i} \cdot \mathbf{u}_{,j3} + \mathbf{u}_{,i} \cdot \bar{\mathbf{x}}_{,j3} + \bar{\mathbf{x}}_{,i3} \cdot \mathbf{u}_{,j}) \quad (8)
\end{aligned}$$

4.2 Remark on bending and twisting

Strains of joints: By construction of our local joint element parameterization, the first order derivatives in bending strains (8), $\bar{\mathbf{x}}_{,j}$, are the joint's axes, and the second order derivatives $\bar{\mathbf{x}}_{,j2}, \bar{\mathbf{x}}_{,j3}$ vanish. Rearranging (8) yields:

$$\begin{aligned}
B^2_{ij} &= \frac{1}{2}(\mathbf{u}_{,i2} \cdot \bar{\mathbf{x}}_{,j} + \bar{\mathbf{x}}_{,i} \cdot \mathbf{u}_{,j2}), \\
B^3_{ij} &= \frac{1}{2}(\mathbf{u}_{,i3} \cdot \bar{\mathbf{x}}_{,j} + \bar{\mathbf{x}}_{,i} \cdot \mathbf{u}_{,j3}), \quad (9)
\end{aligned}$$

where bending strains along two normal directions $\mathbf{d}_2$ and $\mathbf{d}_3$ are $\bar{\mathbf{x}}_{,1} \cdot \mathbf{u}_{,32}$, and $\bar{\mathbf{x}}_{,1} \cdot \mathbf{u}_{,23}$, respectively. The twist of a rod can be computed as $\mathbf{u}_{,12} \cdot \bar{\mathbf{x}}_{,3}$, or $\bar{\mathbf{x}}_{,2} \cdot \mathbf{u}_{,13}$. The Kirchhoff rod conditions state that the centerline of an elastic rod is a Cosserat curve which is inextensible and unshearable. Therefore, the material frame is orthonormal at every point on the curved centerline and the values of the two twists are the same under the Kirchhoff rod conditions. From (9), the bending strains in (9) also incorporate a measurement for twisting deformations. In the appendix, we derive the expression for the bending and twisting strains using the Kirchhoff rod model, resulting in the same strain expressions as our generalized continuum model.

Strains of edges In our 1D rod configurations, the strain of edge segments, e.g bar elements, leads to the known stiffness equivalence rule for springs in series. This is due to the fact that spring's stiffness k is equal to the spring's elastic compliance C divided by its rest length $k = \frac{EA}{L}$, where E is Young's modulus of bar, A is the cross sectional area of bar, and L is the rest length of bar.

Consider two edge bars, one with stiffness k_1 between $\mathbf{x}_0$ and $\mathbf{x}_1$, and the other with stiffness k_2 between $\mathbf{x}_1$ and $\mathbf{x}_2$. With the position of $\mathbf{x}_0$ fixed, the two bars are connected by an elastic joint $\mathbf{j}^0$. The harmonic displacement h, must satisfy the following conditions:

5. FORCES ON THE CENTERLINE

The analytic integration in the normal directions $\mathbf{d}_2$ and $\mathbf{d}_3$ yields the remaining one-dimensional integral of the axial energy density over the centerline, described in the discrete form as:

$$W = \sum_{i=0}^{n-1} \frac{h^2}{2} S_{ij} C_{ijkl} S_{kl} + \frac{r^2}{12} B^2_{ij} C_{ijkl} B^2_{kl} + \frac{r^2}{12} B^3_{ij} C_{ijkl} B^3_{kl}, \qquad (10)$$

The dimension of the joint r is a predefined constant for the thickness of a volumetric joint along two normal directions, e.g. the radius of the rod.

With the finite element implementation of the linear elasticity, displacements are stored in a vector $\mathbf{u}_k$ for each time step and a stiffness matrix $\mathbf{K}$ is assembled so that the potential energy of each elastic joint becomes $\frac{1}{2}(\mathbf{u}_k^T \mathbf{K} \mathbf{u}_k)$. The displacements $\mathbf{u}(x)$ are interpolated inside the elastic joints using a weighted sum of the function values at the nodes $\mathbf{x}_i$, where $u(x) = \sum_i \phi_i(x) u_i$, where the $\phi_i(x)$ are called shape functions. Assuming that thin elastic joints undergo small deformations, we use a linear shape function for the joints. The equations of motion is an ODE:

$$\mathbf{M}\ddot{\mathbf{u}} + \mathbf{D}\dot{\mathbf{u}} + \mathbf{K}\mathbf{u} = \mathbf{F}^{ext} \qquad (11)$$

where $\mathbf{M}$ is the mass matrix, $\mathbf{D}$ is the damping matrix acting on the velocity vector $\dot{\mathbf{u}}$, and $\mathbf{F}^{ext}$ are external forces applied to the rod.

The linear strain measurements in our system leads a fast and stable simulation by co-rotational methods [19, 22]. We employ an efficient update of the rotation matrices $\mathbf{R}$ as proposed by Mezger et al [20]. This method estimates the change of the co-rotation $\mathbf{R}$ of an element and evaluates the difference of deformation gradients between the last time step and the current time step. The force field in the elastic rod thus becomes:

$$\mathbb{F} = \frac{1}{2} \sum_{j=0}^{n} [\mathbf{R}^j \mathbf{K}^j \mathbf{R}^{jT} (\mathbf{u} - \mathbf{a}_j) - 2\mathbf{R}^j \mathbf{K}^j (\bar{\mathbf{x}}_j - \bar{\mathbf{a}}_j)]. \qquad (12)$$

where $\mathbf{a}_j$ and $\bar{\mathbf{a}}_j$ are the center of mass of the edges and the elastic joints in the deformed and undeformed states, respectively.

6. TIME INTEGRATION

We use a cheap explicit Euler time integration scheme for our rod simulation with constant time steps. A mixed explicit/implicit time integration scheme with constant time steps [8] can also be used to improve the simulation accuracy. The advantage is to combine the flexibility and simplicity of explicit methods (such as a Runge-Kutta) with the efficiency of implicit schemes (such as backward Euler). However, we observe no significant noticeable visual artifacts with the explicit integration scheme.

6.1 Enforce inextensibility of the rod

For simulating inextensible rods, edge length constraints for the centerline are enforced. Many approaches were presented in the literature for maintaining constraints acting on a mechanical system. In particular, the penalty method formulates geometric constraints as energy functions and minimizes the energy to satisfy the constraints [1, 30]. The penalty forces are unacceptably stiff and require small time steps to ensure stability. Alternatively, using an augmented Lagrangian formulation introduces additional variables (i.e. Lagrange multipliers)to be solved during the time integration step. In order to ensure more stable simulations, post integration methods such as strain rate limiting method was proposedto enforce inextensibility of springs as a velocity-filtering pass [8]. Another post integration paradigm was manifold projection methods [12], which integrates a mechanical system by alternating between an unconstrained time integration step and a constraint enforcement step. The post integration methods enable the design of modular systems with mix-and-match flexibility [12]. We choose to maintain the length of the edge segments using this approach.

Our inextensibility enforcement procedure can be described in two steps: 1)compute the potential forces with an explicit Euler step to obtain the unconstrained position, $\mathbf{x}_0^{n+1}$, and the center of mass for the edge segment $\mathbf{a}_0^{n+1}$ and the joint element $\mathbf{a}_{j0}^{n+1}$; 2) enforce the constraints by projecting onto the constraint manifold.

Constraints are expressed in quadratic forms:

$$C(\mathbf{x}_{ij}) = \frac{\|\mathbf{a}_i - \mathbf{a}^j\|^2}{4L} - \frac{L}{4} = 0, \qquad (13)$$

We propose a modified fast manifold projection by considering the strain of each joint element along the tangent direction as the constrained gradient to *pull/pushe* the center of mass of the edge segment onto the constrained manifold $\mathbf{a}_0^{n+1} + \delta\mathbf{a}_0^{n+1}$. The two endpoints of each joint are used to project the edge length constrains in just a few enforcement steps.

6.2 Collision detection and response

Deformable collision detection is an essential component in interactive physically-based simulation and animation. Highly flexible structures such as elastic rods have the possibility of self-colliding at multiple places. A stochastic collision approach with a two-steps scheme is used to process collisions and self-collisions. Firstly, computing the local distance minima for edge segments. Secondly, when a collision occurs between two edges, a recursive algorithm is applied to search the neighborhood for possible collisions. In order to provide a robust collision response, collisions are propagated from the collision point to the joints with a

collision response applied to these joints. Collision response is computed as a penalty force.

7. RESULTS

In order to demonstrate the efficacy of thin elastic joints for rod simulation, we test our approach on a number of experiments that are intended to illustrate the physical plausibility, robustness, numerical numerical stability, and computational efficiency of our model.

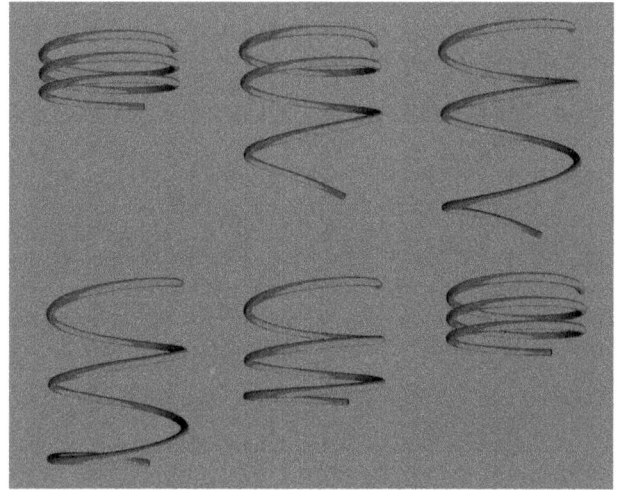

Figure 3: A spring deformation sequence shows the typical helical patterns as the pulling force is released at the distal end of the rod without moving it back towards its rest state.

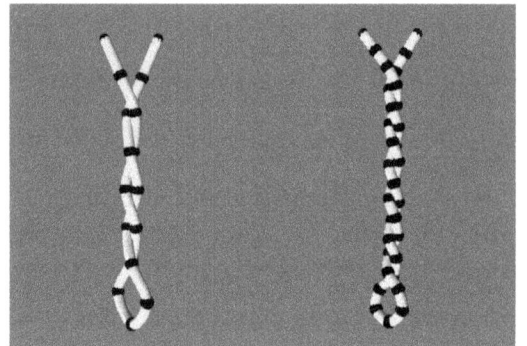

Figure 4: Twisting a rod at both ends generates a plectoneme, regardless of the length of edge segments.

Helical deformation: Fig.3 illustrates the mechanical spatial equilibria of an elastic rod with intrinsic curvatures. The proximal end of an elastic spring is fixed, while its distal end is being pulled away from its rest position for a certain distance. By releasing the pulling force, the spring tends to restore to its mechanical spatial equilibria known as helical form (the transition between helical segments of opposite ends, see Fig.3). We do not move back the distal end towards its unreformed position for shape recovering, instead simply releasing the pulling force to demonstrate

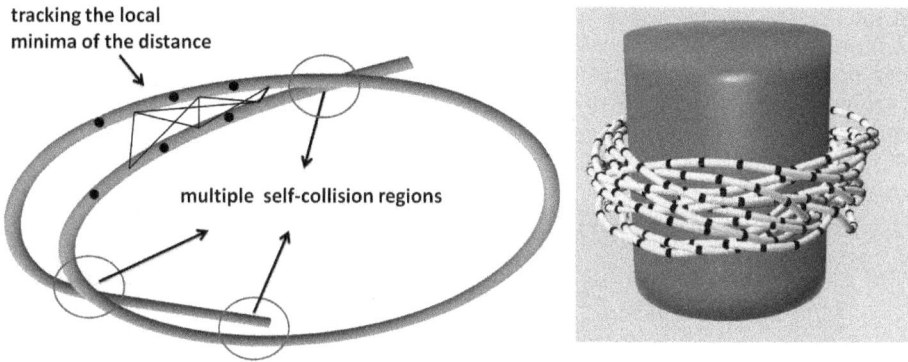

Figure 2: (left) collision and self-collision detection between different folds of rod by tracking the local minima of the distance and performing distance computations between neighboring pairs; (right) example of self-collisions.

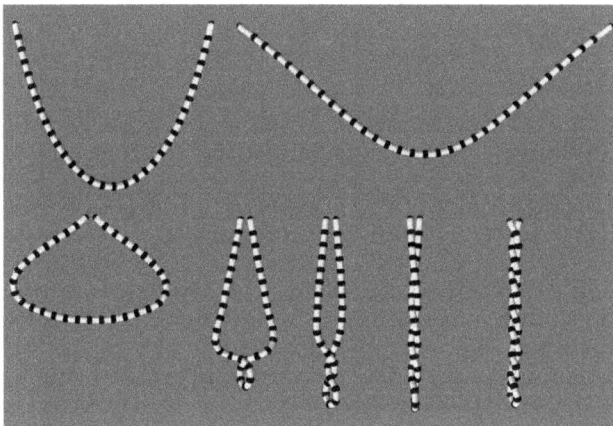

Figure 5: As a rod being held at two ends and being rapidly pulled apart then moved closely together, the balance between the effects of gravity and elastic tension leads to a plectoneme.

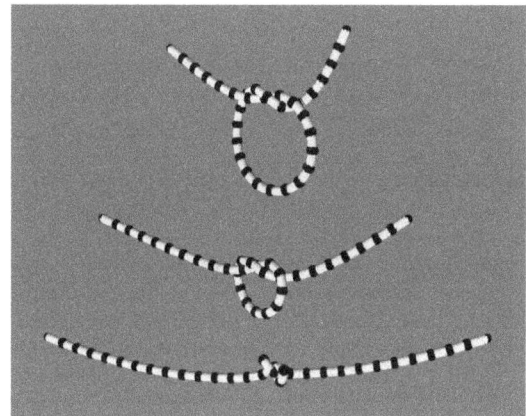

Figure 6: A knot is being tied by a sequence of movements at both ends, then is tighten by pulling the ends apart.

that the volumetric deformation field of the elastic joints can stably and accurately resolve to the stored deformation energy of the elastic rod. The deformation sequence in Fig.3 shows a spring with a high elastic modulus whose shape is recovered to its spatial equilibria near perfectly.

Plectoneme: Twisting a rod at both ends generates a plectoneme. One of benefits of our proposed heterogeneous composition for the centerline is the computational efficiency. The cost of computation for long rods grows linearly with the number of elements [5, 27], while this dependency is quadratic with approaches such as [7]. As shown in Fig.4, our model is capable of generating realistic plectonemes with varied edge lengthes without having a high joint density for simulating such elastic rod behavior.

The numerical stability and edge constraints are illustrated in a sequence of rapid movements acting at both ends of a rod: firstly pulling apart both ends rapidly to straighten the rod and simultaneously lifting the lower part of the rod (top right frame of Fig.5); then quickly putting the ends together (bottom left frame of Fig.5). By twisting at both

ends, as it is sagged under gravity, the rod tends to evolve into a plectoneme. A movement sequence at both ends also generates a knot (see Fig.6). The realism is further enhanced by pulling away the ends of the rod to tighten the knot (bottom frame of Fig.6). In the accompany video we show the visual comparison of the viscous elastic material of a real and the simulated elastic bands.

Rope coiling: When a long rope is twisted and also adding the length from the proximal end at the top, the rope rapidly coils. The radius and frequency of the coil formation depend on the height of the rod being dropped. The existence of local bifurcations along the centerline are also illustrated in Fig.11 (third, fourth and the fifth frames). Our simulation shows a hysteretic effect as the height of both ends are slowly changed by firstly moving them upward and then back down. The simulation shows different stable coiling modes for the same heights (last three frames to the right).

Buckling: When a naturally straight isotropic rod is clamped at its distal end with a constantly applied compressive force at the proximal end, as the force increasing, the rod buckles due to the sudden loss of the load-carrying capacity of elastic joints within the rod structure. The elastic joint model reproduces the buckling effect: the rod sustains the increasing stress load at a certain stage during the state of static equilibrium (top frame), buckling occurs as members of the structure becoming unstable subject to a high compressive load (the force), resulting in a laterally-deformed state and a sudden decreasing of the stress in the rod structure (see Fig.7).

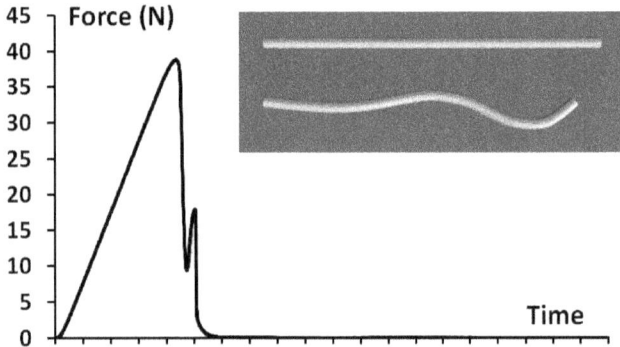

Figure 7: Localized buckling of a naturally straight, isotropic rod with an imposed high compressive force ($E = 1.0317 \times 10^6 M^2/N, r = 3.0mm$).

Viscoelasticity: An example shown in Fig.10 demonstrates a viscoelastic deformation of the rod. Both viscous and elastic characteristics coexist in the rod when undergoing a stretching deformation. An elastic rod deforms instantaneously when a force is applied and returns to its original state immediately once the force is removed. A viscoelastic rod resists strains as the result of the diffusion of the volumetric deformation field of elastic joints embedded inside the rod. When a stretching force is applied, the strain of a viscoelastic rod increases gradually until it reaches a strain limit due to the energy dissipation. Once the force is released, We observe hysteresis effect in the strain rate with time (see Fig.8). Further examples demonstrating the unique hysteresis elasticity property of the elastic rod are shown in Fig.10. To demonstrate the efficacy of the proposed model, we conduct a visual validation experiment to compare deformations of simulated viscous elasticity simulation with that of a real life object.

8. LIMITATIONS AND FUTURE WORK

The elastic joint-based model with the linear elasticity displacement and a centerline discretization offers an alternative approach for further explorations of rod simulation. The result is a nonlinear system backed up by a well established elastic theory. The model is stable and robust for simulating a wide range of rod effects. While real-time for examples presented in the paper, further optimization can improve the system: firstly, our collision handling framework can be further improved by incorporating hierarchical detection accelerations and stochastic methods would be useful for balancing the accuracy and the performance for scenes such as rope coiling.

We assume that the rod is geometrically homogeneous, i.e. it has a constant radius throughout. This assumption leads to limitations of the model for simulating fluid-like threads. The simulation of anisotropic viscous sheets would

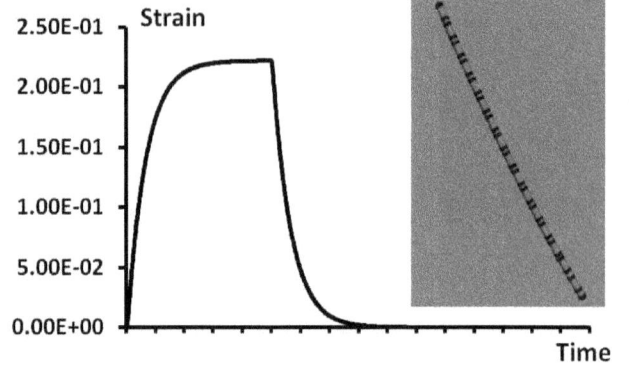

Figure 8: The distal end of a viscoelastic rod is fixed. When a pulling force is applied to its proximal end, the rod displays a time dependent strain rate due to the loss of energy ($E = 7.9365 \times 10^6 M^2/N, r = 3.0mm$).

Example	$t_{integration}$	t_{joints}	$t_{collision}$	t_{total}
Plectoneme (16)	0.26	20.60	0.11	20.98
Plectoneme (32)	0.34	32.11	0.18	32.49
Rope(150)	0.85	81.96	0.57	83.35

Figure 9: Performance table: This table summarizes the timing information (in milliseconds per simulation step) for examples depicted in the figures as measured on a single-threaded application running on a 2.66GHz Core 2 Duo.

be a direction for future work. There are many important applications which this model can be applied to. One of which is in the area of medical simulations.

9. REFERENCES

[1] D. Baraff. Linear-time dynamics using lagrange multipliers. In *Proc. of ACM SIGGRAPH '96*, pages 137–146, 1996.

[2] D. Baraff and A. Witkin. Large steps in cloth simulation. In *Proc. of ACM SIGGRAPH '98*, pages 43–54, 1998.

[3] A. W. Bargteil, C. Wojtan, J. K. Hodgins, and G. Turk. A finite element method for animating large viscoplastic flow. *ACM Trans. on Graphics*, 26(3):16:1–16:8, 2007.

[4] M. Bergou, B. Audoly, E. Vouga, M. Wardetzky, and E. Grinspun. Discrete viscous threads. *ACM Trans. Graph (Proc. SIGGRAPH)*, 29(4), 2010.

[5] M. Bergou, M. Wardetzky, S. Robinson, B. Audoly, and E. Grinspun. Discrete elastic rods. *ACM Transactions on Graphics*, 27(3):63:1–63:12, 2008.

[6] F. Bertails. Linear time super-helices. 28(2):417–426, 2009.

[7] F. Bertails, B. Audoly, M.-P. Cani, B. Querleux, F. Leroy, and J.-L. Lévêque. Super-helices for

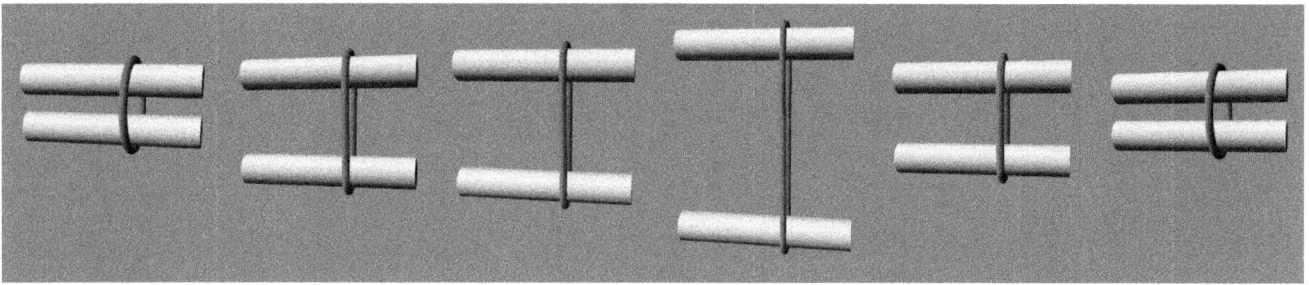

Figure 10: A unique contribution of the proposed simulation mode is the ability to generate the deformation effect of elastic bands, which, as far as authors aware, the hysteresis elasticity property has not been demonstrated in other elastic rod simulation models published in the computer graphics literature. (From left to right) A simulated elastic hair band is stretch by vertical movements of two cylinders, simulating large deformations and viscous elasticity strains. The object rapidly recovers to its relaxed configuration fully as the cylinders returning to their initial setups (see attached movie, and also a visual comparison of this effect with a real life object.

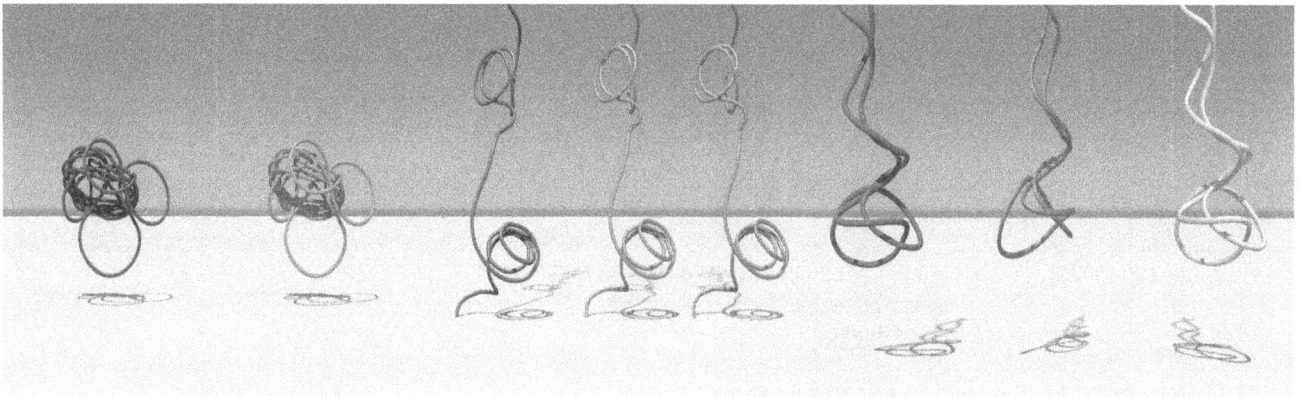

Figure 11: Thin rods are coiled into ropes. Ropes under the gravity with twists at ends create intricate coiling effects simulated by the elastic joint model.

predicting the dynamics of natural hair. *ACM Trans. Graph (Proc. SIGGRAPH)*, 25(3):1180–1187, 2006.

[8] R. Bridson, S. Marino, and R. Fedkiw. Simulation of clothing with folds and wrinkles. In *Proc. of Symp. on Computer Animation '03*, pages 28–36, 2003.

[9] F. Cirak, M. Ortiz, and P. Schröder. Subdivision surfaces: A new paradigm for thin-shell finite-element analysis. *Int. J. Numer. Methods Eng.*, 47(12):2039–2072, 2000.

[10] C. Duriez, S. Cotin, J. Lenoir, and P. Neumann. New approaches to catheter navigation for interventional radiology simulation. *Computer Aided Surgery*, pages 300–308, 2006.

[11] J. Georgii and R. Westermann. Corotated finite elements made fast and stable. In *Proc. of the 5th Workshop on Virtual Reality Interaction and Physical Simulation*, 2008.

[12] R. Goldenthal, D. Harmon, R. Fattal, M. Bercovier, and E. Grinspun. Efficient simulation of inextensible cloth. *tog*, 26(3), 2007.

[13] M. Gregoier and E. Schoer. Interactive simulation of one-dimensional flexible parts. *CAD*, 39(8):694–707, 2007.

[14] E. Grinpun, A. N. Hirani, M. Desbrun, and P. Schröder. Discrete shells. In *Proc. ACM SIGGRAPH/Eurographics Symposium on Computer Animation*, pages 62–67, 2003.

[15] S. Hadap, M. P. Cani, M. Lin, T. Y. Kim, F. Beriails, S. Marschner, K. Ward, and Z. Kacic-alesic. Strands and hair: modeling, animation, and rendering. ACM SIGGRAPH Courses 2007. pages 1–150, 2007.

[16] G. Irving, C. Schröeder, and R. Fedkiw. Volume conserving finite element simulations of deformable models. *ACM Trans. on Graphics*, 26(3):13:1–13:2, 2007.

[17] G. Irving, J. Teran, and R. Fedkiw. Invertible finite elements for robust simulation of large deformation. In *Proc. Eurographics/ACM SIGGRAPH Symposium on Computer Animation'04*, volume 31, 2004.

[18] S. Martin, P. Kaufmann, M. Botsch, E. Grinspun, and M. Gross. Unified simulation of elastic rods, shells,

and solids. *Proc. of ACM SIGGRAPH*,
29(3):39:1–39:10, 2010.

[19] M. Müller, J. Dorsey, L. McMillan, R. Jagnow, and
B. Cutler. Stable real-time deformations. In *Proc. of
the Symposium on Computer Animation*, pages 49–54,
2002.

[20] J. Mezger, B. Thomaszewski, S. Pabst, and
W. Strasser. Interactive physically-based shape
editing. In *Proc. of ACM Symp. on Solid and Physical
Modeling '08*, pages 79–89, 2008.

[21] J. P. Morris, M. B. Rubin, G. I. Block, and M. P.
Bonner. Simulations of fracture and fragmentation of
geologic materials using combined fem/dem analysis.
Hypervelocity Impact Symposium, 2005.

[22] M. Nesme, P. G. Kry, L. Jeřàbková, and F. Faure.
Preserving topology and elasticity for embedded
deformable models. *ACM Trans. Gr.*, 28(3):52:1–52:9,
2009.

[23] J. F. O'Brien and J. K. Hodgins. Graphical modeling
and animation of brittle fracture. In *Proc. ACM
SIGGRAPH*, pages 137–146, 1999.

[24] D. K. Pai. Strands: interactive simulation of thin
solids using cosserat models. 21(3):347–352, 2002.

[25] M. B. Rubin. On the theory of a cosserat point and its
application to the numerical solution of continuum
problems. *Journal of Applied Mechanics*,
52(2):368–372, 1985.

[26] A. Selle, M. Lentine, and R. Fedkiw. A mass spring
model for hair simulation. *ACM Trans. Gr.*,
27(3):64:1–64:11, 2008.

[27] J. Spillmann and M. Harders. Inextensible elastic rods
with torsional friction based on lagrange multipliers.
Computer Animations and Virtual Worlds,
21(6):561–572, 2010.

[28] J. Spillmann and M. Teschner. Corde: Cosserat rod
elements for the dynamic simulation of
one-dimensional elastic objects. In *Proc. ACM
SIGGRAPH/Eurographics Symposium on Computer
Animation*, pages 63–72, 2007.

[29] W. Tang, T. R. Wan, D. A. Gould, T. How, and
N. W. John. A stable and real-time nonlinear elastic
approach to simulating guidewire and catheter
insertions based on cosserat rod. *IEEE Trans. Biomed.
Engineering*, 59(8):2211–2218, 2012.

[30] A. Witkin, K. Fleischer, and A. Barr. Energy
constraints on parameterized models. *Computer
Graphics*, 21(4):225–232, 1987.

APPENDIX

A. DERIVATION OF STRAIN RATES IN TERMS OF THE KIRCHHOFF ROD MODEL

The spatial derivatives of the normal directors $\mathbf{d}_2'$ and $\mathbf{d}_3'$, and the tangent director $\mathbf{d}_1'$ indicate the spatial rate of change in bending and twist. From differential geometry, it is known that the Darboux vector, Ω, measures the strain rates for the bending and twisting and has the relation

$$\mathbf{d}_k^{'} = \Omega \times d_k, \quad k = 1, 2, 3 \qquad (14)$$

Since the $\mathbf{d}_k$ define an orthonormal basis, we write

$$\Omega = (\mathbf{d}_2' \cdot \mathbf{d}_3)\mathbf{d}_1 + (\mathbf{d}_3' \cdot \mathbf{d}_1)\mathbf{d}_2 + (\mathbf{d}_2' \cdot \mathbf{d}_1)\mathbf{d}_3, \qquad (15)$$

The values Ω_2 and Ω_3 measure the bending strain in the two normal directions while Ω_1 measures the twisting strain. Where $\mathbf{d}_2'$ and $\mathbf{d}_3'$ are the centerline's curvature (normal) vector. Let Let $\mathbf{x}(\xi) = \mathbf{x}(\xi_1, \xi_2, \xi_3)$ be a given deformation, the tangent vector to the coordinate curve ξ_k at $\mathbf{x}$ is given by

$$\mathbf{d}_k = \frac{\partial \mathbf{x}}{\partial \xi_k}, \quad k = 1, 2, 3 \qquad (16)$$

We write $\mathbf{d}_2' \cdot \mathbf{d}_3 = \frac{\partial^2 \mathbf{x}}{\partial \xi_1 \partial \xi_2} \cdot \frac{\partial \mathbf{x}}{\partial \xi_3}$, $\mathbf{d}_3' \cdot \mathbf{d}_1 = \frac{\partial^2 \mathbf{x}}{\partial \xi_2 \partial \xi_3} \cdot \frac{\partial \mathbf{x}}{\partial \xi_1}$, and $\mathbf{d}_2' \cdot \mathbf{d}_1 = \frac{\partial^2 \mathbf{x}}{\partial \xi_3 \partial \xi_2} \cdot \frac{\partial \mathbf{x}}{\partial \xi_1}$. Using (1) and linearizing in $\mathbf{u}$ this becomes

$$\mathbf{d}_j' \cdot \mathbf{d}_k = \frac{\partial^2 \mathbf{u}}{\partial \xi_i \partial \xi_j} \cdot \frac{\partial \bar{\mathbf{x}}}{\partial \xi_k}, \quad i, j, k = 1, 2, 3 \qquad (17)$$

We similarly obtain: $\mathbf{d}_3' \cdot \mathbf{d}_2 = \frac{\partial^2 \mathbf{u}}{\partial \xi_1 \partial \xi_3} \cdot \frac{\partial \bar{\mathbf{x}}}{\partial \xi_2}$, $\mathbf{d}_1' \cdot \mathbf{d}_3 = \frac{\partial^2 \mathbf{u}}{\partial \xi_2 \partial \xi_3} \cdot \frac{\partial \bar{\mathbf{x}}}{\partial \xi_1}$, and $\mathbf{d}_1' \cdot \mathbf{d}_2 = \frac{\partial^2 \mathbf{u}}{\partial \xi_3 \partial \xi_1} \cdot \frac{\partial \bar{\mathbf{x}}}{\partial \xi_2}$.

Modifying an Identified Position of Edged Shapes Using Pseudo-Haptic Effects

Yuki Ban
The University of Tokyo
Information Science and
Technology,7-3-1 Hongo
Tokyo, Japan
ban@cyber.t.u-
tokyo.ac.jp

Takuji Narumi
The University of Tokyo
Information Science and
Technology,7-3-1 Hongo
Tokyo, Japan
narumi@cyber.t.u-
tokyo.ac.jp

Tomohiro Tanikawa
The University of Tokyo
Information Science and
Technology,7-3-1 Hongo
Tokyo, Japan
tani@cyber.t.u-
tokyo.ac.jp

Michitaka Hirose
The University of Tokyo
Information Science and
Technology,7-3-1 Hongo
Tokyo, Japan
hirose@cyber.t.u-
tokyo.ac.jp

ABSTRACT

In our research, we are trying to realize the visuo-haptic system which can give users a sense as if they were touching on virtual objects with various shapes, using pseudo-haptic effects. In this paper, we focus on altering the identified position of edges on a object when touching it with a pointing finger, by displacing the visual representation of the user's hand as if they were touching a virtual object, in order to construct a intended visuo-haptic system. To confirm the effect of a visual feedback for altering the identified position of primitives, we composed a video see-through system, which enables us to change the perception of the shape of an object a user is visually touching, when in actuality s/he is touching another shape.

The experiments were conducted with a video see-through system we composed and their results showed the participants perceived positions of edges that was the same as the one they were visually touching, even though the positions of edges they were actually touching was different. These results prove that the perceived positions of edges could be modified, and even if the ratio of the successive distance between edges is $1:1$, we can modify the perception of this ratio from $3:2$ to $2:3$.

Categories and Subject Descriptors

H.5.2 [**User Interfaces**]: Haptic I/O

Keywords

Pseudo-haptics, Visuo-haptic interaction, Identified Shape Modification

1. INTRODUCTION

In recent virtual reality (VR) systems, haptics have become an important modality and several research have developed haptic devices. However, because it is hard to reproduce the force perfectly that we perceive when touching an object, most haptic devices exhibit very complicated problems. As a consequence, haptic devices are hardly applied to widely used systems, because a large amount of preparation work, such as installation and calibration, must be performed for each person.

While thus far in VR systems, research on haptic presentation often concerns active haptics, an increasing number of works rivet their eyes on alternative approaches such as passive haptics, which include pseudo-haptics and sensory substitution. Pseudo-haptics is an illusional phenomenon triggered by the characteristics of our senses, called crossmodal effect between our visual and haptic senses [6]. There is great potential to use these phenomena for generating haptic sensations using only visual feedback, without the need for applying any physical devices.

In our research, we use this cross-modal effect to modify the perception of shape, and construct a simple system that can show a variety of shapes, while the user actually touches only a simple static physical object (Fig.1). In other words, using a visual display and a simple physical device, we aim to exploit visual feedback to widen the range of what can be physically presented by the device. This system provokes a pseudo-haptic effect by displacing and deforming a userAfs hand image which shows that the user touches the static object.

In our system, we set out display complicated shapes that are composed of primitives. To realize this concept, we must develop two capabilities. One is that we need to display primitives, i.e. convex, edge, concave, and so on, near the

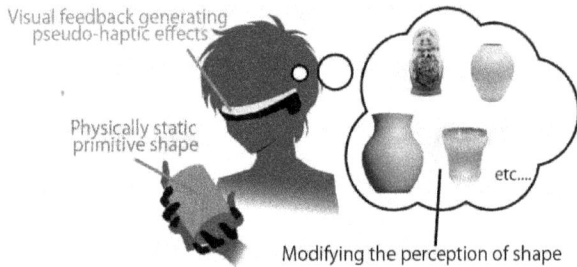

Figure 1: Displaying the shape of an object using the pseudo-haptic effect

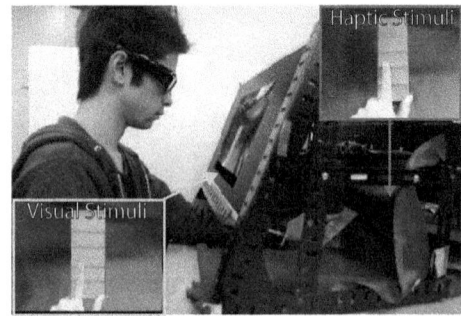

Figure 2: Shape display system using effect of a visuo-haptic interaction

point of contact. The other is that we need to set the relative postures of these primitives in an object. By combining these two capabilities, we can educe the pseudo-haptic effect and display various shapes without any complicated physical devices.

First, we used our simple system to verify the potential of altering shape perception for primitives of areas touched by the user. We have proved that using the pseudo-haptic effect, users can perceive a variety of curved shapes, while touching only a physically static cylinder [3].

The next step in our research is to use our system to examine the capability of utilizing the pseudo-haptic effect to modify an identified placement. We already revealed that the proposed system can modify an identified angle of the placement of primitives on an object [2]. So in this paper, we have experience to confirm the capability of altering an identified position of primitives.

2. RELATED WORK

While much research have been conducted about cross modal effects between our haptic sensation and other sensations, here we mainly focus on effects between our haptic sensation and vision, which we aim to use in our system.

Pseudo-haptics, which is an illusional phenomenon triggered by this characteristic of our senses, was first introduced by Lecuyer [6]. Lecuyer et al. had subjects push their thumbs against a piston, which in turn pushed against an isometric Spaceball device. Simultaneously, subjects were visually presented with a compressed virtual spring. Even though the Spaceball device was not compressed, the virtual spring influenced the perception of stiffness of the subjects. Pusch et al. proposed a pseudo-haptic approach, called hand-displacement-based pseudo-haptics (HEMP), which provides haptic-like sensations by displacing the visual representation of a userÂfs hand [7]. Research has also shown that when we are presented with conflicting sensory stimuli, our vision usually dominates in our perception of a shape. Kohli et al. proved that distorting a pointer showing the position of a device along a flat surface of a desk can change the perception of the shape of the surface [5]. Their work revealed that when subjects traced the device on the flat surface while being presented with the visual presentation as if they were tracing it on a curved surface, they visually perceived the curved one.

For modifying an identified position of primitives, it is important to confirm the influence of visual and haptic stimuli to the perception of length. Several studies were conducted to reveal the effect of visuo-haptic interactions to the perception of length[1, 4]. They examined the contribution of haptic and visual cues to the subjective estimation of object length, and revealed that the visual sense is more influential for the perception of length than the haptic sense.

However, most of these study the contribution of haptic and visual sense to a single length, to realize our proposed shape display system it is required to be able to alter the perception of two or more distances between primitives placed on an object. So in this paper, we confirm the ability of the pseudo-haptic effect to modify the perception of multi successive distances between primitives.

3. ALTERING AN IDENTIFIED PLACEMENT OF EDGES

The video see-through system (Fig.2 [2]) was used to confirmed the possibility that pseudo-haptic effects can assist in generating a perception of a position of a shape. Subjects touched a physical object placed behind a visual monitor and viewed the virtual object through the 3D monitor.

In what follows, we call the shape of the physically static object users touches, $S_{physical}$ which serves as the haptic stimuli. We call the shape of the image of an object users watched on the monitor, S_{visual} which serves as the visual stimuli. The shape of the object reported by the user as the one perceived as touching is defined as $S_{perceived}$. In this system, by changing S_{visual} to a variety of $S_{physical}$ shapes using the pseudo-haptic effect, we set out to change $S_{perceived}$ with the physically static shape of the object. Using this system, we already confirmed that an identified primitive curved surface shape and an identified angle of primitives can be modified [3, 2]. In these two experiments, we revealed that simply showing the shape of a virtual object that is different from the real one is insufficient, while showing the image of the displaced hand image is critical for altering an identified shape. Next, we conducted an experiment to confirm weather the pseudo-haptic effect can modify our perception of position of shapes or not, by displacement of a hand image. The shape of the object chosen to be touched by subjects was selected to contain edges placed at various intervals, because with this shape we could easily measure the differences between $S_{physical}$, S_{visual} and $S_{perceived}$. We constructed an algorithm used to generate the necessary visual feedback to provoke the pseudo-haptic effect, and enable us to perceive a variety of positions of edges with only edges at even intervals. The image for visual feedback was composed from the images taken by the two cameras attached, according to the following procedure.

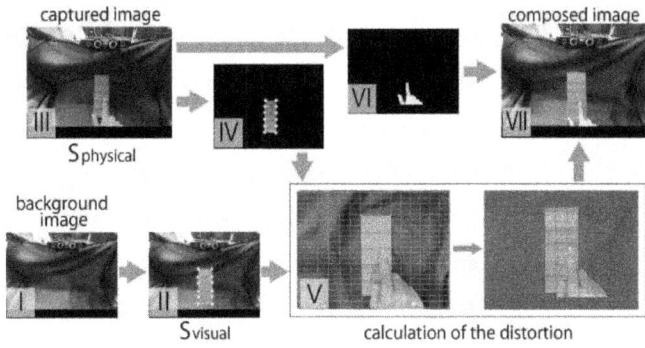

Figure 3: Procedure for manipulating a visual stimulus

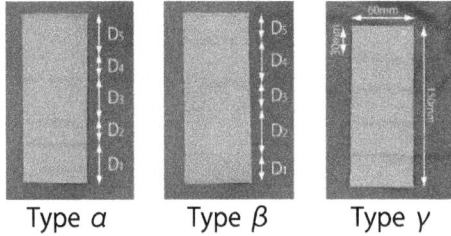

Figure 4: The three types of S_{visual} as the visual stimuli

First, The background image(I in Fig.3) taken in advance was set. From the captured images, using color extraction, we detected the area of the user's hand and the position of his fingertip(VI in Fig.3). Then, on this background image the virtual object S_{visual} was overlaid, and both ends of the angles of S_{visual}(II in Fig.3) were extracted. In a similar way, we extracted both ends of the angles of the physical object $S_{physical}$, from the image taken by the web cameras(III and IV in Fig.3). Comparing the positions of the ends of the edges, the system warped the space for the displacement of the user's hand to synchronize the timing that the finger passes the above of edges(V in Fig.3) [2]. Based on this distortion, we place the image of the user's hand at the corresponding position as if s/he was touching the virtual object(VII in Fig.3).

4. EXPERIMENT

We inspected the capability of our shape-display system to modify the perception of the position of edges. The experiment was conducted to confirm how the effect of S_{visual} altered $S_{physical}$ to $S_{perceived}$, and compared these three shapes. It can be said that we concluded that the visuo-haptic interaction was effectively provoked, meaning that the system worked as we intended, if $S_{perceived}$ was similar to S_{visual} rather than $S_{physical}$.

We chose nine kinds of boards with edges at various intervals shown in Fig.4 denoted as S_{visual}. These boards with edges are classified into three types, the type-α on which the intervals of edges are arranged in order of wide-narrow-wide... , the type-β on which the intervals of edges are arranged in order of narrow-wide-narrow... , and the type-γ on which the edges are arranged at even intervals. The type-α and the type-β have four kinds of combinations of distance between edges like Table.1. Hereinafter, the distance between edges is called $D_i(i = 1, \cdots, 5)$. For virtual bodies which shapes are the type of α_1-α_4, β_1-β_4 and γ, we

Table 1: The distance between two edges on the S_{visual} (mm)

	α_1	α_2	α_3	α_4	γ
$D_1(=D_3=D_5)$	36.5	35	34	32	30
$D_2(=D_4)$	20	22	24	27	30

	β_1	β_2	β_3	β_4
$D_1(=D_3=D_5)$	22.5	24	26	28
$D_2(=D_4)$	41	39	36	33

presented subjects with the $S_{physical}$ which shape is the type of γ in Fig.4. Virtual bodies were presented to the users in a random order. We presented users with edges at various intervals, not with only one interval with two edges. This was because we predicted that the amount of modification of the perception of the position was influenced by the relative difference of successive edges' position.

The subjects slided the edges on the device(Fig.5) and answered about the positions of the edges they felt touching. This device has four edges which can be slided freely, and the size of the board and its edges is the same as $S_{physical}$. The subjects could touch and compare the position of edges on the physical shape and device repeatedly and slided the edges of device to fit to the shape they felt touching. The positional relationship of this device and the eyes of a subject was arranged with the positional relationship of $S_{physical}$ and a subject's eyes in a trial, and the experimenter set the angle at even intervals when one trail finished.

We did not set a time limit for the subjects to answer what shape they felt, and we gave them the following instructions. We told them to watch the image presented on the monitor when touching the object and to touch the object from top to bottom as evenly as possible. Subjects were also told to touch the object with one finger. We did not hold the heads of the subjects with any equipment. Instead, we instructed them not to move their heads from the position that we initially set in realizing the video see-through system. We measured the position of the heads of the subjects, and confirmed that the subjects watched the correct video see-through image on the monitor. Subjects were not aware that they actually touched only one kind of $S_{physical}$. In each trial the experimenter only went through the motions of changing $S_{physical}$. In addition, the experimenter did not indicate whether the hand position in the monitor was actually distorted or not, and thus the subjects did not know whether S_{visual} was the same as $S_{physical}$. Eight men and two women in their twenties participated in this experiment, and two trials were conducted for each S_{visual}.

For this experiment, we conducted a control experiment in which subjects were shown the shapes they were actually touching as S_{visual}. Thus, in this control experiment, $S_{physical}$ was the same as S_{visual}. We call $Ex_{composed}$ the type of experiment in which we show the image of subject's hand on a monitor. The type of experiment that shows S_{visual} as the shape that subjects are actually touching, is called Ex_{real}. A@ During Ex_{real}, we used α_1-α_4, β_1-β_4 and γ as $S_{physical}$ which has edges at same intervals as S_{visual}. Two trials were conducted for each $S_{physical}$ in Ex_{real}. We computed the visuo-haptic effect by distorting the position of the hand touching the object and comparing the results of these experiments. By comparing the results of $Ex_{composed}$ and the result of Ex_{real}, we measured the effectiveness of the system, defined as the ability to modify the identified angle of edges.

Figure 5: Subjects answer the shape they feel by adjusting the edges of this device.

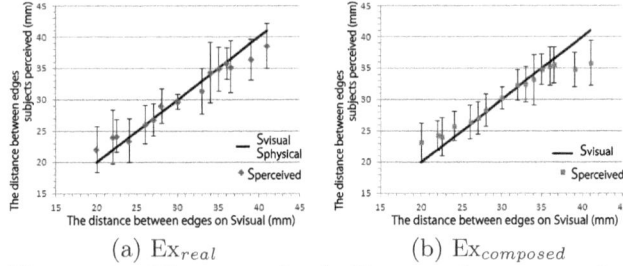

(a) Ex_{real} (b) $\text{Ex}_{composed}$

Figure 6: The perceived distance between edges (means and SDs)

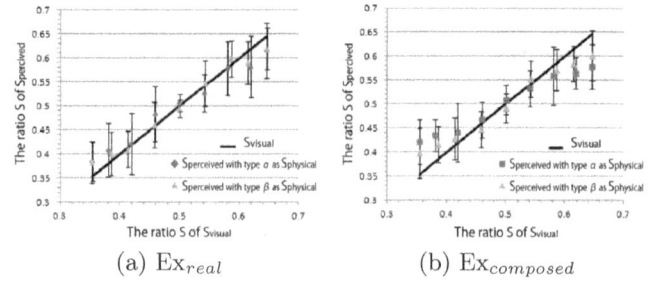

(a) Ex_{real} (b) $\text{Ex}_{composed}$

Figure 7: The ratio S of $S_{perceived}$ (means and SDs)

5. RESULTS AND DISCUSSION

Fig.6(a) shows the result of Ex_{real} and Fig.6(b) shows the result of $\text{Ex}_{composed}$ that are arranged according to the order of the distance between edges of S_{visual}. The comparison of these results shows that even though subjects were actually touching γ containing edges at even intervals, when we displayed the image of the displaced hand, they perceived a shape similar to what they perceived when touching $\alpha_i (i = 1, \cdots, 4)$ or $\beta_i (i = 1, \cdots, 4)$ as $S_{physical}$. These results indicate that even though subjects were touching edges at even intervals, the positions of edges identified by the subjects could be modified.

In these experiments, it was observed that all subjects touched objects in the particular way, that their pointing fingers went back and forth between successive intervals of edges to parallel the length between two successive intervals of edges. It seems that this is because the ratio of the distance between two successive intervals of edges influences the modification of an identified position of edges. So, we arranged these results in the order of the relative difference between two successive intervals of edges of S_{visual}. We named the ratio of the length of two successive intervals of edges as the ratio S ($S = \frac{D_i}{D_i + D_{i+1}}$).

In the $\text{Ex}_{composed}$, the ratio S of $S_{physical}$ is always 0.5, because subjects only touched the shape of γ as $S_{physical}$ in this experiment. Using this ratio S, we arranged the results of Ex_{real} in Fig.7(a), and $\text{Ex}_{composed}$ in Fig.7(b). These two results are almost in agreement if the ratio S is settled in 0.38 to 0.62. On the contrary, using a paired t test, there is a significant difference between the ratio S of S_{visual} and $S_{perceived}$ ($p<0.05$), if the ratio S of S_{visual} is over 0.65 or less than 0.35. So, it can be said that our proposed method can modify an identified position of edges, and even if the ratio of the successive distances between edges on objects they actually touching is 1 : 1, it is possible to modify the ratio 2 : 3 (the ratio S = 0.38) to 3 : 2 (the ratio S = 0.62).

6. CONCLUSION AND FUTURE WORK

This paper evaluate the effectiveness of modifying an iden-

tified position of shapes using a visuo-haptic shape display system. In this study, we focused on modifying an identified position of primitives, edges. We conducted an experiment to evaluate the effectiveness of the proposed system, and a large portion of the subjects felt that they were not touching the shape of the haptic stimuli, but rather the shape of the object visually presented. This proved that our system can modify the perception of the relative difference between two successive distance between edges, and even if the ratio of the successive distance between edges is 1 : 1, we can modify the perception of this ratio from 3 : 2 to 2 : 3. Thus, we conclude that it is possible to modify an identified position of primitives, such as edges, by using visual feedback similar to the one used in our system.

To derive more detailed specifications for the system, we should measure the range of perception of the position that we can generate using pseudo-haptic effects, and examine whether it is possible to modify the identified position and angle of a shape. Based on these measurements, we can decide on the range and accuracy of shapes we should generate with physical devices. Then, we can compose the physical devices and visual display to generate the visual feedback, and construct a system, which give users the sense of touching a variety of shapes.

7. REFERENCES

[1] E. Abravanel. The synthesis of length within and between perceptual systems. *Attention, Perception, & Psychophysics*, 9(4):327—328, 1971.

[2] Y. B. et al. Modifying an identified angle of edged shapes using pseudo-haptic effect. *EuroHaptics2012*, 2012.

[3] Y. B. et al. Modifying an identified curved surface shape using pseudo-haptic effect. *HAPTICS2012*, 2012.

[4] B. Jones. Psychological analyses of haptic and haptic-visual judgements of extent. *The Quarterly Journal of Experimental Psychology*, 35(4):597–606, 1983.

[5] L. Kohli. Exploiting perceptual illusions to enhance passive haptics. *IEEE VR Workshop on Perceptual Illusions in Virtual Environments*, pages 22–24, 2009.

[6] A. Lecuyer. Simuling haptic feedback using vision: A survey of research and applications of pseudo-haptic feedback. *Teleoperators and Virtual Environments*, 18(1):39–53, 2009.

[7] A. Pusch, O. Martin, and S. Coquillart. Hemp–hand-displacement-based pseudo-haptics: A study of a force field application and a behavioural analysis. *International Journal of Human-Computer Studies*, 67(3):256–268, 2009.

CrOS: A Touch Screen Interaction Technique for Cursor Manipulation on 2-manifolds

Manuel Veit
Holo3 – Schiltigheim, France
m.veit@holo3.com

Antonio Capobianco
University of Strasbourg –
LSIIT, CNRS UMR 7005
a.capobianco@unistra.fr

Dominique Bechmann
University of Strasbourg –
LSIIT, CNRS UMR 7005
bechmann@unistra.fr

ABSTRACT

We present a new Virtual Reality (VR) interaction technique for cursor manipulation on 3-D surfaces (2-manifolds) using touch screen input, named Cursor On Surface (CrOS). Its purpose is to easily perform complex modelling operations in VR. CrOS is based on an algorithm which maps 2-D inputs into cursor displacements on 3-D surfaces. Its design rely relies on two principles. Firstly, it restricts the manipulation space to a 2-D space. Secondly, it reduces the complexity of the task through an automatic orientation algorithm that prevent the user from switching between edition task and object repositioning task.

Categories and Subject Descriptors

H.5.1 [**INFORMATION INTERFACES AND PRESENTATION**]: Multimedia Information Systems—*Artificial, augmented, and virtual realities*; I.3.6 [**COMPUTER GRAPHICS**]: Methodology and Techniques Interaction techniques

Keywords

Interaction Technique; Touch Screen Interaction; Virtual Reality; Geometric Modelling

1. INTRODUCTION

In VR, many tasks are similar to moving a point of interest (virtual pointer for editing tasks, camera view-point for navigation tasks) along a constrained or freely defined path. For example, painting on the surface of an object usually requires to be able to draw long strokes on the surface of an object, sometimes on parts of the object that are initially hidden from the view of the user [1]. Sketching tasks also require to edit paths that define the general shape of an object to create, such as in the Terrain Sketching application [2].

In many contexts, navigating is also similar to following a path. Usually, when navigating in 3-D virtual worlds, one freely decides the path to follow, and displaces the camera view-point by moving it on a 2-D surface at the users' view height. In other situations of use, however, the task can be much more complex. For example, multi-scale navigation imply to navigate through 3-D scenes that

extend at many levels: country, city, houses, or even objects laying on a table [3]. Medical applications can also show complex sets of 3-D objects, such as vessels segmentation derived from contrast-enhanced magnetic resonance angiography. Schooten et al. [4] suggest that defining a path for navigation on the objects' surface is an efficient solution to navigate in the 3-D representation of the data .

We propose a new interaction technique named CrOS. Its purpose is to move a Cursor of Interaction (CI) on a 3-D surface using 2-D touch screen input. The displacements on the surface of the touch screen are transformed, through a mapping algorithm, in displacements on the surface of the object. The technique allows to displace a CI to either select an object or define a path on a surface. It also allows to explore the surface of the object by simply moving the CI towards a distant point of interest. In the remaining of this paper, we will focus on the context of path-based interaction for editing tasks, since the work we present here was conducted in the context of Geometric Modelling Applications (GMA). However, we think that the technique can be used in any situation where the task requires to displace a CI along an implicit or explicit surface.

In the next section, we introduce the previous works related to our purpose. Then, in Section 3, we describe the implementation of CrOS. In particular, we describe the two algorithms we propose: the first one which computes the geodesic displacements, the second one which computes the reorientation of the object.

2. PREVIOUS WORKS

Manipulations in 3-D immersive environments are often performed using 6 Degrees of Freedom (DoF) devices and techniques, while the tasks to handle are less complex, causing an unnecessary increase of the cognitive load [5]. To avoid this phenomenon, it has been shown that the control properties of the device should match the perceptual structure of the task [6]. In other words, the dimensions of manipulation must correspond to the particular task at end, and should mirror the mental representation of the task. Moreover, with 6 DoF devices, the manipulation is usually performed in the mid-air, introducing fatigue that can impair users' comfort and limit their precision [7].

To overcome these issues, several techniques propose to use 2-D devices (e.g. a mouse or a touch screen) to perform manipulations in a 3-D environment. The *Balloon Selection* technique, designed by Benko et al. [8], consists of positioning a selection cursor in the 3-D space using touch screen interaction. With this technique, the users can freely position a CI in a 3-D environement, but it is not designed to perform manipulations on the surfaces of the objects. Smith et al. also propose to manipulate objects in a 3-D environment using 2-D devices [9]. To simplify the task, they introduce constraints on the possible positions of objects. They show that their technique is much more efficient than free interaction with 3-D devices.

Using 2-D devices for navigation tasks has also been proposed. The *Navidget* technique uses 2-D inputs for navigating in 3-D environments [10]. The user simply designates the part of an object he/she wants to explore, and the technique automatically computes a position for the camera that will ensure an adequate view of the object. However, it is a flying technique, that does not allow to control the path followed by the user's view-point. Hanson et al. [11] propose a technique based on the idea of a constrained manipulation to navigate in a 3-D space using a mouse. To this purpose, they use a *surface for navigation* to move in a 3-D scene. One major difficulty to implement this technique is to compute the displacements on the surface for navigation. Their approach is quite similar to the approaches used in the parametrisation of surfaces. They unfold the surface over a 2-D surface. By moving on the unfolded surface, the user moves on the original surface. This technique however has been designed for controlling camera viewpoints during navigation tasks and isn't adapted for other tasks (such as modelling tasks for instance). Moreover, this technique has not been tested using complex surfaces, presenting hidden parts, or numerous holes and bends.

The idea of constraining the manipulation to a 2-D surface to match the dimension of the task has also been implemented using haptic devices. The ArtNova technique uses force feedback to apply textures on a 3-D surface [12]. It also implements an automatic orientation algorithm that avoids switching between edition task and camera repositioning task. This is likely to reduce the cognitive load of the task, and Foskey et al. report that an informal study suggested that it was both efficient and intuitive.

In the next section we present the implementation method and the design principles of CrOS, a technique that combines several ideas from the above techniques: the use of a 2-D device for manipulation on a 2-manifold, combined with an automatic reorientation of the manipulated object.

3. CROS

Our objective is to develop an intuitive technique for precise and efficient interaction on the surface of an object. With this technique, we want to perform several complex modelling operations (e.g. sculpting, colouring or topological manipulation) in VR. It must allow to precisely designate a point of interaction or define a path on the surface. It is also important that it is adapted to complex surfaces presenting numerous holes and bends.

To this purpose, we place a CI on the surface of the object. The cursor is then moved using 2-D displacements performed through touch screen interaction. CrOS maps the users' hands movements into geodesic displacements on the surface of the 3-D object. In the remainder of this paper, we consider that this is performed by the *mapping function*. These geodesic displacements are then used to move the CI.

3.1 The mapping function

From a geometrical point of view, mapping 2-D displacements on a 3-D surface is similar to the problem of finding a parameterization of a surface. However, algorithms used to find a local or a global parameterization of a surface [13] are generally time consuming [14] and may introduce latency. This is known to decrease the users' performance by reducing accuracy and increasing achievement times [15]. This is why, with the algorithm we propose, we focus on trying to introduce a low computational time. Moreover, the algorithm tries to comply at best with the princi-

ples of the Directional Stimuli - Response Compatibility (DSRC) (which is not possible when using a parameterization).

In order to reduce the computational cost, our solution is based on a method using only the local geometry of the object around the CI. The idea is that, for a given point on the surface of the object, each direction within the tangent plane to the surface at this point can be projected onto a geodesic path on the surface (see Figure 1). It is important to note that this statement is only true for 2-manifolds (i.e. surfaces that are locally similar to 2-D Euclidean space at each position on the surface).

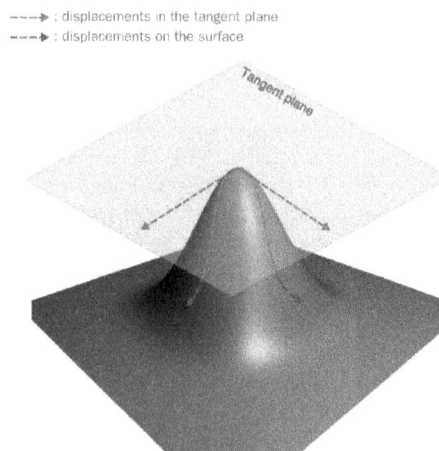

Figure 1: Two 2-D displacements transformed in geodesic displacements on the surface of the object (used to move the cursor located on the top of the bump).

This geodesic path can be considered as a part of the intersection between a plane (called *geodesic plane*) and the surface. To ensure a good compatibility between the displacements performed by the user on the touch screen and the CI, the geodesic plane: is orthogonal to the tangent plane, contains the 2-D movement and passes through the position of the CI (see Figure 2).

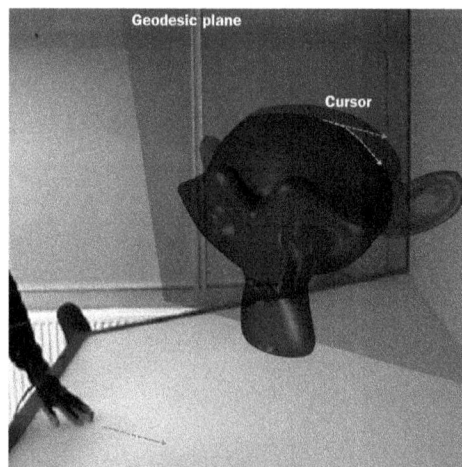

Figure 2: We can see that the geodesic displacement on the surface is defined as a part of the intersection between the 3-D object and the geodesic plane.

To implement the mapping function, we do not make any assumptions on the data structure used to represent the 3-D objects.

In order to be efficient, it is preferable to use a data structure providing information about the topology of the object. More specifically, it is recommended to have access for each face of the object, to all adjacent faces.

3.1.1 Definitions

To formally describe the algorithm, we use the following geometrical entities:

- P_c (the control plane): the plane in which the user performs the 2-D displacements;

- $\vec{N}_c$: the normal associated to the plane P_c. In our case, $\vec{N}_c = (0,1,0)$;

- P_g (the geodesic plane): the plane used to compute the displacement on the surface of the object;

- $\vec{N}_g$: the normal associated to the plane P_g;

- $\vec{D}$: 2-D movement performed by the user on the control plane. In practice, this displacement is represented by a 3-D vector whose y coordinate is considered as null;

- I_{path}: the intersection between P_g and the 3-D object. The intersection is stored as a polygonal line (closed or open) containing the list of intersection points between the edges and vertexes, and the plane.

3.1.2 Geodesic plane computation

The constraints used to define the geodesic plane P_g are the following:

- The plane passes through the CI;

- The plane contains the displacement specified by the user;

- The plane is orthogonal to the tangent plane at the current position of the CI.

From these characteristics, it is possible to define geometrically P_g. First, we define $\vec{N}_g$ as follows:

$$\vec{N}_g = A \times (\vec{D} \times \vec{N}_c)$$

A is the matrix representing the minimum rigid body transformation between $\vec{N}_c$ and the surface's normal at the CI. In other words, if $\vec{N}_s$ is the normal of the surface at the position of the CI, $\vec{N}_s = A \times \vec{N}_c$.

By defining the normal of the plane, we define three of the four unknowns of its equation. The fourth unknown can be easily computed using the fact that the CI is contained in the plane. Using P_g, we are now able to compute the geodesic path.

3.1.3 Computing the intersection

The approach we use to compute the intersection I_{path} is incremental. A naive approach would be to compute the entire intersection between P_g and the 3-D object, to finally select the part of the intersection corresponding to the geodesic path. This calculation would be in $O(n)$ where n is the number of edges of the mesh. We propose an approach where I_{path} is constructed incrementally, reducing the computation time to $O(m)$ where m is the number of vertexes or edges belonging to the geodesic path. This gain is significant especially for objects with a high level of details.

First, we consider that the CI is on a face F. The first vertex of the geodesic path is the CI itself. The intersection between F and

P_g is a line with at least two vertexes that are on the edges of F or are vertexes of F. The question that arises is: "Which vertex belongs to the geodesic path?". By choosing the wrong vertex, we introduce an inversion in the relationship between the direction of the CI's displacement and the direction of the user's movement.

We choose the vertex so that, $\vec{V}_g.\vec{D} > 0$, with $\vec{V}_g = $ tested vertex − position of the CI. This test indicates whether the displacement on the surface induces a movement whose projection on P_c is in the same direction as $\vec{D}$ or not. If the condition is satisfied, the vertex belongs to the geodesic path I_{path}. This condition ensures the DSRC. Now that we found the first vertex of I_{path}, the construction of the rest of the geodesic path can be done incrementally and without ambiguity using the following algorithm:

Algorithm 1 How to compute I_{path}

Ensure: I_{path}
  $geoPathLength = \| \vec{D} \|$
  $firstInter = $ first intersection
  $interEdge = $ edge on which is $firstInter$
  $curFace = $ adjacent face to F and incident to $interEdge$
  $geodesicPath = cursorPosition, firstInter$
  $curGeoPathLength = length(cursorPosition - firstInter)$
  while $curGeoPathLength < geoPathLength$ **do**
    $curInterEdge = $ edge intersected by P_g different of $interEdge$
    $curInter = $ point of intersection between P_g and $curInterEdge$
    $curGeoPathLength += \| curInter - geodesicPath.back() \|$
    add the intersection with $curInterEdge$ to I_{path}
    $interEdge = curInterEdge$
    $curFace = $ face adjacent to $curFace$, incident to $curInterEdge$
  end while

Finally, the position of the CI after the displacement is defined as the position on I_{path} such that the distance between the previous and the current position of the CI is equal to the length of the displacement made by the user on the control plane.

3.2 Automatic orientation

Because of the possible complex geometry of the object, the user might have to repeatedly modify the orientation of the object, introducing multiple switches between the cursor manipulation and the object's orientation correction. To avoid this problem, we propose to add to the technique an orientation algorithm, that automatically rotates the object according to the displacements of the cursor on the surface and the position of the head of the user. This reduces the number of DoF, and thus the complexity of the task. For users, this should mean a reduction of the cognitive load allowing them to achieve higher performances and an increased usability, despite the fact that such a technique reduces predictability.

We implemented an algorithm to automatically orientate the object in order to provide the user with an appropriate point of view toward the cursor. This algorithm follows two rules:

1. When the angular distance between $\vec{N}_c$ and the viewing direction of the user toward the CI is over a threshold (e.g. 85 degrees), we rotate the object to align these two directions;

2. The orientation correction is performed when the above-mentioned criterion is not respected for at least one second.

This mechanism ensures an optimal DSRC during the whole manipulation and provides an appropriate point of view to the cursor being manipulated. To avoid sudden changes of the object, all corrections are progressively and smoothly applied.

4. PROTOTYPE EVALUATION

We developed a proof-of-concept prototype using our VR environment. The apparatus used is a Barco Consul providing stereoscopic display with two screen having a resolution of 1400x1050, with a refresh rate of 120 Hz. The images were generated using two workstations (one for each screen) fit out with a 3GHz Intel Quad Core and a NVIDIA FX 5600. The head and hands tracking was provided by an ART tracking system and optical trackers. The apparatus is completed by two XIST Data Gloves to interact with the environment.

We used the lower screen of the Workbench (which is at arms' reach) as a touch screen interface. Using the pressure sensors placed at the extremities of the fingers of the data gloves, we are able to detect whether the user is touching the screen or not. The displacements of the hands are computed using the optical tracking system, and CrOS transforms the users' hands movements into geodesic displacements on the surface of the object (see Figure 3).

We asked 12 participants, with prior experience with VR environments, to perform 20 selection tasks and 9 curve steering tasks using this prototype and give an informal feedback. We were particularly interested in knowing if the technique was adapted to the tasks and if the automatic orientation was not disturbing.

The participants reported that the technique was pleasant to use, and adapted to the tasks they had to perform. We also asked if the automatic orientation didn't hinder the manipulation, especially during the steering task. However, it seems that they were able to handle this behaviour of CrOS without hindering the manipulation.

5. CONCLUSION AND FUTURE WORK

In this paper, we proposed a new technique of interaction for editing 3-D objects, called CrOS. This technique uses touch screen interaction to control a cursor constrained to the surface of the object. It also implements an orientation algorithm that allows users to focus on the task at hand: the manipulation of the cursor. Based on preliminary users' feedback, we believe that this technique can be efficient to perform complex modelling operations in immersive VR environments using touch screen devices. We have already developed a new prototype using state of the art touch screen devices. We are now working on the formal evaluation of this technique to better assess its advantages for the user, its performance during selection and curve steering tasks, and its potential limits and drawbacks.

6. REFERENCES

[1] CW. Fu, J. Xia, and Y. He. LayerPaint: a multi-layer interactive 3-D painting interface. In Proceedings of the 28th international conference on Human factors in computing systems (CHI '10). ACM, New York, NY, USA, 811-820, 2010.

[2] J. Gain, P. Marais, and W. Straßer. Terrain sketching. In Proceedings of the 2009 symposium on Interactive 3-D graphics and games (I3D '09). ACM, New York, NY, USA, 31-38, 2009.

[3] J. McCrae, I. Mordatch, M. Glueck, A. Khan, Multiscale 3-D navigation, Interactive 3-D Graphics and Games, 7-14 2009.

[4] B. Van Schooten, E. Van Dijk, A.Suinesiaputra, J. Reiber, Interactive navigation of segmented MR angiograms using simultaneous curved planar and volume visualizations. International Journal of Computer Assisted Radiology and Surgery,6,5:591-599, 2011.

[5] D. A. Bowman, E. Kruijff, J.J. LaViola, and I Poupyrev, 3-D

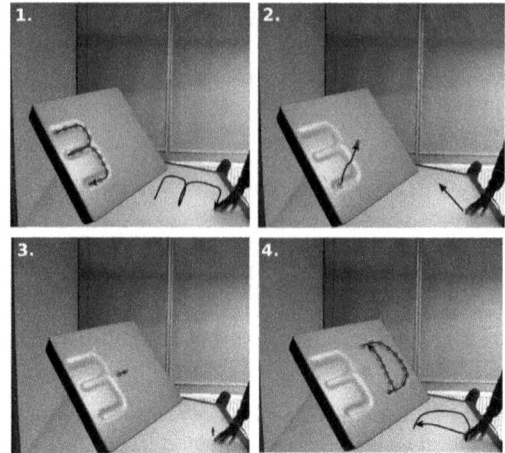

Figure 3: The user utilizes the CrOS technique to sculpt the model.

User Interfaces : Theory and practice. Redwood City, CA, USA : Addison Wesley longman Publishing Co. Inc., 2004.

[6] Robert J. K. Jacob, Linda E. Sibert, Daniel C. McFarlane, and M. Preston Mullen, Jr.. 1994. Integrality and separability of input devices. ACM Trans. Comput.-Hum. Interact. 1, 1 (March 1994), 3-26.

[7] K. Hinckley, R. Pausch, J. Goble and N. Kassell. A Survey of Design Issues in Spatial Input. ACM Symposium on User Interface Software & Technology (UIST'94), 213-222, 1994.

[8] H. Benko and S. Feiner. Balloon Selection: A Multi-Finger Technique for Accurate Low-Fatigue 3-D Selection. IEEE Symposium on 3-D User Interfaces (3DUI'07), 2007.

[9] G. Smith, T. Salzman, W. Stuerzlinger. 3-D Scene Manipulation with 2-D Devices and Constraints, Graphics Interface 2001, pp. 135-142, June 2001.

[10] M. Hachet, F. Decle, S. Knodel, and P. Guitton. Navidget for Easy 3-D Camera Positioning from 2-D Inputs. In Proceedings of IEEE Symposium on 3-D User Interfaces (3DUI), pages 83-89, 2008.

[11] A. Hanson and E. Wernert. Constrained 3-D navigation with 2-D controllers. Conference on Visualization (VIZ'97), 175-183, 1997.

[12] Mark Foskey, Miguel A. Otaduy, and Ming C. Lin. 2005. ArtNova: touch-enabled 3D model design. In ACM SIGGRAPH 2005 Courses (SIGGRAPH'05), John Fujii (Ed.). ACM, New York, NY, USA, , Article 188 .

[13] K. Hormann, K. Polthier and A. Sheffer. Mesh parameterization: theory and practice. ACM SIGGRAPH ASIA courses, 1-87, 2008.

[14] A. Sheffer, E. Praun and K. Rose. Mesh parameterization methods and their applications, Foundations and Trends. Computer Graphics and Vision 2:105-171, 2006.

[15] A. Pavlovych and W. Stuerzlinger. The tradeoff between spatial jitter and latency in pointing tasks. ACM SIGCHI Symposium on Engineering Interactive Computing Systems (EICS'09), 187-196, 2009.

Starfish: a Selection Technique for Dense Virtual Environments

Jonathan Wonner
ENS Cachan - Bretagne
University of Strasbourg -
LSIIT, CNRS UMR 7005
jonathan.wonner@ens-
cachan.org

Jérôme Grosjean
University of Strasbourg -
LSIIT, CNRS UMR 7005
grosjean@unistra.fr

Antonio Capobianco
University of Strasbourg -
LSIIT, CNRS UMR 7005
a.capobianco@unistra.fr

Dominique Bechmann
University of Strasbourg -
LSIIT, CNRS UMR 7005
bechmann@unistra.fr

ABSTRACT

We present Starfish - a new target selection technique for virtual reality (VR) environments. This technique provides a solution to accurately select targets in high-density 3D scenes.

The user controls a 3D pointer surrounded by a starfish-shaped closed surface. The extremity of each branch ends exactly on preselected near targets. The shape is an implicit surface built on the segments going from the pointer to each of these targets. As the pointer moves across the scene, the starfish shape is dynamically rebuilt. When it is locked the pointer is allowed to move inside the volume, slide down the desired branch, reach and select the corresponding target. Since the pointer stays within the shape, targets are easy to reach and select.

Categories and Subject Descriptors

I.3.6 [**Methodology and Techniques**]: Interaction techniques; H.5.1 [**Multimedia Information Systems**]: Artificial, augmented, and virtual realities

Keywords

Virtual reality; 3D interaction; Selection; Implicit surface; Starfish

1. INTRODUCTION

Selecting a target is one of the most fundamental tasks in VR environments [3]. However, this task faces difficulties inherent to such environments, especially at high levels of density. Our work is part of an application focused on

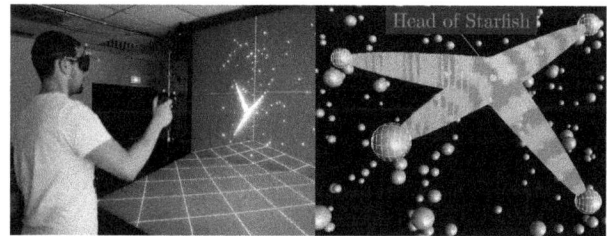

Figure 1: The Starfish selection technique.

editing volumetric meshes. In such a scenario, vertices and edges can partially or totally occlude the target. Moreover, selecting a target closely surrounded by these distractors requires high precision, due to the natural hand tremors [9]. It is also known that the depth perception is biased in VR environments [1]. Thus, precisely locating the depth of the pointer in the scene, or a specific target among others, may be difficult.

The focus of our work is to design a new 3D selection technique, satisfying the following criteria:

- Selection can be performed in sparse or dense scenes.
- The user can effortlessly and quickly select his target.

The technique has to help the user to be precise, and to offer a solution for occluded targets. Basically, our approach was to look for techniques addressing some aspects of these constraints, and to identify their relevant features to design our technique.

Some previous approaches suggest to preselect a subset of targets and then to offer a menu to the user. We think this could be a solution to our first constraint. The SQUAD technique [7] preselects a set of targets using sphere-casting, and then distributes the retained targets into a quad-menu. Since the number of targets is iteratively reduced by intermediate selections, this approach does not require a high level of precision, even in a dense scene, or when the target is initially occulted. However, the SQUAD technique increases the number of necessary selections, and disconnects the scene from the menu [4]. We assume that keeping the local context is important not to disturb the user, especially in the case of targets with the same appearance and only distinguishable by their position in space, like the vertices of a mesh.

About our second guideline, we think that constraining a pointer into a specific-shape volume, is an elegant solution to guide the user during the selection gesture. The Hard-Borders technique [5] is a pie menu whose items are placed on the vertices of a polyhedron. The border of this shape has been made haptically solid, to guide the user within the polyhedron. The C^3 technique [6] is the VR counterpart of a 2D pie-menu. Items are placed around the user's hand, so that the user can quickly select an item by moving a pointer in one specific direction. Whereas the C^3 items are arranged in a regular grid, we can adapt this idea to a more generic 3D scene, by suggesting to the user the directions of a subset of targets, and constraining the pointer in these directions.

All these observations led us to design the Starfish technique (Selection of TARgets From Implicit Surfaces with simulated Haptics), represented in figure 1. The user controls a pointer, surrounded by a starfish-shaped volume: several branches start from the pointer (called the *head* of Starfish) to near preselected targets. At any moment, the shape is rebuilt according to the position of the head. When the desired target is preselected, the user can lock the shape and move the head inside its volume. We graphically constraint the pointer within the shape, so that the user is guided along the branch, which acts as a bottleneck, to reach and stop on the target. In the next section, we describe the design of Starfish.

2. STARFISH

Starfish is based on a closed surface freely positioned by the user. This surface is built on the union of several branches, starting from a pointer (called *head* of Starfish) to a set of near targets. As a result, the surface has the shape of a starfish. The user controls the head of Starfish like a 3D pointer: a direct mapping is used between the user's hand and the head of Starfish. The branches are dynamically rebuilt while the head is moved. At any time, in particular when the desired target is reached (or *captured*) by one of the branches, the user can lock the shape. The head of Starfish is still controlled by the user, but is now virtually constrained within the closed surface. The head can therefore lean on the surface along the branches, reach the target at the extremity of the branch, and select it.

In this section, we first focus on how the user controls Starfish. We then detail the algorithm behind the creation of the shape with an implicit surface [2]. Finally, we explain how we constraint the head of Starfish within the surface.

2.1 Control of Starfish

In our implementation, Starfish requires a tracker device, equipped with two buttons, called Move button and Select button. As long as no button is pressed, the head of Starfish is stationary. This state, called Idle mode, allows the user to rest his arm without moving Starfish. Moreover, to reach distant targets, the user can drag and drop Starfish in the scene. When the Move button is pressed, the position of the head is mapped to the position of the device. We call this state the Move mode. At any moment, the surface is rebuilt to capture targets near the head. When the Select button

is pressed, the surface is locked, and the head of Starfish is constrained within its shape. This state is called the Select mode. When the user releases this button, we first check if a target is selected. If so, the user can interact with it. The target at the extremity of a branch is selected when the head of Starfish has entered deep enough in the branch. In our implementation, the user can select the target when the head has reached 30% of the length of the branch.

2.2 Building of the surface

The goal of Starfish is to locally help the user to select a target. This assistance is provided by preselecting a subset of targets and putting spatial constraints on the head of Starfish, so that these targets can be more easily reached. These two aims are achieved by building a closed surface which captures the preselected targets, and by constraining the head of Starfish inside the volume formed by the surface. We assume that the shape of a starfish (*i.e.* a union of branches), is adequate for that purpose. Thanks to the bottleneck shape of each branch, the head of Starfish slides on the surface, and stops precisely on the target. Moreover, branches indicate to the user in which directions he can move, and help to perceive the relative position of the neighbouring targets.

2.2.1 Preselecting targets

For reasons of visibility and comfort, Starfish should not preselect all the nearest targets, but provides help to the more relevant ones. These targets define the skeleton on which the surface will be built, *i.e.* a set of segments between the head of Starfish, H, and the targets T_i. We follow these intuitive guidelines:

1. **Distance filter:** Starfish is a local assistance, so all targets whose euclidean distance to the pointer is larger than a parameter R_{max} are rejected. Once the desired target is captured, the selection has to be fast. We suggest that the value of R_{max} should be chosen so that the user can reach each preselected targets by moving the device less than 50 cm.

2. **Angle filter:** If the angle between two branches is too small, it may be difficult to enter the chosen one without mistake. To address this issue, we check each couple of targets. If the angle between two segments is smaller than a parameter Θ_{min}, the farthest target is rejected. From preliminary tests, we feel that Starfish is more comfortable when Θ_{min} is larger than or equal to $\frac{\pi}{8}$ rad.

3. **Quantity filter:** Finally, we only accept the N_{max} targets nearest to the head among the remaining, to avoid cluttering the shape with too many branches. In our modelling application, we choose to keep only 3 or 4 branches.

After applying these filters, if the desired target is not the nearest one, it may be rejected. However, since the shape is constantly rebuilt, adjusting the Starfish position to capture the correct target does not require much effort, and is rather fast and intuitive. The set of segments between the head of Starfish and the retained targets is called the *skeleton*.

2.2.2 Building the shape

Each segment starts from the head to a preselected target. To obtain the desired Starfish shape, shown on figure 2A, an implicit surface is used. The surface of Starfish can be seen as the set of points which share a same potential value, in a potential field generated by the skeleton. Each segment of the skeleton generates a branch-shaped potential field, as illustrated in figure 2B. The fields of all the branches are then merged. Finally, the isopotential surface S_0 crossing all the targets at the extremities of the segments of the skeleton is chosen, and displayed as explained in section 2.2.3.

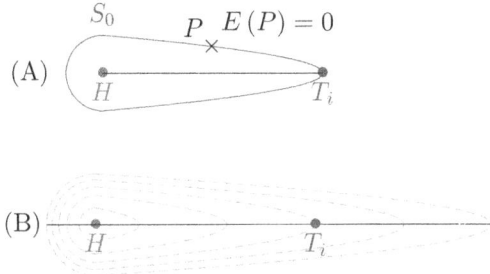

Figure 2: **(A): 2D section of the isopotential surface S_0. This surface crosses the target T_i, and surrounds the head H. (B): The potential field generated by segment $[HT_i]$.**

To generate such an implicit surface, we need a potential function E, and a specific distance function d to the skeleton.

The function E computes the potential of a point P according to its distance to the skeleton. In our implementation, the following function is used:

$$E(P) = \begin{cases} 0 & \text{if } d(P) \geqslant D_{\max}, \\ \left(1 - \dfrac{d(P)^2}{D_{\max}^2}\right)^2 & \text{otherwise.} \end{cases} \quad (1)$$

$D_{\max}$ is a distance which value is the radius of the branch at its base, and sets the thickness of the branch. So that the technique scales when the density increases, we recommend to vary this parameter according to the length of the branch. In our implementation, $D_{\max}$ quadratically depends on this length. All points of the surface S_0 have a distance to the skeleton equal to $D_{\max}$. Therefore, due to the particular desired shape, an euclidean distance is not relevant.

The distance function d is carefully designed so that the isopotential surface S_0 crosses all the targets retained by the filters defined in section 2.2.1, and surrounds the head of Starfish. We define a distance function d_i to each segment $[HT_i]$. These functions are then merged to obtain a distance function to the complete skeleton, as follows:

$$d(P) = \min_{i=1...n} (d_i(P)). \quad (2)$$

The desired appearance of the surface for one single segment, shown on figure 3A, matches the isodistance surface $d_i = D_{\max}$. The head of Starfish is located at the intersection of all branches, and therefore should have a null distance to each segment. Consequently, our functions d_i must verify the following constraints:

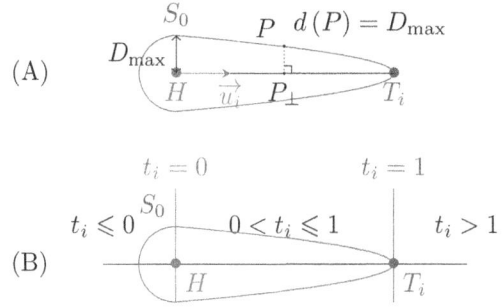

Figure 3: **(A): 2D section of the isodistance surface S_0. (B): Representation of t_i, with $t_i(P)$ between 0 and 1 if $P_\perp$, projection of P on the line (HT_i), is in the segment $[HT_i]$.**

- $d_i(T_i) = D_{\max}$,
- $d_i(H) = 0$,
- the surface has the shape of a bottleneck.

The shape of the surface implies that the distance d_i to the segment $[HT_i]$ is piecewise-defined, and that $d_i(P)$ depends on the coordinate of P along the axis (HT_i). Thus, for each point P, we define a scalar $t_i(P)$ as follows:

$$t_i(P) = \frac{\overrightarrow{HP_\perp} \cdot \overrightarrow{u_i}}{HT_i}, \quad (3)$$

where $\overrightarrow{u_i}$ is a unit direction vector of the line (HT_i), and $P_\perp$ is the orthogonal projection of P on this line. This function verifies $t_i(P) = 0$ if $P_\perp = H$, and $t_i(P) = 1$ if $P_\perp = T_i$. These conditions are represented in figure 3B. For $t_i \leqslant 0$, all points of the surface S_0 have the same euclidean distance to H. In this area, the surface has the shape of an half sphere. For $0 < t_i \leqslant 1$, the surface has the shape of a bottleneck.

From the definition of t_i results the function d_i, representing the distance to the segment $[HT_i]$, or *branch* B_i:

$$d_i(P) = \begin{cases} \dfrac{(HP)^2}{D_{\max}} & \text{if } t_i(P) < 0, \\ \dfrac{(PP_\perp)^2}{D_{\max}} + D_{\max} \cdot t_i(P) & \text{otherwise.} \end{cases} \quad (4)$$

When the skeleton has more than one branch, the distance to the skeleton of a point is defined as its smallest distance-to-branch value, as explained in equation 2. As a result, it looks like branches are merged. Figure 4 shows a representation of this surface for a multi-segment skeleton.

2.2.3 Displaying the surface

In Move mode, the user must ensure that the target is captured by Starfish. We therefore need to display the surface S_0. A Marching Cube algorithm[8] is first applied on the potential field to produce a triangle mesh. Then, a simple implementation consists in displaying the triangles of the mesh with only one color, semi-transparent to see the head. However, we believe that this may be not sufficient to distinguish between branches, and their directions. Some

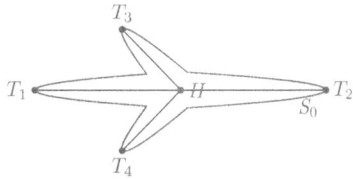

Figure 4: 2D section of the surface generated by Starfish from a skeleton with four segments.

preliminary tests led us to another procedure to color each vertex of the mesh. Basically, the idea is to display a fixed number of stripes for each branch, with a color gradation, as shown in figure 5. We assume that the color gradation helps to disambiguate branches, and the stripes help to understand their orientations. In Select mode, a different color function is used to visually inform the user that the mode has changed. Moreover, the branch containing the captive pointer is highlighted.

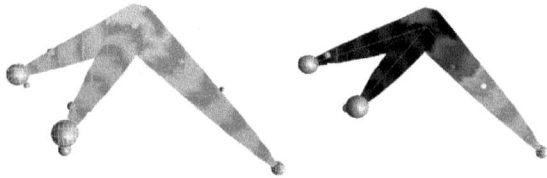

Figure 5: Starfish in Move mode (left) and in Select mode (right).

2.3 Constraints on the pointer

In Select mode, the surface is locked, and we want the head of Starfish to be constrained within the surface, so that it can slide on it, and stop on the desired target (we say that the head becomes a *captive* pointer). Obviously, we cannot prevent the user's hand to cross the surface. To get around this, the position of the user's hand is associated with a second pointer, called *free* pointer, which stays invisible. Initially, when Starfish switches to Select mode, the free pointer is at the same position than the captive one. While both are inside the surface, their positions are identical. When the free pointer moves outside, the captive pointer has to slide along the surface to follow the free pointer.

A simple way to obtain this behaviour is to place the captive pointer on the point of the surface nearest to the free pointer. However, this may involve involuntary "jumps" between two branches, that should not be allowed. The user chooses to enter a branch, then the bottleneck shape ensures that either the captive pointer ends on the target, or the user changes his mind and has to move back to the center to choose another branch. The captive pointer should never jump from branch to branch. We propose a method to follow the surface, based on small successive movements in directions tangential to the surface.

Let P_C be the position of the captive pointer, P_F the position of the free pointer, and $\overrightarrow{D} = \overrightarrow{P_C P_F}$ the direction of the desired movement for the captive pointer. Let also $\overrightarrow{N_s}$

be the normal to the surface at P_C. $\overrightarrow{N_s}$ is easily computed thanks to the gradient of the potential field.

Algorithm: Following the surface

While $\overrightarrow{D}$ and $\overrightarrow{N_s}$ are not collinear:

- The captive pointer is translated by a vector $\delta \cdot \overrightarrow{N_s} \wedge \left(\overrightarrow{D} \wedge \overrightarrow{N_s} \right)$, where δ is an arbitrary small factor.
- The captive pointer is then moved back to the surface, iteratively adjusting its position in the direction of the gradient of the potential field.

EndWhile

3. CONCLUSION AND FUTURE WORK

In this paper, we proposed a new interaction technique for target selection in VR environments, called Starfish. This technique builds a closed implicit surface around the pointer to preselect near targets. Once locked, the surface constrains the pointer, so it can easily slide towards and select the desired target without requiring much precision.

From a preliminary study, Starfish has been deemed comfortable and "fun" to control by the participants, while its performance in terms of selection time and error rate seems promising. Thus, a more formal and complete experience is being developed, to compare Starfish with SQUAD [7].

4. REFERENCES

[1] C. Armbruster, M. Wolter, T. Kuhlen, W. Spijkers, and B. Fimm. Depth perception in virtual reality: distance estimations in peri- and extrapersonal space. *Cyberpsychol Behav.*, 11(1):9–15, 2008.

[2] J. F. Blinn. A generalization of algebraic surface drawing. *SIGGRAPH Comput. Graph.*, 16(3):273–, 1982.

[3] D. A. Bowman, E. Kruijff, J. J. LaViola, and I. Poupyrev. *3D User Interfaces: Theory and Practice.* Addison Wesley, 2004.

[4] J. Cashion, C. Wingrave, and J. J. LaViola Jr. Dense and dynamic 3d selection for game-based virtual environments. *IEEE Trans. on Visualization and Computer Graphics*, 18(4):634–642, 2012.

[5] C. Essert-Villard and A. Capobianco. Hardborders: a new haptic approach for selection tasks in 3d menus. In *Proc. of ACM Symp. on VR Software and Technology*, VRST '09, pages 243–244, 2009.

[6] J. Grosjean, J.-M. Burkhardt, S. Coquillart, and P. Richard. Evaluation of the command and control cube. In *Proc. of Int. Conf. on Multimodal Interfaces*, ICMI '02, pages 473–, 2002.

[7] R. Kopper, F. Bacim, and D. A. Bowman. Rapid and accurate 3d selection by progressive refinement. In *Proc. of IEEE Symp. on 3D User Interfaces*, 3DUI '11, pages 67–74, 2011.

[8] W. E. Lorensen and H. E. Cline. Marching cubes: A high resolution 3d surface construction algorithm. *SIGGRAPH Comput. Graph.*, 21(4):163–169, Aug. 1987.

[9] L. Vanacken, T. Grossman, and K. Coninx. Multimodal selection techniques for dense and occluded 3d virtual environments. *Int. J. Human-Computer Studies*, 67(3):237–255, 2009.

Efficient Selection of Multiple Objects on a Large Scale*

Rasmus Stenholt
Aalborg University
Aalborg
Denmark
rs@create.aau.dk

ABSTRACT

The task of multiple object selection (MOS) in immersive virtual environments is important and still largely unexplored. The difficulty of efficient MOS increases with the number of objects to be selected. E.g. in small-scale MOS, only a few objects need to be simultaneously selected. This may be accomplished by serializing existing single-object selection techniques. In this paper, we explore various MOS tools for large-scale MOS. That is, when the number of objects to be selected are counted in hundreds, or even thousands. This makes serialization of single-object techniques prohibitively time consuming. Instead, we have implemented and tested two of the existing approaches to 3-D MOS, a brush and a lasso, as well as a new technique, a magic wand, which automatically selects objects based on local proximity to other objects. In a formal user evaluation, we have studied how the performance of the MOS tools are affected by the geometric configuration of the objects to be selected. Our studies demonstrate that the performance of MOS techniques is very significantly affected by the geometric scenario facing the user. Furthermore, we demonstrate that a good match between MOS tool shape and the geometric configuration is not always preferable, if the applied tool is complex to use.

Categories and Subject Descriptors

H.5.2 [**Information Systems**]: Information Interfaces and PresentationUser Interfaces; I.3.6 [**Computing Methodologies**]: Computer GraphicsMethodology and Techniques

Keywords

Multiple object selection; virtual reality; HMD; user evaluation

1. INTRODUCTION

Selection of multiple objects (MOS) is a frequent goal of user interactions in desktop environments. The prime example of this is the ubiquitous selection box used for picking multiple icons located

---

*Presented at the VRST '12 in Toronto.

in a contiguous region on a computer desktop. Many image processing applications, such as Adobe Photoshop or GIMP, include tools for selecting a large number of pixels to be the target of further processing. Furthermore, MOS is very often used in computer games, where the player has to efficiently assign the same commands to several characters or units. All of the mentioned tasks, and the techniques used to accomplish them, can collectively be referred to as 2-D MOS, since they are carried out in a 2-D context.

Once MOS moves beyond the 2-D desktop and into 3-D, the case becomes more complex, and fewer studies exist. The added complexity comes from several sources: More degrees-of-freedom (DoF) to control, a lack of standardized MOS tools, and the possibility of occlusion. The lack of studies on 3-D MOS cannot be explained by a lack of potentially useful applications of 3-D MOS. To illustrate this, consider the following example: In data visualizations, there are often thousands of glyphs or voxels floating around in 3-D space [11], each representing a sample of the visualized database. In many cases, it is useful for a user exploring such a visualization to be able to highlight groups of glyphs or voxels that are of particular interest [4], or to be able to add annotations [6] to specific parts of the visualization. The prerequisite operation for this is a MOS task.

The number of selection targets is an important parameter in this context. We shall refer to this as the *scale* of the MOS task. In some applications, serialization of single-object selection techniques may be adequate and efficient, since the number of target objects is often manageable. We henceforth refer to small-scale MOS as SS-MOS. However, in the case of data mining applications, the scale of the MOS increases drastically, since it is not uncommon to work with databases consisting of thousands of records. Thus, this application is an example of large-scale MOS (LS-MOS). Since serialization of single-object techniques unavoidably becomes more and more impractical to use as the task scale increases - e.g. imagine pointing out 1,000 objects one-by-one - the techniques applicable to LS-MOS tasks are potentially quite different from those applicable to SS-MOS. This makes the technical challenge of designing good LS-MOS techniques interesting. Furthermore, efficient LS-MOS techniques in 3-D are currently relatively unexplored. For these reasons, this paper only deals with MOS tasks, where the scale of the task is at least well into the hundreds.

Thus, the main point of this paper is to test and evaluate the usefulness and performance of different 3-D LS-MOS tools. Furthermore, we seek to evaluate how the geometric layout of the objects to be selected affects the efficiency, precision and ease-of-use of the tools. The results gained through this study are therefore useful to future designers of 3-D LS-MOS toolboxes, since they provide information about the trade-offs made when using the tools. That is, recommendations of when to use specific tools, and, just as importantly, when to avoid them.

2. RELATED WORK AND MOS THEORY

The tasks that users perform while immersed inside virtual environments are traditionally split into four categories: Selection, manipulation, navigation, and system control. This distinction of categories is e.g. presented by Bowman et al in [2], where a comprehensive design space for 3-D selection techniques is presented. However, the work only mentions single-object selection techniques. The presented design space for selection tasks includes a category for automatic selection, but does not present any examples of such techniques. Although MOS tasks clearly belong within the well-established selection category, 3-D MOS, and in particular 3-D LS-MOS, does not appear to have been the subject of much study. A few exceptions are presented in [8, 16, 17]. For this reason, much of the related work concerns traditional single-object selection.

2.1 Single-Object Selection

For several reasons, single-object selection (SOS) techniques are of interest in the design of 3-D MOS techniques. First of all, any SOS technique has the potential to be used as a MOS technique, if used serially. However, this becomes prohibitively time-consuming as the scale of the MOS task grows. Secondly, many SOS techniques are inherently MOS techniques with an added disambiguation step. This step is included in order to pick just one of the candidate objects that fall within a selection volume. The inclusion of a disambiguation step modifies a MOS technique into a SOS counterpart. As such, many SOS techniques hold additional potential as MOS techniques by removing or modifying the disambiguation step.

Ray casting is one of the most well-established SOS techniques [10, 1]. In ray casting, the selection volume is a half-line or a very narrow cylinder extending from the user's hand infinitely into 3-D space like the beam of a laser pointer. In many cases, the selection ray intersects more than one object, which calls for the inclusion of a disambiguation step. The potential of ray casting in itself as a non-serialized 3-D LS-MOS technique is limited, however, since the selection volume is very small. This issue may be alleviated by using the selection ray to pick out a single object, after which all similar or nearby objects are automatically included in the selection. The similarity/proximity criterion can be arbitrarily chosen. The idea of automatically expanding the selection from a single object forms the basis of the *magic wand* technique which is introduced and evaluated in this paper (see section 3.3).

2.2 Multiple Object Selection

2.2.1 2-D MOS

In 2-D desktop contexts, MOS tasks are very frequent. As such, the techniques for solving the problem in 2-D are well-established. Wills presents a comprehensive design space for 2-D MOS techniques in [20]. In that paper, a distinction between *brush*-type techniques and *lasso*-type techniques is made. This distinction is also valid for 3-D MOS.

Brushes: With a brush, the selection is made inside a persistent object, called a brush, which the user can manipulate in various ways. One typical manipulation is to drag the brush around. It is possible to add more to the selection simply by moving the brush while making an indication to select (e.g. clicking a button). The brush-metaphor is very clear and intuitive, because dragging the virtual brush around is very similar to painting with a real brush.

It is fairly straightforward to adapt the idea of a selection brush to 3-D MOS, since all that is needed is to 1) use a 3-D shape instead of 2-D shape for the brush and 2) map the controls of the brush to a motion-tracked 3-D interaction device. In this paper, we have chosen to use a spherical 3-D brush with adjustable radius as one of the three evaluated MOS techniques.

Lassos: The lasso category of selection techniques is based on the user defining a temporary selection shape, called a lasso. All objects that lie within the created lasso are selected, after which the lasso disappears. If the user wishes to expand the selection, more lassos must be defined. In 2-D, a lasso can be made in several ways. Desktop selection rectangles are a well-known example of such a method. In other applications, lassos are made by tracing out a closed, free-form contour on the screen using a mouse.

The lasso concept can also be adapted for use in 3-D. However, the case is not as straightforward as with the brush, because the steps involved in creating the actual lasso are non-trivial to convert from 2-D. First of all, the lasso shape must be a closed 3-D volume, or at least an infinite extrusion of a 2-D shape. This means that the desired shape of a 3-D lasso is probably the primary design choice to make. It only becomes possible to design an efficient way of producing the lasso, after deciding on the class of 3-D shape. Efficient creation of 3-D shapes, specifically 3-D boxes - the natural 3-D extension of 2-D rectangles, is discussed in [17, 15]. A box-shaped lasso, created according to the 3C technique introduced in [15] is the second 3D LS-MOS technique evaluated in this paper.

Automatic techniques: The work of Wills [20] does not account for the possibility of automating part of the MOS process, although the proposed design parameters do include the possibility of modifying the selection volume based on the objects inside of it. Nonetheless, automatic 2-D MOS selection tools are very common in desktop applications, especially in image processing. Such tools use region growing algorithms to expand a selection to all similar pixels connected to an initial seed pixel indicated by the user. The similarity of pixels is typically based on their RGB values. This is the approach which we have chosen to evaluate as the third way of performing MOS tasks. In Adobe Photoshop, the automatic selection tool is named a magic wand. This has inspired us to use the same name for our automatic tool in order to give users a metaphor to relate to. However, the region growing method underlying our magic wand is somewhat different from the one found in Photoshop. See section 3.3 for more details. A study based on automatic 2-D group selection based on human perception is found in [3]. This work has also served as inspiration.

2.2.2 3-D MOS

Few studies directly concerning 3-D MOS currently exist. In one of the currently most comprehensive studies on the subject, Lucas et al [8] presents a design space for 3-D MOS techniques. This design space identifies 6 parameters to consider in 3-D MOS design. Subsequently, variations of two of these parameters, concurrency and spatial context, are used in designing and evaluating four different 3-D MOS techniques. One technique was serialized ray casting. Two of the techniques were performed through a 2-D view of the scene on a hand-held tablet, and as such, are more or less clones of well known desktop MOS techniques. The final technique featured a persistent selection box, i.e. a box-shaped brush, which could be scaled, rotated, and positioned arbitrarily through a combination of two techniques: Go-Go [13] and PORT [9]. The box selection technique is the only one of the four techniques tested by Lucas et al which is both compatible with the LS-MOS context of this paper, and with the non-see-through HMD setup used. The number of target objects was in the range from 9 to 64, thus staying reasonably within the realm of SS-MOS, where serialization of SOS techniques is viable. The objects were laid out in a non-randomized, rectangular grid pattern in all cases. Furthermore, the selection task was visualized on a projection screen. These facts differentiate the study of Lucas et al from the one in this paper.

In the work of Ulinski et al [17], the subject of study is MOS using box lassos of arbitrary position, orientation, and scale. Several techniques for creating the lassos were evaluated wrt. two binary factors, density and occlusion. The studies were carried out by users interacting with a monoscopic rendering of the data displayed on a table-top monitor. The spatial layout of the target objects were box-shaped in all cases, meaning that no test of the influence of layout, beyond the mentioned factors, was made. I.e. there were no cases where the target objects' spatial layout did not match the shape of the lasso. No quantitative information about the scale of the task is given. Thus, our work of differentiates itself from Ulinski et al's by virtue of testing several different spatial layouts of target objects, by testing other tools than 3-D box lassos, and by using an immersive display such as an HMD.

The case of automatic 3-D MOS has also been considered previously. However, it seems that existing techniques rely on the existence of a relational data structure, e.g. a scene graph, behind the rendered virtual objects. This for example means that selecting a virtual table also selects all the objects resting on the table. Such techniques are e.g. presented in [12, 7, 21]. These methods seem very attractive for virtual worlds populated by recognizable objects such as architectural visualizations or computer games. However, these techniques are not applicable in the general case, where the visualized objects come from a database without natural structures such as parent-child relations. This is frequently the case in abstract data visualizations.

3. DESIGN OF 3-D MOS TECHNIQUES

In this section, we present the specific design used for the three tested MOS techniques. Two of these, the brush and the lasso, relate directly to some of the studies mentioned above. The magic wand, however, is new in a 3-D MOS context. Therefore, the algorithm used in the implementation of the automatic aspects of the wand is of particular interest. The choice of the control mappings in all techniques is heavily based on the available controllers: Two wireless presenter mice fitted with markers to make them trackable with 6 DoF. This implies that the available controls on the devices apart from the motion tracking are three buttons (left, middle, right) and a scroll wheel. The mice are shown in Figure 1. The designed techniques take advantage of having two controllers either by being bimanual techniques, or by duplicating the same technique to both hands, giving the users a free choice of which hand to use. Furthermore, the two primary concerns addressed as design criteria are that the techniques must be usable in an HMD context, and that they must be applicable as 3-D LS-MOS techniques.

3.1 Brush

The two primary decisions to make when designing a 3-D brush is the shape of the brush and its control mappings.

In this study, we have chosen to use a spherical brush. The main motivations for this choice are twofold. First of all, a sphere is a well-known shape which should be easy to control for the average user. A spherical brush has a maximum of 4 DoF, i.e. a 3-D position and a radius. This fact is important to this study, where the time available for familiarizing oneself with the tool is fairly limited. Secondly, a spherical brush with adjustable radius should be applicable and relatively precise in many contexts.

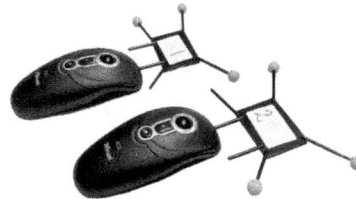

Figure 1: The mice used in the experiment. Each mouse is fitted with reflective markers to make it detectable by an infrared camera system. The mice are equipped with the three usual mouse buttons as well as a scroll wheel.

The main disadvantage is expected to be that it will be difficult to select targets located at the edges of a non-spherical volume, e.g. a box shape, where clutter is present close to the targets. E.g. it is difficult to use a sphere to select target objects in the corner of a box surrounded by undesired objects (clutter), without also selecting some of the clutter.

The choice of a spherical shape also has direct implications on the control scheme used. Since the sphere is a closed volume in space, unlike a ray or a cone, the actual brushing process becomes local and direct. I.e. the users must place the brush at the desired targets before doing the brushing. We decided to go with a sphere and the resulting control scheme, because a cone is impractical in scenarios where clutter is obstructing a clear path of pointing. This is the case in several of the scenarios we have tested.

For the same reasons, we have also chosen to go with the same control scheme for the other MOS techniques. This not only has the mentioned benefit of working well in cluttered scenarios, it also reduces the amount of different interaction schemes that the test subjects will have to learn. Furthermore, it puts the tested techniques on even ground in the evaluation, meaning that the control scheme is not a factor of the study.

Therefore, the controls are a direct mapping of the positions of the user's two hands to the positions of two virtual brush spheres, based on the information provided by a motion tracking system. The brush spheres are made semi-transparent in order to allow better perception of the objects inside the brush. This design choice is in line with previous work by Zhai et al [22]. The adjustable radius is controlled by scrolling the wheel on the controller. Selecting the objects currently inside the brush is mapped to the left buttons. That is, clicking the left button once selects all objects inside the brush, while holding the left button allows the user to keep selecting objects while sweeping the brush through the volume of objects. The brushes in action are shown in Figure 2.A and Figure 2.E.

In order to allow the user to correct mistakes, clicking the right button toggles from the basic selection mode to a deselection mode, where the brushing removes objects from the selection set. The current mode of operation is indicated by the colour of the brushes. This mode toggling feature is also available for the lasso, whereas deselection works differently with the magic wand.

The user can select or deselect objects by repeating the process as many times as desired. Thus, the designed techniques are examples of parallel 3-D MOS tools in the terminology of [8], which can be used in a serial fashion to refine or expand a selection.

3.2 Lasso

For the lasso metaphor, we chose to use a 3-D version of the well-known 2-D selection box lasso from the desktop. Since an arbitrary 3-D box has 9 DoF, the construction technique for the lasso has to comply with this fact. Control of all 9 DoF is needed

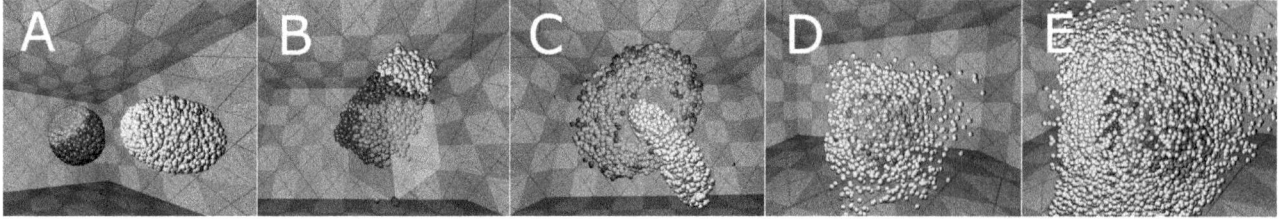

Figure 2: Screenshots of various experimental conditions and techniques. Blue glyphs are targets, yellow ones are clutter. Correctly selected glyphs are highlighted in green, incorrect ones in red. (A) The separated clouds scenario with the 3-D spherical brush shown as faint, semi-transparent green spheres. (B) The adjacent clouds scenario with the 3-D box lasso technique in use. (C) The entangled clouds with the magic wand technique in use. The magic wand has been used once to select most of the blue cloud without adjusting its proximity threshold. (D) The embedded nucleus scenario with the magic wand as selection tool. As in part C, the wand has been used once here to make a selection. A few false positives are showing as red glyphs. (E) The uniform embedding scenario with a large 3-D brush in use. This scenario is difficult due to the amount of visual occlusion, and the proximity of the clutter and target glyphs.

to allow for full control of the flexibility offered by the box shape. This makes the technique somewhat more difficult to use than the 4 DoF spherical brush. However, it also has the potential to be a better match for the presented cloud of target objects, if the cloud has angular corners or planar surfaces. Controlling 9 DoF in an efficient manner is non-trivial. For this reason, we have chosen to implement the existing 3C technique, which provides the greatest degree of precision according to [15].

The 3C technique requires the user to indicate the positions of 3 corners on the desired box in a specific pattern. We have chosen to go with the variant of 3C named 3+3+3 DoF 3C in [15]. This suits the direct interaction pattern chosen for the brush technique well, since it is simple to point out specific points in space, in this case box corners, in a direct way. I.e. the user has to place a hand at a desired corner position, after which a click places the corner there. The hand positions are indicated by small spheres. After making three clicks, the lasso is completed, and all objects inside the lasso are selected. The user can interactively see the lasso currently resulting from the positions of the hands as soon as the first lasso corner has been placed. As was the case with the brush, the lassos are rendered as semi-transparent boxes. An example of a box lasso in use is shown in Figure 2.B.

As was the case with the brush, the user has the option to right-click in order to toggle to a deselection mode, where the boxes remove objects from the selection set. Similarly, the user is allowed to make as many selection/deselection boxes as desired to reach the end result.

3.3 Magic Wand

The magic wand is based on its namesake technique used in 2-D image processing applications. The main idea is that the user indicates a single object, the seed, which is representative of the objects in the desired selection. An algorithm then takes care of expanding the selection from the seed to all objects which are similar enough to the seed according to some criterion. In general terms, any selection technique, SOS or MOS - automatic or manual, can be viewed as a binary classification task, where the objects of the scene are split into two clusters, the target and the clutter. In the special case of SOS, the target cluster only contains one object. Thus, the type of algorithm needed for the magic wand belongs to the category of clustering algorithms. Many clustering algorithms are based on knowing the expected distribution of the objects to be clustered. However, in the general case of MOS, nothing is known a priori about such distributions. I.e. the spatial layout of the objects varies much from case to case. Therefore, we have aimed to

design a magic wand algorithm which does not make any assumptions about the overall shape of the clouds to be selected.

Instead, the assumption that we make is based on human perception. People tend to think of densely packed groups of objects as a whole instead of invidual constituents. This is a well-established fact in the gestalt laws of human visual perception [19]. The gestalt law of proximity is of special interest here, since it provides a proven theoretical background to base the automatic techniques on. As such, our magic wand technique is designed to select all objects that feature high proximity to other objects in the cluster, and ultimately to the seed. Furthermore, to be applicable as an interaction technique, the clustering algorithm should not be so computationally expensive that it prevents the clustering from happening in real-time with the scales of MOS tasks used in our study.

Such a procedure is e.g. presented as the initial grouping step of the clustering algorithm introduced in [5]. In our case, where we want to base the algorithm on the gestalt law of proximity, the closeness of cluster members is based on Euclidean distance in 3-D. More dimensions can also be taken into account to make the clustering sensitive to other cues than spatial proximity (e.g. colour or shape), corresponding to the gestalt law of similarity.

It is worth noting that the use of Euclidean distance as proximity criterion does not necessarily lead to spherical clusters: When viewed on a global level, it is not the Euclidean distance from the seed to the other members of the cluster that matters. Instead, all members have in common that there is at least one other member located somewhere within local proximity. I.e. clusters can have members very far from the seed, as long as there exists a path of sufficiently small jumps through the cluster from the seed to the distant cluster members. This principle maintains the idea that the selected objects should be in a region of similar density/proximity between the objects. This is illustrated in Figure 3.

Mapping the above to user controls has the following implications: 1) The user must be able to select the seed object. 2) The user must be able to adjust the proximity threshold used when deciding which objects belong to the selection set. Pointing out the seed is done directly using a small, spherical cursor - just like the indication of the corners of the 3-D box lasso. Furthermore, adjustment of the maximum allowed distance between cluster members and their closest neighbour in the cluster is mapped to the scroll wheel. This means that the magic wand is a 4 DoF tool. Increasing the threshold value has the effect of lowering the requirements of cluster membership, i.e. expanding the selection. The opposite is true when decreasing the threshold value. At the minimum value of 0, only the seed is admitted into the cluster, effectively making

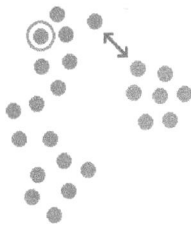

Figure 3: Example of two preceptually distinct clusters that can be individually selected using the proposed clustering method. Selecting a seed (green circle) in one cluster will not cause a selection of objects in the other cluster because the internal distances in the cluster containing the seed are smaller than the minimum distance separating the two clusters (red arrow). The other cluster is also selectable in the same way for the same reasons.

the magic wand a simple SOS tool. Figure 2.C and 2.D show the the magic wand being used.

Thus, selection and deselection with the magic wand happens when the scroll wheel is used. As with the brush and the lasso, the user is allowed to add to the selection by adding new seeds. This implies that in some difficult cases, the user has the option to keep the proximity threshold at a low level, in order to serially add new seeds with small clusters to the selection set without much risk of accidentally selecting any clutter.

There are many possible modifications to the basic magic wand technique. Some examples are: Including an upper limit on the size of the selection set, limiting the number of allowed jumps from the seed, increasing the linkage requirement from a single neighbour to more neighbours, etc. However, in this study we have chosen to go with the basic scheme as outlined above.

4. EXPERIMENT

With the three MOS techniques outlined and motivated, the performed experiment can be explained.

4.1 Geometric Scenarios

The main purpose of the experiment is to test how the three chosen MOS techniques fare in scenarios of different geometric layout. In choosing scenarios, we have aimed to include some that represent a broad range of all possible scenarios, and to design the scenarios such that they potentially hightlight the strengths and weaknesses of each technique. As such, scenarios encountered in real applications should conceptually match a combination of those tested in this study. A geometric scenario consists of two randomized clouds of glyphs: A target cloud rendered as blue glyphs, and clutter rendered in yellow. The glyphs temporarily change colours to green (target) or red (clutter) upon entering a selection volume, and permanently so upon being committed to the selection set. Examples of all 5 chosen scenarios are shown in Figure 2.

The randomization is performed such that the overall shape of the clouds adheres to the design of the scenario. Both clouds are typically created with an average density of $50,000$ glyphs/m^3, which makes it straightforward to perceive the overall shape of the clouds from the visualized glyphs. The chosen density implied that the mean number of target glyphs was approx. 1700, while the mean amount of clutter was app. 3300. The glyphs were rendered as Phong-shaded, spherical point sprites in the experiment. The goal of the user task was to select all target glyphs while avoid-

ing selection of clutter. The best possible result, i.e. one where all targets are selected without any of the clutter being selected, is referred to as a perfect selection.

4.1.1 Separated Clouds (SC)

The separated clouds scenario is the baseline best-case scenario, which is expected to be straightforward for all techniques. It consists of two spherical clouds, which are spatially well-separated. As such it should be simple to make a perfect selection no matter which technique is used.

4.1.2 Adjacent Clouds (AC)

In the adjacent clouds scenario, two box-shaped clouds are placed adjacent to each other with only a very small separation distance. This layout poses considerable difficulty for the magic wand, because the local proximity criterion can easily cause the clustering algorithm to bridge the gap between the two clouds. Furthermore, the spherical brush can be difficult to use in the region close to the boundary between the two clouds without accidentally selecting some of the clutter. The box lasso shape is a perfect fit for this scenario.

4.1.3 Entangled Clouds (EC)

In this scenario, the clouds are shaped as two tori. The tori are oriented such that the plane of one is perpendicular to that of the other. Furthermore, they are offset from each other such that one runs through the centre of the other. The two tori are well separated everywhere. This is a perfect case for the magic wand, since the local proximity criterion allows the clustering to walk all around one torus without ever jumping to the other one. Using the brush is also expected to be somewhat straightforward. The entangled clouds are problematic with box shaped lassos. It is impossible to achieve perfect selection using a single box, since any volume completely containing one of the tori also contains part of the other torus.

4.1.4 Embedded Nucleus (EN)

In the target nucleus scenario, the target is presented as a dense nucleus completely embedded in a more sparse cloud of clutter. There is no clutter inside the volume spanned by the target nucleus. Both the targets and the clutter are box-shaped. This scenario is expected to be straightforward with the magic wand, since local proximity essentially is the same as density. This allows the automatic selection to reach good results with only a few false positives within a short amount of time. The brush will probably have problems avoiding false positives, and will likely begin to suffer from occlusion problems, where the clutter gets in the way of properly controlling the brush. The box lasso perfectly matches the task, however, visual occlusion problems may degrade its precision.

4.1.5 Uniform Embedding (UE)

The UE scenario is almost identical to the EN scenario. The only difference is that the clutter and the target are equally dense. The UE scenario is a worst-case scenario. The only possible worse situation would be the case, where the target and clutter volumes are overlapping in space. None of the techniques are expected to perform well here, however, a uniform embedding is a particularly challenging scenario for the magic wand and the brush. The box lasso has the potential to make a perfect selection in just one selection operation, however, this requires that the user is not hindered too much by the amount of visual occlusion present.

4.2 Design Matrix

Having 5 geometric scenarios and 3 different MOS techniques, produces a total of 15 different conditions to make up the 2-factorial randomized complete block design, which we have chosen to use. All conditions are outlined in Table 1.

Table 1: All combinations of the two factors of the experiment. The numbers in the table will be used to refer to the specific combinations of the two factors in the analysis of the results. The (+), (.) and (-) labels indicate if the technique is expected to perform well (+), average (.), or badly (-) in the given scenario.

Technique	Scenario				
	SC	AC	EC	EN	UE
Lasso	0 (+)	1 (+)	2 (-)	3 (+)	4 (-)
Brush	5 (+)	6 (.)	7 (+)	8 (.)	9 (-)
Wand	10 (+)	11 (-)	12 (+)	13 (+)	14 (-)

4.3 Hypotheses

Based on the preceding analysis of MOS techniques, and the presentation of the scenarios above, the hypotheses of the experiment are:

H1 The combination of MOS tool and geometric scenario significantly affects the selection performance.

H2 The box lasso is better than the other techniques in the adjacent clouds (AC) scenario.

H3 The magic wand is better than the other techniques in the entangled clouds (EC) and the embedded nucleus (EN) scenarios.

H4 Overall, the magic wand is faster to use than the other techniques.

H5 Overall, the brush is easier to use than the other techniques.

4.4 Response Variables

The notion of performance can be measured in several ways for a MOS task. There are three main categories of response variables, which are relevant to the hypotheses: Completion time, selection quality, and ease-of-use.

The most basic approach to measuring MOS performance is to count the number of true positives (TP), false negatives (FN), true negatives (TN), and false positives (FP). The goal of any MOS task is to maximize the TP and TN counts while minimizing the FP and FN counts. Instead of using the raw counts, we have chosen to use the scale independent quantities of sensitivity and specificity. The sensitivity is the amount of targets selected out of the total number of targets. Conversely, the specificity expresses how much of the clutter has been correctly avoided relative to the total amount clutter. As such, the perfect solution to a MOS task reaches 100% sensitivity while maintaining 100% specificity.

The concept of ease-of-use is a subjective assessment. This assessment can be given in a multitude of ways, e.g. through post-test questionnaires, structured interviews, informal discussions, etc. In order to facilitate statistical analysis along with the other response variables, we have chosen a quantitative approach, where participants are asked to subjectively quantify their perception of task difficulty on a discrete 1 (trivial) to 10 (impossible) scale after completing the trials of each test condition. The specific question asked was "How difficult do you think it was to solve the task well?". To supplement the subjective measurement, we also decided to count the number of operations used in each trial to get an objective measurement of the ease-of-use. Operations were counted through the number of selection/deselection indications (i.e. lasso completions, brush strokes, or magic wand seed selections), and adjustments made on the scroll wheels.

4.5 Experimental Procedure & Equipment

The experiment was run on an Intel Core i7-2600 3.4 GHz PC with 8 GB of memory and an nVidia GeForce GTX 590 graphics card. The experimental software was a custom made OpenGL renderer running under 64-bit Microsoft Windows 7. For head and hand tracking, a 24 camera OptiTrack system was used, which allowed unrestricted user motion inside a 2.25 m radius. The HMD was an nVisor SX111 featuring a $102 \times 64°$ total field-of-view at a resolution of 1280×1024 pixels per eye. Two wireless presenter mice fitted with trackable markers were used as interaction devices (see Figure 1).

In the experiment, the participants first received an introduction to the equipment. Then a few basic, demographic questions (age, gender, 3DUI experience) followed. All participants were instructed that they could stop the experiment at any time, and that they could request breaks. A total of 18 people, 16 males and 2 females, participated in the study. All of the participants were recruited among local university staff and students. The mean age was 27 years ($\sigma = 6.55$ years), and the median self-reported 3DUI experience level on a 1 (novice) to 5 (expert) scale was 3. No payment was offered, apart from some light refreshments during the experiment.

After donning the HMD, the participants were presented with a few practice scenarios to familiarize themselves with all of the techniques and controls. These practice scenarios were all of the SC and AC types. Once the subjects were comfortable with all three techniques, the experiment commenced. The participants were instructed to select all of the blue glyphs, and to avoid selecting the yellow glyphs *as well as possible* in all scenarios. Not requiring perfect selections was a necessity, since far from all combinations of techniques and scenarios would be perfectly solvable, at least within reasonable time. Furthermore, this approach means that the quality parameters of sensitivity and specificity become meaningful quantities to measure, since they are not always at 100%. The subjects were instructed to let the experimenter know as soon as they felt that they were done with a trial. The experimenter would then press a button, the completion time would be logged, and the experiment proceeded to the next trial.

The sequence of the test conditions was randomized for each subject to counterbalance any effects caused by the sequence. Furthermore, all test conditions were repeated 3 times for all subjects. Thus, each subject went through a total of 45 trials during the experiment, which was doable for most subjects in less than an hour. At the end of the experiment, an informal debriefing was made.

5. RESULTS

5.1 Analysis of Hypotheses

All analyses have been made using the statistical software package R [14] using a significance level of $\alpha = 0.05$. Before doing a pre-analysis of the data, three extra response variables were computed from ratios of the directly measured responses. The three ratios were: 1) the sensitivity/operation count ratio, 2) the operation count/completion time ratio, and 3) the sensitivity/completion time ratio. These ratios provide new insights, i.e. 1) the amount of sensitivity gained per operation performed, 2) the speed of each opera-

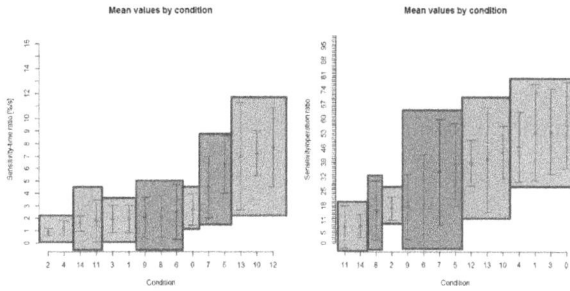

Figure 4: Illustration of mean values and standard devations for each experimental condition. The coloured boxes show which technique each condition belongs to. (Left) The sensitivity gained per second. Here, the magic wand (blue) performs well, except in the AC and UE scenarios. Overall, the brush (red) is slower than the wand, while the box lasso (green) is slowest. (Right) The sensitivity gained per operation. The box lasso performs well, while the magic wand shows a bimodal tendency. The brush technique requires the most operations, implying that many brush strokes are needed to get the desired results.

tion, and 3) the speed of sensitivity gain. As such, these ratios represent the extent to which selection quality, ease-of-use, and speed are traded off. We have included these variables, because they highlight several important differences between the techniques.

A pre-analysis of the data was carried out to check if it conformed to the requirements of analysis of variance (ANOVA). The assumption of independence is satisfied by the fact that independent subjects were used. The normality of the residuals was checked using quantile-quantile (Q-Q) plots. No big problems were detected, however, the sensitivity, specificity, and operation count responses all have some outlier values in their Q-Q plots. The homoscedasticity requirement was not fulfilled for any of the response variables, and attempts to correct this through the use of variance stabilizing transformations failed. We did, however, observe that a logarithm transformation on all of the response variables involving completion time, made the histograms conform much better to a normal distribution bell curve. Therefore, we have used log transformations on all completion time-dependent variables. To be sure that we are not reaching the wrong conclusions, we verified that a non-parametric Friedman test reaches the same conclusions as the performed ANOVA. For this reason, we chose to use ANOVA in spite of the violation of a basic ANOVA assumption. All pairwise post-hoc tests were carried out using the Tukey's honest significant difference method. Some of the results are illustrated in Figure 4.

5.1.1 Hypothesis 1

The hypothesis H1 stated that there would be a significant effect of the combination of MOS tool and geometric scenario. This hypothesis is unambiguously supported no matter which response variable is considered. The p-values are all $\ll 0.001$. This means that the choice of MOS tool makes a big difference depending on the geometric scenario facing the user, both in terms of the quality of selection, completion time, and the subjective judgment of ease-of-use.

5.1.2 Hypothesis 2

H2 hypothesized that the box lasso was the best tool to use in the AC scenario. This means that test conditions 1 (lasso), 6 (brush), and 11 (wand) must be compared. The performance of the box

lasso in the AC scenario relative to the other techniques depends on the response variable chosen. Wrt. subjective difficulty, the lasso is deemed significantly easier to use than the magic wand ($p < 0.001$), but there is no significant difference between the brush and the lasso. With respect to completion time, there are no significant differences among the techniques. In the case of sensitivity, the lasso does outperform the magic wand ($p < 0.001$), but not the brush. The same result is the case wrt. specificity. If the tradeoff ratios are considered, no significant difference is found wrt. the sensitivity achieved per time unit. However, if the sensitivity achieved per operation is considered, the lasso is superior to both the brush and the magic wand (both $p < 0.001$). I.e. the lasso is very good in the adjacent scenario, if judged by the quality it achieves relative to the number of lassos that you have to use. The fact that the lasso is not performing any better is surprising, or at least contrary to current speculation on the topic, e.g. on pp. 20-21 of [18] where it is stated that it is desirable to use a flexible MOS shape that fits the shape of the targets. It is likely, however, that extensive training in the usage of the complex tool modifies this result. The main impact of this result is that users may actually *not* subjectively or objectively prefer to use a tool which is perfectly shaped for the job, *if* the tool is too complex to use compared to using a simpler tool multiple times.

5.1.3 Hypothesis 3

This hypothesis deals with the performance of the magic wand in the EC and EN scenarios. The test conditions of interest are 12 and 13 (wand) compared to 2 and 3 (lasso) and 7 and 8 (brush). Specifically, H3 hypothesizes that the magic wand will outperform the other techniques in those scenarios. With respect to subjective difficulty, the magic wand is better than the lasso ($p < 0.001$ and $p = 0.013$). However, there is no significant difference between the wand and the brush. The response variable that really sets the wand apart from the other two techniques is completion time, where the wand is significantly faster to use than any of the others (p-values in the range from 0.023 to < 0.001). There is not much difference wrt. sensitivity and specificity, the only signficant result being that the wand reaches significantly higher sensitivity in the EN scenario. If the sensitivity gained per time unit is considered, the wand is significantly better than the other two techniques ($p < 0.001$), except when compared to the brush in the EC scenario. The overall conclusion wrt. H3 is therefore that in EC and EN scenarios, the wand mainly outperforms the other techniques wrt. speed, but in terms of selection quality, all techniques achieve similar results.

5.1.4 Hypothesis 4

H4 states that the magic wand is faster than the other techniques in general. The results of H3 already supports H4. Inspecting the completion time response variable across all geometric scenarios, reveals that H4 is supported. The magic wand is significantly faster than the brush ($p < 0.001$), which in turn is significantly faster than the lasso ($p < 0.001$). This is also true, if the amount of sensitivity gained per second using the wand is considered. Here, the wand is significantly better than the brush ($p = 0.020$) and the lasso ($p < 0.001$).

5.1.5 Hypothesis 5

In the final hypothesis, we conjectured that the brush would be judged to be easier to use than the other techniques, viewed across all tested scenarios. The motivation of H5 being true was that the brush featured fewer DoF than the lasso (4 vs. 9), which provides for easier control. At the same time, some of the scenarios were designed to be nearly impossible to do well using the magic wand.

Thus, the brush has potential to be a jack-of-all-trades tool, which users would find easy to use. H5 is supported by the data, based on the subjective ratings of difficulty. Thus, the brush is evaluated to be easier to use than the other two tested techniques, $p = 0.026$ (wand) and $p < 0.001$ (lasso). However, if we evaluate ease-of-use in terms of the number of operations needed to accomplish the tasks, then the picture very different. In terms of number of operations, the box lasso uses significantly fewer operations than any of the other two techniques, $p = 0.0026$ (brush) and $p < 0.001$ (wand). This provides even more evidence that users prefer to use a simple tool many times rather than using a better fitting, complex tool a few times.

6. CONCLUSION & PERSPECTIVES

In this paper, we have presented the following contributions in relation to 3-D MOS tasks. We have presented a thorough analysis of the field of 3-D MOS, including the distinction between the requirements of small and large-scale MOS tasks. We have presented and evaluated a new technique, the magic wand, for partially automating 3-D LS-MOS tasks. Furthermore, we have made a rigourous experiment demonstrating that:

1. Tool efficiency is very geometry dependent. The best 3-D MOS approach in future applications must be to be to include an ensemble of complementary MOS tools.

2. The use of a 3-D magic wand is a very fast technique, but also very sensitive to the geometric scenario, making it either very easy or completely impractical to use.

3. The natural 3-D extension of the 2-D rectangular lasso is not preferred by participants over simpler techniques, even when the simpler options are less suitable for the geometric scenario.

4. The 3-D spherical brush is a good candidate for a simple, general 3-D MOS tool applicable to many scenarios.

Overall, we believe that the results of this experiment should be of interest to any future investigators of 3-D MOS tasks, especially those performed on a large scale, i.e. with too many objects to make serial single-object selection practical.

7. REFERENCES

[1] D. A. Bowman and L. F. Hodges. An evaluation of techniques for grabbing and manipulating remote objects in immersive virtual environments. In *Proceedings of the 1997 symposium on Interactive 3D graphics*, I3D '97, pages 35–ff., New York, NY, USA, 1997. ACM.

[2] D. A. Bowman, E. Kruijff, J. J. LaViola, and I. Poupyrev. *3D User Interfaces: Theory and Practice*. Addison Wesley, first edition, 2005.

[3] H. Dehmeshki and W. Stuerzlinger. Design and evaluation of a perceptual-based object group selection technique. In *Proceedings of the 24th BCS Interaction Specialist Group Conference*, BCS '10, pages 365–373, Swinton, UK, UK, 2010. British Computer Society.

[4] R. Fuchs, V. Welker, and J. Hornegger. Non-convex polyhedral volume of interest selection. *Computerized Medical Imaging and Graphics*, 34(2):105 – 113, 2010.

[5] E. Gokcay and J. C. Principe. Information theoretic clustering. *IEEE Transactions on Pattern Analysis and Machine Intelligence*, 24:158–171, 2002.

[6] R. Harmon, W. Patterson, W. Ribarsky, and J. Bolter. The virtual annotation system. In *Virtual Reality Annual International Symposium, 1996., Proceedings of the IEEE 1996*, pages 239 –245, 270, mar-3 apr 1996.

[7] J. Jang and J. R. Rossignac. Multiple object selection in pattern hierarchies. Technical report, Georgia Institute of Technology, 2007.

[8] J. F. Lucas. Design and evaluation of 3d multiple object selection techniques. Master's thesis, Virginia Polytechnic Institute and State University, 2005.

[9] J. F. Lucas, J.-S. Kim, and D. A. Bowman. Resizing beyond widgets: object resizing techniques for immersive virtual environments. In *CHI '05 extended abstracts on Human factors in computing systems*, CHI EA '05, pages 1601–1604, New York, NY, USA, 2005. ACM.

[10] M. Mine. Virtual environment interaction techniques. Technical report, UNC Chapel Hill CS Dept, 1995.

[11] H. R. Nagel. *Exploratory Visual Data Mining in Spatio-Temporal Virtual Reality*. PhD thesis, Faculty of Engineering and Science, Aalborg University, 2005.

[12] J.-Y. Oh, W. Stuerzlinger, and D. Dadgari. Group selection techniques for efficient 3d modeling. *3D User Interfaces*, 0:95–102, 2006.

[13] I. Poupyrev, M. Billinghurst, S. Weghorst, and T. Ichikawa. The go-go interaction technique: non-linear mapping for direct manipulation in vr. In *Proceedings of the 9th annual ACM symposium on User interface software and technology*, UIST '96, pages 79–80, New York, NY, USA, 1996. ACM.

[14] R Development Core Team. *R: A Language and Environment for Statistical Computing*. R Foundation for Statistical Computing, Vienna, Austria, 2011. ISBN 3-900051-07-0.

[15] R. Stenholt and C. B. Madsen. Shaping 3-d boxes: A full 9-degree-of-freedom docking experiment. In *Virtual Reality Conference (VR), 2011 IEEE*, pages 103–110, March 2011.

[16] W. Stuerzlinger and G. Smith. Efficient manipulation of object groups in virtual environments. In *Virtual Reality, 2002. Proceedings. IEEE*, pages 251 –258, 2002.

[17] A. Ulinski, C. Zanbaka, Z. Wartell, P. Goolkasian, and L. Hodges. Two handed selection techniques for volumetric data. *3D User Interfaces, 2007. 3DUI '07. IEEE Symposium on*, mar. 2007.

[18] A. C. Ulinski. *Taxonomy and experimental evaluation of two-handed selection techniques for volumetric data*. PhD thesis, University of North Carolina at Charlotte, Charlotte, NC, USA, 2008. Adviser-Hodges, Larry F.

[19] C. Ware. *Information Visualization: Perception for Design*. Morgan Kaufmann Publishers, second edition, 2004.

[20] G. Wills. Selection: 524,288 ways to say "this is interesting". In *Information Visualization '96, Proceedings IEEE Symposium on*, pages 54 –60, 120, oct 1996.

[21] R. C. Zeleznik, K. P. Herndon, and J. F. Hughes. Sketch: an interface for sketching 3d scenes. In *ACM SIGGRAPH 2006 Courses*, SIGGRAPH '06, New York, NY, USA, 2006. ACM.

[22] S. Zhai, W. Buxton, and P. Milgram. The "silk cursor": investigating transparency for 3d target acquisition. In *Proceedings of the SIGCHI conference on Human factors in computing systems: celebrating interdependence*, CHI '94, pages 459–464, New York, NY, USA, 1994. ACM.

Brain Computer Interface Vs Walking Interface in VR: The Impact of Motor Activity on Spatial Transfer

Florian Larrue[1][2][3]
flo.larrue@gmail.com

Hélène Sauzéon[2]
helene.sauzeon@u-bordeaux2.fr

Lioubov Aguilova[2]
aguilova@gmail.com

Fabien Lotte[3][1]
fabien.lotte@inria.fr

Martin Hachet[3][1]
martin.hachet@inria.fr

Bernard NKaoua[2]
bernard.nkaoua@u-bordeaux2.fr

(1) University of Bordeaux, LaBRI,UMR 5800
F-33400 Talence, France.
CNRS, LaBRI, UMR 5800,33400 Talence,
France.

(2) University of Bordeaux Victor Segalen
EA 4136, Handicap & Système Nerveux
33076 Bordeaux Cedex, France.

(3) INRIA, F-33400 Talence, France.

ABSTRACT

The goal of this study is to explore new navigation methods in Virtual Reality (VR) and to understand the impact of motor activity on spatial cognition, and more precisely the question of the spatial learning transfer. We present a user study comparing two interfaces with different motor activities: the first one, a walking interface (a treadmill with rotation) gives the user a high level of sensorimotor activity (especially body-based and vestibular information). The second one, a brain computer interface (BCI), enables the user to navigate in a virtual environment (VE) without any motor activity, by using brain activity only. The task consisted in learning a path in a virtual city built from a 3D model of a real city with either one of these two interfaces (named treadmill condition and BCI condition), or in the real city directly (the real condition). Then, participants had to recall spatial knowledge, according to six different tasks assessing spatial memory and transfer. We also evaluated the ergonomics of these two interfaces and the presence felt by participants. Surprisingly, contrary to expectations, our results showed similar performances whatever the spatial restitution tasks or the interfaces used, very close to that of the real condition, which tends to indicate that motor activity is not essential to learn and transfer spatial knowledge. Even if BCI seems to be less natural to use than the treadmill, our study suggests that BCI is a promising interface for studying spatial cognition.

Categories and Subject Descriptors

H.1.2 [**Information Systems**]: Models and Principles, User/Machine Systems - *Human factors, Human information processing, Software psychology*; H.5.2 [**Information Systems**]: User interfaces – *Ergonomics, Evaluation/methodology, Theory and method, User-centered design*.

General Terms

Human Factors, Measurement, Performance, Experimentation.

Keywords

Interfaces, Navigation, Virtual Reality, Spatial Cognition, Treadmill, Brain Computer Interface, User Study.

1. INTRODUCTION

One future goal of the Virtual Reality (VR) technologies for neuropsychologists is to place patients in virtual situations that are similar to real-life situations, in order to improve the diagnostic or the effects of virtual learning on daily living activities [18]. VR is also important for example, to train people in airplane simulators, and to increase their performances, where real training is difficult, due to the cost and the availability of equipments. So, one question is to identify the variables that promote the knowledge transfer from a virtual to a real environment. In this paper, we focused more precisely on the role of motor activity and the interfaces on spatial cognition. Indeed, the impact and the amount of motor activity in VR that is necessary to successfully learn and recall spatial knowledge learning are still undefined. Spatial cognition involves cognitive processes which are necessary for many daily life situations, such as shopping in supermarkets (e.g., finding a product in a section) or driving. These cognitive processes are often affected by neurological diseases, brain trauma, etc. [18]. According to Montello [13], spatial cognition refers to two components: the first one, the cognitive component named wayfinding, corresponds to the processes necessary to plan an itinerary, to take a direction, to store and restitute spatial knowledge. The second component is a sensorimotor one which concerns all the displacements, and visual, vestibular and kinesthetic information, informing on the position and direction of our own body/head in an environment [19]. In real environments, it has been shown that body-based and vestibular information are important to learn and restore spatial knowledge. However, motor and cognitive component are often studied at the same time, and little research focused only on the cognitive component, due to the difficulty to isolate it. With VR technology, we proposed to isolate the motor component with the use of a Brain Computer Interface (BCI). BCI are communication devices that enable users to send command to a computer application by using brain activity only. This activity is generally measured using ElectroEncephaloGraphy (EEG) [14]. While initial BCI research was mostly targeted at severely paralyzed users, e.g., to design brain-controlled prostheses or wheelchairs [3], more recent works have also identified promising applications for healthy users, in areas such as video games or VR, among many others [9, 23]. In this work, we focus on the impact of the (sensori) motor component on the cognitive component of spatial transfer using two interfaces in VR. More precisely, we used for a spatial transfer task, 1) a treadmill with rotation, which provides vestibular, full–body based information and a motor activity near to real walking, and 2) a BCI, which permits to navigate in a Virtual Environment (VE) without motor activity, by brain activity only. These two learning conditions in VR were compared to a real condition where participants performed the same learning task in a comparable real environment. We used different spatial restitution tests to evaluate spatial acquisition levels and transfer. To our knowledge, this is the first user study which proposed a method to distinguish the motor from the cognitive component for spatial cognition. This is also the first study which compares a BCI to a walking interface, more particularly addressing the transfer question.

2. RELATED WORK

2.1 Spatial Cognition and cognitive processes

Several models of spatial knowledge acquisition exist. One of the most cited is the Landmark Route Survey (L-R-S) model of Siegel and White [22] which advances that spatial knowledge is acquired by steps: first, landmarks are stored, then the route survey (fixed sequences of landmarks and action). The last stage concerns survey knowledge, comparable to a map view of the environment. The two first levels are egocentric (i.e. involves the person's point of view) while the last stage is allocentric (i.e. spatial information are integrated independently from the personal point of view). The survey knowledge is more difficult to achieve and requires the repetition of spatial information. But currently, this model is questioned in particular the fact that spatial information may not be acquired only by steps but also in parallel [6].

2.2 Spatial Cognition and motor processes

One theory of spatial knowledge acquisition concerns path integration [12]. This theory admits that it is possible to acquire spatial knowledge without optic flow, only based on body-based information generated by our motor activity, updating away information of position and translation of the body. In real environments, the impact of body based-information, and more precisely vestibular information on spatial knowledge, have been deeply studied. For example, Loomis et al. [10] showed that when only optic flow is involved, performances on directional responses were much poorer than when walking. Mittelstaedt and Mittelstaedt [12] also found that vestibular information is essential, specifically when visual information is not present. Vestibular information would be necessary for the perception of distances, angles, and for route knowledge (i.e. egocentric spatial updating [2]), while allocentric knowledge would use position and orientation of visual cues.

2.3 Spatial Cognition and VR studies

Our real question is: do interactions in VE and associated motor activity have an impact on spatial knowledge? The majority of the spatial cognition experiments use a joystick for the navigation, which provides little motor activity due to low displacement and the force applied by the hand (no vestibular information). But different authors [21,5] found that motor activity, body-based and vestibular information given by walking in VR (with treadmill or direct walking with a Head Mounted Display –HMD- for rotational movement and direction of the head) gave better results when vestibular information was present than when no vestibular information was provided. Ruddle and Lessels [20], for example, compared different interfaces (walking in VE/HMD, Keyboard/HMD and mouse/Keyboard) and found that the walking VR group performed better than the other groups for navigational search tasks (finding targets hidden inside boxes in a room-sized space). This was also consistent with the findings by Grant and Magee [5], which is, to our knowledge, the only research about walking motor activity and spatial transfer. The authors showed that people performed better on a wayfinding task in the real world if they had previously been exposed to a VE using a walking interface rather than a joystick. For Waller [24], the use of a joystick requires different attention levels which would interfere on spatial representations of a VE. Ruddle et al. [21] recently addressed the role of both translational and rotational vestibular information in VE on the accuracy of participants' cognitive maps (survey knowledge). To do so, they used different locomotion interfaces (translational displacements with walking or treadmill vs. no translational displacements with joystick), sometimes with the possibility of really turning the head (i.e., rotational vestibular condition or not) during rotational movement. They reported that walking, as well as the treadmill condition, significantly improved the accuracy of participants' survey knowledge, but, that vestibular rotational-based information had no effect. To summarize, results on interfaces and motor activity in a VE are sporadic and contrasted.

2.4 Spatial Cognition and BCI

As for as we know, there is no user study which focused on spatial cognition with BCI. However it has been shown that BCI could be used to navigate and explore real and VE by using only brain activity. For instance some groups have reported that a BCI could be used to freely navigate along a virtual street [7], in a virtual apartment [8] or in a virtual museum [11]. Navigation in real environments has also been achieved using a brain-controlled wheelchair [3]. This demonstrates that a BCI is a suitable input device to perform navigation tasks. For Lecuyer et al. [9], BCI have the same properties as a classical interface, as such it could be used to distinguish the cognitive component from the motor component in spatial cognition. But currently, no study addressed the impact of BCI use on spatial knowledge, most BCI research being focused on signal processing and assistive applications.

2.5 Spatial knowledge transfer from virtual to real environments

When VR is used as a medium for spatial learning, one key challenge is to understand what spatial knowledge learned from the VE is transferred into real life, and to identify the factors that promote these transfers. Previous findings indicated that spatial learning from a VE was similar to knowledge acquired in a real environment, irrespective of the type of participants [26], or even if patients suffer from traumatic brain injury. Different authors have also found a significant impact of the motor activity of the joystick. However, certain factors such as visual fidelity, retention delay, navigation mode [25, 26, 27], or video game experience [16] can also have an impact on spatial transfer. In the end, we found few experiments that studied spatial transfer from virtual to real by comparing different interfaces and associated level of motor activity.

3. METHOD

VR was used as a spatial learning medium using a spatial learning paradigm that involves acquiring a path, either in a real environment or its virtual replica [26, 27]. The acquisition path was assessed according to three conditions of navigation modes: in VR with either 1) a Treadmill (all body-based information); 2) a BCI (no body displacement and no body-based information), or 3) in real condition where participants learned the path in the real environment (all body-based information). After path acquisition, participants completed tasks for assessing their spatial knowledge.

3.1 Setup

3.1.1 The environment

The real environment was a 9km^2 area near a hospital. The VE was a 3D scale model of the real environment, with realistic rendering (photos of several building facades were applied to 3D geometric surfaces) and urban sounds to make the simulation more realistic. Significant landmarks (e.g., signposts, signs, and urban furniture) were also included in the VE. The VE was laboratory-developed using Virtools 3.5™. Irrespective of the learning conditions, the itinerary was presented to participants on the basis of an egocentric frame of reference, at head height. It was characterized by an irregular closed loop, 780 m in length, with 13 crossroads and 11 directional changes.

3.2   Material

The material used in the darkened laboratory room was a DELL Precision M6300 laptop computer (RAM: 3GHz; processor: Intel Core 2 Duo T9500 2.60 Ghz) with an Nvidia Quadro FX 1600M graphics card (256Mo) and a resolution of 1024 x 768, a 2 x 1.88 meter screen, a projector (Optoma/ThemeScene from Texas Instrument) with rear projection. The participants were located two meters away from the display screen.

Description of the treadmill and the BCI Interfaces

The treadmill condition included an HP COSCOM programmable (speed, declination and acceleration) treadmill and a MS-EZ1 sonar telemeter. This interface enabled users to modify the VE's visual display in real time to match his/her walking speed, with a maximum speed of 6 km/h. The Sonar MS-EZ1 telemeter monitored the participant's movements on the treadmill which was divided into three parts (see Figure 1): one for accelerating (the front of the treadmill), one for walking normally (the middle of the treadmill), and one for decelerating (the back of the treadmill). Neither acceleration nor deceleration information was sent to the treadmill when the participant was in the walk zone. In contrast, when the participant walked into the acceleration or deceleration zone, the sonar detected length changes in the participant's position, and instructed the computer to accelerate or decelerate until the participant returned to the walk zone. Finally, the participant remaining in the deceleration zone for a prolonged period induced a stop in the VE. Participants were able to walk, accelerate, decelerate, and stop in the VE, thus receiving body-based information induced by the physical displacement of the participant on the treadmill. For rotational movement (and rotational vestibular information), the participant walked on the treadmill and was informed that his/her point of view in the VE would be controlled in real time by head rotations captured by motion capture (analyzed with 12 cameras OPTITRACK system, Motion point™): when the participant turned his/her head, the system updated the visual optic flow at a rate correlated with the head movement rotation angle (the greater the rotation angle was, the faster the modification in rotational optic flow was, reflecting natural head movements).

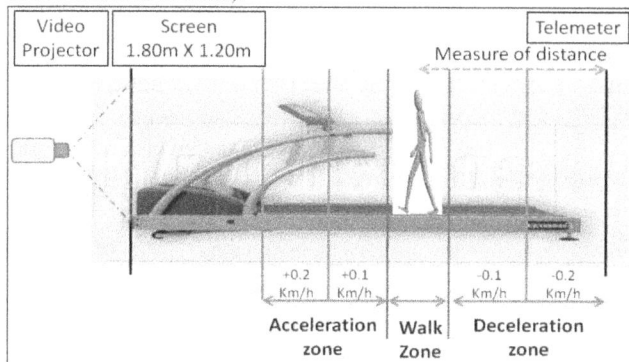

Figure 1: Treadmill interface and interaction techniques To accelerate, decelerate or stop in the VE.

Our BCI system was a two-class system, based on motor imagery tasks [14]. More precisely, participants had to imagine a left (or right) hand movement, which the BCI had to detect, to turn left (or right) in the VE. Our BCI was thus synchronous, which means that the EEG data analysis was performed at a specific time points and not continuously. Indeed, participants cannot interact any time but only on computer demand. Interaction was possible with the BCI system only when an arrow was presented at each intersection, indicating which hand motor imagery (left or right) the participant had to perform. Speed displacement in the VE was fixed to 4 km/h.

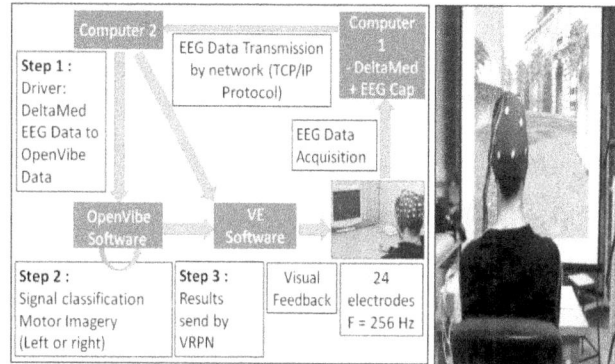

Figure 2: On the left, our OpenVibe BCI system. On the right, A participant with our BCI during a VR spatial learning task.

Our BCI was based on the OpenVibE software [15] which allows implementing easily a BCI with little knowledge on signal processing. Brain signals acquisition was done by a PC X86 equipped with an EEG Deltamed System composed of a 24 electrode cap. Communication between the VE and Deltamed system acquisition relies on the VRPN protocol, based on TCP/IP (see Figure 2). EEG corresponding to left or right hand motor imagery were identified using a classical processing pipeline [14, 15]. Precisely, band power features in the mu and beta bands (8-30 Hz) were extracted from laplacian channels over electrodes C3 and C4 and classified using a Support Vector Machine (SVM).

3.3   Procedure

Each participant completed a three-phase procedure: (1) spatial ability tests and immersion propensity, orientation, shortcuts, map questionnaires, to assess the participant's characteristics (see below); (2) learning phase: training interface and the route-learning task under one of the three conditions (BCI vs. treadmill vs. real); (3) restitution phase with six spatial knowledge tasks.

3.3.1 Spatial ability tests, immersion propensity, orientation, shortcuts, map questionnaires:

The GZ5 test was used to measure spatial ability of participants. The Mental Rotation Test (MRT) was administered to measure spatial mental rotation abilities. The Corsi's block-tapping test was employed to measure the visual-spatial memory span. Three self-administrated questionnaires were filled in by the participants. One focused on spatial orientation in everyday life, the second one evaluated the ability to take shortcuts, and the third one, the ability to use maps, including seven questions each (for each responses were given on a 7-point scale). The higher the score the higher the subject's difficulties on one of these different themes. Measures of the immersion propensity were based on the questionnaire used by Girard and Turcotte [4].

3.3.2 Learning phase

- Real condition: Route learning under real conditions was the baseline, providing referential performances by learning a real route in an urban environment. The participants walked at their own speed, were instructed which direction to take at each corner, and were free to visually explore their surroundings. Learning position data was acquired using a Magellan™ GPS CrossOver, and a video was recorded using an AIPTEK™ DV8900 camera mounted on a bicycle helmet worn by the participant.

- Treadmill condition (VR):

Before VR exposition, each participant participated to a training phase, to get used to interacting with the treadmill. The initial training phase was considered to be completed when the participant was able to use the interface in another VE. Route learning in the treadmill condition was similar to the real condition. The directions were indicated verbally by an experimenter situated behind the participant. Position, time, collisions and interactions (acceleration, deceleration, turning left and right) were captured.

- BCI condition (VR):

Step 1) Learning to use a BCI:

The BCI use requires a long training time because participants had to learn to control their brain activity, and the computer has to learn this brain activity. The participants were equipped with the EEG cap (see Figure 2). The training was composed of six sessions distributed over three days (about three hours of training by session). The learning protocol was based on a standard protocol (see [14] for more details), which consisted to imagine movements of the left (or right) hand when a left (or right) arrow was presented on the screen. A visual feedback in a VE informed the participant about the motor imagery detected.

Step 2) Learning the path with the BCI:

Directions in route learning were given at each intersection by an arrow indicating the direction of the motor imagery that the participant had to execute. If the recognized computer command was incorrect (for example, if the system detected a right motor imagery while a left arrow was presented), the participant was redirected by the experimenter in the correct direction with a joystick.

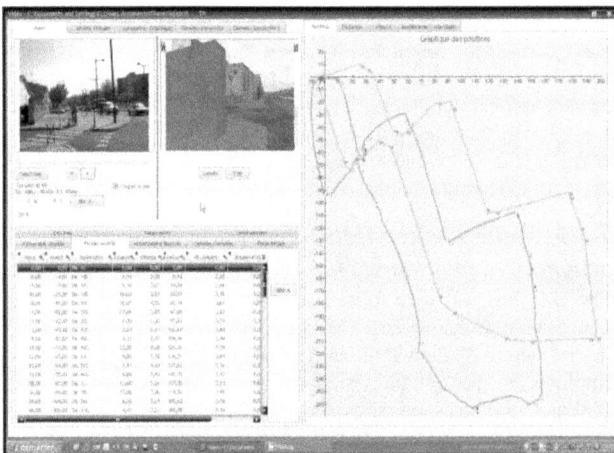

**Figure 3: Analysis software to compare
Virtual and real conditions.**

In addition, after VR exposure (for the BCI and treadmill condition), the participants completed 1) a simplified simulator sickness questionnaire (SSQ) to measure the negative side effects of being immersed in graphically-rendered virtual worlds, 2) a questionnaire concerning the ergonomics of the interface used, and 3) a presence the questionnaire proposed by Girard and Turcotte [4]. Moreover, a software tool (see Figure 3) was developed to analyze the participant's positions, interactions, speed and time data in the VE or in the real condition, to ensure the similarity of path learning in real and virtual conditions.

3.3.3 Restitution phase

Six tasks were performed by each participant, in an order counterbalanced across participants.

Photograph classification task: twelve real photographs of intersections of the path followed were presented to the participants in a random order. Participants were required to arrange the photographs in chronological order along the path they had learned (the time allowed was ten minutes). The results were scored as follows: one point for a photo in the correct position and 0.5 point for each photo in a correct sequence, but not correctly placed along the path (e.g., positioning photos 4-5-6 in the right order but not placing them correctly in the overall sequence earned 1.5 points). This paper-pencil task assessed the participants' ability to recall landmarks and route knowledge within an egocentric framework [26, 27].

Distance estimation task: Each participant was asked to give a verbal estimation of the distance walked in the VE (in meters).

Directional estimation task (see Figure 4): This task was computer-based and consisted of presenting a series of twelve pictures of real intersections, taken from a walker's perspective, in random order. Each photograph was displayed at the top of the screen, above an 8-point compass. The participant had to select the compass direction they were facing on the learned path. We noted the percentage of errors and the angular error were averaged. Directional estimations are expected to be accurate when participants have acquired well-developed route knowledge.

**Figure 4: Screenshot of the directional estimation task
And the starting point estimation task.**

Sketch-mapping task: Participants had to draw a freehand sketch of the visualized route. The time limit was ten minutes. One point was scored for each correct change of direction. This paper-pencil task is known to measure survey knowledge [26, 27].

Point starting estimation task (see Figure 4): This computer-based task consisted of presenting a series of twelve pictures of real intersections, taken from a walker's point of view, in random order. Each photograph was displayed at the top of the screen, above an 8-point compass. For each photograph, the participant had to select the compass direction of the starting point of the learned path. We noted the percentage of errors and the number of angular errors was averaged. These direction estimations are expected to be accurate when participants have memorized a well-developed, map-like representation of the walked environment and measures survey knowledge.

Real wayfinding task: this task consisted of reproducing the learned path in the real environment. Direction errors were calculated and expressed in percentages. When a participant made a mistake, s/he was stopped and invited to turn in the right direction. This task may be considered as a naturalistic assessment of navigational abilities and spatial knowledge transfer, based on the use of landmarks, as well as route and survey knowledge [27]. In addition, restitution path software included the participant's position and time data analyses, in order to measure restitution speed (the same Magellan GPS CrossOver and helmet-mounted video camera were used for data capture).

3.4 Participants

Participants were 48 student volunteers from our university (24 men and 24 women): 20 students were assigned to the real condition, 20 to the treadmill condition and only 8 to the BCI condition, due to the time required to learn to use this interface (about 10 hours per subject), and the difficulties in having subjects on 3 different days and closely spaced in time. All participants had normal or corrected-to- normal vision and were right-handed, and had at least an A-level or equivalent degree. Their ages ranged from 18 to 30 years. We controlled the video game experience of subjects: half of each condition was constituted of video game players (who played a minimum of three hours by week during more than one year), and the other half of non video game players (who never played regularly to video games, and who were not old video gamers). The three composed conditions were balanced for gender and for video game experience (χ^2 procedure p>0.05). In addition, there was no significant difference in spatial abilities among the three conditions, as assessed with the GZ-5, the Mental Rotation Test (MRT) and the Corsi's block-tapping (respectively, p>0.300; p>0.800; p>0.900). No differences were found concerning the orientation, shortcuts and map questionnaires (p>0.200, p>0.400, p>0.400). For the VR conditions, no differences were found for immersion propensity (p>0.600).

4. RESULTS

Dependent measurements and statistical analyses: each of the dependent measurements presented above were submitted to a one-way ANOVA analysis (3 learning condition: BCI, treadmill with rotation, real), with between-subject measures (see Table 1). Post-hoc analyses were carried out using Fisher's procedure. A Pearson's correlation was used to assess the relationships between the performances in the spatial restitution tasks, the tasks assessing spatial abilities, the presence questionnaire, the self-reporting questionnaire about spatial difficulties, the SSQ and the questionnaire about the interface ergonomics.

For the *Photograph classification task*, the ANOVA revealed a significant effect of the learning condition ($F(2,45)$=4.01; $p<0.05$; $\eta^2=0.15$) where results were better in the real condition than the two virtual conditions. Results in VR conditions were very close and post hoc comparisons showed a significant difference for the real condition compared to the treadmill condition ($p<0.05$), and a tendency between the real and the BCI condition ($p=0.06$).

No significant effect (p>0.100) was found for the *Distance estimation task*.

For the *directional estimation task*, no differences were found for errors percentage (p>0.200) or for mean angular errors (p>0.300). For the *Sketch-mapping task*, the statistical analyses revealed no significant differences (p>0.200).

Concerning the *point starting estimation task*, no differences were found for the percentage errors (p>0.600) or for the mean angular error (p>0.900).

For the *Real wayfinding task*, the ANOVA analyses for the restitution speed revealed a significant difference ($F(2,45)$=3.99; $p<0.05$; $\eta^2=0.15$). Restitution speed was the slowest for the BCI condition, followed by the treadmill condition, and the real condition was the fastest. Post hoc comparisons showed only a significant difference between the real condition and the BCI condition, where restitution speed was significantly lowest for the BCI condition ($p<0.001$). For the errors direction percentage, the ANOVA analysis revealed no significant differences (p>0.100).

Table 1: Results of the spatial restitution tasks according to The learning conditions (real, treadmill or BCI).

		Real Environment	Treadmill	BCI
Wayfinding Task	Mean Speed	3.66	3.1	2.93
	(SD)	0.26	0.32	0.31
	Percentage Error	4.99	8.5	8.65
	(SD)	6.72	5.99	6.41
Photograph classification task	Correct Score	8.6	5.85	6
	(SD)	3.46	2.88	3.65
Directional estimation task	Percentage Error	19.23	28.07	22.11
	(SD)	14.22	19.7	16.16
	Mean angular error	104.86	87.09	81.02
	(SD)	56.81	42.85	25.38
Distance estimation task	Distance	865.1	1063	1355.62
	(SD)	636.28	587.43	544.61
Starting point estimation task	Percentage Error	45.83	50.83	46.87
	(SD)	17.62	17.91	19.38
	Mean angular error	82.59	81.43	81.95
	(SD)	29.51	15.5	25.38
Sketch-mapping task	Correct responses	11.15	10.45	11.87
	(SD)	2.41	2.26	1.45

For the last results, we compared the treadmill and the BCI condition using an unpaired two-tailed Student's t-test (with dof=26), the real condition was excluded because no interface was used in this condition.

SSQ and ergonomics of the interface used (see figure 5):
Concerning the SSQ questionnaire (based on only the two VR conditions, see Figure 5), no differences were found for discomfort, fatigue, eye pain, headaches, stomachache (respectively, p=0.07, p=0.44, p=0.93, p=0.48, p=0.39).
Concerning the ergonomics questionnaire about the interface used, the Student's t-test analysis revealed a significant difference for the possibility to rotate (t(-11.40); $p<0.0001$; $\eta^2=0.83$) in favor of the treadmill condition. To the question "The interface used was easy to use", statistical analyses revealed a significant difference for the treadmill condition compared to the BCI condition (t(5.41); $p<0.0001$; $\eta^2=0.53$). For the tiring question, the statistical analyses revealed no differences (p=0.52). It should be noted that for the BCI condition, 3 participants (out of 8) found

that it was a tiring interface. Concerning the last questions, we used a 7 point scale (0 = the worst and 7 = the best). All participants in VR conditions thought that the two interfaces were easy to learn; statistical analyses revealed a significant difference in favor of the treadmill condition (t(3.30); p=0.028; η^2=0.30) for the learning of the interface used and for the understanding of the interface (t(3.56); p=0.0015; η^2=0.32). 4 participants in the BCI condition found difficulties due to the precision of the interface, but no significant difference was found about it (p=0.18).

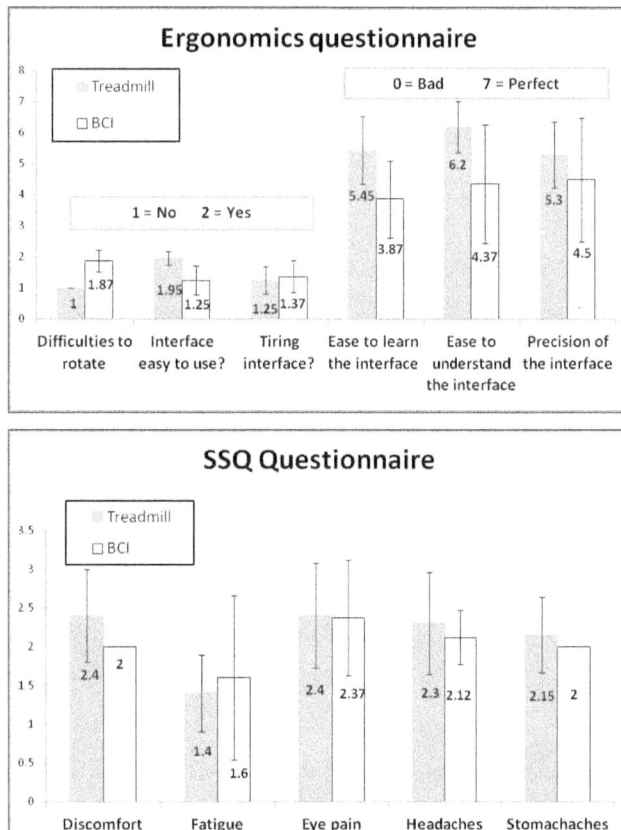

Figure 5: Ergonomics and SSQ questionnaire according to The treadmill and the BCI condition.

Presence questionnaire (see results on Figure 6):
The authors have decomposed this test in sub-scales and a global score. Concerning the realism sub-score, no difference was found (p=0.35). For the acting possibility subscale, a difference was found in favor of the treadmill condition (t(3.37) ; p=0.002; η^2=0.30). The Student's t-test revealed no differences concerning interface quality (p=0.85), but a significant difference for the treadmill condition concerning the possibility to examine the environment (t(2.10); p=0.04; η^2=0.14). No differences were found on the auditory presence (p=0.83) or for the haptic presence (p=0.45). Finally, the Student's t-test revealed a significant effect in favor of the treadmill condition (t(2.66); p=0.013; η^2=0.21) for the global presence score.

Correlations:
For the *Orientation, shortcuts and maps questionnaire*, negative correlations were found between the percentage of errors for the starting point estimation task and the general orientation questionnaire. A negative correlation was also found between the shortcuts questionnaire and all the dependent variables of the starting point estimation task. Finally, a negative correlation was

found between the percentage of errors for the starting point estimation task and the maps questionnaire.
Concerning the *SSQ and the ergonomics questionnaire*, no correlations were found with the scores of the spatial tasks.
Finally, for the *Presence questionnaire*, while we found correlations between the different subscales (not presented here), we did not found significant correlations between these subscales and the spatial knowledge measures of our different tasks.

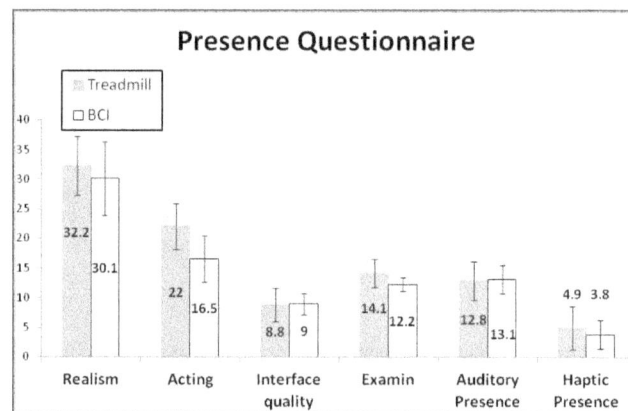

Figure 6: Presence questionnaire according to the treadmill And the BCI condition.

5. DISCUSSION

To recall, our study focuses on the impact of a motor activity on the transfer of spatial knowledge from virtual to real environments, by comparing two virtual learning conditions: 1) a treadmill condition which provided body-based information very close to a real waking activity, 2) a BCI condition where displacements were performed by brain activity (without any motor activity), to a real condition where participants learned a path while walking in the real environment. Six different restitution tasks were presented to the participant in order to evaluate if the motor activity had an impact on these tasks, known to measure transfer, egocentric and allocentric knowledge.

5.1 Motor activity and spatial transfer

For the photograph classification task, our results showed a significant difference in favor of the real condition compared to the two others conditions. Post hoc comparisons also showed a significant difference between the real condition and the treadmill condition and a tendency between the real condition and the BCI condition, but none between the BCI and the treadmill condition. This task consisted in measuring chronological sequences of intersections photographs of the real environment with an egocentric point of view, which would involve the episodic memory, and more precisely the temporal component. Our results suggest that motor activity (the treadmill condition) does not improve performances compared to a condition without motor activity (BCI). However, the best results are for the real condition, which should mean that the visual information provided by this last condition seems to be more important than motor activity for this task. Our results are in accordance with Wallet et al. [27] who found for the same task, that the visual fidelity of an environment is more important than the interaction (passive -no interaction- vs. active mode -joystick interaction). Efforts to improve the visual rendering of our VE to make it close to the real environment could confirm these results.
Surprisingly, for the distance estimation task, no differences were found, whatever the learning conditions used, meaning that motor activity would not be important for this type of task. For certain

authors, in VE [21] or real environments, body displacement are important to evaluate egocentric tasks such as distance estimations. But for others [17], visual information would be sufficient. Three explanations can be summarized as follow: 1) visual information may be sufficient for spatial knowledge transfer 2) the neuromuscular theory of Abernethy et al. [1] affirms that there would be a similitude between a performed movement and an imagined movement; in our BCI condition, the motor activity would be "symbolic", meaning that body-based information would be stimulated without the effective displacement 3) For the BCI condition, only eight participants are presented; it would be interesting to increase the number of participants in order to confirm our results.

No differences were found for the directional estimation task. This task consisted in the reminding of an egocentric point of view of a real intersection associated to an action. Once again, the motor activity provided by the real walking or walking on the treadmill does not improve performances compared to the BCI condition. One other explanation could be that BCI participants had a long training period where they saw arrows to indicate a hand movement to imagine. Maybe these indications could increase the learning by combining an arrow to a direction. A solution would be to use a verbal BCI system to delete this visual aid.

No differences were found concerning the measures of allocentric knowledge (i.e. the starting point estimation task, and the sketch mapping task), knowledge acquired with repetitions and manipulations of spatial information. Nevertheless, most of the dependant variables of these two tasks were correlated with our questionnaire about self-reporting of using maps, shortcuts or general orientation. These results mean that allocentric knowledge would be more linked to cognitive processes and real life experience than the motor activity or the tasks used. Once again, BCI seems to be sufficient to acquire this type of knowledge.

Concerning the wayfinding task, our results showed no significant differences between the three conditions for the percentage of errors, meaning that motor activity and body-based information induced by walking are not essential to increase spatial knowledge transfer. Our results for the treadmill condition are in accordance with other experiments which showed that body-based information is important [21] when walking in a VE (not a transfer task). Nevertheless, our BCI condition could be compared to a passive exploration mode, with the participants not moving except that they could interact. Here, our BCI condition proposed results similar with the treadmill or the real condition, meaning that the possibility to interact in the VE seems to be more important than motor activity. Different authors who compared active exploration to a passive exploration [25, 26, 27] often showed that the real condition was the best condition to acquire and to recall spatial knowledge, but also that active exploration (often with a joystick or a keyboard and a mouse for the displacement, which do not provide body-based information or vestibular information) was better than a passive exploration. Maybe joystick or mouse interfaces involve an important learning phase and large attention as already said by Waller [24] which had a bad impact on spatial cognitive processes. Or maybe our BCI and the absence of motor displacement permitted to be more vigilant than with a joystick where motor activity is required. Indeed, even if participants had to limit their motor movements during BCI use, they might have still done some minor movements. In the future, a joystick condition could provide information about a small motor activity during a spatial navigation task. It is to note that statistical analyses showed that the restitution speed was the worst for the BCI condition in comparison to the real condition, indicating that the interface used

could have an impact on the speed of spatial transfer. More precisely, the motor activity of the treadmill condition enabled to obtain time and spatial performances that were very close to the real condition, while no motor activity provided by the BCI condition allows similar spatial transfer performances but in a longer time. Maybe the fact that the displacement speed in the BCI condition was fixed and not controlled by the user and the interactions occurred only at the intersections, may have an impact on the spatial information acquisition. A new BCI condition with the possibility to modify the displacement speed and to choose its orientation (an asynchronous three-class BCI) at any time may give new information about the impact of motor activity on spatial restitution time.

Of course, our BCI condition contained only eight participants. Moreover, the learning phase of this interface was longer than the treadmill condition and could have an impact on performances. But our results are the first ones which compared a BCI to another interface. Moreover, we tried to clearly distinguish the motor component of the cognitive component in spatial cognition, and tried to evaluate the impact of the motor activity during a navigational task in a VE. Results pointed that motor activity and body-based information are not essential if the cognitive processes, the ability to act and to understand its interaction are not interfered by motor processes. It is also important to note that is unlikely that gaming or interface experience played a major role because these two VR interactions were totally novel and unknown of all the participants. It would be interesting now, to increase the number of participants in the BCI condition, and to compare the performances of the treadmill and the BCI conditions to a joystick condition, in order to confirm our results about the motor activity of a less natural interface than the treadmill.

5.2 Ergonomics and presence questionnaires

This section concerns more precisely self-report of users about the two VR interfaces. The goals here are to determine the differences between the walking interface and a BCI, in order to give some guidelines concerning navigational interactions in a VE.

For the realism of the simulation, we did not found significant differences, meaning that the high level of motor activity of the treadmill condition had little impact on the realism compared to the BCI condition. It is to note that there was no difference for the haptic and auditory feedback, meaning also that the motor activity was natural for the treadmill condition, and similar to the BCI. Maybe a less natural and transparent interface such as a joystick may give new information about realism perception.

In contrast, the possibility to act, and to examine the VE were significantly better for the treadmill compared to the BCI condition. These results showed that our walking VR condition allowed the participants to explore and to navigate more easily in the VE. Our results also showed that the treadmill condition was easier to learn, to understand, to use and to perform than the BCI condition. The use of the treadmill seems to be more natural and transparent to use than the BCI. This may be due to the fact that 1) the treadmill is a walking interface where the interaction is very close to real walking and participants did not have a long training to use it strongly; 2) the interactions in the BCI condition were synchronous, i.e., participants had to perform their mental tasks very few times and should not do so when they want but only at the intersections. Therefore, it seems that the possibility to act and to examine the VE were the worst for this condition. But for this last condition, maybe attention processes were less used due to the little amount of interactions, improving the processes necessary to acquire spatial knowledge, and explaining similar results between the two VR conditions.

A significant difference was found concerning the total presence score in favor of the treadmill condition. Finally, the presence may be more strongly related to the navigational possibilities offered to the users than to the interface they used. But even if the treadmill condition permitted the users to explore more easily and more naturally the VE than the BCI condition, performances in term of spatial navigation were equivalent. This means that even if the sense of presence is high, it does not improve performances. Moreover, it seems that cognitive processes are more important than motor processes for spatial cognition. It is also important to note that whatever the interfaces used, no significant statistical differences were found concerning the SSQ, and no correlations were revealed with the spatial restitution tasks, and the SSQ or the presence questionnaire. So, performances on spatial tasks cannot be explained by the limitations of the interface used.

A natural interface such as the treadmill condition, which is easier to use, would not be necessary better than another navigational interface, maybe less intuitive. These results could be supported by the statistical analyses concerning the quality, the precision, or the fatigue caused by the interface used, which were not different between the treadmill and the BCI. Even if some differences appeared concerning the presence and the ergonomics of the two interfaces in favor of the treadmill condition, results in term of spatial transfer performances are equivalent, and not correlated with the ergonomics score. We may wonder whether it is necessary to use more complex BCI (e.g. asynchronous and/or three-class BCI) given that the transfer performances achieved with a simple BCI seem satisfactory.

6. CONCLUSION

Whatever the tasks performed, our results showed two surprising and important points: 1) walking in a VE with a treadmill permits users to acquire and to transfer spatial knowledge [5] in a similar manner as a real condition; 2) Our BCI condition also showed that it was possible to store and to recall spatial knowledge as in a real condition, only based on visual information and mental interactions. This suggests that the motor activity, vestibular information and body-based information are not essential to acquire and to recall spatial knowledge. Future work could consist in comparing our results with an interface less transparent and natural than our walking interface as a joystick, and to increase the number of subjects in the BCI condition, which could further support our results. Finally, it seems to be more important to favor the understanding of the interactions, the VE, and the cognitive processes adapted to people using the interface than the motor activity. But more generally, our results suggest that the BCI could be a promising tool to study and diagnose diseases where spatial cognition or motor processes are altered, such as the Parkinson's disease. Indeed, it could enable researchers to detect and diagnose what processes (cognitive and motor) are damaged and impact spatial cognition and/or daily activities, and thus to propose adapted solutions.

7. REFERENCES

[1] Abernethy, B., Hanrahan, S., Kippers, V., Mackinnon, L., and Pandy, M. 2005. *The Biophysical Foundations of Human Movement.* Palgrave Macmillan, 2 ed., 285-288.

[2] Chance, S. S., Gaunet, F., Beall, A. C., and Loomis, J. M. 1998. Locomotion Mode Affects the Updating of Objects Encountered During Travel: The Contribution of Vestibular and Proprioceptive Inputs to Path Integration. *Presence-Teleop Virt*, 7(2), 168-178.

[3] Galan, F.; Nuttin, M.; Lew, E.; Ferrez, P.; Vanacker, G.; Philips, J., and del R. Millán, J. 2008. A brain-actuated wheelchair: Asynchronous and non-invasive Brain–computer interfaces for continuous control of robots. *Clin Neurophysiol*, 119, 2159-216.

[4] Girard, B., and Turcotte, V. 2007. A Virtual Arm to Stop Smoking, A Pilot Perceptual Learning Experiment. In *Annual Review of CyberTherapy and Medicine*, B. K. Wiederhold, 5, 65-74.

[5] Grant, S. C., and Magee, L. E. 1998. Contributions of proprioception to navigation in virtual environments. *Hum Factors*, 40, 489-497.

[6] Ishikawa, T., and Montello, D. R. 2006. Spatial knowledge acquisition from direct experience in the environment: individual differences in the development of metric knowledge and the integration of separately learned places. *Cognitive Psychol*, 52(2), 93-129.

[7] Leeb, R.; Keinrath, C.; Friedman, D.; Guger, C.; Scherer, R.; Neuper, C.; Garau, M.; Antley, A.; Steed, A.; Slater, M., and Pfurtscheller, G. 2006. Walking by thinking: The brainwaves are crucial, not the muscles! *Presence-Teleop Virt*, 15, 500-51.

[8] Leeb, R.; Lee, F.; Keinrath, C.; Scherer, R.; Bischof, H., and Pfurtscheller, G. 2007. Brain-Computer Communication: Motivation, aim and impact of exploring a virtual apartment. In *IEEE T Neur Sys Reh*, 15, 473-482.

[9] Lecuyer, A., Lotte, F., Reilly, R. B., Leeb, R., Hirose, M., and Slater, M. 2008. Brain-Computer Interfaces, Virtual Reality, and Videogames. *IEEE Comput*, 41(10), 66-72.

[10] Loomis, J. M., Da Silva, J. A., Philbeck, J. W., and Fukusima, S. S.,1996. Visual perception of location and distance.*Curr Dir Psychol Sci*. 5(3), 72–77.

[11] Lotte, F., Van Langhenhove, A., Lamarche, F., Ernest, T., Renard, Y., Arnaldi, B., and Lecuyer, A. 2010. Exploring Large Virtual Environments by Thoughts Using a Brain–Computer Interface Based on Motor Imagery and High-Level Commands. *Presence-Teleop Virt*, 19(1), 54-70.

[12] Mittelstaedt, M.-L., and Mittelstaedt, H. 2001. Idiothetic navigation in humans: estimation of path length. *Exp Brain Res*, 139(3), 318-332.

[13] Montello, D.R. 2005. Navigation. In *The Cambridge handbook of visuospatial thinking*, P. Shah and A. Miyake, Cambridge: Cambridge University, 257-294.

[14] Pfurtscheller, G., and Neuper, C. 2001. Motor imagery and direct brain-computer communication. *P IEEE*, 89(7), 1123-1134.

[15] Renard, Y., Lotte, F., Gibert, G., Congedo, M., Maby, E., Delannoy, V., Bertrand, O., and al. 2010. OpenViBE: An Open-Source Software Platform to Design, Test, and Use Brain–Computer Interfaces in Real and Virtual Environments. . *Presence-Teleop Virt*, 19(1), 35-53.

[16] Richardson, A. E., Powers, M. E., and Bousquet, L. G. 2011. Video game experience predicts virtual, but not real navigation performance. *Comput Hum Behav*, 27(1), 552-560.

[17] Riecke, B. E., Cunningham, D. W., and Bülthoff, H. H. 2007. Spatial updating in virtual reality: the sufficiency of visual information. *Psychol Res*, 71(3), 298-313.

[18] Rizzo, A. A., and Buckwalter, J. G. 1997. Virtual reality and cognitive assessment and rehabilitation: the state of the art. *St Heal T*, 44, 123-45.

[19] Ruddle, R., and Peruch, P. 2004. Effects of proprioceptive feedback and environmental characteristics on spatial learning in virtual environments. *Int J Hum-Comput St*, 60(3), 299-326.

[20] Ruddle, R. A., and Lessels, S. 2009. The benefits of using a walking interface to navigate virtual environments. *Acm T Comput-Hum Int*, 16(1), 1-18.

[21] Ruddle, R. A., Volkova, E., and Bülthoff, H. H. 2011. Walking improves your cognitive map in environments that are large-scale and large in extent. *ACM T Comput-Hum Int*, 18(2), 1-20.

[22] Siegel, A. W., and White, S. H. 1975. The development of spatial representations of large-scale environments. *Adv Child Dev Behav*, 10, 9-55.

[23] Van Erp, J., Lotte, F., and Tangermann, M. 2012. Brain-Computer Interfaces: Beyond Medical Applications. *IEEE Comput*, 45(4), 26-34.

[24] Waller, D. 2000. Individual differences in spatial learning from computer-simulated environments. *J Exp Psychol-Appl*, 6(4), 307-321.

[25] Wallet, G., Sauzeon, H., Rodrigues, J., and N'Kaoua, B. 2008. Use of virtual reality for spatial knowledge transfer: effects of passive/active exploration mode in simple and complex routes for three different recall tasks In *Proceedings of the 2008 ACM symposium on Virtual reality software and technology* (VRST '08). ACM, New York, NY, USA, 175-178.

[26] Wallet, G., Sauzeon, H., Rodrigues, J., Larrue, F., and N'Kaoua, B. 2010. Virtual / Real Transfer of Spatial Learning: Impact of Activity According to the Retention Delay. *St Heal*, 154:145-9.

[27] Wallet, G., Sauzeon, H., Pala, P. A., Larrue, F., Zheng, X., and N'Kaoua, B. 2011. Virtual/Real transfer of spatial knowledge: benefit from visual fidelity provided in a virtual environment and impact of active navigation. *Cyberpsychology, behavior and social networking*, 14(7-8), 417-23.

Leaning-Based Travel Interfaces Revisited: Frontal versus Sidewise Stances for Flying in 3D Virtual Spaces

Jia Wang   Robert W. Lindeman

HIVE Lab
Worcester Polytechnic Institute

ABSTRACT

In this paper we revisit the design of leaning-based travel interfaces and propose a design space to categorize existing implementations. Within the design space, frontal and sidewise stances when using a flying surfboard interface were compared through a user study. The interfaces were adapted and improved from our previous designs using a body-mounted, multi-touch touchpad. Two different experiments were designed and conducted that focus on user performance and virtual world cognition, respectively. The results suggest better user performance and user experience when using the frontal stance, although no better spatial orientation or virtual world cognition was identified. Further, user interviews revealed that despite the realistic simulation of skateboarding/snowboarding, the sidewise stance suffers from poor usability due to inefficient and inaccurate turning control and confusion between the viewing and movement directions. Based on these results, several guidelines are proposed to aid the design of leaning-based travel interfaces for immersive virtual reality applications.

Categories and Subject Descriptors

H.5.1 [**Information Interfaces and Presentation**]: Multimedia Information Systems – *artificial, augmented, and virtual realities*; H.5.2 [**Information Interfaces and Presentation**]: User Interfaces – *evaluation/methodology, input devices and strategies, interaction styles, user-centered design*.

Keywords

Leaning-based travel interface; Stance; Navigation; 3D virtual spaces.

1. INTRODUCTION

Navigation, together with object selection and manipulation, system control, and symbolic input, is one of the basic building blocks of 3D user interaction in immersive virtual environments (VEs) [2]. A satisfactory travel experience is critical for the overall immersive experience a virtual reality (VR) application provides to the user. Although in many applications navigation is not the main goal, when a user is able to intuitively, efficiently, and easily travel in the VE, the portion of the user's cognitive load devoted to travel can be greatly reduced, freeing more

WPI CS Dept., 100 Institute Road, Worcester, MA 01609, USA
{wangjia, gogo}@cs.wpi.edu

resources to invest on more important tasks such as the inspection of a virtual urban area or the training of cooperation skills on a virtual battlefield. Navigation in VEs combines the mental process of wayfinding and the physical process of transporting one's virtual body [2]. In terms of interface design, the latter is more challenging, mainly due to the demand of mapping from user motions in the limited real world space to a possibly infinite virtual world space. Based on the way the travel direction is specified, travel interfaces have been categorized into gaze-directed, pointing-directed, torso-directed, steering-based, and walking interfaces [2].

Inspired by real life transporters such as the skateboard, the snowboard, and the Segway, several leaning-based travel interfaces (LTIs) have been proposed that allow standing users to control virtual locomotion through leaning his/her body [8] or shifting his/her center of gravity (COG) [16]. The 2-DOF data from the devices are usually mapped to forward/backward motion and left/right turning in the VE to enable travelling on a terrain surface, although a flying surfboard interface has been proposed by adding an extra DOF [19]. LTIs are steering-based travel interfaces because the travel direction is always aligned with the platform, regardless of the user's body orientation. Prior work in this area has mainly focused on the design and implementation of the hardware and control laws, but little work has been done to systematically explore the various design options of LTIs except for our previous study that compared isometric and elastic implementations of the flying surfboard interface [19].

In this paper, we revisit the design space of LTIs with a focus on a comparison between the frontal and sidewise stances of using the interface. In skiing/snowboarding people can adapt to, and even master, both stances through practice. However in VR, stance may have a significant influence on task performance and VE cognition because of the degraded physical simulation of the real life metaphor, the narrow field of view of the display, and the lack of haptic and vestibular feedback that indicate the ongoing motion. In this paper, we raise this question to the level of 4-DOF flying control using an improved flying surfboard interface [19]. The goal is not only to find the better of these two design options, but more importantly, also to investigate the fundamental factors that affect the usability of LTIs in VR to provide guidelines that aid the selection and realization of LTIs for future VR research and applications.

2. RELATED WORK

Travel in VEs can be reduced to the continuous specification of a 3D vector. The aforementioned gaze-directed, pointing-directed, and torso-directed travel interfaces all use orientation sensors mounted on the user's head, hand, or torso to specify the direction of this vector in the VE [2]. The magnitude (the travel speed) can be controlled by buttons, hand gestures, voice commands, and so on [7]. These abstractions have been proven to be efficient by empirical studies in different travel scenarios [1]. However they do not represent how people travel in the real world and may therefore degrade the sense of presence in the VE.

Using vehicles in real life, people are able to travel long distances by applying body motion in a much more limited local space. This metaphor motivated the design and development of various vehicle simulators in VR for military training and entertainment purposes. LTIs are a sub-category of such interfaces and are mostly inspired by real life personal transporters, such as the PemRam motion base [4], the Hawai'i surf simulator, the virtual Segway Patroller [16], the Joyman interface [8], and the flying surfboard interface [19]. It should be stressed that our discussion of LTIs in this paper does not apply to interfaces that require users to turn their bodies [10], or make upper body postures to travel in the VE [5][18]. In other words, a LTI is defined only when whole body or at least lower body leaning is involved in controlling the virtual locomotion. Such LTIs can provide users with appropriate affordances and feedback without occupying large spaces.

On the other hand, to approach real walking in VR, walking-in-place (WIP) travel interfaces have been proposed in which the user wears multiple acceleration, orientation, and pressure sensors on special locations of the body, and steps, turns, and strafes in-place to control locomotion in the VE [14]. By designing the gestures to mimic real walking, WIP interfaces offer high proprioceptive but insufficient vestibular feedback because the user does not actually displace in the real world. Inspired by the treadmill, sophisticated mechanical systems have been built to rotate floor pieces from the back of the user to the front where he/she is going to step next [6]. These interfaces enabled limitless walking in a limited space. However, the systems were very expensive to build and maintain, very noisy to operate, and the user is forced to step very slowly and carefully to compensate for the time delay to mechanically displace the floor tiles.

The invention of large area tracking systems fully realized real walking in VR by tracking the user's position and orientation in a relatively large space to travel in a VE of the same size. Empirical user studies showed that this real walking technique significantly increases the sense of presence and the cognition of virtual spaces compared to WIP and joystick in immersive VEs [15][20]. To expand the reachable space in the VE, several redirected walking techniques have been proposed and evaluated which explore the effect of visual dominance [12] and change blindness [13] in VR. By imperceptibly manipulating the structure or the user's visual perception of the VE, such techniques are able to redirect the user to walk curved paths within a limited lab space without breaking presence in the virtual world. Despite the high cost to distribute the hardware systems, redirected walking techniques are by far the most successful solutions for terrain based VR navigation, especially in indoor VEs.

3. INTERFACE DESIGN
3.1 Leaning-Based Travel Interfaces
The motivations for using LTIs for travel in VE mainly include:

- **Hands-free navigation**: The lower-body controlled locomotion frees the hands for other tasks in the VE. For example, the virtual Segway Patroller frees both hands to do map navigation (wayfinding) on a multi-touch surface presented as a podium in front of the user [16]. However, the hands-free benefit is not available when designers choose to include hands as part of the travel interface design, either for safety concerns [8] or to extend the 2-DOF terrain travel to 3-DOF flying [19].

- **Ease of learning**: Because LTIs simulate real life personal transporters, they may require less time to learn, especially

for users with prior experience with skateboards, snowboards, or the Segway Patroller.

- **Rich equilibrioceptive feedback**: Because LTIs involve the user's whole body motion to control the platform, the user is able to perceive equilibrioceptive feedback from his/her balance system and become more aware of the state of the interaction, which results in more efficient travel control and a higher level of presence in the VE [8][19].

- **Space and cost effectiveness**: The building and maintenance costs and space requirements of LTIs are much lower than other types of travel interfaces such as real walking.

The challenges to making LTIs more usable mainly include:

- **Ergonomics**: Since the immersed user does not have vision of the real world, the consequences of falling off the platform can be very dangerous. Therefore designers have to include proper protection mechanisms, such as larger platform surfaces, surrounding guard bars, or handrails [8].

- **Fatigue**: Since most LTIs require the user to stand and use his/her whole body or at least lower body motion to control VE travel, fatigue becomes a significant problem in cluttered VEs that demand frequent changes in direction to navigate, or applications that require a long immersion time.

- **Lack of precision**: Because leaning is controlled by whole body motion, most LTIs have poor accuracy compared to gaze-, pointing-, or torso-directed interfaces in which more dexterous muscle groups are used.

It should be mentioned that the benefits and challenges listed above are targeted at general LTIs, and not specific implementations. When implementing a specific LTI, the designers have the following design options:

- **Isometric, elastic, and isotonic** platforms offer different types of equilibrioceptive feedback to the users [19]. One example of an isometric LTI is the virtual Segway Patroller [16] which uses the Nintendo Wii Fit Balance Board. The user has to apply isometric muscle tension to shift his/her COG on the static platform. On the other hand, isotonic LTIs, such as the Hawaii Surf Simulator and the Tony Hawk RIDE game board, tilt freely in all directions without giving any resistive feedback to the user. Between isometric and isotonic, elastic LTIs, such as the flying surfboard interface based on the Reebok Core Board [19], increase the strength of elastic resistant force as they tilt. Isometric and elastic implementations of the flying surfboard interface have been compared by the authors, and better user experience and presence were identified for the latter, although no performance difference was found [19].

- **Rate control, position control, the Go-go technique [11], and physics-based models** are all control laws that govern the mapping from the raw motion data from the devices to locomotion variables in the VE. The virtual Segway Simulator [16] and the Joyman interface [8] both proposed innovative control laws based the physical rules of their metaphors. The separation of rate controlled and position controlled pitch and yaw was addressed in the design of the flying surfboard interface through a pilot study [19]. The selection of control laws is highly relevant to the DOFs implemented in the VE and no single option can be concluded to be the best for all scenarios.

- **The DOF mapping** from the devices to virtual travel is highly relevant to the target application and is usually determined together with the control laws for each DOF. Most LTIs offer 2-DOF data (leaning in all directions on a horizontal surface) although by detecting a torque gesture, an extra DOF data can be extracted from the Nintendo Wii Fit Balance Board to control elevation of the virtual body [16]. Therefore, the possible DOF mappings for LTIs are 3-DOF (2-DOF leaning and 1-DOF torque) data from the device to 6-DOF control of the virtual locomotion (pitch, roll, yaw, and translation in three dimensions). It should be mentioned however, that including rolling in VE has been shown to be inappropriate because of motion sickness [17].

- **Passive and active** LTIs are different in whether the platform contains actuators in addition to sensors. An example of an active LTI is the PemRam motion base [4], while most other LTIs are passive devices driven only by user motion. Essentially, active LTIs open the tactile feedback channel for developers to program and can therefore provide a more realistic simulation of real life scenarios.

- **Frontal and sidewise stances** are the least discussed design pairs so far in LTIs. Most LTIs (with the exception of the flying surfboard interface [19]) use the frontal stance because people are used to walking frontally. However, no study has been done to investigate this assumption, which is also the focal point of this paper.

The design space above can be used to categorize LTIs. For example, the Joyman interface [8] is an elastic, passive, frontally used LTI that maps 2-DOF leaning data to a velocity vector on the terrain surface through a control law based on the Joyman metaphor. Different combinations in this design space can result in very different user performance and experience and may create additional benefits and problems. For example, an isometric, passive, sidewise used LTI that maps 2-DOF leaning to pitch and yaw in the VE made some users become nauseated. However, the possibility of motion sickness is lower when the isometric platform is replaced with an elastic one [19].

3.2 The Improved Flying Surfboard Interface

Figure 1 illustrates the DOF mapping and control law of the original flying surfboard interface [19]. The user wears an accelerometer on one arm to control speed by lifting the arm, and stands sidewise on the COG-sensing board to control his/her pitch and yaw in the VE. The speed control uses a control law adapted from the Go-go technique [11] to allow fine-grained control in local spaces and efficient navigation over long distances. Leaning on the long axis (B_x) maps to pitch by position control (PC) and leaning on the short axis (B_y) maps to yaw by rate control (RC).

The original interface had three main criticisms:

- **Fatiguing and unrealistic speed control**: In order to maintain a travel speed, the user had to keep his/her arm lifted. When the user relaxed the arm, the speed returned to zero instantly without any inertia, unlike in real life.

- **Inefficient elevation control**: The only way to change elevation was to pitch the board up and down while moving forward. This was very inefficient when the travel target was

right above or below the virtual body, in which case the user had to zigzag to reach the destination.

- **Inaccurate location control**: Although the Go-go-like technique [11] control law made speed control more fine grained in local spaces, the user still did not have direct control of his/her virtual body's location. Additionally, the method only supported moving forward. When the user's target was in a cluttered, small space and his/her initial moving direction was slightly off target, it was very easy to overshoot due to the lack of PC and very hard to readjust due to the lack of backward movement.

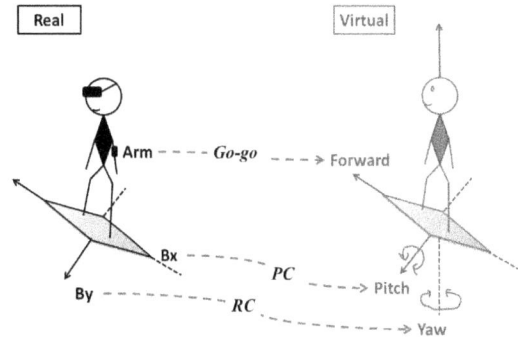

Figure 1. The original flying surfboard interface

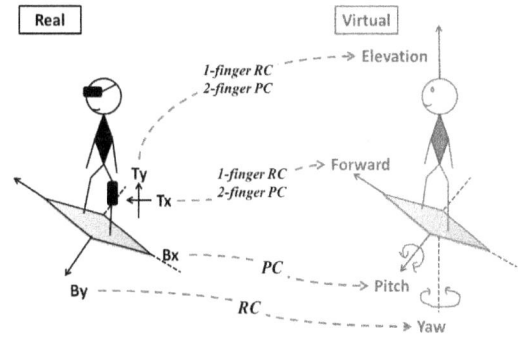

(a)

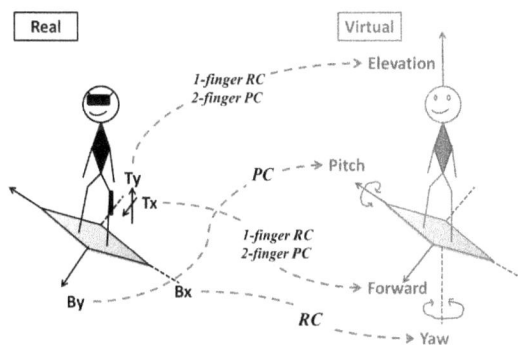

(b)

Figure 2. The improved flying surfboard interface using the (a) sidewise and (b) the frontal stances

These issues are all addressed in our improved design of the flying surfboard interface, as illustrated in Figure 2, by replacing the arm-mounted accelerometer with a multi-touch touchpad. The Bamboo tablet being used is a rectangular, two-finger, multi-touch surface. The touchpad is always attached vertically with the long edge pointing downwards. For each user, the touchpad location is adjusted so that the corresponding hand can cover the whole surface easily when the arm is at rest, which greatly reduces the fatigue of operating the touchpad. To make the best use of proprioception [8], the touchpad is also always aligned with the travel direction so that touching the touchpad (T_x and T_y) also moves the virtual body in the same direction. In other words, for the sidewise stance, the touchpad is attached to the front of the thigh (Figure 2(a)) whereas for the frontal stance, it is attached to the side of the thigh (Figure 2(b)).

The control laws of the touchpad are explained in Figure 2, Figure 3, and Equation (1) and (2). Vectors are represented in **bold** and *italic*. The touch position data on the touchpad is normalized to [0.0, 1.0] from the top-left corner to the bottom-right corner so that delta touch position is a vector T ranging from (-1.0, -1.0) to (1.0, 1.0). The x and y components of this vector are mapped to forward/backward movement and direct elevation (moving straight up and down) using the body as a reference. Two gestures are defined to enable control over both the travel speed (one-finger RC) and the location of the virtual body (two-finger PC). As shown in Figure 3(a) and Equation (1), the one-finger RC mode maps T linearly to the travel speed S in the VE as long as the finger is in contact with the touchpad. A scale factor of 2 helps accommodate users who are used to starting touch gestures in the center of the touchpad, so that they can reach the maximum speed (S_{max} = 150 meters/second in our system) in all four directions while only covering half of the touch space. When the touch release event is detected, the last travel speed S_{last} decays linearly to 0 in t_d (t_d = 2 in our system) seconds.

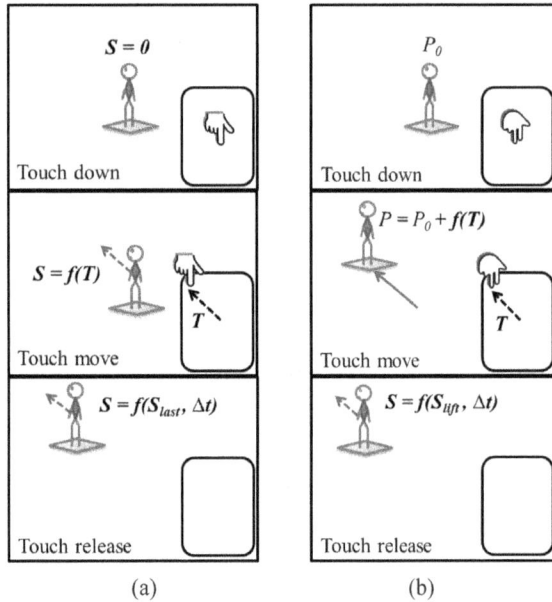

(a)   (b)

Figure 3. (a) One-finger RC mode controls travel speed. (b) Two-finger PC mode controls virtual body location.

Figure 3(b) and Equation (2) explain the two-finger PC mode designed to resolve the inaccurate location control issue of the previous interface. T is linearly mapped to virtual body translation (ΔP_{max} = 25 meters in our system) in the VE as long as both fingers stay on the touchpad. When two fingers are released together, an instant speed S_{lift} is given to the virtual body based on the change between the last two reported touch positions, i.e., the touch releasing speed. This speed will also decay to 0 in t_d (t_d = 2 in our system) seconds. The purpose of including inertia when a

touch session ends is to make the speed control more realistic, answering the first criticism of the original interface.

$$\begin{cases} S = \hat{T}\max\left(2\|T\|S_{max}, S_{max}\right) & , (-1.0, -1.0) < T < (1.0, 1.0) \\ S = \hat{S}_{last}\max\left(\|S_{last}\| - \Delta t * \frac{\|S_{last}\|}{t_d}, 0.0\right) & , when\ touch\ released \end{cases} \quad (1)$$

$$\begin{cases} P = P_0 + \hat{T}\max(2\|T\|\Delta P_{max}, \Delta P_{max}) & , (-1.0, -1.0) < T < (1.0, 1.0) \\ S = \hat{S}_{lift}\max\left(\|S_{lift}\| - \Delta t * \frac{\|S_{lift}\|}{t_d}, 0.0\right) & , when\ touch\ released \end{cases} \quad (2)$$

The DOF mapping and the control laws of the board interface are kept the same as the original interface, meaning that leaning in the movement direction (B_x in sidewise stance and B_y in frontal stance) will pitch the virtual board using PC and leaning in the other direction will turn the virtual board using RC. Lastly, the input and output devices are all the same as the original interface. We use an elastic platform made by attaching a Nintendo Wii Fit Balance Board on top of a Reebok Core Board as the board interface, an eMagin Z800 head-mounted display (HMD) as the visual display, a SpacePoint Fusion sensor as the head tracker, and the TactaCage system to provide wind feedback. Figure 4 shows the complete system of both stances.

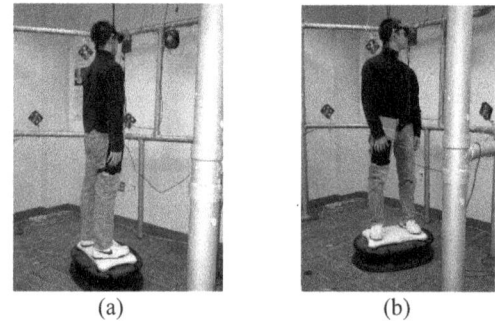

(a)   (b)

Figure 4. The complete system setup of (a) the frontal stance and (b) the sidewise stance

4. USER STUDY

4.1 Hypotheses

Both the frontal stance and the sidewise stance bear appropriate affordances and feedback based on their real life metaphors (skiing/Segway and snowboarding/skateboarding, respectively). However, we hypothesize a preference for the frontal stance, since the sidewise stance forces the user to twist his/her neck to one side in order to align the viewport with the movement direction, which more-negatively influences the user experience and even travel performance. Formally stated, we hypothesize the frontal stance will outscore the sidewise stance in questionnaire ratings, spatial orientation tests, VE cognition tests, and performance on 3D VE travel tasks.

4.2 Experiment Design

The VE in our experiments was created using the Unity3D game engine. Several graphical user interface (GUI) components were added to help the user with wayfinding [3]. In Figure 5(a), the 3D arrow at the lower center of the screen always pointed to the next target, the top left timer showed the elapsed time, and the bottom right counter showed the number of targets left in the current trial. In the zoomed-in view of the radar (Figure 5(b)), the yellow cone rotated around the center to show the direction of the viewport, the blue rectangle represented the surfboard, the red bar indicated the current travel speed, and the letter "N" gave the North direction within the VE. The red triangle indicated the location of the next target relative to the user with its pointing direction showing its relative height, below the user when pointing down and above when pointing up.

Figure 5. (a) The performance experiment. (b) The radar

Two experiments were designed and conducted to test our hypotheses. The first experiment compared user performance of the two stances on a simple reach-target task [1]. As illustrated in Figure 5(a), the targets were presented one after another to the subject in a specific order. When the virtual body and the current target collided, the target disappeared, and both the 3D arrow and the radar pointed to the next target positioned at a different 3D location. The task was complete when all targets had been visited. The total time was recorded as the metric of user performance. The VE for this experiment was a 2,000m X 2,000m flat textured terrain contained in a cube that was 2,000m X 2,000m X 500m. The inside faces of the cube were impenetrable cloud walls to assure the subject could focus on the task in a contained 3D space.

The second experiment was presented to the subject in the form of a mini game. The purpose was to investigate spatial orientation and VE cognition when navigating a large-scale 3D virtual world using the two stances. The role of the subject within the game was a mechanic whose job was to maintain windmills installed at different locations in the mountains. Figure 6 illustrates the task in detailed steps. The subject started from his/her base station, and used the 3D arrow and radar to move to the next windmill (Figure 6(a)). As the subject approached the windmill, he/she saw and heard the name of the windmill and corresponding feature objects (such as the wild flowers in Figure 6(b) and wood piles in Figure 6(c)). The blades of the windmill, as well as the cloud in the front, indicated the status of the windmill (red cloud and static blades for broken windmill, and white cloud and turning blades for working windmill). Regardless of its status, the subject needed to arrive at the cloud, which then froze the motion of his/her virtual body (turning was still enabled by leaning on the board). If the windmill was broken, the "fixing process" was triggered, which was a three-second timer. Otherwise, this step was skipped. Lastly the subject was asked to look in the direction of the previous station and confirm the answer with the experimenter (Figure 6(d)). Since the VE was large and complex and the view of the previous station was always occluded by mountains, we did not turn off the display or reduce the visibility of the VE while subjects were answering this spatial-orientation question. When the question was answered, the subject's virtual body was unfrozen so he/she could continue to the next windmill. Once all the windmills were visited, the subject returned to the base station, after which he/she had three minutes to freely explore the VE. The session ended when the timer expired. The VE of this experiment was a 4,000m X 4,000m X 600m mountainous terrain. Landmarks in the VE included houses, roads, rivers, bridges, and tall standing rocks.

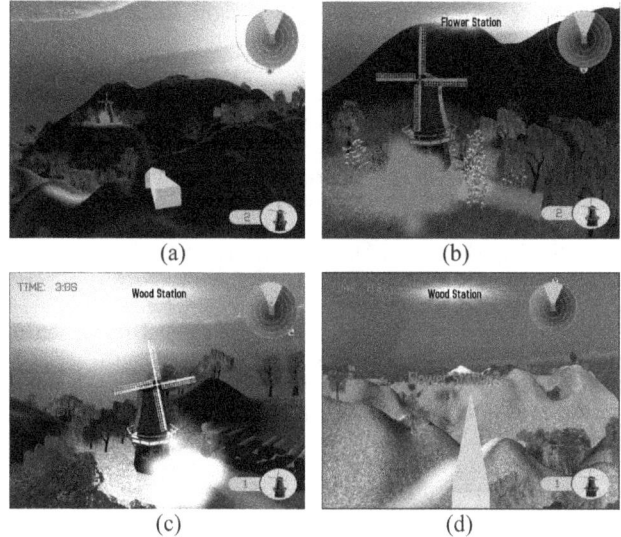

Figure 6. The cognition experiment in steps. (a) The user travels to the next windmill. (b) The user approaches a broken windmill. (c) The user approaches a working windmill. (d) The user indicates the direction to the previous windmill.

4.3 Study Procedure

The user study employed a within-subjects design, so each subject performed both experiments using both stances. The order of the stances was the same for both experiments for a given subject, but different between subjects to eliminate learning effects. When the study began, the subject completed a demographic form which included questions such as gender, age, dominant hand, height, weight, surfing stance (goofy or regular), real life Segway experience, real life board surfing experience, surfing-type video game experience, first person shooter video game experience, multi-touch interface experience, and VR experience. After that, the experimenter explained the flying surfboard interface and the experiment, and helped the subject to calibrate the board. The subject then traveled in a simple VE to test the calibration for both stances. The performance experiments started whenever the board was well calibrated (leaning in all directions was balanced). For each stance there were two trials, one training trial with five targets, and one study trial with ten targets to reach. The subject was asked to complete the task as fast as possible. When all four trials were completed, the subject took a five-minute break while the experimenter explained the cognition experiment.

After the break the subject began the cognition experiment, performing one training trial and one study trial for each stance. The training trial had a smaller VE (2,000m X 2,000m X 400m mountainous terrain) with one river, one wood bridge, one rock, one base station, and two windmills. The study trial had the normal size VE mentioned in the previous section with two rivers, five wood bridges, two stone bridges, three rocks, one base station, and four windmills. The geographical structure of the VE and the locations of the windmills were designed to be different between the two study trials to eliminate learning effects. The subject was asked to first complete the windmill task as fast as possible and then explore the VE for three minutes. After each study trial, the subject answered a cognitive questionnaire to test recollection of the VE. The first question listed ten windmill names and asked the subject to indicate if they were broken, working, or not visited, and also for the ones visited, the order of visitation. The second question gave a top-down view of the VE in black and white with the bridges, the rocks, the windmills, and the base station removed. The subject needed to add the missing components as well as to specify the North direction. The last question asked the subject to rate his/her sense of orientation, feeling of being lost, and understanding of the VE during the experiment on six-point scales. Eventually after finishing all experiments, the subject was asked to answer a post-questionnaire to indicate his/her favorite stance and to rate the two stances on six-point scales about efficiency, accuracy, intuitiveness, ease of learning, ease of use, sense of presence, after effects (e.g., loss of balance), motion sickness, fatigue, and fun for traveling within the 3D VE. The whole study took about one and a half hours on average.

The user study was approved by the institutional review board (IRB) and 12 male students from the Computer Science Department at Worcester Polytechnic Institute were recruited with no remuneration. Three subjects had difficulty understanding the interface and started to show motion sickness symptoms after the training session, and were therefore stopped immediately. It should be mentioned that two of the three subjects had no first-person shooter video games experience and reported more severe discomfort when learning the sidewise stance due to confusion between the viewing and the movement directions. Furthermore, one subject spent quadruple the maximum time of the rest subjects on the performance experiment was therefore removed as an outlier during data analysis. The rest of the eight subjects successfully completed the study and the experimenter was able to balance the stance assignment so that half of them started with the frontal stance while the other half started with the sidewise stance. Of these eight subjects, four surfed using a goofy stance (right foot forward) and four with a regular stance (left foot forward), and seven used the touchpad using their right hands and one using the left hand (all subjects were right-hand dominant). Ages ranged from 18 to 32 years (mean = 24.0, SD = 3.9), height from 173 to 188 centimeters (mean = 178.8, SD = 4.4), and weight from 59 to 100 kilograms (mean = 79.3, SD = 11.9). Two subjects reported board surfing in real life once and the rest never. One subject used a Segway in real life yearly and the rest never. One subject played first-person shooter video games daily, four weekly, two monthly, and one once. Two subjects played surfing-type video games once (Wii Sports Resort) and the rest never. Six subjects used multi-touch interfaces daily, one weekly, and one monthly. One subject had VR experience yearly, six once, and one never.

4.4 Data Analysis

4.4.1 Questionnaire Measures
The six-point scale rating scores of the two stances were analyzed using two-sided Wilcoxon signed-rank tests with a threshold of 0.05 for significance on all questions. The three presence questions respectively asked the subjects about the sense of "being there", whether "the virtual world became the reality", and the sense of "not seeing, but visiting the virtual world". The average scores and p-values are listed in Table 1 with statistically significant differences marked by stars (*) and shown in **bold**. The frontal stance was rated to be more efficient, more accurate, more intuitive, more fun, less tiring to use, and easier to learn. There was also a trend (p < 0.1) of easier to learn and more of a feeling of "the virtual world became the reality," however these results were not significant. In addition, seven of the eight subjects preferred the frontal stance in general.

For scoring the windmill-status question and the windmill-visiting-order question, each of the four correctly answered windmills was worth two and one point, respectively. Because structured questions were used, the answers were graded by only one rater. On the other hand, the windmill map was graded by two raters, whose results were averaged as the final scores. The subject needed to specify the positions of three rocks, seven bridges, four windmills, and one base station, as well as the North direction. Each of these components was worth two points adding up to 32 points in total. The inter-rater reliability was evaluated using Pearson's correlation analysis and the result shows high agreement (R = 0.975). Lastly, the three subjective ratings regarding sense of orientation, feeling of being lost, and understanding the VE were analyzed using two-sided Wilcoxon signed-rank tests with a threshold of 0.05 for significance. The average scores and p-values are listed in Table 2. No statistically significant results were discovered in this part, although it is worth mentioning that seven of the eight subjects answered the windmill order question correctly when using the frontal stance compared to four when using the sidewise stance.

Table 1. The analysis result of the comparative rating scores

Ratings (1-6 scale)	Front	Side	Ratings (1-6 scale)	Front	Side
Efficiency*	**4.6**	2.9	Dizziness	1.3	1.6
	p = 0.021			p = 0.371	
Accuracy*	**4.4**	2.5	Nauseated	1.1	1.1
	p = 0.033			p = 1.000	
Intuitiveness*	**4.8**	3.1	Presence Question-1	4.4	4.1
	p = 0.034			p = 0.346	
Ease of Learning	4.8	3.4	Presence Question-2	3.6	3.0
	p = 0.099			p = 0.089	
Ease of Use*	**5.0**	3.3	Presence Question-3	3.8	3.5
	p = 0.034			p = 0.346	
Fatigue*	2.3	**3.8**	Loss of Balance	1.6	1.6
	p = 0.048			p = 1.000	
Fun*	**4.5**	3.3			
	p = 0.044				

Table 2. The analysis result of the windmill questionnaires

Ratings (1-6 scale)	Front	Side	Scores (min-max)	Front	Side
Oriented in VE	4.4	3.9	Windmill Order (0-4)	3.9	3.1
	p = 0.387			p = 0.181	
VE Understanding	4.1	3.9	Windmill Status (0-8)	7.1	6.8
	p = 0.784			p = 0.657	
Lost in VE	4.9	4.0	Windmill Map (0-32)	24.8	20.5
	p = 0.269			p = 0.167	

4.4.2 Performance Measures
The performance measures were analyzed using a single-factor ANOVA with a threshold of 0.05 for significance. The results are shown in Table 3. The total time spent to reach all 10 targets in the performance experiment was significantly shorter when using the frontal stance. For the cognition experiment, the time spent on travel was extracted from the total time by removing the time spent on exploration, fixing windmills, and pointing at previous stations. Additionally, the system recorded the pointing directions when the subject indicated the last visited windmills and computed the angular errors from the correct answer. The averaged angular errors were analyzed using a single-factor ANOVA. However, the differences between the two stances were not significant as shown in Table 3.

Table 3. The analysis result of the task performance data

	Front	Side
Time to reach all targets (seconds)*	**214.3**	280.3
	p = 0.002	
Time to reach all windmills (seconds)	189.4	221.4
	p = 0.438	
Average pointing deviation (degrees)	22.0	26.7
	p = 0.423	

5. DISCUSSION

Although only eight subjects successfully completed the study, the results clearly show advantages when using the frontal stance both objectively (shorter task completion time) and subjectively (rated as significantly more efficient, accurate, intuitive, easier to use, more fun, and less tiring). However, against our hypothesis, the use of different stances did not result in different levels of presence, spatial orientation, and VE cognition. To explore the causes of these results and gain a deeper understanding of LTI, we interviewed all subjects including the four who dropped out. Only one subject preferred the sidewise stance because of its realistic simulation of real life board surfing. According to this subject, it felt more like flying when using the sidewise stance to travel through large landscapes. However, like other subjects, he was frustrated by the sidewise stance when approaching targets.

From the comments of seven subjects, the causes of the sidewise stance's poor usability in local spaces can be summarized into three points. Firstly, left and right turning (yaw) in the VE was very difficult to control. This is because leaning forward and backward (as in sidewise stance) is harder to do than leaning side to side (as in frontal stance) and the rate control mechanism made it very slow to initiate turning and very easy to overshoot once reaching the desired direction. What was worse is that even when the desired heading was reached through careful maneuvering, it was very difficult to maintain it because the virtual board could not be "locked" and keeping the body balance absolutely centered on the board was very difficult. Secondly, the subjects felt easily confused and frustrated when the view and travel directions were not aligned. According to five subjects, it was not intuitive to figure out the heading of the board when starting to touch the touchpad. The virtual board indicated this information but it was far below eye level. The radar also showed the difference between the two directions but was hard to notice. The 3D arrow which pointed to the next target actually seemed to make things worse because sometimes the users thought it was an indication of travel direction. Consequently, the experimenter observed some extreme cases when a user was looking at a target and the 3D arrow was pointing at the same target. The user thought he/she would move towards the target and hence speeded up. However since the board was actually heading to the side of the view, movement dragged the user further from the target. To solve this problem, one subject suggested replacing the HMD with a TV or projection screen set up to the side of the board interface. Another subject suggested adding a cursor to the VE that was aligned with the front of the board, essentially bringing the virtual board to eye level, providing a constant visual cue about the forward direction.

On the other hand, seven subjects preferred the frontal stance because it partly resolved the two main issues of using the sidewise stance. Turning was still slow and easy to overshoot but leaning side to side was more accurate and less tiring to control. In addition, the movement direction was better predicated when the user was looking forward. However, one subject did mention that standing on the heels (leaning backward) seemed harder for him when using the frontal stance, making pitch-up control slightly harder to use compared to elevation using the touchpad.

Regarding the two experiments, all eight subjects who completed both tasks commented that the advantages of the frontal stance were obvious in the first task because fine-grained, local-space maneuvering was necessary to reach the targets. However, the two stances seemed equal when performing the windmill task because of the large-scale VE. This explained the lack of differences in the corresponding data analysis. It is worth mentioning that based on these conclusions one may suggest a hybrid design to use the sidewise stance for long distance travel and the frontal stance for local space maneuvering. This would create problems as three subjects mentioned confusion when switching from one stance to the other during the user study.

Summarizing the discussions above, we make the following suggestions to designers who consider using similar LTIs in their immersive VR applications:

- **Fit to use cases**: Avoid using LTIs for applications which feature a small or indoor VE or which require high travel efficiency or accuracy. On the other hand, consider using LTIs to simulate realistic navigation in large-scale outdoor virtual worlds. Exemplary use cases include racing arcade games or virtual tourism such as Google Earth navigation.

- **Hybrid interfaces**: Consider mixing LTIs with local-space efficient travel interfaces. For example, the flying surfboard interface can be combined with real walking so that users can step on the board to fly through large landscapes as well as walk around in small local spaces to inspect details.

- **Better sidewise board surfing**: When using board-directed travel interfaces with an HMD, include visual cues at eye level to indicate the moving direction and pay special attention to existing visual cues to avoid confusing the user. Alternatively, replace the HMD with a projection screen installed in the moving direction. The fitness of CAVE systems in this scenario still needs further investigation.

- **Orientation lock**: When possible (not hindering intended orientation control), add a mechanism to lock the current travel direction to increase travel efficiency and precision.

Lastly, despite its complex control laws, the touchpad was complimented by all subjects to be a highly successful addition to the board interface. Seven subjects claimed that the two touch gestures were both necessary and complemented each other perfectly. The observed use pattern in the user study was one finger RC mode for long-distance travel (about 80% of time) followed by two-finger PC mode for local-space fine adjustment (about 20% of time). One subject suggested using the touchpad alone for controlling all DOFs. Two subjects liked the rich proprioception when the touchpad was aligned with the stance. Criticisms of the touchpad included its slippery surface and unclear touching boundaries.

6. CONCLUSION AND FUTURE WORK

To conclude, we revisited LTIs and proposed a design space to categorize their implementations. Within this design space the two stances of using LTIs were selected for further investigation through a user study. The frontal and sidewise stances for using an improved flying surfboard interface were compared in the context of a performance task and a cognition task. The result revealed poor performance when using the latter to travel within local spaces because of inefficient and inaccurate turning control and confusion between looking and moving directions. Based on these findings we suggested six guidelines for using LTIs in immersive VR applications. For future work, we will further investigate the design space of LTIs and explore hybrid solutions such as combining LTIs and real walking in a CAVE. We will also consider using body-mounted multi-touch surfaces for other tasks in VR such as object manipulation and system control.

7. REFERENCES

[1] Bowman, D. A., Koller, D., and Hodges, L. F. 1997. Travel in Immersive Virtual Environments: an Evaluation of Viewpoint Motion Control Techniques, In *Proceedings of IEEE Virtual Reality Conference'97* (Albuquerque, NM, USA). VR'97, IEEE, 45-52.

[2] Bowman, D. A., Kruijff, E., LaViola, J. J., and Poupyrev, I. 2004. *3D User Interfaces: Theory and Practice.* 1 ed. Addison-Wesley Professional, Aug.

[3] Burigat, S. and Chittaro, L. 2007. Navigation in 3D Virtual Environments: Effects of User Experience and Location-Pointing Navigation Aids. *International Journal of Human-Computer Studies.* 65, 11 (Nov. 2007), 945-958.

[4] Denne, P.R.M. 1996. The PemRam – an Electromagnetic Linear Actuator. *IEE Colloquium on Actuator Technology: Current Practice and New Developments* (London, UK).

[5] Doulis, M., Zwimpfer, V., Pfluger, J., Simon, A., Stem, C., Haldimann, T., Jenni, C. 2006. SpaceActor – Interface Prototypes for Virtual Environments. In *Proceedings of IEEE Symposium on 3D User Interfaces'06* (Alexandria, VA, USA). 3DUI'06, IEEE, 171-174.

[6] Iwata, H., Yano, H., Fukushima, H., and Noma, H. 2005. CirculaFloor: a Locomotion Interface Using Circulation of Movable Tiles. In *Proceedings of IEEE Virtual Reality Conference'05* (Bonn, Germany). VR'05, IEEE, 223-230.

[7] Jeong, D. H., Song, C. G., Chang, R., and Hodges, L. 2009. User Experimentation: an Evaluation of Velocity Control Techniques in Immersive Virtual Environments. *Virtual Reality.* 13, 1 (Aug. 2008), 41-50.

[8] Marchal, M., Pettré, J., and Lécuyer, A. 2011. Joyman: a Human-Scale Joystick for Navigating in Virtual Worlds. In *Proceedings of IEEE Symposium on 3D User Interfaces'11* (Singapore). 3DUI'11, IEEE, 19-26.

[9] Mine, M. R., Brooks, F. P., and Sequin, C. H. 1997. Moving Objects in Space: Exploiting Proprioception in Virtual-Environment Interaction. In *Proceedings of the 24th Annual Conference on Computer Graphics and Interactive Techniques* (Los Angeles, CA, USA). SIGGRAPH'97. ACM, New York, NY, 19-26.

[10] Peterson, B., Wells, M., Furness, T. A., and Hunt, E. 1998. The Effects of the Interface on Navigation in Virtual Environments. In *Proceedings of Human Factors and Ergonomics Society Annual Meeting.* 42, 21 (Oct. 1998), 1496-1500.

[11] Poupyrev, I., Billinghurst, M., Weghorst, S., and Ichikawa, T. 1996. The Go-Go Interaction Technique: Non-linear Mapping for Direct Manipulation in VR. In *Proceedings of the 9th Annual ACM Symposium on User Interface Software and Technology* (Seattle, WA, USA). UIST '03. ACM, New York, NY, 79-80.

[12] Razzaque, S., Kohn, Z., and Whitton, M. C. 2001. Redirected Walking. In *Proceedings of Eurographics'01* (Manchester, UK).

[13] Suma, E. A., Lipps, Z., Finkelstein, S., Krum, D. M., and Bolas, M. 2012. Impossible Spaces: Maximizing Natural Walking in Virtual Environments with Self-overlapping Architecture. *IEEE Transactions on Visualization and Computer Graphics.* 18, 4 (Apr. 2012), 555-564.

[14] Templeman, J. N., Denbrook, P. S., and Sibert, L. E. 1999. Virtual Locomotion: Walking in Place through Virtual Environments, *Presence: Tele-operators and Virtual Environments,* 8, 6 (Dec. 1999), 598-617.

[15] Usoh, M., Arthur, K., Whitton, M. C., Bastos, R., Steed, A., Slater, M., and Brooks, F. P. 1999. Walking > Walking-in-Place > Flying, in Virtual Environments. In *Proceedings of the 26th Annual Conference on Computer Graphics and Interactive Techniques* (Los Angeles, CA, USA). SIGGRAPH'99. ACM, New York, NY, 359-364.

[16] Valkov, D., Steinicke, F., Bruder, G., and Hinrichs, K. H. 2010. Traveling in 3D Virtual Environments with Foot Gestures and a Multi-Touch enabled WIM. In *Proceedings of IEEE Virtual Reality Conference'10* (Waltham, MA, USA). VR'10. IEEE, 171–180.

[17] Vidal, M., Amorim, M., and Berthoz, A. 2004. Navigating in a Virtual Three-dimensional Maze: How do Egocentric and Allocentric Reference Frames Interact? *Cognitive Brain Research,* 19, 3 (May 2004), 244–258.

[18] Von Kapri, A., Rick, T., and Feiner, S. 2011. Comparing Steering-Based Travel Techniques for Search Tasks in a CAVE. In *Proceedings of IEEE Virtual Reality Conference'11* (Singapore). VR'11. IEEE, 91-94.

[19] Wang, J. and Lindeman, R.W. 2012. Comparing Isometric and Elastic Surfboard Interfaces for Leaning-Based Travel in 3D Virtual Environments. In *Proceedings of IEEE Symposium on 3D User Interfaces'12* (Orange County, CA, USA). 3DUI'12. IEEE, 31-38.

[20] Zanbaka, C. A., Lok, B. C., Babu, S. V., Ulinski, A. C., and Hodges, L. F. 2005. Comparison of Path Visualizations and Cognitive Measures Relative to Travel Techniques in a Virtual Environment. *IEEE Transactions on Visualization and Computer Graphics.* 11, 6 (Nov. 2005), 694-705.

Evaluation of Remote Collaborative Manipulation for Scientific Data Analysis

Cédric Fleury
Insa de Rennes
IRISA, UMR CNRS 6074
UEB, Rennes, France
fleury@cs.unc.edu

Thierry Duval
Université de Rennes 1
IRISA, UMR CNRS 6074
UEB, Rennes, France
thierry.duval@irisa.fr

Valérie Gouranton
Insa de Rennes
IRISA, UMR CNRS 6074
UEB, Rennes, France
valerie.gouranton@irisa.fr

Anthony Steed
Department of
Computer Science
University College London
A.Steed@cs.ucl.ac.uk

ABSTRACT

In the context of scientific data analysis, we propose to compare a remote collaborative manipulation technique with a single user manipulation technique. The manipulation task consists in positioning a clipping plane in order to perform cross-sections of scientific data that show several points of interest located inside these data. For the remote collaborative manipulation, we have chosen to use the 3-hand manipulation technique proposed by Aguerreche et al. [1], which is very suitable with a remote manipulation of a plane. We ran two experiments to compare the two manipulation techniques with some participants located in two different countries. These experiments has shown that the remote collaborative manipulation technique was significantly more efficient than the single user manipulation when the 3 points of interest were far apart inside the scientific data and, consequently, when the manipulation task was more difficult and required more precision. When the 3 points of interest were close together, there was not significant difference between the two manipulation techniques.

Categories and Subject Descriptors

H.5.3 [**Informations Interfaces and Presentation**]: Group and Organization Interfaces—*Evaluation/methodology, Computer-supported cooperative work, Synchronous interaction*; H.5.1 [**Informations Interfaces and Presentation**]: Multimedia Information Systems—*Artificial, augmented, and virtual realities*

General Terms

Experimentation, Human Factors, Performance

Keywords

Scientific data analysis, Remote collaborative manipulation, Virtual environment, VR experiments

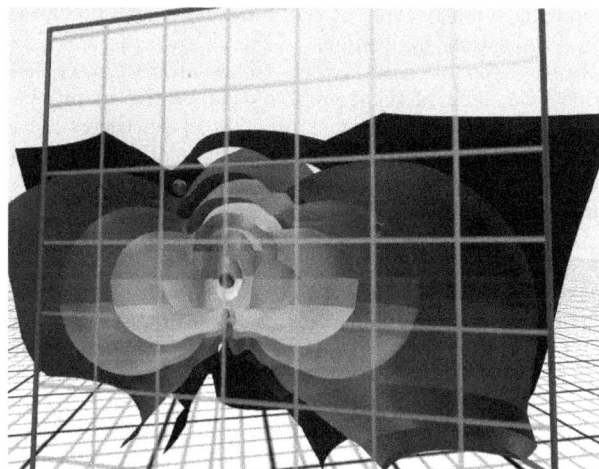

Figure 1: Cross-section of scientific data that shows the 3 points of interest (red spheres).

1. INTRODUCTION

Virtual reality is often used to visualise and to interact with scientific data. However, analysing scientific data can be a difficult task and it requires, sometimes, the knowledge of several remote experts. Distributed virtual reality enables remote experts to meet themselves in a virtual environment to perform joint review of scientific data. Most of the time, this joint review is limited to a simple observation of the scientific data and, when the users can interact, interactions are only sequential (just one user can access to tools at the same time). However, we think that collaborative interactions (parallel access to tools) could be useful for these experts to analyse together scientific data. On the one hand, if they are able to act together, it will increase their involvement in the task and their understanding of the data analysis. On the other hand, it can be helpful to perform some difficult manipulation tasks that require a good precision. So we propose to compare a remote collaborative manipulation technique with a single user manipulation technique for precisely positioning a clipping plane used to perform cross-sections of scientific data (see figure 1).

In this paper, we describe two experiments realised in order to compare these two kinds of manipulation techniques. For the single user manipulation, we have used a classical six degrees of freedom manipulation technique and, for the remote collaborative manipulation, we have chosen to use the 3-hand manipulation technique proposed by Aguerreche et al. [1]. Together the two experiments help us to determine situations when collaborative manipulation is useful.

This paper starts with an overview of related work focusing on scientific data analysis and collaborative interactions. It is followed by a description of the experimental context and the two manipulation techniques used. Part 4 presents the two experiments, their results, and a general discussion on these results. Then, the paper ends with a conclusion on this study and some perspectives for future experiments.

2. RELATED WORK

Lots of previous works use virtual reality for visualising scientific data as stated by Bryson [3]. Part 2.1 presents some applications in which a user analyses scientific data by making cross-sections of the data and some collaborative visualisation applications. Even if some visualisation applications enable several users to visualise together scientific data, none of them propose collaborative manipulations for exploring the data. Part 2.2 analyses the existing techniques for remote collaborative manipulation in virtual reality according to the requirements of the clipping plane manipulation.

2.1 Scientific Data Analysis

Several VR applications enable users to make cross-sections of scientific data. Hinckley et al. [8] propose to use a head and a cutting plane props to intuitively make a cross-section of brain MRI data. A props-based interaction device called the "cubic mouse" is also used by Fröhlich et al. [7] to position 3 orthogonal sections in geo-scientific data. Moreover, the 3D Sketch Slice [14] uses a tracked tablet to enable a user to control the position of a slice of seismic data using a 6 degrees of freedom manipulation. The tablet makes also possible to add some annotations inside the data. Even if these applications propose interesting techniques to make cross-sections of scientific data, none of them enables several users to make it collaboratively.

Leigh et al. [9] describe a range of examples of collaborative visualisation applications using immersive devices, but most of the time the users just observe the data and the only collaborative interaction consists in showing something to the others. Steed et al. [15] propose a interactive and collaborative system for the visualisation of medical data. Users can directly interact with the visualisation in order to drive an offline computation of the medical data. However, each user interacts alone and there is no collaborative manipulation.

2.2 Collaborative Manipulation

There are two categories of techniques that allow remote users to manipulate together a virtual object jointly: the techniques that split the degrees of freedom of a virtual object and the techniques that manage the concurrent access to the same degrees of freedom of a virtual object.

2.2.1 Splitting the degrees of freedom

As proposed by Pinho et al. [10], each user can control only some particular degrees of freedom of the virtual object. For example, one user can control the translation while another one can control the rotation. To perform this kind of manipulation, each user can use a particular tool more relevant for the degrees of freedom that he controls. For example, one user can use a virtual ray to move a virtual object while another one can use a virtual hand to rotate it and translate it along the virtual ray. However, this kind of collaborative manipulation is not relevant for the clipping plane manipulation because the users have very asymmetric role and none of the users can focus his action on finding particular points of interest without help of the others.

2.2.2 Managing concurrent access to the same DOF

Several techniques can be used to combine actions of several users to manipulate a virtual object as stated by Ruddle et al. [13]. A first solution consists in adding actions of these users, a second solution is to average their actions and a third solution proposes to keep only the common part of the actions (intersection). However, none of these solutions are ideal for the clipping plane manipulation because, if the users want to explore different parts of the data, they may perform contrary actions, which could disturb the others.

The Bent Pick Ray [11] technique enables several users to simultaneously manipulate a virtual object using virtual rays. This technique merges actions of all users by interpolating translations and rotations provided by the virtual rays. These virtual rays are also deformed according to their action on the virtual object to enable the users to understand the action of each user. This technique may be close to the average technique and the use of virtual rays does not seem to be very convenient for the clipping plane manipulation.

The SkeweR [5] technique enables two users to simultaneously grab any part of a virtual object. This technique determines the translation and the rotation of this grabbed object according to the positions of the 2 "grabbing points". A similar technique is used in a collaborative experiment that aims to construct a virtual gazebo [12]. Two users can manipulate a beam by grabbing its extremities using 2 virtual hands (one for each user). When the beam position cannot be resolved because the positions of the 2 virtual hands are not consistent, a red line is displayed between the beam and each virtual hands to show that the virtual hands are too far from the beam. However, these two techniques do not propose a solution to determine the rotation along the axis defined by the 2 "grabbing points". Since the clipping plane has to be rotated along each axis, these techniques seem not to be relevant for the clipping plane manipulation.

To avoid rotation issues, Aguerreche et al. [1] propose to add a third control point to manipulate virtual objects. In this 3-hand manipulation technique, virtual objects can be manipulated by 2 or 3 users together: either one user manipulates 2 control points and another one manipulates the third one, or each of 3 users manipulates one control point. The 3 translations of control points are sufficient to determine the resulting 6 degrees of freedom motion of manipulated objects. This technique coupled with a tangible interface (the 3 control points are attached to a tangible device) has been compared with the mean technique and the separation of degrees of freedom [2]. This evaluation has shown that the 3-hand manipulation technique (using a tangible interface) is more accurate, more realistic and preferred by users. But, the technique had not yet been evaluated with remote users. We propose to use this technique for the remote collaborative manipulation of the clipping plane, because it is particularly well adapted to a precise manipulation of a plane (the positions of the 3 control points define a plane that can be the clipping plane).

(a)	(b)

Figure 2: Collaborative manipulation of the clipping plane with the 3-hand manipulation technique : (a) the participant located in Rennes manipulated 2 control points (green cubes) and (b) the participant located in London manipulated one control point (yellow cube on the floor).

3. CONTEXT

During the experiments, participants had to manipulate a clipping plane that can be used to interactively perform cross-sections of scientific data. To manipulate this clipping plane, participants used either a single user manipulation technique or a collaborative manipulation technique which involved another remote participant. To avoid disturbing the manipulation task with a navigation task, navigation (locomotion) was turned off. However, users were tracked inside the immersive device and they could move in the virtual environment by using their physical movements.

3.1 Single User Manipulation

For the single user manipulation, a participant manipulated alone the clipping plane using a target tracked by a tracking system. The target was directly attached to the centre of the clipping plane (see figure 3). The participant could thus apply translations and rotations to the centre of the clipping plane with 6 degrees of freedom. This kind of manipulation was similar to the slice manipulation using a tracked tablet in the 3D Sketch Slice [14] application.

Figure 3: Single user manipulation of the centre of the clipping plane (yellow cube).

3.2 Collaborative Manipulation

For the collaborative manipulation, we have chosen to use the 3-hand manipulation technique proposed by Aguerreche et al. [1]. The participant located in Rennes manipulated 2 control points, using his two hands tracked by a tracking system. The participant located in London manipulated one control points, using one of his hands tracked by a tracking system. The positions of these 3 control points (2 in Rennes, 1 in London) defined the position of the clipping plane. So these control points enabled the two participants to move together the clipping plane (see figure 2).

Each participant was represented in the virtual world by his viewing frustum to enable the other to understand what he was seeing. His control point(s) used to manipulate the clipping plane was(were) also represented in the virtual world to enable the other to understand what he was doing (see figure 2). Moreover, the two participants could communicate by the voice with a microphone put on each participant and some speakers located in each immersive device.

3.3 Technical Specifications

To realise these experiments, a collaborative virtual environment has been deployed between Rennes and London. We first describe the immersive device used on each site, then we explain how the data of the virtual environment have been distributed for the collaborative manipulation.

3.3.1 Immersive Devices

On each side, participants used a specific immersive device to manipulate the clipping plane:

- **In Rennes:** the VR room is composed of 2 big screens (9,6 by 3m) with a resolution of 6240x2016 for the front and 3502x1050 for the floor. The front screen is back-projected by 8 projectors controlled by 2 *Nvidia® Quatro® Plex 2200*, while the floor is projected from above by 3 projectors controlled by 1 *Nvidia® Quatro® Plex 2200*. An *ART* tracking system based on infra-red cameras is used to track the user's head and hands inside the parallelepiped defined by the 2 screens.

- **In London:** the VR room is composed of 4 big screens (3 by 2,1m) with a resolution of 1400x1050 each (front, right, left and floor). Each of the front, right and left screens are back-projected by 1 projector controlled by a separate computer, while the floor is projected from above by 1 projector controlled by a 4th computer. An *InterSense* tracking system based on ultra-sonic sensors is used to track the user's head and one of his hands inside the parallelepiped defined by the 4 screens.

On each side, the *jReality* graphical library [16] was used to render the virtual environment. This library makes possible to distribute the scene graph on the different computers managing the projectors of each VR room, to display stereoscopic images, and to deform the user's viewing frustum according to his head position (head tracking).

3.3.2 Network Distribution

For the single user manipulation, the data of the virtual environment were managed locally on each side. But, for the collaborative manipulation, these data were distributed on the network. We used a client/server architecture with a server located in Rennes. The two clients (one in Rennes, one in London) were connected to this server using TCP connections. The network latency between the server in Rennes and the client in London could be up to 50 ms. We used the model proposed by Fleury et al. [6] to distribute the data of the virtual environment between the server and the two clients. This model makes it possible to choose a particular data distribution for each virtual object. We chose to process the scientific data, the points of interest, the clipping plane and the viewing frustum representations on the server to ensure a strong consistency between the two participants' view. However, we chose to process the control points of the clipping plane on each client to ensure a good responsiveness when the participants were moving these points.

With this data distribution, a small gap could occur between the control points and the clipping plane due to the network latency. However, it was less disturbing for the participants that this gap occurred between the control points and the clipping plane than between the participant real hands and the control points. Moreover, it occurred only when the participants moved very quickly the clipping plane and not when they moved slowly the clipping plane to perform precise manipulation tasks. None of the participants complained about this small gap during the experiments.

4. EXPERIMENTS

We ran two experiments to compare the single user manipulation with the remote collaborative manipulation of the clipping plane. Even if the first experiment has not shown significant difference between the two manipulation techniques, the observations performed during this experiment have allowed us to formulate two interesting new hypotheses. The second experiment aimed to validate these hypotheses by modifying the experimental conditions.

4.1 First Experiment

To compare the two manipulation techniques for scientific data analysis, we ran a first experiment in which the participants had to examine some real scientific data.

4.1.1 Description

The scientific data were seismic data from a physical simulation of an earthquake near Nice in France [4]. This earthquake is not real, but it is realistic according to localisation and intensity. Data used in the experiment were iso-surfaces of the PGD (Peak Ground Displacement) computed during the simulation. The iso-surfaces were organised on a concentric way around the earthquake's epicentre (see figure 1).

Task to Perform.
Participants had to find 3 points of interest inside the scientific data. For the experiments, these points of interest were represented by small red spheres. To find the points of interest, participants manipulated the clipping plane using either the single user manipulation (part 3.1) or the collaborative manipulation with a remote participant (part 3.2). When participants had found the 3 points of interest, they had to precisely move the clipping plane in order to reach the 3 points at the same time and to make a cross-section that showed the 3 points at the same time (see figure 1).

Population.
10 participants in Rennes (1 female and 9 males) aged from 20 to 39 (mean: 24, standard deviation: 5,63) took part in this experiment. They performed the collaborative manipulation with a confederate in London (always the same co-author). One of two participants performed first the single user manipulation and then the collaboration manipulation, and vice versa for the other half of the participants.

Procedure.
After a training period, each participant performed 5 trials for each manipulation technique. For each trial, the positions of the 3 points of interest were randomly chosen in a set of 5 interesting configurations of the points. When one configuration was chosen for a trial, it was removed from the set. The same set of configurations was used for each of the two techniques and for each participant.

Collected Data.
For each trial and each participant, we recorded the completion time. Time recording started when the participant activated the manipulation of the clipping plane by pressing a control button, and was automatically stopped when the clipping plane reached the 3 points at the same time.

4.1.2 Results

This experiment showed that the difference between the two manipulation techniques was not significant. First, the mean completion times of all the participants for the two techniques were very close: 71.66 sec with the single user manipulation and 67.66 sec with the collaborative manipulation. Second, there was an important participant variability: standard deviation of the mean completion time was equal to 89.14 sec for the single user manipulation and to 32.49 sec for the collaborative manipulation. A Student's test (t-test) showed that the difference between the two techniques was not significant ($t(18) = 0.13$, $p = 0.9$). This not significant difference can be explained by the following observations:

1. The distance between the 3 points of interest was too small (and stayed always similar on each trial). Indeed, for some participants, the task to complete was very easy and took them just few seconds. So, for these participants, it was difficult to make a difference between the two manipulation techniques. Moreover, if the task is too easy, the time required by the two par-

ticipants to synchronise themselves at the beginning of a collaborative manipulation penalises this technique.

2. The search of the 3 points of interest inside the scientific data introduced a bias in the evaluation of the two manipulation techniques. Indeed, the participants did not have particular knowledge in analysing scientific data and, for some of them, it was very difficult to find the 3 points of interest inside the data. For these participants, it was impossible to compare the two techniques together, because the completion time depended more on the "luck" of finding quickly the points of interest than on the time required to well adjust the clipping plane position.

3. The training period was maybe too short. Indeed, we noticed that the completion time was shorter for the last trials than for the first trials. It was even more noticeable for the collaborative manipulation technique.

Observations 2 and 3 have been identified as sources of bias that required to be controlled in next experiment, while first observation could be used to formulate two hypotheses:

- **H1**: when the 3 points of interest are close together (and the task is almost easy), the single user manipulation is as efficient as the collaborative manipulation.

- **H2**: if the distance between the 3 points of interest increases (and thus the task becomes more difficult), then the collaborative manipulation will be more efficient than the single user manipulation.

4.2 Second Experiment

To test the hypothesis **H1** and **H2** formulated in the first experiment, we have performed a second experiment by adapting the experimental protocol.

4.2.1 Description

First, to avoid the bias described in the observations 2 and 3, we have decided, respectively, to remove the scientific data in order to not mix the manipulation task with a search task, and to increase the training period for the two manipulation techniques. Second, we have decided to keep some similar configurations of the 3 points of interest to test **H1**, and to introduce some new configurations with a significantly bigger distance between the 3 points of interest to test **H2**.

Task to Perform.

Even if the scientific data had been removed, participants still had to manipulate a clipping plane in order to reach 3 points of the virtual world at the same time (see figure 4). To manipulate this plane, participants used either the single user manipulation (part 3.1) or the collaborative manipulation with a remote participant (part 3.2). Some new configurations of the 3 points with a bigger distance between the points had been added, and all the configurations used for the experiment had been divided into two groups according to the distance between the points (mean of the distances two by two between the 3 points):

- a "**Close**" group with the configurations for which the mean of the distances was less than 0,6 m,

- a "**Far**" group with the configurations for which the mean of the distances was more than 1,4 m.

Figure 4: 2nd experiment that consisted in manipulating the clipping plane without the scientific data.

Population.

32 participants (6 females and 26 males) aged from 18 to 50 (mean: 26, standard deviation: 6,72) took part in this experiment. None of these participants had been involved in the first experiment. They were divided in two groups:

- a group **G1** of 16 participants in Rennes who performed the collaborative manipulation with a confederate in London (always the same co-author). Only the 16 participants in Rennes performed the single user manipulation (the confederate did not perform the single user manipulation), and 16 teams (each participant in Rennes with the confederate in London) performed the collaborative manipulation.

- a group **G2** of 16 participants (8 in Rennes, 8 in London) who performed the collaborative manipulation with another real participant of this group. The 16 participants, both in Rennes and London, performed separately the single user manipulation, but only 8 teams (one participant in Rennes with one participant in London) performed the collaborative manipulation.

In each group, one of two participants performed first the single user manipulation and then the collaboration manipulation, and vice versa for the other half of the group.

Procedure.

After time to familiarise themselves with the virtual environment, participants realised first a training for the two techniques in the same order than for the real experiment. The training consisted in performing 4 trials for each technique. When participants had finished the training, they started the real experiment. They had to performed 10 trials for each manipulation technique: 5 used a configuration of 3 **Close** points and 5 used a configuration of 3 **Far** points. The 5 trials with the **Close** points were randomly mixed with the 5 trials with the **Far** points. The experiment lasted about 45 minutes including training trials.

Collected Data.

For each trial and each participant, we recorded the completion time in the same way as in the first experiment. After the experiment, participants filled out a subjective questionnaire about the two manipulation techniques. Obviously, the confederate did not fill out this questionnaire.

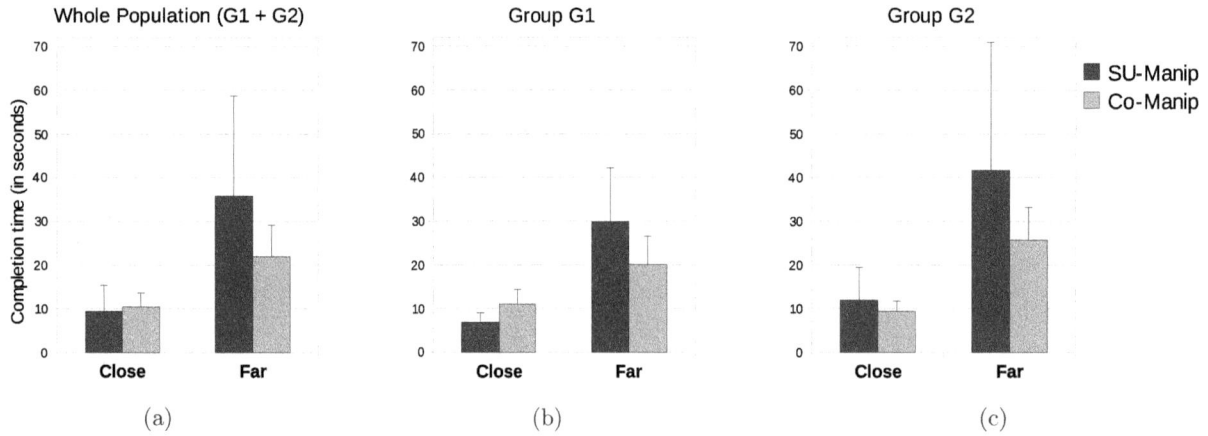

Figure 5: Means and standard deviations of the completion time for the two techniques for the whole population (a), for group G1 (b) and for group G2 (c).

4.2.2 Results

Using the data collected during the experiment, we conducted statistic analysis to compare the single user manipulation (SU-Manip) with the collaborative manipulation (Co-Manip). For these statistic analysis, we separated the cases when the 3 points were **Close** together and the cases when the 3 points were **Far** apart.

Completion Time.

For each participant, we computed the mean completion time on the 5 trials for each group of points and for each manipulation technique (4 cases). Then, we performed a Student's test (t-test) on these mean values (in seconds) to compare the two techniques (SU-Manip, Co-Manip). We also computed the mean values (M) and the standard deviation (SD) of the mean completion times of all the participant, for each one of the 4 cases.

First, we considered the whole population **G1+G2** (see figure 5(a)). When the 3 points were **Close** together, the mean completion time was almost the same with the SU-Manip technique ($M = 9.38$ sec, $SD = 6.06$ sec) and with the Co-Manip technique ($M = 10.42$ sec, $SD = 3.19$ sec), and the difference between both techniques was not significant ($t(54) = -0.76$, $p = 0.44$). However, when the 3 points were **Far** apart, the mean completion time was shorter with the Co-Manip technique ($M = 22$ sec, $SD = 7.15$ sec) than with the SU-Manip technique ($M = 35.78$ sec, $SD = 22.88$ sec), and this difference was significant ($t(54) = 2.84$, $p = 0.006$).

Second, we only considered the group **G1** of the participants who had performed the Co-Manip with the same confederate in London (see figure 5(b)). When the 3 points were **Close** together, the mean completion time was slightly shorter with the SU-Manip technique ($M = 6.88$ sec, $SD = 2.13$ sec) than with the Co-Manip technique ($M = 10.94$ sec, $SD = 3.45$ sec), and this difference was significant ($t(30) = -44.01$, $p < 0.001$). When the 3 points were **Far** apart, the mean completion time was shorter with the Co-Manip technique ($M = 20.13$ sec, $SD = 6.43$ sec) than with the SU-Manip technique ($M = 29.88$ sec, $SD = 12.25$ sec), and this difference was significant ($t(30) = 2.82$, $p = 0.008$).

Finally, we only considered the group **G2** of the par-

ticipants who had performed the Co-Manip with another real participant of the group (see figure 5(c)). When the 3 points were **Close** together, the mean completion time was slightly shorter with the Co-Manip technique ($M = 9.38$ sec, $SD = 2.45$ sec) than with the SU-Manip technique ($M = 12$ sec, $SD = 7.5$ sec), but this difference was not significant ($t(22) = 0.96$, $p = 0.35$). When the 3 points were **Far** apart, the mean completion time was shorter with the Co-Manip technique ($M = 25.75$ sec, $SD = 7.44$ sec) than with the SU-Manip technique ($M = 41.63$ sec, $SD = 29.27$ sec), however this difference was not significant ($t(22) = 1.49$, $p = 0.149$). We thought that, even if there was a big difference between the mean completion time for the two techniques, this difference was not significant for the farther apart points because:

- Some participants had lot of difficulties to perform the task with the SU-Manip technique when the 3 points were **Far** apart (it could explain the big standard deviation for the **Far** points).

- Some two-person teams in the group **G2** had difficulties to synchronise themselves at the beginning of the Co-Manip (language barrier, etc.). It induced some big differences between the completion time of each two-person team.

- In the group **G2**, each participant performed the task alone for SU-Manip (16 participants) and with another participant of the group for the Co-Manip (8 teams). Thus, the number of samples for the SU-Manip was twice the number of samples for the Co-Manip.

Subjective Questionnaire.

After the experiment, a preference questionnaire was proposed in which the participants had to grade from 1 to 7 (7-point Likert scale) the two manipulation techniques for each group of point configurations (**Close** or **Far**) according to 5 subjective criteria: *fatigue, ease* of use, *precision, naturalness* and a *global appreciation* of the technique. Moreover, for the Co-Manip, they had to grade from 1 to 7 for each group of point configurations their feeling of *collaborating* with another real participant. We computed the mean values and the standard deviation on ratings given by the whole

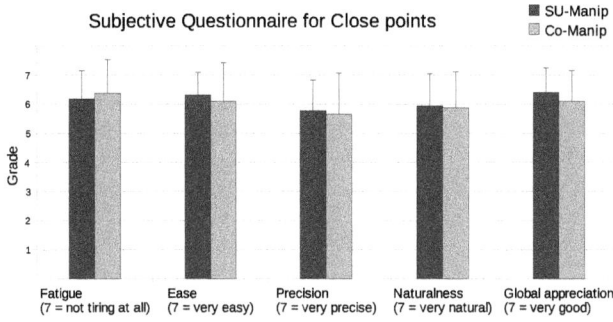

Figure 6: Means and standard deviations of subjective ratings for the two techniques when the 3 points were Close together.

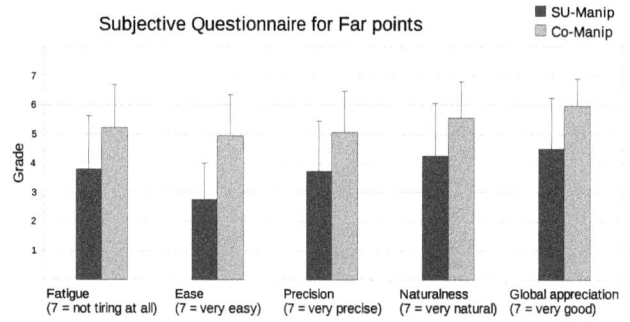

Figure 7: Means and standard deviations of subjective ratings for the two techniques when the 3 points were Far apart.

population **G1** + **G2** for each one of the 4 cases. Then, to compare the two manipulation techniques, we computed the differences (Δ) between the mean values of the two techniques and we performed a Wilcoxon signed rank test on ratings given by the participants to determine if these differences were significant.

First, we considered the subjective ratings given when the 3 points were **Close** together (see figure 6): it did not seem to have particular preferences for one or the other manipulation technique. Indeed, the differences between the mean values of the two techniques were very low and the statistical analysis showed that these differences were not significant: *fatigue* ($\Delta = 0.19$, $p = 0.21$), *ease* ($\Delta = 0.22$, $p = 0.58$), *precision* ($\Delta = 0.13$, $p = 0.77$), *naturalness* ($\Delta = 0.06$, $p = 1$) and global appreciation ($\Delta = 0.31$, $p = 0.08$).

Second, we considered the subjective ratings given when the 3 points were **Far** apart (see figure 7): it seemed that the Co-Manip technique was more preferred than the SU-Manip technique. Indeed, the differences between the mean values of the two techniques were substantial (more than 1 point) for each criterion and for the *global appreciation*. The statistical analysis showed that these differences were highly significant: *fatigue* ($\Delta = 1.44$, $p < 0.001$), *ease* ($\Delta = 2.19$, $p < 0.001$), *precision* ($\Delta = 1.34$, $p < 0.001$), *naturalness* ($\Delta = 1.31$, $p < 0.001$) and *global appreciation* ($\Delta = 1.47$, $p < 0.001$).

Finally, whatever the distance between the 3 points, it seemed that the participants had a strong feeling of *collaborating* with another remote participant: for the **Close** points ($M = 5.69$, $SD = 1.18$) and for the **Far** points ($M = 6.34$, $SD = 0.97$). Moreover, it is interesting to notice that the feeling of *collaboration* was slightly stronger when the 3 points were **Far** apart and the statistic analysis showed that this difference was significant ($\Delta = 0.66$, $p = 0.007$). We can think that the participants felt more the need to collaborate when the task to perform was more difficult (i.e. when the 3 points were farther apart).

4.3 Discussion

The results obtained in the second experiment showed that there was not a significant difference between the two manipulation techniques when the 3 points were closer together. Indeed, the completion time was shorter either with the single user manipulation technique or with the collaborative manipulation technique according to the studied population, and these differences were not significant. Moreover, the subjective questionnaire did not show particular preferences for one or the other manipulation technique when the 3 points were closer together. This lack of significant differences between the two techniques validated hypothesis **H1** stated in the first experiment.

When the 3 points were far apart, the second experiment showed that a collaborative manipulation between two remote users was more efficient than a single user manipulation to analyse the scientific data. It can be explained by two factors: when the 3 points were farther apart, first, the task of positioning the clipping plane required more precision and, second, the participants could not see all the 3 points at the same time in their field of view and they had to rotate the head to adjust the clipping plane position. These two factors globally increased the difficulty of performing the task when the 3 points were farther apart. With the collaborative manipulation technique, each user could focus on adjusting the clipping position to reach only one or two points and let the other do the same for the other points. So, the completion time was significantly shorter with the collaborative manipulation technique than with the single user manipulation technique. Moreover, the subjective questionnaire showed that the participants globally preferred the collaborative manipulation technique when the 3 points were farther apart, and they also found this technique less tiring, easier, more precise and more natural for these point configurations. Consequently, hypothesis **H2** stated in the first experiment was validated.

For the second experiment, there were not noticeable evolution of the completion time between the first trials and the last trials. So we could conclude that the observation 3 of the first experiment was true, and that the training period in the second experiment was sufficient. However, nothing enabled us to corroborate the observation 2 stated in the first experiment. It would be interesting to realise a new experiment with the scientific data and the farther apart points to determine if the presence of the scientific data impacts the manipulation task. Moreover, it could also be interesting to propose some solutions to enable participants to take advantage of the collaboration for searching the points of interest inside the data.

Finally, the less significant results obtained for the group **G2** in the second experiment showed that collaborative experiments are difficult to design because so many parameters are involved. Indeed, when remote participants who do not know each other collaborate together, some additional difficulties can occur according to the participants' language, their vocabularies, their predispositions for the collaborative work or their goodwill to work with someone else.

5. CONCLUSION

These experiments aimed to compare a single user manipulation technique with a collaborative manipulation technique between two remote users (one located in Rennes and the other located in London) for analysing some scientific data. The task consisted in positioning a clipping plane in order to show, at the same time, 3 points of interest located inside the scientific data. For the single user manipulation, a participant manipulated alone the clipping plane by rotating and translating its centre (6 degrees of freedom). For the collaborative manipulation, two participants manipulated together the clipping plane by using the 3-hand manipulation technique proposed by Aguerreche et al. [1]. Even if there were not significant differences between the two manipulation techniques when the 3 points of interests were close together, the experiments showed that the remote collaborative manipulation was more efficient than the single user manipulation when the 3 points were far apart and, consequently, when the task to perform was more difficult.

In future work, we would like to perform a new experiment to determine the threshold of the distance between the points of interest from which it becomes more efficient to use the remote collaborative manipulation technique than the single user manipulation technique. It would also be interesting to run experiment with the scientific data and the farther apart points as explained in the discussion part. In this new experiment with scientific data and farther apart points, we guess that maybe the manipulation of a clipping plane could interfere with the individuals' visualisation of the scientific data. Indeed, the manipulation of one user could lead sometimes to "put" the other inside the data (by reversing the clipping plane for instance). In this case, the second user loses track of the points of interest on which he is focusing. There are thus some potential rendering challenges to address in order to allow this user to continue his interaction even if he is inside the scientific data.

ACKNOWLEDGMENTS

We wish to thank the Visionair European infrastructure project, the Foundation Rennes 1 "Progress, Innovation, Entrepreneurship" and the French Research National Agency project named Collaviz for their support.

REFERENCES

[1] L. Aguerreche, T. Duval, and A. Lécuyer. Short paper: 3-Hand Manipulation of Virtual Objects. In *Proc. of the Joint Virtual Reality Conf. of EGVE - ICAT - EuroVR*, pages 153–156, 2009.

[2] L. Aguerreche, T. Duval, and A. Lécuyer. Evaluation of a Reconfigurable Tangible Device for Collaborative Manipulation of Objects in Virtual Reality. In *Proceedings of Theory and Practice of Computer Graphics Conference*, pages 81–88, 2011.

[3] S. Bryson. Virtual reality in scientific visualization. *Communications of the ACM*, 39(5):62–71, may 1996.

[4] F. Dupros, F. D. Martin, E. Foerster, D. Komatitsch, and J. Roman. High-performance finite-element simulations of seismic wave propagation in three-dimensional nonlinear inelastic geological media. *Parallel Computing*, 36(5-6):308–325, 2010.

[5] T. Duval, A. Lecuyer, and S. Thomas. SkeweR: a 3D Interaction Technique for 2-User Collaborative Manipulation of Objects in Virtual Environments. In *Proceedings of the IEEE symposium on 3D User Interfaces*, pages 69–72, 2006.

[6] C. Fleury, T. Duval, V. Gouranton, and B. Arnaldi. A New Adaptive Data Distribution Model for Consistency Maintenance in Collaborative Virtual Environments. In *Proc. of the Joint Virtual Reality Conf. of EuroVR - EGVE - VEC*, pages 29–36, 2010.

[7] B. Fröhlich, S. Barrass, B. Zehner, J. Plate, and M. Göbel. Exploring geo-scientific data in virtual environments. In *Proceedings of the conference on Visualization*, pages 169–173, 1999.

[8] K. Hinckley, R. Pausch, J. C. Goble, and N. F. Kassell. Passive real-world interface props for neurosurgical visualization. In *Proceedings of the SIGCHI conference on Human factors in computing systems*, pages 452–458, 1994.

[9] J. Leigh, A. E. Johnson, M. Brown, D. J. Sandin, and T. A. DeFanti. Visualization in Teleimmersive Environments. *Computer*, 32(12):66–73, Dec. 1999.

[10] M. S. Pinho, D. A. Bowman, and C. M. Freitas. Cooperative object manipulation in immersive virtual environments: framework and techniques. In *Proc. of the ACM symposium on Virtual Reality Software and Technology*, pages 171–178, 2002.

[11] K. Riege, T. Holtkamper, G. Wesche, and B. Frohlich. The Bent Pick Ray: An Extended Pointing Technique for Multi-User Interaction. In *Proc. of the IEEE symp. on 3D User Interfaces*, pages 62–65, 2006.

[12] D. Roberts, R. Wolff, O. Otto, and A. Steed. Constructing a Gazebo: supporting teamwork in a tightly coupled, distributed task in virtual reality. *Presence: Teleoperators and Virtual Environments*, 12(6):644–657, Dec. 2003.

[13] R. A. Ruddle, J. C. D. Savage, and D. M. Jones. Symmetric and asymmetric action integration during cooperative object manipulation in virtual environments. *ACM Transaction Computer-Human Interaction*, 9(4):285–308, Dec. 2002.

[14] J. Schild, T. Holtkämper, and M. Bogen. The 3D Sketch Slice: Precise 3D Volume Annotations in Virtual Environments. In *Proceedings of the Joint Virtual Reality Conference of EGVE - ICAT - EuroVR*, pages 65–72, 2009.

[15] A. Steed, D. Alexander, P. Cook, and C. Parker. Visualizing Diffusion-Weighted MRI Data Using Collaborative Virtual Environment and Grid Technologies. In *Proceedings of the Theory and Practice of Computer Graphics*, pages 156–161, 2003.

[16] S. Weißmann, C. Gunn, P. Brinkmann, T. Hoffmann, and U. Pinkall. jReality: a java library for real-time interactive 3D graphics and audio. In *Proc. of the ACM conference on Multimedia*, pages 927–928, 2009.

CaveUDK: A VR Game Engine Middleware

Jean-Luc Lugrin[†],
Fred Charles, Marc Cavazza,
Teesside University,
School of Computing,
Middlesbrough, TS1 3BA
j-l.lugrin@tees.ac.uk

Marc Le Renard
ESIEA
38 rue des docteurs Calmette
et Guérin, Parc Universitaire,
Laval, 53000
marc.lerenard@esiea-ouest.fr

Jonathan Freeman,
Jane Lessiter
Psychology Department, Goldsmiths,
University of London,
London, SE14 6NW
j.freeman@gold.ac.uk

ABSTRACT

Previous attempts at developing immersive versions of game engines have faced difficulties in achieving both overall high performance and preserving reusability of software developments. In this paper, we present a high-level VR middleware based on one of the most successful commercial game engines: the Unreal® Engine 3.0 (UE3). We describe a VR framework implemented as an extension to the Unreal® Development Kit (UDK) supporting CAVE™-like installations. Our approach relies on a distributed architecture reinforced by specific replication patterns to synchronize the user's point of view and interactions within a multi-screen installation. Our performance benchmarks indicated that our immersive port does not affect the game engine performance, even with complex real-time applications, such as fast-paced multiplayer First Person Shooter (FPS) games or high-resolution graphical environments with 2M+ polygons. A user study also demonstrated the capacity of our VR middleware to elicit high spatial presence while maintaining low cybersickness effects. With free distribution, we believe such a platform can support future entertainment and VR research.

Categories and Subject Descriptors

H.5.1 [**Multimedia Information Systems**]: Artificial, Augmented and Virtual Reality - Virtual Reality for Art and Entertainment

General Terms

Algorithms, Design, Performance.

Keywords

Immersive Display, Virtual Reality, Game Engine, Framework.

1. INTRODUCTION AND RATIONALE

Game engines have emerged as a unique platform providing increased interactivity and compelling graphics performance [10] [24] [28] [31]. This situation had led several researchers to explore the use of game engines to support high-end VR, in particular immersive displays such as CAVE™-like [6] systems. For instance, Paul Rajlich's *CAVE Quake II*, developed at NCSA, is probably the first immersive implementation of a popular computer game. It has been followed by *CAVE Quake III Arena*, based on the open source Aftershock engine. Juarez et al. [19] have ported the CryEngine2 game engine to a CAVE™-like

[†]*Current Affiliation: Universität Würzburg, HCI, Germany*

installation, through their *CryVE* system. However, they have reported average frame rates < 20 fps, which may not be sufficient to support a comfortable viewing and interaction experience. *CAVEUT* was originally developed at the University of Pittsburgh [15] and later extended to include stereoscopy [16], but its version of the Unreal® Engine is now out of date. *BlenderCave* [7] is the VR extension of the open-source Blender engine but its VR version demonstrated limited rendering performances, without support for dedicated I/O VR peripherals. *MiddleVR* [27] offers a VR port of the Unity Game Engine [37], but its visual performances do not reach that of the most advanced commercial game engines like the CryEngine [5] or the Unreal® Engine [38]. Performances achieved by game engines are the results of extremely complex and optimised architectures. One major challenge faced by this endeavor is the preservation of game engine performances and content synchronization within a multi-screen stereoscopic displays, since game engine optimizations have not been developed with multi-screen displays in mind. Another important aspect of high-end multi-screen VR systems, not originally part of game engines, is the integration of a mechanism for the inclusion of tracker input and the configuration of individual screens. VR systems typically propose large field of view (multiple surrounding screens), accurate motion tracking (tracker devices) and depth perception (3D rendering and head motion parallax). One important technical requirement of a multi-screen system is to preserve visualisation and interaction consistency in between screens while delivering a comfortable refresh rate and low end-to-end tracking latency. Multi-screen consistency mostly represents the preservation of the virtual object alignment when visualised over different focal planes (i.e. screens). This is especially important when the user moves an object across multiple screen borders via a virtual hand (such as a virtual weapon held by the user in a typical FPS game). Traditional VR frameworks implement asymmetric frustum, homography correction and accurate distributed object synchronization protocols to ensure the best visualisation coherence and interactivity over different screens. However, game engines typically do not include such features. Their complex architecture and implementation, as well as their proprietary source code and optimization, often make them very opaque to such transformation. In this paper, we present CaveUDK as a high-level VR middleware for CAVE™-like platforms developed on top of a state-of-the-art game engine, Unreal® Development Kit (UDK) [38]. It constitutes the natural follow-up of CaveUT [16], while providing more advanced and generic UnrealScript VR Class framework and set of software tools for multi-screen visualisation, interaction, conversion, calibration and deployment (Figure 1). Here, we discuss its implementation, performances and reusability, where *reusability* refers to its extensible high-level class framework and the presence of conversion, calibration and deployment systems.

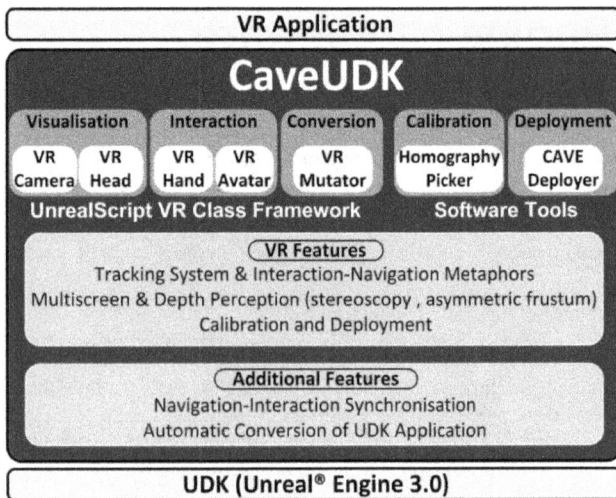

Figure 1. The CaveUDK Framework (a layer of VR objects and tools in-between the VR hardware and the application).

2. SYSTEM OVERVIEW

2.1 Choice of Game Engine

UDK is a free professional authoring toolset based on UE3, which is now adopted by a large development and research community. It has been installed on more than 1.4 million unique machines, and showcases numerous applications in training simulation, games, architecture and construction simulations [39]. Epic Games has allowed us to access the game engine's C++ source code to gain necessary knowledge and efficiently integrate VR features at a low level. However, one key aspect of our approach was to maximize the flexibility and extensibility of the system by keeping a major part of the project open source via a DLL plug-in architecture (for tracker integration and screen calibration) and an open-source UnrealScript classes framework (for rapid development over existing or new Unreal®-based application). CaveUDK exposes the VR system features without requesting the acquisition and recompilation of the game engine source code.

2.2 Target Hardware Platforms

Our target platforms for CaveUDK are multi-screen, immersive display installations such as CAVE™. Our own CAVE™ platform is a four-screen cubic-shape structure of 3.0×3.0×2.25 meters (Figure 2). Our PC cluster is composed of 5 image generators running Windows 7 Ultimate 64 bit, 2×Xeon E5606 Processor *(Quad Core, 2.13 GHz, 4MB Cache, 4.80 GT/s Intel®)*, 12Gb DDR3 RAM 1333Mhz and 2.5GB GDDR5 NVIDIA Quadro 5000 with G-Sync. One of the image generators is used as the game server; while each of the four others are connected to a projector *(Christie Digital Mirage S+6K SXGA+ DLP 3D)* generating 1400×1050×100Hz. For 3D vision, the user wears stereoactive shutter glasses *(NVIDIA Vision Pro Kit [29])*, while stereo signals and rendering synchronisation are handled at 50 Hz by the NVIDIA cards and drivers). Real-time tracking is operated by an Intersense™ IS900 system [14] for both head and wand tracking, using a VRPN *(Virtual Reality Peripheral Network [40])* server.

3. FRAMEWORK AND FEATURES

In order to integrate our middleware on top of the Unreal® Game engine, we modeled our architecture using a distributed approach, whereby each VR Client (game client) represents a different screen synchronised with the VR Server (game server) connected to a Tracker Server (Figure 2). Our VR framework, proposes a set of UnrealScript classes, called VR Objects, supporting consistent multi-screen visualisation *(VR-Camera* and *VR-Head* classes) and interactions *(VR-Hand* and *VR-Avatar* classes) in a multi-screen context. These classes are internally connected to VR Trackers through a module, called *VR Interface* (C++ DLL) directly integrated to the game engine source code. They also implement a specific replication process to synchronize user's point of view and interactions across all VR Clients (i.e. on all screens). We rely on a customized Master-Proxy object replication approach [25] which benefitted from the fast Unreal® network system to ensure position and states synchronicity.

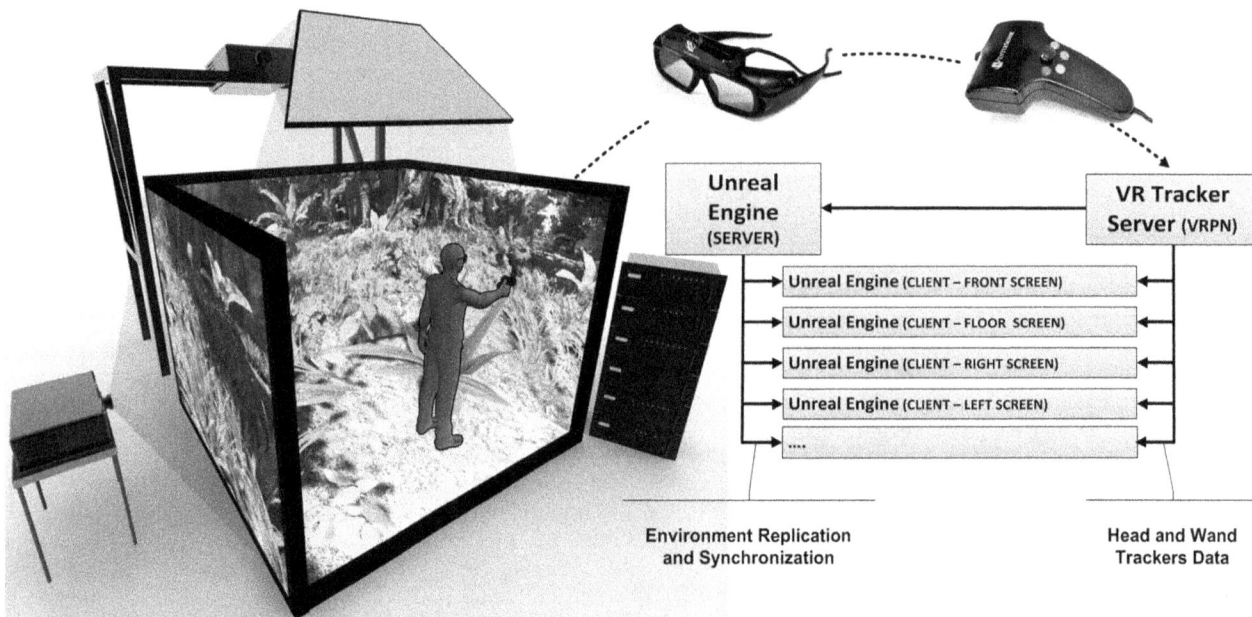

Figure 2. CaveUDK Architecture within a CAVE™-like Platform (2M+ triangles per screen on average).

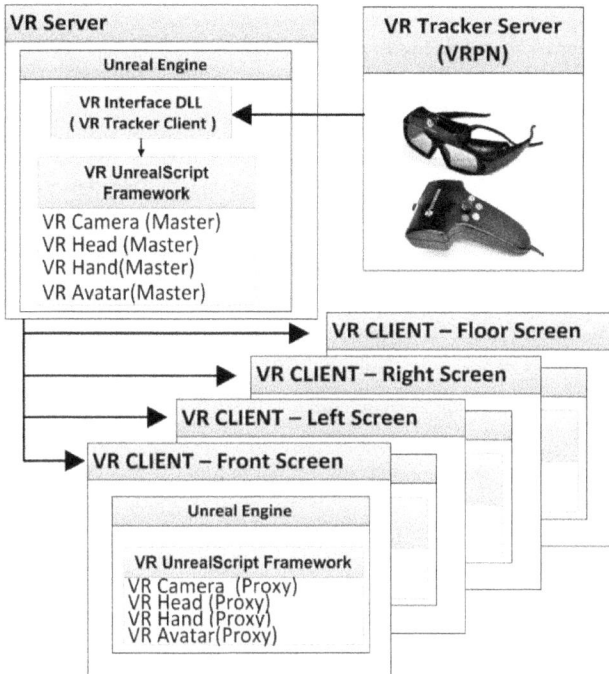

Figure 3. VR Framework Integration and Replication.

3.1 Visualization: *VR Camera* and *VR Head*

Conveying depth and layout is a key element of a VR system. In a multi–view projection system with a strong user centric paradigm such as a CAVE™, egocentric depth perception is simulated using binocular stereopsis and motion parallax. Meanwhile, creating egocentric depth perception in a multi-screen environment using a distributed architecture requires the implementation of a specific camera system. Our VR framework (Figure 3) relies on a *Virtual Camera Cluster* [7] system to map the topology and geometry of a projection system to different game clients. The location of the *Virtual Camera*s running on each game client *(i.e. VR-Camera Proxy)* are synchronised with a virtual camera *(i.e. VR-Camera Master)* controlled by the user on the game server (Figure 3). The movements of the master camera are replicated on the game client, simulating the user's motion on all screens. Meanwhile, each VR Client computes its own camera direction and viewing frustum using this origin, their respective display topology (i.e. Front, Left, Floor, Right screen) and head tracker position. Stereoscopic visualisation is achieved via specific graphics drivers synchronised with a 3D compatible projection system and glasses. We adopted the NVIDIA 3D vision system [30] which provides a generic and low cost solution, capable of adding 3D perspectives to numerous existing graphics applications. The implementation of motion parallax is also important, as it faithfully reproduces the illusion of depth by adding depth cues to artificial stereopsis [8] [17]. Motion parallax adapts each screen projection perspective to match the user's point of view as he/she moves inside the CAVE™. Therefore, the virtual world camera position and perspective matrix need to be constantly adjusted for each screen to provide the correct viewpoint. Cameras should thus compute an asymmetric viewing frustum [1] as shown on Figure 4 for each screen and for each frame using exact location of the user's head within the CAVE™ (head tracker information). A dynamic asymmetric frustum system allows the coverage of the entire visible volume in the VR scene, while preventing frustum intersections. In addition, an off-axis projection matrix allows a comfortable 3D viewing

Figure 4. VR Client viewpoint using asymmetric frustum with head tracking (horizontal /vertical FOV in dashed lines).

experience which notably reduce the window violation effect by covering a larger part of the screen for each eye [3] [33]. Our system supports an off axis perspective implementation as the one proposed by the OpenGL wrapper library, called VRGL (by Willem de Jonge). However, we implemented such an asymmetric projection matrix computation directly at the core of the game engine rendering system[1]. The *VR-Head* object is responsible for computing the asymmetric frustum and applying user head position offset to the *VR-Camera*. As the *VR-Head* object is replicated, each client has access to the exact location of the user's head within the CAVE™, allowing them to perform their own frustum modifications. Motion parallax is then simulated by attaching the master *VR-Camera* to the head tracker with a combination of dynamic viewing frustum computed locally by each VR Client.

Therefore, multi-screen depth perception is rendered through a combination of binocular stereopsis, handled by the NVIDIA drivers and graphics cards, and motion parallax, managed by our distributed camera system. Nevertheless, with a distributed approach, it is essential to accurately synchronise camera motions on the VR Clients to achieve a smooth and consistent multi-screen visualisation when navigating in the virtual environment. The mechanisms ensuring VR Client camera synchronisation are discussed in the Navigation-Interaction synchronisation section.

3.2 Interaction: *VR Avatar* and *VR Hand*

User interaction in CAVE™-like environments often resorts to the explicit visualization of a virtual hand supporting interaction-navigation metaphors [33] [34].Our system supports user virtual representation through the *VR-Hand* and *VR-Avatar* objects. The *VR-Hand* represents the wand tracker, which is constantly converting the tracker physical position to its position transposed within the virtual world. It continuously receives tracker data from the *VR Interface* and triggers associated tracker events (button, analog, position and orientations updates). The *VR-Hand* facilitates high-level programming of navigation and interaction aspects by redefining the tracker events responses (Figure 5) and by using its positional data as the actual wand tracker position. It

---

[1] For confidentiality reasons, the integration of the dynamic frustum computations inside the game engine could not be discussed here.

thus enables developers to easily attach virtual objects to the wand tracker and program interaction while automatically ensuring synchronization across all screens. The synchronization of virtual hand position and orientation is explained in the following section.

```
event TrackerInputs(TrackerInput _Input)
{
  switch(_Input.buttonId)
  {
  case 1 :  if(_Input.action == ePressed)
                GetALocalPlayerController().startfire(0);
            if(_Input.action == eReleased)
                GetALocalPlayerController().stopfire(0);
            break;
  //...
```

Figure 5. Example of Tracker Event Overriding in *VR-Hand*.

The *VR-Hand* class also proposes a default mapping tracker event to keyboard/mouse inputs for fast conversion between desktop and immersive settings. The default navigation-interaction paradigm supported by our system is the "moving-by-pointing" navigation model [4] and the Virtual Hand/Ray-Casting [22] for interaction model. The user navigates in the virtual environment by pointing the wand tracker to a direction and moving the wand analogue stick. Consequently, the user's avatar *(VR-Avatar)* on the game server is moving in the specified direction. The avatar motion is then applied to the master *VR-Camera* also running on the server. The movements of the master camera are automatically replicated to all game clients, simulating the user's motion across all CAVE™ screens (Figure 3). To simulate user collision on clients, a collision cylinder is attached to the *VR-Avatar* proxies running on all individual clients. The *VR-Avatar* proxies are invisible to prevent them to appear in the CAVE™ and occlude the user's vision. As previously mentioned, for motion parallax simulation, when the user is moving inside the CAVE™ (i.e. walking), the master VR-Avatar position is automatically adjusted to match the offset detected by the VR-Head.

3.3 Synchronising Navigation-Interaction

As observed in our previous versions of CaveUT [6], the native Unreal® replication system would generate perceptible latency/ jitter during motion, and object misalignment in-between screens. Latency and jitter have been proven to diminish performance and increase simulator sickness [32]. Therefore, in order to considerably reduce the translation and rotation latency/jitters and synchronize interaction, we developed our own Navigation-Interaction replication systems i) removing native replicated variable aggregation and ii) forcing replication updates for certain data types.

The Unreal® Engine provides a high level networking and replication system [36] which relies on a very flexible and rapid distributed object approach. It maximises the responsiveness and consistency of the shared virtual environment using an optimised UDP-based network protocol, in combination with lock-step prediction/correction algorithms (e.g. dead-reckoning), area of interest management (AOI) and data quantization (compression). The location/acceleration vectors and quaternions are quantized to single 32-bit variables before being replicated. Therefore, the data loss from the compression or inaccuracy from the prediction could lead to slight differences in terms of object spatial or animation state between clients. Such a lack of accuracy or delay is acceptable in multiplayer games, where users do not share the same screen. However in our multi-screen context, they are perceptible and so could generate multi-screen object

misalignments, breaking multi-screen consistency and so compromising the immersive experience. One crucial point in avoiding such misalignment is to first provide accurate virtual camera synchronization for each screen. Subsequently, all virtual objects manipulated by the user should also support accurate and low latency replication. This is especially important when the user moves an object across multiple screen borders via the Virtual Hand (such as a virtual weapon held by the user in a FPS game). A slight difference in position from one screen to another could result in the user perceiving two or three different virtual objects instead of a single one.

Therefore, our VR Object replication implementation takes advantage of the fast Unreal® network layer to synchronize client views, using a customized high-frequency network replication pattern for our *VR-Camera*, *VR-Head* and *VR-Hand* objects. The UnrealScript code samples (Figures 6-7-8) illustrate our replication pattern based on *asynchronous unreliable remote function calls* to prevent data quantization and reduce replication latency.

```
simulated state VIRTUAL_MASTER_CAMERA_UPDATE
{
    simulated event Tick (float deltatime)
    {
    //...
    CaveUDkPlayerController(CavePlayerController)
    .ServerReplicatePosition(newCamLoc,  newCamRot,
        VirtualHand.location,  VirtualHand.rotation,
        VirtualHead.location,  VirtualHead.rotation );
    //...
```

Figure 6. *VR-Object* replication process via an asynchronous unreliable remote function call (in *VR-Camera* class).

The replication process is handled by the *VR-Camera* object running on the server (Figure 6). For every frame (aka game tick), the *VR-Camera* evaluates if the position and rotation of the virtual camera, head and hand need to be updated on VR Clients (e.g. when the user moves the virtual hand using the wand). In case of discrepancies, the *ServerReplicatePosition* function is executed on the server, hence the keyword *server*.

```
unreliable server function ServerReplicatePosition(
vector cam_v,rotator cam_r,vector hand_v,rotator hand_r,
vector head_v ,rotator head_r)
{
local CaveUDKSpectatorController PC;
foreach AllControllers(class'CaveUDKSpectatorController', PC)
{
 PC.ClientReceivedPosition (cam_v.X,cam_v.Y,cam_v.Z,
                    cam_r.Pitch,cam_r.Yaw,cam_r.Roll,
                    hand_v.X,hand_v.Y,hand_v.Z,
                    hand_r.Pitch,hand_r.Yaw,hand_r.Roll,
                    head_v.X,head_v.Y,head_v.Z,
                    head_r.Pitch,head_r.Yaw,head_r.Roll);
//...
```

Figure 7. *Server* function accessing game clients and triggering an instantaneous remote function call on clients (Note the uncompressed basic variables as parameter).

This function accesses the list of player spectators (i.e. a VR Client registered as non-playing game client) connected to the server, and requests them to execute the *ClientReceivePosition* function using the master *VR-Camera*, *VR-Head* and *VR-Hand* positions as parameters (Figure 7). The *ClientReceivePosition* function is declared as a *Client* function, which will force the function to run on the game clients. Function replication in Unreal® is asynchronous, meaning that remote function calls are executed immediately rather than at the end of the game tick as for replicated class variables. In addition, by passing floating values instead of vector and rotator variables we avoid the engine native data compression associated with such structures. Consequently, the *ClientReceivePosition* function is executed on the client as fast as possible, and maps its local copy of the *VR-Camera*, *VR-Head* and *VR-Hand* to an exact match of the positions present on the server (Figure 8).

```
unreliable client function ClientReceivedPosition(
float c_x ,float c_y ,float c_z ,int c_p ,int c_yaw , int c_r,
float ha_x,float ha_y,float ha_z,int ha_p,int ha_yaw, int ha_r,
float he_x,float he_y,float he_z,int he_p,int he_yaw, int he_r)
{
  if( LocalPlayer(Player).CaveCamera !=none)
  {
    LocalPlayer(Player).CaveCamera.setBaseActorCameraPos(
      c_x ,c_y ,c_z ,c_p,c_yaw,c_r,
      ha_x,ha_y,ha_z,ha_p,ha_yaw,ha_r,
      he_x,he_y,he_z,he_p,he_yaw,he_r);
//...
```

Figure 8. *Client* function executed by a game client in order to update their own copy of the user's camera, head and hand.

It is important to understand that an *unreliable* function replication makes no guarantee about the ordering of the remote function call (similar to a UDP protocol approach). Within our context, where the user's camera location and rotation need to be replicated at a high frequently to preserve multiscreen consistency and smooth navigation, using a *reliable* function would overload the network and cause latency. The *reliable* function guarantees delivery and ordering, but creates a delay due to acknowledgement waiting-time. Missing a replication update is not critical with a high refresh rate (50Hz) on a LAN. However, to avoid network congestion and to adapt to different hardware capacity, the replication frequency is adjustable from a configuration file (10 ms in our installation).This replication pattern is thus able to efficiently achieve smooth and accurate camera transition among multiple screens with no latency or jitter perceptible. It also permits the system to have a perfect multi-screen motion synchronisation for virtual objects attached to the wand tracker, such as virtual hand or weapon mesh (as shown in Figure 12 during in our immersive game usability study).

4. VR DEVELOPMENT WITH CAVEUDK

CaveUDK provides a high-level framework of VR Object and software tools for rapid development of VR application on the top of UDK. The following section describes its features and overall approach to hardware integration and software development.

4.1 Hardware Integration and Calibration

Because most multi-screen installations are custom-built, a VR Middleware should be able to adapt to different screens and tracker configurations. Our VRPN Client approach, directly integrated at the game engine level, enable to easily plug most of the VR devices available, while our simple screen configuration and homography correction supports different screen layout. The software calibration of the screen alignment is also essential to rapidly adapt the system to particular screen and projector configurations. The screen spatial configuration is easily handled via a text file specifying the coordinates of the screen corners in the tracker referential (Figure 9). However, to facilitate screen matching alignment, the system also includes a homography correction [2], providing a projective distortion matrix to perfectly match a particular screen projection geometry without manually adjusting the projector calibration settings and physical position for a perfect multi-screen alignment.

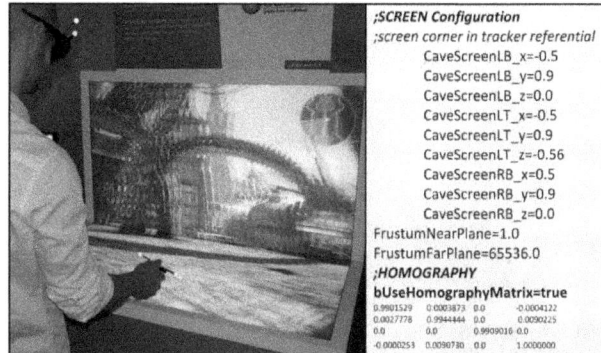

Figure 9. Screen calibration on Workbench (homography).

The tool delivered with the system is *Homography Picker* [12], and the homography matrix is also configured via a text file, read by the *VR Interface*. Figure 9 illustrates the porting of CaveUDK under Workbench-like screen configuration using an Optitrack V120: Trio tracker system [30]. Theoretically, CaveUDK supports up to 16-32 screens (Unreal Server maximum capacity), depending on application complexity. However, further evaluation should be carried to identify the actual screen limitation preserving application responsiveness and consistency.

4.2 Software Development and Deployment

4.2.1 Interaction Programming
The reusability of the system mostly relies on the ease of extension of the VR framework classes and its associated tracker-events and functions overriding. As previously demonstrated (Figure 5), custom interactions could be implemented by simply extending the *VR-Hand* or *VR-Head* classes and redefining their initial properties or tracker events. The redefinition of those classes is easily specified in the *VR-Camera* Class as shown on Figure 10. In addition, the inclusion of a high-level event system on the top of a high-level OO scripting language (i.e. UnrealScript) also constitutes a critical feature for the VR community in terms of rapid development and interaction programming. Developer can redefine their own VR object classes and apply them to a UDK environment using our Conversion System as discussed in the next section.

```
class CaveUDKTCaveCamera extends CaveUDKCaveCamera;
//...
DefaultProperties
{
  //...
  VirtualHandClass=class'CaveUDKVirtualHand'
  VirtualHeadClass=class'CaveUDKVirtualHead'
  //...
```

Figure 10. Redefining Custom Classes within CaveUDK.

4.2.2 Conversion and Integration: VR-Mutator
Adapting the game engine ensures that the approach is generic and compatible with all other applications developed with the same game engine. An application or game developed with UDK should be portable with minimum effort to an immersive context using our approach. Consequently, we designed a non-intrusive conversion system making our system reusable for many existing VR applications without any modification. The integration of the VR system to an Unreal® application requires the simple addition of an Unreal® *Mutator* to the game engine launching process. The Unreal® *Mutator* system allows the modification of certain classes or events in an existing Unreal® game level without modifying the

Figure 11. Automatic Desktop (top)-Immersive (bottom) conversion using the VR-Mutator System.

actual source code. Our specific CAVE™ *Mutator* automatically instantiates and activates our VR Objects within a UDK environment at run-time. This activation overrides the default camera system, activates the frustum modification and tracker event generation. Figure 11 illustrates the automatic porting of a compelling complex graphical environment (DirectX 11.0) [29] into an immersive version using our CAVE™ *Mutator* and its default control setting.

4.2.3 Deployment: Cave Launcher

Adopting a distributed approach results in the need to control remote game client and deploy new scripts, assets and maps to a group of machines before being able to connect to a game server. For security and anti-cheating issues, Unreal® maps and asset packages are digitally signed, forcing every game client to execute the exact same copy of the UnrealScript and environment as the one running on the game server. In addition, the screen calibration files for each client also need to be deployed with minimal effort. Consequently, we developed a Java-based deployment software tool named *CaveLauncher*. It automatically transfers asset packages and screen configuration files from the server to all clients at once, while enabling to remotely control the game clients execution.

In sum, interactions programming, conversion and deployment of VR application is considerably simplified and transparent to UDK developer using CaveUDK framework and tools.

5. EVALUATION

5.1 System Performances

Low latency is a critical feature of a VR system, as it is not only a negative factor in simulator sickness, but also considerably affects interaction [35]. Consequently, VR systems should support both high rendering refresh rates (>=30Hz) and high interaction responsiveness (<=150 ms for digital games [18]). For environments of a complexity equivalent to current high-quality 3D games rendering (200k to 2M triangles per frame), our immersive system reproduces similar rendering rates ($\approx$ 50Hz) as normal 3D desktop configurations (Table 1). Our system only presents a lower frame rate (< 20 Hz) for complex layouts such as

the last UE3 tech-demo, *NightAndDay,* displaying up to 6M triangles per frame. To measure responsiveness, we also performed video-based measurements of the end-to-end input latency using a frame-counting method as described in [9], which is better adapted to direct in-game measurements, but less accurate than the pendulum method discussed in [32]. As illustrated in Table 2 our results within a FPS game context (UT3 game map over 600K and 2M polygons) demonstrated an average response time of $\approx$ 82 ms for user interaction, which is the average delay between a tracker event (e.g. button pressed) and its associated virtual world events (e.g. The weapon firing on all four CAVE™ screens). In term of Navigation latency, the movements inside the virtual environment triggered by the tracker analogue stick are slower on average ($\approx$137 ms). The virtual hand motion transcribing the motion of the wand tracker inside the CAVE is also presenting a similar latency ($\approx$126 ms), considering our Intersense IS900 tracker 4 ms latency. The difference in response time between firing and camera/virtual hand movement is due to the optimized native mechanism for firing events replication in UT3 (crucial element for an online multiplayer FPS), while our camera/virtual hand replication going through function replication has a lesser priority within the unreal network system. The difference in latency measurements between camera and virtual hand motion, despite relying on the same replication system, could be explained by the lack of accuracy of the frame counting method. Future work should include less error-prone measurement methods as discussed in [32]. However, our system responsiveness remains below the 150-200 ms threshold given by the current literature in digital games [18] and standard causal perception studies [26] [35]. Overall, the performance results of our system demonstrated the appropriateness of our VR framework implementation regarding rendering performance and end-to-end latency.

Table 1: Comparison of desktop-immersive performances

Map	Triangles in Field of View	3D Desktop FPS	3D CAVE FPS
DM- Deck	$\approx$ 200-600K	$\approx$ 50	$\approx$ 50
Foliage	$\approx$ 1500-2500K	$\approx$ 50-45	$\approx$ 45-40
NightAndDay	$\approx$ 2500-6000K	$\approx$ 35-30	$\approx$ 20-15

Table 2: End-to-end Latency performances (Immersive)

Interactions within UT3 environments (3D/ 50Hz)	Av. Frame at 220 Hz (10 samples)	Av. in ms
Firing weapon (Button)	17.9 ($\sigma \approx$2.02)	$\approx$82
Move Camera (Analog)	30.1 ($\sigma \approx$ 4.43)	$\approx$136
Move Virtual Hand (wand)	27.7 ($\sigma \approx$ 5.36)	$\approx$126

5.2 User Experience

Prolonged exposure to stereoscopic VR can lead to adverse effects such as cybersickness or visual discomfort, through a variety of mechanisms [11] [13] [21]. Therefore, we conducted measurements of Cybersickness in a user study comparing desktop and immersive version of the same FPS game: Unreal® Tournament 3 (UT3) as illustrated by Figure 12. Before and after each session, participants completed the Simulator Sickness Questionnaire (SSQ), developed by Kennedy et al [20]. At the end of each session, users were presented with the ITC-SOPI Presence questionnaires proposed by Lessiter et al. [23]. Amongst our 40 participants, the different SSQ scores obtained for each of the

Figure 12. Immersive 3D gaming with FPS game (weapon attached to virtual hand – in blue).

cybersickness components (Nausea, Oculomotor and Disorientation) are low (around 5-7%), giving an overall score of 19.5% for an average exposure time of 10 min. It is important to note that the desktop game session revealed an average of 7.33 % SSQ score, creating only a 12% gap with the immersive version. All participants felt comfortable having completed the whole experiment. Meanwhile, the average of Negative Effects expressed in the ITC-SOPI questionnaire (mostly visual discomfort) increased by 23% in the immersive condition. As expected the immersive settings resulted in superior levels of Spatial Presence (+20%), Ecological Validity (+14%) and Engagement (+4%). A series of paired samples t-tests were conducted to explore whether these differences were statistically significant across the two experimental conditions (Desktop *vs.* CAVE™). Results for all four subscales revealed that significantly higher presence related ratings were given for the CAVE™ setting compared with the desktop setting: Spatial Presence $(t(38) = 9.51, p < 0.01)$, Engagement $(t(38) = 3.59, p < 0.01)$, Ecological Validity $(t(38) = 6.65, p < 0.01)$, while Negative Effects remained moderate $(t(38) = 9.10, p < 0.01)$.

In conclusion, the navigation-interaction replication pattern employed appears to provide a comfortable multi-screen visualization while having little impact on the performances (real-time interaction response time and overall frame rate close to desktop performances). CaveUDK is thus capable of supporting state-of-the-art real-world applications, providing real-time response, multi-screen consistency, and convincing 3D rendering. In addition, our preference questionnaire results also demonstrated a strong preference from users towards the immersive setting (72% of users expressed a clear preference), which is also confirmed by their self-reporting (*"It made me feel part of the world, easy to get immersed", "The immersion was so complete that towards the end of the second round, I forgot the walls were separated and just saw the environment around me"*).

6. CONCLUSIONS

CaveUDK offers a high-level VR middleware for the rapid deployment of immersive applications developed with UDK. It brings the benefits of developing with game engines to the VR community: an unmatched performance/cost ratio for visual rendering, sophisticated built-in Physics engines and advanced mechanisms for environment and characters behavior. The reusability of our system resides in its extensible high-level class framework and the integration of an automatic conversion, calibration and deployment systems. Custom interactions can be implemented by simply extending our UnrealScript classes and redefining their initial properties or tracker events. Our performance benchmarks also indicated that our implementation

does not significantly affect the baseline performance characteristics of the game engine, even with complex real-time applications such as fast-paced multiplayer FPS games and high-resolution graphic environments (2M+ polygons). The user study demonstrated the capacity of the resulting system to elicit high spatial presence without introducing significant cyber sickness effects. The free, open source distribution of CaveUDK should open interesting perspectives for VR technology, especially concerning the usability and development of future immersive entertainment, serious games or virtual training applications.

One important feature missing from the framework is the presence of a multi-screen compatible 3D head-up displays (HUD) system, which would allow a quick conversion of 2D Desktop HUD to 3D Immersive HUD and follow the user's head position while adjusting horizontal screen parallax to limit visual fatigue. This feature would be primarily needed for immersive gaming, which would constitute a natural application of our system. Further work also should investigate the factors of such visual fatigue, and explore possible solutions to reduce it such as "Dynamic Parallax Separation" with content-adaptive adjustment [13].

7. ACKNOWLEDGEMENTS
Epic Games (Mark Rein) and Public VR (Jeff Jacobson) are thanked for granted us access to the Unreal® engine source code. Matthew Laverick provided the visuals of Figure 1. This work has been funded (in part) by the European Commission through the CEEDS project (FP7-ICT-258749).

8. REFERENCES
[1] Arthur, K. W. 3D Task performance using head-coupled stereo displays. M.Sc. Thesis. University of British Columbia, 1993.

[2] Bimber, O. and Raskar, R., 2005. *Spatial Augmented Reality: Merging Real and Virtual Worlds.* AK Peters, CRC Press.

[3] Bourke, P., 1999. *Calculating Stereo Pairs.* URL: http://local.wasp.uwa.edu.au/~pbourke/miscellaneous/stereographics/stereorender/

[4] Bowman, D. A., Johnson, D. B. and Hodges, L. F., 1999. Testbed evaluation of virtual environment interaction techniques. In *Proceedings of the ACM symposium on Virtual reality software and technology (VRST '99).* ACM, New York, NY, USA, 26-33.

[5] *CryENGINE®3.* URL: http://mycryengine.com/

[6] Cruz-Neira, C., Sandin, D. J. and DeFanti, T. A., 1993. Surround-screen projection-based virtual reality: the design and implementation of the CAVE. In *Proceedings of the 20th annual conference on Computer graphics and interactive techniques.* (Anaheim, CA, USA). ACM, New York, NY, USA, 135-142.

[7] Gascón, G., José M. Bayona, José Miguel Espadero, Miguel A. Otaduy, 2011. BlenderCAVE: Easy VR Authoring for Multi-Screen Displays. *SIACG 2011: Ibero-American Symposium in Computer Graphics .*

[8] Hassaine, D., Nicolas S. Holliman, and Simon P. Liversedge., 2010. Investigating the performance of path-searching tasks in depth on multiview displays. *ACM Trans. Appl. Percept. 8, 1, Article 8* (November 2010), 18 pages.

[9] He, D., Liu, F., Pape, D., Dawe, G. and Sandin. D., 2000. Video-Based Measurement of System Latency, *International Immersive Projection Technology Workshop,* Ames IA, USA.

[10] Herrlich, M., 2007. A Tool for Landscape Architecture Based on Computer Game Technology. In *Proceedings of the 17th International Conference on Artificial Reality and Telexistence*, IEEE, 264-268.

[11] Hoffman, D., Girshick, A., Akeley, K., and Banks, M., 2008. Vergence–accommodation conflicts hinder visual performance and cause visual fatigue. *Journal of Vision, volume 8(3)*.

[12] *Homography Picker*. URL: https://sites.google.com/site/jeromeardouin/projects/homography-picker

[13] Hughes, J., 2011. *Automatic Dynamic Stereoscopic 3D. Game Engine Gems 2, Chapter 9*, Eric Lengyel AK Peters/CRC Press 2011, 135–149.

[14] *Intersense IS 900*. URL: http://www.intersense.com/pages/20/14

[15] Jacobson, J., 2003. Using CaveUT to build immersive displays with the unreal tournament engine and a PC cluster. In *Proceedings of the 2003 symposium on Interactive 3D graphics*. (Monterey, California, USA). ACM, New York, NY, USA, 221-222.

[16] Jacobson, J., Le Renard, M., Lugrin, J-L. and Cavazza, M., 2005. The CaveUT system: immersive entertainment based on a game engine. *In Proceedings of the 2005 ACM SIGCHI International Conference on Advances in computer entertainment technology* (ACE '05). ACM, New York, NY, USA, 184-187.

[17] Jones, J. A., Swan, J. E., Singh, G., Kolstad, E., and Ellis, S. R., 2008. The effects of virtual reality, augmented reality, and motion parallax on egocentric depth perception. In *Proceedings of the 5th symposium on Applied perception in graphics and visualization (APGV '08)*. ACM, New York, NY, USA, 9-14.

[18] Jörg, S., Normoyle, A. and Safonova, A., 2012. How responsiveness affects players' perception in digital games. *In Proceedings of the ACM Symposium on Applied Perception (SAP '12)*. ACM, New York, NY, USA, 33-38.

[19] Juarez, A., Schonenberg, W. and Bartneck, C., 2010. Implementing a low-cost CAVE system using the CryEngine2. *Entertainment Computing*, 1(3-4), (December 2010), 157–164.

[20] Kennedy, R., Lane, N., Berbaum, K. and Lilienthal, M., 1993. Simulator Sickness Questionnaire: An Enhanced Method for Quantifying Simulator Sickness. *The International Journal of Aviation Psychology*, Vol. 3, Issue 3, 203-220.

[21] Lambooij, M., Fortuin, M., IJsselsteijn, W. A., & Heynderickx, I., 2009. Measuring Visual Discomfort associated with 3D displays. In *Proceedings of SPIE, 7237*, San Jose, CA, USA.

[22] Lee, G. A., Kim, G. J. and Park, C., 2002. Modeling virtual object behavior within virtual environment. In *Proceedings of the ACM Symposium on Virtual Reality Software and Technology (VRST '02)*. ACM, New York, NY, 41-48.

[23] Lessiter, J., Freeman, J., Keogh, E., and Davidoff, J. A 2011. Cross-Media Presence Questionnaire: The ITC-Sense of Presence Inventory. *Presence: Teleoperators and Virtual Environments*, 10:3, 282-297.

[24] Lewis, M., and Jacobson, J., 2002. Game Engines In Scientific Research. *Communications of the ACM*, 45, 1, 2002, 27-31.

[25] Li, F.W.B., Lau, R.W.H., Kilis, D. and Li, L.W. F., 2011. Game-on-demand: An online game engine based on geometry streaming. *ACM Trans. Multimedia Comput. Commun. Appl. 7, 3, Article 19)*, 22 pages.

[26] Michotte, A. (1963). *The perception of causality*. New York: Basic Books. Translated from the French by T. R. and E.Miles

[27] *MiddleVR*. URL: http://www.imin.fr/middlevr-for-unity/

[28] Noh, S. S., Hong, S. D., & Park, J. W., 2006. Using a Game Engine Technique to Produce 3D Entertainment Contents. In *Proceedings of the 16th international Conference on Artificial Reality and Telexistence--Workshops* (November 29 - December 01, 2006). IEEE Computer Society, 246-251.

[29] *NVIDIA*. URL: http://www.nvidia.com

[30] *OptiTrack V120-Trio*. URL: http://www.naturalpoint.com/optitrack/products/v120-trio/

[31] Richie, A., Lindstrom, P. and Duggan, B., 2006. Using the Source engine for Serious Games. In *Proceedings of the 9th International Conference on Computer Games: AI, Animation, Mobile, Educational & Serious Games*, November 2006, Dublin Institute of Technology, Ireland.

[32] Steed, A., 2008. A simple method for estimating the latency of interactive, real-time graphics simulations. In *Proceedings of the 2008 ACM Symposium on Virtual Reality Software and Technology (VRST '08)*. NY, 123-129.

[33] Sherstyuk, A. and State, A., 2010. Dynamic eye convergence for head-mounted displays. In *Proceedings of the 17th ACM Symposium on Virtual Reality Software and Technology (VRST '10)*. ACM, New York,, USA, 43-46.

[34] Sutcliffe, A., Gault, B., Fernando, T. and Tan, K., 2006. Investigating interaction in CAVE virtual environments. *ACM Trans. Comput.-Hum. Interact. 13, 2, 235-267*.

[35] Teather, R.J., Pavlovych, A., Stuerzlinger, W. and MacKenzie, I.S., 2009. Effects of tracking technology, latency, and spatial jitter on object movement. In *Proceedings of the 2009 IEEE Symposium on 3D User Interfaces (3DUI '09)*. Washington, DC, USA, 43-50.

[36] *UDK Networking and Replication*. URL: http://udn.epicgames.com/Three/ReplicationHome.html

[37] *Unity® Game Engine*. URL: http://unity3d.com/

[38] *Unreal® Development Kit (UDK)*. URL: http://www.unrealengine.com/udk/

[39] *Unreal® Engine Technology Awards*. URL: http://www.unrealengine.com/awards_accolades/

[40] *Virtual Reality Peripheral Network (VRPN)*. URL: http://www.cs.unc.edu/Research/vrpn/

VINS - Shared Memory Space for Definition of Interactive Techniques

Dimitar Valkov, Alexander Giesler and Klaus Hinrichs
Visualization and Computer Graphics (VisCG) Research Group
University of Münster, Germany
[dimitar.valkov, alexander.giesler, khh]@uni-muenster.de

ABSTRACT

Traditionally, interaction techniques for virtual reality applications are implemented in a proprietary way on specific target platforms, e. g., requiring specific hardware, physics or rendering libraries, which hinders reusability and portability. Even though abstraction layers for hardware devices are provided by numerous virtual reality libraries, they are usually tightly bound to a particular rendering environment and hardware configuration.

In this paper we introduce *VINS (Virtual Interactive Namespace)* a seamless distributed memory space, which provides a hierarchical structure to support reusable design of interactive techniques. With VINS an interaction metaphor, whether it is implemented as function or class in the main application thread, uses its own thread or runs as its own process on another computer, can be transferred from one application to another without modifications.

We describe the underlying concepts and present examples on how to integrate VINS with different frameworks or already implemented interactive techniques.

Categories and Subject Descriptors

H.5.1 [**Information Interfaces and Presentation**]: Multimedia Information Systems: Artificial, augmented, and virtual realities; I.3.7 [**Computer Graphics**]: Three-Dimensional Graphics and Realism: Virtual reality

Keywords

library; virtual reality; distributed interactive systems

1. INTRODUCTION

The field of virtual reality (VR) encompasses research on various aspects of semi-immersive or immersive virtual environments (IVEs), including the development of multi-modal interaction, computer graphics techniques as well as hardware technology. In most VR applications a computer-generated graphical environment is presented to the user by mapping tracked head movements to camera motions in the virtual world. In addition, many applications include auditory and haptic rendering. Thus IVEs are often complex

hardware and software systems that require application developers to be knowledgeable in different areas of computer science, engineering and psychology, and to integrate or implement libraries or frameworks in extensive software engineering projects.

Nevertheless, graphical environments, hardware configurations and programming languages differ significantly between and within research groups, being constantly adapted for shifted research requirements and often replaced due to rapid developments in the computer graphics community. In addition, interaction techniques in VEs are often implemented as prototypes for a specific laboratory setup and are therefore tightly coupled to particular hardware configurations and rendering frameworks, often based on a research group's locally developed libraries and depending on the group's experience and preferences. For these reasons, VR applications usually lack portability and reusability, which hinders collaborative work and progress in the field of complex interaction techniques, e. g., making it nearly impossible to develop interaction code collaboratively with multiple research groups and VR laboratories or to exchange readily developed code.

Obvious effects of this situation can be observed in numerous VR demonstrations. Usually, these systems are based on immersive or semi-immersive displays and tracking systems combining head tracking and view-dependent rendering with virtual object interaction via various input devices. While such kinds of multimodal user interfaces provide compelling immersive experiences, they often lack state-of-the-art rendering technologies, i. e., the visual appearance of the VE is often antiquated in contrast to current efforts in the game or movie industry and thus does not reflect the perceptual importance of visual stimulation in multimodal environments. Often this can be traced to developers integrating hardware technology and interaction concepts designed for locally developed graphics libraries based directly on *OpenGL* or *DirectX*, or open source graphics engines such as *OGRE*, *OSG* or *IrrLicht*. Many VR libraries and toolkits have been developed on top of these rendering engines, which allow to abstract the hardware interface from the application, but cause significant re-implementation when porting a VR application to another graphics engine.

The same situation may be observed with the support for emerging input devices. While virtually all VR frameworks, whether fully integrated or modular, implement a hardware abstraction layer to wrap the data from different input devices into higher level events, extending those layers to support new devices or event types is usually a complex and time consuming task. Furthermore, because of the event-oriented design of most VR frameworks, it is usually very difficult and sometimes even impossible to find a proper integration of streaming device output, e. g., a sound-stream from a microphone or a depth image stream from Microsoft's Kinect.

As a result, migration of VR interaction techniques from one environment to another usually leads to dropping support for many of the implementations, causing transfer of interaction techniques between researchers to be usually limited to general descriptions of the concepts which are sufficiently simple for easy reimplementation but may also cause loss of features on the target system.

In this paper we introduce VINS[1] (*Virtual Interaction Namespace*), a framework which provides seamless access to a dedicated distributed shared memory space designed to support modular and reusable design of interactive systems. Conceptually, the VINS shared memory space consists of very small data blocks called *variables*, which are hierarchically grouped into *namespaces*. The functional blocks of the application, e.g., threads or processes on the same or different computers, can create, read and update variables in this data space and thus exchange internal states and results in a seamless and modular way, allowing easy transfer of interaction code between different graphics or game engines, VR laboratories and research groups. Since the API of the VINS framework is kept as minimalistic as possible (single library and header files, and an end user API consisting of 3 classes with few methods) it could easily be ported to another programming or scripting language; it is currently implemented in C++.

2. RELATED WORK

Many VR software systems and VR toolkits have been proposed to support the development of VR applications, e.g., [1, 4, 9, 10]. These systems usually provide interfaces for specification of VEs or interaction, abstracting hardware device handling from the layout and the dynamics of the virtual scene. However, many of these systems do not provide sufficient modularity for rapid integration of the currently most advanced rendering systems and cannot be integrated easily in existing VR hardware or software environments.

Examples of traditional VR software systems that provide high-level interfaces for developers are *VPL's Body Electric* [1] and *SGI's Open Inventor* [9]. These systems allow users to specify relations between virtual objects and input or output devices in a dataflow diagram editor, but have limited program modularity [4] and in particular do not provide a dedicated interface for integrating existing interaction techniques. Various other VR software systems provide rapid prototyping environments for creating interactive computer graphics applications without requiring a strong technical background by abstracting control of graphics and rendering [12]. Other VR libraries focus on specific display technologies or applications, making it difficult to share interaction techniques [6]. For instance, some libraries are based on specific rendering platforms [5, 19] or focus on particular areas of virtual or augmented reality, such as the Studierstube project [13] or ARToolkit [15].

Integrated software systems, such as VRJuggler [4], Vizard [27] or Virtools [23], allow building high-end VR applications and have been designed to overcome the drawbacks of some of the previous systems. For instance, the DIVERSE framework [10] provides an elegant solution for abstracting the particular display configurations, interaction techniques and devices. By dynamically loading and unloading pre-compiled shared modules, the framework allows to port an application from one hardware setup to another with minimal or no modifications and to easily exchange readily programmed DIVERSE modules. Many of these systems allow to choose from multiple wrapped rendering frameworks or provide plugins for different libraries, DIVERSE for instance provides rendering back-ends based on OpenGL Performer [14], VTK [25] or directly on OpenGL. However, some experience with low-level

programming in these environments is required for being able to write a plugin for state-of-the-art graphics rendering or game development environments. Moreover, developed interaction techniques often cannot be shared with other research groups due to incompatible versions, licensing issues or customizations.

As discussed above, VR developments often lack standardization of the system components and architecture, but incorporate abstractions of hardware device handling, e.g., [18]. Some research was recently conducted on flexible abstraction for interaction metaphors or interface definitions, such as the VITAL [7] abstraction layer, or InTml [8] or CHASM [21] systems. In addition, some recent reviews on VR software architecture [16, 17, 22] provide valuable guidelines for building re-usable and flexible VR applications. In contrast, we are interested in designing an infrastructure to connect independent (already developed) VR modules in a seamless data pool, which would foster modular design and re-usability and allow application developers to easily share their work.

The idea of sharing memory space or *computer resources* in general between multiple computers connected in a network cluster is not new. Maybe the most prominent example for such a system is the MOSIX [26] project, which originated in the year 1977 (later branched to openMosix which continued as LinuxPMI [11]). MOSIX is a UNIX/Linux based operating system which allows multiple computers in a cluster to be abstracted as a single "supercomputer" and seamlessly share all available resources between them. Although appealing, the idea to connect all computers in a VR laboratory to a single super-computer and let the operating system manage communication and distribution issues is most often not suitable for VR applications. Distributed VR frameworks such as FlowVR [2] or Avocado [20] usually provide more adequate solutions in this context. FlowVR, for example, abstracts functional blocks into *modules*, which work in their own threads or processes without being aware of each other. The modules exchange high level messages and meta-data with light-weight *daemons* installed on each node of the cluster, which then forward those messages to other modules if needed. The messages could also be preprocessed and modified while passing through *filters* between the modules. Even though such systems provide a superior solution for implementation of distributed, high performance VR applications, their message-oriented communication approach makes the definition of flexible and extendible I/O semantics a challenging task. Another interesting example in this context is the DIVERSE framework [10], which uses the shared memory space not only for communication, but also loads its system modules in this space. In particular, this allows to change or reconfigure the system on the fly. For example one may redirect an input handler from a particular hardware device to some "fake" input provider, which benefits application development and debugging considerably. Furthermore, since DIVERSE's display formats are also handled in the same way, existing applications may be reconfigured for arbitrary (supported) display setups without the need to change anything in the application itself. Nevertheless, the building blocks of the framework are usually tightly coupled with a particular rendering back-end which hinders the integration of up-to-date rendering techniques or the usage of alternative rendering packages.

In effect, although many systems are available for creating and developing VR-based applications, due to compatibility and customization issues universities and research institutions tend to write their own VR-based extensions to existing frameworks.

In the next sections we present an alternative approach for encapsulating VR interaction metaphors in an easily shareable and integrable interaction subsystem.

---

[1] Available under LGPL license on *http://vins.uni.muenster.de/*

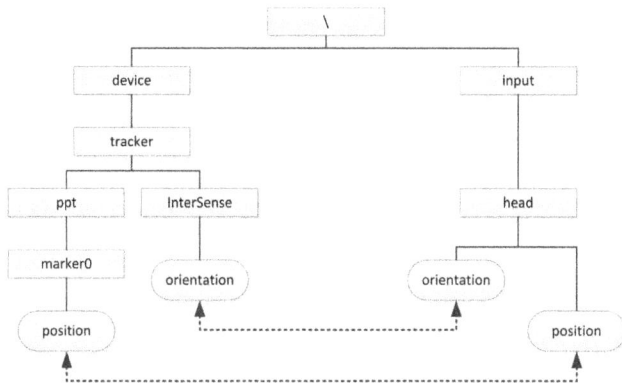

Figure 1: Example of a hierarchically structured virtual namespace. The path of the *variable* "position" reveals that it is the position of a tracked marker with id 0. An *alias* name of the same variable reveals additional semantics, here - the head position.

3. SHARED INTERACTION SPACE

In this chapter we discuss a flexible framework concept capable of providing a suitable balance between common demands of the VR systems. In particular, we are looking for a way to extend *already implemented* interaction techniques by only a few lines of code, so that they become portable from one hardware or software configuration to another without modification, while keeping the complexity of the system hidden from the user and the performance penalties and latency at a minimum. A concrete implementation of the concept, i. e., the VINS open source framework, is presented in Section 4.

3.1 Overall Concept

As main concept of our framework we propose to use a shared memory space with named variables, which are structured in a hierarchical manner suitable for interactive applications. Thus a hardware device could create a named variable or a set of variables and update them, sharing in this way its output data with other components of the system. An interaction technique would then read the input variable provided by the device and write to an output variable to communicate changes. Finally, the application could read a set of output variables and update its state accordingly. Existing flowgraph based frameworks, e. g., FlowVR [2], usually use a processing module as central building block. In such frameworks an application is considered as a set of connected modules, which exchange complex messages and attributes in some synchronized manner in order to communicate. In contrast, in our concept we concentrate on the organisation of the data itself and not on the way it is created or used. In particular, we propose the use of very simple and easily understandable data types, e. g., simple numeric types, strings and vector structs, which are hierarchically grouped in *namespaces*. The semantics of a variable could then be anticipated by tracking the path from the variable to the root-namespace. Consider for instance the example structure shown in Figure 1. The meaning of the variables `position` and `orientation` could easily be anticipated by their *address path*, i. e., `\device\tracker\ppt\marker0\position` means that `position` (a `vec3f` type) is the position of marker 0, which is detected with PPT, which is a tracker device. In a similar manner `\device\tracker\InterSense\orientation` means, that `orientation` (a `Quaternion` type) is detected with a tracker device named InterSense. By adding *aliases*, i. e., alternative names or address patterns for the same data

unit, one could extend the semantics of a variable, e. g., the aliases `\input\head\position` and `\input\head\orientation` reveal that the same variables are representing the position and orientation of the user's head and allow the interaction developer to abstract from the concrete hardware implementation of the tracking setup.

In order to keep the framework as simple and flexible as possible, we consider the following requirements:

- **User interface**:
  The API must be kept as small as possible, still providing understandable and transparent functionality.

- **Transparent data transfer**:
  The framework should provide a shared data pool in which every element could be accessed in the same way, no matter if it is provided from the same thread, process or computer.

- **Temporal traceability**:
  The data must be provided on demand, be always available (if the provider exists), and its temporal properties (e. g., last update time, previous values) must be easily traceable.

- **Hierarchical structure**:
  The data pool has to provide suitable and easily extensible internal structure to support interactive applications.

- **Access to the application's internal states or structure**:
  In a modular system every module should be self-contained and independent from all other modules. Nevertheless, for interaction with components of the virtual environment, certain parts of this environment must be made available. For instance, certain interaction techniques require an interface for casting a ray through the virtual scene in order to select an object.

Since the proposed framework is essentially a shared memory space the API would ideally contain only two functions with simple semantic, i. e., the `get` function

```
T get(string variableName);
```

which retrieves the most recent value of the variable with the name `variableName` and the `set` function

```
void set(string variableName, const T& value);
```

which sets a new value of the variable. Nevertheless, usually some additional functions, e. g., `create`, `request` or `initialize`, are required. Section 4 gives a more thorough presentation of the API and particular implementation details of the VINS system, which implements this concept.

Since we want to keep the latency as small as possible, it is clear that different data transfer techniques must be engaged if the variables are updated and read by the same application or by different processes on different computers. Nevertheless, in order to provide easily transferable and modular interaction techniques this complexity has to be hidden from the interaction developer. The *temporal traceability* condition allows in particular to check if the current value is up-to-date or not. Moreover, since previous values can be retrieved, interaction techniques with complex gesture recognition algorithms can be implemented.

The last two conditions, *hierarchical structure* and *access to application states* are in the core of our concept and are discussed in more detail in the following section.

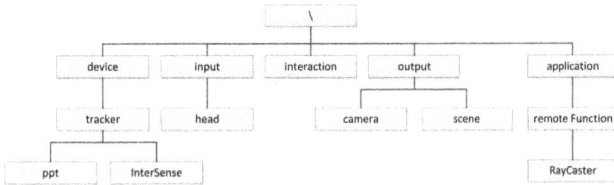

Figure 2: Conceptual structure of the virtual interaction namespace. The input device data is mapped under \device, which is then remapped under \input. The \interaction provides a space for the interactive techniques to share internal states, before the results are written to the \output namespace and remapped in the \application namespace.

3.2 Hierarchical Structure

As already discussed, the core idea in our conceptual framework is to group the basic data units, i. e., the *variables*, in semantically meaningful groups which we call *namespaces*. For that we consider the basic structure shown in Figure 2. The structure consists of five main namespaces which are children of the root namespace "\".

Device namespace

All hardware devices should be mapped to the \device namespace. Thus all devices needed for interaction should create their own subspaces and variables and write their output data in those variables. The namespace might be further subdivided into device types or classes, or just by device name.

Input namespace

The input semantics for the interaction techniques must be mapped to the \input namespace. In particular, the structure of this namespace should reflect the meaning of the input data and not how it is acquired. The variables within the namespace are usually either simple aliases for input device data, as shown in Figure 1, or they are created and updated from simple transformer functions, e. g., converting handedness and up-vector of a matrix or vector. Nevertheless, there is no constraint for the functionality or complexity of the transformers nor for their implementation. For instance, one could create an application, which reads the data from \device \kinect\frame, determines the user's head position and orientation with sophisticated computer vision algorithms and writes the results to the variables \input\head\position and \input \head\orientation. Since the virtual space is shared among all computers connected in a network, this application could then be easily moved to another machine to reduce the overall load on the target computer.

An instant benefit of the separation in device and input namespaces is that input sources could be redirected or manipulated on the fly, without affecting the functionality of the subsequent processing units. Indeed, similar to DIVERSE [10], one could remap an input variable (e. g. \input\head\position) from a tracker device to, for instance, a slider or some other "fake" input generator, by just changing the appropriate alias. This could allow a programmer to develop an interactive application in her office or laboratory and only test and fine tune it on the target platform, and would significantly benefit testing and debugging of the application, since the input states and dynamics cold be easily simulated.

Interaction namespace

The substructure of the \interaction namespace is deliberately left unspecified. In this namespace functional blocks, which imple-

ment interaction techniques, could share their internal states or, if an interaction technique is designed to be modular, their intermediate data.

Output namespace

In analogy to the \input namespace the \output namespace provides semantic abstraction of the interaction output and its mapping in the application. For instance, it might be appropriate for an interaction technique to create and manipulate the position and orientation of an "avatar" object, while the application is using a complex, animated "player" object for a visually appealing representation. Thus the variable \output\avatar\position should be mapped to \application\player\gotoPosition. Again the output mapping variables are usually created and maintained by simple functional blocks or are simply aliases of the application's variables. An appropriate initial structure of this namespace is given in [17, 22].

Application namespace

The \application namespace is the domain in which application specific variables reside. In this namespace a set of variables should be provided which allow the application to synchronize its internal state in the most convenient way. More interesting is the subspace remoteFunction, which is aimed to allow access to the application's internal states. As an example a RayCaster function is shown in Figure 2. To use the function a functional block creates the variables \application\remoteFunction\RayCaster \<block-name>\ray and \application\remoteFunction\ RayCaster\<block-name>\run. If the functional block then sets the variable ray to the ray to be casted and the variable run to true the application implementing the function should constantly update all variables under the \application\remoteFunction \RayCaster\<block-name>\result namespace, i. e., position and orientation of the first intersecting object, intersection point, etc.

The type and number of input and output parameters as well as a sufficient set of remote functions is subject of specification and is currently under development.

3.3 Application Scope and Limitations

As mentioned previously the main objective of the concept is to provide an infrastructure to easily connect existing modules to a functional application. While this gives an application developer the freedom to design the application as she finds it best, it also means that the appropriate low-level components must be either already available or developed in the first place. In order to simplify initial development a package, which implements this concept, should provide a suitable and extensible set of pre-compiled modules. On the other hand, since the shared interaction space supports design modularity, the modules themselves are usually considerably simpler as if they were implemented as part of a single application, where commonly threading and synchronisation issues arise. In addition, already developed modules could easily be reused without modification.

When talking about distributed VR frameworks, it is sometimes tempting to generalize the use of a single tool or concept for each level of the distribution. However, the granularity of an IVE might differ significantly between and within applications, ranging from distributed rendering or simulation running on a multi-processor grid through inter-process communication on the application level to collaborative applications having parts updating with tremendous latency. In our current focus, the presented concepts are perfectly suited for seamless communication between processes and threads running on a low latency network, as provided in most VR laboratories. While distributed rendering is also a crucial part of many VE applications, sharing named variables to communicate low level graphic primitives is usually not adequate, and there are some dedicated frameworks, e. g., FlowVR's Balzac [2] or EQUAL-IZER [24], which provide more appropriate solutions in this context. Scaling a level up in the granularity, i. e., supporting distribution over low-latency networks to foster collaborative VR applications, is currently not supported by the VINS implementation, but will be addressed in the future.

4. IMPLEMENTATION OF THE VINS FRAMEWORK

VINS is an open source, platform independent framework, which implements the concepts described in the previous section. An application using the VINS framework does not need to be distributed, but, if needed, it could easily be extended to run on multiple computers by just modifying functions or threads to run as their own process.

4.1 API

One of the main objectives for developing this framework was to provide a simple and transparent, but still powerful API, while hiding the complexity in the background. In the current implementation, the API is provided by 3 main classes, i. e., `Variable`, `Namespace` and `Timestamp`, and few static functions encapsulated in the class `Root`.

Before the framework can be used it has to be initialized by calling `Root:initialize(...)`. Once initialized the framework can be used to create variables, to request access to variables or entire namespaces and to read from or write to the variables. An example of using the API is shown in Listing 1. Usually an application or thread would execute some infinite loop, constantly reading the values of the variables and writing the results. To keep this example simple, we refrained from such a loop. The classes `vec{234}{ifd}`, `mat{34}{fd}` and `quat{fd}` are simple utility classes to encapsulate vectors, matrices and quaternions. Since most graphic systems already implement their own classes for this, we are providing alternative implementations, which write in a `type*` buffer provided by the user, e. g., `Root::get(string, float*)`.

```
#include <vins.h>
using namespace vins;

int main(int argc, char* argv[]) {

    // initialize the framework
    Root:initialize("myWalkingMetaphor", ...);

    // request access to variables
    Root::request("\\input\\head\\position");
    Variable& slider = Root::request(
        "\\input\\slider\\value");

    // create some variables
    Root::create<vec3f>(
        "\\output\\camera\\main\\position");

    Variable& visible = Root::create<bool>(
        "\\output\\mainMenu\\visible");

    // get the most current values
    // of the variables
    vec3f headPos = vec3f(Root::get(
        "\\input\\head\\position"));
    float sliderValue = float(slider);
```

```
    // ... do something

    // write the output
    Root::set("\\output\\camera\\main\\position",
        headPos);
    visible = bool(sliderValue >= 0.5f);

    return 0;
}
```

Listing 1: Example usage of the VINS API.

During the initialization the process creates its own empty representation of the global namespace. The calls of `request(...)` are needed, in order to allow the process create its own copies of the variables and connect them with their sources, which then take care of updating those copies. The call of the `create(...)` function puts a new variable with the specified type in the global namespace. If the variable is then needed by another unit, this unit gets connected to it and then receives asynchronously updates at each call of `set(...)`. As it can be seen from the example, variables can be accessed directly by calling the `Root::get(...)` and `Root::set(...)` functions. While this makes a variable accessible at each point of the program without the need for forward references between different functions and threads, it will result in traversing the namespace tree each time a variable is needed. Therefore, if more frequent access is needed, one can save the reference returned by `Root::request(...)` or `Root::get(...)`. Alternatively, one can get access to entire namespaces and address the variables within. An example for this is given in Listing 2.

```
// request access to namespace
Namespace& input = Root::requestNamespace(
    "\\input\\");
Namespace& head = input.getNamespace("\\head\\");

// get/set values
vec3f headPos = vec3f(head.get("position"));
float sliderValue = float(input.get(
    "\\slider\\position"));
```

Listing 2: Example of using namespaces.

Using namespaces gives the programmer an option to reduce the number of namespace tree traversals to a minimum, while still maintaining a "reasonable" amount of references.

The third and last class in the VINS API is the `Timestamp` class which is used for temporal synchronisation between the variables. By default, calling the `get(...)` method will return the most up-to-date value of a variable. Nevertheless, sometimes it is desirable to retrieve the values of a variable, which are most coherent with other related variables. Consider for example a hardware setup in which the user's head position is tracked with an optical tracking system, working (for some reason) with $25fps$, while her head orientation is tracked with an InterSence sensor with $120Hz$ refresh rate. Calling the function `get("\\input\\head\\position")` and then `get("\\input\\head\\orientation")` will result in getting the most recent value of the user's head position and orientation. Nevertheless, the value of the orientation might be offset up to $40ms$ from the value of the position. To make it even worse, there are no constraints for retrieving the variables' values at the same time; thus an application developer could, for example, retrieve the head position at the start of a function and its orientation, say $20ms$, later. To address such issues, VINS uses *timestamps*. Two example cases of using timestamps for synchronisation are given in Listing 3.

```
Variable& headPos = Root::request("\\input\\head
    \\position");
Variable& headOri = Root::request("\\input\\head
    \\orientation");

// get the values at specific point in time
Timestamp& ts = headPos.getTimestamp();
ts.setConstraints(-5.0f, 5.0f, BEST_FIT);
ts.sample();    // lock the time

// get the value in locked time
vec3f pos = vec3f(headPos(ts));
quatf ori = quatf(headOri(ts));

// ...

// get values relative to each other
Timestamp& ts2 = headPos.getTimestamp();
ts2.setConstraints(-5.0f, 5.0f, MOST_RECENT);
headOri.setTimestamp(ts2);

pos = vec3f(headPos); // auto lock the time
// get the value in locked time
ori = quatf(headOri);

headOri.removeTimestamp();

//...
```

Listing 3: Example of using timestamps for synchronisation

In both cases the variable `headPos` is used to provide a timestamp for synchronisation. In the first case, the point in time is explicitly locked and used to retrieve the values of both variables. The sample time could then be locked again by just calling `sample()`. The first and second parameter of the `setConstraints(...)` function specify the maximal deviation of the sample's time from the locked time (here $\pm 5ms$), and the third parameter specifies the selection strategy if multiple samples satisfy the range, i.e., the sample closest to the locked time, the most recent sample within the range, etc. An exception is thrown, if no sample could satisfy the constraints.

In the second case the timestamp `ts2` is not locked explicitly, but registered to the `headOri` variable. Therefore, the timestamp "knows" to lock itself by the call of `headPos.get()` (here implemented as cast operator) and the variable `headOri` "knows" to return its timestamped value, and not the most recent one. The time constraint can then be released by calling `removeTimestamp()`.

In all examples until now the values of the variables were pooled by some thread. Although one can simply check if a variable has changed since the last call of `get()` by calling its `changed()` method, in many cases an event mechanism is desired. One could implement this in VINS by just registering callback functions or methods to the framework. By default each variable or namespace is set to not fire callbacks, whether there are any registered or not. Thus this should be explicitly enabled for each variable or namespace. An example of using event callbacks is given in Listing 4.

```
class SomeClass {
  public:
    // class member callbacks
    void handleValueChanged(string path);
    void anotherValueChanged(Variable& v);

    // or static
    static void handleStructureChanged(
        string path);
    static void anotherStructureChanged(
        Namespace& ns);
};
```

```
SomeClass inst(...);

// register the callbacks
Root::addValueChangedCallback("someName", &inst,
    SomeClass::handleValueChanged);
Root::addValueChangedCallback("anotherName",
    &inst, SomeClass::anotherValueChanged);

Root::addStructureChangedCallback("name",
    SomeClass::handleStructureChanged);
Root::addStructureChangedCallback("yaName",
    SomeClass::anotherStructureChanged);

// ...
Variable& headPos = Root::request("\\input\\head
    \\position");
Variable& headOri = Root::request("\\input\\head
    \\orientation");

Namespace& input  = Root::requestNamespace(
    "\\input\\");
Namespace& output = Root::requestNamespace(
    "\\output\\");

// enable callbacks
// call handleValueChanged on change
headPos.reportValueChanged("someName");

// all input variables should use
// anotherValueChanged, this overrides
// previous settings on headPos
input.reportValueChanged("anotherName");

// headOri reports nothing
headOri.reportValueChanged("");

// the same could be made with namespaces
// to report structure changes
output.reportStructureChanged("name");
output.getNamespace("\\head\\").
    reportStructureChanged("yaName");

//...
```

Listing 4: Example of using callbacks

The callbacks could either be global functions or *functors*, or members of a class. The appropriate "valueChanged" callback is called each time the value of a variable gets updated. Similarly the appropriate "structureChanged" callback is called to communicate changes in the structure of the namespace, i.e., adding or removing a variable or namespace. If an empty string is set as name of the callback, the reports are efficiently suppressed for this variable or namespace, which is the default behaviour.

4.2 Network

From a networking point of view, the implementation could be considered as a peer-to-peer network with global coordination between one or more processes running on the same or different nodes of a cluster. The coordination server rules the connection between the processing units as well as the creation of and access to all variables and namespaces. Setting and updating of the variables' values is achieved via direct connections between the peers. Common distributed frameworks avoid depending on a global coordination server, since disconnecting the node on which the server is running would lead to disrupting all already running programs. Nevertheless, in VR applications where most of the nodes are connected to some specific hardware device which is usually crucial for the system, e.g., a tracking server or a rendering node, simultaneous and hassle-free functioning of all nodes at all times is usually required.

(a)

(b)

Figure 3: Examples of student projects using VINS. (a) A Demo of the NeoAxis game engine updated to work with HMD and optical head tracking. (b) City visualization rendered with the IrrLicht engine in our 3-Wall CAVE. Nintendo's Wii controller is used for navigation and the user's head position is tracked with Kinect (not in the picture).

On the other hand, single coordination could provide some benefits against a "true" distributed architecture. For instance, in our system the coordination server is the only point at which the entire namespace with all variables (but not their values) and all connected processing units is visible. Therefore it is a suitable place for implementation of a user interface to control or debug the network. Furthermore, such an architecture allows to reduce the number of broadcasts to a minimum.

Each processing unit must first register itself to the coordination server and inform it about its *peer coordination port* and name. The name of a unit is a composition of a user defined string and the unit's host IP, process ID and thread ID, thus it allows unambiguous identification of this unit. The peer coordination port is a TCP port, which other peers should use to coordinate the data transfer with this peer. Since we want to minimize the communication latency, we are using different communication channels for data transfer between the processing units, depending on the expected data volume and refresh rates and whether they are in the same process, in different processes on the same node or on different nodes. If the processing units reside within the same process, they simply access the same internal data structure, representing the part of the namespace needed by the process. For communication between processes on the same node *named memory files* are used. Finally, for communication between processes running on different nodes a UDP connection between the nodes is used. The processing units, which need to transfer data, coordinate the connection type and endpoints via TCP connection on the peer coordination ports. In particular, if a unit wants to create a variable, it sends a request to the coordination server with information about the variable address path and its type. The coordination server then checks if a variable with the same name already exists, and if not registers it to the namespace, creating all namespaces in the address path if not already existing. If then another unit requests access to the variable, the coordination server checks if it exists, and if this is the case sends the connection information of the creator to the requesting unit. The two units can then connect through TCP on their peer coordination ports and exchange information about available and needed communication channels and, in the case of success, the variable owner can start sending updates to the requesting peer. Although somehow complex, this multi-handshaking process ensures the best communication between the components of the system and allows flexibility to extend the number of available communication channels. Adding support for new communication protocols or networks, for example, would not make already compiled modules unusable, since they could simply reject the request for a communication channel and search for another one supported on both sides.

5. INITIAL FEEDBACK

Since a few months we are using VINS in the context of our research projects, but also in some student projects (cf. Figure 3). In the scope of those student projects, several students have used VINS for developing their applications using a variety of hardware systems (e. g., CAVEs, multi-touch walls, hand-held devices, Microsoft Kinects). To receive feedback from different users, we encouraged the students to inform us about any problems and to give comments about the VINS framework. In addition, we performed informal interviews and questionnaires with students, who have worked at least 3 months with VINS. The major observations concerning the requirements in terms of performance, flexibility and ease-of-use, as described in [3], as well as problems with the use of the VINS framework are discussed in the following.

Students were able to adopt existing interaction metaphors and to program custom interaction metaphors without significant effort. For instance, object selection and manipulation (i. e., translation, rotation and scaling) metaphors as well as camera manipulation metaphors could be implemented within few hours. Furthermore, students stated that VINS provides an easy to use interface to the hardware, i. e., instead of directly processing the low-level data in different formats or writing their own networking code the shared memory space allowed them to use various devices without knowing the underlying low-level data format or network connections.

As expected by using abstract data space, students were able to easily exchange their interaction metaphors independently of the used hardware. For instance, an interaction metaphor for mapping a skeletal posture onto a virtual avatar was transferred from tracking using active LED markers to tracking using the Microsoft Kinect. Moreover, students were able to easily integrate new hardware libraries, such as the Microsoft's Kinect SDK or Wiigle.

The majority of problems or inconveniences that occurred were caused by difficulties with API syntax or conceptual ideas. For example, some students, mostly used to the Java programming language, had difficulties with the overloaded cast, assignment and function call operators, commonly confusing them with constructor or reference copy semantics. Some students had also difficulties with the network connection itself, e. g., firewall setting issues or port ranges, but less with the implementation of VINS itself. However, most of these issues were easily fixed by providing the students with instructions to avoid such pitfalls.

6. CONCLUSIONS AND FUTURE WORK

In this paper we introduced VINS, which provides a seamless distributed data pool, in which user defined named variables reside in hierarchically grouped namespaces. Although an initial structure of this shared space was discussed, there is still a long way to go until this structure becomes clean and systematized enough to provide sufficient support for a large number of VR applications. Furthermore, a suitable set of "standard" remote functions has to be defined, which are sufficient for multiple cases. And while the current implementation is performing sufficiently, there is still enough space for improvements. These issues as well as provision of sufficient community support will be addressed in the future.

7. ACKNOWLEDGMENTS

We would like to thank all students for their feedback and evaluations. This work was supported by a grant from the Deutsche Forschungsgemeinschaft in the scope of the iMUTS project.

8. REFERENCES

[1] Y. Adachi, T. Kumano, and K. Ogino. Intermediate Representation for Stiff Virtual Objects. In *Proceedings of IEEE VRAIS*, pages 195–203, 1995.

[2] J. Allard and B. Raffin. Distributed physical based simulations for large vr applications. In *IEEE Proceedings of VR*, Alexandria, USA, March 2006.

[3] A. Bierbaum and C. Just. Software Tools for Virtual Reality Application Development. In *Course Notes for SIGGRAPH 98 Course 14, Applied Virtual Reality*, 1998.

[4] A. Bierbaum, C. Just, P. Hartling, K. Meinert, A. Baker, and C. Cruz-Neira. VR Juggler: A Virtual Platform for Virtual Reality Application Development. In *IEEE Proceedings of VR*, pages 89–96, 2001.

[5] R. Blach, J. Landauer, A. Roesch, and A. Simon. A Flexible Prototyping Tool for 3D Real-Time User Interaction. *ACM Proceedings of Eurographics Workshop of Virtual Environments (VE'98)*, pages 195–203, 1998.

[6] C. Cruz-Neira. *Virtual Reality based on Multiple Projection Screens: The CAVE and Its Applications to Computational Science and Engineering*. PhD thesis, University of Illinois at Chicago, 1995.

[7] M. Csisinko and H. Kaufmann. Vital - the virtual environment interaction technique abstraction layer. In *Proceedings of IEEE VR SEARIS Workshop*, pages 77–86. Shaker Verlag, 2010.

[8] P. Figueroa, W. F. Bischof, P. Boulanger, H. J. Hoover, and R. Taylor. Intml: A dataflow oriented development system for virtual reality applications. *Presence: Teleoper. Virtual Environ.*, 17:492–511, October 2008.

[9] O. I. A. Group. *Open Inventor C++ Reference Manual*. Addison-Wesley, 2005.

[10] J. Kelso, L. Arsenault, S. Satterfield, and R. Kriz. DIVERSE: A Framework for Building Extensible and Reconfigurable Device Independent Virtual Environments. In *IEEE Proceedings of VR*, pages 183–190. IEEE, 2002.

[11] linuxpmi.org. Linuxpmi project. 2011.

[12] R. Pausch, T. Burnette, A. C. Capehar, M. Conway, D. Cosgrove, R. DeLine, J. Durbin, R. Gossweiler, S. Koga, and J. White. A Brief Architectural Overview of Alice, a Rapid Prototyping System for Virtual Reality. In *IEEE Computer Graphics and Applications*, pages 195–203, 1995.

[13] D. Schmalstieg, A. Fuhrmann, G. Hesina, Z. Szalavari, M. Encarnação, M. Gervautz, and W. Purgathofer. The Studierstube Augmented Reality Project. In *PRESENCE - Teleoperators and Virtual Environments 11(1)*, pages 32–45, 2002.

[14] SGI. *A Technical Overview of OpenGL Performer 3.1*. SGI White Paper, 2004.

[15] C. Shaw, M. Green, J. Liang, and Y. Sun. Decoupled Simulation in Virtual Reality with the MR Toolkit. *ACM Transactions on Information Systems*, 11(3):287–317, 1993.

[16] A. Steed. Some useful abstractions for re-usable virtual environment platform. In *Proceedings of the IEEE VR SEARIS Workshop*, 2008.

[17] R. M. Taylor, J. Jerald, C. VanderKnyff, J. Wendt, D. Borland, D. Marshburn, W. R. Sherman, and M. C. Whitton. Lessons about virtual environment software systems from 20 years of ve building. *Presence: Teleoper. Virtual Environ.*, 19(2):162–178.

[18] R. M. Taylor, II, T. C. Hudson, A. Seeger, H. Weber, J. Juliano, and A. T. Helser. Vrpn: a device-independent, network-transparent vr peripheral system. In *ACM Proceedings of VRST*, VRST '01, pages 55–61. ACM, 2001.

[19] H. Tramberend. AVANGO: A distributed virtual reality framework. In *IEEE Proceedings of VR*, 1999.

[20] H. Tramberend. Avocado: a distributed virtual reality framework. In *IEEE Proceedings of VR*, pages 14–21, 1999.

[21] C. Wingrave and D. Bowman. Tiered developer-centric representations for 3d interfaces: Concept-oriented design in chasm. In *IEEE Proceedings of VR*, pages 193–200, 2008.

[22] C. A. Wingrave and J. J. LaViola. Reflecting on the design and implementation issues of virtual environments. *Presence: Teleoper. Virtual Environ.*, 19(2):179–195.

[23] www.3dviavirtools.com. 3dvia virtools vr library. 2011.

[24] www.equalizergraphics.com/index.html. The equalizer parallel rendering framework. 2011.

[25] www.kitware.com. Kitware's visualization toolkit (vtk). 2011.

[26] www.mosix.cs.huji.ac.il. M o s i x cluster operating system. 2011.

[27] www.worldviz.com/products/vizard. Vizard vr toolkit - rapid prototyping for novices. 2011.

Evaluating Scala, Actors, & Ontologies for Intelligent Realtime Interactive Systems

Dennis Wiebusch
Würzburg University
Am Hubland
97074 Würzburg, Germany
dennis.wiebusch@
uni-wuerzburg.de

Martin Fischbach
Würzburg University
Am Hubland
97074 Würzburg, Germany
martin.fischbach@
uni-wuerzburg.de

Marc Erich Latoschik
Würzburg University
Am Hubland
97074 Würzburg, Germany
marc.latoschik@
uni-wuerzburg.de

Henrik Tramberend
Beuth Hochschule
Luxemburger Straße 10
13353 Berlin, Germany
tramberend@
beuth-hochschule.de

ABSTRACT

This article evaluates the utility of three technical design approaches implemented during the development of a Realtime Interactive Systems (RIS) architecture focusing on the areas of Virtual and Augmented Reality (VR and AR), Robotics, and Human-Computer Interaction (HCI). The design decisions are (1) the choice of the Scala programming language, (2) the implementation of the actor computational model, and (3) the central incorporation of ontologies as a base for semantic modeling, required for several Artificial Intelligence (AI) methods. A white-box expert review is applied to a detailed use case illustrating an interactive and multimodal game scenario, which requires a number of complex functional features like speech and gesture processing and instruction mapping. The review matches the three design decisions against three comprehensive non-functional requirements from software engineering: Reusability, scalability, and extensibility. The qualitative evaluation is condensed to a semi-quantitative summary, pointing out the benefits of the chosen technical design.

Categories and Subject Descriptors

D.2.11 [**Software Engineering**]: Software Architectures—*Domain-specific architectures*; D.2.13 [**Software Engineering**]: Reusable Software; I.3.7 [**Computer Graphics**]: Three-Dimensional Graphics and Realism—*Virtual reality*; H.5.2 [**Information interfaces and presentation**]: User Interfaces

Keywords

Scala, Actor Model, Ontology, Intelligent Realtime Interactive Systems, Multimodal Interaction, Domain Specific Languages, Smart Objects

1. INTRODUCTION

Realtime Interactive Systems (RIS), required for Virtual and Augmented Reality (VR and AR), Robotics, or Human-Computer Interaction (HCI) in general, have been developed for several decades now. The underlying requirements of simultaneously processing multimodal input and output to generate a coherent and possibly immersive user experience and a successful interaction flow cause diverse engineering and development challenges. RIS architectures have to fulfill several functional requirements depending on the feature set an application has to provide: Graphics, physics, haptics, audio, direct input, multimodal interaction, artificial intelligence (AI), or behavior simulation are commonly found in several applications. In turn, most of these features can be—or sometimes must be—realized by multiple approaches, leading to a plethora of possible combinations.

Non-functional requirements started to play an increasingly important role for RIS architectures. All necessary functional requirements can seldomly be met by developments from scratch anymore. Existing software parts, libraries, and tools already solve reoccurring and often quite complex tasks. These must be adapted and reused. Due to their underlying nature, functional modules in RIS architectures often establish a close coupling on both the execution schemes as well as the data management. Temporal and data dependencies as well as synchronization occur on all levels to guarantee a coherent simulation. Maintenance and further developments are affected by the resulting processing and code complexity, hindering scientific progress as well as economical benefits.

This article presents three technical design approaches and their application during a RIS architecture development:

d_1 **Scala**, a programming language providing object-oriented as well as functional paradigms.

d_2 **Actors**, a computation model providing a flexible concurrent programming paradigm.

d_3 **Ontologies**, as Knowledge Representation Layer (KRL), providing semantic content modeling paradigms.

The three approaches are evaluated using a well established software quality method: White-box testing by expert review. Several demo applications (e.g., [9, 10]) utilizing the designed architecture have been evaluated and the experiences of >10 software developers are summarized by development experts. All of those applications included physical simulation, 3D-rendering, and sound output. The user-input was dependent on the used hardware, ranging from standard desktop environments (mouse/keyboard input) to CAVE-like setups (speech-gesture input). The three design decisions d_{1-3} are evaluated against the following three non-functional requirements, considered prominently important as qualities that oppose problems which are induced by processing- and code-complexity:

r_1 **Reusability** of code parts and libraries; includes parametrization and platform portability.

r_2 **Scalability** of a developed application; regarding both the simulation's size and its performance.

r_3 **Extensibility** in terms of new functional requirements; includes software-based exchangeability of features.

The article provides a detailed walkthrough of a complex use case, an agent-oriented multimodal—speech and gesture driven—interaction application. The evaluation will analyze the realization of four mission critical functional requirements to illustrate the benefits of the design decisions with respect to the three non-functional requirements r_{1-3}.

We will begin with a brief description of the use case, followed by a short introduction of the underlying design decisions and their implementation in our current software architecture research platform *Simulator X* [16, 17], pointing out their general benefits. This is followed by the detailed walkthrough and completed by a discussion of a concluding summary with respect to the related work.

2. USE CASE

The use case is taken from an interactive and immersive entertainment application [9]. It uses one or more stereoscopic large screen displays, a sound system, a 6 degrees of freedom tracking system for head-tracking and gesture input, and a dedicated speech recognition system.

The user, or player in that scenario, has to defend a medieval city from being destroyed by a group of evil ghosts. The ghosts follow a plan, which ultimately results in the destruction of city buildings. To achieve their goal, they will use a number of scattered powder kegs, which they will search, collect, and carry to designated target spots for detonation.

The user, in his role of a wizard protecting the city, is given the ability to cast multimodal spells to hinder the ghosts in succeeding their evil plan. One of these spells allows him to gain temporal control over a previously designated ghost. The ghost may then be commanded to assist the user, e.g.,

to gather mana or to find healing for injuries caused to the user by the haunting ghosts.

The use case is built around the processing of the following interaction sequence, occurring sometimes during an ongoing game session. It describes the multimodal ghost designation and task assignment. A ghost is seen by the user in the vicinity. The user intervenes:

1. *Hey* [pointing gesture at ghost] *you!*

2. [symmetric hand rotation] *Serve me!*

3. *Bring me mana!*

The gesture in 2. is a specific spell-dedicated iconic gesture, indicating a fictitious half-sphere in front of the user. The multimodal spells will only succeed if the concurrent timing of certain speech and gesture parts is successful. This is a typical—and hence required—characteristic found in natural speech and gesture utterances as well. The interaction will make one particular ghost search for a mana source, collect mana and return with its findings to the wizard.

To realize the use case, the application has to provide several high-level functional features processed in successive stages:

1. Multimodal input processing.

2. Multimodal fusion, generation of action descriptions.

3. Action planning based on action descriptions.

4. Execution of generated plans.

The given use case is based on an entertainment application, which in itself is of high economic relevance. The results are certainly transferable to similar intelligent real-time interactive systems (IRISs), which require a close integration of AI methods, e.g., for natural interaction, agent behavior, or AI-enhanced simulation purposes. The presented methods and their evaluation are of equal relevance to a much broader area of RIS applications and scientific work depending on multiple functional features, which have to outlast a mere prototype stadium.

3. SYSTEM DESIGN

A central core concept of our IRIS research platform uses so called state variables. State variables mimic a global and coherent state. They are ultimately realized on top of an actor-based distributed data management providing read/write and observation features to the core architecture and application layers. An entity model utilizes the state variables as property containers while it combines these with ontologically grounded symbols for property access. This establishes unique identification and semantic world representation at a core level. A loosely coupled component model is provided to fit typical RIS requirements, i.e., the fulfillment of commonly needed tasks like rendering, physics simulation, AI, etc. The independence of components from each other is facilitated by the use of an automated type conversion mechanism, which is also supported by the ontology. The research platform is implemented using the Scala programming language while it supports additional language bindings existing for the respective virtual machine (VM) in use.

3.1 The Scala Programming Language

The Scala programming language [21] has multiple RIS-relevant features. The integrated actor library (see section 3.2) facilitates the creation of concurrent software. Scala code can be compiled to run either on the Java VM or the .Net VM, which guarantees wide portability and a high amount of directly usable libraries. In addition, Scala's functional concepts have proven to be very effective for the definition of reactions or call-backs in application-dependent or configurable parts of RIS software.

Included syntax variants—Scala allows to omit the dot operator for member-variables and methods—in combination with implicit functions, on top of clever scoping rules with a guaranteed type safety, provide built-in domain-specific language (DSL) support. A DSL implementation using the syntax of the underlying programming language enables the use of existing editors and features for content creation, like syntax highlighting or code completion. Dynamic class loading features of the underlying virtual machines allow to compile and load terms written in such DSLs at runtime. In this work, the gesture descriptions as well as actions are specified using DSLs (see sections 4.1 and 4.3).

3.2 Actors

The actor model [12] provides an alternative concurrency paradigm which avoids several pitfalls and drawbacks of well-known shared state concurrency concepts [18]. Actors are universal primitives of concurrent computation, representing independent flows of control while communicating exclusively via messages. In response to a message that it receives, an actor can make local decisions, create additional actors, send messages, and determine how to respond to the next message. The actor model's message passing is also used to implement a publish/subscribe event system for asynchronous inter-actor communication (see section 3.3).

On a coarse grained level, actor-driven components are used to facilitate decoupling. At the same time the use of the actor model supports scalability on all levels of granularity: Any computational task can be parallelized easily, from primitive animations to elaborated AI methods (see section 4). Hence, the utilized actor model provides a uniform and consistent concurrency paradigm and communication interface.

3.3 Ontological Grounding

The ontology and KRL is realized using the Web Ontology Language (OWL [25]). The stored information covers used datatypes as well as descriptions of entities and their properties. The human-readable identifiers for those concepts constitute GROUNDED SYMBOLS, which are used throughout a whole application. Two major features, based on the ontological grounding, are especially important for the presented work: A worldinterface and an automatic type conversion mechanism [27].

The worldinterface is a central core component. It serves as a registry for all elements of an application. This includes technical components, like a physics engine or a renderer, as well as content-related entities residing in the Virtual Environment (VE). Since entities provide direct access to all of their attributes via grounded symbols, the worldinterface allows to query the current state of the simulation at any given point in time. It also serves as a registry for event handlers and event providers. Therefore, the developer can create

events without knowing which component will request them and request events without knowing which component creates them. Ontologically grounded symbols greatly enhance the identification of events and their semantics by content developers. Automatic type conversion is provided using the ontology and a semantic reflection paradigm.

The ontology decouples components, as the only remaining connection is the agreement on grounded symbols. Inconsistent use of symbols is prevented by the permission of exactly one ontology per application. The automatic type conversion in combination with the entity-centered data representation facilitates the creation of action objects (see section 4.3). These become independent from the data types used by related components, while a consistent view on the current world state is maintained.

4. USE CASE WALKTHROUGH

The following section presents a detailed walk through the use case from section 2. It focuses on the four functional requirements: Multimodal input processing, multimodal fusion, action planning, and the execution of plans. The impact of the taken design decisions d_{1-3} on the emphasized software-requirements r_{1-3} is discussed after each section.

4.1 Multimodal Input Processing

Description: Gesture Recognition

Following input processing and time stamping, a gesture processing component extracts higher order movement features from the incoming frame-based spatiotemporal data. Features might be based on trajectory, velocity or acceleration profiles, or certain user defined attributes considered important for a later classification and interpretation. Such spatiotemporal pre-processing is a typical example of functions, often considered of less importance and too often directly coded into systems. Here, features are externally defined by an application programmer or interaction designer using a specifically developed DSL.

```
1  define vec "vel" as { (s, t) =>
2    ((get "pos" from s at t)-(get "pos" from s at (t-1))/
3    (deltaT between t and (t-1)) }
4
5  get "vel" from "RIGHT_HAND" at lastFrame
```

Listing 1: Definition and usage of one feature extraction function, implemented by solely using Scala's native language constructs.

Listing 1 exemplifies the definition and use of a feature extraction function: The velocity of a tracking target `s` at time `t` is calculated from the position of `s` at `t` and `t-1`. The identifier `"vel"` is afterwards used to extract the current velocity of the right hand target.

```
1  object define {def vec(name: String) = Vec(name)}
2  case class Vec(name: String){
3    def as(extrFunc: (String, Float) => Vec3f) {...}}
```

Listing 2: Excerpt of the underlying implementation of the DSL shown in listing 1.

Listing 2 illustrates the underlying Scala implementation of this DSL: The singleton **define** and its method **vec** form the first two keywords of the definition of `"vel"` in listing 1. **vec** is therein called passing the parameter `"vel"`. Note that Scala's language option to omit the dot operator and the parentheses is utilized. The return value of this method call is an instance of the class `Vec`. Its methods (e.g., `as`) represent valid successive nonterminal symbols of the modeled DSL. Further DSL elements are defined accordingly.

The extracted features are passed to a classification component that uses a connectionistic learning paradigm based on a neural network. Output of the classification is the dominant gesture over a predefined time window, augmented with selected expression features, e.g., the pointing direction in case of a pointing gesture. The output is published by the gesture recognition component to respective subscribers. It is represented by an ontologically grounded feature structure, a nested attribute-value matrix typically applied by computer linguistics:

$$\begin{bmatrix} \text{SEMANTICS} & \text{GESTURE} \\ \text{TYPE} & \text{POINTING} \\ \text{DIRECTION} & \begin{bmatrix} \text{X} & 3.20 \\ \text{Y} & 1.02 \\ \text{Z} & 12.25 \end{bmatrix} \\ \text{TIME} & 12102.012 \end{bmatrix}$$

Description: Speech Recognition

The actual speech recognition is currently performed by an external software, i.e., Nuance's commercial product Dragon NaturallySpeaking or the open source software Sphinx-4 [26]. Similar to the gesture processing, a speech processing component publishes feature structures representing recognized speech tokens. A subsequent parts-of-speech tagging step identifies base form as well as the lexical and grammatical category. The following semantic analysis uses the ontology to map tagged utterances to their meanings. For example, the first token of the spoken sentence "*Bring me mana!*" is identified as verb (imperative case) *to bring* and associated with the ontology concept BRING. This results in the publication of the following feature structure:

$$\begin{bmatrix} \text{SEMANTICS} & \text{TOKEN} \\ \text{LEX\_CAT} & \text{VERB} \\ \text{GRAM\_CAT} & \begin{bmatrix} \text{CASE} & \text{IMPERATIVE} \\ \text{TENSE} & \text{PRESENT} \end{bmatrix} \\ \text{BASE\_FORM} & bring \\ \text{ACTION} & \text{BRING} \\ \text{TIME} & 12102.824 \end{bmatrix}$$

Analysis

The Scala programming language greatly supports the implementation of the utilized DSL. Other programming languages, e.g., C or C++, oftentimes require the additional implementation of auxiliary concepts, like parsers and interpreters. Here Scala's native language concepts provide a non-verbose syntax for the definition of application-dependent functions, e.g., the feature extraction functions used by the gesture recognition component (see section 3.1 as well as listings 1 and 2). Altogether, this results in support of reusability and extensibility.

The underlying actor model allows time consuming tasks, like the evaluation of the neural network or the speech recognition, to easily run in parallel. At the same time, the actor implementation makes sure that available CPU resources are fully utilized. This guarantees high scalability. New required

actors, e.g., for the handling of input sources, can seamlessly be integrated into the system. This contributes to extensibility. Existing actors can be reused effectively, due to the message interface. This directly supports reusability.

The availability of system-wide ontologically grounded symbols is especially beneficial for the early categorization of speech and gesture input (see example feature structures). It can thus be reused more easily. On the one hand, the ontologically grounded symbols provide a general interface to add respectively exchange speech or gesture components. On the other hand, they allow the definition of further interactions without the need of new functional requirements. This results in a contribution to scalability. Table 1 presents a summary of the discussed advantages.

	d_1 Scala	d_2 Actors	d_3 Ontology
r_1 reusability	+	+	+
r_2 scalability	o	+	+
r_3 extensibility	+	+	+

Table 1: **Impact of the taken design decisions on the emphasized software-requirements in relation to the gesture and speech recognition.**

4.2 Multimodal Fusion

Description

The multimodal fusion mechanism operates on the feature structures published by the gesture and speech recognition components. A unification component uses an extended chart parser and a unificator approach to parse and integrate incoming input. The integration is based on a predefined grammar and goal feature structures, representing possible actions and their logical requirements.

The chart parser serves as an aggregator of incoming feature structures. It runs passes on input arrival to dynamically fill the chart. A chart clearing timeout mechanism is implemented to distinguish between a failed fusion and a successive attempt. The chart parser attempts to match the incoming input onto productions of the given grammar. Additionally, it is extended to perform a unification operation after a successful scan of an input token. During the parsing process, feature structures are thus completed towards a goal feature structure. A beneficial side-effect of this approach is the reduction of the overall number of otherwise required, typically time consuming unification operations.

The unification operation has also been extended from the typical exact feature-match which is based on equality, to fit the requirements of processing the underlying variety of natural multimodal expressions. A loosely coupled function factory provides predefined unification functions, based on the types of the attributes to match. The obtained functions are applied accordingly during the unification process to determine its outcome. The current unification applies fuzzy matches, e.g., on acceptable time frames between gestures and parts of speech, as well as semantic matches. The latter exploit the built-in ontology in combination with the worldinterface to match synonyms or concepts residing in an inheritance relation. A successful fusion of a filled goal feature structure represents an action and its necessary attributes:

$$\begin{bmatrix} \text{SEMANTICS} & \text{ACTION-DESCRIPTION} \\ \text{ACTION} & \text{BRING} \\ \text{SUBJECT} & ghost\#2 \\ \text{TARGET} & user\#1 \\ \text{OBJECT} & \text{MANA} \end{bmatrix}$$

Analysis

In analogy to the Scala analysis in section 4.1, the general grammar definition, the type based unification functions, and application-dependent functions are heavily facilitated by Scala features, in particular due to the DSL support. This increases reusability and extensibility.

The actor model provides a flexible interface to process expensive tasks concurrently. Besides the unification process itself, additional disambiguation processes are necessary. For example, the spatial disambiguation of a pointing direction to a set of contemplable entities can implicate quite complex intersection and weighting algorithms. A dedicated component performs such tasks concurrently and publishes its results to the unification component on demand. Altogether the actor model enhances the scalability and extensibility of the multimodal fusion.

The availability of a general KRL in terms of an ontology enables the implementation of a semantic match during the unification process. The grammar definition required for the parsing process benefits from the established semantic concepts. This facilitates the reuse and extension of semantics-based structures. Table 2 presents a summary of the discussed advantages.

	d_1 Scala	d_2 Actors	d_3 Ontology
r_1 reusability	+	∘	+
r_2 scalability	∘	+	∘
r_3 extensibility	+	+	+

Table 2: Impact of the taken design decisions on the emphasized software-requirements in relation to multimodal fusion.

4.3 Action Planning

Goal feature structures (see section 4.2) are mapped onto a sequence of executable actions in the VE to realize the identified instruction. The goal feature structure's high-level action concept BRING is defined in the ontology. But a high-level action often cannot be carried out directly. It requires a plan of sub-steps based on preconditions for each step: The ghost probably does not carry mana, wherefore it first has to find some and take it to the user. To provide a mapping between the actions defined in the ontology and those that may be performed in the VE, action objects are introduced.

```
1  val goalState = Carries(user1, manapotion1) and
       Not(Carries(ghost2, manapotion1))
2
3  action bring affecting Subject and Target and Object
4    requires canCarry(Target, Object)
5    requires carries(Subject, Object)
6    removes carries(Subject, Object)
7    adds carries(Target, Object)
```

Listing 3: Example definition of a (goal) state and an action using a DSL.

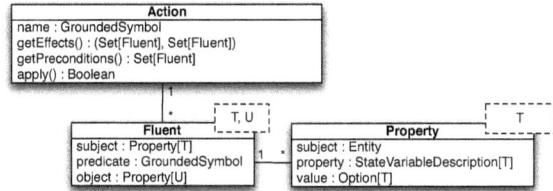

Figure 1: Relations between action, fluent and property classes.

Description: Action Objects

As shown in figure 1, an action object is defined by its preconditions and effects. A grounded symbol, (usually) reflecting the action's semantics, is assigned for identification purposes. This symbol is directly associated with the high-level ontology concept (see section 4.1), ensuring singular and therefore consistent concept definitions.

Effects and preconditions of an action object may depend on the entity which the action shall be applied to. E.g., a standard door might require its doorknob to be used, whereas an automatic sliding door opens when it is approached. On instantiation, each action object is bound to the entities to which it shall be applied, to support entity-specific preconditions. The role (e.g., subject or object) of each entity is specified using definitions from the global ontology. An action object can access all properties of an entity and accordingly adjust its preconditions and effects. For example, the action open will return different preconditions depending on the entity it shall be applied to. This results in different plans being created to open the respective door.

The integration with the framework is achieved by means of the Fluent and the Property class (see figure 1): Preconditions and effects are represented by fluents, which basically consist of a symbol that describes the relation of two objects. To ensure consistency and the correct use of symbols, instances of the Fluent class are specified as subclasses of the concept FLUENT in the OWL ontology and directly transformed into Scala source code. Instances of the Property class connect the architecture elements with fluents.

The generation of plans is modeled based on the fluent calculus [23], which describes transitions between situations by the effects of the respective actions. This representation allows the current world representation to be incomplete, which is advantageous for complex VEs.

A Scala-native DSL simplifies the definition of actions and states. For example, a fluent-calculus state representation in first-order logic may be given as:

$$\exists z \, [State(S_n) = carries(user\#1, manapotion\#1) \circ z$$
$$\wedge \forall z' \, [z \neq carries(ghost\#2, manapotion\#1) \circ z']]$$

The corresponding DSL maps the $State(S_n)$ definition to goalState in line 1 of listing 3. Lines 3–7 illustrate the definition of the bring action (cf. actions in table 3) in Scala.

In contrast to [1], the action objects defined here are independent from their graphical representation but solely describe the action itself. They can be combined with any compatible entity in an intelligent virtual environment (IVE). Just like other architecture elements, action objects are registered with the worldinterface. This enables the developer to add, access, and remove them at run-time.

Action	effects	preconditions
bring	$+(carries(t,o))$ $-(carries(s,o))$	$carries(s,o)$ $equals(s.pos, t.pos)$
goto	$+(equals(s.pos, o.pos))$	$canMove(s,s)$
pickup	$+(carries(s,o))$	$canCarry(s,o)$ $equals(s.pos, o.pos)$

Table 3: Actions available in the given example.

Description: Planning

In the given example, an action object named bring exists. It is based on the respective concept BRING that is defined in the ontology. The feature structure for the bring action, used by the unification component, as well as the corresponding action object are defined in the same place (the ontology). Therefore, the information contained in the filled feature structure exactly matches the information needed to instantiate the bring action object.

A plan consists of actions that are executed consecutively. By means of the respective action object a plan to fulfill the action bring(ghost#2, user#1, mana) is calculated. This is achieved by recursively identifying actions that satisfy some of the preconditions for a given state and generating a new state for each of them (see figure 2). Alternatively, an external fluent calculus compliant reasoner (e.g., [23]) can be applied, fostered by the framework's component model.

The current simulation state is dynamically accessed via the worldinterface to create initial states for the reasoning process. This allows to easily exchange the underlying database, since the implementation is decoupled by means of the worldinterface: A fluent $canCarry(ghost, mana)$ could be stored in a static knowledge base. On the other hand, if the evaluation of the fluent would require additional computation, it could be evaluated by some additional component. This is especially interesting for tasks like path-planning: A goto action could require the precondition $canGoto(s, o)$ to be met, which might be evaluated using a path-planning algorithm. Depending on the results of that algorithm additional preconditions (like $isOpen(door\#1)$) might arise.

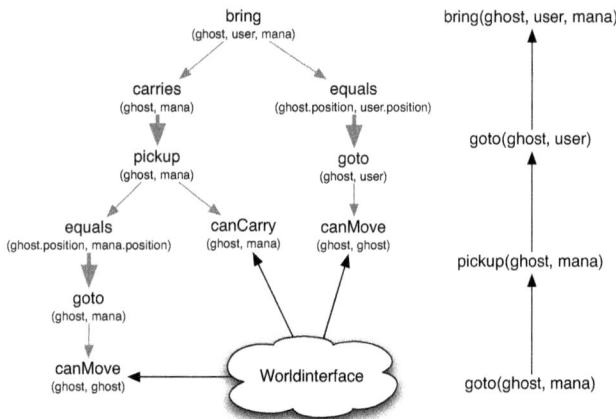

Figure 2: Planning steps (left) and resulting plan (right). Red arrows mark preconditions, green ones the chosen actions to meet these.

Analysis

The extension of an application by the definition of new action objects is supported by Scala's potential to create domain specific languages.

Since each branch in the planning graph (see figure 2) can be evaluated concurrently using the actor model, the scalability of the planning process is increased. The message based communication between actors enforces an interface in form of the used messages, which allows to easily exchange the employed planning component.

Action planning especially benefits from the integrated ontology. Action objects can easily be integrated and reused without the need for changes in any other part of the system. The underlying knowledge base can easily be exchanged. Both of this is owed to the design decisions regarding features that facilitate the decoupling of components, i.e., automatic data conversion and implementation of grounded symbols. This results in highly extensible applications. The fact that more information in the ontology leads to improved planning capabilities implies its benefits regarding scalability. Table 4 presents a summary of these advantages.

	d_1 Scala	d_2 Actors	d_3 Ontology
r_1 reusability	○	○	+
r_2 scalability	○	+	+
r_3 extensibility	+	+	+

Table 4: Impact of the taken design decisions on the emphasized software-requirements in relation to the task planning process.

4.4 Execution of Plans

Description

Assuming the plan shown in figure 2 is generated to execute a bring task: The ghost will first go to a place where it can pick up some mana, then approach the user and finally pass the collected mana. Such a plan is implemented as the consecutive execution of a sequence of actions objects. At any time during this execution the properties of each involved entity may be accessed. This is essential if those properties are mutable. For example, the location of a mana source tends to be static, whereas the user may have moved while the ghost carried out the first parts of the plan. Runtime information on the properties of the respective entities can be accessed during the actual execution of an action since the actions were bound to the entities they are applied to during the planning phase. The same grounded symbols that were used therein are applied in this context as well.

Additionally, action objects can be executed independently without any kind of planning and precondition/effect tests. For example, the user could command the application to move an entity somewhere, which might result in the execution of a single goto or moveto action. Depending on the action's nature, it can be executed by an existing component or independently operate on an entity. In the above example, the process of moving the ghost could be animated by means of a physics component, by an actor that is spawned for that purpose, or simply put into its new place by setting its transformation property. In general, actions and plans can either be executed by a designated actor (e.g., a moveto action could be controlled by an actor that is spawned to send waypoints to a character animation component) or by a component itself (e.g., a hover action object could be sent to a physics component which integrates it in its simulation loop).

Analysis

The functional aspects of the Scala programming language, e.g., currying and closures, foster reusability and extensibility of functions and therefore of action objects.

The actor model is advantageous for the use of action objects with regard to scalability, since one actor can be spawned for the execution of each plan.

The execution of action objects greatly benefits from the ontology that is incorporated into the framework: On the one hand, plans and actions can be reused in combination with any entity, because the framework's automatic type conversion feature reduces the coupling of action objects to the use of grounded symbols. On the other hand, action objects are easily extensible and exchangeable for the same reasons. Table 5 presents a summary of these advantages.

	d_1 Scala	d_2 Actors	d_3 Ontology
r_1 reusability	+	○	+
r_2 scalability	○	+	○
r_3 extensibility	+	○	+

Table 5: Impact of the taken design decisions on the emphasized software-requirements in relation to the execution of plans.

5. CONCLUSION & RELATED WORK

This article evaluated three technical design approaches: The use of the Scala programming language, the implementation of the actor model, and the core-level integration of ontologies in the RIS domain. These were matched against the non-functional requirements reusability, scalability, and extensibility on the basis of a white-box expert review examining a complex use case. Table 6 summarizes the results in condensed form.

d_1: **Scala** facilitates the efficient implementation of auxiliary concepts, e.g., DSLs and callbacks, thereby highly supporting reusability and extensibility. RIS architectures are commonly implemented in C or C++ (e.g., [3, 5, 11, 15]). The most prominent reason for this choice is speed. Speed is certainly an important RIS factor one has to consider when using virtual machine languages like Scala. But a cost-benefit analysis reveals additional key factors relevant for the non-functional requirements. To value the utility of a programming language, the provided abstraction concepts are of equal importance: A concise language facilitates compact code of high reusability and low maintenance costs.

The Scala language performs exceptionally well with respect to abstraction and compact representation. Its functional programming concepts reduce typical maintenance nightmares caused by side-effects. Its integrated support of human-readable DSLs (as in [7, 13]) fosters declarativity and externalization of application logic, only too often hidden inside rather complex low-level code snippets. Besides the application of scripting languages (e.g., in [20]), DSLs are an interesting approach to software modularity. The

	d_1 Scala	d_2 Actors	d_3 Ontology
r_1 reusability	+++	+	++++
r_2 scalability	○	++++	++
r_3 extensibility	++++	+++	++++

Table 6: Accumulated semi-quantitative summary relating the design approaches d_{1-3} to the software-requirements r_{1-3}.

concept is not new to computer science but Scala facilitates an easy integration into native code. A similar approach using C or C++ requires a deep understanding of compiler technology and/or the utilization of supporting tools like yacc or bison, thereby drastically increasing complexity.

d_2: **The actor model** provides a unified interface to meet typical RIS concurrency requirements, while effectively utilizing available hardware resources. This results in high scalability and extensibility. The latter is especially fostered by the message-based interface, which is induced by the actor model. Several alternative approaches have targeted distributed and cluster-based applications (e.g., [2, 6, 24]). But node-based concurrency still is largely the domain of multi-thread or multi-process paradigms, known to cause major problems like race conditions and deadlocks [18]. The actor model encompasses inter-node and cluster-based as well as node-based concurrency. A unified concept drastically reduces the different programming paradigms developers have to know and maintain. In addition, the drawbacks in terms of speed are largely reduced by a node-based concurrency, which natively supports multi-core applications.

d_3: **The ontology**, realized in form of a KRL fosters decoupling and increases reusability and extensibility and even scalability to some extend. For IVEs [4] and IRIS applications there is often no conceptual alternative to the utilization of a KRL. A mapping between the domain specific entities and their procedural behavior has to be established somehow (e.g., [14, 20, 22]). A common approach uses a rather loose coupling between the simulation software, e.g., a game engine, and an ontology [8, 19]. This is beneficial since it fosters a clean decoupling, but it is disadvantageous with respect to an ontological reach-through. That is, the semantic grounding depends on the aspects the simulation software provides to the outside. This often is restricted to mere entities and some of their properties. A deeper access, e.g., to the procedural realization of a certain entity capability, is prevented. A close integration of a semantic binding on all simulation layers in turn supports reflective programming paradigms based on semantic primitives (semantic reflection) and hence enhances decoupling and extensibility.

In addition, several independent features might require ontology access (see use case). A loosely coupled scheme here often results in ontology redundancies, since each module uses its own representation and data model. But coherence on the ontology level is mandatory to guarantee a successful processing. Keeping multiple ontologies in sync, especially during modifications, is error-prone and well-known as the multiple-database problem.

Future work will further utilize the benefits of ontologies by mapping procedural behavior to a semantic description, which would be very beneficial for story telling etc. In addition, the multimodal processing components will undergo an evaluation against alternative approaches like state machines or probabilistic approaches.

6. ACKNOWLEDGMENTS

The presented work was supported by the German Federal Ministry of Education and Research, program *Ingenieur*Nachwuchs, project SIRIS (#17N4409).

7. REFERENCES

[1] T. Abaci, J. Ciger, and D. Thalmann. Planning with smart objects. *WSCG*, pages 25–28, 2005.

[2] J. Allard, V. Gouranton, L. Lecointre, E. Melin, and B. Raffin. Net Juggler: Running VR Juggler with Multiple Displays on a Commodity Component Cluster. In *Proceedings of the IEEE Virtual Reality Conference*, page 273. IEEE, 2002.

[3] J. Allard, J.-D. Lesage, and B. Raffin. Modularity for Large Virtual Reality Applications. *Presence: Teleoperators and Virtual Environments*, 19(2):142–162, 2010.

[4] R. Aylett and M. Luck. Applying Artificial Intelligence to Virtual Reality: Intelligent Virtual Environments. *Applied Artificial Intelligence*, 14(1):3–32, 2000.

[5] A. D. Bierbaum, C. Just, P. Hartling, K. Meinert, A. Baker, and C. Cruz-Neira. VR Juggler: A Virtual Platform for Virtual Reality Application Development. In *Proceedings of the IEEE Virtual Reality Conference*, pages 89–96. IEEE, 2001.

[6] M. Bues, T. Gleue, and R. Blach. Lightning: Dataflow in motion. In *Proceedings of the IEEE Virtual Reality SEARIS Workshop*, pages 7–11, 2008.

[7] H. Chafi, A. Sujeeth, K. Brown, H. Lee, A. Atreya, and K. Olukotun. A domain-specific approach to heterogeneous parallelism. *Principles and Practices of Parallel Programming, PPoPP*, 11, 2011.

[8] P. Chevaillier, T. Trinh, M. Barange, F. Devillers, J. Soler, P. Loor, and R. Querrec. Semantic modelling of virtual environments using MASCARET. In *Proceedings of the IEEE Virtual Reality SEARIS Workshop*. IEEE, 2011.

[9] M. Fischbach, D. Wiebusch, A. Giebler-Schubert, M. E. Latoschik, S. Rehfeld, and H. Tramberend. SiXton's curse - Simulator X demonstration. In *Proceedings of the IEEE VR*, pages 255–256, 2011.

[10] M. Fischbach, D. Wiebusch, M. E. Latoschik, G. Bruder, and F. Steinicke. Blending Real and Virtual Worlds using Self-Reflection and Fiducials. In *Proceedings of the ICEC, Demo Papers*, 2012.

[11] J. Herling and W. Broll. The Ocean framework: providing the basis for next-gen MR applications. In *Proceedings of the IEEE Virtual Reality SEARIS Workshop*. IEEE, 2010.

[12] C. Hewitt, P. Bishop, and R. Steiger. A universal modular ACTOR formalism for artificial intelligence. In *Proceedings of the International Joint Conference on Artificial Intelligence*, pages 235–245, 1973.

[13] C. Hofer and K. Ostermann. Modular domain-specific language components in Scala. In *SIGPLAN Notices*, volume 46, pages 83–92. ACM, 2010.

[14] P. Kapahnke, P. Liedtke, S. Nesbigall, S. Warwas, and M. Klusch. ISReal: An Open Platform for Semantic-Based 3D Simulations in the 3D Internet. *The Semantic Web–ISWC*, pages 161–176, 2010.

[15] J. Kelso and L. E. Arsenault. Diverse: A framework for building extensible and reconfigurable device independent virtual environments. In *IEEE Virtual Reality*, pages 183–190, 2002.

[16] M. Latoschik and H. Tramberend. A scala-based actor-entity architecture for intelligent interactive simulations. In *Proceedings of the Virtual Reality SEARIS Workshop*, pages 9–17, 2012.

[17] M. E. Latoschik and H. Tramberend. Simulator X: A Scalable and Concurrent Software Platform for Intelligent Realtime Interactive Systems. In *Proceedings of the IEEE VR*, 2011.

[18] E. A. Lee. The problem with threads. *IEEE Computer*, 39(5):33–42, 2006.

[19] J.-L. Lugrin and M. Cavazza. Making Sense of Virtual Environments: Action Representation, Grounding and Common Sense. In *Proceedings of the Intelligent User Interfaces*, 2007.

[20] J.-L. Lugrin and M. Cavazza. Towards AR Game Engines. In *Proceedings of the IEEE Virtual Reality SEARIS Workshop*. IEEE, 2010.

[21] M. Odersky, L. Spoon, and B. Venners. *Programming in Scala*. Artima Inc, 2nd edition, 2010.

[22] B. Pellens, F. Kleinermann, and O. De Troyer. An Approach Facilitating 3D/VR System Development Using Behavior Design Patterns. In *Proceedings of the IEEE Virtual Reality SEARIS Workshop*. IEEE, 2010.

[23] M. Thielscher. FLUX: A logic programming method for reasoning agents. *Theory and Practice of Logic Programming*, 5(4-5):533–565, 2005.

[24] H. Tramberend. Avocado: A Distributed Virtual Reality Framework. In *IEEE Virtual Reality Conference*, pages 14–21, 1999.

[25] W3C OWL Working Group. OWL 2 Web Ontology Language Document Overview. Technical report, W3C, October 2009.

[26] W. Walker, P. Lamere, P. Kwok, B. Raj, R. Singh, E. Gouvea, P. Wolf, and J. Woelfel. Sphinx-4: A flexible open source framework for speech recognition. Technical report, Sun Microsystems, Inc., 2004.

[27] D. Wiebusch and M. E. Latoschik. Enhanced Decoupling of Components in Intelligent Realtime Interactive Systems using Ontologies. In *Proceedings of the Virtual Reality SEARIS Workshop*, pages 43–51. IEEE, 2012.

Tracking of Manufacturing Tools with Cylindrical Markers

Jan-Patrick Hülß
ART GmbH
Am Öferl 6
82362 Weilheim, Germany
jan-patrick.huelss@ar-
tracking.de

Bastian Müller
ART GmbH
Am Öferl 6
82362 Weilheim, Germany
bastian.mueller@ar-
tracking.de

Daniel Pustka
ART GmbH
Am Öferl 6
82362 Weilheim, Germany
daniel.pustka@ar-
tracking.de

Jochen Willneff
ART GmbH
Am Öferl 6
82362 Weilheim, Germany
jochen.willneff@ar-
tracking.de

Konrad Zürl
ART GmbH
Am Öferl 6
82362 Weilheim, Germany
k.zuerl@ar-tracking.de

ABSTRACT

In industrial manufacturing processes, targets for infrared marker based tracking have to be robust and must integrate into the tools without disturbing the work flow. In this paper, we propose cylindrical markers attached directly to the tool. We show that, targets equipped with cylindrical markers can be tracked with about the same precision as targets equipped with spherical markers, if a correction for the reduced symmetry is applied. Additionally, the markers can be placed on different parts of a tool with a flexible connection, which is also considered in this paper.

Categories and Subject Descriptors

I.4.8 [**Image Processing and Computer Vision**]: Scene Analysis—*Tracking*; I.4.9 [**Image Processing and Computer Vision**]: Applications

General Terms

Algorithms, Measurement, Reliability

Keywords

tracking, input devices, engineering, training

1. INTRODUCTION

Outside-In tracking with infrared markers is used in a large variety of applications. It delivers high precision measurements of position and rotation of an object in 3D space. Standard systems are a cave installation for virtual reality or a power wall as 3D monitor with 6D input device. Usual

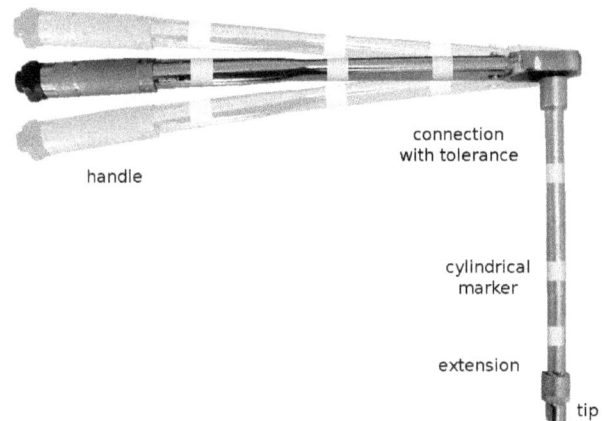

Figure 1: Torque wrench consisting of handle and extension. Due to the construction the torque wrench has tolerance in the connection. To enable tracking, it is equipped with six cylindrical markers

applications are development, design, data analysis and presentations. They are carried out in a designated area with the VR system.

A field where infrared tracking is rarely used are manufacturing processes (for example at an assembly line). A promising application is quality assurance. Tracking a manufacturing tool (e.g. a torque wrench as shown in figure 1) during assembly gives essential information about its proper operation. During the regular work process all steps are tracked and recorded. All mistakes (e.g. wrong screw, wrong torque, and more) are documented. This saves time in the post-treatment: Less time has to be spent searching for mistakes. We tested an application in an assembly line with a robot. If the robot fails on a screw, a worker fixes the error. The whole procedure is documented by the tracking system.

Another application is the training of workers in a VR environment. Training in a VR environment saves materials, otherwise wasted in conventional processes. For example,

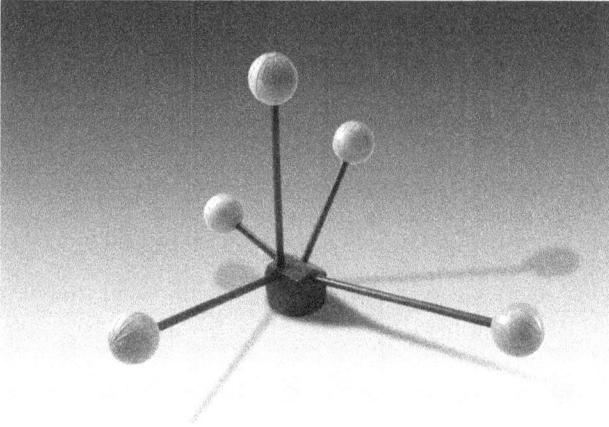

Figure 2: Typical target for marker based infrared tracking. Five retro-reflecting spheres arranged to a unique geometry.

handling a welding gun could be trained on a screen. It is important that the training tool is identical to the one used in the manufacturing process. Only then, the trained movements can be directly applied to the real work situation.

For these applications infrared tracking offers high precision and reliability. The main issues are targets which are too bulky and their lack of robustness [10]. Usual targets consists of several markers with a retro-reflecting foil (an example is shown in figure 2). Tools equipped with such a target are bulky and the target can easily be damaged. Putting it down without care can already effect the target severely. This is not tolerable for manufacturing environments dedicated to mechanical work with time pressure.

In addition, the retro-reflecting foil is open-pored and looses its reflectivity quickly when it is touched or gets dirty. The foil can be destroyed within a few uses of the tool. Thus, the wearout is too fast for any manufacturing application.

The proposed solution to these problems is to remove the targets and attach the markers directly to the tool. Therefore, stripes of reflective foil are directly wrapped around the metal bars of the tool creating cylindrical markers. These cylindrical markers are for several reasons a good concept:

- Many tools have metal bars. They offer the suitable locations to attach cylindrical markers without increasing the size of the tool, avoiding bulkiness.

- Cylindrical markers are visible from all around the bar, avoiding occlusions by the tool itself.

- For cylindrical markers the foil is bent only in one direction. Therefore, a less flexible and more robust foil can be used. Dirt is a lesser problem.

In addition, cylindrical markers can decrease the size of targets frequently used in VR systems. For example, a target for shutter glasses (usually as big as the glasses) is reduced to essentially one bar with cylindrical markers.

Besides these advantages, the image of a cylindrical marker depends on the observation direction. To utilize cylindrical markers we present a correction for this effect. Additionally, applying markers directly to a tool adds a complication: Tools are not always manufactured as one piece. They

can have tolerances and/or flexible connections. This issue of flexible targets is addressed and solved in this paper, too.

2. MARKER BASED TRACKING

In this section the basic concepts of infrared tracking of targets is summarized. These are the base for the later discussion of flexible targets and targets with cylindrical markers. Marker based tracking is a well studied field: Madritsch and Gervautz [6] used a two-camera system, Dorfmüller [3] describes a system of synchronized cameras which can distinguish targets and also Pintaric and Kaufmann [8] present a tracking system.

Tracking is possible in a volume viewed by two or more cameras with known position, orientation and optical properties. These cameras synchronously record infrared images of the scenery with constant frequency (here 60 Hz). A set of these images is called a *frame*. Additionally, they are equipped with infrared flashes to illuminate the scene.

The images of all cameras are used to determine the position and orientation of the target in 3D space. The single processing steps of the procedure are described in the following subsections.

2.1 Marker Algorithm

In each image of a camera the 2D positions of the observed markers are determined. Here, only the information available in the image is used. The 2D position of a marker is determined as the center of gravity of connected image pixels above a threshold. In the following this is called the *image position* and the corresponding point on the marker is called *observed position O*. The straight line through the camera position, the *image position* and the *observed position* of the marker is called *ray*.

2.2 3D Marker Tracking

3D Markers are calculated from the images of each *frame*. By epipolar constraints, corresponding *image points* are identified [4]. For spherical markers the *rays* of all observations intersect at the center of the sphere. This point is the position of the 3D marker.

Statistical uncertainties and imprecision create small distances between the *rays*. Thus, also *rays* with distances smaller than ϵ_{3D} are combined. In a volume of several cubic meters a value of $\epsilon_{3D} = 4$ mm for spherical markers appears to be a practical choice.

2.3 Target Recognition

The recognition of a target is based on the relative positions of its markers. These positions are calibrated in a previous step (section 2.5). The relative marker positions are searched in the cloud of calculated 3D markers. The procedure is similar to [8]. From the group of matching 3D markers the position $\vec{t}_t$ and rotation R_t of the target are estimated as described in [2, 14].

Here, again a certain tolerance ϵ_{6D} is necessary:

$$\epsilon_{6D} > \epsilon = \frac{1}{N} \sum_i^N \left| R_t \cdot \vec{x}_i + \vec{t}_t - \vec{x}_{3Di} \right|^2 . \quad (1)$$

N is the number of markers in the target, $\vec{x}_i$ the position of a marker in the target and $\vec{x}_{3Di}$ the position of a 3D marker. In a volume of several cubic meter a value of $\epsilon_{6D} = 4$ mm for spherical markers appears to be a practical choice.

2.4 Target Tracking

Once recognized, the target is tracked from one *frame* to the next. Therefore, the position and rotation of the target are extrapolated and the marker positions are projected into the camera images.

$$p_i(\vec{x}_i) = C_c \cdot R_c^T \left(R_t \cdot \vec{x}_i + \vec{t}_t - \vec{t}_c \right) , \qquad (2)$$

p_i is the position of the marker i in the image, C_c represents the optical properties of the camera, R_c and $\vec{t}_c$ the rotation and position of the camera. For R_t and t_t the extrapolated rotation and position of the target are used.

Now, the *image points* of the next *frame* are directly assigned to the extrapolated points and the corresponding marker of the target if

$$p_i - m_j = v_i < \epsilon_{2D} . \qquad (3)$$

m_j is a measured image point and ϵ_{2D} an upper bound for the assignment. For spherical markers a value of $\epsilon_{2D} \sim 1.4$ pixel is used.

With the measured and assigned image points an iterative adjustment of the target position and rotation is performed (see [7], [4] for the method and [9] for details). The optimization minimizes the projection errors v_i using the Jacobian of the projection (equation 2).

2.5 Target Calibration

In advance of the tracking of a target the relative positions of its markers are calibrated. Therefore, 3D markers are determined as described in section 2.2. In the first *frame* all observed 3D markers are added to a temporary target. In the next frames the target recognition (section 2.3) is used to determine the pose of the temporary target and the matching 3D markers. Usually, only some of the markers in the temporary target have matching 3D markers. Based on this identification, for each marker the amount of *frames* it is visible is counted. New markers are added to the temporary target if an unmatched 3D marker with a fixed position relative to the target is observed in a number of successive *frames*. After a certain time (here 30 s) the new calibrated target is composed from all markers of the temporary target visible more than 30 % of the *frames*. For each marker the average position in the target is used.

3. CYLINDRICAL MARKERS

Compared to spherical markers cylindrical markers have a rotation symmetry only for the cylinder axis. Thus, the image of the marker in a camera differs depending on the angle θ between the cylinder axis and the observation direction. As described in section 2.1 the *image point* is determined as the 2D center of gravity of the marker image. The projected *observed position* O on the marker for such an *image point* is not on the same *ray* as the 3D center of gravity of the cylindrical marker. Figure 3 illustrates this. This shift between the *observed position* O and the 3D center of gravity S is the main challenge for the precise tracking of cylindrical markers. These shifts do not occur for spherical markers.

Due to this shift *rays* of observations of cylindrical markers from cameras at different positions do not intersect. This, has to be taken into account to enable the tracking of cylindrical markers.

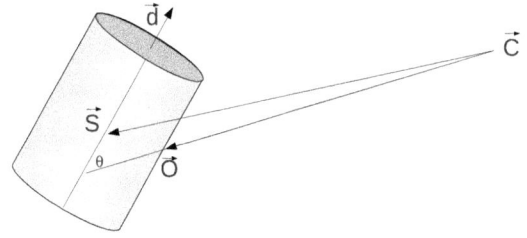

Figure 3: Observation of a cylindrical marker with a camera C (not to scale). The 3D center of gravity S of the marker is not on the same line of sight as the *observed position* O. θ is the angle between the cylinder axis and the observation direction.

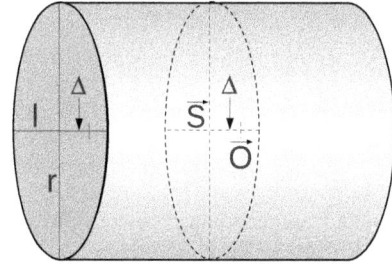

Figure 4: Image of a cylindrical marker (without perspective distortion). The image of the 3D center of gravity S is shifted by Δ to the *observed position* O. r is the radius of the cylinder.

The difference between the *observed position* O and the 3D center of gravity S is computed using the seen ellipse of the cylinder end. The rotation of the cylinder changes the length l of the minor axis:

$$l = r \cdot \cos(\theta). \qquad (4)$$

Here, r is the radius of the cylinder. Figure 4 illustrates the geometrical properties. To compute the shift Δ the center of gravity in the image is considered. It is calculated from the geometrical properties of the ellipse as

$$\Delta = \frac{4l}{3\pi} = r \cdot \frac{4\cos(\theta)}{3\pi} . \qquad (5)$$

With this shift the *observed position* is

$$\vec{O} = \vec{S} + \vec{d} \cdot \Delta \cdot \alpha . \qquad (6)$$

$\vec{d}$ is the direction of the cylinder axis projected to the image plane. Here, α is introduced as an additional factor to the size of the shift. Depending on the reflecting properties of the foil of the marker, usually not the complete cylinder is observed. The edges of the cylinder appear darker or disappear in the image, because the foil becomes close to parallel to the observation direction and thus less light is reflected towards the camera. This effect increases the shift to a maximum of l/Δ:

$$1 < \alpha < \frac{l}{\Delta} = \frac{3\pi}{4} \ . \qquad (7)$$

An additional shift due to perspective distortion is negligible (assuming that the distance between camera and marker is large compared to the height of the cylinder). To compute the image point for a given cylindrical marker the projection (equation 2) is extended by equation 6

$$p_i(\vec{x}_i) = C_c[R_c^T \left(R_t \cdot \vec{x}_i + \vec{t}_t - \vec{t}_c\right) + \vec{d} \cdot \Delta \cdot \alpha] \ . \qquad (8)$$

Using this result it is possible to compute the image point for a cylindrical marker with known position, radius and axis direction. Note, the height of the cylinder is not required.

3.1 Recognition and Tracking

Recognition and tracking of cylindrical markers is analog to spherical markers. For the marker algorithm (compare section 2.1) and the calculation of 3D markers (section 2.2) no information about an expected shape is available and all markers are treated in the same way. A decision whether a marker is spherical based on the image information is not applicable due to small marker images (down to a few pixel) and occlusions. The larger distance between the *rays* of one 3D marker causes an increased value of ϵ_{3D}.

Also the recognition of a target with cylindrical markers is identical to the recognition of a target with spherical markers, but with an increased tolerance ϵ_{6D}. For typical targets the shift fulfills

$$\Delta \le r \ll d_{\text{marker}} \ . \qquad (9)$$

The first inequality is directly derived from equation 6. The second inequality utilizes that the distance between two markers d_{marker} is larger than the radius of the cylinders. Thus, it is sufficient and possible to increase the tolerances to the scale of the radius of the cylindrical markers.

After recognition the tracking is straightforward. The *image positions* of the markers are determined using equation 8 and the same adjustment process as for spherical markers is used (again applying equation 2 instead of 8).

3.2 Calibration of Cylindrical Markers

The calibration of a target consisting of several cylindrical markers starts assuming a target with spherical markers using the calibration procedure described in section 2.5. Additionally, the 3D markers are recorded together with their *image points* in each camera.

After this initial step, an iterative optimization procedure is applied determining the three additional degrees of freedom: two for the orientation and one for the radius. Here, the radius and additional factor α are simply treated as one parameter $r' = r\alpha$.

The parameters are optimized in an iterative procedure using the recorded correspondences between markers and *image points*. Here, a two step procedure is iteratively executed. This procedure is similar to a bundle adjustment which alternates between intersecting and resecting described in [13].

- For each *frame* the target position and rotation is calculated by an adjustment procedure relying on the current values of the marker positions, rotations and the radius.

- For each marker its position, rotation and radius are determined in an adjustment procedure using the current values of the target position and rotation.

This process relies on the projection of cylindrical markers in equation 8 and its Jacobian with respect to the adjusted parameters in the corresponding step. The two adjustment procedures are similar to the adjustment used for the tracking (section 2.4), which minimizes the errors of the projections (equation 3).

The additional degrees of freedom for each marker increase the total number of degrees of freedom for the optimization procedure. Prior knowledge about the target can be used to reduce this number again and increase the speed of the convergence. For many tools used in industrial environments the geometry is known accurately. In case of the torque wrench shown in figure 1 with six markers the degrees of freedom can be reduced from 36 to 12. For each marker only the radius and the position along the handle or extension are determined.

4. FLEXIBLE TARGETS

For articulated objects, flexibility is added to the target description. This issue is frequently studied in the field of motion capture. However, the motion capture problem is far more complex [12] due to several flexible joints. Anyhow, the task here is similar to fitting a skeleton to observed 3D markers [5][11].

In equation 2 and equation 8, all markers of a target are described by their position $\vec{x}$ within the target. This description is extended to

$$\vec{x} = R_r \cdot \vec{x}' + \vec{t}_r \ . \qquad (10)$$

$\vec{x}'$ is the position of the marker within a rigid part of the target. R_r and $\vec{t}_r$ are the relative rotation and position of the rigid block with respect to the first rigid block. R_r and $\vec{t}_r$ represent six degrees of freedom for each rigid block after the first.

For tools, usually two rigid parts connected at a fixed position and rotating around a given axis is an adequate description. For example, the torque wrench in figure 1 has handle and extension as rigid parts. $\vec{t}_r$ is fixed at the connection point and R_r varies due to the tolerance of the connection. Thus, the position $\vec{t}_r$ is determined during the calibration while R_r is determined during the tracking on a *frame* to *frame* basis.

4.1 Target Recognition and Tracking

The recognition of a flexible target is identical to the standard procedure described in section 2.3. The required relative positions of the markers are determined by default values for the position $\vec{t}_r$ and rotation R_r between the rigid blocks.

For the tracking, the projection (equation 2 or equation 8 for targets with cylindrical markers) is combined with the additional freedom of the rigid parts (equation 10)

$$p_i(\vec{x}_i) = p_i(R_r \cdot \vec{x}_i' + \vec{t}_r) \qquad (11)$$

This extended equation is used in the adjustment procedure. The variable parameters of R_r and t_r are optimized simultaneously within the adjustment. Respectively the Jacobian is increased in its dimensions.

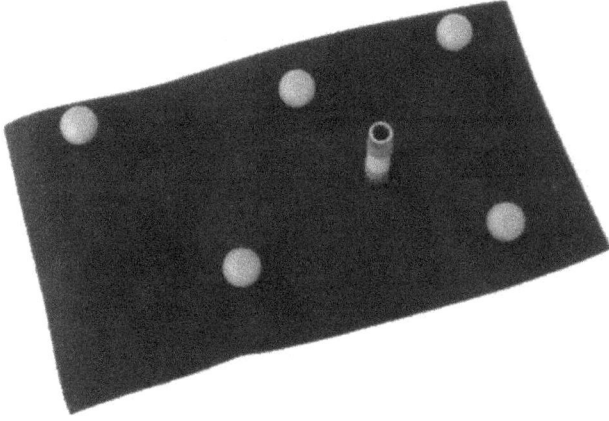

Figure 5: Target for the test of the shift: Five spherical markers on an even plane and one additional cylindrical marker with its axis perpendicular to the plane.

4.2 Calibration of Flexible Targets

The calibration of flexible targets is based on the same procedure as the calibration for targets with cylindrical markers (section 3.2): first the standard target calibration followed by an optimization to determine the additional parameters. Here, these are the parameters of the position t_r and rotation R_r of the connection.

For some conditions, a reliable determination of the parameters might be numerically unstable. This is especially the case if only small changes in the parameters are possible. In case of the torque wrench (fig. 1), a precise calibration of the connection point is not possible, due to the small tolerance at this point.

Parameters which are numerically unstable can be extracted from the known object geometry. For the torque wrench the connection point and the rotation axis are extracted. Additionally, the marker positions are reduced to one degree of freedom (plus degrees of freedom for the cylindrical markers): the distance to the connection.

With this procedure, flexible tools are accurately calibrated. If the tools have cylindrical markers, the optimization step for the cylindrical markers is directly combined with the optimization for the parameters of the rigid blocks.

5. TEST AND PRECISION

The following subsections show tests for the precision and applicability of the discussed flexible targets with cylindrical markers.

5.1 Measured Shift of Cylindrical Markers

Using the correct shift (equation 6) for the cylindrical markers is crucial for the precision of the tracking. To compare the analytically determined shift with the shift measured when using a cylindrical marker, a special target is constructed. It consists of five spherical markers and one cylindrical marker ($r = 13$ cm) mounted on an even plane (fig. 5). The axis of the cylindrical marker is perpendicular to the plane.

The target cannot be calibrated with the procedure for cylindrical markers as described in section 3.2, because this calibration approach relies on the shift tested here. Thus, it can not be used for an independent test. Instead, the cylindrical marker is replaced by a spherical marker during the calibration. The mount is constructed such that the center of the spherical marker is on the axis of the original cylindrical marker. After the target calibration the cylindrical marker is re-mounted. The calibrated marker position in the plane of the target is now also valid for the cylindrical marker. Only the height above the plane is unknown.

Now the target moved and rotated by hand in a volume observed by a system of six ARTtrack2 cameras [1] using only the five spherical markers and ignoring the mounted cylindrical marker. For each time the cameras record images the position of the cylindrical marker is

$$\vec{c} = R_t \cdot \vec{x} - \vec{t}_t + \vec{\delta} \,. \tag{12}$$

R_t and $\vec{t}_t$ are rotation and position of the target. $\vec{x}$ is the position of the spherical marker calibrated at the position of the cylindrical marker. $\vec{\delta}$ is the unknown offset along the cylinder axis.

For all observations of the cylindrical marker the closest approach point $\vec{c}_a$ of the *ray* on the cylinder axis is determined. The measured shift is

$$\sigma = |\vec{c}_a - \vec{c}| = |\vec{c}_a - R_t \cdot \vec{x} + \vec{t}_t + \vec{\delta}| \,. \tag{13}$$

Additionally, the angle between the cylinder axis and the observation direction is calculated

$$\cos(\theta) = \frac{\vec{d} \cdot (\vec{t}_c - \vec{c'})}{|\vec{d}||\vec{t}_c - \vec{c'}|} \quad \text{with} \tag{14}$$

$$\vec{c'} = R_t \cdot \vec{x} - \vec{t}_t \approx \vec{c} \,. \tag{15}$$

$\vec{d}$ and $\vec{t}_c$ as defined in section 3. Due to $|\vec{\delta}| \ll |\vec{t}_c - \vec{c'}|$ the offset $\vec{\delta}$ it is neglected here. Using the known property $\sigma(90°) = 0$, the offset $\vec{\delta}$ is determined from the measurement. Figure 6 shows the results of this procedure compared to the analytically determined shift. To fit the measurements, the radius is increased by $\alpha \approx 1.53$.

In the range from $20°$ to $90°$ the measured shifts fit the analytical expectation. At smaller angles no observations exist. Here, the cylindrical marker is observed from the top where no reflecting foil is placed. The width of the curve of measured shifts is caused by measurement uncertainties and the neglected offset in the angle calculation. In addition some not matching shifts are measured in the range between $10°$ and $40°$. Their systematic arrangement (two lines) indicates associations of wrong observations to the cylindrical marker.

This test shows that the analytically determined shift reflects the shift observed in the images if the product $r\alpha$ is chosen properly. Using the shift (equation 6) the projection of cylindrical markers is almost as precise as for spherical markers.

5.2 3D Marker Generation and Recognition

The 3D markers are the base for the target recognition. Important is, that the *rays* of the observations of cylindrical markers are combined to 3D markers. This is quantified by

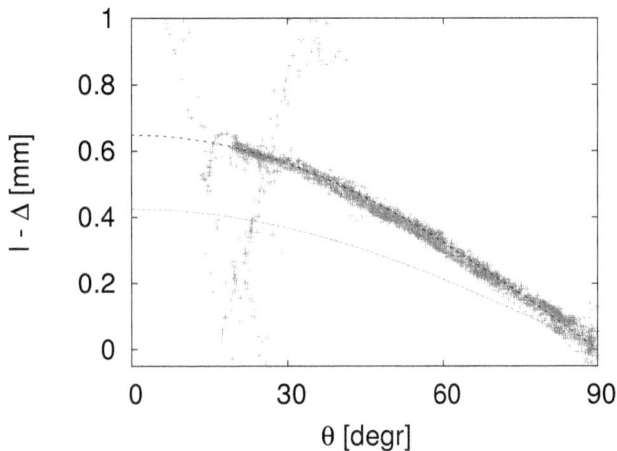

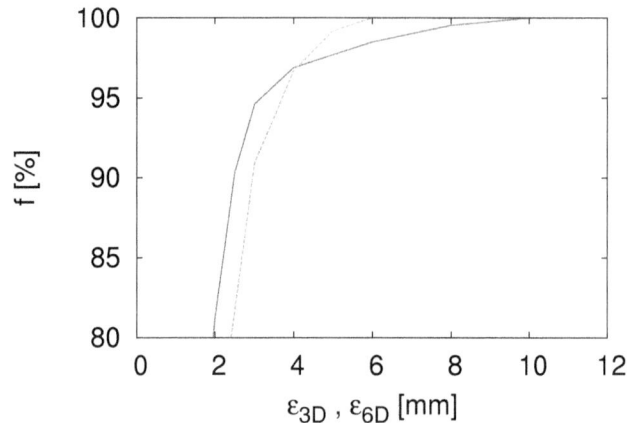

Figure 6: Measured shift (red crosses) compared to the expected shift (green fine dotted, equation 6) depending on the angle between cylinder axis and observation direction θ normalized to radius $r = 1$ ($\alpha = 1$). Additionally, the expected shift for $\alpha \approx 1.53$ is shown (black dashed).

Figure 7: Relative amount of generated 3D markers (solid red) depending on the tolerance ϵ_{3D} for the identification for a cylindrical marker with radius $r = 12$ mm. Additionally, the relative amount of recognized targets (green dashed) depending on the tolerance ϵ_{6D} is shown. The shape of both curves also depends on the movement of the marker in front of the cameras. Here, all possible observation angles are included.

the number of 3D markers N_{3D} compared to the number of 3D markers with two or more observations N_{2Obs}.

$$f = \frac{N_{3D}}{N_{2Obs}} \qquad (16)$$

Figure 7 shows f depending on the 3D tolerance ϵ_{3D} for a cylindrical marker with radius 12 mm. For $\epsilon_{3D} \geq 10$ mm all candidates are combined to a 3D marker. The shape of the curve shown in figure 7 depends on the movement of the marker in front of the camera. Here, the same data set as for the analysis of the shift is used (section 5.1). Figure 6 shows that all possible observation angles and shifts are included.

Figure 7 also shows the target recognition efficiency depending on ϵ_{6D}. It is defined as:

$$f = \frac{N_{6D}}{N_4} \qquad (17)$$

N_{6D} is the amount of *frames* with a recognized target and N_4 is the amount of *frames* with four 3D markers corresponding to the target. For the target recognition full efficiency is already reached at $\epsilon_{6D} \geq 5$ mm. This value is smaller than the required value for ϵ_{3D} because the 3D markers average the shifts and reduce the discrepancies. Additionally, 3D markers corresponding to cylindrical markers with the same orientation are displaced in the same direction.

Both tests show that using the increased tolerances the generation of 3D markers and the recognition of the target work with full efficiency.

5.3 Precision of the Estimated Position

The precision is the core feature of the marker based infrared tracking. Flexible targets with cylindrical markers are only applicable for tracking if their pose estimation yields precisions comparable to standard targets.

Here, we demonstrate the precision in an application orientated setup using the torque wrench (fig. 1) to fix screws on an engine block (fig. 8). The engine block is at the center of an approximately 2 m x 2 m x 2 m tracking volume equipped with eight ARTtrack2 cameras [1] in each corner. Goal of the application is to record which screws on a work piece are fixed. Thus, the position of the torque wrench tip is tracked while a user fixes five screws and compared to the expected screw positions. The precision of the measured reference screw positions is better than 0.1 mm. To achieve this, a standard tracking device is used and the recorded data is averaged.

The test is done with four targets:

(1) the torque wrench with cylindrical markers,

(2) a torque wrench with a tree target (fig. 2) mounted on the handle,

(3) a torque wrench with a tree target mounted on the extension and

(4) a torque wrench mock-up. It consists of two metal rods which are connected by a flexible rubber joint. The rather thin metal rods pierce through spherical markers replicating the same target geometry as the cylindrical markers on the torque wrench.

Additionally the measurement for target (1) is computed with four different combinations of algorithms: using cylindrical or spherical markers and considering the target as rigid or flexible.

The measurement of the accuracy in the above described setup uses only the tip positions recorded while the tip is on the screw. Here, the tip is defined to be on the screw if the difference in the z-coordinate (parallel to the screw axis) is

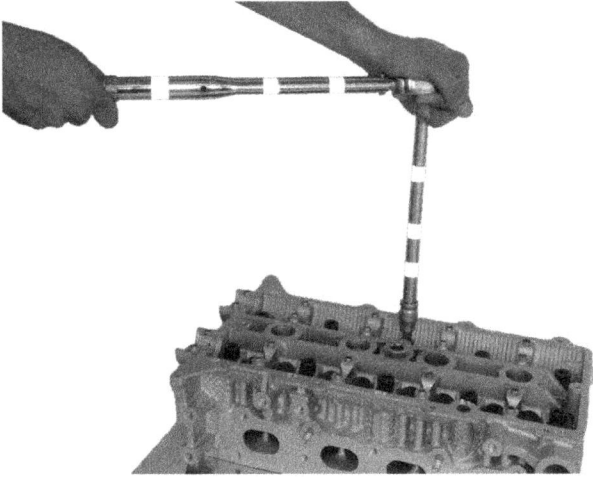

Figure 8: Application of the torque wrench, to fix screws on an engine block.

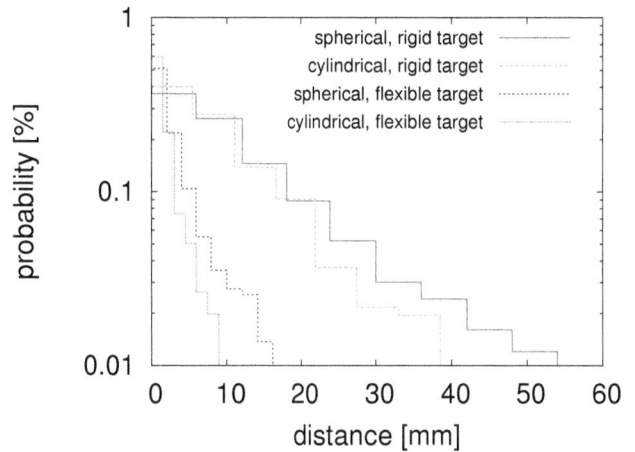

Figure 9: Normalized distributions of the distance between the measured tip position and the screw position using target (1) and different algorithms on the same measured data: assuming spherical or cylindrical, with and without tolerance. (The bin size depends on the width of the distribution.)

Table 1: Combined accuracy of the tip position measured at five screw positions. Targets are described in the text. Either the algorithm for spherical or for cylindrical markers is used. Additionally the algorithm considering the flexibility is applied in some cases.

target	algorithm	RMS[mm]
(2)	spherical	±35
(1)	spherical	±17
(1)	cylinders	±12
(1)	spherical, flexible	±3.9
(1)	cylinders, flexible	±2.5
(3)	spherical	±2.5
(4)	spherical, flexible	±1.5

less than 5 mm. Additionally, the first and last 10 recorded positions fulfilling this criterion are discarded to exclude all positions where the tip is not on the screw.

The accuracy is measured by the distance between the tip position of the torque wrench and the known screw positions. Figure 9 shows the distribution of these distances for target (1) and the different algorithms. For a direct comparison the RMS of the distances is calculated. This is given in table 1.

If the flexibility is not considered (table 1, line 1-3) the RMS is above 12 mm. Here, smaller RMS values are achieved, if markers are placed on the extension, and if the algorithm for cylindrical markers (section 3) is applied.

When accounting for the flexibility as described in section 4, the RMS is below 4 mm. Comparing the measurement for target (1) using the standard algorithm for spherical markers and the algorithm for cylindrical markers (section 3), a clear improvement in the accuracy is visible (table 1, line 4, 5 and figure 9, blue, pink). Applying the algorithm for cylindrical markers, the same precision as for target (3) is archived: 2.5 mm. However, the best precision is achieved with target (4) the torque wrench mock-up. This is due to the combination of the advantages of slightly more precise spherical markers (target (3)) and a minimal distance between markers and the tool tip (target (1)). Anyway, it is not possible to use

a tool with a bulky target (target (2) and target (3)) or to design a tool using a target like the mock-up (target (4)).

Figure 10 shows example measurements of five screws fixed with the torque wrench with cylindrical markers. Calculation is performed assuming spherical markers and no flexibility as well as cylindrical markers and a flexible connection. The torque wrench tip approaches the screw (sometimes misses on the first try), fixes the screw and is removed. With the assumption of spherical markers, general shifts as well as errors of more than 1 cm are observed. Changing to cylindrical markers, the precision increases and the general shift disappears.

Thus, a high precision measurement of the tip of a tool is possible with robust cylindrical markers and without mounting a bulky target.

5.4 Reliability and Visibility

Reliable tracking is only possible if sufficient markers of the target are visible. In difference to spherical markers, cylindrical markers are invisible from certain directions (fig. 6), although this effect is small. The observation range from 30° to 90° allows an observation from 86 % (full sphere minus two caps) of all possible viewing directions.

Occlusions are highly setup-dependent and less affected by the marker type itself, anyhow, an advantageous placement of the markers on the tool improves the visibility. A slightly decreased visibility of the cylindrical markers outweighs the disadvantages of a bulky tool.

6. CONCLUSIONS

Cylindrical markers attached directly to tools can overcome the issues of bulky and fragile targets for infrared tracking. Size, shape and handling of the tool remain the same. The work flow is not affected.

The reduced symmetry of the cylindrical marker causes a shift between the 3D center of gravity of the marker and

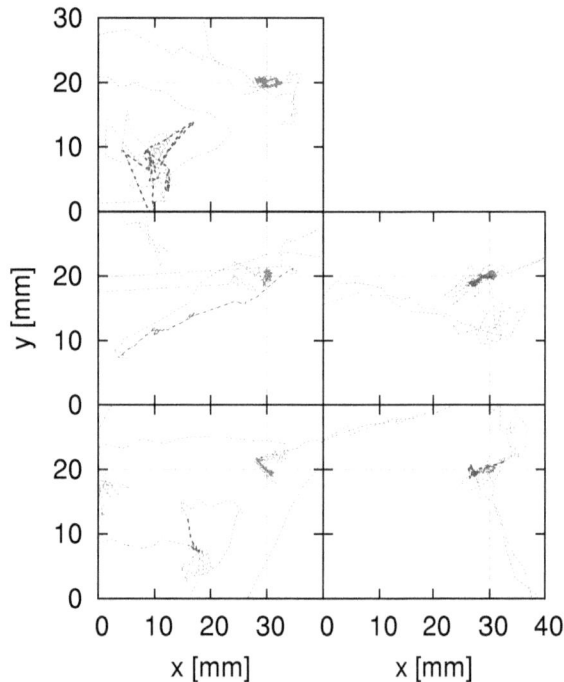

Figure 10: Comparison: tracking the tip of the torque wrench (target (1)) while fixing five screws. Blue dashed line: using the algorithms for spherical markers and a rigid tool. Red solid line: using the here developed algorithms for cylindrical markers and two rigid parts. Gray dashed lines: torque wrench is not on the screw. The screw is at $x = 30$ mm and $y = 20$ mm.

the *observed position*. This shift is calculated analytically from the geometrical properties of a cylinder and fits the measurements. Applying the analytical calculation allows accurate tracking of targets with cylindrical markers.

The treatment of targets composed of several rigid blocks reduces the requirements for a tool to be equipped with markers. It basically requires very little amount of space on a metal bar.

Combining both features, a high precision tracking of many tools becomes possible with robust markers and handy targets. The functionality of the algorithms is demonstrated using a torque wrench. Also, we already have successfully applied the technique to other tools: a welding gun, usual screw drivers, an EC-screw driver and targets for glasses.

For the future, an improved target recognition is desirable. A flexible target is only recognized by the relative default position of its markers. Reduced requirements for the relative positions for markers on different rigid blocks would increase the recognition capabilities.

7. ACKNOWLEDGMENTS

This work was supported by the Bundesministerium für Bildung und Forschung, project AVILUS - Angewandte Virtuelle Technologien im Produkt- und Produktionsmittellebenszyklus (FKZ: 01IM08001C).

8. REFERENCES

[1] Advanced Realtime Tracking GmbH. http://www.ar-tracking.com.

[2] K. S. Arun, T. S. Huang, and S. D. Blostein. Least-squares fitting of two 3-d point sets. *IEEE Trans. Pattern Anal. Mach. Intell.*, 9(5):698–700, May 1987.

[3] K. Dorfmüller. An Optical Tracking System for VR/AR-Applications. In *Virtual Environments '99, Proceedings of the Virtual Environments Conference and fifth Eurographics Workshop*, pages 33–42. Springer Verlag, 1999.

[4] R. I. Hartley and A. Zisserman. *Multiple View Geometry in Computer Vision*. Cambridge University Press, June 2000.

[5] L. Herda, P. Fua, R. Plankers, R. Boulic, and D. Thalmann. Skeleton-based motion capture for robust reconstruction of human motion. In *Computer Animation (CA)*, pages 77–83. IEEE, 2000.

[6] F. Madritsch and M. Gervautz. CCD-Camera Based Optical Beacon Tracking for Virtual and Augmented Reality. In *Computer Graphics Forum (Proc. Eurographics 96)*, volume 15, pages 207–216, 1996.

[7] W. Niemeier. *Ausgleichsrechnung, Statistische Auswertemethoden*. de Gruyter Textbook, 2nd edition, 2008.

[8] T. Pintaric and H. Kaufmann. Affordable Infrared-Optical Pose Tracking for Virtual and Augmented Reality. In *Proceedings of IEEE VR Workshop on Trends and Issues in Tracking for Virtual Environments*, March 2007.

[9] D. Pustka, J. Willneff, O. Wenisch, P. Lukewille, K. Achatz, P. Keitler, and G. Klinker. Determining the point of minimum error for 6dof pose uncertainty representation. In *ISMAR*, pages 37–45. IEEE, 2010.

[10] W. Schreiber and P. Zimmermann. *Virtuelle Techniken im industriellen Umfeld*. Springer Verlag, Berlin Heidelberg, Germany, 2011.

[11] M.-C. Silaghi, R. Plänkers, R. Boulic, P. Fua, and D. Thalmann. Local and global skeleton fitting techniques for optical motion capture. In N. Magnenat-Thalmann and D. Thalmann, editors, *Modelling and Motion Capture Techniques for Virtual Environments*, volume 1537 of *LNCS*, pages 26–40. Springer Berlin / Heidelberg, 1998.

[12] D. Tolani, A. Goswami, and N. I. Badler. Real-time inverse kinematics techniques for anthropomorphic limbs. *Graphical Models*, 62(5):353 – 388, 2000.

[13] B. Triggs, P. McLauchlan, R. Hartley, and A. Fitzgibbon. Bundle adjustment - a modern synthesis. In B. Triggs, A. Zisserman, and R. Szeliski, editors, *Vision Algorithms: Theory and Practice*, volume 1883 of *Lecture Notes in Computer Science*, pages 153–177. Springer Berlin / Heidelberg, 2000.

[14] S. Umeyama. Least-squares estimation of transformation parameters between two point patterns. *IEEE Trans. Pattern Anal. Mach. Intell.*, 13(4):376–380, Apr. 1991.

Random Model Variation for Universal Feature Tracking

Jan Herling
Ilmenau University of Technology
jan.herling@tu-ilmenau.de

Wolfgang Broll
Ilmenau University of Technology
wolfgang.broll@tu-ilmenau.de

ABSTRACT

Feature based tracking approaches become more and more common for Augmented Reality (AR). However, most upcoming AR solutions are designed for mobile devices, in particular for smartphones and tablet computers, lacking sufficient performance for the execution of state-of-the art feature based approaches at interactive frame rates.

In this paper we will present our approach significantly increasing the speed of feature based tracking, thus allowing for real-time applications even on mobile devices. Our approach applies a randomized pose initialization, is applicable to any feature detector and does not require any feature appearance attributes, such as descriptors or ferns.

Categories and Subject Descriptors

I.4.8 [**Image processing and computer vision**]: Scene analysis-Motion, Photometry, Sensor fusion, Tracking; I.3.m [**Computer graphics**]: Miscellaneous-Augmented Reality; I.5.5 [**Pattern recognition**]: Applications-Computer vision

Keywords

Tracking, features, descriptor-free, real-time, mobile phones, no RANSAC, Augmented Reality

1. INTRODUCTION

Ubiquitous Augmented Reality (AR) has only recently come within reach by the introduction of sufficiently powerful personal devices such as smartphones and tablets. For a long time, fiducial markers have dominated AR tracking solutions. Meanwhile, we can increasingly observe that feature based vision approaches are used for this task. The projection between the 3D features in the environment and the 2D features in the camera frame allows for calculating the current pose. Several feature detectors have been proposed for detecting interest points in an image, mainly, corner or point detectors, and blob-like feature detectors.

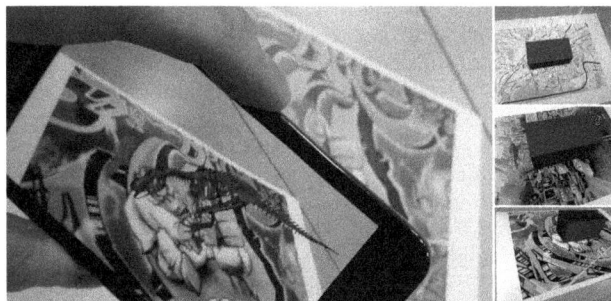

Figure 1: Descriptor-less feature tracking.

Feature based pose calculation requires to find correspondences between 3D object features onto 2D image feature in the video frame. Feature descriptors based on an investigation of the immediate environment of a feature point can be used to distinguish between them. Unfortunately, reliable feature descriptors such as the SURF feature descriptor are computationally expensive. Other approaches apply skewed image patches instead [5]. Ferns [13] provide another alternative here, but require an additional pre-processing step, which additionally is memory intensive. Thus, even on recent mobile devices, these approaches are computationally too expensive, barely allowing for tracking results at sufficient framerates and/or accuracy.

In this paper we will present our approach to universal feature tracking applying a randomized approach for finding initial correspondences. We will show, how this approach allows us to speed up the overall tracking dramatically. In section 2 we will review recent previous work. In section 3 we will present our approach. Section 4 introduces our approach on initialization, while section 5 deals with the actual tracking. The accuracy and the reliability of the tracking approach is evaluated in section 6. In section 7 we discuss the overall performance, before concluding and providing a look into future work.

2. RELATED WORK

One of the first feature based trackers for AR has been proposed by Gordon and Lowe [3]. Their approach applied SIFT features to track real 3D objects by matching SIFT descriptors between model and camera features. The first feature based tracker for mobile phones solely using natural feature points has been proposed by Wagner et al. [13] applying ferns and modified SIFT descriptors for distinguishing natural features. The FAST detector was used for feature detection. However, as ferns need to be trained for each individual tracking object, such training is usually performed on a more powerful platform. SIFT descriptors can be applied without pre-processing step but need more performance during the tracking. The simultaneous localization and mapping approach by Klein [5] detects FAST features and matches them with skewed image patches. This work was also demonstrated to achieve interactive framerates on mobile phones [6]. Recently we had proposed an approach [4] solely applying SURF features instead of using the faster but less robust FAST features. That system performed fast enough for smartphones without applying any pre-processing. However, all those approaches require a description of the stored and live detected feature points for feature matching. In contrast, our new approach relies on feature detectors only, not requiring any pre-processing.

SoftPOSIT has been proposed by [2] solving the well-known POSIT algorithm without any information about feature correspondences. Therefore, a huge correspondence matrix is iteratively updated eventually providing unique correspondences due to almost unique assignments given by the matrix. However, this approach is far away from real-time performance. Moreno et al. [7] proposed a Blind PnP algorithm. They apply a Gaussian Mixture Model that is initialized by a set of rough poses already known. By application of a Kalman Filter these poses are refined and a final accurate pose is determined. The performance is comparable to SoftPOSIT but still far too slow for real-time applications. The Blind PnP algorithm has been extended by Sanchez et al. [10] allowing to detect non-rigid and deformable shapes. However, their approach needs up to half an hour to proceed. Another extension of Blind PnP has been introduced by Sarradell et al. [11] allowing to determine a homography between to images under difficult viewing conditions. However, they additionally use ferns shrinking their search space significantly. Although, this approach is faster than the original one, it still does not seem to be real-time capable. Rodriguez et al. [9] realized a descriptor-less tracker to estimate sparse optical flow in long video sequences. They applied PROSAC [1] in combination with a motion estimation model. However, they do not provide a 6DOF pose but apply a simple 2D/2D tracking only.

3. OUR APPROACH

Similar to other tracking approaches, we determine the camera pose by finding reliable feature correspondences between 2D image features and 3D features of an already known feature map. However, all previously proposed approaches mainly determine these correspondences by applying constraints with respect to the appearance of feature points. These tracking approaches find matching features by individual descriptors, image patches or probabilistic structures such as ferns. However, even correspondences matched by time intensive descriptors may be wrong. Those false correspondences have to be identified and removed, typically by applying RANSAC.

Our approach entirely avoids the usage of structures describing the appearance of feature points and thus may not apply RANSAC. The only additionally information we use upon availability is the strength of the features detected. This information typically is a result of the feature detection process, thus not requiring any additional processing. However, once the features are sorted, even the strength

parameter is not used any further. Thus, the overall data structure of the tracker shrinks to a simple set of 3D object points and 2D image points. The 3D points define a feature map used as tracking reference and live detected image camera features define the 2D points. The algorithm tries to align two 2D points clouds. The first point clouds results from the projected 3D feature map points. The second cloud is defined by the current live image feature points. Once, an extrinsic camera matrix aligning the two point clouds is determined, candidates for feature correspondences are extracted by investigating 2D points with similar positions. Afterwards, these correspondence candidates are used for fine-tuning the camera pose. As the feature points do not contain any further information except their positions, the validation has to rely on geometric constrains only.

Let $T = [R \,|\, t]$ be a 3×4 homogenous transformation matrix with a 3×3 orthonormal rotation matrix R and a translation vector $t = (t_x, t_y, t_z)^\top$ [12]. T transforms points defined in world coordinates into points defined in camera coordinates. Therefore, a pair of a 3D feature point p and a 2D image feature q is stated to be a reliable correspondence regarding to T and a 3×3 intrinsic camera matrix K [12], if the projected 3D point p' is sufficiently close to q.

$$\left| q - p' \right|^2 < \epsilon, \quad \text{with } s \begin{pmatrix} p' \\ 1 \end{pmatrix} = KT \cdot \begin{pmatrix} p \\ 1 \end{pmatrix} \qquad (1)$$

with scalar scaling factor s and maximal projection error ϵ. In the following an homogenous coordinate is expected to be de-homogenized automatically if necessary in the mathematical context and vice versa. Thus for better readability (1) could also be written as

$$\left| q - KTp \right|^2 < \epsilon \qquad (2)$$

The probability that several hundred 3D features precisely project to individual 2D features while the applied extrinsic camera matrix is inaccurate or even wrong is very low. This rexplains why the approach is well suited for feature tracking. Our approach simply seeks randomly for a sufficient number of reliable correspondences in each camera frame and calculates a resulting pose.

Our tracker may use any feature detector including but not limited to FAST features, Harris corners, SURF or SIFT features. The pose accuracy then depends on the reliability and the quality of the applied detector. The strength parameters of detected features are used to sort the 3D feature map points as well as the live camera features. Thus, if any tracker routine takes a subset of the first features, it can be expected that these features are at least as strong as the following features.

4. INITIALIZATION

The most time consuming part of the tracking pipeline typically is the determination of the initial camera pose when no further information about its position or orientation is available. Although the initialization or a re-initialization are required rather seldom (e.g. if the camera has not captured the tracking object in the previous frame), an applicable tracking solution needs a fast (re-)initialization method. In section 6 the break condition forcing a re-initialization is explained in detail. Thus this issue is investigated in detail. Independent of the tracking approach applied, a brute force search in the entire data set usually cannot be

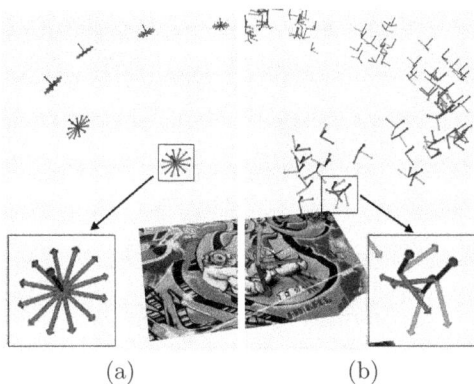

Figure 2: Comparison of regular, equally distributed camera poses (a) and randomized poses (b).

avoided for initialization. This search space increases dramatically, when possible candidates for correspondences cannot be compared directly due to missing descriptors.

In our approach we applied some minor constraints, using a user centric or user empathic approach, assuming that a user will usually start investigating the entire object to be tracked. Our approach allows a real-time initialization as long as an adequate extent of the object to be tracked is visible. While the orientation and position of the camera may be arbitrary, the only constraint is that the distance to the object should be inside a given range, which has to be specified before the actual tracking starts.

The initialization is a three step approach: First, 2D image point positions of the projected (3D) feature map describing the object to be tracked are generated for a set of different virtual camera poses. Second, the current live camera features are compared to these sets of projected feature points and the best matching set is selected. Third, the real extrinsic camera matrix is determined by finding the transformation between the live features and those from the selected set. If no transformation can be calculated, the tracking object may be claimed to be invisible or the next best sets of projected 2D features may be used as long as a given time period has not been exceeded. In the following a more detailed description is provided.

4.1 Randomly Created Virtual Camera Poses

The sets of projected 2D points (point clouds) from the 3D feature map can be created very efficiently. They only have to be created once when the feature map of an object to be tracked is provided to the system. Thus, the sets of projected 2D points may be considered an extension to the feature map. Measurements showed that the point clouds can be created within 3ms on a Samsung Galaxy S2 smartphone. Further, the memory, necessary to store the 2D pixel information of the projection sets is negligible compared to the memory necessary for feature descriptors or ferns. For planar tracking objects like images or posters the virtual camera poses are calculated assuming that the camera points into the direction of the object. More precisely, the virtual poses are distributed on a hemisphere above the object. Test showed that slightly randomized poses provide even better results than regularly distributed poses. Figure 2 shows the distribution of a sample of initial poses for a planar tracking object.

4.2 Matching of Point Sets

The average distance calculation between a set of 3D object points $P = \{p_0, p_1, \ldots, p_{n-1}\}$ and a set of corresponding 2D image points $Q = \{q_0, q_1, \ldots, q_{n-1}\}$ with known and sorted correspondences is straight forward:

$$\delta = \frac{1}{n} \sum_{i=0}^{n-1} |q_i - KTp_i|^2 \qquad (3)$$

for a given matrices T and K.

However, in our approach neither the number of elements in the two point sets is identical nor any information about possible correspondences is available. Thus, a different distance measure has to be applied. Basically, our approach estimates the similarity of two arbitrary point clouds by calculating the minimal distances between all points from one cloud to those of the other one:

$$\delta \approx \frac{1}{n} \sum_{i=0}^{n-1} \left(\min_{j=0}^{m-1} |q_i - KTp_j|^2 \right) \qquad (4)$$

The influence of outliers (e.g. features existing in the projected feature map cloud but currently not visible in the current camera image and vice versa) is negligible as the worst point distances are ignored. Further, the errors of the final average minimal point distances are calculated by an M-estimator [8] to reduce the effect of false correspondences. Due to performance reasons three different measurement functions are applied.

4.2.1 Precise distance

The precise procedure determines the averaged minimal distances between all m points from cloud A to all n points from cloud B. The $m \cdot n$ distance results are stored and sorted. Afterwards, the two points with minimal distance are selected and both are masked to avoid their usage again. The algorithm then takes the next two unmasked points with the second best distance, masks those points, and so on. The algorithm terminates when no point pairs with two unmasked points are left.

Finally, the minimal k distances are weighted according to a specified M-estimator and summed up providing the final result. The closer the parameter k matches the number of inliers the better the final distance measurement.

4.2.2 Approximated distance

The approximated distance measurement function calculates an approximated result rather than the absolute averaged minimum. The algorithm starts with the first point in cloud A and finds the point in cloud B with minimal distance and masks it. For the next point in cloud A only unmasked points from cloud B are investigated. The iterations stops when all approximated minimal distances have been determined or no unmasked points are left.

Finally, the determined distances need to be sorted. Again the best k results are forwarded to the M-estimator. Therefore, the number of distance calculations and the number of elements to be sorted can be reduced while the measurement results stay acceptable.

4.2.3 Rough distance

The rough distance measurement function finds the minimal distance for each point from cloud A to any point from cloud B without masking them. Therefore, this function has the highest performance but would not prevent that all points from cloud A have the minimal distance to exactly one point in cloud B.

As especially the point clouds of the projected 3D feature points are modified several times during the mapping process, the application of kd-trees would not improve the matching performance. Thus, the performance of the above approach is increased by separating one point cloud into a regular matrix of points with 10×10 elements. Therefore, only points lying in the corresponding matrix element or in one of the corresponding eight-neighborhood are considered as possible candidates.

In the following the error function $err_2(\cdot)$ determining the average error between two 2D point clouds will be a placeholder for one of the three methods introduced above.

4.3 Random Model Variation

Once the projected point cloud best matching to the current camera features is found, the transformation between these two points clouds must be determined, resulting in the initial camera pose. Therefore, we developed a novel approach for real-time retrieval of the transformation between two point clouds holding inaccurate feature positions only. The algorithm iteratively reduces the average minimal error between the two point clouds without having knowledge about any valid or invalid point correspondence. As no correspondences are given, a non-linear optimization [12] cannot be applied at this point.

Let a set of object points $P = \{p_0, p_1, \ldots, p_{m-1}\}$ be transformed into a set of projected image points with same cardinality $\acute{P} = \{\acute{p}_0, \acute{p}_1, \ldots, \acute{p}_{m-1}\}$ by the following notation:

$$
\begin{aligned}
\acute{P} &= KT \cdot P = KT \cdot \{p_0, p_1, \ldots, p_{m-1}\} \\
&= \{KTp_0, KTp_1, \ldots, KTp_{m-1}\} \\
&= \{\acute{p}_0, \acute{p}_1, \ldots, \acute{p}_{m-1}\}
\end{aligned}
\tag{5}
$$

with T and K as in (1). Thus, the average error between a given set of 3D object points $P = \{p_0, p_1, \ldots, p_{m-1}\}$ and a set of 2D image points $Q = \{q_0, q_1, \ldots, q_{n-1}\}$ regarding to a transformation T, a camera matrix K and a control parameter k may be expressed by

$$
err_3(P, Q, T, K, k) = err_2(Q, KT \cdot P, k)
\tag{6}
$$

Further let $\forall \alpha : 0 \le \alpha \le \pi$

$$
R = rand_R(\alpha)
\tag{7}
$$

create a random 3×3 orthonormal and scale free rotation matrix R with maximal rotation angle α so that

$$
v \cdot Rv \ge \cos(\alpha), \quad \forall v \in \mathbb{R}^3 : |v| = 1
\tag{8}
$$

holds. Further, let

$$
t = rand_t(o), \quad o \in \mathbb{R}^3_+
\tag{9}
$$

create a random translation vector $t = (t_x, t_y, t_z)^\top$ with maximal translation offset $o = (o_x, o_y, o_z)^\top$ with $o_x \ge 0$, $o_y \ge 0$, $o_z \ge 0$ so that

$$
|t_x| \le o_x \quad \wedge \quad |t_y| \le o_y \quad \wedge \quad |t_z| \le o_z
\tag{10}
$$

holds. Thus, a random 4×4 homogenous transformation T_r with maximal rotation offset α and maximal translation offset $o \in \mathbb{R}^3_+$ may be created by

$$
T_r = rand_T(\alpha, o) = \left[\begin{array}{c|c} rand_R(\alpha) & rand_t(o) \\ \hline 0 & 1 \end{array} \right]
\tag{11}
$$

Our point cloud fusing algorithm begins with a very rough initial transformation $\hat{T}$ providing an initial error $\hat{\delta}$

$$
\hat{\delta} = err_3(P, Q, \hat{T}, K, k)
\tag{12}
$$

Thus, the task is to find a transformation function T with error δ below or equal to a specified threshold τ:

$$
\delta = err_3(P, Q, T, K, k) \le \tau
\tag{13}
$$

Therefore, within several iterations 4×4 transformations T_j are sought providing a lower error than the iteration before. The sought transformations are concatenated and therefore can be understood as small transformation offsets. With each new iteration the new found transformation must reduce the overall error compared to the previous iterations. The iterative process stops after i iterations when the threshold τ is reached:

$$
\begin{aligned}
\hat{\delta} &= err_3(P, Q, \hat{T}, K, k) \\
&> err_3(P, Q, \hat{T} \cdot T_0, K, k) \\
&> err_3(P, Q, \hat{T} \cdot T_0 \cdot T_1, K, k) \\
&\qquad \cdots \\
&> err_3(P, Q, \hat{T} \cdot T_0 \cdot T_1 \cdots T_{i-1}, K, k) \\
&= err_3(P, Q, T, K, k) = \delta \le \tau
\end{aligned}
\tag{14}
$$

with $T = \hat{T} \cdot T_0 \cdot T_1 \cdots T_{i-1}$.

Let the constants α_{max} and o_{max} define the maximal allowed (and expected) offsets between the initial transformation $\hat{T}$ and the final concatenated transformation T. Further, let α_j and o_j be the maximal ranges a randomized offset transformation may have in the jth-iteration.

Therefore, a transformation offset candidate T_j for the jth-iteration is determined by:

$$
\begin{gathered}
T_j = rand_T(\alpha_j, o_j), \quad \text{for that holds} \\
r(T_0 \cdot T_1 \cdots T_j) \le \alpha_{max} \quad \wedge \quad t(T_0 \cdot T_1 \cdots T_j) \le o_{max}
\end{gathered}
\tag{15}
$$

With $r(\cdot)$ determining the minimal rotation angle of a homogenous transformation T in relation to the identity and $t(\cdot)$ determining the translation part of T.

Afterwards, the candidate T_j is tested according to (14). If T_j produces a larger error a new random candidate T_j' is randomly created and tested. In the case the candidate confirms (14), the current iterations stops and a new iteration begins seeking a new random transformation T_{j+1}. However, for the new iteration the range parameters are updated by:

$$
\alpha_{j+1} = \omega \cdot \alpha_j, \quad o_{j+1} = \omega \cdot o_j, \quad 0 \le \omega \le 1
\tag{16}
$$

The static damping parameter $\omega = 0.95$ successively shrinks the offset of the random transformation candidates with each new valid transformation. Therefore, the algorithm is able to provide a result close to the optimum without determining any feature correspondences. The parameters α_{max} and o_{max} are chosen in relation to the accuracy of the initial transformation and are also used for the initial range values $\alpha_0 = \alpha_{max}$ and $o_0 = o_{max}$.

Finally, when the cloud distance is calculated for a new model, the applied distance function has to be carefully selected. The rough distance function for instance, my not be used from the beginning, as it would allow a model transforming all points from one cloud to exactly one point in the other cloud. However, the closer the fusion of the two point clouds, the more inaccurate the distance measurement

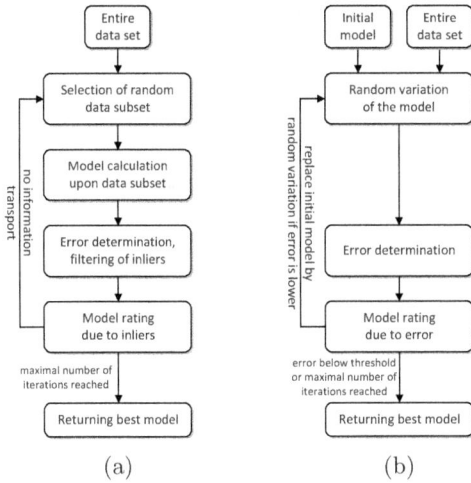

Figure 3: Comparison of the well-known RANSAC (a) and our random model variation approach (b).

Table 1: Definition of individual reliability classes of correspondences regarding to d_{max} and d_{accur}.

Reliability	Property
High	$d_i^a \le d_{accur} \wedge d_i^b > d_{max}$
Medium	$d_i^a \le d_{max} \quad \wedge d_i^b > d_{max}$
Low	$d_i^a \le d_{accur} \wedge d_i^b \le d_{accur},$ with $\frac{d_i^b}{d_i^a} \gg 1$
No	$d_i^a \le d_{accur} \wedge d_i^b \le d_{accur},$ with $\frac{d_i^b}{d_i^a} \approx 1$

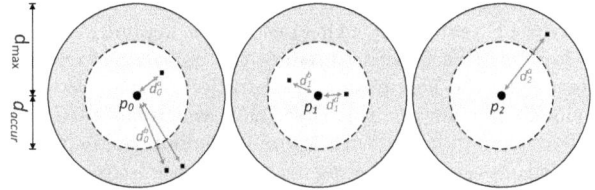

Figure 4: From left to right: Accurate correspondence, ambiguous correspondences, unique but inaccurate correspondence.

method may be. Therefore, once the two clouds match pretty well to each other, the rough method will result in almost the same distance measurement as the precise version while performing several times faster. Finally, if the cloud measurement distance falls below a specified threshold, the point clouds can be expected to coincide. Thus, point correspondences can now be extracted for all points lying close enough together. Only those correspondences are then used to improve the accuracy of the pose further by minimizing the projection error with a non-linear least squares (NLLS) [12] optimization. If the specified distance threshold τ from (13) cannot be reached within a specified time period, both point clouds are considered not to coincide. Thus another point cloud may be tested or finally, the object to be tracked has to considered to be invisible in the current frame.

Test showed that depending on the feature detector used the false positive feature ratio ϕ (see section 6) in the point clouds may be too high (higher than 60%) to allow for the initialization algorithm to succeed. In our tests the SURF detector provided significant better than the FAST feature detector due to the bad scale invariance and lighting robustness properties of FAST. However, this issue can be solved by reducing the image resolution of the tracking frame while applying the cloud distance measurement with a reduced number of expected inliers.

In figure 3 the scheme of the random model variation is depicted and directly compared to the RANSAC algorithm commonly applied for feature tracking.

5. TRACKING

In the following the actual tracking and pose determination algorithm of our approach is introduced.

5.1 Correspondences

Although the random model variation approach provides the camera pose for the current camera frame, its accuracy is not sufficient for AR applications. Therefore, actual feature correspondences have to be determined, allowing for the refinement of the extrinsic camera matrix by an NLLS optimization. Please note, that feature correspondences between object features and image features have to be deter-

mined by geometric constraints only (offsets between camera points and projected map points), as no additional feature information is available. Although a large amount of possible candidates usually can be discarded due to the previous poses, the number of remaining candidates is still large.

Thus, a fast approach is proposed allowing to find geometrical correspondences for a given set of features. The algorithms starts with a set of 3D object features, a set with the current 2D image features, a given extrinsic camera matrix T and an intrinsic camera matrix K. The 3D points $P = \{p_0, p_1, \dots\}$ are projected into the camera image. For each image feature $Q = \{q_0, q_1, \dots\}$ the nearest projected object features are detected and the two nearest ones are stored. The search space for each image point is narrowed by a predefined search radius d_{max}. Only projected object points inside the radius d_{max} are considered. Thus, for each image point $q_i \in Q$ a data structure with a nearest projected distance d_i^a according to an object point $p_a \in P$ and a second nearest distance d_i^b according to $p_b \in P$ is determined.

We apply a simple grid separation of all projected object points. When applied in advance this speeds up the nearest neighbor search significantly, even more than a kd-tree does. Correspondences may be extracted applying individual uniqueness and accuracy criteria using the same data structure. However, an additional threshold radius d_{accur} with $d_{accur} < d_{max}$ is necessary, which is constant for each correspondence search.

In table 1 correspondences are separated into four individual reliability classes according to $q_i, d_i^a, d_i^b, d_{max}$ and d_{accur}. Figure 4 depicts the different types of correspondences. The predefined maximal search radius d_{max} has a significant influence on the final result. A larger radius reduces the number of unique correspondences while a small radius may result in an insufficient amount.

5.2 Tracking with a Rough Pose

If a rough camera pose is known for the current frame the accuracy must be improved to stabilize the pose. First, our approach applies a random model variation as described in subsection 4.3. Thus, compared to an initialization phase without any knowledge, a significantly smaller number of iterations for determining a valid model are required. Afterwards, the extracted feature correspondences are used to refine the pose based on an NLLS optimization with respect to the projection error. The pose determined is then used to find additional feature correspondences by applying the rating mechanism as described in subsection 5.1.

In a first iteration, correspondences retrieved must have a high reliability, while d_{accur} is chosen to be slightly smaller than d_{max}. The (typically) larger set of correspondences is then used to find a more precise pose by applying another NLLS refinement. An M-estimator applying the Huber loss function is used to reduce the influence of outliers. Afterwards, the new pose is used to find even more correspondences. However, this time the search area is reduced, while correspondences with low and medium reliability are included. Several alternating correspondence search and refinement steps are applied until a suitable number of accurate correspondences has been found to allow for the calculation of the final (accurate) pose.

5.3 Frame to Frame Tracking

The descriptor-less tracker can apply all performance benefits if an accurate pose and the applied feature correspondences defining this pose are known from the previous frame. Randomly, features are selected in the current frame which can be expected to be the new positions of the old correspondences. The accuracy of the newly selected correspondences is immediately approved or new correspondences are selected. A linear motion model is applied predicting the new pose for the current frame [5]. The randomized tracker supports two kinds of frame to frame tracking which are introduced in the next two subsections.

5.3.1 Tracking with Strong Correspondences

Strong correspondences in the previous frame have a small confusion probability allowing to reliably recovering them in the current frame. Correspondences are considered to be strong only, if their projection error between feature map points and image points is small. Additionally, the direct neighborhood of the image feature point should provide no further features. Therefore, it can be expected that in the following camera frame these features can be detected again while having an almost empty neighborhood. Two individual classes of strong features are defined. Class A holds features with medium and high reliability having high strength values, low projection errors and large empty neighborhoods. Class B stores correspondences with medium reliability having weakened thresholds. First, correspondences from class A are used in the subsequent camera frame. Only, if no valid pose can be determined, correspondences from class B are taken into account as well. The class separation improves the performance and the accuracy significantly. Further, whenever a strong feature map point is used for pose calculation, an internal counter is increased. This counter allows for an individual error weighting during NLLS iterations. Thus, features used frequently, which already proved to be stable and to be easily detectable have a higher influence to the final pose than features used occasionally. Several combinations of robust NLLS improvements of the extrinsic camera matrix are followed by search iterations for further correspondences to end up with a final and accurate pose.

5.3.2 Tracking with Arbitrary Correspondences

Sometimes the number of strong and reliable feature correspondences found is not sufficient to determine a new pose. Thus, also previous correspondences with a low reliability have to be investigated to determine the pose for the new frame. Therefore, the search mechanism as described in subsection 5.1 is used to find weak correspondence candidates between the two point clouds. However, this time more than two candidates are stored for each feature. Afterwards, RANSAC (indeed the solely application in our approach) randomly selects one point candidate of each correspondence and tries to calculate a new pose for the subset by applying an NLLS refinement in combination with a Huber driven M-estimator. After several RANSAC iterations the best matching model is forwarded to the next refinement step, if a sufficient number of correspondences can be reliably recovered.

6. QUANTITATIVE EVALUATION

In this section we provide a quantitative evaluation of the reliability and the accuracy of our tracker. Therefore, artificial ground-truth data has been generated to allow for precise and repeatable measurements. A bitmap of the graffiti image as depicted in figure 8a) has been used for the creation of a planar and a volumetric 3D feature map. The FAST detector is applied to detect feature map points. We also did a ground-truth evaluation using SURF feature points and Harris corners. However, the results did not differ significantly from those using the FAST detector.

The planar feature map is determined by assigning the z coordinate of all feature map points to zero. The volumetric map is created by randomly moving the z coordinates of the individual planar feature map points perpendicular to the xy plane within a range of +/- 50% of the diagonal map size. For the evaluation the strongest 600 feature map points and 400 camera feature points are used. During the initialization a subset of the two point sets is used only: 120 feature map points and 80 camera feature points. The ground-truth data is created by a virtual camera with a resolution of 640×480 pixels and a $60°$ horizontal field of view for projecting the 3D feature map points into the virtual camera plane. Further, to create realistic ground-truth data each virtually created camera feature point is white noised by a Gaussian distribution with $\sigma = 1$ pixel. Finally, we simulate false positive camera features by replacing a certain amount ϕ of virtually projected feature map points in the camera plane by random feature points.

We measure the reliability and the accuracy by executing the initialization process (section 4) followed by an NLLS pose refinements (subsection 5.1). Therefore a very rough initial pose of the virtual camera is created randomly. The random translation error is within a range of +/- 30% of the diagonal of the feature map size. The random rotation error is within a range of +/- 20°. However, the randomly created rough camera pose is used as test pose only, if more than 75% of the virtual feature map points are visible in the feature map. We created 500 test poses and averaged the measurements. As described in subsection 4.2.1 the individual cloud distance functions determines the distance for the nearest k point pairs only. In the following the ratio between k and the entire number of virtual camera feature points is

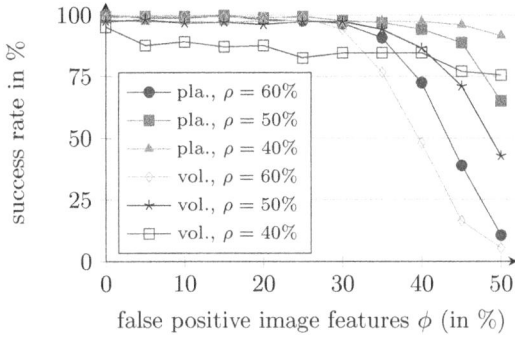

Figure 5: Overall success rate.

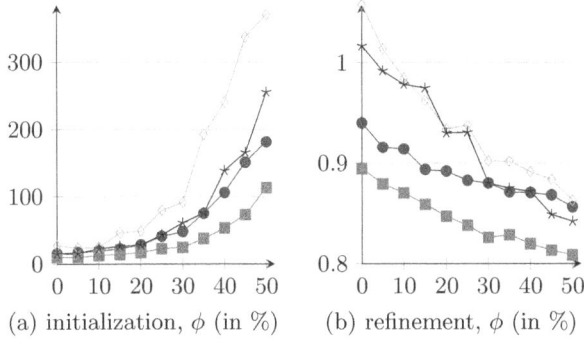

(a) initialization, ϕ (in %)   (b) refinement, ϕ (in %)

Figure 6: Performance in ms. Description see fig. 5.

denoted by ρ. Thus, a $\rho = 60\%$ expects that 40% of the camera points are false positive features.

In figure 5 the success rate regarding the number of false positive camera features is depicted for a planar and volumetric feature map. One tracking iteration succeeds if a) the initialization step (section 4) determines a transformation fusing both point clouds with an average pixel error of $\sqrt{2}$ wrt. ρ; and b) a following refinement step (subsection 5.1) provides enough reliable correspondences with sufficiently small projection errors. Figure 6 shows the performance values for the initialization step and the refinement step (subsequently after the initialization) on a i7 2.13GHz CPU. Figure 7a) shows the maximal angular error between the final (initialized and refined) pose and the exact test pose. Further the relative translation error (in relation to the diagonal of the feature map dimension) is depicted in figure (7b). An translation error of 0.5% equals an absolute error of approximately 1.5 millimeter for an object to be tracked at the size of a DIN A4 page (with Gaussian distributed noise with $\sigma = 1$ pixel).

The evaluation shows that the tracker is able to handle individual ratios of false positive feature points depending on the estimated camera feature reliability ρ. Thus, the higher ρ, the higher the success rate of the tracker. However, as depicted in figure 7 the higher the success rate of the tracker, the lower the final pose accuracy for the planar feature map.

Further, the graph shows that the random model variation approach is able to track volumetric 3D objects, even with a higher accuracy compared to simple planar tracking objcts.

7. PERFORMANCE ISSUES

In the following subsections performance results of our ap-

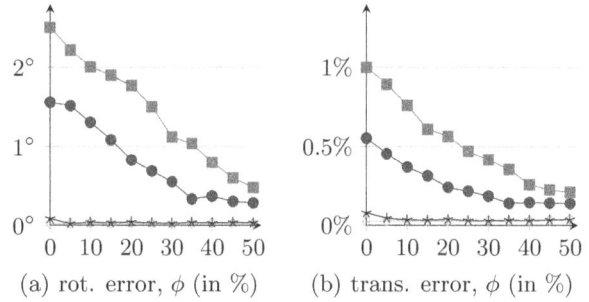

(a) rot. error, ϕ (in %)   (b) trans. error, ϕ (in %)

Figure 7: Pose accuracy. Description see fig. 5.

(a)   (b)   (c)   (d)

Figure 8: Four applied tracking objects.

proach are provided. The entire code has been implemented in C++ and is applied on desktop and mobile devices without any modification.

7.1 Initialization

To evaluate the initialization performance and success rate we deactivated all tracking routines using information from previous frames. Thus, the tracker has to re-initialize in each new frame to determine the final pose. Four different tracking patterns with individual characteristics have been used as tracking objects (see figure 8). Therefore, digital bitmaps of the tracking objects have been applied to create a static feature map in a pre-processing step. A free hand webcam has been used showing almost the entire tracking object in each camera frame. Extreme camera movements have been applied to observe the tracking object from the entire surrounding with varying orientations. The measurements have been done on a sequence of 1000 frames. In each frame 120 Harris corners features from the feature map and 80 corners in the camera frame with resolution 640×480 have been used. Table 2 shows the success rate and the average performance measured on a laptop Intel i7 Nehalem Core with 2.13GHz running Windows 7. The success rate is the ratio between the number of video frames for which a valid and accurate pose could be determined and the total number of video frames. Thus, in average, initialization has a success rate of almost 90% and terminates within 50ms. However, (re-)initialization is rarely used and has less influence on the overall tracking performance.

7.2 Tracking on Laptop Computers

The overall performance of the randomized tracker has been evaluated for two individual camera movements. In the

Table 2: Averaged initialization performances.

Tracking object	Success rate	Performance
Graffiti (figure 8a)	90.6%	23.6ms
Cars (figure 8b)	89.8%	44.9ms
Satellite (figure 8c)	91.5%	41.3ms
Street map (figure 8d)	87.1%	46.8ms

Table 3: Averaged performance on a Laptop.

	1st sequence	2nd sequence
Initialization	42.1ms	15.7ms
Failing frames	0%	2.8%
Gray scale image	0.31ms	0.32ms
Feature detection	1.59ms	1.59ms
Feature tracking and pose determination	1.41ms	1.47ms
Overall process	3.31ms	3.37ms

Table 4: Averaged performance on a smartphone.

	FAST	SURF
Samsung Galaxy S2		
Feature detection	7.44ms	16.75ms
Feature tracking and pose determination	10.16ms	8.43ms
Overall process	17.60ms	25.18ms
Samsung Galaxy S1		
Feature detection	15.64ms	54.58ms
Feature tracking and pose determination	27.34ms	23.64ms
Overall process	42.98ms	78.22ms

first test sequence the camera was smoothly moved without strong velocity changes. The camera movement complies with the behavior of a user in a standard AR application. The second evaluation sequence applied rough camera movements and strong velocity changes not typical for AR. Table 3 shows the performance measurements for an image sequence of 1000 frames captured with a live camera at 30Hz using a resolution of 640×480. 600 FAST features are stored in the already known feature map and 400 features are detected in each camera frame. Not considering the time required for image conversion, tracking requires about 3ms.

7.3 Tracking on Smartphones

Further, the performance for smartphone devices has been evaluated. Table 4 provides the performance figures applying FAST respectively SURF feature points. A Samsung Galaxy S2 (1.2GHz) and a Galaxy S1 (1.0GHz) were used for performance measurements. Tracking is based on 400 feature map points and 200 live camera image points. The entire sequence consisted of 1000 test frames, using a camera resolution of 320×240. For both detectors the initialization succeeded within three frames. Each initialization procedure required about 60ms per frame. Obviously, the detection of FAST features perform significantly faster than the detection of SURF feature points. However, when using the SURF detector, the tracking and pose calculations are significantly faster. While additional time is required to find the more robust SURF features, even more time during the following tracking iterations is saved. Grayscale image conversion is not required here as the YVU format of the image already provides direct access to the grayscale information.

8. CONCLUSION

In this paper we presented our approach on universal randomized feature tracking. We showed that our approach allows for real-time tracking even on mobile devices. This is achieved by avoiding the computation of additional feature descriptors or similar types of information. Further, we re-use existing information from previous frames as far

as possible resulting in a staggered approach. For initialization, the distance of two point clouds are estimated, the underlying model is randomly modified, and the distance for the model is evaluated, finally resulting in a rough initial pose. Afterwards, the initial pose is used to find unique feature correspondences allowing to calculate a precise camera pose. Frame to frame tracking is realized by a similar approach, performing significantly faster due to the knowledge of the previous pose.

As we showed, our approach provides real-time performance as well as a very stable pose estimation (see also accompanying video). Current limitations are in particular regarding the initialization distance and the extent to which the object to be tracked has to be visible. A further restriction is the limited suitability for regular patterns. In our future work we will make up for tests with volumetric (not planar) 3D feature maps. Further we will investigate into extending the approach to allow for map creation in a SLAM like manner.

9. REFERENCES

[1] O. Chum and J. Matas. Matching with prosac - progressive sample consensus. In *Proc. of CVPR'05 - Volume 1 - Volume 01*, pages 220–226, 2005.

[2] P. David, D. Dementhon, R. Duraiswami, and H. Samet. Softposit: Simultaneous pose and correspondence determination. *Int. J. Comput. Vision*, 59(3):259–284, Sept. 2004.

[3] I. Gordon and D. G. Lowe. What and where: 3d object recognition with accurate pose. In *Toward Category-Level Object Recognition*, pages 67–82, 2006.

[4] J. Herling and W. Broll. An adaptive training-free feature tracker for mobile phones. In *Proc. of VRST'10*, pages 35–42, New York, 2010. ACM.

[5] G. Klein and D. Murray. Parallel tracking and mapping for small ar workspaces. In *Proc. of ISMAR '07*, pages 1–10, Washington, DC, USA, 2007.

[6] G. Klein and D. Murray. Parallel tracking and mapping on a camera phone. In *Proc. of ISMAR '09*, pages 83–86, Washington, DC, USA, 2009.

[7] F. Moreno-Noguer, V. Lepetit, and P. Fua. Pose priors for simultaneously solving alignment and correspondence. In *Proc. of ECCV '08*, 2008.

[8] W. H. Press, S. A. Teukolsky, W. T. Vetterling, and B. P. Flannery. *Numerical Recipes 3rd Edition: The Art of Scientific Computing*. Cambridge, 2007.

[9] A. L. Rodríguez, P. E. López-De-Teruel, and A. Ruiz. Real-time descriptorless feature tracking. In *Proc. of ICIAP '09*, pages 853–862. Springer-Verlag, 2009.

[10] J. Sanchez-R., J. Östlund, P. Fua, and F. Moreno-N. Simultaneous pose, correspondence and non-rigid shape. In *Proc. of CVPR*, pages 1189–1196, 2010.

[11] E. Serradell, M. Özuysal, V. Lepetit, P. Fua, and F. Moreno-Noguer. Combining geometric and appearance priors for robust homography estimation. In *Proc. of ECCV'10*, pages 58–72, 2010.

[12] R. Szeliski. *Computer Vision: Algorithms and Applications*. Springer, 2010.

[13] D. Wagner, G. Reitmayr, A. Mulloni, T. Drummond, and D. Schmalstieg. Pose tracking from natural features on mobile phones. In *Proc. of ISMAR '08*, pages 125–134, Washington, DC, USA, 2008.

Static Pose Reconstruction with an Instrumented Bouldering Wall

Rami Aladdin
Computer Graphics and Animation Lab, School
of Computer Science, McGill University
rami.aladdin@mail.mcgill.ca

Paul G. Kry
Computer Graphics and Animation Lab, School
of Computer Science, McGill University
kry@cs.mcgill.ca

ABSTRACT

This paper describes the design and construction of an instrumented bouldering wall, and a technique for estimating poses by optimizing an objective function involving contact forces. We describe the design and calibration of the wall, which can capture the contact forces and torques during climbing while motion capture (MoCap) records the climber pose, and present a solution for identifying static poses for a given set of holds and forces. We show results of our calibration process and static poses estimated for different measured forces. To estimate poses from forces, we use optimization and start with an inexpensive objective to guide the solver toward the optimal solution. When good candidates are encountered, the full objective function is evaluated with a physics-based simulation to determine physical plausibility while meeting additional constraints. Comparison between our reconstructed poses and MoCap show that our objective function is a good model for human posture.

Categories and Subject Descriptors

I.3.7 [**Computer Graphics**]: Three-Dimensional Graphics and Realism—*Virtual reality*

Keywords

Motion Capture; Force Capture; Physics-Based Simulation; Optimization

1. INTRODUCTION

Producing physically plausible computer animation of virtual humans is difficult because of the complexity and subtleties of how real humans control posture and motion. While it is easy to write down the equations of motion for an articulated character, it is difficult to model how this character should move or what constitutes a natural pose. One way to deal with this is to devise an optimization problem and design a set of terms for the objective function based on reasonable assumptions and approximations, such as terms

that minimize metabolic energy, that keep the head level, or that guide the center of mass (COM) to a location above the feet. Another way to generate plausible postures for virtual humans is to simply use MoCap and record the poses of a real person. MoCap can be challenging to modify, however, and we must ultimately come up with a computational model that lets us edit the motion for new purposes.

In this paper, we build on the idea of bringing together physics, optimization, and MoCap, which is a popular approach in research on virtual humans. However, we also recognize that MoCap alone is only part of the picture, and that contact forces are critical for building up a clear understanding of how posture and motion are produced: contact forces let us resolve the ambiguity in determining the torques applied at different joints. Contacts and contact forces are often critical, whether in the context of standing balance, object manipulation, or during climbing. We see climbing motion and posture as an interesting example to focus on because it combines locomotion and object manipulation, where the object being manipulated is the body as a whole.

With our desire to study posture and movement of humans in interaction with their surroundings, and the goal of developing improved virtual humans, we have designed an instrumented climbing wall that allows forces and torques to be measured at the holds. In this investigation, we focus on static and slow moving, near-static postures in order to simplify the problem. While we can capture both motion and contact forces simultaneously, another goal of this work is to have a method for reconstructing the posture of a climber from the force capture alone. We use optimization to find a pose that meets the contact constraints while being valid for the measured forces and minimizing additional plausibility requirements, such as wall contact, joint limits, and facing direction. The objective function is quite complex, and uses a physics-based simulation as a black box for its evaluation. We use Covariance Matrix Adaptation Evolution Strategy (CMA-ES) to compute the solution as it alleviates the need for a derivative in the objective function. We accelerate the optimization process with a simple objective function that guides the hips of the character to a location predicted from the forces by a linear regression. This helps bring our optimization to the neighborhood of the optimal solution quickly, and reduces the number of computationally expensive evaluations of our full objective function. Our posture optimization method is beneficial because MoCap of climbing can be challenging due to occlusions, and we can instead produce posture estimates for a climb without requiring the capture subject to wear a MoCap suit.

Our three main contributions are: an instrumented climbing wall design, a calibration process for this wall, and a new optimization-based method for estimating posture from contact forces. Our climbing wall design permits forces and torques to be measured at the holds, and allows a variety of different experiments to be conducted. The pitch of the wall is adjustable, and hold positions are easily reconfigurable in pockets of the torsion box. Also, the wall is easily disassembled for transport or long term storage. The calibration process for force sensors mounted in arbitrary locations is presented, in addition to a convenient calibration based on known mounting locations. Finally, our estimates of posture from recorded forces combine physics, capture, and optimization to produce plausible poses which we validate with ground truth MoCap measurements.

2. RELATED WORK

We first review related work in biomechanics involving climbing and the use of instrumented climbing holds. Then, we focus on the field of animation, on works that combine motion and forces, and on works revolving around the use of optimization for physics-based simulations.

Climbing has been studied by various research groups in the field of biomechanics using instrumented holds. Rougier et al. [15] describe the first instrumented wall designed to measure the amplitude of forces at the holds in 1991. Testa et al. [17] use 3-Degrees of Freedom (3DoF) sensors. Quaine et al. [12] use two video cameras to record two 2-D views of the climber while recording forces on 3DoF transducers to include postural information. A more recent instrumented bouldering wall design is described by Fuss et al. [4], where eight holds are equipped with 6DoF sensors. Works using these setups mainly focus on analyzing the performance of a climb and the climbers' level of expertise [4, 3, 15, 16], and on studying the effects of specific posture changes or constraints on forces at the holds [13, 12, 17]. Our setup is different in that it incorporates MoCap to offer full 3D reconstruction of forces, torques and posture synchronized in time and space. The objective of our approach is also different as we are looking at the amount of information contained in forces to explain a pose.

Pfeil et al. [11] provide a tool for quickly designing and testing different hold configurations on a virtual climbing wall. While the tool provides a good means of visualizing possible routes, our approach differs as it relies on a physically simulated model of the climber.

A wide range of contributions to capture and synthesis of posture or force data is found in computer animation. Similarly to Brubaker et al. [1], who look at the converse problem of estimating forces acting on the system from given motion, we use a simulated character to model the subject and constraints. Rosenhahn et al. [14] also use simulation to enforce constraints found through analytics in MoCap of special interactions.

MoCap and force sensing is used by Kry et al. [9] to capture interactions, focusing on hands and grasping. Joint compliance is estimated from small time windows just before and after contacts, and used along with the reference trajectory to synthesize new interactions. While it would be interesting to look at how this method could be applied to climbing to synthesize new postures with different wall configurations, the focus of our research is to look at the relationship between static poses and forces at the holds.

Closer to our work, Yin et al. [18] and Kry et al. [8] look at how full body poses and grasp configurations can be estimated using force measurements from respectively a foot-ground pressure sensor pad and a graspable device. These approaches use a database consisting of pairs of MoCap and force data to find the pose for the closest set of measured forces. We, on the other hand, learn reduced features from recorded data and use a physics-based approach to find a pose that best explains the forces.

A similar approach is used by Ha et al. [5] to reconstruct human motion from consumer-grade force sensors, and while they also use a form of MoCap to obtain hand positions, one can argue that because of the constrained nature of climbing, end effector positions are given by the holds whereas only feet locations can be obtained in the case of standing on a platform. A fundamental difference is that our work focuses on statics and looks at how climbing-specific constraints can drive the reconstruction through the optimization of an objective function that we introduce as a means of characterizing static poses.

Another body of relevant research in animation concerns the use of optimization for physics-based simulations. de Lasa et al. [2] describe a means of expressing locomotion using a small number of features. Jain et al. [7] also look at constrained optimization for virtual characters to design controllers by formulating high-level objectives, and use those constraints to generate, among other controllers, a climbing controller. Using CMA-ES [6] with simple penalties around the main objective is also a method we share with Nunes et al. [10]. However, these authors look at generating plausible motion through the optimization of selected objectives, while we are interested in optimizing the physical quality of a static pose reconstruction for a set of forces.

3. WALL DESIGN

The instrumented bouldering wall's main structure is an 8'×8' torsion box. The wall doesn't need to be fixed to a second supporting wall as four additional beams offer support for the box and climber's weight. This configuration allows for easy movement of the wall and offers control over the desired tilt of the climbing path, as shown in Figure 1.

Each climbing hold is mounted onto a front plate, in turn attached to a 6-axis force torque sensor. The sensor is fixed to a back plate that is mounted on the wall. The hold, front plate, sensor and back plate form a "sensor sandwich" shown in Figure 3a. The torsion box design will ultimately allow us to hide sensors and wires inside and behind the pockets, leaving sensitive material out of harm's way and giving the climber the same freedom they would have on a regular wall.

The sensor sandwiches can be inserted into each pocket in four different orientations, providing good freedom for designing climbing routes. The design also makes reconfiguration easy. Moving a hold or changing its shape can be done by respectively unscrewing the sensor from one of the 144 possible positions, or unscrewing the hold from the sensor.

The sensors are multi-component transducers with 6 channels for linear and angular forces expressed in a local coordinate frame. Each sensor is connected to a 6-channel strain gage amplifier with adjustable excitation voltage and gain. Sensors can therefore easily be calibrated for maximum sensitivity depending on the climber's weight, or, in the case of dynamic motions, the planned motion. The sensors are

Figure 1: The instrumented bouldering wall.

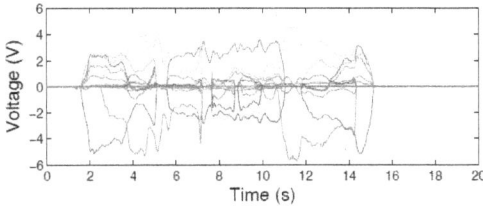

Figure 2: Voltages recorded for an example session.

sensitive enough to capture small tremors of muscle fatigue, as well as contact forces as light as 0.05 N.

The calibration matrices to convert raw voltage data to wrenches are close to diagonal and real-time visualization is enough to evaluate excitation voltage and gain choices for sensor sensitivity, as shown in Figure 2.

4. CALIBRATION AND CAPTURE

The main challenge in capturing data from both the Mo-Cap and force sensing equipment is to find the relationship between the two independently recorded data sets, both in time and space. In this section, we describe the calibration process, present the major steps involved in capturing synchronized data, and show a sample visualization.

4.1 Calibration

Each sensor possesses its own local frame in which the force measurements are expressed as voltages, while skeleton reconstruction is expressed in the MoCap world frame. Below, we describe two techniques for calibrating the position and orientation of the sensors, which allow the force and torque measurements to be expressed in the MoCap world reference frame. We also describe a simple technique for synchronizing the two data sets in time.

4.1.1 Converting the raw data to forces

As shown in Figure 2, sensors provide voltages for each of the 6 channels. Using the inverse sensitivity matrices that are provided with each sensor, we compute the forces and torques from these voltages while taking into consideration possible cross-talk. The forces and torques are given by

$$F = SV, \qquad (1)$$

where F is the vector containing the forces and torques, S the inverse cross-talk sensitivity matrix for the sensor and

V the vector containing normalized voltages for the corresponding channels. Normalized voltages for a channel are found by dividing measured values by the appropriate gain and excitation voltage, which are configured on the amplifier boards for each individual channel, for each sensor.

4.1.2 Optimization-based space calibration

In order to visualize the force and motion data and to be able to relate the different coordinate frames in which the different measurements are made, we need to find the appropriate transforms. Our goal is to find the transform

$$^w_s E = \begin{bmatrix} ^w_s R & ^w p_s \\ \mathbf{0} & 1 \end{bmatrix} \qquad (2)$$

that converts coordinates expressed in the local frame of the sensor to coordinates in the world MoCap frame. Here s denotes the sensor frame, w the world frame, $^w p_s$ the origin of the sensor frame in world coordinates, and $^w_s R$ is the rotation matrix that aligns the axis in the sensor frame with the corresponding axis in the world frame. In order to find $^w p_s$ and $^w_s R$, we look at the influences of force and contact location on sensor measurements. We will show how precise contact locations are found, and how these positions are used along with recorded forces to compute the sensor frames.

To obtain contact locations, a calibration tool consisting of a rigid body with a sharp tip is tracked with MoCap as it is rotated around the contact point, as shown in Figure 3b. For a recorded set of orientations of our rigid body, the contact point is found using a least-squares approach by finding the pair $(^b p_c, {}^w p_c)$ that minimizes

$$\sum_{j=1}^{n} \left\| {}^w_b E_j \; {}^b p_c - {}^w p_c \right\|^2, \qquad (3)$$

where b is the body frame, n the number of collected samples, $^w p_c$ is the position of the contact point in world coordinates, and $^w_b E_j$ is the calibration tool coordinate frame for sample j in the recorded MoCap trajectory. In other words, we are looking for the point p_c that is invariant for $^w_b E$ over the data. That is the point that best describes a center of rotation for all individual frames, which is the location of the contact between the tip and surface. Using the position of the tip in body coordinates, we can thereafter find any contact location in world coordinates from the captured calibration tool frame.

We can now look at how a set of linear forces (with no torque) applied at different contact points are measured by the sensor. More specifically, and assuming that the contact coordinate frame is aligned with the world coordinate frame, the measured torque can be expressed as

$$^c\tau = {}^w_s R \; {}^s\tau + ({}^w p_s - {}^w p_c) \times {}^w_s R \; {}^s f, \qquad (4)$$

where $^c\tau$ is the torque in the contact frame, and $^s f$ and $^s\tau$ are respectively the forces and torques in the sensor frame. Since we are not applying a torque at the contact point, $^c\tau = 0$. Thus, finding the origin and orientation of the sensor's local frame given a wide variety of contacts and associated measured forces becomes an optimization problem where we are trying to find the pair $(^w_s R, {}^w p_s)$ that minimizes

$$\sum_{i=1}^{k} \sum_{j=1}^{m} \left\| {}^w_s R \; {}^s\tau_{ij} + ({}^w p_s - {}^w p_{ci}) \times {}^w_s R \; {}^s f_{ij} \right\|^2, \qquad (5)$$

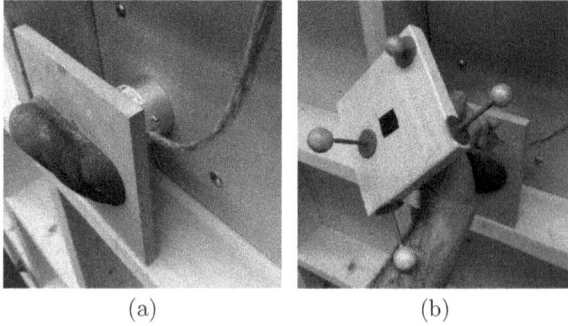

(a)   (b)

Figure 3: Close-up on a "sensor sandwich" (a) and the calibration tool in action (b).

where k is the number of contacts and m is the number of recorded force samples per contact. Put simply, we are looking for the sensor frame that can best explain force and torque measurements for every given contact point. We find $^w p_c$ using the calibration tool and MoCap, and $^s \tau$ and $^s f$ are given by the sensors. In order to perform this calibration, we then need a wide set of forces applied at various contact points to ensure that the problem is not under-constrained.

We use MoCap to track the calibration tool while applying linear forces at a contact point, with the sensors recording forces and torques. For a set of contact points, and the forces and torques recorded during the contact, we use Equation 5 to solve for $^w_s R$ and $^w p_s$. The equation is nonlinear due to rotations, and once linearized (as we describe later), it is quartic. For that reason, we use an iterative and alternating least squares approach. We set $^w_s R$ and $^w p_s$ to initial approximations and then solve for one of the unknowns while fixing the other. Then, we alternate and repeat until we converge to an acceptable error. In practice, three different contact points are enough to find good solutions.

With $^w_s R$ fixed, $^w p_s$ can be easily computed as the least squares solution of Equation 5. Solving for the best rotation is trickier. We choose to solve for a small change in rotation R such that our estimate at iteration $l + 1$ is updated from the estimate at iteration l using

$$^w_s R_{l+1} = {}^w_s R_l \ R \ . \qquad (6)$$

We parameterize R in exponential coordinates, $R = \exp([\omega])$, where $[\omega]$ is the skew symmetric matrix that performs the cross product operation $\omega \times$, and we linearize the rotation with a first order approximation of the exponential,

$$^w_s R_{l+1} \approx {}^w_s R_l \ (I + [\omega]). \qquad (7)$$

When solving for $^w_s R$ with a fixed $^w p_s$, we consequently solve for ω that minimizes Equation 5, where $^w_s R$ becomes $^w_s R_l (I + [\omega])$ and $^w_s R_l$ is the most recent estimate. With the least squares solution ω, we use Equation 6 to update the estimate for $^w_s R$ using the exponential map $R = \exp([\omega])$ computed with Rodrigues' formula. To limit the error induced by the linearization, we bound the norm of ω so that the update is no more than 0.1 radians.

In sum, the calibration process consists of calibrating the calibration tool to have accurate contact positions, recording motion and forces as the tool is used to apply linear forces at different contact locations rigidly attached to the sensor and computing a least-squares estimate for the frame using an iterative method and first-order approximation.

4.1.3 Pocket-based space calibration

Although time consuming as it requires several MoCap and force recordings for each sensor to be calibrated, the last approach is accurate and indispensable when sensors are not in specific locations. In cases where sensors are attached in pockets in known orientations, a speedier calibration method is to place markers on known locations on the wall and define a wall coordinate frame in which a sensor position and orientation can be expressed. The origin of each sensor frame can be computed from its location in a given corner of the pocket where it is mounted, while the orientation can be set to a combination of 90-degree rotations about the axis of the wall frame. The positions and orientations are then easily expressed in the world frame using the position of the wall, determined by the markers attached to it and MoCap.

4.1.4 Measurement synchronization

Since our equipment does not easily permit a synchronous recording of motion and forces, an extra step of measurement synchronization is needed. Similarly to what is done to synchronize sound and video in cinema, we hit one of the sensors with an object tracked with MoCap. The post-processing step consists of finding the frame with a sharp peak at the beginning of the raw voltage data visualization, and the frame where the tracked body used for synchronization has its momentum change in the MoCap data. For simplicity, we capture forces and motion at the same rate, even though forces can be sampled at a much higher frequency.

4.2 Capture

As in any system involving MoCap, one of the main challenges when it comes to collecting quality data is camera placement to avoid occlusion. When capturing a climber, the front is mostly occluded as the body is facing the wall. For that reason, most markers on the subject are placed carefully to face away from the wall during a climbing session. Sometimes marker positions are only chosen after several trials, especially when recording new dynamic motions. Our MoCap setup consists of 24 cameras, 6 of which have wide-angle lenses; these are placed close to the wall, above and on each side and are critical because they cover all the regions occluded from the other cameras.

For the force sensors, the only concern is to choose gain and excitation parameters that will allow for high sensitivity while preventing sensor overload. This is also done by trial and error but is far less time consuming. Typically, more torque is exerted by hands as the holds need to allow for grasping and tend to protrude more, as shown in Figure 3a.

The pre-processing to perform a successful capture session consists of calibrating the cameras to avoid occlusions, finding the origins and orientations of the sensor frames using one of the two space calibration methods, and carefully choosing marker positions and sensor sensitivities to have quality data. During the capture session, the subject uses a rigid object to hit sensors prior to climbing and performs the desired task. The post-processing consists of using the hit to synchronize the two data streams in time, using the calibration matrices to convert the recorded voltages to force measurements, and using the estimated sensor frames to express the measured forces in the MoCap world frame. Figure 4 depicts the results of a successful capture, where squares represent the sensors, and red and green arrows represent forces and torques measured by each sensor.

(a)   (b)

Figure 4: Climber during a trial (a) and visualization (b).

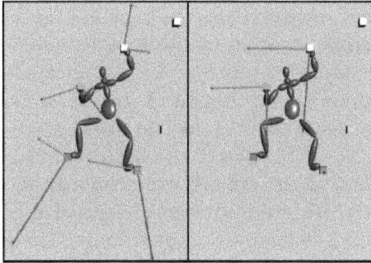

Figure 5: Subject generating a range of arbitrary forces at the sensors while maintaining the same pose.

5. RECONSTRUCTION OF STATIC POSES

In order to look at the relationship between motion and forces, several capture trials with male and female participants of various skill levels were recorded. Finding a relationship between measured forces and observed pose is difficult, and we distinguish between two forms of ambiguity: similar poses can generate different forces, as shown in Figure 5, and similar forces can be generated by different poses. To limit ambiguity, we restrict our focus to simpler problems where data consists of static poses and quasi-static transitions. To ensure as little dynamic movements as possible, participants were asked to move slowly while performing natural and controlled movements.

5.1 Statistical analysis

We took a preliminary look at the data to see how much of the posture and force spaces was exploited by various climbers. We investigated the correspondence between forces and static poses by performing linear regression and canonical correlation analysis. In static or quasi-static poses, the forces offer a lot of information on the location of the COM: without momentum, forces at the holds are highly dependent on the distribution of the climber's weight, as shown in Figure 6. For simplicity, and because we do not know the exact mass of the different links, the position of the COM is approximated by the root of the skeleton (the hips). The location of the root can be predicted using linear regression with a maximum error around 10 cm. However, the models failed to predict entire poses from forces. A likely explanation is strong non-linearities in the correlation due to joint angles. A principal component analysis of the two data sets reveals that only a few components are necessary to capture most of the variation in the data in both cases, as shown in

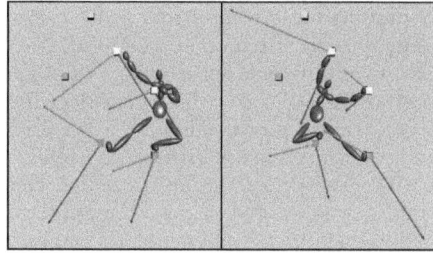

Figure 6: Correlation between forces at the sensors and COM position for static poses.

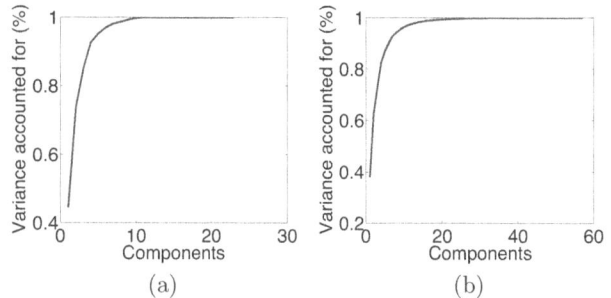

(a)   (b)

Figure 7: Variance explained against number of components for (a) forces and torques and (b) MoCap joint angles.

Figure 7. The lower dimensionality of both data sets can be explained by the highly constrained nature of the problem.

5.2 Physical simulation and CMA-ES

In order to take advantage of these constraints and to account for physical plausibility, we use a physics-based simulation. Specifically, hands and feet are constrained to locations given by the four sensors at which forces are non-zero, the climber must face the wall, he cannot penetrate it, and has joint angle limits. The virtual character used to simulate the climber has its dimensions defined by the captured climber (stored in the Biovision Hierarchy format). The skeleton is a set of rigid bodies attached using different types of joints. Joints are also used to constrain hands and feet to proper hold locations, determined by assuming the climber is facing the wall, is upright and is exerting force on the holds. Joint angle limits and weight distribution are chosen to match that of the climber, while contacts with the simulated wall prevent unnatural poses. The simulation is built using the Open Dynamics Engine (ODE).

We want to find a pose that best explains an arbitrary function – which we define in Sections 5.3 and 5.4 – of forces at the holds. Treating this as an optimization, we want the pose that minimizes our objective while taking into account the hard constraints enforced by the simulation. In other words, we are looking for the set of joint angles

$$\underset{\phi' \in \Phi^*}{\operatorname{argmin}} f(\phi', F_S), \qquad (8)$$

where Φ^* is the manifold of joint angles that describe poses respecting the constraints, f is the objective function, and F_S is the measured set of forces. We choose CMA-ES, which uses sample fitness to update the sampling distribution, because we evaluate our objective functions via simulation.

181

CMA-ES produces sets of arbitrary joint angles ϕ using a multi-variate normal distribution, and we devise a projection step $\Gamma(\phi)$ to find, for a given arbitrary set of joint angles ϕ, the closest set of angles $\phi' = \Gamma(\phi)$ that describes a valid pose on the constrained pose manifold Φ^*. This projection is achieved using a proportional-derivative controller, by starting with a valid pose (from MoCap data) and treating the produced angles ϕ as desired angles. We apply torques at each joint individually to try and match the angles produced by CMA-ES, using differences in orientations, as well as stiffness and damping parameters that offer a trade-off between speed and stability. After a small amount of time, the simulation stabilizes into a new pose with joint angles ϕ' that is treated as the projection of the pose described by angles ϕ onto the constraint manifold. The fitness of the original sample ϕ is computed using the projected pose given by ϕ'.

5.3 Physical Plausibility as an Objective

In order to find the pose that best explains forces at the holds, our objective function evaluates the fitness of a sample ϕ by computing the physical plausibility of the pose given by $\phi' = \Gamma(\phi)$, with the additional physical constraints that the pose is static and generates the contact forces measured by the sensors. The plausibility is computed as

$$\rho(\phi', F_S) = \|\tau_r\|^2 \qquad (9)$$

where τ_r is the torque generated at the root (or hips), where the contact forces F_S at the sensors and gravity are acting on the system, and where the system is static. In other words, we look at the constraint torque generated to enforce statics for the pose given by ϕ' when the forces acting on the system are gravity and the forces measured by the sensors.

We find the plausibility ρ using the ODE simulation. Rigid constraints are set on skeleton joint angles to enforce the pose given by ϕ', while another fixed constraint is applied to the root position and orientation in the world to enforce statics. In order to simulate the forces generated by the holds on the hands and feet, the opposite of the forces measured by the sensors are applied to the appropriate end effectors. Gravity is also taken into account.

The wrench applied to the root to enforce statics contains information on the physical plausibility of the pose for F_S. For a static pose, resultant forces and torques at the root are zero as gravity and the sum of the forces generated by the holds cancel out. Assuming forces at the holds are explained by the position of the COM, as illustrated by Figure 6, we can always hope to find a pose that minimizes torque at the root by distributing the skeleton's weight appropriately. Linear force at the root however is the difference between the weight of the simulated skeleton and the sum of forces at the holds and is therefore pose-invariant.

Torques at the inner joints describe the necessary effort to maintain the pose given by ϕ'. A small total inner torque is in general a good measure of high human plausibility. However, the simplicity of our simulated model makes it difficult to interpret inner torques, as it does not capture the shape of the holds or model the strategies used by different climbers to distribute effort among different muscle groups.

Therefore, we only use the torque that needs to be applied to the root to enforce statics as a measure of the quality of the pose given by ϕ' for explaining F_S. The closer the torque is to zero, the more plausible the pose. Consequently, finding a unique pose with physical plausibility as an objective is

under-constrained: the set of COM positions that minimize the said torque lie on a line parallel to the linear part of the wrench applied to the root to enforce statics. To incorporate the missing information on human plausibility and guide our optimizer toward a smaller set of good solutions, we use statistical information gathered on the position of the root for a given set of forces.

5.4 Hint Objective for improved optimization

As mentionned earlier, linear regression can be used to accurately estimate root position with a maximum error in the order of 10 cm. The model to predict the position of the hips for a given set of forces is input into CMA-ES and used to help reduce ambiguity. During initialization, r', the expected root position, is computed with the regression model given the forces measured by the sensors. The distance between the current location of the hips for a candidate pose and the estimated root position for the sensor forces is used as a hint to guide the optimization toward a good solution. Since the regression error is in the order of 10 cm, we use r' to guide CMA-ES toward the set of poses with a root position inside a 10 cm sphere from the estimate.

Conceptually, we guide our pose toward a configuration where the COM, which we approximate as root position, lies in a sphere, and use physical plausibility to project that COM onto the line that minimizes constraint torque applied to the root. In practice, the optimal solution is described as the most physically plausible pose where the hips are within a 10 cm radius of the expected hips position.

In sum, the optimization procedure starts with an arbitrary initial pose that satisfies the constraints. Linear regression is used to find r', the predicted root position for forces F_S. For a new CMA-ES sample ϕ, the projection $\phi' = \Gamma(\phi)$ on the constrained manifold is found using a proportional-derivative controller. The actual position of the root r is given by the pose described with ϕ'. The fitness – which we want to minimize – of the sample ϕ for explaining F_S is defined as

$$\zeta(\phi) = \begin{cases} k\,\|r - r'\|^2 + G(\phi') & \text{if } \|r - r'\| > t \\ \rho(\phi', F_S) + G(\phi') & \text{otherwise} \end{cases}, \qquad (10)$$

where t is an estimate of the maximum regression error, used to determine the significance of the information provided by r', $G(\phi')$ is a set of linear penalties that grow as the skeleton faces away from the wall, and k is a large weight that ensures CMA-ES discards samples where the hips lie outside the sphere given by the regression. Since the distance between actual and expected root positions r and r' is inexpensive to compute for a given pose, the physical plausibility ρ is only evaluated when the solution is promising in terms of human plausibility. Figure 8 illustrates the exploration of pose space by CMA-ES, where each picture contains the population cloud for the indicated iteration. Our projection method enables an easy exploration of the set of valid poses, and the optimization converges when in the vicinity of the optimal solution by progressively lowering the variance for the CMA-ES sampling variables (the desired joint angles ϕ).

6. RESULTS AND DISCUSSION

Our calibration methods were used to capture nine subjects and collect close to an hour of climbing data. Two routes were designed and each subject was asked to perform

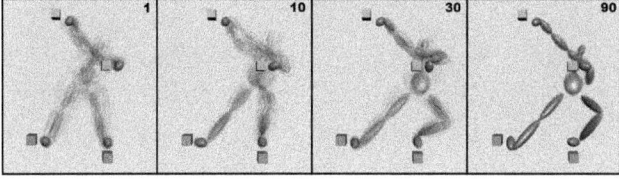

Figure 8: Vizualisation of the optimization process.

several takes with objectives such as shifting COM position and completing routes following different progressions.

6.1 Calibration

Our setup supports the expedient calibration procedure: in practice, most of the capture sessions were recorded using the pocket-based procedure. Markers are placed in corners of the wall to define the coordinate frame in which sensor frames are expressed as a function of pocket placement.

However, a number of tests as well as a full wall calibration were performed for the optimization-based calibration. For each sensor, three contact point locations were considered. For each contact location, 20 seconds of MoCap and 20 seconds of force measurements were recorded. Using Matlab, calibrating the calibration tool from 2500 frames of MoCap took less than a second, while estimating the position and orientation of a sensor with the iterative and alternating method from 2000 samples per point and 3 contact locations took less than a minute.

Contact point estimate error is expressed as the mean error for the least-squares estimate ${}^b p_c^*$. For each frame, ${}^w_b E_j$ is used to compute the contact location in world coordinates. Based on Equation 3, we describe the error as

$$\epsilon_c = \frac{1}{n} \sum_{j=1}^{n} \left\| {}^w_b E_j \, {}^b p_c^* - {}^w p_c^* \right\|, \quad (11)$$

where ${}^w p_c^*$ is the average of ${}^w_b E_j \, {}^b p_c^*$ over all samples. This quantity can be seen as the size of the point cloud where the actual contact point lies in world coordinates. Table 1 shows average errors for contact point estimates at each hold for a full calibration procedure. The high errors can be explained by the use of the matrices ${}^w_b E_j$, which are estimated by the software from the position of four markers, each of which has an individual reconstruction error in the order of 0.3 mm.

Sensor frame estimate error ϵ_s is expressed as

$$\frac{1}{km} \sum_{i=1}^{k} \sum_{j=1}^{m} \left\| {}^w_s R^* \, {}^s \tau_{ij} + ({}^w p_s^* - {}^w p_{ci}^*) \times {}^w_s R^* \, {}^s f_{ij} \right\|, \quad (12)$$

where ${}^w_s R^*$ and ${}^w p_s^*$ are the least-squares estimates for the sensor frames. Table 1 shows average errors with a contact point estimation error in the order of 4 mm, and sensor noise in the order of 0.1 N for forces and 1 Nmm for torques. Since a torque is a force applied at a distance, and given that in our setup contacts with holds occur approximately 15 cm from the origin of the sensors, an error of 75 Nmm represents a weight discrepancy of a mere 50 grams at the sensor. The iterative solver stops when the change in error is less than 0.01 Nmm per iteration.

A simple validation technique is to compare the climber's weight to the weight derived from measured forces expressed in the world frame for static poses. While this does not give any indication of the calibration precision, it is a good means

Sensor	Average ϵ_c (mm)	ϵ_s (Nmm)
1	4.3	75
2	3.3	55
3	4.6	92
4	3.4	87
5	4.4	102
6	4.1	96

Table 1: Average error accross the three contact point estimates and error for sensor frame estimate for each sensor.

Test	Best (cm)	Average (cm)	Worst (cm)
1	0.95	5.99	10.49
2	0.72	3.37	7.94
3	2.03	5.44	11.07
4	2.59	7.11	12.60
5	1.31	5.72	9.39
6	0.53	5.42	13.64

Table 2: Root position regression error.

of detecting errors in recorded gains, excitation voltages and sensor orientations with respect to the wall.

6.2 Reconstruction of static poses

Using a data set containing a wide variety of static poses and over 4000 frames of synchronized MoCap and force data, we looked at how well linear regression on the position of the root generalizes. We trained the model on 90% of the samples and tested it on the remainder. Table 2 shows the distance between predicted and actual root position for 6 such 90/10 partitions. As expected, dynamic motions and higher errors coincide, confirming our hypothesis that the correlation is more pronounced in the static case.

Pose reconstruction was run on several, varied static poses. The reconstruction is compared to ground truth for 5 of these poses in Figure 9, and timings as well as error measurements for those runs are given in Table 3. Reconstruction error is computed as the average distance between geometric centers of two corresponding bodies from the optimal pose and the ground truth. Examples were run using ODE and Java, on a dual-core 3 GHz Intel i3 CPU with 4 GB RAM. CMA-ES runs for 100 iterations with 10 samples per iteration, and the parameters for evaluating the fitness of a pose are the desired angles for hips, knees, ankles, chest, shoulders, elbows and wrists. The threshold to stop applying penalties pertaining to the distance between actual and predicted root position is 10 cm. Average reconstruction error is near that threshold for all bodies, indicating that our method for computing the optimality of the pose for a given set of forces provides an accurate model for reconstructing the remaining degrees of freedom.

7. CONCLUSIONS

We present an instrumented climbing wall, its design, and calibration procedures. We also present new ideas in computing postures during climbing from forces alone, using optimization to find a physically valid pose while meeting other important plausibility constraints. While linear regression cannot directly provide good estimates of posture from forces, it is useful for identifying the location of the

Figure 9: Reconstruction examples. At the bottom, the ground truth. At the top, the result of the optimization.

Example	Time (min)	ϵ_r (cm)
1	24.1	11.19
2	30.0	7.77
3	26.5	8.17
4	26.0	8.88
5	33.1	8.67

Table 3: Durations and reconstruction errors for the pose reconstruction examples.

hips, which we use as an inexpensive hint to guide our optimization towards the optimal solution. Comparison between our reconstructed poses and MoCap show that our objective function is a good model for human posture.

In the future, several avenues can be explored, such as automating the calibration procedure and improving the calibration tool, as well as expanding the framework to study dynamics using the physical simulation.

Climbing and bouldering are difficult skills to learn because the actions and postures involved depend not only on body position but also on how forces are applied. We believe that our methods for estimating posture from forces will be useful for augmented reality applications. For instance, in learning or rehabilitation, data projectors could be used to provide real-time visual feedback directly on the wall as a person is climbing.

8. REFERENCES

[1] M. A. Brubaker, L. Sigal, and D. J. Fleet. Estimating Contact Dynamics. In *International Conference on Computer Vision*, pages 2389–2396, 2009.

[2] M. de Lasa, I. Mordatch, and A. Hertzmann. Feature-Based Locomotion Controllers. In *ACM SIGGRAPH*, 2010.

[3] F. K. Fuss and G. Niegl. Instrumented Climbing Holds and Dynamics of Sport Climbing. In *The Engineering of Sport 6*, pages 57–62. Springer New York, 2006.

[4] F. K. Fuss and G. Niegl. *The Impact of Technology on Sport II*, chapter The Fully Instrumented Climbing Wall: Performance Analysis, Route Grading and Vector Diagrams – a Preliminary Study, pages 677–682. Taylor and Francis, 2007.

[5] S. Ha, Y. Bai, and K. C. Liu. Human Motion Reconstruction from Force Sensors. In *Proceedings of SIGGRAPH/SCA*, pages 129–138, 2011.

[6] N. Hansen. The CMA Evolution Strategy: A Comparing Review. In *Towards a New Evolutionary Computation*, volume 192, pages 75–102. Springer Berlin / Heidelberg, 2006.

[7] S. Jain, Y. Ye, and K. C. Liu. Optimization-Based Interactive Motion Synthesis. *ACM Transactions on Graphics*, 28(1):10:1–10:12, 2009.

[8] P. G. Kry and D. K. Pai. Grasp Recognition and Manipulation with the Tango. In *ISER*, volume 10. Springer, 2006.

[9] P. G. Kry and D. K. Pai. Interaction Capture and Synthesis. In *ACM SIGGRAPH*, pages 872–880, 2006.

[10] R. F. Nunes, J. B. Cavalcante-Neto, C. A. Vidal, P. G. Kry, and V. B. Zordan. Using Natural Vibrations to Guide Control for Locomotion. In *Proceedings of the ACM SIGGRAPH Symposium on Interactive 3D Graphics and Games*, pages 87–94, 2012.

[11] J. Pfeil, J. Mitani, and T. Igarashi. Interactive Climbing Route Design Using a Simulated Virtual Climber. In *SIGGRAPH Asia Sketches*, pages 2:1–2:2, 2011.

[12] F. Quaine, L. Martin, and J.-P. Blanchi. Effect of a Leg Movement on the Organisation of the Forces at the Holds in a Climbing Position. *Human Movement Science*, 16(2–3):337–346, 1997.

[13] F. Quaine, L. Martin, and J.-P. Blanchi. The Effect of Body Position and Number of Supports on Wall Reaction Forces in Rock Climbing. *Journal of Applied Biomechanics*, 13:14 – 23, 1997.

[14] B. Rosenhahn, C. Schmaltz, T. Brox, J. Weickert, D. Cremers, and H.-P. Seidel. Markerless Motion Capture of Man-Machine Interaction. In *Computer Vision and Pattern Recognition*, pages 1–8, 2008.

[15] P. Rougier, R. Billat, R. Merlin, and J.-P. Blanchi. Conception d'un Système pour Étudier la Relation Posturo-Cinétique dans un Plan Vertical. *ITBM*, 12:568 – 580, 1991.

[16] P. Rougier and J.-P. Blanchi. Mesure de la Force Maximale Volontaire à partir d'une Posture Quadrupodale en Escalade : Influence du Niveau d'Expertise. *Science and Sports*, 7(1):19–25, 1992.

[17] M. Testa, L. Martin, and B. Debû. Effects of the Type of Holds and Movement Amplitude on Postural Control associated with a Climbing Task. *Gait and Posture*, 9(1):57–64, 1999.

[18] K. Yin and D. K. Pai. FootSee: An Interactive Animation System. In *Proceedings of ACM SIGGRAPH/Eurographics SCA*, pages 329–338, 2003.

Pinch-n-Paste: Direct Texture Transfer Interaction in Augmented Reality

Atsushi Umakatsu
Osaka University, Japan
umakatsu@lab.ime.cmc.
osaka-u.ac.jp

Tomohiro Mashita
Osaka University, Japan
mashita@ime.cmc.osaka-
u.ac.jp

Kiyoshi Kiyokawa
Osaka University, Japan
kiyo@ime.cmc.osaka-
u.ac.jp

Haruo Takemura
Osaka University, Japan
takemura@ime.cmc.osaka-
u.ac.jp

ABSTRACT

Our Pinch-n-Paste allows a user to touch or pinch one part of an object, copy and move its texture, and paste it onto another object, directly with his or her hand, in an augmented reality environment. To transfer texture appropriately from one part of an object to another, two texture images are generated by the Least Square Conformal Map (LSCM) technique. Two regions in the texture images corresponding to source and target areas of interest are then obtained using cross-boundary brushes. Target texel values are sampled from corresponding source texels by Moving Least Squares (MLS), and are finally mapped onto the target object.

Categories and Subject Descriptors

H.5.1 [**Information Interfaces and Presentation**]: Multimedia Information Systems; I.3.7 [**Computer Graphics**]: Three-dimensional Graphics and Realism

Keywords

Augmented Reality; 3D Interaction.

1. INTRODUCTION

We aim to develop an intuitive and flexible in-situ AR authoring system, where a user is able to alter real objects' appearance and to create a novel object, by copying, modifying, and combining parts of the real objects in the scene. In this demo, we show a novel interaction technique called Pinch-n-Paste, as a function in a larger in-situ AR authoring project. Our Pinch-n-Paste can be used for an arbitrary texture-mapped object in an AR environment with physics-based, direct hand interaction. For example, in the case of interior design, a user grabs a texture of a real chair and

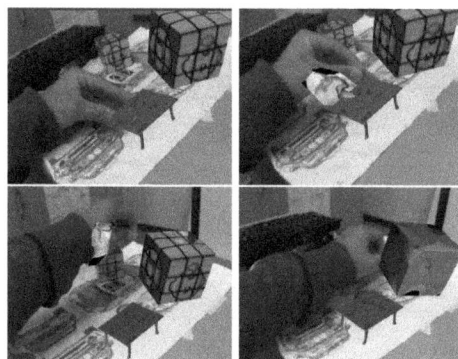

Figure 1: The Pinch-n-Paste interaction in action.

paste it to a nearby real sofa to examine how the sofa with a new texture suits his or her room.

2. INTERACTIVE TEXTURE TRANSFER

Pinch-n-Paste interaction technique is implemented in two main modules. The texture transfer module [2] is responsible for identifying source and target texture regions, and texel conversion between them. The natural hand interaction module [1] is responsible for collision detection between the user hand and the objects.

A user can interactively change and modify object textures in the scene using textures of existing objects. Fig. 1 shows Pinch-n-Paste interation in aciton. User pinches a part of a virtual table (Fig. 1, top-left). User extracts the pinched part of the texture as a virtual handkerchief with his hand (Fig. 1, top-right). User is now able to drag the virtual handkerchief (Fig. 1, bottom-left). User pastes the texture to another object (a reconstructed Rubic's Cube) (Fig. 1, bottom-right).

3. REFERENCES

[1] T. Piumsomboon et al. Poster: Physically-based natural hand and tangible AR interaction for face-to-face collaboration on a tabletop. In *3DUI'12*, pages 155–156, 2012.

[2] A. Umakatsu et al. Touch-n-paste: Direct texture transfer interaction in ar environments. In *ISMAR'12*, 2012 (to appear).

Underwater Augmented Reality Game using the DOLPHYN

Abdelkader Bellarbi
CDTA
Algiers, Algeria
abellarbi@cdta.dz

Christophe Domingues
IBISC EA 4526
University of Evry, France
Christophe.domingues@univ-evry.fr

Samir Otmane
IBISC EA 4526
University of Evry, France
Samir.Otmane@univ-evry.fr

Samir Benbelkacem CDTA
Algiers, Algeria
sbenbelkacem @cdta.dz

Alain Dinis
VirtualDive
Morainvilliers, France
adnis@virtualdive.com

ABSTRACT
The introduction of virtual and mixed realities in aquatic leisure activities constitutes a technological rupture when compared with the status of related technologies. With the extension of Internet to underwater applications, the innovative character of the project becomes evident, and the impact of this development in the littoral and beach tourism may be considerable.

Categories and Subject Descriptors
H.5.1 [**H.5.1 Multimedia Information Systems**]: Artificial, augmented, and virtual realities

Keywords
Underwater, Augmented Reality, User Interaction

1. INTRODUCTION
In fact, there are recent developments to extend the use of computers and computer components, such as the mouse, to underwater uses [1]. Dolphyn is an underwater-computerized display system with various sensors and devices conceived for existing swimming pools and for beach shores, associating computer functions, video gaming and simulations [2].

2. DOLPHYN
The DOLPHYN is using an x86 tablet running Windows 7, this device is dedicated to the underwater world with various sensors and devices: user interface device, web camera, GPS, thermometer and flow-meter that measure the displacement of the swimmer in the water. In addition, the Dolphyn has a wireless antenna for extended multiplayer game play and therefore multi-Dolphyns. Our device is composed by two modules, the waterproof case, which contains the tablet, and the electronic case that is used to manage all connected devices.

3. AR SERIOUS GAME
The game idea is to explore the ocean and to discover its different species through surviving, performing tasks and collaboration. The main objective of the game is educational. It allows the divers to know the different underwater creatures, and how to preserve their environment. Thus, augmented reality techniques can be used to develop this game. By this way, we have placed ArtoolkitPlus markers [3] in the diving site. The recognition of the markers enables the Dolphyn's user (diver) to view virtual fishes, virtual marine-plants and virtual submarines. In our case study, two scenarios of game are established: The first one consists in protecting fishes and plants by eliminating submarines that kill the fishes and cut the plants, by pulling with virtual missiles using the Dolphyn's joysticks. The player moves underwater and handles a Dolphyn device. He can see, through the Dolphyn, fishes, plants and submarines in augmentation form. Particularly, the augmented fishes move in various directions and speeds. The player is subjected to some constraints. First, he should not shoot the fishes neither the plants. So, the player should be more accurate as possible when he aims the submarines. The second scenario is educational. The user may see a variety of fishes and plants existing underwater. Annotations (e.g. fish's name, origin) are displayed besides each virtual fish or plant visible by the Dolphyn's camera.

4. CONCLUSION
In this paper, an underwater AR Game using the Dolphyn devices is developed. We are focused on serious and educational games. It is shown that Augmented Reality techniques can be used to extend a usual diving site with virtual objects. The developed application facilitates the AR application control using integrated joysticks. The positive results of this work, give us new ideas to develop more sophisticated applications and to enhance new technical aspects of the hardware prototype.

5. REFERENCES

[1] Blum L., Broll W. and Müller S. 2009. Augmented Reality under water. *ACM SIGGRAPH '09*. (New York, NY, USA).

[2] Domingues C., Otmane S. and Dinis A. 2012. A new Device for Virtual or Augmented Underwater Diving. *In Proceedings of the IEEE Symposium on 3D User Interface* (Orange County, USA). (3DUI 2012).

[3] Wagner D. and Schmalstieg D. 2007. ARToolKitPlus for Pose Tracking on Mobile Devices. *In the Proceedings of 12th Computer Vision Winter Workshop*. (CVWW'07), pp. 139-146, 2007.

Multimodal Virtual Environment Subserving the Design of Electronic Orientation Aids for the Blind

Slim Kammoun
IRIT, CNRS & Univ. of Toulouse
slim.kammoun@irit.fr

Marc J-M Macé
IRIT, CNRS & Univ. of Toulouse
marc.mace@irit.fr

Christophe Jouffrais
IRIT, CNRS & Univ. of Toulouse
christophe.jouffrais@irit.fr

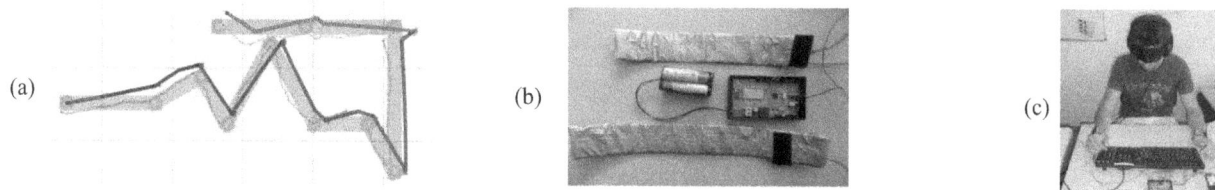

Figure 1: (a) Representation of a recorded trajectory, (b) The BT Arduino board and bracelets, (c) A blindfolded subject during a test session

Categories and Subject Descriptors

H.5.1 [**Information Interfaces and Presentation**] Multimedia Information Systems – *Artificial, augmented, and virtual realities, Evaluation/methodology.*

General Terms

Experimentation, Human Factors

Keywords

Virtual environment, Multimodal interaction, Blind, Guidance.

1. INTRODUCTION & MOTIVATION

In the last few decades, a growing number of Electronic Orientation Aids (EOA) has been developed with the purpose of improving the autonomy of visually impaired people. However, the majority of those systems are not used by the blind due to limited usability. The main challenges to be addressed are about interaction and guidance. To address these issues, we designed a multimodal (input and output) Virtual Environment (VE) that simulates different interactions that could be used for space perception and guidance in an EOA. This platform subserves two goals: help designers to systematically test guidance strategies (i.e. for the development of new EOAs) and train blind people to use interactive EOAs, with an emphasis on cognitive mapping enhancement. In a multimodal VE, both objectives are assessed in a controlled, cost-effective, safe and flexible environment.

2. OVERVIEW OF THE SIMULATOR

The platform presents two distinct modes: a *Control* mode and an *Exploration* mode. The *Control* mode is used by designers, researchers, and O&M instructors. This mode allows designers to create and modify VEs. A key feature of the Control mode is the ability to import an XML file from Open Street Map to create a new 3D virtual map and to manually or automatically select a path between two points. This makes it easy to import maps of different places. The Control mode also includes a feedback editor to assign arbitrary tactile & auditory feedbacks to any event in the VE. The *Evaluation* mode allows researchers and O&M instructors to record and replay the events and user's behavior.

During a session, the system logs in a text file all the information concerning the interaction (keystrokes, joystick, audio, haptic stimuli), as well as the avatar position, orientation and speed. In a real environment, a blind pedestrian who intends to

move along a straight path typically deviates about 10% to the right or to the left. An adjustable drift has been added to the avatar's displacement to simulate this behavior. EOAs usually rely on GNSS positioning. An adjustable error was also added to the location of the avatar in the VE to account for positioning inaccuracy. The visual output of the VE (for the experimenter only) displays different textures applied to the surfaces (building, etc.) or the objects (e.g. tar texture for roads) encountered in the VE. Fig 1a shows a representation of a recorded journey. The platform was implemented in C++ and the rendering was performed with OGRE 3D engine.

3. GUIDANCE AND FEEDBACK EDITOR

In EOAs, guidance consists in rendering instructions and descriptions that help the user to understand the environment and reach a desired destination. Several strategies can be adapted depending on two main factors: 1/ it is easier to guide the user when the global positioning accuracy is good; 2/ the verbosity can be adapted to the task and the user. It is easy to systematically modify these factors in the VE to evaluate different strategies.

The interaction between the user and the VE is managed through a feedback editor. Single/combined auditory and somatosensory feedbacks (a BT Arduino board and bracelets, see Fig 1b, c) were triggered depending on the actions performed by the avatar (e.g. a footstep sound related to the walking surface and speed, etc.). The guidance instructions were triggered according to the desired strategy. For instance a virtual 3D sound may be positioned on the next point to reach, and TTS or spatialized TTS may be used to describe points of interests, etc.

4. CONCLUSION & PERSPECTIVE

In this paper, we proposed an experimental platform to subserve the design of EOAs for the Blind. Such platform is not absolutely realistic but allows the systematic evaluation and benchmark of several guidance strategies in a controlled, cost-effective, safe and flexible manner. A first evaluation has been conducted for the NAVIG system [1].

5. REFERENCES

[1] Katz, B.F.G., Kammoun, S. Parseihian, G., Gutierrez, O., Brilhault, A., Auvray, M., Truillet, P., Denis, M., Thorpe, S., Jouffrais, C . Augmented reality guidance system for the visually impaired: Combining object localization, GNSS, and spatial audio. Virtual Reality, in press, DOI:10.1007/s10055-012-0213-6, 2012.

Elastic Connections: Separating and Observation Methods for Complex Virtual Objects

Mai Otsuki, Tsutomu Oshita, Asako Kimura Fumihisa Shibata, and Hideyuki Tamura
Ritsumeikan University, Japan.
otsuki@rm.is.ritsumei.ac.jp

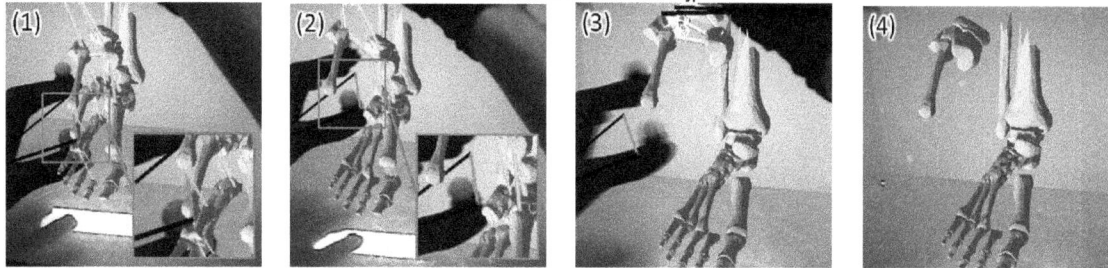

Figure 1. Lifting and separating the group of parts by cutting virtual rubber bands between parts. After the user releases the parts, separation is complete.

Categories and Subject Descriptors

H5.2 [**Information interfaces and presentation**]: User Interfaces
- *Interaction styles*

Keywords

3D interaction; VR; MR; AR; Observation; Ungroup; Connection; Relationship; Gesture.

1. INTRODUCTION

Today's technology enables users to manipulate complex, multi-part 3D virtual objects such as industrial products, structures designed by CAD, and models of the human body in 3D space. In some modeling software, parts of such objects are grouped and manipulated together, but not individually, for efficient operation. However, separating operations are often necessary for partial observation or manipulation. We propose a system that realizes gesture-based separation and observation of a group of parts from complex virtual objects in 3D space. One practical application of our system is for training, such as learning the structures of the human body or industrial products.

Volume cursors [1, 2] are simple ways to select multiple targets simultaneously; however, in highly complex multi-part objects, it is difficult to avoid selecting unnecessary parts. Our method allows users to flexibly select objects using the connections between parts. There are existing techniques that utilize geometric relationships [3, 4] to automatically select multiple parts as a single group; however, these studies did not consider the connection strength between associated parts. We believe that the connection strength between parts is important when observing and separating the varied structures of complex objects, in which the size and shape of parts may vary significantly. For example, if bone, muscle, and blood vessels are interconnected in the geometric relationships within a model of the human body, and the user needs only bone structures, the connection strength based on semantic relationships is required. For example, the connections between parts of the same category may be stronger than the connections between parts in a different category.

2. PROPOSED METHOD

Figure 1 shows the operations required for a user to separate the parts of a foot bone model using our method. In our system, parts are connected by a "virtual rubber band," and the width of this band indicates the connection strength between connected parts. When the user lifts a part, the connected parts are also gradually lifted, relative to the distance of the user's hands movement. The user can observe the connections and the strength between the parts in detail through visual feedback that illustrate the expansion and contraction of the virtual rubber band. To assist understanding, the visual feedback is accompanied by auditory feedback, such as the stretching sounds of a rubber band.

If all parts are expanded at once, users will lose the original shape of the object, and it can become unclear which parts they wanted to separate. This is why we expand gradually relative to a user's hand movement. This method is based on Shiozawa's method [5]. Users can separate a group of parts freely by cutting the connections with their other hand, observing connections. However, even though the user lifts a single part, other parts will stay in contact with each other. In other words, the user cannot cut all connections between parts. Therefore, to create space between parts, we implemented a force-based algorithm [6], and use elastic and Coulomb forces for calculating the behavior of the parts.

3. FUTURE WORK

Through student trials, we found that the suitable spacing size varies depending on the user. We plan to implement a function for adjusting this spacing size. Currently, the connection strength is mapped to the virtual rubber band width. We also plan to map it to the spacing between the parts; for example, by making the space where the connection strength is strong short, a user can easily understand each group. Additionally, we are going to demonstrate the user study, evaluate the usefulness of our method, and examine the appropriateness of the interactions in detail.

REFERENCES

[1] Forsberg, A. *et al.* Aperture based selection for immersive virtual environments, In *Proc. UIST 1996*, pp. 95-96, 1996.
[2] Zhai, S. *et al.* The "Silk Cursor": Investigating transparency for 3D target acquisition, In *Proc. CHI 94*, pp. 459-464, 1994.
[3] Stuerzlinger, W. *et al.* Efficient manipulation of object groups in virtual environments, In *Proc. VR '02*, pp. 251-258, 2002.
[4] Oh, J. Y. *et al.* Group selection techniques for efficient 3D modeling, In *Proc. 3DUI '06*, pp. 95-102, 2006.
[5] Shiozawa, H. *et al.* WWW visualization giving meanings to interactive manipulations, In *Proc. HCI Int'97*, pp. 791-794, 1997.
[6] Eades, P. A heuristic for graph drawing. *Congressus Numerantium,* Vol. 42, pp. 149-160, 1984.

VRST'12, December 10–12, 2012, Toronto, Ontario, Canada.
ACM 978-1-4503-1469-5/12/12.

Supporting Data Collection in Virtual Worlds

Hiep Luong, Dipesh Gautam, John Gauch, Susan Gauch
University of Arkansas
Fayetteville, AR 72701, U.S.A
{hluong, dgautam, jgauch, sgauch}@uark.edu

ABSTRACT

This paper presents a new services paradigm for virtual world crawler interaction that is co-operative and exploits information about 3D objects in the virtual world. Our approach supports analyzing redundant information crawled from virtual worlds in order to decrease the amount of data collected by crawlers, keep search engine collections up to date, and provide an efficient mechanism for collecting and searching information from multiple virtual worlds.

Categories and Subject Descriptors

H.5.1 **[Information Interfaces and Presentation]**: Multimedia Information Systems; Artificial, augmented, and virtual realities

General Terms

Measurement, Performance, Design, Experimentation.

Keywords

Virtual World, Distributed Search, Data Crawling, Bandwidth

1. CRAWLING IN VIRTUAL WORLDS

Virtual worlds present problems in content collection that differ significantly from traditional crawlers, making this an open field for further research. As it travels in a region, the crawler may encounter objects have already been collected by previous crawls. Thus, the crawler will consume bandwidth needlessly by collecting these redundant objects. Our goal in this work is to explore a more efficient and exhaustive method of collecting content from virtual worlds. We investigate the potential bandwidth savings that a collaborative crawling approach could achieve. In addition, this collaborative approach could be used to direct the crawler to a list of unvisited regions or a region in the virtual world that has a high rate of change.

1.1 Bandwidth Consumption Saving

We have developed a focused crawler allowing us to collect data from the Second Life and/or OpenSimuator virtual worlds. The content collection is done by a set of virtual world client emulators interacting with the virtual world servers [1]. Once we gather data, we explore how frequently content changes in different regions to build a model of the rate of change in virtual worlds. We propose the development of a web service for each virtual world server and that shares object metadata in XML format with a collaborative crawler (Figure 1). We present measures that estimate data redundancy (DR) and the potential savings in bandwidth consumed (BS) by the crawler using the proposed architecture.

$$DR = \frac{UC}{TC} * 100 \quad BS = \frac{TC-UC}{TC} * 100$$

where UC is the number of unchanged objects which are crawled in a region; and TC is total number of objects crawled from that region.

The average data redundancy is calculated using the average UC and TC values over all regions that are crawled.

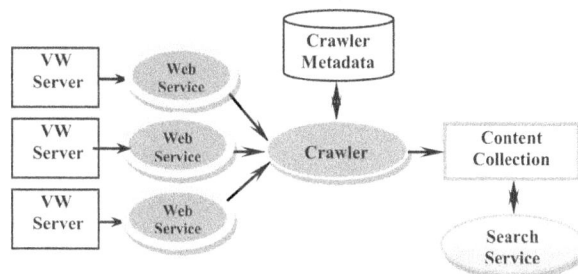

Figure 1. System Architecture Overview

1.2 Experiments and Results

After collecting and investigating the data collected (~450,000 objects) from our four weekly crawls of 100 regions of Second Life, we have analyzed in detail the number of objects added, deleted and modified in each region. We calculated the bandwidth savings that would be provided by our proposed architecture. Table 1 shows a summary of the 25th, 50th, and 75th percentile values of bandwidth saving over four weeks. These values are very consistent from week to week. The bandwidth savings for the 25th percentile region averaged 48.50%, which indicates that roughly half of the objects in these regions remain unchanged from week to week. The 50th percentile region had an average bandwidth saving of 31.70%, which is a significant drop from the 25th percentile region. Finally, the 75th percentile region only had a bandwidth saving of 16.37%, which is only 1/3 of the 25th percentile value.

Table 1. Percentile of bandwidth savings over 4 weeks

Percentile	BS_Week2	BS_Week3	BS_Week4	Average_BS
25th	45.86%	46.31%	49.70%	48.50%
50th	29.61%	30.14%	31.45%	31.70%
75th	15.16%	14.89%	16.50%	16.37%

According to our investigation, the crawler got redundant data over weeks because the majority of the content in virtual worlds is static objects like chairs, trees, towers, buildings, etc.

1.3 Conclusion

The goal of this research study is to implement and validate an intelligent crawler that collects data from virtual worlds. We have demonstrated that the crawler performance can be significantly enhanced with bandwidth consumption saving as the crawling results are well investigated and analyzed after each download. Our approach has analyzed the data redundancy due to the overlapping content that are retuned by the crawler. Experimental results with data crawled from Second Life servers demonstrate that our approach provides the ability to save crawling bandwidth consumption, to explore more hidden objects and new regions to be crawled that facilitate the search service in virtual worlds.

2. REFERENCES

[1] Eno, J., Gauch, S. and Thompson, C. 2009. Intelligent Crawling in Virtual Worlds. In *Proc. IEEE/WIC/ACM (WI-IAT '09)*, Washington, DC, USA, Vol. 3, pp. 555-558.

Optical Illusion in Augmented Reality

Maryam Khademi
University of California, Irvine
mkhademi@ics.uci.edu

Hossein Mousavi Hondori
University of California, Irvine
hossein.mousavi@ieee.org

Cristina Videira Lopes
University of California, Irvine
lopes@ics.uci.edu

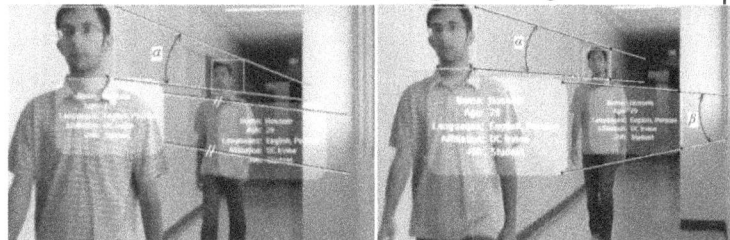

Figure 1. The Social AR case study where personal information appears next to the individual's face.

ABSTRACT

While developers are mainly tackling primary problems in developing augmented reality systems [1-2], perceptually-correct augmentation rests a critical challenge. In this paper, we focus on how to correctly display and accurately convey the augmented virtual object's size with respect to real-world objects. We conducted a user study to examine how subjects would verify relative size of virtual objects, augmented in a real scene. The results confirmed that optical illusion occurs in AR applications if comparative size of virtual objects to real-world ones is not considered.

Categories and Subject Descriptors

H5.2 [Information interfaces and presentation]: User Interfaces, Graphical user interfaces.

Keywords

Augmented Reality, Optical Illusion, Human Perception

1. INTRODUCTION

A fundamental problem in AR is characterizing how it affects the perception of spatial layout, depth, and size [3]. Kruijff et al. [4] determined and classified AR perceptual issues based on various AR platforms. They treated these issues in the context of a visual processing and interpretation pipeline, which consists of problems, originating from environment, capturing, augmentation, display device, and user. As the final stage of this perceptual pipeline, user's visual system could be a source of problem in perception. As a deeper examination of user's visual system in AR perception, we verify the effect of relative size of virtual objects with respect to real-world objects and how users judged their differences.

2. METHODOLOGY

We process every frame to recognize the person's face and enclose it with a face rectangle as shown in Figure 1. As a virtual object, we augment an information box including personal information next to the face rectangle. As the person approaches the camera, the rectangle enlarges. Figure 1(a) shows case *E1* where the information box remains the same size whereas Figure 1(b) illustrates case *E2* where it enlarges based on linear perspective, i.e., with the same order as the face (green rectangle) expands. Figure 2 illustrates how area of the information box changes corresponding to the face rectangle's area when it moves toward the camera for both cases of E1 and E2.

3. USER STUDY

20 subjects were asked about any change in size of the information box conveying the above information in E1 and E2. We decided to investigate the following hypotheses: (i) users will have an illusion about the information box' size as if it is shrinking in case of E1; (ii) overall users will favor having the information box enlarged as a more natural perception.

4. RESULTS

In case of E1, although size of the information box did not scale, 70% of subjects had the illusion that it shrank. What occurs in this situation is recognized as Ebbinghaus illusion, which originates from relative size perception. Since relative size of the information box compared to the face rectangle is decreasing, it creates the illusion that actual size of the information box is shrinking. In case of E2, where we scaled up the information box, 80% of users believed it feels more natural than case E1. Therefore, our both hypotheses were satisfied.

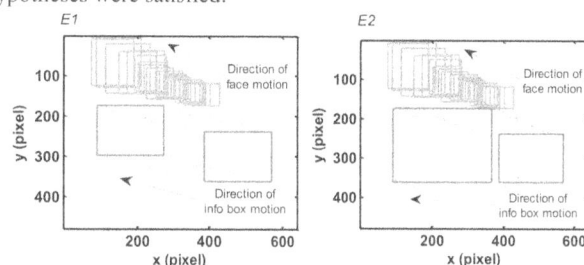

Figure 2. The face rectangle (green) and information box (red) in every 5 frame as the person approaches the camera.

5. REFERENCES

H. M. HONDORI, A.W. TECH, M. KHADEMI, AND C. V. LOPES. Real-time Measurement of Arm's Mechanical Impedance with Augmented Reality Illustration. *2012 Annual International Conference of the IEEE Engineering in Medicine and Biology Society (EMBC)*, Sep 2012.

M. KHADEMI, H. M. HONDORI, C. V. LOPES, L. DODAKIAN, AND S. C. CRAMER. Haptic Augmented Reality to Monitor Human Arm's Stiffness in Rehabilitation. *IEEE EMBS Conference on Biomedical Engineering and Sciences, IECBES*, Dec 2012.

J. SWAN, A. JONES, E. KOLSTAD, M. LIVINGSTON, AND H. S. SMALLMAN. Egocentric Depth Judgments in Optical, See-Through Augmented Reality. *IEEE Transactions on Visualization and Computer Graphics*, vol. 13, no. 3, pp. 429–442, Jun 2007.

E. KRUIJFF, J. E. SWAN, AND S. FEINER. Perceptual issues in augmented reality revisited. *9th IEEE International Symposium on Mixed and Augmented Reality (ISMAR)*, 2010, pp. 3–12.

Falling Water with Key Particle and Envelope Surface for Virtual Liquid Manipulation Model

Shunsuke Miyashita
Nagoya Institute of Technology
Gokiso-cho, showa-ku, Nagoya 466-8555 Japan
miyasita@center.nitech.ac.jp

Kenji Funahashi
Nagoya Institute of Technology
Gokiso-cho, showa-ku, Nagoya 466-8555 Japan
Kenji@nitech.ac.jp

Categories and Subject Descriptors

H.5.1 [**Information Interfaces and Presentation**]: Multimedia Information Systems—*Artificial, augmented, and virtual realities*

Author Keywords

liquid manipulation model; key particle; envelope surface

1. INTRODUCTION

We have proposed a liquid manipulation model based on particle and volume, and a VR chemical laboratory system [1]. In the CG field, although researchers usually use particle method to simulate realistic fluid, it needs enormous computation time and usually needs parallel processing to realize real-time simulation [2]. One of our main goal is to provide the VR-learning system for the people, i.e., who have to stay in the hospital. Therefore we have already proposed an interactive model of virtual liquid like water which focus on user impression and real-time processing rather than exact behavior simulation. The model can make user feel realistic sensation from the water behavior manipulated by user's container. However free fall water was simulated and rendered with particles simply. The processing speed is influenced by a lot of particles, and CG quality is insufficient. In this paper, we propose an efficient and effective method of free fall water with key particles instead of conventional particles. The envelope surface is rendered around the key particles as a surface of the water. The new model can make more realistic sensation with higher processing speed.

2. VOLUME & PARTICLE BASED MODEL

We usually manipulate water with container, and count it as "a cup of water." So we represent the water in our proposed model as following two conditions to simplify calculation; the stay condition which exists in a container and the free fall condition which flows from/to container. The former is treated with volume value, and the latter is treated as a simple particle system that particles do not interfere each other. Although water is not one object, we treat the water in a container as one object, and calculate water surface level from volume and its tilt. We have also developed the method to express wave, vortex and color diffusion on the surface. However the free fall condition water is represented

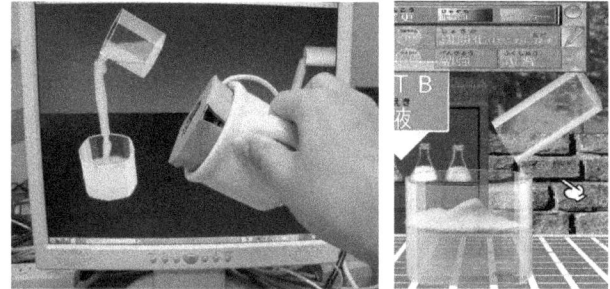

Figure 1: Experimental system

as just particles and rendered as simple square transparent polygons. Using this model, an interactive water manipulation is realized in real-time.

3. KEY PARTICLE BASED MODEL

In our new model, key particles are proposed to represent falling water behavior. They have their own location, volume and color parameters, and do not interfere each other as same as conventional particles. While water is flowing, key particles are generated at regular intervals, then each particle moves according to gravity and inertia. So the number of key particles is less than the conventional ones. When the flow is stopped, the particle segment is separated. Finally, envelope surfaces are rendered around each segment of the key particles. The surface is constructed as a frustum for each pair of adjoining key particles, base area is decided by the volume parameter of the particle.

4. CONCLUSIONS

We proposed the new model which represents falling liquid with key particles and an envelope surface as a part of the virtual liquid manipulation model. It can make more realistic sensation with higher speed (Fig. 1). As a future work, we should implement a VR chemical laboratory system on a mobile computer, and evaluate its validity from students.
Acknowledgments: This work was supported in part by JSPS KAKENHI Grant Number 24501186.

5. REFERENCES

[1] Natsume, et al. The virtual chemical laboratory using particle and volume based liquid model. Proc. SCIS & ISIS, 1354–1359, 2010.

[2] Losasso, et al. Two-way coupled SPH and particle level set fluid simulation. IEEE TVCG, 14(4):797–804, 2008.

Are Immersive FPS Games Enjoyable?

Jean-Luc Lugrin [†],
Fred Charles, Marc Cavazza,
Teesside University,
School of Computing,
Middlesbrough, TS1 3BA
j-l.lugrin@tees.ac.uk

Marc Le Renard
ESIEA
38 rue des docteurs Calmette
et Guérin, Parc Universitaire,
Laval, 53000
marc.lerenard@esiea-ouest.fr

Jonathan Freeman,
Jane Lessiter
Psychology Department, Goldsmiths,
University of London,
London, SE14 6NW
j.freeman@gold.ac.uk

ABSTRACT

This paper describes an experiment comparing immersive and non-immersive gaming using a state-of-the-art first person shooter game (FPS) in which we analyse user experience and performance through a combination of in-game metrics, questionnaires and subjective reports. Our results show an overwhelming subjective preference for the immersive version despite a decrease in performance attributed to a more realistic aiming mechanism. Interaction metrics suggest that users took full advantage of the immersive context rather than simply transposing their desktop gaming skills.

Categories and Subject Descriptors

H.5.1 [**Multimedia Information Systems**]: Artificial, Augmented and Virtual Reality - Virtual Reality for Art and Entertainment.

General Terms

Measurement, Performance, Experimentation, Human Factors.

Keywords

Immersive Gaming, User Experience, Presence.

1. EXPERIMENTS

We report the evaluation of a major commercial computer game, Unreal® Tournament 3, as a real-time immersive stereoscopic experience based on a four-screen CAVE™-like installation. Thirty-nine experienced FPS players (avg. 21.5 years) participated in our experiment, composed of two main parts: a Desktop and a CAVE™ session (~20 minutes each). Both versions of the game were identical (i.e. matching gameplay, rendering performances (50Hz in 3D) and end-to-end latency (Interaction: <=82ms; Navigation controls: <=136ms), with differences only attributable to the immersive nature of the VR version (i.e. large field of view, active stereoscopy, and wand tracker interactions (Figure 1) instead of desktop monitor and keyboard/mouse input). Our questionnaire demonstrates a strong preference of users for the immersive setting (72%), which is also confirmed by their self-reporting (*"It made me feel part of the world, easy to get immersed"*). This preference contrasts with a higher performance level in the desktop configuration (*"The CAVE was a lot harder but it was much more fun"*). The immersive settings resulted in significantly lower performances than Desktop settings (Table 1). We noted important differences regarding the average number of kills (33.7 in desktop and 4.5 in immersive) and shooting accuracy (73.6% and 92.2% of missed shoots)

[†]*Current Affiliation: Universität Würzburg, HCI, Germany*

Figure 1. Immersive FPS Session (Unreal® Tournament 3).

However, the close percentages of time having an enemy in the player's field of view (12.9% and 15.7%), the similar average walking distance covered in-between player's death (27.8m and 24.4m) as well as the similar overall number of player's death (22.6 and 20.5), suggest a lack of accuracy in shooting rather than navigation difficulty or lower target detection. Results from the Presence questionnaire (ITC-SOPI) are also in line with expectations, where the immersive configuration revealed significantly higher scores (Table 2). Interestingly, the majority of the participants seem to adapt almost immediately to a large field of view (multi-screen); users were facing at least two screens 40% of the time and switched screen on average 25 times per 10 minutes session. We thus observed an interesting dissociation between in-game performance and player satisfaction, where players expressed a clear preference for the immersive setting, despite moderate cybersickness effects and lower aiming accuracy with the wand tracker, a finding which is however consistent with previous literature [1].

Table 1: Lower Performance in the immersive session.

Accuracy	$t(39) = -13.76$	$p < 0.001$
Number of Kills	$t(39) = -21.032$	$p < 0.001$
Player Deaths	$t(39) = 3.53$	$p < 0.01$

Table 2: Higher Presence in the immersive session.

Spatial Presence	$t(39) = 9.51$	$p < 0.01$
Engagement	$t(39) = 3.59$	$p < 0.01$
Ecological Validity	$t(39) = 6.65$	$p < 0.01$
Negative Effects	$t(39) = 9.10$	$p < 0.01$

2. REFERENCES

[1] Klimmt, C., Blake, C., Hefner, D., Vorderer, P. and Roth, C. 2009. Player Performance, Satisfaction, and Video Game Enjoyment. In *Proceedings of the 8th International Conference on Entertainment Computing.* (Paris, France). Springer-Verlag, Berlin, Heidelberg, 1-12.

A Semantic Reasoning Engine for Context-Awareness: Detection and Enhancement of 3D Interaction Interests

Yannick Dennemont, Guillaume Bouyer, Samir Otmane, Malik Mallem
IBISC Laboratory
40 rue du Pelvoux, Evry, France
FirstName.LastName@ibisc.fr

ABSTRACT

We propose a semantic reasoning engine for context-awareness in classic VR environments. It is currently used to automatically detect user's interests and manage visual enhancements depending on the user's movement.

Categories and Subject Descriptors

I.3.6 [**Methodology and Techniques Subjects**]: Interaction Techniques; I.3.7 [**Computer Graphics**]: Virtual reality; I.2.4 [**Computing Methodologies**]: Knowledge Representation Formalism and Methods

Keywords

Context-awareness, 3D interaction assistance, Adaptive 3D interaction,

1. INTRODUCTION

Tasks in immersive virtual environments are associated to 3D interaction (3DI) techniques and devices. As tasks and environments become more and more complex, these techniques can no longer be the same for every application. Our work focuses on 3DI assistance by adding adaptivity depending on the interaction context. To reach context-awareness, an engine has been designed, implemented with the Amine platform and tested with a Virtools application.

2. A SEMANTIC REASONING ENGINE

The engine uses rules to take decisions regarding a stored context (knowledge, events etc.). Context and decisions concern the user, the interaction and the environment. They communicate with the engine through a set of tools with a semantic description by using Open Sound Control. Tools can be actuators with perceivable multimodal effects (environment modifications etc.) or sensors that retrieve information (by monitoring the interaction, etc.). The engine uses Conceptual Graphs (CGs) which provide a good expressiveness and usability. CGs link concepts with relations, both classified in an ontology. They are used to describe rules and facts. Decision request seeks a true reaction applicable by a tool. Then, the engine aggregates its global *confidence* (degree of sureness) and *impact* (degree of perceived repercussion). A CG global *confidence* depends on all paths leading to a true expression of the described situation using facts, events and rules. A CG fact is certain by default or can supply its own *confidence* (e.g. provided by a sensor). Events *confidence* decreases with the ratio of their remaining validity. Rule effects *confidence* is equal to the rule causes average *confidence*, times the rule *confidence* itself. Finally the global *confidence* of a CG expression is obtained by a fusion function. With n paths and *Mean* as their average confidence value: $Globalconfidence = (1 - Mean) \times (1 - \frac{1}{n}) \times Mean + Mean$.

Next, the engine aggregates the decisions *impact*. Each tool has an initial *impact* which can be modified given specific cases. Initial *impact* equals to 0 (without any impacts) or 1 (with the most impact) are not modified. Otherwise at each applicable case, the *impact* is altered with a weight (W, 25% if not valued) $impact(n) = impact(n - 1) - W \times impact(n - 1)$ for a decrease or $impact(n) = impact(n - 1) + W \times (1 - impact(n - 1))$ for a increase. An acceptable total *impact* limits the decisions that can be made, which induces a knapsack problem as a last classification.

3. 3D INTERACTION ASSISTANCE

The engine is applied in a case study to automatically acquire and enhance user's interests. Sensors describe user movement, gestures and Zones of Interest (ZOI) content. Actuators create the ZOI, change objects color or add an attraction. The engine triggers adaptations using internal rules and those tools. Thereby, a object is colored red when the user passes by or points at it and reset when the user moves far away or after time. An attraction is added to the virtual hand when the object is detected several times as an interest or when the user stands next to it and removed when the user tries to resist. Attraction can not be added again for a time while coloring reactivations occur as the decision has less impact. An object (e.g. suddenly abandoned by the user) can flicker for a while. This is an unplanned mean to attract the user attention: the object is both still interesting enough to be colored and not enough to avoid the color reset. When several objects are close to the hand, a group logic usually emerged by distributing the available impact using the less impacting adaptation (coloring) on a maximum of objects. Thus the rules are combined, with outcomes not fully planned. In fact, the engine can release the designer from the prediction of every situation. Besides, it acquires and manages context to assist the user. This work is supported by the AP7 DigitalOcean project.

VRST'12, December 10–12, 2012, Toronto, Ontario, Canada.
ACM 978-1-4503-1469-5/12/12.

Gaze and Gesture Based Object Manipulation in Virtual Worlds

Dana Slambekova
Rochester Institute of
Technology
Rochester, NY, USA
dxs4659@rit.edu

Reynold Bailey
Rochester Institute of
Technology
Rochester, NY, USA
rjb@cs.rit.edu

Joe Geigel
Rochester Institute of
Technology
Rochester, NY, USA
jmg@cs.rit.edu

ABSTRACT

In this work we present a framework for enabling the use of both eye gaze and hand gestures for interaction within a 3D virtual world. We define a set of natural interaction mechanisms for manipulation of objects within the 3D space and describe a prototype implementation based on Second Life that allows these mechanisms to be used in that world. We also explore how these mechanisms can be extended to other spatial tasks such as camera positioning and motion.

Categories and Subject Descriptors

I.3.7 [**Computer Graphics**]: Three-Dimensional Graphics and Realism - Virtual reality

Keywords

virtual reality;gesture recognition;eye tracking; Kinect

1. INTRODUCTION

Motivated by interfaces depicted in films such as *Minority Report*, much attention has been placed on the use of spatial gestures for interactions in 3D virtual spaces [1, 2]. Research on natural gaze behavior and hand-eye coordination during object manipulation suggests that the use of gaze data, in addition to gesture based methods, may increase the effectiveness of performing these tasks in a virtual space.

2. ARCHITECTURE & INTERACTION

The system (Figure 1) provides two paths for user interaction: detection and recognition of 3D gestures and the tracking the eye gaze of the user. Together, these signals are used to trigger actions from a set of predefined mappings: from gesture / gaze to controllable events within the virtual space. These events are then realized within a particular virtual world environment using the mechanisms available in that environment.

We combine a "look at" mechanism for choosing objects with a handle bar metaphor[2] for object manipulation. Hand state is used as a trigger for selection and deselection of objects while eye gaze data is used to determine the object on which to apply the selection. Once selected, objects can be translated, rotated, and scaled by use of intuitive 3D gestures as shown in Figure 2. For translation, eye gaze is also used to locate a target position for the translated object.

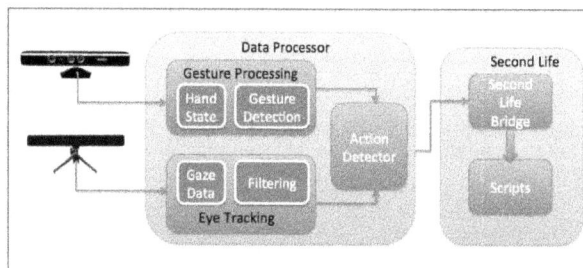

Figure 1: System Architecture

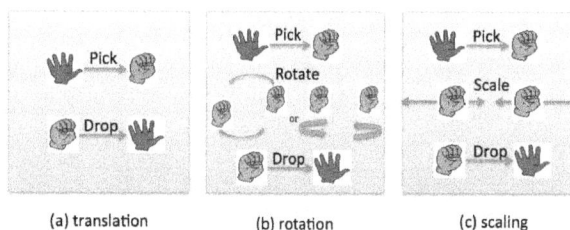

(a) translation (b) rotation (c) scaling

Figure 2: Interaction Mechanisms

We have implemented a prototype of the system using a Microsoft Kinect sensor for gesture capture, a Mirametrix eye tracker to detect eye gaze and Second Life as the target virtual world platform. The prototype serves as a proof of concept and a framework for testing other kinds of interaction based on gesture and gaze (e.g. camera motion).

3. REFERENCES

[1] G. Hackenberg, R. McCall, and W. Broll. Lightweight palm and finger tracking for real-time 3d gesture control. In *Virtual Reality Conference (VR), 2011 IEEE*, pages 19 –26, march 2011.

[2] P. Song, W. B. Goh, W. Hutama, C.-W. Fu, and X. Liu. A handle bar metaphor for virtual object manipulation with mid-air interaction. In *Proceedings of the 2012 ACM annual conference on Human Factors in Computing Systems*, CHI '12, pages 1297–1306, New York, NY, USA, 2012. ACM.

Collaborative Approach for Dynamic Adjustment of Selection Areas in Polygonal Modelling

Adrien Girard *
Paris-Sud University
CNRS-LIMSI

Yacine Bellik *
Paris-Sud University
CNRS-LIMSI

Malika Auvray *
CNRS-LIMSI

Mehdi Ammi *
Paris-Sud University
CNRS-LIMSI

ABSTRACT

Mutual awareness between users working in collaborative virtual environments is an important factor for efficient collaboration. This article presents a collaborative metaphor dedicated to the dynamic adjustment of selection area in polygonal modelling.

Categories and Subject Descriptors

H.5.3 [**Information Interface and Presentation**]: Group and Organization Interfaces Computer-supported cooperative work

Keywords

Collaborative polygonal modelling, Selection adjustment

1. INTRODUCTION

Collaborative Virtual Environments (CVEs) introduce new working methods, allowing multiple users to work simultaneously in the same virtual space from different spatial locations. However, CVEs are not able to reflect the richness of real world communication. Indeed, these environments limit the mutual awareness (degree of similarity between each member's perception of a same given situation) and may lead to a reduction in efficiency of the group.

Nova et al. [1] showed that using awareness tools improves performance in collaborative task. These awareness tools provide relevant information about the position of a partner in the virtual environment. We choose a different solution to support awareness. Instead of providing more information about users, we developed an interaction method which depends on the partner's actions in order to forces each partner to be aware of the partner's activity.

2. PROPOSED APPROACH

In the context of a collaborative polygonal modelling, the standard approach to adjust the size of the selection area (i.e., the number of selected faces) is an individual function which is independent of the partner's actions. In order to support mutual awareness, we propose to link the size of the selection area with the distance separating the two partners. The proposed approach dynamically increases or reduces the selected areas according to the number of faces separating

*e-mail: surname.name@limsi.fr

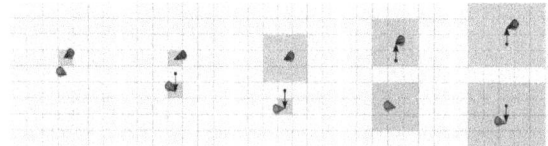

Figure 1: Size of the selection according the cursors' position.

the two partners on the mesh. To overcome the overlapping of selections, one face separates the two selection areas.

Figure 1 shows different selection sizes according to the number of faces separating the two cursors. On a flat plan with a uniform distribution of square faces (see Figure 1), the number of faces selected by each partner is defined by: $F_1 = (N + 1 - N(mod\ 2))^2$ and $F_2 = (N - 1 + N(mod\ 2)))^2$, where N is the number of faces separating the users, F_i is the number of faces selected by the user i and $a(mod\ b)$ is the modulo operation of a by b.

3. RESULTS AND CONCLUSION

The proposed method for Collaborative Selection Adjustment (CSA) was compared with the classic and Individual method of Selection Adjustment (ISA). In these two conditions, pairs of participants are asked to deform shapes in order to turn them into new pre-defined shapes.

The experimental results revealed that performance are rather close between the two conditions. The average completion time is 127s for the ISA condition and 113(s) for the CSA condition (p-value = 0.06). However, the evaluation of the crossed distance showed that the involved effort is reduced under the CSA condition. Indeed, the distance travelled by the two cursors during the experiment was significantly lower in the CSA condition (28.5 m) than in the ISA condition (37.2m; p-value=0.001).

Moreover the difference of the distances crossed by each user during the deformation phase shows an important reduction under the CSA condition. It decreases from 0.8 m for ISA condition to 0.38 m for CSA condition (p-value = 0.035). The workload is thus more balanced under the CSA condition. In summary, the results of this experiment reveal that CSA method improves the team efficiency and provides a better workload distribution.

4. REFERENCES

[1] N. Nova, *et al.* Collaboration in a multi-user game: impacts of an awareness tool on mutual modeling. *Multimedia Tools and Applications*, 32(2):161–183, Nov. 2006.

Spatial Augmented Reality based Tangible CAD System

Hyeon Joon Joo*   Ross Smith **   Bruce Thomas **   Jun Park*

*School of Information & Computer Engineering, Hong-ik University, Mapo-Gu, Seoul, Republic of Korea
**School of computer and Information Science, University of South Australia, Mawson Lakes, Australia

Abstract

In current Computer Aided Design (CAD) systems, designers are commonly restricted to a traditional workstation environment with mouse and keyboard. This environment is indirect from the physical object they are designing, and as such they may lose the one to one correspondence between the virtual and physical magnification of the design. In order to reduce this, we propose a Spatial Augmented Reality (SAR) based CAD system which consists of a fixed camera-projector pair, a Light Emitting Diode (LED) pen with two buttons, a wireless communication module, and a physical drawing board.

Categories and Subject Descriptors: H.5.1

[Information Interfaces and Presentation]: Multimedia Information Systems - Artificial, augmented, and virtual realities; J.6 [Computer-Aided Engineering]: Computer-Aided Design (CAD)

Keywords: Spatial Augmented Reality, Computer Aided Design

1. Introduction

We envision SAR to be used in the near future as a design tool to facilitate the rapid design of new products [1]. CAD and CAD-like drawing tools are a predominate method which designers use to capture their concepts into a computer. We are interested in extending interactive SAR systems with user interfaces that capture CAD operations. Jones et al. introduced various interactions such as game control and a photo viewer on a complex surface using an Infrared LED stylus [2]. Our system was developed for assisting the design process by providing various convenient functionalities in a SAR environment similar to traditional drawing tools. We are interested in the research question: "How does a designer perform CAD interactions in an intuitive manner within a SAR environment?"

2. Interaction and Example Use of SAR CAD

Our SAR CAD system provides users with several novel methods to increase performance of the design process. While we wish to support direct manipulation of CAD operations, we had to overcome the tracking limitations of our SAR CAD system because of errors and jitters in LED tracking. To overcome the limitations of the technology, we provide six methods: Firstly, we set a range within which the LED pen's coordinates remain unchanged, which prevented unwanted jitters. Secondly, we provided snatching capability allowing graphic primitive positions to be aligned previously drawn objects. Guiding lines are also displayed (Fig. 1.b). Thirdly, we provide users with four novel functionalities: magnifying glass, mirroring, replication, and ruler detection. The magnifying glass assists users to accurately and precisely draw graphic primitives such as lines, circles, and rectangles while drawing in millimeter units (Fig.1.a). Mirroring

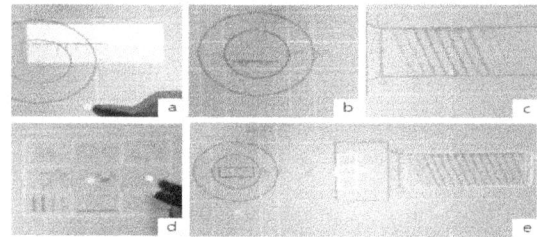

Figure 1. (a) Magnifying Glass Tool. (b) Mirroring Tool. (c) Replication tool. (d) Ruler detection. (e) the Example Use

brings a default option to users for drawing a graphic primitive in a reflective position from an existing one (Fig.1.b). To reduce designers' repeated actions, we provide the replication operation (Fig 1.c). Due to errors and jitters in LED tracking, our system adjusts the coordinate of the LED pen on the detected ruler's position when a user activates drawing a line function (Fig 1.d).

An example of using our SAR CAD is to draw the side view and the front view of a bolt (Fig 1.e). The result highlights some of the advantages and limitations. Our SAR CAD facilitates design performance through our functions. Compared to current CAD system, our system provides actual drawing experience. However, we experienced a slight difference between the coordinates of the camera and projected or augmented images, so we tried several times to detect ruler on the correct position.

3. Conclusion and Future work

We described our SAR CAD system with an example use. We believe our SAR CAD is an alternative design tool to existing CAD systems. We added a variety of design functions to make our system more accurate and convenient to perform CAD drawing operations. We have a plan to support habitual behaviors of designers such as doodling and drawing diagrams while they are using our SAR CAD system. More importantly, we will investigate how our SAR CAD may be used as a collaborative design tool which allows designers, and stakeholders to participate in a design process to share various opinions.

4. Acknowledgement

This work was supported by the Industrial Strategic Technology Development Program (10041656, Open Platform Development for See-Through Smart Glasses with Smart Vision) funded by the Ministry of Knowledge Economy (MKE, Korea)

5. References

[1] G.S.V. Itzstein, B.H. Thomas, R.T. Smith, and S. Walker, "Using spatial augmented reality for appliance design", in Proc. PerCom Workshops, 2011, pp.316-318.

[2] Jones, B., Sodhi, R., Campbell, R., Garnett, G. and Bailey, B. P. , "Build your world and play in it: Interacting with surface particles on complex objects", In Proc. of IEEE International Symposium on Mixed and Augmented, (2010), pp.165-174

* e-mail: tensaiijoo@gmail.com

A System for Evaluating 3D Pointing Techniques

Robert J. Teather, Wolfgang Stuerzlinger
York University, Toronto, Canada
rteather@cse.yorku.ca

ABSTRACT

This demo presents a desktop VR system for evaluating human performance in 3D pointing tasks. The system supports different input devices (e.g., mouse and 6DOF remote pointer), pointing techniques (e.g., screen-plane and depth cursors), and cursor visualization styles (e.g., one-eyed and stereo 3D cursors). The objective is to comprehensively compare all combinations of these conditions. We especially focus in on fair and direct comparisons between 2D and 3D pointing tasks. Finally, our system includes a new pointing technique that outperforms standard ray pointing.

Categories and Subject Descriptors

H.5.1 [Information Interfaces and Presentation]: Multimedia Information Systems – virtual reality. H.5.2 [Information Interfaces and Presentation]: User Interfaces – input devices, interaction styles.

Keywords

3D pointing; cursors; selection; Fitts' law.

1. INTRODUCTION

Three-dimensional pointing in VR systems is analogous to 2D pointing commonly used with a mouse on desktop systems. While 2D pointing tasks are well-studied and well-understood [1], 3D pointing is relatively less well understood and direct comparisons between 2D and 3D pointing are rare. Hence we developed a system to both evaluate 3D pointing tasks, and to permit direct comparison between 2D and 3D pointing tasks under a variety of test conditions. Our main objective is to identify better methods for evaluating 3D pointing techniques using methodology commonly employed in the evaluation of 2D techniques.

2. The System

Our system runs on a 3 GHz PC, with an Nvidia Quadro 4400, and a 24" 120Hz stereo LCD. Stereo graphics are enabled using NVidia 3DVision Pro shutter glasses. Five NaturalPoint Optitrack S250e cameras are used for 3D tracking. The system can display the scene in both stereo and mono. It can also render the cursor in stereo or mono, see e.g., Ware's work on one-eyed cursors [5].

We use a 3D extension of the ISO 9241-9 standard for evaluating pointing devices [2], based on Fitts' law [1]. The scene is a 30 cm deep box matching the display size, see Figure 1a. Textures and cylinders are used to facilitate spatial perception of the 3D scene. Target spheres are centered on top of cylinders arranged in a circle. The active target highlights blue and targets highlight red when selected. The cursor is a small 3D crosshair, either at the screen plane or in the 3D scene, depending on the current condition. In one-eyed mode, the cursor is displayed only to the viewer's dominant eye. In ray mode, the 3D device ray is also displayed. While the 2D experimental paradigm varies only target size and distance, our system supports any combination of target size, distance, and depth within the limitations of the screen geometry, tracking volume size, and device characteristics.

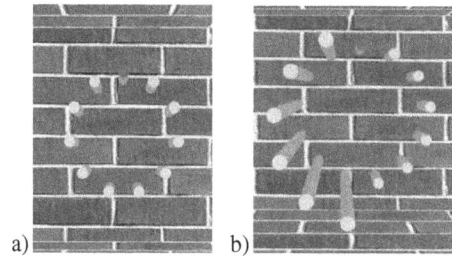

Figure 1 (a). A target circle at constant (flat) -20 cm depth. (b) Mixed depth targets – those on the right are farther.

3. Pointing Techniques

We currently support two different cursor modes with each of the mouse and remote pointing devices. The first mode employs a screen plane cursor and the second a sliding cursor. All four cursor/device combinations are depicted in Figure 2.

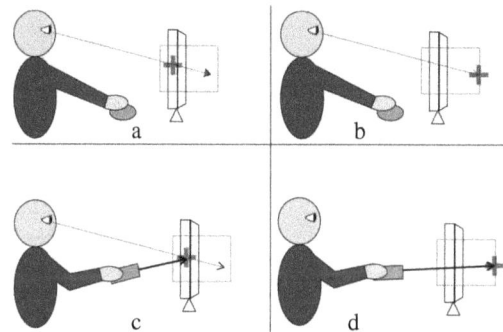

Figure 2. The pointing techniques supported by the system.

The mouse technique (Figure 2a) uses a screen cursor. The sliding mouse cursor (Figure 2b) instead displays the cursor at the ray/scene intersection, so the cursor slides across geometry. Our novel "ray-screen" technique (Figure 2c) displays a screen cursor where the device ray intersects the screen, and uses the eye-to-cursor ray for selection. The final technique (Figure 2d) is standard ray pointing. Our evaluations [3, 4] show the mouse is best, but also that ray-screen outperformed ray pointing.

4. REFERENCES

[1] Fitts, P. M., The information capacity of the human motor system in controlling the amplitude of movement, *Journal of Experimental Psychology*, 47, 1954, 381-391.

[2] International Organization for Standardization, ISO 9241-9 Ergonomic requirements for office work with visual display terminals (VDTs) - Part 9: Requirements for non-keyboard input devices. *International Standard*, 2000.

[3] Teather, R. J. and Stuerzlinger, W., Pointing at 3D targets in a stereo head-tracked virtual environment, *3DUI 2011*, 87-94.

[4] Teather, R. J. and Stuerzlinger, W., Cursors for 3D pointing, *3DCHI Workshop*, 2012.

[5] Ware, C. and Lowther, K., Selection using a one-eyed cursor in a fish tank VR environment, *ACM TOCHI*, 4, 1997, 309-322.

Exploration of Fused Multi-Volume Images Using User-Defined Binary Masks

Ryan Armstrong
Western University
London, Ontario

rarmst2@uwo.ca

Roy Eagleson
Western University
London, Ontario

eagleson@uwo.ca

Sandrine de Ribaupierre
Western University
London, Ontario

sderibau@uwo.ca

Categories and Subject Descriptors

H.5.2 [**Information Interfaces and Presenting**]: User Interfaces; I.3.7 [**Computer Graphics**]: Three-Dimensional Graphics and Realism;

Keywords

Direct Volume Rendering, Computer-Human Interaction, Multi-Modal Rendering, Medical Image Visualization

1. INTRODUCTION

Acquisition and fusion of multiple imaging modalities is becoming an increasingly desired clinical practice. This is particularly the case in radiation therapy, where dosage must be determined using CT images, which lack the contrast to resolve soft-tissue structures. This often necessitates the fusion of corresponding MRI images in order to plot radiation trajectories safely around critical tissues. Simultaneous visualization of multiple volumes using direct volume rendering (DVR) techniques offers a number of advantages over traditional visualization methods. Specifically, fused visualization enhances the relational aspects of volumes, providing improved context [cite the first one]. However, there are many challenges involved in implementing DVR using fused data sets. The primary challenge is determining how images overlap to provide meaningful information. Additionally, there is increased computational complexity beyond standard DVR techniques, threatening real-time applications of fused DVR. These difficulties are evident to users of such systems as they must manage complex user interfaces and poor application performance. In this work, we introduce a user-centric multi-volume DVR technique which addresses issues of performance and ease of use. Through an intuitive interface, users are able to spatially define regions of interest, determining the relative contributions of each modality in the output rendering.

2. APPROACH

Our volume renderer is implemented using a custom GPU-based ray casting algorithm with the CUDA API. Images are loaded into texture memory at initialization, using either a single image, or two pre-registered images of differing modalities. In addition to the images, a third texture with the same extents is created to be used as a volumetric binary mask. This volume is initialized to zero values. During rendering, the sampling technique at each sample position is dependent on the binary value at that position. The corresponding sampling techniques can be set by the user, but a simple example would involve sampling only the first image for false values and only the second image for true values. In this way, two volumes can be rendered in conjunction with minimal computational overhead by dividing the volume into two regions.

Users modify the binary mask using an axial-aligned, slice-based interface familiar to clinicians. There are two tools available to the user for this task: region painting and spherical clipping. Region painting allows the user to paint on each axial slice, transforming the corresponding bits of the binary mask along the plane. In order to view a feature of interest from one image within the context of another, the user must simply paint the desired regions on each slice of the volume. Additionally, the spherical clipping tool allows the user to identify a region of interest and place a point to transform all bits within a desired Euclidean distance from the point.

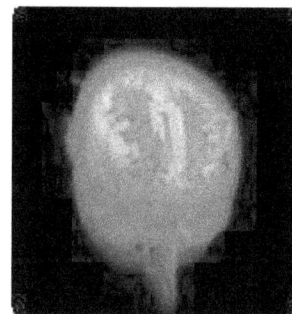

Figure 1. Multi-modality rendering of skin from CT and brain from Visible Human 2.0 [2] cryo-section volume.

3. FUTURE WORK

Future work will involve expanding the functionality and accessibility of the software. A clinical application is also being explored with the goal of incorporating physician-defined contours in order to validate segmentation visually against volumetric renderings for the purpose of guiding radiation therapy. Current validation methods neglect to examine contours against original structures in spatial contexts, injecting an amount of uncertainty into the process.

4. ACKNOWLEDGEMENTS

This work has been partially funded by GRAND-NCE as well as the CAMI program.

5. REFERENCES

[1] Beyer, J., HadWiger, M., Wolfsberger, S., Buhler, K. High-quality multimodal volume rendering for preoperative planning of neurosurgical interventions. IEEE Transactions on Visualization and Computer Graphics, 13(6), (2007).

[2] Ratui, P., Hillen, B., Glaser, J., Jenkins, D.P. Visible Human 2.0 – the next generation. Stud. Health Technol. Inform. 94, (2003), 275-281.

Gesture-Based Interaction with 3D Visualizations of Document Collections for Exploration and Search

Angélica de Antonio, Cristian Moral, Daniel Klepel, Martín J. Abente
Facultad de Informática, Campus de Montegancedo, Universidad Politécnica de Madrid
{angelica, cmoral, dklepel, mabente}@fi.upm.es

1. INTRODUCTION

Despite the powerful tools which are available nowadays to make easy the access to information contained in huge document collections, like WWW, satisfactory solutions haven't been found yet which allow not only to easily locate potentially interesting documents but also to help users to build a mental model on a set of documents, and to allow users to explore and interact intuitively with a corpus and to reorganize it according to their interests and preferences. Three-dimensional representations of document collections have shown their usefulness in helping users visualize the thematic structure of the collection. However, a 3D visualization is not enough. New interaction paradigms and techniques need to be investigated.

2. THE PROTOTYPE SYSTEM

A prototype has been developed fully automating the visualization pipeline for unstructured document collections. A set of input documents are transformed into a conceptual representation that can be further analyzed through the Vector Space Model [4], where a multidimensional vector is computed for each document, each position corresponding to a concept appearing in the document. Several options have been proposed in the literature to compute the thematic pairwise document similarity based on this vector representation [3]. The next step is reducing this n-dimensional representation into a 3D representation allowing to locate the document spatially. A Force Directed Placement [2] approach is selected for this step, with an improvement proposed to enhance the user's capability to adapt the visualization according to its current goal and personal preferences. A clustering algorithm is also applied to the conceptual representation in order to group documents into thematic clusters visualized in different colors. For this step the k-means algorithm [1] is selected as it allows the user to select the number k of clusters to generate. Besides the location and the color, a meaningful keyword is associated to and shown beside every document (see Figure 1a). A gestural interaction mechanism (see Figure 1b) is developed to allow users to navigate throughout the 3D space, select a single document or a whole cluster, invert or hide a selection, open an excerpt of a single document, change the number of clusters, strengthen the attraction force among similar documents or strengthen the intra-cluster attraction force.

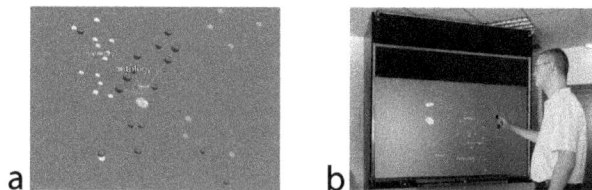

Figure 1: a) 3D user interface; b) User interaction

3. EXPERIMENT

In order to evaluate our prototype, we have carried out an experiment where users have been asked to perform some exploration and search tasks to determine if the prototype facilitates the obtaining of a mental model of a corpus of documents. We have also asked the users to provide us with a subjective opinion about the prototype. Both users and the screen have been recorded during the experiment for further analysis of their gestures and behaviour while interacting with the prototype.

4. CONCLUSIONS

The results of the experiment allow us to conclude that users liked the visual metaphor representing the documents and appreciated the metadata attached to them (color and keyword). Additionally many of them declared that the spatial closeness between similar documents helped them to figure out the thematic hierarchy of the corpus. However, some of them indicated that they had too little time to train with the system, which influenced negatively their handling skills and then the results. Nevertheless, these users stated that with a longer training time they would perform the tasks faster.

5. REFERENCES

[1] I. S. Dhillon and D. S. Modha. Concept decompositions for large sparse text data using clustering. *Mach. Learn.*, 42(1-2):143–175, jan 2001.

[2] T. M. J. Fruchterman and E. M. Reingold. Graph drawing by force-directed placement. *Softw. Pract. Exper.*, 21(11):1129–1164, nov 1991.

[3] G. Salton and M. J. Mcgill. *Introduction to Modern Information Retrieval*. McGraw-Hill, Inc., New York, NY, USA, 1986.

[4] G. Salton, A. Wong, and C. S. Yang. A vector space model for automatic indexing. *Commun. ACM*, 18(11):613–620, nov 1975.

Author Index